D1271664

Frank O'Connor: New Perspectives

LOCUST HILL LITERARY STUDIES
No. 23

The Locust Hill Literary Studies Series

Frank O'Connor:
New Perspectives

Edited by

Robert C. Evans
and
Richard Harp

LOCUST HILL PRESS
West Cornwall, CT
1998

Library of Congress Cataloging-in-Publication Data

Frank O'Connor : new perspectives / edited by Robert C. Evans and
Richard Harp.
    470p.   cm. -- (Locust Hill literary studies ; no. 23)
    Includes bibliographical references (p. 397-446) and index.
    ISBN 0-933951-79-5 (alk. paper)
    1. O'Connor, Frank, 1903-1966--Criticism and interpretation.
2. Ireland--In literature. I. Evans, Robert C. II. Harp, Richard.
III. Series.
PR6029.D58Z67 1998
823'.912--dc21   97-32626
                                              CIP

Printed on acid-free, 250-year-life paper
Manufactured in the United States of America

Acknowledgments

Since a primary interest of both editors has been to encourage interest among students in the work of Frank O'Connor, both of them wish to thank the many students—some of them published here—who have contributed so much to the editors' enthusiasm for this project. In this volume particularly, artificial distinctions between "teachers" and "students" have tended to collapse, as we have all worked together as colleagues. We offer the book as an outgrowth of an effort at truly collaborative learning.

The editors also thank *all* the contributors for the goodwill, good spirits, and exemplary patience they demonstrated as this project creeped to its conclusion. The book is now at least twice the size of the volume originally planned, and preparation of it took at least twice as long as originally anticipated, but the delays have allowed us to include a variety of features that will (we hope) make the volume more useful to readers and scholars of O'Connor's work.

We are extremely grateful for the cooperation of Mrs. Harriet O'Donovan Sheehy—Frank O'Connor's widow. Dealing with her has been a true delight, and we will greatly miss the regular arrival of sprightly e-mails from Dublin. Although we realize that answering all our questions and handling all our requests must have been exasperating at times, the only thing Harriet never permitted was a flagging of her friendly demeanor.

Finally, we are both extraordinarily grateful to Tom Bechtle of Locust Hill Press. Our dealings with him have helped us sense what it must have been like for Frank O'Connor to deal with his own generous and conscientious editor, William Maxwell. Gracious, patient, and constantly encouraging, Tom is a man in love with books—and, as it happens, with Ireland and the Irish. To him we owe too much to say.

***

Robert Evans: I am especially grateful to Alan Gribben for unstinting encouragement in this project and in everything else. Alan has been more than an exemplary colleague and administrator; he has been an exemplary human being, whose decency, kindness, and generosity are constant and are especially felt by his wife Irene and his children, Walter and Valerie (two of the best young folk ever).

Of the many other colleagues and friends who deserve special thanks, let the following stand as representatives: Joe Crowley (and the whole Crowley crew); Ann Depas-Orange (she of the threatening phone calls); Anne Little (and her helpmate, Bob); Eric Sterling (and his wife Jill and new son, Scott, perhaps the most cheerful baby on the planet); and Roberta J. Walker (a notoriously "outspoken woman").

Special thanks are owed to the Andrew W. Mellon Foundation, which funded a special summer seminar on Critical Pluralism that helped contribute to the completion of this project; and to Fariba Deravi, whose help with the details of the seminar (and whose cheerful help in general) causes smiles not only at the time but also in retrospect.

Of the many teachers whose encouragement and confidence over the years have helped lead to this book, let Alvin Kernan serve as the symbol and embodiment of them all. He has led a truly dramatic life, in which I am very grateful to have had a small walk-on role.

Finally, I thank my sisters (Darla and Betty), my in-laws (Claramae, Carol, Bill, Penny, Brendan, and Shannon), the other members of my family, my other friends, my wife (Ruth), and above all my *best* friend (Ruth).

***

Richard Harp: I would like to thank the late Frank Nelick for his great generosity in stimulating my interest in Irish studies and for introducing me to the wonderful O'Hegarty collection at the University of Kansas. I would also like to thank Donncha O'Haodh, Seamus Grimes, and Gearoid O'Tuathaogh for their hospitality during a sabbatical stay at University College, Galway, which further developed my interst in Irish literature, as well as Fr. Walter Macken, Bryan MacMahon, and Benedict Kiley for their help during that visit.

Dedications

For Margaret, my wife and sweetheart.—RH

For all who have meant so much,
especially Ruth—RCE

and especially for

HARRIET O'DONOVAN SHEEHY
and
WILLIAM MAXWELL

"I have an absolutely clear memory of the voices
of the two men at the table
working on the proofs.
Such a pleasure it was to listen to them—
Bill's voice quiet, soft, almost hesitant—
Michael's deep, strong, more insistent—
but the ease and admiration between them
creating a harmonious atmosphere.
Michael never failed to marvel
at Bill's skills as an editor—
the way changing a word here
or rearranging a phrase there
would make the meaning
which Michael had intended clear.
I never heard a cross word."

—Harriet O'Donovan Sheehy
on the friendship between
Frank O'Connor (Michael O'Donovan)
and William Maxwell,
his editor at *The New Yorker*

I am especially grateful to Chris Hudgins, Joe McCullough, and John Bowers for their encouragement to develop courses in Irish literature at the University of Nevada, Las Vegas, and to my students in those courses, especially John Kerrigan, Bob Fuhrel, Lisa Montagne, Megan Denio, Joe Csicsila, Jan MacIntyre, and Madelyn Montgomery. And I am always aware of the debt I owe to my teachers, Frank Nelick, John Senior, and Dennis Quinn of the University of Kansas and John Mahoney, Richard Hughes, and the late Edward Hirsh of Boston College, to all of whom "I owe / All that I am in arts, all that I know / (How nothing's that?)."

My deepest personal gratitude is to my parents, Martha Sue and Dick, my children, Rebecca, Matthew, and Adam, and last, but far from least, my wife, Margaret, herself of Irish heritage and from whom I have gained much knowledge about Ireland, and our soon-to-be-born child.

Contents

Comparisons and Contrasts

Critical Kaleidoscope

Some Final Words

Contents

Facts and Figures

Introduction

Richard Harp and Robert C. Evans

This collection has been inspired by a desire to create and re-
new interest in the brilliant literary artistry of Frank O'Connor.
Perhaps Ireland's most complete man of letters, best known for his
varied and comprehensive short stories but also a notable literary
critic, essayist, travel writer, translator and biographer, O'Connor
at his death in 1966 seemed assured of a lasting place in the pan-
theon of twentieth-century Irish writers. For many that is still now
the case. O'Connor's *Collected Stories*, edited by Richard Ellmann,
has been in print since 1981, and the past several years have seen
new collections of O'Connor's work in *The Collar: Stories of Irish
Priests*, published in Belfast in 1993, *A Frank O'Connor Reader*,
edited by Michael Steinman in 1994, and the exchange of letters between O'Connor and his New Yorker editor William Maxwell, also
edited by Steinman and published in 1996. In addition, at least one
of O'Connor's stories has recently reached a large audience in the
always coveted crossover medium of cinema, as "Guests of the
Nation" was the basis for the widely-seen movie *The Crying Game*.
There is also interest in O'Connor in non-English speaking coun-
tries, as the interview with his widow Harriet Sheehy in this volume will attest. Academic interest in O'Connor's work, however,
has somewhat flagged in the decades since his death; there have
been revivals in appreciation of the stories of Flann O'Brien (died
1966), for example, and of the poetry of Patrick Kavanagh (died
1967), but nothing similar for O'Connor, whose work was certainly
as incisive and much more far reaching. The only full-scale biography, that by James Matthews in 1983, has the fullness of detail
and narrative richness which a great writer deserves (and which
many lesser writers often get as well), yet its appreciation of the
man is continually undercut by what Matthews regards as his
subject's personal failings. Such failings, be they as they may, have

seldom detracted from critical appreciation of the work of a Joyce or a Yeats, much less from the work of those writers and artists whose lives Paul Johnson recounts in such particular detail in *Intellectuals* (O'Connor is a champion of the moral life compared to most of Johnson's rogues' gallery). O'Connor attempted to live his life without cant or hypocrisy; his frailties and controversies were often public—his bitter disillusionment with the failure of Irish republicanism, his outrage over Irish censorship in the 1930s and 1940s, his divorce in the 1950s—and he said and acted the way he thought. This brought him considerable grief in Ireland, yet he did not seek safety in permanent exile as did Joyce or in an outright rejection of religion as did modern writers too numerous to mention. Robert Frost said that he had a "lover's quarrel with the world"; O'Connor had a lover's quarrel with Ireland, and he never stopped loving her even when she bloodied him up.

If O'Connor's life occasionally embroiled him in controversy, then, he was willing to live those controversies and not observe them from afar. It is part, surely, of what gives his stories their powerful sense of life. For those who were not Irish contemporaries of O'Connor, however, his artistic credo may be one of the more controversial things about him. For O'Connor was neither an aesthete nor a writer of experimental fiction. He was a great devotee of realistic nineteenth-century fiction, who, as Yeats said, did for Ireland what Chekhov did for Russia. While this may endear him to ordinary readers and students, it will not necessarily make him popular amongst the critics and university scholars who have beat the drum for modernism as the only acceptable way for literature to follow this century. O'Connor characteristically took this literary controversy head-on, not fearing to attack Joyce for abandoning a depiction of life as it is really lived by most people. This is heresy of a particularly rank order for those who think modern literature must be difficult and obscure and experimental and has given O'Connor a position among fiction writers perhaps not unlike that of Frost or (in years past) George Herbert in poetry. But as Herbert counseled seventeenth-century writers of poetry to avoid useless ornament and rhetorical decoration so that they could find that "there is in love a sweetness ready penned / Copy only that and save expense" ("Jordan II"), O'Connor was a tireless searcher for the right word or phrase, for the right fable or plot, for, finally, that most difficult of all techniques, the art which might appear to his readers to be achieved without effort.

Insofar as postmodernism is a liberation from the notion that modern art must be "difficult," as T.S. Eliot famously prescribed, O'Connor's work is likely to grow considerably in popularity at all levels. His fiction alone has the range of the greatest of writers. The most frequently anthologized stories are those about children— "My Oedipus Complex," "The Drunkard," "My First Confession"—which achieve the difficult end of seeing the world through a child's eyes without being childish. Such stories are amusing but, like children themselves, demand to be taken seriously. The moral of "My Oedipus Complex," for example, is the interesting one that "Of course the Oedipus Complex exists—and it is not such a bad thing." Other stories about childhood are considerably less amusing and capture the extreme sensitivity and cruelty which children may be given to—"The Pretender" is an example. There are few gender stereotypes in O'Connor's stories. Women play the most diverse roles and when they do act capriciously or wantonly O'-Connor makes clear the reasons why—quite frequently it is because the men they have taken pity on are too stolid or too much the bumpkin to allow them many other options. The wonder and independence of a woman's beauty may be explored or her capacity for self-sacrifice, which comes at a price, without O'Connor feeling that he must give the final explanation for such mysteries. There are superlative stories of the Irish middle class (written decades before this became the general interest of journalism or sociology) which still unravel the complexities of their subject with a concreteness that other disciplines find difficult. There are stories of religion which do not condescend to either those who believe or to those who imperfectly embody their belief or to those who do not believe at all, stories of war that make clear there are causes worth fighting for and innumerable ways in which those causes may be betrayed, stories of the Irish peasantry meeting their urban cousins, who are pursuing education, religion, or business, which make clear the strangeness of the encounter and the manner in which each side may maintain (or not) their dignity.

O'Connor was born in 1903 and has recounted the early years of his life in one of his best books, *An Only Child*, a memoir not published until 1961 but which has the immediacy of a precocious diary. His childhood was shaped in part by his saintly mother, who supplied much of the family's income because his father was unable to keep steady employment because of the demon drink. His father, Mick O'Donovan, was also at times a terror around the house to both mother and child. That O'Connor could portray his father as compassionately as he does in stories such as "My Oedipus Complex" and even "The Drunkard" is testimony to his own generosity. O'Connor read voraciously but with little direction as a child; consequently one of the profound influences on his early life was that of his schoolmaster Daniel Corkery, who aroused and deepened his love for the allied causes of Irish culture and political independence. O'Connor then fought on the side of the Republicans in the 1921–22 Civil War, those who favored rejection of the treaty which brought peace between Ireland and Britain but at the cost of a divided island. The Republicans lost the civil war—the treaty's division of Ireland into a twenty-six county "Free State" and a six-county territory in Ulster (Northern Ireland) which would remain part of the United Kingdom was made permanent— and this led to bitterness and disillusionment for O'Connor, as it did for countless other Irish. But his anguish was directed not only against the British or the Free Staters but also against those with whom he had fought, as he discovered in them a romantic naiveté and a spirit of repression and ignorance as inhumane as their enemies (see, for example, his stories "Guests of a Nation" and "Freedom"). This largeness of vision is characteristic of O'Connor and, as always, was won in the crucible of experience rather than through exile or aestheticism or ideology. His stories about this, as well as his account in *An Only Child*, are more moving than those, for example, of the disillusioned soldiers of World War I that Hemingway describes, whose remoteness from the cause they are engaged in undercuts the passion of their experience. They also feature an engagement superior to that of Yeats's famous question in the poem "The Man and the Echo" where he wonders, "Did that play of mine [*Cathleen Ni Houlihan*] send out / Certain men the English shot?" For O'Connor, it was not art which gave rise to life, but life which produced art. One American work on the First World War that does have both O'Connor's passion and humor is e.e. cummings' *The Enormous Room*, an account of cummings' imprisonment in France.

O'Connor's first book of stories was *Guests of the Nation*, published in 1931. A number of these stories concern military life and many of them he did not choose to reprint. This was notable, as O'Connor would characteristically rewrite stories innumerable times and later republish the new versions in an attempt to get them right. Harriet Sheehy has said that one of her services to literary history after she married O'Connor in 1953 was retrieving multiple drafts of stories from his wastebasket so that his process of revision could be studied. In the 1930s he also worked with Yeats at the Abbey Theater, serving as Director there from 1937 to 1939. Among the plays he wrote during this period was a version of his well-known short story "In the Train." In 1937 he also published a biography of the leader of the Irish rebellion against the British, Michael Collins, who later led the forces of the Free State in the civil war. He was continuously at work on his fiction, publishing six collections between 1931 and 1951, with more to come until he died in 1966. Several collections were published posthumously. All told he wrote more than two hundred stories, many of them first appearing in magazines. James Alexander examines the stories that he published in *The New Yorker* in this volume of essays; that most munificent of magazines paid its writers $1.00 a word in the 1950s.

O'Connor's translations of poetry from Irish began in 1932 and continued steadily until the 1960s; they probably achieved their widest circulation in 1959 with the publication of *Kings, Lords & Commons* by Knopf in New York and, in 1961, by Macmillan in London. The annotated bibliography at the end of this book indicates the high regard in which these translations have been held. And, indeed, it is to that bibliography that one should turn to best appreciate the extent and quality of O'Connor's achievement. For he deserves as his literary epitaph the tribute Dr. Johnson paid to Oliver Goldsmith: *"Qui nullum fere scribendi genus non tetigit; nullum quod tetigit non ornavit"*—"he left scarcely any kind of writing untouched, and he touched none that he did not adorn."— **R.H.**

***

Our volume opens, appropriately, with an interview of Harriet O'Donovan Sheehy, Frank O'Connor's widow, who discusses his private personality and public personae, his attraction to short fiction, his attitudes toward priests, the origins of his stories, and how his personal qualities affected their marriage. Mrs. Sheehy shares not only her fond memories of the man but also her thoughtful appreciation of his art.

In the first regular essay, written in a lively style that O'Connor himself would surely have enjoyed, Alan Titley discusses O'-Connor's views of the Irish literary tradition, paying particular attention to his book *The Backward Look*. John C. Kerrigan also makes that book his focus, exploring O'Connor's views of his forebears and contemporaries, particularly Yeats and Joyce. Both Titley and

Introduction

Kerrigan discuss O'Connor's poetry and translations—topics not often explored in studies of this famous master of short fiction. Meanwhile, Shawn O'Hare looks at a work almost unknown even to O'Connor specialists—his unpublished book on dreams. O'Hare suggests that the evidence provided by this text implies that O'-Connor's fiction may have been more "modernist" than is commonly supposed.

Richard Harp turns to that fiction itself, discussing especially its great themes of loneliness, freedom, self-knowledge, love, conversion, and achieved satisfaction. Michael Neary, on the other hand, looks at the stories from a different perspective, examining the tensions between the events presented and the narrators' interpretations of those same events. As often as not (according to Neary), O'Connor encourages readers to question rather than merely accept his narrators' views. Julianne White's essay also discusses the reliability of O'Connor's narrators as well as the major theme of human isolation, particularly in the stories entitled "The Grand Vizier's Daughters" and "The Duke's Children."

The latter work, first published in *The New Yorker*, was one of forty-five tales by O'Connor first printed in that famous magazine. These stories are the subject of James D. Alexander's essay, which argues that O'Connor's *New Yorker* fiction is far less light and comic, far more dark and serious, than has often been assumed. Its depictions of Irish culture and Irish lives—particularly the lives of children and priests—is much more disturbing (in Alexander's view) than many readers might expect. Owene Weber, meanwhile, examines O'Connor's presentations of the lives of another important group of characters—women. She discusses his depiction of tomboys, "quicksilver girls," married women, and "bold crones," clearly demonstrating his intense interest in lively female characters. Priests, another group in whom O'Connor took great interest, are the major concern of Megan L. Denio's essay, which focuses especially on one priest in particular: Father Jerry Fogarty. A recurring character in many of O'Connor's later stories, Fogarty exemplifies (Denio argues) both the disappointments and the hopes, the loneliness and the love, that O'Connor considered central to the human condition. According to Denio, Fogarty combines and embodies two of O'Connor's favorite kinds of character—the child and the priest. Finally, in another essay covering several stories, Katie Magaw and Robert C. Evans turn from discussions of theme and character to a discussion of style and technique, arguing that the irony and paradox so often found in O'Connor's stories contribute not only to the richness of their artistry but to the complexity of their implied view of life.

The volume's next section, which compares and contrasts individual stories, either in their various versions or with other writings, begins with Michael Steinman's detailed examination of the early and late texts of "The Procession of Life." O'Connor constantly revised (a point stressed by many contributors), and Steinman shows how the two versions of "Procession" reflect two distinct stages of O'Connor's life as man and artist. Robert Fuhrel, on the other hand, compares and contrasts not two versions of one O'Connor story but rather one work by O'Connor ("The Man of the House") with a similar work by James Joyce ("Araby"). The differences between these works (Fuhrel contends) typify the larger differences of style, theme, and purpose between O'Connor and his great colleague and rival. Lastly, this section devoted to comparing and contrasting individual works turns to O'Connor's masterpiece, "Guests of the Nation." One of O'Connor's earliest stories and one of his best, "Guests" is also widely considered one of the finest short stories ever written. Robert Evans and Michael Probst examine the points of contact between the story and *An Only Child*, the highly effective first volume of O'Connor's autobiography. The essayists consider whether the story influenced the life, whether the life influenced the story, or whether the connections are far more complicated than such simple alternatives imply. Lastly, Katie Magaw and Evans compare and contrast "Guests of the Nation" (the story) with *Guests of the Nation* (the dramatic adaptation prepared by Neil McKenzie). Studying the two works side by side, they argue, helps illustrate the particular qualities of each.

The next section of this volume (a "Critical Kaleidoscope") offers several distinctive features which we hope will make the book especially useful to students, scholars, teachers, and even other writers. Thus, John M. Burdett, Michael Probst, Claudia Wilsch, and Carolyn T. Young first provide paraphrased samplings of O'-Connor's own comments about writers and writings—comments culled from several of his books of criticism and from personal interviews. These are intended to offer a quick sense of his thinking on a variety of topics, partly so that readers can better perceive the intentions underlying his own fiction. Next, Kathleen B. Durrer, Scott Johnson, Katie Magaw, and Claire Skowronski present a concise introduction to the various critical approaches (especially modern theories) often used to interpret literary texts. These theo-

ries are then used to provide a kaleidoscopic survey of two of O'-
Connor's best short stories—the well-known "Guests of the Nation" as well as another work, "The Bridal Night," that deserves
much more attention than it has yet received. The same focus on
theory is then applied to an O'Connor story that is almost completely unknown: "Lady Brenda." This work has never before been
published in book form and was printed only once in a magazine.
The story is used here partly as a test case for assessing how easily
O'Connor's fiction can be analyzed from a variety of theoretical
perspectives. Brief analytical comments on the work are offered by
Patricia Angley, Kathleen B. Durrer, Timothy Francisco, Ashley
Gordon, Karen Worley Pirnie, Michael Probst, Claire Skowronski,
Ondra Thomas-Krouse, Claudia Wilsch, and Jonathan Wright—all
of whom participated in a special seminar on "Critical Pluralism"
sponsored in 1997 by the Andrew W. Mellon Foundation. Their
work suggests the possible advantages of a "pluralistic" critical
approach to O'Connor's writings.

From brief comments on an obscure story, we next turn to ex-
haustive analysis (by Robert Evans) of O'Connor's most famous
piece of fiction—"Guests of the Nation." Evans tries to pay close
attention to the style, structure, and detailed craftsmanship of this
tale, hoping thereby to illuminate as precisely as possible some
factors that help make this work so powerfully compelling. Finally, this "Critical Kaleidoscope" ends with a very lengthy listing
of most of O'Connor's published fiction, collected and uncollected.
Each entry provides publication details, a brief plot synopsis, and
brisk summaries of some pertinent critical commentary. We hope
that this part of the volume will give readers a handy guide to
O'Connor's characteristic themes and subjects, the issues his critics
have debated, and the stories they may most want to explore on
their own.

As the book reaches its conclusion, we offer three pieces of
new primary data. The first is a conversation between Harriet
Sheehy (O'Connor's widow) and Valentina Tenedini, who has
recently translated one of O'Connor's novels, *Dutch Interiors*, into
Italian. This conversation not only provides new glimpses of
O'Connor's life from the perspective of Mrs. Sheehy but also offers
an informal discussion of the main features of one of O'Connor's
two attempts at long fiction. Harriet Sheehy herself then offers a
fascinating "Postscript" in which she comments on many of the
issues raised (implicitly or explicitly) by the other essays in this
book. Next, we present a previously unpublished text by

O'Connor himself—his 1959 adaptation for radio of "Guests of the Nation," perhaps his finest story.

Finally, the closing portion of the volume offers a detailed chronology of O'Connor's life (prepared by John M. Burdett and Robert Evans); an extremely lengthy bibliography of works by and about O'Connor (prepared by John C. Kerrigan); and several indices designed to make the information in the book as accessible and useful as possible. All in all, we hope that our book will help to stimulate even more interest in a writer whose stature is likely to grow as a new century provides new perspectives on the era now ending.—**R.C.E**

Contexts

The Frank O'Connor I Knew

Harriet O'Donovan Sheehy

(The following are edited excerpts from two interviews which took place between the widow of Frank O'Connor and two different Italian graduate students in Dublin in 1995 and 1996. Gaia Rizzato, the first student, is finishing her master's degree, the main focus of which is O'Connor's short stories. Valentina Tenedini hopes to complete her doctorate soon; her focus is "Frank O'Connor: the writer, the Irishman, the man." The selection of questions and the editing are entirely Harriet Sheehy's.)

Q. Would you tell me something about the difference between Frank O'Connor and Michael O'Donovan—in other words, between the public and the private person?

A. Frank O'Connor was the public person. He was a brilliant actor and, on public occasions, would give quite a performance. He didn't particularly enjoy doing this, and would actually feel rather sick beforehand. But once he got started he could be a spell binder. Although he wasn't arrogant and never thought of himself as an important person or a great writer he would often, at such times, say very controversial things in a most emphatic manner. To him this seemed the best way to get people to think about what he considered important issues. These varied over the years, but while we were married he wrote and talked about the neglect and destruction of Irish national monuments (particularly the remains of early churches and monastic buildings); the authenticity of the Casement Diaries (he firmly believed they were forged); and making the learning of Irish compulsory and a requirement for certain jobs, so that people hated something he thought beautifully rich. Of course in the early days, before I knew him, he was fighting against the censorship (particularly of books like *The Tailor and Anstey* or books by other Irish writers like O'Faolain, Kate O'Brien or Patrick Kavanagh). And there was the famous article in *Holiday* magazine which infuriated not only the Irish, but also the Irish Americans because he actually wrote that there was not only poverty in Ireland but also illiteracy and even (dare we mention it) illegitimacy. The best way I can describe his attitude is to say that he was very intolerant of and impatient with the hypocrisy which resulted in Irish society's denial of many of the real problems of the day. Obviously this sort of attitude brought him into conflict with the Church, the government and those who were happy with the status quo. So he got the reputation (particularly among people who had never met him) of being a very opinionated character who was always trying to stir up trouble. As I said, this was largely a pose which he adopted because he really cared about these issues; he thought they were important for the country as a whole, and he wanted people to PAY ATTENTION. (This was the same sort of controversy which was created by *The Bell*. It is fascinating to read old issues of that magazine and to see how amazingly Ireland has changed in the last 40 years. And it helps put the controversial writing of Frank O'Connor into a historical context.) As another aspect of the public side of his personality, he thoroughly enjoyed teaching, and was very comfortable in his role of Frank O'Connor when he was in the classroom—whether at Stanford or Harvard or Trinity. The students loved him, which is not surprising since he often said that he learned as much from them as they did from him. A former student, Philip Levine, now a well known poet, wrote recently about his experience of being in Professor O'Connor's class. Will I read you what he said? I was very moved by it. "He was astonishing: direct, resourceful, honest, [and] wonderfully entertaining.... He would read from a student story and then suggest more fruitful ways of going about the building of a scene or the construction of a character. The two hours passed in a blink, and I came away with a renewed love of what I hoped some day would be my craft." So that was Frank O'Connor—the public man. Michael O'Donovan, on the other hand, was the man to whom I was very happily married. He was an enormously empathic, sensitive, kind person who was intensely loyal to his friends and would go to great lengths to help them. He was actually rather shy and nervous about meeting new people, though he generally hid this fairly well. He knew a great deal about all forms of art—music, architecture, poetry, painting—and cared passionately about all of them. He was warm and funny but could get in a flaming rage when he came across injustice. He was

totally bored by people who put on airs, but could listen endlessly
to somebody talking about a job they loved, no matter what it was,
so long as they were really committed to it. He was intolerant and
dismissive of the second rate and shoddy and had no hesitation in
saying so. He was extremely sensitive to voices and had almost no
memory for physical details. This caused me no end of frustration
when he went somewhere without me and I asked him afterwards
about the things women always want to know—the color of someone's dress or whether a particular person was "attractive." "I
don't know," he'd say. "All I know is that she had a terrible
screechy voice and I couldn't place her accent." Michael O'Donovan was glad that Frank O'Connor was a successful writer because
it vindicated his mother's faith in him. But I never felt that he
thought being famous gave him the right to be arrogant or superior. There was a phrase his mother used to use about someone
who had behaved badly: "Ah, he has no word." "Word" meant
"honour" and Michael never wanted to behave in a way which
would earn that condemnation.

Q. Why do you think he was drawn to writing short stories rather
than novels?

A. I think it was a question both of temperament and of the society
he grew up in. He started writing poetry at a young age and his
innate outlook and understanding were more poetic than they
were novelistic. He also loved to draw, and used to say that he
might have been a painter if he had had enough money to buy
paints. A copy book and a pencil were within his reach and that is
exactly what his earliest stories were written in. An ordinary
school child's copybook. I think that he felt the short story had the
intensity of poetry; that at its best it focused on an important moment in somebody's life—a moment when something happened
which meant that everything changed. Do you remember the last
line of "Guests of the Nation"? "And anything that ever happened
to me afterward, I never felt the same about again." That more or
less sums up his feeling as to what a short story should be about.
He wrote about all of this in the introduction to *The Lonely Voice*. If
you haven't already read that you should take a look at it, because
he explains all this much better than I can. Also, you have to remember that when he began writing, the social situation in Ireland
was so constricting, the Church's influence so strong, that in order
to have a life worth writing about, the hero or heroine of a novel
would have to go to England. As he was fond of quoting: "An

Irishman's private life begins at Holyhead." This situation has changed radically since then, but at the time writers like Joyce went into exile and there were many more Irish short stories than there were Irish novels.

Q. You talk about the power of the Catholic Church. Could you tell me what his own attitude to it was? And in particular how he felt about priests?

A. He did not like the institutional church and after being excommunicated during the Troubles was never again a practicing Catholic. But he was a believer, and despite the fact that someone wrote that "the sight of the collar was enough to make his hair stand on end" he had great sympathy for priests. If you don't mind, I'd like to read you what I wrote in my introduction to *The Collar* (a collection of his stories about priests, published in England by Blackstaff): "towards those called 'father' by people who are not their children he had an attitude compounded of amusement, respect, curiosity and, above all, compassion." I really believe that this is illustrated very clearly in these stories, which show a deeply sympathetic understanding of the difficulties of trying to live by "standards other than those of this world." This was not just a theoretical understanding on his part: for years he was a close friend of a priest named Tim Traynor (who turns up as Father Fogarty in some of his best stories) and in his later years he was great friends with my second husband, Maurice Sheehy, who was a priest at the time. He and Maurice used to argue quite fiercely about some of the more arcane utterances of Archbishop John Charles McQuaid (for whom Michael had no time at all), but he never failed to listen very carefully when Maurice described the vestments worn for a certain ritual or the correct ecclesiastical protocol for important occasions. Priests often came to call, and I will never forget the Jesuit who said to him, "Wait a minute, Mr. O'Connor. We've got things backwards. You are attacking Joyce on moral grounds while I am attacking him on aesthetic grounds." So I think it is fair to say that while he was quite antagonistic to the institution as institution, he was bored by priests only when they too rigorously toed the institutional line. Interestingly, a young American named Shawn O'Hare has recently done his master's thesis on the subject of O'Connor's stories about priests. You should try to get it if you want to explore this whole area of Michael's relationship with the church. I was very impressed by it, and think he really understands the whole feeling behind the priest stories.

Q. What was the source of his stories—where did he get the ideas for them?

A. Mostly he got the ideas for his stories from incidents in his own life (as well as the lives of his family and friends), but also he got them from things that other people told him. He had a little notebook which he called his "theme" book and he would write down, in three or four lines, what he considered the kernel of the story. When he was teaching the short story class he used to ask the students to bring in themes, and I remember that he would sometimes come home saying "so and so brought in a brilliant theme today. I'd really love to write it myself, but I don't think he wants to part with it." He might write a theme in his book and then not go near it for months, or he might start on it the very next day. It seemed to depend on his frame of mind at the time and whether the story fit in with something else he was already thinking about or wanting to write. Most of his stories came from Irish people, but some of them he heard in America or from me or my friends. No matter what the source, however, they were always written in an Irish context, and not just an Irish context, but very often a Cork one. He was, of course, deeply influenced by Cork and we spent a lot of time there visiting, but once he had moved away for good he never wanted to go back there to live. It would have been too claustrophobic. Dublin was bad enough (in that sense) because people would stop him on the street and tell him how he should have ended this or that story or (even worse from his point of view) tell him that they had a story they just knew he would want to write. But though it sometimes drove him crazy, he needed the intimacy of Ireland; he felt that was the only way he could be sure his stories would be true to life. Though he travelled a lot and lived for extended periods in both England and the U.S., he never wanted to be out of the country for too long. He used to talk about the way Irish Americans sentimentalized the country and this was something he *never* wanted to do. He really hated sentimentality and wanted to write about people and conditions as they were and not as they might appear in some nostalgic memory of home. His stories about children came almost entirely from his own life and from his observations of his own children. He was endlessly fascinated by children—perhaps because their emotions are so intense, their experience of life so immediate and their reactions so transparent. Perfect material for the short story and particularly for someone like Michael, whose own memory of the way he felt as a child was so clear.

Q. If you don't mind I would like to ask you some personal questions. In the first place, how did you feel about taking second place to him? Did people ask you, "And what do you do, Mrs. O'Connor?"

A. Yes, often. It always surprised me, because they would also ask if I wrote too. I always answered that I couldn't imagine two writers in one house (at the time the only ones I knew of were Pamela Hansford Johnson and Charles Snow, though I gather there are more now). I think the people who asked that question felt rather sorry for me—that I was just the poor old housewife making things easy for the great writer, but it wasn't like that at all. I had a multifaceted job. Sometimes I acted as secretary—answering business letters or adding long postscripts to letters he wrote to mutual friends. (When I was collecting the material for the recently published book of letters between himself and William Maxwell—*The Happiness of Getting It Down Right*—I found that I sometimes even answered editorial queries about how things worked in Ireland.) Sometimes I acted as resident critic—reading his reviews or articles—or having the stories in progress read to me. One of my favorite jobs was saving his discarded manuscripts. He was notorious for re-writing his stories and he would throw the old version in the wastepaper basket. I would retrieve it, and put all the versions in a file in chronological order. (I think there were something like fourteen versions of "A Set of Variations.") One day he caught me at this and laughed and said: "When I am dead and gone, graduate students are going to rise up and call you blessed for all the work you've done for them." Perhaps the greatest compliment he ever gave me was in a story which he wrote to tease me. Because he was so much older than I, I was always worrying about his health and nagging him to stop smoking or to carry an identification card in his wallet, so that if anything happened to him while he was out walking, I'd be notified immediately. He used to laugh and tease me about all this and one day he said: "I'm going to write a story against you, and in this one you are going to die before I do." He did, and in the story is a line which I still can't read without tears coming into my eyes. I think it is the greatest compliment I've ever been given. It goes like this: "What she had given Jim, though she did not recognize it, was precisely the thing whose consequences she deplored, the desire to live and be happy."

Q. Perhaps I should have asked this first of all. You are American. He was Irish. Where did you meet him?

A. At Harvard Summer School where he was teaching a course in Anglo-Irish Literature. I had read a story by him in *Mademoiselle* magazine and liked the light way he wrote about the difficulties of being a Roman Catholic. (I had been considering marrying a man who was very serious about his Catholicism and was surprised to discover that it was possible to be funny about serious Catholicism. It seemed as good a reason as any for taking his course.) I was a "mature student" majoring in English and it was O'Connor and the Irish or Leon Edel and Henry James. O'Connor sounded like more fun. He was an absolute spellbinder of a teacher and we all loved the course and spent a lot of time discussing what he had said. One day I was talking to a fellow student about a play we had been studying and said: "Well I don't care what Mr. O'Connor says, I still think Deidre was a bitch." When I turned around I saw he had heard me and I was so overcome by confusion and chagrin that I didn't accept his amused invitation to "Come for coffee and tell us why you think that." It wasn't until near the end of the course, when there was a party for him in a student's house, that I got to know him. The person giving the party asked if I would collect O'Connor (I happened to have a car) and bring him along. I did and we got to talking and he asked me to have supper with him and this time I said yes. I felt more comfortable with him than I had ever felt with anybody in my life, and after that we spent a lot of time together, eventually marrying a year and a half later.

Q. What did you like about him most?

A. Well, that's a terrible question! How do I know? He was a man I loved deeply and completely and it is hard to think which of his many good qualities I most valued. But I suppose it was the way he always made me feel that I was smarter and funnier and indeed even nicer than I really am, and by doing that somehow made it possible for me to be a better person than I would have been otherwise. He never put me down, always treated me as his equal. He made me laugh, and he made me happy. He showed me that the world was incredibly interesting and that other people were not only fascinating, but also admirable and lovable. He opened my eyes (and ears) to so much and yet never acted as though he knew more than I did. He asked my opinion about important things and would read the second or third drafts of his stories to me. He made me feel that my opinions and concerns mattered. Of course he was human and one time he regretted letting me read an early draft of a story. I remember frowning as I was reading it, and he immediately said, "What's wrong with it?" "Well," I answered blithely, "I'm just surprised that you are writing about such a cliché." "What do you mean?" and this time his tone was definitely testy. "Well, it is just the old double standard. It's OK for a man to do something but not for a woman to do the same thing." "Well, thank you very much. I never heard of the double standard as you call it, but you've certainly ruined that story for me." He was really quite cross (and he really never *had* heard of the double standard) and it was some time before he could make a joke of it and tell people how I'd ruined his story. So from then on I was a little more circumspect in my criticisms!

Q. Did he ever tell you which of his stories was his favorite?

A. Yes, he did. It's "The Luceys," and when he first said this I was very surprised. I had read it and hadn't really been terribly impressed by it. But then I heard him read it on Radio Eireann and it was extraordinary how it came alive. I think the thing that appealed to him was the problem of trying to create a sympathetic portrait of somebody who was a victim of his own personality. Tom Lucey *had* to act as he did even though his actions were making the people nearest and dearest to him terribly unhappy. There is a great line in that story which hints at the central dilemma: "we love the dead according to our own natures and not theirs, or else how would we feel remorse?" I also think he liked "The Luceys" because, as an only child, he never experienced the conflicts that can arise between siblings, yet felt that he had got it right in the story. But this is only a guess on my part. If you think about it, a lot of his stories are about the kinds of misunderstandings that occur when people misread each other: I think of "The Cheat" (which is one of my favorite stories) and "Peasants" (which is another). And then there are the childrens' stories in which the question is "Who am I?" like "The Duke's Children" and "The Face of Evil" and "A Minority." I think he cared more about those stories than he did about the universally popular "First Confession" or "My Oedipus Complex." I remember one day someone went on and on about "First Confession" and he smiled rather wearily and replied, "As Yeats used to say whenever people praised 'The Lake Isle of Inisfree'—'Yes. That is my undoubted masterpiece.'"

Q. Why did you decide to edit your husband's work when he died?

A. To tell the truth, I think I didn't trust anybody else to do it. After all, I had spent a lot of time taking drafts of stories out of the wastepaper basket and putting them in order in files so I had a very possessive feeling about those files. Also I thought I knew how he worked and what he liked and didn't like. I thought I knew how important it was to get a certain order for the way stories were placed in a collection. He used to say that if you got the order right the stories would reflect off each other and in some cases even enhance each other. Vanity. Maybe that's what it was. Just plain pride on my part. But also I wanted something to do that would keep me close to him. He didn't seem quite so far away when I had his work in front of me and could immerse myself in it.

Q. [Considering all the times you've been interviewed], what is the most sensible question that the interviewer should have asked and hasn't asked about Frank O'Connor?

A. An interesting question! I think probably something like "What would you like to see happen to make his work better known?" I know that writers go through ups and downs and I feel that, at the moment, his reputation is suffering a bit. I am not sure why, but I suspect it is that some critics think he is too "easy" a writer, that he is not trendy enough. It is funny, because he is in almost every important anthology of short stories, and in an awful lot of school textbooks. And his work has been translated into German and Danish and Italian and, just this year, there is a new French collection (*Les Hôtes de la Nation*) published by Calmann-Levy. I think—I believe—that there is a timeless quality to his best work which means that it will just go on and on quietly being read and appreciated, and maybe that is a better situation than if he were hugely popular for a short time.

Q. Finally, I was wondering if you have a special memory you haven't yet told that, if it were told, would cast a new light on Frank O'Connor, letting one know something new about him?

A. So many memories ... it is hard to choose one. I remember that he would know how I was feeling without my having to tell him.

When we first moved to Ireland I found it very hard because we were living in a flat without central heating, and I couldn't find the things for the house I was used to, and one day he looked up from something he was working on, frowned, and said: "Sweetie—you look downright blue mouldy. You're missing home, aren't you? Here—here's some money. Go down to Brown Thomas and buy yourself something you don't need, but want. You deserve a treat." Another time, when I had a migraine he said: "There's something I can do to make you feel better. I'll read you the best book in the world for times when one feels as you feel now." "What is it?" I asked doubtfully. "James Stephens' *The Charwoman's Daughter*. It's a lovely, life affirming book. You'll feel better, I promise." As he read, I fell asleep, and when I woke up the migraine was gone. That was typical of him. He couldn't drive, he was hopeless around the house, but he knew how you were feeling and he was marvelously imaginative about doing things that made you feel better. He was also very funny. He used to write little verses against me. The one I remember best was occasioned by my asking to borrow his pen to write a check and then putting it in my own pocket. He never said a word, but that night as we were going to bed he intoned (in a Yeatsian manner): "Hallie Rich stole a pen / never gave it back again / punish her, O lord. Amen." How could I resist a man like that? The answer is, of course, that I couldn't.

The Interpretation of Tradition

Alan Titley

In the introduction to his survey of Irish literature, *The Backward Look*, Frank O'Connor asks, "Is there such a thing as an Irish literature, or is it merely two unrelated subjects linked together by a geographical accident?"[1] This question has been central to studies of literature in Ireland for more than a hundred years and has been answered, as could be expected, in at least two different ways. On the one hand scholars of the Irish language or of what is sometimes quaintly called "The Gaelic Tradition" have tended to ignore writing in English; while those involved in what used to be known as "The Anglo-Irish Tradition" generally treat writing in Irish as a kind of background which validates but doesn't disturb their own point of view. Thus standard works such as Douglas Hyde's *A Literary History of Ireland* or Robin Flower's *The Irish Tradition* and Seamus Deane's *A Short History of Irish Literature* or Maurice Harmon's *Modern Irish Literature 1800–1967* seem to be dealing with entirely different universes. It doth seem that "Irish" in these interminable debates can mean anything the author chooses it to mean within a clearly defined ideological position.

Although Frank O'Connor was never one to shirk a good row or hide his heart up his sleeve, it appears that his wrestling with this problem of one or two Irish literatures was genuine. He was ideally equipped to deal with the dilemma. Not only did he speak English and modern Irish, but he also was a considerable scholar of old Irish, which he learned out of his passion for the country's literature and civilization. This love is evident in all that he wrote about it, but most especially in his many translations of Irish poetry from the earliest times down unto the nineteenth century. Unlike most other writers on this topic, O'Connor concluded that he

---

[1] Frank O'Connor, *The Backward Look* (London: Macmillan, 1967), 1.

was dealing with one subject and that this merited a unified approach. Very few people have followed him down this road, although recent work by Declan Kiberd on modern Irish literature[2] and Robert Welch's *Oxford Companion to Irish Literature* straddle both traditions with generosity and honor.

To treat of literature in the Irish language from its beginning and to do so outside the academy of accepted scholars might have been a foolhardy thing to do. Scholars can be a notoriously prickly bunch, guarding their borders with as much zeal as any armed functionary; and scholars of old Irish in particular can be notoriously aggressive in defending their *tuath* with adzes and spears against encroaching blow-ins. O'Connor, although sufficiently knowledgeable and tough-skinned to beat off any attack, had the good fortune to be supported in some of his ventures by one of the high kings of Irish scholarship, Professor David Greene.[3] He may also have been seen to be at a disadvantage in approaching the critical enterprise as a mere writer, but mere writers, as we know, get inside the skin of craft and of wonder in ways that nobody else can.

Writers of English in Ireland have oft been required to stake out their position with regard both to the vast bulk of writing in Irish which preceded them and to the not inconsiderable stream which flows parallel to them. They can ignore it as many do, exploit it as Yeats did, parody it as Synge did, weave through it as Joyce did, have good fun with it as Myles na gCopaleen did, or worry over it as Thomas Kinsella does. There can also be the relationship of ambiguity which Frank O'Connor had. On the one hand he stated that literature in the Irish language "may be said to have died" with Brian Merriman in 1805[4]; on the other, he wrote stories in it himself and translated poetry composed well after the

---

[2]See in particular Declan Kiberd, *Inventing Ireland: The Literature of the Modern Nation* (London: Cape, 1995) and *Idir Dhá Chultúr* (Dublin: n.p., 1993).

[3]David Greene and Frank O'Connor, *A Golden Treasury of Irish Poetry AD. 600–1200* (London: Macmillan, 1967). He also says in his introduction to *The Backward Look* that in his discussions on Irish literature with Professor Greene "I have long ceased to remember whose ideas I have put forward, his or my own."

[4]Frank O'Connor, *Kings, Lords and Commons* (London: Macmillan, 1961), xiii.

death of Merriman.[5] Whatever he thought about his relationship to writing in Irish during his own time—and most of his life he simply kept his mouth shut about it—he saw it as a necessary duty to translate as much as possible of the earlier literature in order to make it known both at home and abroad. His books *The Wild Bird's Nest*, *Lords and Commons*, *The Fountain of Magic* and *The Midnight Court*, later variously selected to make *Kings, Lords and Commons* (1961), are among the very best translations of Irish poetry that we have. This is in itself curious because I am not aware of any success or much interest in original poetry by O'Connor himself.

It is doubly curious because any translator of poetry must have a lively and sympathetic understanding of the society and of the people who produced it. I cannot argue that O'Connor didn't have this, but he had a decidedly quirky and sometimes even batty judgment of writers and works of literature which is both his glory and his weakness. He can be at turns brilliantly insightful, searingly imaginative, and then just plain wrong. But we are always aware of an intense and personal engagement with the literature. He shows no tiresome detachment, no two-handed objectivity, and when he gets bored he just tells us straight on up. The result is to draw us into the debate, and when we disagree with him, as I do again and again with equal vehemence, we feel that he would thoroughly enjoy a robust altercation about the nature of Irish literature and the possibilities of translation.

In *The Backward Look*, for example, he has a wonderful way with sweeping generalizations. "The Irish had the choice between imagination and intellect," he declares, "and they chose imagination" (5). Matthew Arnold and Lord Macauley and purveyors of the myth of the helpless, hapless Celt would agree. "Unlike Daniel Corkery, who wrote a very lyrical and wrongheaded book on it, I can see nothing to admire in Irish eighteenth-century poetry" (*Backward Look* 114). This is an awful lot of poetry, and poets, and matters, and genres not to admire. Of twelfth-century Irish litera-

---

[5]*Kings, Lords, and Commons*, 131 and 132–35. Also Frank O'Connor, *The Fountain of Magic* (London: Macmillan, 1939), 64, 67, 68, 72. For one of his short stories in Irish see "Darcy i dTír na nÓg" in Tomás de Bhaldraithe, *Nuascéalaíocht* (Dublin: n.p., 1952), 24–32. Some of his radio essays or reminiscences which are very similar to his short stories appear in *Aeriris* (Dublin: n.p., 1976), edited by Proinsias Mac Aonghusa, under the titles "Fiche bliain d'óige," "Nodlaig as baile," "Leabhar a theastaigh uaim," and "Oíche shamhraidh."

ture he says, "It has no real prose, and consequently no intellectual content" (*Backward Look* 86). This will be grating music to the ears of our thousands of poets. Ranging over more than a thousand years, he refers to "the Irish type of mind, which is largely the mind of primitive man everywhere" (*Backward Look* 11). This could be construed as being an insult to the Irish or more seriously to those primitive men wheresoever they might dwell.

As against such opinions, his critical comments which depend on taste and judgment are often brave and incisive. He does argue that "scholars who are also men of letters should trust their instincts" (*Backward Look* 33), and we suspect he might be referring to himself. His opinion of the *Táin* or "Cattle Raid of Cooley" as "a simply appalling text" and a "rambling tedious account" of a long-forgotten war strike chords in honest readers (*Backward Look* 33). He captures the mood of what most aristocratic poets must have felt when poetry deteriorated from syllabic to accentual in the seventeenth century: "Every peasant poet was hammering it out with hobnailed boots like an ignorant audience listening to a Mozart minuet. It is no wonder if it offended O'Hussey's delicate ear; it often offends mine" (*Backward Look* 107). We know that O'Connor despised the poetry of vassals and churls composed in the misery of their hutments. And his assertion that the golden era of early Irish literature "ended with what I may call the Cistercian invasion, which in intellectual matters was direr than the Norman Invasion" may seem like the sweep of another totalizing impulse, but it does have pith and substance (*Backward Look* 256).

These whanging declarations make us wake up and take note. The exaggerating posture usually contains a big truth. His humorous description of the early Irish noun having twenty-five different cases with beautiful scholarly names such as the "neglective, desidative, fundative, privative, comitative, ascensive, augmentative, ingressive, depositive, parentative, progenitive, circumdative, and trespassive" (*Backward Look* 19–20) has its echoes in the professor who wondered how anybody could speak Old Irish at all since its verbal system was so complicated. O'Connor set himself the task of interpreting this tradition (which he often claimed to find "weird" and "strange") to a modern audience through his own translations.

There is no need again to revisit the difficulties or even the impossibilities of translation. The translator must choose either sounds or sense or meter or rhyme or a combination of them, or must interpret or crib or rewrite or whatever, but everything altogether can not be done. No matter what you do, finally and in sum, a translation is not the original poem. It may be a shadow, or an echo, or a ghost, or an excretion, or alike to a discursive description of live music, or a flat photograph of a once-pulsing multidimensional image, but the real thing it ain't. For any decent writer, words are physical, tactile, sensual things and the living stuff cannot be scraped away or washed off. The translator of Lorca's *Poet in New York*, Ben Belitt, argues that

> words, in whatever language, have a history which is not Esperanto or Sanskrit, or "the history of mankind," but the cultural consequence of their activity in the linguistic experience of the group—that words must be shouted into, like wells, rather than joined in a series like pipe-lengths; and finally, that for the poet, the momentum of words is as important and mysterious a trust as their matter, and that their momentum—their brio, their capacity to reveal the spirit at work within the letter—is rooted irrationally in the densities and ambiguities of the individual language.[6]

A translator will usually have the humility to acknowledge that cooking the original poetic goose leaves most of the sauce ungarnered and simply go for whatever is possible.

O'Connor's best translations from the early period of Irish literature are of those brief sententious poems occasionally written on the margins of manuscripts by either bored or frightened monks.

In the Ireland of the ninth century the monasteries feared the barbarian Vikings who terrorised western Europe as well as their own patch. One scribe wrote in O'Connor's version:

> Since tonight the wind is high,
> The sea's white mane a fury
> I need not fear the hordes of Hell
> Coursing the Irish Channel.
>   (*Kings, Lords and Commons* 45)

Brendan Kennelly's translation reads:

> There's a wicked wind tonight
> Wild upheaval in the sea;

---

[6]Ben Belitt, "Introduction," *Poet in New York/Un poeta en Nueva York* (New York: Grove Press, 1955), n.p.

No fear now that the Viking hordes
Will terrify me.[7]

It is very difficult to compare both of these verses and entirely unnecessary to do so. They are epigrams that depend for their effect
on our knowledge of what they are about and on their quick
brevity. There is the added simplicity that the original does not
carry any echoes that we can now grasp. Even though we can discern modern Irish lurking within the old, there is no way we can
extract its feel or touch its tenor. The emotional impact of Old Irish
is very largely a closed book. We can make a good guess at imitating its sound system but it reverberates nowhere; nothing sticks to
it. Translators of the earlier poetry have generally gone for these
brief marginal pieces because they circumvent the cultural battle of
dealing with longer legal or encomiastic or quasi-official verse
which did have echoes and did have all manner of cultural bag-
gage and dingleberries hanging out of it. Even though very few
people ever read these marginal poems for a thousand years between the ninth and the nineteenth century—perhaps nobody at
all in most cases—they appeal to a modern sensibility which
smells the pristine and the fresh-from-the-birth-of-the-Irish-world
off them, a dewy voice from the dawn of civilization. This is still
hard to resist and the religious verse in their midst gives succour
to tired twentieth-century Catholics in search of a coffee-table
Celtic spirituality.

A different cultural problem faced O'Connor in his wrestlings
with the later middle ages. The poetry of courtly love was common to Ireland, Britain, France and elsewhere in Western Europe.
Although he was sceptical of "vague suggestions of influence from
Provencal and Norman-French" (*Backward Look* 97), it is generally
accepted now that if the jongleurs themselves didn't bring their
wares ashore then somebody certainly did jongle them into Ireland. The difficulty here is not one of making the strange accessible
but rather a technical turn of getting complicated Irish verse into
English. In a note on his own translations from the same period,
Robin Flower comments that "Some apology is perhaps necessary
for the substitution of simpler English lyrical measures for the
intricate and subtly interwoven harmonies of alliteration and
internal rhyme in the Irish. But the attempt to borrow those qualities of verse could only end in a mechanic exercise, which might be

---

[7]Brendan Kennelly, *Love of Ireland: Poems from the Irish* (Cork and
Dublin: Mercier, 1989), 17.

a metrical commentary, but could not be poetry. And to translate poetry by less than poetry is a sin beyond absolution."[8] One feels that O'Connor would entirely concur. He solves the metrical problems by simply ignoring them, apart from giving his poems the shape and cut of what the originals looked like on the page. And yet in many cases, the point of these poems was their metrical ingenuity. Our age would accuse them of being all technique and no feeling, whereas the truth might be that the feeling resided in the perfection of the technique. It appears to be poetry of the starched collar, but within it bulges a powerful and sinewy neck. If we compare O'Connor's "Hugh Maguire" to James Clarence Mangan's "Ode to the Maguire,"[9] both of which are a translation of Eochaidh Ó hEoghusa's poem to his chief and patron composed in 1601 while he was on a campaign against the troops of the strengthening English conquistadores, we can see that O'Connor at least keeps the cut of the original. He hints at tautness and makes the requisite nods towards the coiled and smoldering passion of Ó hEoghusa. Mangan on the other hand is wild and diffuse and cumulative and exclamatory and turns the author into a Jacobean mad dog.

A translation can do only what a translation can do. If it is the vector of something, even anything, of the original we can be a mite happy. If O'Connor had a knack it was to get at the spirit of the thing and let that spirit sing if it could. In translating most Irish poetry from the late middle ages until the present century, the translator simply has to dump any notion of getting the meter right. There is not much point in being a life-support system for a piece of scaffolding. A good translator must soften hard facts, and a good reader must take these boobs to be self-evident. O'Connor cottoned on to this early on and chose poetry which answered his own nature and sensibility. He was distinctly uncomfortable with the literary poetry from the mid-seventeenth century on, perceiving in it too many lumpen elements with neither the craft nor sullen art of the Bardic era, or the artless facility of the folk song. Consequently, we only get the very best of Ó Rathaille from him, one solitary poem by the great word-musician Eoghan Rua Ó

---

[8]Robin Flower, *Poems and Translations* (Dublin: Lilliput Press, 1994; orig. pub. London 1931), 109.

[9]In Fiana Griffin, *Extracts from Irish Literature* (Dublin: Linguaviva Centre, 1992), 24–25. O'Connor describes it as "a torrent of nineteenth century romantic eloquence" in *The Backward Look* (101).

Súilleabháin, and nothing at all by the who of whos of Irish poetry
in the late seventeenth century, Dáibhí Ó Bruadair. Scrubbed from
the record also, to name but seven more luminaries amongst
dozens well translated by others, were Pádraigín Haicéad, Seán
Clárach Mac Domhnaill, Séamas Mac Cuarta, Donnchadh Rua Mac
Con Mara, Mícheál Óg Ó Longain, Cathal Buí Mac Giolla Gunna,
and Peadar Ó Doirnín. This seems all the stranger when we note
his love of Anthony Raftery, a person whose works he describes as
being "as close as genuine poetry has ever come to doggerel"
(*Kings, Lords and Commons* 132). O'Connor, however, being the independent spirit he was, did not suffer from a literary-academic
complex and hoisted from the tradition just precisely what he
liked and nothing else.

He did like the two greatest poems of the last decades of the
eighteenth century, and his versions of them are his finest and
most important as a translator. "Caoineadh Airt Uí Laoghaire"
("The Lament for Art O'Leary") and "Cúirt an Mheán Oíche"
("The Midnight Court") were composed within seven years of
each other but are about as different as the proverbial chalk from
the legendary cheese. "The Lament for Art O'Leary" is a traditional keen or funeral poem composed in an extempore fashion in
honor of the dead person. In this case, it was sung or chanted by
Eileen O'Connell on the discovery of the body of her murdered
husband, and perhaps added to by herself and by others for some
time afterwards. Arthur O'Leary was an officer in the Austrian
Army—the Irish having none of their own and certainly not wishing to enlist in the British one—and when on leave at home treated
the authorities with much less than the obsequious respect which
they thought was their due as a ruling caste. They did what all
great powers do with the annoying little gadflies who nip at them.
They shot him. There is some rich irony to be had in the fact that
one of the great poems of the western world about death and
blood-letting was occasioned by the agents of the British Vampire.
The former professor of poetry at Oxford University, Peter Levi,
called it "the greatest poem written in these islands in the whole of
the eighteenth century" and opined that "Goethe, and Thomas
Gray, and Wordsworth, and Matthew Arnold … might all have
thought so."[10] Whatever about the opinion, he errs a little when he

---

[10]Peter Levi, *The Lamentation of the Dead with "The Lament for Arthur
O'Leary" by Eileen O'Connell translated by Eilís Dillon* (London: Anvil P. Poetry, 1984), 18.

refers to it being *written*. It was, of course, an oral artifact and survived beyond all those countless thousands of other laments because of the force of the poetry and the tragedy of the story.

Its orality presents its own problems to the translator. And not just the fact of its being spoken, or rather sung, or chanted, or wailed, but the fact of its being torn from its natural surroundings of death and performance. "Natural" here is also difficult. The lament was generally composed and performed at the wake of the dead soul. These wakes were, more or less, a party for the departing person (and a celebration of life for those still around) accompanied by booze and whatever passed for debauchery at that time. The corpses themselves were often brought into the music or the card games or even the dance (which is probably the origin of the stiffness of Irish stepdancers). This pagan relic was, not surprisingly, in constant conflict with the church, which viewed death as a much more solemn occasion. The traditional lament was a composition without prayer or angels or devils or intimations of the other world. It was an explosion of remembered life in the presence of death. And while there were probably no fun and games at Art's wake, because of the unnatural nature of his murder, it had its origin and its being in this strange ritual as exotic to us now as the burning of Hindu widows or the binding of Chinese female feet.

O'Connor could only translate the words ripped from their sockets. He gets the rhythm dead-on, so to speak. It is a rhythm based on a long breath and on a single thought. When the breath gives out and the thought finishes, the stanza, if that's what they are, dies. A kind of pantometer. There would have been some break in a longer piece like this, which speaks for itself:

> My love and my mate
> That I never thought dead
> Till your horse came to me
> With bridle trailing,
> All blood from forehead
> To polished saddle
> Where you should be,
> Either sitting or standing;
> I gave one leap to the threshold,
> A second to the gate,
> A third upon its back.
> I clapped my hands
> And off at a gallop;
> I never lingered

Till I found you lying
By a little furze-bush
Without pope or bishop
Or priest or cleric
One prayer to whisper
But an old, old woman,
And her cloak about you,
And your blood in torrents—
Art O'Leary—
I did not wipe it off,
I drank it from my palms.[11]

The original is as simple as that also, and as direct, and as uncompromising. It is difficult to foul up on the headlong rush of the poem and most translators have simply opened the gates and let it rip. The only infelicities take place with exclamations and endearments, which can be very culturally and linguistically specific. O'-Connor, for example, translated Eileen's *mo chara is mo lao thu!* as "my love and my calf." *Cara* is certainly more colloquially "friend" than "love," although it is analogous with other Indo-European languages that have the 'Car' bit linked with love; *lao* is certainly and literally a calf, but it hardly has romantic echoes for the normal twentieth-century English speaker who might not appreciate being compared with a young cow. Eilis Dillon gets round it differently by speaking of "My friend and my treasure," or "My friend and my heart,"[12] while Brendan Kennelly makes do with "My lover" or "My man," which may not be accurate but are at least sayable (*Love of Ireland* 57–64). On the other hand, O'Connor can hardly be faulted for a line such as "You gave me everything," which later became the first line of an early Beatles song and now jingles in the head accordingly.

"The Midnight Court," which Frank O'Connor published in a separate volume,[13] has a much more sensibility-friendly look to it. It is a poem of more than a thousand lines of rhyming couplets in which the women of Ireland put their men on trial for being sexu-

---

[11]*Kings, Lords and Commons* (111–12). This is a slightly different version from that published originally in *The Fountain of Magic* (London: Macmillan, 1939), 75–85.

[12]See Levi, *The Lamentation of the Dead*, 23–35.

[13]Frank O'Connor, *The Midnight Court, a Rhythmical Bacchanalia from the Irish of Bryan Merryman, translated by Frank O'Connor* (London and Dublin: Fridberg, 1945).

ally timid, or just plain no good. It is funny, bawdy, explicit, dramatic and intelligent and in one declamation seems to destroy the stereotype of the repressed and puritanical peasant. That is to say, it is a poem which represents the direct opposite of the regnant assumptions of those ignorant of Irish culture. Apart from it being instantly attractive, and instantly accessible to people without any background in Irish society or history or literature, people are drawn to it because it is an endless source of ammunition for cultural and ideological battles. To the anti-clerical it is anti-clerical; to the libertarian it is libertarian; to the nativist native; to the Europhile Europhiliac; to the modernist modern; to the feminist it is pro-women or anti-women, depending on which side of that particular Paglian-Dworkish camp they belong. This is partly because we know so little about the intentions of its author, Brian Merriman, and, intentional fallacies apart, so very little again about his life, origins, or literary circle. It is the kind of debate Frank O'-Connor jumped into with his two feet flying and his two fists flailing.

His translation was published in 1945 and was promptly banned. This lengthy quote from his introduction gives a fair idea of the flavor of the ideas he was furthering and the battles he was fighting with this work:

> There is no tablet in Clare Street to mark where Bryan Merriman, the author of *The Midnight Court* died, nor is there ever likely to be, for Limerick has a reputation for piety. Merryman [sic] was born about the middle of the eighteenth century in a part of Ireland which must then have been as barbarous as any in Europe—it isn't exactly what one would call civilized today. He earned five or ten pounds a year by teaching school in a god-forsaken village called Feakle in the hills above the Shannon, eked it out with a little farming, and somehow or other managed to read and translate a great deal of contemporary literature, English and French. Even with compulsory education, the English language, and public libraries you would be hard set to find a young Clareman of Merryman's class today who knew as much of Lawrence and Gide as he knew of Savage, Swift, Goldsmith and, most of all, Rousseau. How he managed it in an Irish-speaking community is a mystery. He was obviously a man of powerful objective intelligence; his obituary describes him as a "teacher of mathematics" which may explain something; and though his use of "Ego Vos" for the marriage service suggests a Catholic upbringing, the religious background of *The Midnight Court* is protestant, which may explain more. He certainly had

> intellectual independence. In *The Midnight Court* he imitated
> contemporary English verse, and it is clear that he had resolved
> to cut adrift entirely from traditional Gaelic forms. His
> language—that is its principal glory—is also a complete break
> with literary Irish. It is the spoken Irish of Clare.... Intellectually
> Irish literature did not exist. What Merryman aimed at was
> something that had never been guessed at in Gaelic Ireland; a
> perfectly proportioned work of art on a contemporary subject,
> with every detail subordinated to the central theme. The poem is
> as classical as the Limerick Custom House; and fortunately, the
> Board of Works has not been able to get at it. (*Midnight Court* 1–
> 2)

There is very little in that chunk above that is defensible on even
mildly scholarly grounds. Even if we allow the entirely understandable barbs against Limerick and do not deconstruct the idea
of a "powerful objective intelligence" there is enough bullshivism
in it to keep us busy for years to come. O'Connor's picture of an
Irish-speaking world completely cut off from the rest of the universe is a picture of his own invention, and his assertion that Merriman imitated contemporary English verse has been easily
demonstrated to be false. It can only have been because he was at
constant war with the kind of Victorian Catholicism which held
sway in Ireland that he imagined Merriman to be an "intellectual
Protestant," even though others might see that to be a contradiction in terms. There was always a kind of lapsed Irish Catholic
having recovered from their scars who confused tepid Protes-
tantism with a liberal point of view. Add to that O'Connor's (let us
call it) hatred of de Valera, whom he saw as a severe, controlling,
puritanical figure and whom he associated with devotion to the
Irish language, and we can follow his train of thought that Merriman had to be influenced by English literature and by the philosophy of the Enlightenment. He went further and asserted that Merriman's ideas and spirit came directly to him from Robbie Burns;
when it was pointed out to him that Merriman came first he simply declared: "On his own statements the scholars believe he came
before Burns, but the thing is impossible. He must derive from
Burns!"[14] A classic case of if you don't like the evidence, deny it.

---

[14]*Kings, Lords and Commons* (xii). O'Connor sees revolutionary mores
and boldness of spirit where others simply see good rustic fun. David
Daiches in his *Robert Burns and his World* (London: Thames and Hudson,
1971), writes, "But though Burns' sexual problems proved to be unique,
he was far from unique in his country fornications. The simple fact is that

There is nothing in "The Midnight Court" that is not the common stock-in-trade of European medieval literatures. All of the themes of free-love, unmarried bachelors, horny priests, unfulfilled women, lusty young men, deceived cuckolds, healthy love-children and dicey marriages were as much part of literature in Irish as of literature in any other tongue. What made Merriman different is that he bound it all together in one large dramatic and poetic work of art which was driven by a bonking swashbuttoning style. If O'Connor's judgments were simply wrong, he gained a kind of victory when his translation was banned. It gave him publicity which he would never have got otherwise and proved once again that too much moral fiber produces a lot of crap. Consequent on the Censorship Board's banning, O'Connor wrote to *The Irish Times* and his letter was published on 17 July 1946. Part of it read:

> Under the Censorship Act imposed on Irish writers by the Cosgrave government there was established a secret tribunal, empowered, without hearing evidence and without having to answer for its actions in law, to inflict some of the penalties of a court of law: to deprive an Irish writer of his good name, to seize his property and destroy his livelihood in so far as any writer earns a livelihood in this country. Thus, murderers, abortionists, bookies and publicans continued to retain the protection of the law, while literary men—some, like Mr. Shaw, the glory of their country—were outlawed.... The Censorship Board banned my translation; they did not ban the original.... The implication of this was clear; that I had deliberately introduced material which was not to be found in any other edition, and that this material was sufficiently indecent to justify the banning of the whole work.[15]

If O'Connor wanted a debate on the specific question of his translation of *Cúirt an Mheán Oíche* and on the more general one of censorship, he certainly got it. The correspondence continued through July and August of 1946 and is one of the very few examples of a lengthy discussion of the merits of a work of Irish literature carried out in the public domain of a newspaper. One reader from County Mayo wondered what all the fuss was about:

---

such activity was one of the few pleasures available to the Scottish peasantry, and in spite of the thundering of the kirk ... it remained extremely common throughout Burns' lifetime" (29).

[15]Frank O'Connor, letter to *The Irish Times* under the title "Justice—How are you?" (17 July 1946).

The more I read the correspondence on this subject, the more I admire the sturdy virtue of my grandmother. For everybody who knows that famous, but disastrous, poem knows that the original is far more hectic than Frank O'Connor's (more or less) bowdlerized translation. Yet that heroic woman (my grandmother) must have heard that poem recited scores of times at wakes and weddings (as I have) and with additions more lurid than any lines which have been printed. Yet somehow she managed to go to her grave with her character intact.[16]

More seriously and to the point the Censorship Board itself was drawn into the fray and required to defend its actions. James Hogan was its chairman and had little enough time for Merriman and probably less for O'Connor:

His [i.e. O'Connor's] letter is a typically arrogant production. No one, apparently, unless he is a minor poet, or at least of Mr. O'-Connor's literati, can possibly rise to the level of one of Mr. O'-Connor's masterpieces.... He would like them to regard him as the modern Irish literary equivalent of a Servetus or a Voltaire, a sublime victim to a wretched clique of obscurantists.... it was not enough that Merriman's Cúirt is an immoral poem (to put it very mildly). It must also be made to sound a note of blasphemy.[17]

He went on to accuse Merriman of "searching for what he would like to find in the way of scandalous and offensive meanings" but he really dug his canines into O'Connor: "I would also like to make it clear ... that altogether apart from Mr. O'Connor's gross mistranslations, his *Midnight Court* is, in my opinion a book which should not be allowed in public circulation.... I do not think there is a magistrate in Ireland who would allow this book to pass." This was not the kind of letter designed to cool the atmosphere, and O'Connor replied that "Whatever one may say of Merryman's poem, it is not immoral. Mr. de Valera's favourite author, Machiavelli, is."[18] Hogan returned serve with: "Mr. O'Connor was ill-advised to call his *Midnight Court* a translation. As an adaptation to

---

[16]J.B.S. Co. Mayo, Letters to the Editor, "The Midnight Court," *The Irish Times*, 1 August 1946.

[17]James Hogan, Letters to the Editor, "The Midnight Court," *The Irish Times*, 27 July 1946.

[18]Frank O'Connor, Letters to the Editor, "The Midnight Court," *The Irish Times*, 3 August 1946.

his own humour and prejudice, his *Midnight Court* may have some merit here and there; as a translation it has none."[19]

This was one of the first references to the merit of the work *as a translation*. Much of the discussion had been predicated on the belief that a translation is a faithful rendering of an original, a kind of surrender and regrant which only changed the outer appearances. James Hogan drew the line between them. Then the editor of the original poem (who had produced an excellent scholarly edition in 1912 on which O'Connor's translation was based) entered the lists. In his letter he said that he had met O'Connor on College Green and they fell to discussing the *Court* and the correspondence in the papers. And then:

> On my asking why he had not made a close translation, which might be of use to some, his reply was: "Were I to do that, I should only be trotting after Merriman." So we may conclude that what he has produced is the result of a trot on his own account, and a most miserable result it is. I have no hesitation in declaring that it is a misrepresentation, a distortion of the sense, a false picture, and in one line in particular, theologically offensive.... Altogether, it is enough to cause Merriman to turn in his grave.[20]

It was probably quite unusual to have the contents of a private conversation aired so publicly. O'Connor denied what had happened but added, "But I now perceive the value of my wife's remark that in a country like Ireland a man who values his reputation will use an elaborate filing system."[21] The editor, Risteárd Ó Foghludha, was not at all happy to be accused of lying and reasserted his version of events. He said of O'Connor: "He must be the victim of a most serious lapse of memory, but he might remember a particular question which he put to me, viz., 'When are you bringing out a new edition (of the original) so that I may crib?' These are his actual words: my memory is excellent."[22]

---

[19]James Hogan, Letters to the Editor, "The Midnight Court," *The Irish Times*, 9 August 1946.

[20]Fiachra Éilgeach, Letters to the Editor, "The Midnight Court," *The Irish Times*, 9 August 1946.

[21]Frank O'Connor, Letters to the Editor, "The Midnight Court," *The Irish Times*, 10 August 1946.

[22]Fiachra Éilgeach, Letters to the Editor, "The Midnight Court," *The Irish Times*, 11 August 1946.

Although this debate solved nothing it at least raised publicly, however tangentially, the important issues of the morality of literature and the nature of translation. And even if O'Connor's own evaluation of the nature of the poem is generally dotty, he managed to access enough of the spirit of Merriman to make the finest of the (at least) ten full translations of the poem that have so far been done. The frabjous love of life, the Rabelaisian pisstake, the spirited admixture of the comic and the serious is not confined to any one culture or era. It is a universal cast of mind. Some have it, some don't. In the end it does not matter much what *The Midnight Court* is supposed to be about. Some Irish culturists have a vested interest in the primitive, the pagan, the folk, the poets in their darkened booths with stones upon their bellies pumping their brains; others wish to see the Irish world as utterly cosmopolitan, ultimately derivative, a part of the main. O'Connor veered between these depending on when he wrote and who was the enemy. His idea of Irish being a primary literature, meaning one "that is in the main original" (which he put forward in *The Backward Look* [41]) has some credence for the earlier period. His assertion that "the only significant element is English" in the Irish literature of the eighteenth century is pure tosh (*The Backward Look* 109).

What can never be denied is his passionate love for the thousand and a half years of literature in the Irish language. His translations lift the cloak of time and give the general reader an entrance into the Gaelic Irish tradition. Prescinding from all that stuff about stylistic equivalences, and how much a cultural conduit can carry, and what is or is not spirited away in translation, he presents the Gaelic world through time and form with an energy and courage that creates its own validity and truth. And he does this because behind every poet he translates we can clearly hear his own integral voice growling unmistakably away. Whatever gets lost in translation, Frank O'Connor certainly does not.

O'Connor's "Backward Look": The Irish Writer's Struggle for Identity and an Irish Tradition

John C. Kerrigan

Probably the best and most memorable comment on Frank O'Connor's critical capacity remains that of his old friend, Sean O'Faolain:

> [O'Connor] was like a man who takes a machine gun to a shooting gallery. Everybody falls flat on his face, the proprietor at once takes to the hills, and when it is all over, and [you] cautiously peep up, you will find that he has wrecked the place but got three perfect bull's-eyes.[1]

Indeed, the bulk of O'Connor's critical writings has long been considered suspect for the very reason to which O'Faolain alludes: O'Connor was a writer of short stories who lacked discipline and consistency as a critic.[2] Throughout his six books of literary criticism, O'Connor conceded these faults, repeatedly confessing to being opinionated, untrained, and instinctive as a critic. His formal education did not extend beyond grade school, and what he knew was almost wholly the result of what he taught himself. Still, as such, he was free from institutional preconceptions and conformity, and at his best, Frank O'Connor the literary critic was incisive, honest, and original.

Flawed as O'Connor's criticism is, it is certainly not without value; nor, for that matter, is it excessively dated. O'Connor's ear-

---

[1] *Vive Moi!* (Boston: Little, Brown, and Co., 1964), 369.

[2] See, for example, "A Cargo of Impure Art," the fifth chapter of Maurice Wohlgelernter's *Frank O'Connor: An Introduction* (New York: Columbia University Press, 1977) and James Matthews's biography of O'-Connor, *Voices* (New York: Atheneum, 1983), 302, 341.

liest critical efforts, *The Art of the Theatre* and *Towards an Appreciation for Literature*, which were written over fifty years ago, remain readable as general introductory approaches. The theories he expressed in *The Mirror in the Roadway* and *The Lonely Voice*, studies of the modern novel and the short story, respectively, remain speculative and controversial, often unprovable yet not disproved. Among these, O'Connor's term "submerged population group" and disapproval of James Joyce's later work[3] are theoretical assertions which have remained particularly relevant in criticism since O'Connor's death. Although his critical writings have often been considered in terms of their failure as objective criticism, still his attempts provoke readers with every turn of the page and occasionally produce flashes of brilliant insight, "bull's-eyes," as O'-Faolain called them.

O'Connor's last and arguably his most significant scholarly endeavor, *A Short History of Irish Literature: A Backward Look*,[4] like his books on the novel and the short story, was conceived from a series of university lectures which were diligently prepared, well-attended, and well-received. O'Connor's *Backward Look* is still not entirely free from the deficiencies of his earlier critical works, but in this last critical effort, he seems to have had a more vested interest in the material he presented. Whereas in earlier critical efforts he had referred to himself as a mere "'belletristic trifler'"[5] and had very rarely cited more than a few critical texts on which he had gauged his own speculations, in *A Short History* he was on much more solid ground. Far more than any other of his critical works, *A Short History* relies on a significant number of scholarly sources

---

[3]"Submerged population group" was a term O'Connor used to describe the particular set of characters which inhabits the territory of any given short story writer's corpus. See *The Lonely Voice* (New York: World Publishing Co., 1963), 20. For the most recent and most complete scholarly engagement with O'Connor's view of Joyce, see James D. Alexander's essay, "Frank O'Connor's Joyce Criticism," in *The Journal of Irish Literature* 21 (May 1992): 40–53.

[4](New York: G.P. Putnam's Sons, 1967). This is the American edition of *The Backward Look: A Survey of Irish Literature* (London: Macmillan, 1967). Abbreviated versions of these titles, *A Short History* and *The Backward Look*, will be used interchangeably throughout this essay. All references to page numbers within the essay refer to *A Short History of Irish Literature*, unless otherwise indicated.

[5]O'Connor in Maurice Wohlgelernter's *Frank O'Connor*, 109.

(listed in a "Selected Bibliography"), and his speculations were verified by (or at least tested on) friends who were among the foremost Celtic scholars of his day—Daniel Binchy, Philip Edwards, and David Greene.[6] Perhaps most important, as O'Connor's final completed work, published posthumously in 1967, *The Backward Look* capped a career which was, in many ways, a struggle to justify the very notion of Irish literature.

Indeed, in setting out to write a short history of Irish literature, O'Connor faced a theoretical challenge from the start: scholars of his day barely acknowledged that Ireland had a literature worthy of critical study. Irish universities, for example, did not offer a formal course on Irish literature (or on any aspect of Irish culture, for that matter). Furthermore, respected scholarship seriously questioned the notion of an Irish literary tradition. Vivian Mercier's *The Irish Comic Tradition*, in 1962, had rather cautiously posited the existence of a tradition, declaring (for example) that "the reader should ... be wary of assuming a greater homogeneity between the two literatures than actually exists" and, ultimately, that

> the whole subject of the relationship between Gaelic and Anglo-Irish literature has been bedeviled by so many intemperate generalizations on both sides of the argument that I was determined not to force my own views upon the reader.[7]

Mercier's book was hailed as a standard for Irish literary criticism,[8] and thus it is hardly surprising that the most extensive review of O'Connor's *Short History*, American professor Kevin Sullivan's, cites Mercier's book as the "best attempt" to write Irish literary history. Sullivan declares that proving that Ireland has a literary history would require its author to demonstrate a continuity between the ancient Irish-language literature and the twentieth-cen-

---

[6]James Matthews refers to Osborn Bergin and Binchy as the "foremost Celtic scholars" in *Voices: A Life of Frank O'Connor* (New York: Atheneum, 1983), 88. Binchy, Greene, and Edwards are acknowledged as having specifically collaborated on the theorizing for *A Short History* (8).

[7]Vivian Mercier, *The Irish Comic Tradition* (London: Clarendon Press, 1962; Souvenir Press, 1991), xi–xii.

[8]Indeed, according to the billing for the 1991 edition, Mercier's is "The key book of Irish literary criticism," one that "has never been superseded and remains a key work for any student of Irish and Anglo-Irish literature."

tury English-language literature, but identifying such continuity seems an "impossible task" to him, since Ireland's literature is so "various, complicated and obscure."[9]

Even if the task of creating a literary history of Ireland seemed virtually impossible by critics' standards, O'Connor believed that his "backward look" was an absolute necessity, not for the critics, but for the Irish people:

> The abandonment of every mark of cultural identity by the Irish people during the nineteenth century has left a historical gap that is hard to span. Ours is probably the only civilized country which has no such thing as a chair of national literature; thousands of students pass through our universities each year with less knowledge of their own culture than one would expect to find among American students. The literature of the past is simply ignored; the literature of our own time is either ignored or banned by law. (1)

What O'Connor did, then, in constructing his *Backward Look*, was to purposefully impose a continuity upon Ireland's past. Sullivan charged that O'Connor was writing a story, creating a myth, rather than objectively portraying Ireland's past; there is some truth to this claim. Even if O'Connor did perceive his task in a serious, scholarly way, his aim was only partially motivated by objectivity; he also, and perhaps more importantly, hoped to awaken and restore the cultural memory of the Irish. O'Connor consciously subsumed the multiple literatures of Ireland under the singular name of Irish literature, although he was mindful of the generalizations, particularly the essentialized version of Irishness, upon which previous generations had relied. His formulation of history showed Irish literature to have a continuity in terms of phases of colonization such that survival, the cultural memory itself, was the predominant theme. In this way, O'Connor's history of Irish literature is a series of recurrent, perhaps even cyclical, struggles with colonial identity.

O'Connor's purpose in this short history can be more clearly understood in light of his seemingly inconsistent comments on Matthew Arnold's *On the Study of Celtic Literature*: he simultaneously praises it as "excellent criticism" and damns it as much "bad work in the 'Celtic Twilight' manner" (159). More importantly than either of these statements, and no matter what he or anyone

---

[9]Kevin Sullivan, "A Labor of Love and Learning," *The Nation* (28 August 1967), 149.

else thinks of Arnold's work, O'Connor insists that Irish scholars should recognize the importance of *On the Study of Celtic Literature* in "making Ireland and things Irish dignified in the eyes of our own people" (159). To help the Irish respect and cherish their past struggles in the hope that it might provide inspiration to subsequent generations: this was O'Connor's reason for lecturing at Trinity and Maynooth, for translating Irish poetry into English, and for writing *A Short History of Irish Literature*.

It must be said, as well, that O'Connor believed inspiration could only come from knowledge, and that, without a knowledge of the past, "we have nothing and are nothing" (230). Literature, for O'Connor, played a most significant role in the cultural memory of the people, for it not only inspired, it also helped to bridge the gaps in one's cultural knowledge. The Irish Literary Renaissance served both of these ends, but the revival itself by the early 1940s "was all over and done with," according to O'Connor (229). The revival had restored interest in Ireland's early literature, primarily by making Irish-language works available to an English-speaking audience either through direct translation or through figurative transposition into a contemporary context (in a play like Yeats's *Cathleen Ni Houlihan*, for example). However, once the revival ended, Ireland's knowledge of its literary past was once again threatened. Particularly, poems from earlier periods of the island's history faced extinction by virtue of the continuing decline of knowledge of the Irish language. Consequently, at various stages of his life, O'Connor devoted a significant effort to learning and translating Old and Middle Irish poetry for the sake of the Irish people.[10] Still, one should not assume that O'Connor was *merely* carrying on an outdated, unfashionable, retrogressive crusade or embracing the literary revival and its goals *in toto*. His *Short History* may seem a mere extension of the "backward look" undertaken by the revivalists forty years earlier, but O'Connor drew some clear distinctions in this regard, as closer analysis will show.

Simultaneous with the threat to language posed by the end of the revival, a puritanical environment began to prevail in the new nation, such that censorship rendered a great deal of modern literature—and some earlier literatures—inaccessible to the Irish people. O'Connor and O'Faolain became prominent figures in the Ire-

---

[10]Julia Carlson, ed., *Banned in Ireland: Censorship and the Irish Writer* (Athens: University of Georgia Press, 1990), 14.

land of the 1940s largely due to their protests against censorship.[11] These battles raged on for the rest of O'Connor's life; in one such protest, just a few years before his *Short History* was published, O'Connor declared that

> To me the most awful thing about the censorship is the way it perpetuates the negative attitude we oppose to every manifesta- tion of intellect and scholarship.... We have a Censorship Board, but we have no publishers. We have a great literature, published by Englishmen and Americans, and, thanks to our censors, ninety-nine percent of it is out of print and unobtainable, so that, as I have said before, we have brought up a country which knows nothing of its own country, or its own literature.[12]

Given this impetus, O'Connor proceeded in *A Short History* to tell a story characterized by great shifts of colonial upheaval. His useful distinctions between periods are mostly categorized in terms of historical occurrences, so that chapters such as "The Norse and After," "Romanesque and Gothic," "The Renaissance in Ireland," and "Anglo-Irish Literature" are named according to the several invasions of the Norse, the Normans, and the British—in- vasions which had a direct influence on the literature of the day. The history itself is in many ways the key to O'Connor's literary interpretation. He approaches each literary work by taking into ac- count the two things he said should always be considered in summing up any man's achievement: "the man's character and the character of the circumstances he had to deal with."[13] The first half of the book, in particular, places much greater emphasis on the cir- cumstances. Thus, it is not surprising that the first few chapters of *A Short History* are as anthropological as they are literary, or that a chapter titled "The Background of Modern Irish Literature" fo- cuses on the circumstances of the Irish potato famine.

Equally relevant to O'Connor's approach throughout is the objective he sets for the book on the first page of the first chapter. After discussing Rudolf Thurneysen's theory of the Irish mind, O'Connor claims that "with certain qualifications," what Thurney-

---

[11]James Alexander, "The Artist at Home," *Twentieth Century Literature* 36 (Fall 1990): 347.

[12]"Frank O'Connor on Censorship," in *Banned in Ireland: Censorship and the Irish Writer*, 155–56; rpt. from *The Dubliner* (March 1962), 39–44.

[13]From O'Connor's speech at Yeats's graveside in 1965, quoted from Sean O'Faolain's "A World of Fitzies," a review of Maurice Wohlgelern- ter's *Frank O'Connor*, in *Times Literary Supplement* (29 April 1977), 503.

sen says is true, although "he does not discuss why things were so, which is part of my story." O'Connor's intention to account for "why things were so" is significant, not only because it epitomizes his approach but because it reveals where his speculations deviate from the facts provided by his sources.

O'Connor's causal speculations seem predominantly linked to his comment that foreign rule has produced, for the Irish and other colonized peoples, a certain stubbornness about the past (7). Thus, his initial attempt to understand the people of early Ireland quickly becomes a more general attempt to enter into "the Irish type of mind, which is largely the mind of primitive man everywhere. To primitive man the greatest possible nightmare is the loss of his identity" (11). Perhaps intending to be provocative, O'Connor chooses a stereotypical and even pejorative word to imply a commonality between "primitive" humans and the Irish: the threat of the loss of identity of a colonized people. O'Connor even seems to define the Irish by no other characteristic than their having been perpetually colonized. He comments, for example, that it "is the tragedy of colonialism that it is self-perpetuating, and that each generation of exploiters considers the previous one fair game" (85).

From this perspective, O'Connor examines the literary remains of Ireland from the Middle Ages to his own day with a keen eye toward the impact of political circumstances on the literature. Though early Ireland was often somewhat chaotic politically, with its host of invaders and constant threat of invasion, at least Ireland maintained something of a cultural continuity in that its colonizers, particularly the Normans, assimilated into Irish society rather than imposing their values upon the subjugated people. O'Connor argues, uniquely, that a feudal system permitting Irish identity was maintained for years because of class differences between the colonizers and the colonized—and that the loss of Irish cultural identity was ultimately the result of the changing class-based influence in British society. O'Connor maintains that the most severe and most successful British efforts to destroy Irish cultural identity were a consequence of the Cromwellian wars and the harsh Penal Laws which followed them—the product of an English lower- and middle-class political movement (109).

Throughout, even in discussing the "Olympian" figures of the literary revival, O'Connor continually refers to the peculiarly political nature of Irish literature. He identifies, for example, the first masterpiece of Irish literature written in English as Swift's "A Modest Proposal," adding,

> and I would ask you to remember that it is a political tract. That political note, I would suggest, is characteristic of all Anglo-Irish literature. I know no other literature so closely linked to the immediate reality of politics. (121)

O'Connor likewise regards O'Casey's *The Plough and the Stars* as perhaps the greatest of modern Irish plays, not because of its political subject matter, but because it so finely captures the immediate reality of Irish experience (219). Even the literary works of minor Irish writers O'Connor addresses by virtue of the burden of the circumstances they faced. William Carleton is a prime example: O'Connor perceives him as a writer of great promise and natural genius who was thwarted by the tensions of a divided and politically-charged audience. Carleton's ambitions to succeed as a writer and to become a classical scholar were complicated by a number of obstacles. Mainly, there was a religious difficulty. He became a Protestant, perhaps to gain admittance to the learned classes, but his writing thus necessarily involved a constant struggle "between Protestants who wanted his work to be a denunciation of Catholicism and Catholics who wanted to read nothing about themselves that was not treacle" (140). O'Connor also describes the linguistic barriers of Carleton's day in a particularly cogent fashion:

> If the people were to survive they had to speak English, and any little knowledge they had was based upon Latin. Accordingly they tended to avoid Anglo-Saxon words, the connotations of which they were not familiar with; were chary of Norman-French words, and as often as possible opted for Latin. (139)

In contrast to a writer like Carleton was one like Brian Merryman, the last important Irish-language poet, who had the advantage, at least, of not having to choose between languages, not having to worry whether what he wrote was Irish or not (130).

The most careful and most significant historical distinction O'Connor makes in *A Short History of Irish Literature* relates directly to the gap between writers like Merryman and Carleton, and more broadly, to the question of the continuity of the Irish literary tradition raised by Vivian Mercier and Kevin Sullivan, among others. In the chapter titled "The Background of Modern Irish Literature," O'Connor states that

> In 1901 the Act of Union put an end to the independent parliament of Ireland and made the country part of the United King-

dom. This produced such a profound change in the whole life of
the community that it makes the literature that followed it seem
more like a new subject than a new phase.... If Irish literature can
be said to have continued after this period, it can have done so
only in a very different way. (132)

O'Connor's qualification here is of tremendous import, for it indicates that he is not unaware of the problems associated with the
notion of an Irish literary tradition. Nonetheless, if in the eyes of
critics Ireland has only an illusory sense of a tradition, it does at
least maintain a continuity in its colonial struggle for the survival
of identity.

On the other hand, Irish literature may not uphold a standard
of linear historical continuity exactly as British or American literature does (as defined by American or British critics)—but it does
uphold the rather different standard of "relevance" posited by
Frank O'Connor. O'Connor defines Irish writing in a somewhat
unique, though perfectly logical, way: not by virtue of an author's
race, creed, or language, but in terms of his or her relevance to a
geographically-defined Irish audience. Thus, *A Short History* argues for the relevance of writers such as Goldsmith and Swift
(whom critics have usually classified as British writers) to the Irish
tradition, while neglecting less "relevant" authors such as Shaw
and Wilde. Relevance is defined by readership, by subject matter,
and by influence, but O'Connor recognizes it as a necessarily contingent standard, being based upon "the reader's frame of reference."[14]

Still, O'Connor's position is further complicated by the fact
that, in his introduction, for the final word on the Irish obsession
with the past, he declares that our attitude toward history must be
that of

the twelfth-century scribe of "The Cattle Raid of Cooley," who
added wistfully to his text: "But I who wrote this history or
rather fable put no trust in this history or fable, for some of these
things are the feats of devils, some poetic figments, some apparently true, some not, and some for the delectation of fools." (2)

O'Connor may be cautioning readers not to trust objective notions
of history too fully because they are necessarily dependent on
one's frame of reference. O'Connor is, after all, telling a story and,
ultimately, telling his "own story" (222) of the history of Irish lit-

---

[14]For O'Connor's discussion of "relevance" in terms of Goldsmith, see
A Short History, 122–25.

erature. He has commented that "in Ireland it is always the personal element that counts,"[15] and his "backward look" is necessarily personal. Moreover, *A Short History* levels its own criticism at Irish literary histories written by Americans and Englishmen, precisely because they tend to disregard the complex personal tensions which are often integral to understanding Irish history and Irish literature. O'Connor, for example, cites the end of the friendship between Synge and Yeats (with Synge's death resulting in a bitter disillusionment for Yeats) as the end of an era, the effective end of the most productive years of the literary revival—a circumstance largely overlooked by critics (176).

In a different manner, one of *A Short History*'s strongest points is its repeated refutation of the Irish racial myth recorded in Matthew Arnold's *On the Study of Celtic Literature* and often used to assert an "essential" Irish identity, as it was by the "Irish Ireland" movement of the Celtic Revival. Unlike popular histories, such as Seamus MacManus's *The Story of the Irish Race*, which perpetuate myths of the Irish as a single, glorious, storied race, O'-Connor's is a more scholarly history in that it begins not with some mythic, homogeneous "first" people of Ireland, but with the known, recorded history of the Middle Ages. Furthermore, O'-Connor acknowledges that a number of "races" formed the population of this time. He does assert that all of Ireland's people, no matter what their "race," derive from one source around the Mediterranean basin, but he also concedes that "I am afraid I do not believe much in Normans, Anglo-Saxons or Celts" (159). Thus, in discussing his nation's Celtic past, O'Connor suggests that "perhaps we can escape [our past] only ... by confronting it and so robbing it of its mystique" (8). *The Backward Look* confronts this past repeatedly, demystifying the notion of an "essential" Irish identity which would exclude such groups as the Anglo-Irish.

O'Connor's first chapter sets the tone for this confrontation. He states that

> From the very beginning we are faced with a contradiction which seems to call for some ... explanation. Politically the country was anarchic, but culturally it was quite homogeneous.... Though we know we are dealing with scores of tribes, with different races, perhaps even with different

---

[15]"Ireland" in *A Frank O'Connor Reader*, edited by Michael Steinman (Syracuse: Syracuse University Press, 1994), 395. Reprinted from the American magazine *Holiday* (Dec. 1949): 34–65.

> languages, so far as the professional classes are concerned there
> is only one nationality—Irish, whatever that might mean at any
> given time—and only one language, and that without a trace of
> dialect.
>
> One can only assume that the professional classes, particularly
> the poets ... all subscribed to a common fiction of racial identity
> that changed as the dominant race changed, while everything
> that conflicted with this fiction was suppressed or distorted. (17)

O'Connor's subtle qualifications ("whatever that might mean at
any given time" and "fiction ... that changed as the dominant race
changed") are significant, for he is suggesting that "Irishness" is
defined by geography, not by race. These distinctions in themselves free O'Connor from two diametrically opposed traps of
Irish history:

> The English myth ... that the Irish were rescued from barbarism
> by the Norman invasion and have displayed disgraceful ingrati-
> tude ... [and the Irish myth that] "the greatest civilization the
> world had ever known was destroyed in the 17th Century by
> English barbarians."[16]

O'Connor's mediation of these oppositions is likely what allows
him to define Irish writers in his unique way, not by virtue of the
author's race, creed, or language, but in terms of his or her relevance to an Irish audience (124–25).

From a somewhat anomalous position, then, O'Connor could
point to Arnold's wholehearted acceptance of racialism as the primary source of his weakness as a critic, while also calling attention
to the fact that Sean O'Faolain perpetuates the same sort of racial
argument in his book entitled *The Irish* (158–59). Then, just as easily as he could scorn such arguments, O'Connor could show a remarkable capacity for sympathy. His *New Yorker* editor William
Maxwell, in a 1966 letter to O'Connor's American agent, marvelled
at O'Connor's mysterious vision, which could embrace indignation and sympathy even when discussing a single subject. Maxwell
specifically refers to the following story from *A Short History*, a
story quoted from Father Peter O'Leary's autobiography, in which
a family of four freezes to death during the Famine:

> Next day a neighbor came to the hut. He saw the two of them
> dead and his wife's feet clasped in Paddy's bosom as though he
> were trying to warm them. It would seem that he felt the death

---

[16]Ibid., 379.

agony come on Kate and her legs grow cold, so he put them inside his own shirt to take the chill from them.[17]

Maxwell wonders

how, for example, the man who produced that quotation from
the Autobiography of Father Peter O'Leary ... could at the same
time be so utterly without indignation. At me, I mean, and all de-
scendants of Anglo-Saxon Protestants. In a way that is so sweet it
is almost baffling, people are people to him, even in this often
indignant book.[18]

In discussing the Famine, as in treating most topics, O'Connor
tended to value the personal while scorning abstraction. This may
be cited as his greatest impediment as a critic, but it may also be
seen as a great advantage, for it allowed him to mediate conflicting
positions and interpretations with the understanding and compassion he felt were demanded. If critical compassion was an impediment, it was one of which he was fully aware.

O'Connor begins the last chapter of *The Backward Look* by consciously freeing his narrative from its scholarly pretensions:

"And now that our story approaches the end" my own position
becomes anomalous, because it becomes my own story, which
must be classed as autobiography, not as literary history or criticism; and yet to keep the narrative all in one tone and pretend a
detachment I do not feel would merely falsify the record. (222)

Still, in openly declaring his subjective stance, O'Connor is revealing something that a careful reader would have noticed as early as
his first chapter on Yeats. O'Connor never directly places himself
within the narrative—that is to say, he never actually discusses
any of his own accomplishments within this history of Irish literature. But the people he knew firsthand are painted unmistakably
by memory more than by critical detachment in the last six chapters.

The two figures who loom over these final chapters most
prominently are the figures with whom O'Connor the writer (and
indeed every other twentieth-century Irish writer) struggled

---

[17]*A Short History*, 142. The Maxwell letter appears in *The Happiness of
Getting It Down Right: Letters of Frank O'Connor and William Maxwell, 1945–
1966*, edited by Michael Steinman (New York: Alfred A. Knopf, 1996), 247,
and reference to the specific passage is supplied by Steinman's note on
page 248.

[18]*The Happiness of Getting It Down Right*, 247.

throughout his career—William Butler Yeats and James Joyce. O'-Connor wrote of them in *The Backward Look* as thesis and antithesis, "the idealist and the realist, the countryman and the townsman, the dead past and the unborn future" (162). Yeats and Joyce as figureheads were yet another set of diametrical oppositions which form a frame of reference—and from which the Irish writer must negotiate his or her place within the literary tradition—yet even they became figureheads only because they had made conscious choices about their relationship to Ireland's colonial past.

O'Connor's personal attachments seem to cloud his judgments of Yeats and Joyce, just as they do not cloud his response to historical matters to which he is more abstractly linked. He can much more readily offer insightful commentary on Lady Gregory's "Victorian complacency" and her limited but genuine tragic sense, or on Synge's Wordsworthian, anti-political nature[19]—precisely because he knew Gregory very little and Synge not at all. O'Connor met Joyce only once, but it is from that storied meeting that he derived his theory of Joyce's "dissociated metaphor":

> Sir Desmond MacCarthy describes in one of his essays how I first came to notice the peculiar cast of Joyce's mind. The incident concerned a picture of Cork in his hallway. I could not detect what the frame was made of. "What is that?" I asked. "Cork," he replied. "Yes," I said, "I know it's Cork, but what's the frame?" "Cork," he replied with a smile. "I had the greatest difficulty in finding a French frame-maker who would make it."[20]

O'Connor could acknowledge that Joyce was "the greatest master of rhetoric who ever lived" (202), but in what mattered most to O'Connor—the reader, the sense of community and of communication—he disagreed with Joyce. Mainly, O'Connor objected to Joyce's reconfiguration of the relationship between writer, reader, and object, which relegated the reader to a "third party, present only by courtesy" (199). To O'Connor, Joyce's last writings were insanity—driven by an associative mania and by deep self-absorption. O'Connor could be realistic about his criticism of Joyce: "Nothing that I or anyone else can say will change the fact

---

[19]For O'Connor's full discussion of Synge, see *A Short History*, 184–89; for his discussion of Lady Gregory, see 188–93.

[20]*The Mirror in the Roadway* (Freeport, NY: Books for Libraries Press, 1970), 301.

that *Ulysses* is one of the great monuments of Irish literature." He could also be extremely wrongheaded:

> What I would suggest to you is that [*Ulysses*] is at its greatest not in its construction, which is haphazard ... but in its description of the poetry of everyday life in Dublin in the first decade of this century; and as that Dublin fades into history, this aspect will seem more and more important. (209)

But just as easily (though not nearly so often), Frank O'Connor as critic could suggest the germ of some significant means of evaluating a writer of James Joyce's stature: for example, Joyce's early departure from Dublin, coupled with the fact that this city remained the primary setting for his fiction, suggests not only that his fiction detailed a rather limited scope but that it continually presented a static view of an Ireland that was changing significantly over the course of Joyce's life.

W.B. Yeats was to O'Connor, variously, friend, father-figure, and hero. It is as hero that Yeats emerges most prominently in *A Short History of Irish Literature*, particularly if one considers the chapter "All the Olympians" the climax of O'Connor's "story." O'Connor claims Yeats was the ideal leader for a revival and chronicles the revival's achievements by framing them as Yeats's grand scheme. O'Connor mentions how Yeats pushed others to suit his needs, telling Synge, for example, to go to the Aran Islands for inspiration; how Yeats's work was often collaborative, with Yeats blending his artistic vision with the visions of a group of people as diverse as Douglas Hyde, George Moore, Synge, Lady Gregory, Oliver Gogarty, and O'Connor himself; and how Yeats's disillusionment after the death of Synge in 1909 effectively halted the creative energy and optimism of the revival movement.

On a more personal level, Yeats was to O'Connor a poet of friendship whom O'Connor emulated in some respects. Both had first-rate intellects, even if at times it appeared they did not, and both willfully suspended their critical faculties to indulge their intuitive natures. Yet at times O'Connor would seem to be even too close to Yeats, for whereas he ceaselessly attacks the self-indulgent chords of Joyce's writings, when he comes across a similar self-referential strain in Yeats's "Lapis Lazuli," he merely questions it:

> In the poem the lapis and the Chinese scenes, the bombardment and my own advice to the players are all rendered in strict chronological order as though copied from a diary.... To me, for

once, the sequence of ideas is perfectly clear as it is not clear in other poems of Yeats, but is it equally clear to readers who are unfamiliar with the voices speaking in the poem? (174–75)

O'Connor's friendship with Yeats allowed for such artistic liberties, but did O'Connor then pattern his own artistic career after Yeats's thesis, the return to the past, or Joyce's antithesis, to forge a new and untracked path? O'Connor chose to embrace both of these possibilities: as a fiction writer he followed the realistic path laid out by Joyce's early work, and in poetry and criticism he more clearly advocated the path championed by Yeats. In fact, one might even say that O'Connor exhausted his possibilities, given the limited resources with which he was provided in postcolonial Ireland. Thus, in the last paragraphs of *A Short History*, O'Connor fumbles for a solution to the problems facing Irish artists of his day, particularly the gap between the writer and Irish readers created by governmentally imposed censorship. He sees himself, O'-Faolain, Austin Clarke, and Patrick Kavanagh as "strayed revellers" of the literary revival, although one may argue that their literary endeavors are more rightly characterized as responses to the revival expressing the concrete reality of the modern Irish experience. O'Connor does propose an alternative to the present situation—"the revival of Irish as a spoken language, [to] give writers a centre, a viewpoint sufficiently different from those of other writers in the English language" (229)—but this seems a vain attempt to synthesize the ambitions of Irish writers and the government's Irish-language program, so that at least the Irish reading public would have some access to Irish literature. O'Connor is asking, "what else can be done?" but he leaves this question unanswered. If these thoughts seem somewhat vague and disillusioned, O'Connor finally returns to the illuminated vision of an Irish future which will come to terms with its past—neither in the mythic, fictionalized accounts of the revivalists, nor in the depressing factual accounts of Irish historians, but rather, in embracing the past in retrospective enjoyment. This, he says,

is the thing we have never been able to do.... Literature in Irish is still a subject unknown, nor except in America is there such a thing as a chair of Irish literature.... I am not sure that any country can afford to discard what I have called "the backward look," but we in Ireland can afford it less than any other because without it we have nothing and are nothing, and we must not cease to remember Yeats' final words:

> Cast your mind on other days
> That we in coming days may be
> Still the indomitable Irishry.[21]

It does not seem entirely coincidental that O'Connor's "backward look" is dedicated to an idealistic revisionism somewhat in accordance with Terence Brown's discussion in a 1988 essay on contemporary history and literature. Brown claims that

> In both the Nationalist and Unionist versions of the Irish past there is ... a profound sense of history as a given, as a nightmare from which it is impossible to awake.
> It need not, of course, be so. The nationalist view of the past could highlight the progressive developments of Irish life, the uneven but undeniable advancement of the people from feudalism to modern democratic government, but so profound have been the traumata endured by the Irish since the seventeenth century, and so painful is much contemporary Irish experience ... that such a revisionist interpretation would seem fanciful to most Irish nationalists, if not downright impertinent.... [The] Nationalist feels his present to be linked to a "continuous past." To be Irish is to endure the nightmare of historical stasis.[22]

O'Connor's short history, even if "fanciful" and "impertinent," does not present an Ireland engulfed in a "nightmare of historical stasis." *A Short History* does, on the other hand, engage issues which remain relevant in present-day Ireland. One of the most important of contemporary Irish critics, Seamus Deane, has himself written a short history of Irish literature—a history which begins with the same premises as O'Connor's, that defining Irish literature requires a negotiation between Irish-language and English-language writings, and that Irish literature has always been "a politically charged activity."[23] Yet Deane does not even allude to O'Connor's criticism. An equally significant work of recent Irish criticism, David Lloyd's 1993 *Anomalous States: Irish Writing and the Post-Colonial Movement*, mentions O'Connor only briefly, and, it would seem, backhandedly, at that: "Paradoxically, then, the tra-

---

[21]*A Short History*, 230. The Yeats excerpt is from "Under Ben Bulben."

[22]*Ireland's Literature* (Totowa, NJ: Barnes & Noble Books, 1988), 245–46.

[23]Seamus Deane's *A Short History of Irish Literature* (Notre Dame, IN: University of Notre Dame Press, 1986), 7.

jectory of these essays has enacted what Frank O'Connor once called a 'backward look.'"[24]

These critics, in passing over O'Connor's work so expediently, fail to account for the dual nature of O'Connor's career. While most critics do acknowledge that O'Connor the short story writer had a foot firmly planted in the immediate realities of modern Irish life, few are able to reconcile that fact with the fact that his other foot was at the same moment stretched back toward the Irish past by way of his poetry and criticism. Particularly, critics have neglected to acknowledge the enduring value of the legacy of Frank O'Connor's criticism of Ireland in its many forms.[25] If O'-Connor's short history achieved nothing else, it at least made apparent and legitimized the notion that Ireland had a literary tradition worth studying. Philip Edwards, a Trinity College professor, has acknowledged the role O'Connor played in initiating the idea of an "Irish Studies" program within Irish universities[26]—which ultimately (though indirectly) led to the establishment of the first such program at University College, Dublin within two years.[27] But O'Connor achieved much more than this. At a time when it was much easier, much more popular, and much more financially wise to compromise one's standards, O'Connor's willingness to challenge his given circumstances was a thirty-year battle which sustained artistic integrity in modern Ireland. His unbowdlerized

---

[24](Durham, NC: Duke University Press, 1993), 6.

[25]Besides the scholarly criticism of *The Backward Look*, O'Connor wrote articles critical of Ireland in leading Irish, British, and American magazines and newspapers, and his critical views were broadcast over the radio airwaves of the BBC as well. O'Connor became so notorious a critic of Irish society that the Irish government actually conducted a campaign to keep him off of the airwaves in both Britain and Ireland (*Voices*, 188-89). By 1943, a series of articles in *The Sunday Independent* required him to use a pseudonym since the name of Frank O'Connor was so "unofficially" frowned upon (*Voices*, 196–97).

[26]"Frank O'Connor at Trinity," in *Michael/Frank: Studies on Frank O'-Connor*, edited by Maurice Sheehy (New York: Alfred A. Knopf, 1969), 131–33. Edwards reports that O'Connor's initial idea and his subsequent campaigning for a coordinated course of studies in Irish literature, language, architecture, art, and sociology gained widespread approval and support at Trinity College—though, ultimately, government funding for this project fell through.

[27]*Voices*, 360.

translations, such as the 1945 rendering of *The Midnight Court*, paved the way for Thomas Kinsella's important translation of *The Tain* in its entirety, and preserved for future generations, "with the intuition of the supreme craftsman,"[28] much otherwise inaccessible Irish poetry. Although it was not his best work, and not even written in a genre in which he excelled, *The Backward Look* provided an apt ending to his career, for it was not just the final chapter of Frank O'Connor's career as literary critic; it was his concluding, and, at the same time, most substantive commentary on the ancient Irish poetry he had been translating into English since his twenties. More than this, it was the final statement of a career devoted to communication and to community; to provoking and sparking the imagination of the Irish people; and to looking back in order to look forward.

---

[28]David Greene, "Poet of the People," in *Michael/Frank*, 138.

Frank O'Connor's Book of Dreams and the Road to Modernity

Shawn O'Hare

In the preface to *The Mirror in the Roadway: A Study of the Modern Novel* (published in 1956), Frank O'Connor momentarily drifts from the thesis of the work to note:

> For some years I have been working on the problem of dream language, not as a psychologist, but as a writer interested in the problem of language. This study seemed to me to support none of the psychoanalytical theories. Instead, it seemed to emphasize the classical distinction between judgement and instinct, which in dreams is represented by the father and mother.[1]

That O'Connor would mention dreams in a critical work on fiction may, at first, seem out of place; in fact, it is not. For much of the 1940s, 50s, and 60s, O'Connor had an intense interest in dream interpretation, and though only one article was eventually published on the topic ("In Dreams Does Seven Mean Conception" in the November 1, 1967 issue of *Vogue*), "the problem of dream language" was an important consideration for the Irish writer. Indeed, O'Connor was so absorbed by his interest in dreams that "sometime between 1954 or 1955," his biographer James Matthews notes, he began working on his own book of dream analysis.[2] Though the text—with the curious, Joycean working title *Here Comes Everybody*—has never been published, it is an important segment in O'Connor's *œuvre*.

Here Comes Everybody, in fact, illustrates that O'Connor is more of a Modernist than is generally recognized. The Modern writer,

---

[1]*The Mirror in the Roadway: A Study of the Modern Novel* (New York: Alfred A. Knopf, 1956), v.

[2]*Voices: A Life of Frank O'Connor* (New York: Atheneum, 1987), 315.

47

Malcolm Bradbury explains, is an artist who is concerned with the
creative conscience, the anxieties of the creative consciousness, the
angle of vision, and point of view; in short, the individual.[3] In her
essay "Modern Fiction," Virginia Woolf posits that "For the mod-
erns, the point of interest lies very likely in the dark places of psychology."[4] The very nature of O'Connor's work—particularly his
short fiction—might seem remote from Bradbury's or Woolf's
definitions. Yet O'Connor's stories do in fact often possess a psychological depth that has been unjustly overlooked.

O'Connor's interest in dreams formed an important link to
Modernism. In fact, for a number of years dreams were his preoc-
cupation, if not obsession. In the article "In Dreams Does Seven
Mean Conception," O'Connor opens by reporting:

> Years ago, my wife overheard my small boy (as he then was) say
> sadly to another small boy, "Daddy isn't just interested in
> dreams. They're a disease with him." He is not the only one who
> has thought that, for a famous novelist [Sean O'Faolain] once re-
> proved me for what he thought was an aberration and said "It
> doesn't go with your sort of work." Which, of course, is true.[5]
> (164)

In *Here Comes Everybody*, however, O'Connor explains his interest
in dreams by arguing, "If we want to understand the mind at all,
we have to reconcile ourselves to its speech" (A/16).[6] For a writer
who readily admits to being one of the "old-fashioned realists who
believe[s] that the close observation of character produces the closest approximation to truth of which literature is capable" ("In
Dreams" 164), dreams offered an alternative way to examine the
"truth" of humanity.

---

[3]*The Novel Today* (Oxford: Manchester University Press, 1977), 9.

[4]In *The Common Reader* (New York: Harcourt, Brace & Company,
1925), 215.

[5]See *Vogue* (1 November 1967): 164–65, 167–68.

[6]For the purpose of this essay, references to the various stages of *Here
Comes Everybody* are based on the University of Florida's O'Connor Papers
categorization. That is, citations will note the specific file letter (A, D, E, G,
and H) followed by O'Connor's page number of that section. Thus the reference (A/16) denotes that the information is from the A file, page 16. The
manuscript was purchased from O'Connor's widow, Harriet O'Donovan
Sheehy, in 1988 and is part of the University of Florida's Frank O'Connor
Papers, Department of Special Collections, Rare Books & Manuscripts,
Manuscript Group 92.

Despite the brevity of *Here Comes Everybody* and the fact that it was never completed, such "outside projects" (non-creative writings) and short, introductory critical works are important elements of his canon. Although O'Connor wrote fully developed books of criticism which were often the product of university lectures, including *The Road to Stratford* (1948, republished in the United States in 1960 as *Shakespeare's Progress*), *The Mirror in the Roadway: A Study of the Modern Novel* (1956), and *A Short History of Irish Literature: A Backward Look* (1967), he also produced brief works such as *Towards an Appreciation of Literature* (1945) and *The Lonely Voice* (1961). In appearance and aim, *Here Comes Everybody* is most similar to *Towards an Appreciation of Literature*, a 58-page monograph that, as the title implies, argues that literature should be important to all people, not just university professors and students. In both *Here Comes Everybody* and *Towards an Appreciation of Literature* O'-Connor's goal is to demystify the subjects, dreams and literature, for a lay audience.

At the time O'Connor was reading and collecting material for his "dreambook," from the late 1940s through the early 1960s, treatises on dream psychology were very popular. While many works from that time were dominated by psychoanalytic jargon, O'Connor dealt with the subject in his typical plain-speaking fashion, much as fellow dream devotee William Archer did in *On Dreams*, a text that O'Connor knew well and used often in his own analysis. O'Connor's primary goal with *Here Comes Everybody* is to make understanding and translating dreams accessible for the novice dream enthusiast.

"Dreaming is a process half-way between consciousness and unconsciousness, and partakes of the qualities of both," O'Connor writes in the opening chapter of *Here Comes Everybody* (A/1). Yet, for O'Connor, dreams surpass any clinical, physiological definition. What intrigued him most about dreams was, indeed, what intrigued him most about waking life: the language. For O'Connor, it was this language that offered so many possibilities in understanding the human condition:

> Unless one has entirely shut one's mind to the inescapable premisses of human experience, one cannot but enjoy much of the artless prattle of dreams. But pretty or ugly, this is the language in which the dreaming mind chooses to express itself, and it may be in the very lingo of the gutter that it describes spiritual regeneration. If we want to understand the mind at all, we have to reconcile ourself to its speech. (A/10)

At the center of O'Connor's thesis is that dreams have a language of their own, and, with proper study, can be understood. The key, of course, is to rely on a knowledge of the structure of the dream language, because, as he notes, "When we move out of the physiological world into the psychological, we move from the known to the unknown. We move, in fact, into the happy hunting grounds of charlatans" (A/11). For O'Connor, understanding dreams was not based on interpreting them, but rather, on *translating* them; interpretation, in his view, left too much to subjective speculation. Translating, on the other hand, was based on certain "facts." In an early draft he simply states, "If I cannot translate dreams I prefer to have nothing to do with them" (F/1). That he should think this is not entirely surprising, as in fact he worked with translations (especially of poetry) his entire career. While on the surface dreams might seem like a hodge-podge of actions, emotions, and sensory feelings, O'Connor believed that in fact the mind was speaking to the dreamer—or the subconscious to consciousness—albeit in a language and process that may at first seem confusing. "The dreaming mind deals less with specific problems than with unsuspected analogies," O'Connor notes in *Here Comes Everybody*. "Its genius is its capacity for grouping and association" (A/12). In *On Dreams*, Sigmund Freud's follow-up to *The Interpretation of Dreams* designed to be more accessible to the lay reader, Freud makes similar claims:

> Each element in the content of a dream is "overdetermined" by material in dream thoughts; it is not derived from a *single* element in the dream thoughts, but may be traced back to a whole number. These elements need not necessarily be closely related to each other in the dream thoughts themselves; they may belong to the most widely separated regions of the fabric of those thoughts.[7]

Freud later argues that (for the purpose of analysis) a "dream that resembles a heap of disconnected fragments is just as valuable as one that has been beautifully polished and provided with a surface" (*On Dreams* 49).

If many of O'Connor's theories seem unduly Freudian, that is because they are. Freud's fondness for organization, rules, and steps is attractive to O'Connor's categorized sensibility. In fact, O'Connor breaks down dreaming into three Freudian stages: (1)

---

[7]*On Dreams*, trans. and ed. James Strachey (1901; New York: W.W. Norton, 1989), 32.

the dream proper—a stream of words, which Freud called "ideograms"; (2) the stream of images when the dreamer visualizes the words, though the visualization seems autonomous—Freud's "pictographic script"; and (3) the stream of rationalization—"the dreamer tries to interpret logically the very illogical dream pictures," called "secondary revision" by Freud (A/6,8). When one understands how the dream processes fit together, O'-Connor argues, an accurate form of translation can begin. Structure is important because it provides a solidly based "system" that, in theory, will provide a translation for any dream. In fact, O'Connor assumes that there is an "international language of dreams," a Jungian-influenced phrase O'Connor often uses to support his claims (e.g., in dreams, one's mother appears as a queen, empress, instructress, nurse, someone else's mother, or a servant, regardless of the cultural context) (A/5). The "international language of dreams" doctrine is crucial to O'Connor's contention that dream content connects all humans. The magnificence of dreams, and what attracted O'Connor to them most, is that they are essentially unpolluted thoughts. That is, dreams are what we are really thinking and feeling, before the conscious mind interferes by imposing socially acceptable thoughts. The primary purpose of studying dreams, O'Connor makes clear throughout *Here Comes Everybody*, is that in understanding that somnolent activity, one can better understand one's self.

While O'Connor contends that the language of dreams is universal, he does not think a dream can be translated in only one way. In *Sex and Dreams: The Language of Dreams*, Wilhelm Stekel, second only to Freud in influencing O'Connor's dream theories, argues that "Every dream has multiple meanings," a premise that O'Connor accepts.[8] The most challenging aspect of translating dreams, and the one that gives O'Connor the most trouble, is working with symbols. The fault of many would-be dream interpreters, O'Connor feels, is an incorrect emphasis on symbols, a point he emphasizes in *Here Comes Everybody*:

> I must make it plain that, so far as I can see, the symbol in the accepted sense of the word does not exist in dreams at all; the dream thought usually lies too deep for symbolic representation, and it is visible only as a constellation of allusions, like bubbles rising to the surface of a pond. We can only say definitely that a

[8]*Sex and Dreams: The Language of Dreams*, trans. James Van Teslaar (Boston: Richard G. Badger, 1922), 93.

particular person or activity is being described when three or four of the dream equivalents are combined in such a way as to make the meaning unmistakable.... Anything else is mere guess-work. (A/14)

O'Connor shares this apprehension of symbols with Freud, who noted that "it must be confessed that the presence of symbols in dreams not only facilitates their interpretation but also makes it more difficult."[9] O'Connor's image of "bubbles rising to the sur-face of a pond" clearly echoes Freud's Condensation Theory. O'-Connor's "bubbles" are Freud's "latent thoughts." Freud points out in *The Interpretation of Dreams* that most dream thoughts are so "compressed" that it is often "impossible to determine the amount of condensation" (313) and that "Dreams make use of this symbol-ism for the disguised representation of their latent thoughts" (387). What O'Connor sees as "a constellation of allusions," Freud sees as one of the "fundamental principles confirmed: the elements of the dream are constructed out of the whole mass of dream thoughts and each one of those elements is shown to have been determined many times over in relation to the dream thoughts" (*Interpretation* 318). Even though O'Connor does not directly acknowledge Freud's Condensation Theory, it is obvious that Freud's writings directly affected the amateur dream enthusiast's own dream trans-lation theories. Although he professed to have, at times, difficulty with symbolism in dreams, O'Connor believed that the presence of an "international dream language" proved that symbols were im-portant. Clearly there is an inconsistency in O'Connor's thinking. Although O'Connor repeatedly criticizes an emphasis on symbols, whether it is in dream analysis or in literature, he discusses and examines symbols throughout *Here Comes Everybody*. His belief in "universal symbols" is held by many dream psychologists, most notably Carl Jung (who posited a "collective consciousness"), Stekel, and, to a lesser extent, Freud. In his essay "On the Nature of Dreams," Jung argues that even dreams by children as young as three years old "contain symbolic images which we also come across in the mental history of mankind."[10] Stekel cites the um-brella as a phallic symbol in *The Language of Dreams* (79), and in *The Interpretation of Dreams*, Freud asserts that "boxes, cases, chests,

---

[9]See Sigmund Freud, *The Interpretation of Dreams*, trans. and ed. James Strachey (1899; New York: Avon Books, 1965), 388.

[10]"On the Nature of Dreams." *Dreams*. Trans. R.F.C. Hull. (1948; Princeton: Princeton University Press, 1974), 67–83; see 77.

cupboards and ovens represent the uterus" (389) and that "in men's dreams a necktie often appears as a symbol for the penis" (391). In *Here Comes Everyone*, O'Connor argues that "we should expect that this instinct for association ought to hold for the psychological world as well as the physical one, and that what is true of a physical unit like the body should be equally true for a psychological unit like the family" (A/11). Thus in dreams, fathers or figures of power often surface "in various fairly transparent disguises such as king, emperor, master, orchestral conductor, bus conductor ..." (A/12), a claim that Stekel makes as well (84). O'Connor is, however, quick to warn that "Dreams are analogies, not representations" (A/23), which suggests that the translator should not over-emphasize symbols and other elements (such as physical discomfort and emotional anxiety) when examining a dream. Freud, not surprisingly, also believed that too much emphasis on symbolism could lead to erroneous interpretations:

> I should like to utter an express warning against over-estimating the importance of symbols in dream-interpretation, against restricting the work of translating dreams merely to translating symbols and against abandoning the technique of making use of the dreamer's associations. The two techniques of dream interpretation must be complementary to each other. (*Interpretation* 395)

Once again, O'Connor's theories are overtly Freudian, proving that the Viennese doctor is O'Connor's greatest influence.

If an analyst, however, understands the international dream language and knows how the mind groups symbols, and if the analyst is willing to try to understand his or her own thoughts and emotions, O'Connor feels that translating dreams is an achievable task. The danger, he points out, is translating dreams without following those guidelines. Early in the text, he cautions the reader that "no one should be fool enough to try and interpret psychological dreams who has not trained himself in these" (A/4). Jung warns that "experience has taught me that a slight knowledge of dream psychology is apt to lead to an overrating of the unconscious which impairs the power of conscious decision" (*Dreams* 82). In his work titled *The Interpretation of Dreams* (1943) Stekel, however, takes the admonition a step further and argues against the dreamer analyzing his/her own dream: "It is impossible for a man to analyze himself as it is for a man to play chess against himself. One cannot at the same time be accusing counsel, judge, defending counsel, and reporter. Every attempt at auto-analysis leads swiftly to a frontier which the would-be auto-analyst cannot cross."[11] O'Connor, steeped in Freud, Jung, Stekel, and other dream psychologists, spent the better part of three decades training himself, blending twenty years of scientific reading with a lifetime of microcosmic observation essential to the Realist writer. *Here Comes Everybody*, then, is not just a regurgitation of popular dream theories, nor is it just an artist's rumination on what dreams mean to him. Rather, the text, written in a manner that is easily understood, is an attempt to make sense of dreams.

Although O'Connor never completed *Here Comes Everybody*, the text has many qualities that suggest it is publishable and significant. Chief among those is its organization. Broken down into eight chapters, *Here Comes Everybody* addresses the primary concerns of dream analysis. Because O'Connor worked on the text over a number of years, he was able to build a stockpile of dreams to analyze. Dreams in *Here Comes Everybody* range from those in Archer's *On Dreams*, to those of O'Connor's friends and relatives, to those of Sigmund Freud and other psychoanalysts, and, of course, O'Connor's own.

O'Connor's first goal was to sort out the dreams and try to make sense of them. It is impossible, he notes, to recall a complete dream fully. "What I am examining here is not the dreams themselves but snapshots of them, caught in that brief moment before they dissolved," he writes. "Certain details I can never question because they have vanished forever" (A/2). By examining aspects that form a pattern, one can credibly evaluate the dream. The problem is that quite often dreams seemingly make little sense. That, according to O'Connor, is to be expected and should not deter the analyst. As he notes, "There is a mass of evidence that the confusion does not obey regular laws," the "confusion" being, not surprisingly, the dream (A/2). In many ways, the pages of *Here Comes Everybody* suggest that O'Connor is both clarifying his own dream-reading skills (perhaps illustrating his competence) and instructing novice analysts.

Here Comes Everybody, however, is also important and valuable because O'Connor's beliefs about dreams and their symbols eventually affected his own writing. While no evidence suggests that he ever directly turned a dream into a short story, his work in

---

[11]See Wilhelm Stekel, *The Interpretation of Dreams: New Developments and Techniques*, trans. Eden and Cedar Paul (1943; New York: Washington Square Press, 1967), 142.

dream interpretation certainly affected his craft, even though he denies such Modernist influences. Indeed, the very presence of symbols in dreams is antithetical to O'Connor's stated view of writing. In *The Mirror in the Roadway*, he proudly argues that he is a nineteenth-century realist and liberal, contrasting that ideology with twentieth-century aesthetics:

> I am not sure that either realism or liberalism is a good thing in itself, but at least I believe that they are aspects of the same attitude of mind. I have an idea that conservatism and romanticism may be aspects of the same attitude of mind. I even fancy that symbolism and naturalism in literature, fascism and communism in politics, represent substantially similar attitudes. And being, as I am, a realist and liberal, I must maintain in my mild, muddled, liberal way that, on the whole, they seem to me bad attitudes. (*Mirror* 15–16)

Despite his concerns about symbolism, much evidence suggests that O'Connor's passion for dreams directly and significantly affected his stories. In fact, many of his works are filled with latent and repressed symbols and themes. William Tomory misjudges the depth of the stories when he argues that "The unconscious plays an insignificant role in his fiction; it is the conscious actions, the deliberately spoken words—as well as the unspoken ones held back—which are his concern."[12] *Here Comes Everybody* and a closer look at the stories prove that O'Connor in fact uses the unconscious natures of characters to tell as much of the story as their words and actions do.

Debra A. Moddelmog has argued that "twentieth-century writers have been fascinated with myth and its possibilities in fiction."[13] Although O'Connor receives only three mentions in Moddelmog's work, he certainly acknowledged the power and universality of emotions and desires associated with the Oedipal myth. Moddelmog defines myth as "a narrative, recurring in various forms throughout a significant period of cultural history, which has acquired, and continues to invite, a number of diverse meanings as readers seek to identify the psychic, social, or sexual unknown that the myth expresses" (4). For O'Connor the Oedipus story identified a very natural part of growing up, and the fact that

---

[12]*Frank O'Connor* (Boston: Twayne, 1980), 60.

[13]See *Readers and Mythic Signs: The Oedipus Myth in Twentieth-Century Fiction* (Carbondale: Southern Illinois University Press, 1993), xi.

it was a part of our dream world—often in a much more direct and some would say repugnant way—underscores its validity.

Interestingly, though, evidence in O'Connor's stories suggests that he was not always aware of the Oedipal themes in his writing. A survey of his work reveals two kinds of Oedipal stories: conscious and subconscious. The conscious Oedipal stories, such as "The Study of History," are obviously in the Freudian/Oedipal tradition, where a son has possessive and sexual desires for his mother. In those stories, O'Connor uses manifest and latent content to emphasize the Oedipal theme. The manifest content in "The Study of History" is a simple storyline underscored with clear statements such as "Mummy, I promise that I never wanted anyone but you."[14] The latent content, however, requires closer reading, and in fact would be impossible to discern without an understanding of O'Connor's preoccupations in *Here Comes Everybody*.

"The Study of History" first appeared in book form in the 1956 publication *Domestic Relations*, two years after O'Connor began writing *Here Comes Everybody*. In *Voices*, James Matthews contends that the story reflects "O'Connor's obsessive quest to understand his dreams" (314). "The Study of History" is a story about Larry's uncovering his parents' past. Larry begins the story by telling the reader,

> The discovery of where babies came from filled my life with excitement and interest. Not in the way it's generally supposed to, of course. Oh, no! I never seem to have done anything like a natural child in a standard textbook. I merely discovered the fascination of history. Up to this, I had lived in a country of my own that had no history, and accepted my parents' marriage as an event ordained from the creation; now, when I considered it in this new, scientific way, I began to see it merely as one of the turning points of history, one of those apparently trivial events that are little more than accidents but have the effect of changing the destiny of humanity. (422)

For Larry, discovering that his parents had lives before he was born was shocking and fascinating. When he quizzed them about their pasts (his father was more interested in talking about his former girlfriends than his mother was about her ex-beaus), he reveled in thoughts of who he would be if his mother or father had

---

[14]See Frank O'Connor, *Collected Stories* (New York: Alfred A. Knopf, 1981), 314. Subsequent citations from the story will be noted in parentheses.

married someone else. "Mother's past was the richer subject for study," Larry declares, mostly because of the three suitors who had proposed to her: a plasterer's apprentice, a French chef, and an elderly but wealthy shopkeeper from the Sunday's Well section of Cork (422).

Of the three father-prospects, Larry favored the shopkeeper, especially since he died shortly after marrying his real wife. Larry therefore thinks that if his mother had married the shopkeeper, they would now be wealthy. In fact, Larry is so obsessed with fantasies about being the shopkeeper's son that one afternoon he walks to Sunday's Well and imagines what such a prosperous life would have been like (425). Unfortunately, Larry would never get the chance to meet Mr. Riordan, or the French chef, or the plasterer's apprentice. His father's old flame, however, is more accessible.

Mick Delaney is more than willing to talk about May Cadogan, now Mrs. O'Brien, much to the dismay of Larry's mother. In fact, Mick takes great delight in talking about his past and how he had to choose between May and Larry's mother. When Larry learns that Mrs. O'Brien, now the mother of six, lives on Douglas Road, he admits that it was "the place that had the greatest attraction of all for me" (426). While walking home one day, Larry asks a group of boys playing on Douglas Road if they know where Mrs. O'Brien lives. When one of them, Gussie O'Brien, asks Larry why he wants to know about his mother, Larry tries to explain that his father was a good friend of the boy's mother. Before he knows it, Larry is introduced to Mrs. O'Brien. When she learns that he is Mick Delaney's son, Mrs. O'Brien fawns over him, and he is clearly pleased by discovering who his mother could have been (427). Indeed, Mrs. O'Brien adopts the mother role by bringing Larry into her house and feeding him. When he leaves, she even gives him money, and her role as a surrogate mother is complete.

When Larry returns home late, his parents question him about his tardiness. They are surprised to hear that Larry just "happened" to meet Mrs. O'Brien. Mick, of course, is pleased to hear that Mrs. O'Brien still remembers him fondly, and is especially glad to hear that his former girlfriend recalls the shape of his head. Larry's story, understandably, does not have the same kind of impact on his mother. "But I knew for the first time I had managed to produce in Mother the unrest that Father could produce, and I felt wretched and guilty and didn't know why," Larry laments (430).

That night, preparing for sleep, Larry imagines what it would be like to *be* Gussie O'Brien and have Mrs. O'Brien as his mother. He soon realizes, however, that he could not be his present self if he were the son of Mrs. O'Brien, a much coarser woman than his mother. "Being good at reading would never satisfy her," Larry realizes. "She would almost compel you to be as Gussie was: flattering, impertinent, and exacting" (430). For the first time in his life, however, Larry cannot escape from his self-imposed trance, even though he tries to talk himself out of it. Finally, he is rescued by his mother:

> ... I was away in the middle of empty space, divorced from my mother and home and everything permanent and familiar. Suddenly I found myself sobbing. The door opened and Mother came in in her nightdress, shivering, her hair over her face.
>
> "You're not sleeping, child," she said in a wan and complaining voice.
>
> I snivelled, and she put her hand on my forehead.
>
> "You're hot," she said. "What ails you?"
>
> I could not tell her of the nightmare in which I was lost. Instead, I took her hand, and gradually the terror retreated, and I became myself again, shrank into my little skin of identity, and left infinity and all its anguish behind.
>
> "Mummy," I said. "I promise I never wanted anyone but you." (431)

"The Study of History" is an example of O'Connor writing with a complete understanding of the power of latent symbols. The story uses such symbols to underscore the Oedipus theme, and *Here Comes Everybody* makes it possible to see where O'Connor's fiction is influenced by his dream text.

O'Connor's first symbol, representing the manifest content to him and the latent content to the reader, is the number eleven. Larry's mother tells the young boy that Mr. Riordan was rumored to be worth eleven thousand pounds (423). This sum suggests that Riordan is twice the man that Larry's father is, for in O'Connor's international dream language the number "1" represents the father (A/30). Though Larry does not hate his father (as the Larry of "My Oedipus Complex" does), the numbers imply that he thinks that his mother (and he) would have benefited from being the wife and son of the wealthy merchant. O'Connor suggests this by having Larry say that eleven thousand pounds is "twenty-seven times greater" than any salary he knew (423). The "2" in twenty-seven represents Larry's mother, and though O'Connor never assigns a meaning for "7," it does fall between "6" (sex) and "8" (conception) (A/41, 42) suggesting that "7" may represent Larry if he had been born Larry Riordan.

O'Connor also subtly uses symbols to suggest Larry's Oedipal feelings for his mother. For example, Larry recounts how he often goes to Sunday's Well to see where his mother lived before she married Mick and had Larry. The boy calls Sunday's Well a "second home" (for O'Connor the number two represents the mother), and Larry's description leaves no doubt that he yearns to be back in his mother's womb. "I stood for a while at the garden gate of the house where Mother had been working when she was proposed to by Mr. Riordan," Larry remarks, "and then went and studied the shop itself" (425). The "garden gate," the "house," and the "shop" all symbolize Larry's Oedipal desires; he wants to be physically close to his mother again. Even though Larry thinks that Mr. Riordan would have been a better father than Mick Delaney, O'Connor implies that Larry also believes that even Mr. Riordan was not good enough for his mother, especially when Larry observes Riordan's store. "It wasn't like one of the big stores on Patrick Street," Larry comments, "but at the same time, in size and fittings, it was well above the level of a village shop" (425). Larry thus suggests that while Riordan does not quite fulfill the expectations of a father—"Patrick," O'Connor contends, suggests the father figure (A/12), and Riordan's shop is not as masculine or powerful as those on Patrick Street—the dead man's shop is better than nothing. For Larry, Riordan's shortcomings would ironically allow the imaginative boy to supplant Riordan and take his rightful place in his mother's life.

When Larry decides to try and see May O'Brien, he transfers his Oedipal feelings from his birth mother to his would-be mother. At this point he desires Mrs. O'Brien as much as he desires his own mother. Perhaps it is the thrill of something new or simply the opportunity to "have" another woman—Bruno Bettelheim suggests that the child older than age five "is struggling to extricate himself by partly repressing the conflict, partly solving it by forming emotional attachments to others beside his parents, and partly sublimating it"[15]—because the interaction between Larry and Mrs. O'Brien is very sexually charged in its symbolism.

---

[15]See *The Uses of Enchantment: The Meaning and Importance of Fairy Tales* (New York: Alfred A. Knopf, 1976), 38.

When Larry finally does go to see Mrs. O'Brien, he does so on his way home from the library. From the perspective of *Here Comes Everybody*, he is going from one womb to another. When he first sees Mrs. O'Brien, he notices that she is "small and untidy looking" (426). O'Connor's treatise on dreams translates a dream that takes place in an "untidy and messy" cellar as an "inspection dream" that depicts the dreamer's sexual curiosity (A/28). The book that Larry is carrying when he meets Mrs. O'Brien represents her genitals, a point that O'Connor makes in *Here Comes Everybody* when he examines a woman's dream that features hymn-books which represent the dreamer's thighs (A/29). O'Connor makes the sexual symbolism even stronger when Mrs. O'Brien asks if the book is for Larry's mother, and he tells her that the book is in fact for him. Mrs. O'Brien is surprised that the boy could read "such a big book" and Larry is happy to "prove it to her by reading aloud" (428). Symbolically, Larry is showing that he is masculine and powerful enough to fulfill his substitute mother's sexual needs. Their pseudo-relationship is further symbolized when Mrs. O'Brien gives Larry a slice of bread "smothered with jam" and a "big mug of milk" (428). As the mother figure, Mrs. O'Brien dutifully provides Larry with sustenance (bread), sweetness (the jam), and nutrition (the milk, which represents mother's milk).

Such sexual tension is further illustrated when Larry prepares to go home. Mrs. O'Brien tries to give him "a sixpence" and, when he refuses it, she "thrust[s] it" into his pants pocket. O'Connor's choice of a "sixpence"—"six" equals "sex"— suggests the Oedipal theme, and the use of the word "thrust" certainly underscores that idea. Eventually, however, Larry decides that he does not want Mrs. O'Brien, and by the end of the story it is clear that despite his Oedipal excursion, he still desires his mother. His declaration that "I promise I never wanted anyone but you" (431) is the most Oedipal sentence in the story and demonstrates that the work is more about Larry's Oedipal feelings than about a boy curious about his parents' past and who he might have been. However, it is the latent content of the story, provided by O'Connor's symbols, that strengthens the Oedipal theme of "The Study of History." Without a knowledge of *Here Comes Everybody* it is all but impossible to recognize consciously what O'Connor is trying to accomplish with the details of the story. Indeed, if the story did not contain such symbols, if there were no latent content for the reader to discover, "The Study of History" might seem just another charming tale of Irish childhood. Seen from the vantage point of *Here*

Comes Everybody, however, it is a story whose multiple levels imply a complexity previously unexplored in O'Connor's short fiction.

In the thirty years since Frank O'Connor's death, he has been remembered mainly for *New Yorker* stories—witty, humorous tales of a sleepy, backward island. Seamus Deane calls such stories "conventional and formulaic."[16] O'Connor, however, appears to be a more complex artist than critics like Deane suggest, and his dream text *Here Comes Everybody* shows how deeply involved he was with the twentieth century's and Modernism's great passion, psychology. Now that it is possible to read his stories in a different light—through *Here Comes Everybody*—it is clear that O'Connor's use of subconscious and latent content in his stories, especially those with Oedipal themes, helps make him, in the tradition of Joyce, Woolf, and Lawrence, a Modernist writer.

O'Connor's blind spot concerning Modernism was that he thought in all-or-nothing terms. For him, Modernism was Joyce, and O'Connor simply did not want to write like Joyce. His primary objection to Joyce's work, and indeed his principal criticism of modern fiction, was that the reader was forced to hunt for answers. Still, the fact that O'Connor's working-title for his dream project directly refers to *Finnegans Wake* suggests that he at least grudgingly recognized what Joyce was trying to accomplish with his art. O'Connor did not mind symbols, as long as they were clearly, universally understood. That, in fact, is what attracted him to studying dreams—the plausibility of an international dream language—and he eventually, consciously, incorporated a variety of symbols into his later writing, as stories such as "The Study of History" illustrate. For all his diatribes against symbolism and Modernism, O'Connor failed to realize that symbols are, and always have been, an important foundation of all writing, his own included.

Eventually, *Here Comes Everybody* may prove to be one of the most important works in O'Connor's corpus because it can help us see the depth and complexity of his art. Although the dream book certainly is one of the least known of his projects, to view O'Connor in an accurate historical and literary context it is an essential document because it provides a new Frank O'Connor to consider. Although he sometimes attacked Modernist writing for underem-

---

[16]*The Field Day Anthology of Irish Writing*, 3 vols. (Derry: Field Day Publications, 1991), 3:127.

phasizing human autonomy (see *The Mirror in the Roadway*, 227), O'Connor ignored the ways in which so many of his own characters lack such freedom. If *Here Comes Everybody* reveals anything to us, it is that Frank O'Connor is an artist in need of a reevaluation. His use of the conscious and subconscious, as well as manifest and latent content, makes him an important figure in twentieth-century literary Modernism. He might not have liked to admit it, but Frank O'Connor was a Modern writer, even if that Modernity was repressed.

The Stories:
Themes and Techniques

Frank O'Connor's Stories:
Epiphanies of the Heart

Richard Harp

Loneliness has been much discussed as a major theme in Frank O'Connor's short stories, and rightly so. It appears in many guises in his fiction, and in addition, of course, he entitled his fine study of the short story *The Lonely Voice*, taking as his epigraph for this work the famous *pensée* of Pascal, "The eternal silence of those infinite spaces terrifies me." But loneliness is a two-edged sword. It is not, for example, necessarily the same thing as "being alone." Loneliness may lead, of course, to sorrow and depression, to that sense of isolation from one's fellows and community that is so familiar in modern fiction. But it is equally, and more positively, the inevitable result of a maturity which insists on a man's freedom to act in the world and which accepts the consequences of that freedom. Loneliness in this sense, as the condition for and consequence of freedom, may set one apart from community, but it does not involve a rejection of community. Instead, it allows one to see his true relationship to his neighbors, a self-knowledge that is hard-won, may be harder to accept, but which is distinctively human and by no means leads to pessimism. Such, at any rate, is the dynamic to be seen in O'Connor's stories, one that aligns them just as properly with another of Pascal's famous *pensées*, that modern man must be able to remain in his room at night alone.[1]

To live by means of his own resources was an ability O'Connor certainly possessed. His wonderful autobiography *An Only Child* dramatized the extent to which he lived as a boy a rich interior life, peopled with a chaotic mix of ancient Irish heroes, wildly

---

[1]"I have often said that the sole cause of man's unhappiness is that he does not know how to stay quietly in his room." *Pensées* (London: Penguin, 1966), 67.

colorful neighborhood characters, and snatches of foreign literature and languages (he says that he may have been the only person
who made translations in his youth from one language that he did
not know into another language that he did not know). This extreme adolescent romanticism met disillusion after disillusion as
he grew to be a man. The earliest of these disillusionments are described in his memoir (his experiences in the Irish Civil War), with
later ones reflected in his fictions; but his sense that life was an adventure he never really lost. He cites Cuchulain's acceptance of the
prophecy he received when he was only seven years old that he
would lead a short life—"Little I care though I were to live but a
day and a night if only my fame and adventures lived after me"[2]—
as a perfect summation of his own view of life, and it is an attitude
that he never really lost.

Discouraged as a boy in never being able to find a suitable job
that would indulge his bookishness while still paying him a wage,
he never thought about giving up; instead, he recalls the game he
played with his friends when they came upon an orchard wall that
seemed too high to climb: "we took off our caps and tossed them
over the wall, and then we had no choice but to follow them." So,
too, he says, he "tossed my cap over the wall of life, and I knew I
must follow it, wherever it had fallen" (144).

Such a sense of adventure causes one to insist on his freedom,
and this O'Connor certainly did. At the end of his autobiography
he recalls telling his saintly mother, then near her death, that he
might have to leave Ireland and live elsewhere, saying he could
get her a place in Cork, as he knew she hated the thought of leaving home. Her response surprised him: "'Of course I'll go with
you.... I know you must be free. Life without freedom is nothing'"
(228). Three of the neighborhood characters in the book that O'-
Connor recalls with clear-eyed but fond recollection, Minnie Connolly, Ellen Farrell, and Gertie Twomey, each spectacularly different in their vices and sanctities, were united in that "each of them
knew exactly where she was going. Ellen was going to hell.... Minnie was going to Heaven.... [and] Gertie, of course, was merely going to London" (91). The persons in O'Connor's fictions quite often
do not know where they are going, but what he insists upon is that
they are going someplace. Occasionally they will glimpse this fact
and as readers we are usually able to see exactly when they make

---

[2](London: Pan Books, 1970), 124. *An Only Child* was first published in
1958. Subsequent references are included in the text.

or refuse the decisive choices of their lives. And they are almost never exempt from the knowledge of what they have done. Not everyone's cap goes over the wall but they do all at least go up into the air.

Freedom, and the self-knowledge that it brings, runs through nearly all of the thematic groupings of O'Connor's stories, those dealing, for example, with childhood, courtship, death, or religion. It is perhaps most conspicuously presented in some of the stories about the law. One of the greatest of these, "The Majesty of the Law," portrays an isolated and lonely old man, Dan Bride, at home in his remote cottage, surrounded by his ancient dog and the decaying home furnishings provided by his dead mother. He is visited by an old acquaintance, a sergeant in the local village police force, who has come to arrest Dan for cracking open the head of an "unmannerly" neighbor in an argument. The facts of the case are not in dispute and what is apparently a routine assignment turns out to be an occasion when each man exercises the greatest tact and skill to illuminate what is the spirit of the law, which is its freedom, as opposed to its mere letter, which is its necessity. That is to say, O'Connor accomplishes the difficult task in this story of showing the romance of law when it is being applied in an official way. Other writers have tried this. G.K. Chesterton's novel *The Man Who Was Thursday*, for example, makes six policemen impersonate criminals so that they may experience the romance of the anarchist as well as the orderliness of policemen. In so doing Chesterton tries to illustrate that law itself is more romantic than the attempt to subvert it. But O'Connor employs in his story that most characteristic of Irish traits, the "personal touch," to do something both simpler and more realistic: Old Dan Bride and the sergeant show the majesty of the law simply by being who they are.

When the two men first meet at Dan's cottage they exchange compliments and maintain through what turns out to be their long afternoon together the most careful yet genuine politeness. What Jerome F. O'Malley calls "the broken pattern of ritual"[3] in O'Connor's stories is at least in this instance repaired. When Dan, for example, starts to make tea, the sergeant protests that he doesn't

---

[3]See his article, "The Broken Pattern of Ritual in the Stories of Frank O'Connor," *Eire-Ireland* 23 (Spring 1988): 45–59.

want Dan to be "'putting yourself out,'"[4] to which the old man considerately replies, "'I am not making it for you, indeed; I am making it for myself and I'll take it very bad of you if you won't have a cup'" (322). After which, "the policemen unbuttoned his tunic, opened his belt, took a pipe and a plug of tobacco from his breast pocket, and crossing his legs in an easy posture, began to cut the tobacco slowly and carefully with his pocket knife" (322). Manners and courtesy are used throughout the story to regulate the respect due between two old friends who might potentially be brought into conflict because of the business between them— which in fact is never mentioned until the end of the story. The word "courtesy," in fact, is derived ultimately from the Latin *cor*, "heart," and the sergeant's professional duty does not detract in this story from the obligations of cordiality (another word meaning "heart" in derivation) between friends.

It also turns out that if the sergeant is to embody the majesty of the law, he, like Dan, will have to violate its letter. For when the old man offers him a glass of *poteen*, he, "concealing whatever qualms he might have felt at the idea of drinking illegal whiskey," tells Dan that it "'tastes good.'" Dan replies that it is not all that good, "not wishing," the narrator notes, "to praise his own hospitality in his own house" (322). The sergeant comments, "'You'd be a good judge, I'd say,'" a remark, the narrator says, made "without irony" (323). The sergeant goes so far as to say, "'I think sometimes 'twas a great mistake of the law to set its hand against'" *poteen*; Dan's reply was to be found only in his eyes, as it was not "in nature for a man to criticize the occupation of a guest in his own home" (323). The sergeant, then, is willing to violate the law in the interest of friendship—and his own thirst—even as he discharges his professional responsibility. All men are equal before the law: that is, all men break it. When, finally, the two men get down to business, both try to accommodate the other. The policeman does not require that Dan go back to town with him, saying if it would be "'convenient'" he could turn himself in in "'two or three days,'" and Dan replies that when he did so, he would like to feel that he would be among friends at the jailhouse; the sergeant assures him this will be the case (326–27). Going to jail is in fact what Dan wants to do, for this will allow him to shame the neighbor with whom he fought. To the sergeant's suggestion that Dan pay a fine

---

[4]Unless otherwise indicated, all quotations from O'Connor's fiction are from *Collected Stories* (New York: Vintage Books, 1982).

rather than be jailed, the old man replies, ""'tisn't the money so much, as giving that fellow the satisfaction of paying. Because he angered me, sergeant'" (326). And later as the sergeant leaves for the last time, Dan tells him: "'I'll punish him. I'll lie on bare boards for him. I'll suffer for him, sergeant, so that neither he nor any of his children after him will be able to raise their heads for the shame of it'" (327). Even going to jail is an extension of Dan's freedom, and in the end this fine story reconciles what today we almost always assume are opposites—friendship versus duty, the country and its customs versus the city and its legalisms, even home versus jail—and does so by respecting absolutely the integrity of its characters.

O'Connor comments in *An Only Child* that to his mother "'freedom' did not mean freedom to do what one pleased—that was a conception that never crossed her mind—but freedom to do what one thought 'right,' whatever the consequences" (281). The two are not divorced in O'Connor's fiction, either. For to bear the consequences of freedom is also part of the majesty of the law. Caddy O'Driscoll is acquitted of the murder of her husband in "In the Train" because her village neighbors perjure themselves in court in a distant city to protect her—one of their own is not to be subject to the judgment of strangers—but on the train ride home Caddy realizes that even though she will not go to jail, "the flame of life had narrowed in her to a pin-point" (and that she will not realize the liberation that she had anticipated from her act).[5] It is not, as is sometimes suggested, that the villagers who had protected her will now ostracize her but rather that the act of murder has hardened her own heart. Enough is said of the villagers in the train to indicate that many of them have deficiencies in their own lives to make them less than perfect executors of justice, and one of the policemen who arrested her even congratulates her on her acquittal, saying, "'You're a clever woman, a remarkable woman, and I give you full credit for it'" (27). In this case, legal machinery fails but the law itself does not.

In the stories about romantic love, freedom and justice do not always operate with such apparent external equilibrium but in most instances the loneliness which results from romantic confusion is balanced by a self-knowledge which is genuinely compen-

---

[5]This story is printed in *A Frank O'Connor Reader*, ed. Michael Steinman (Syracuse: Syracuse University Press, 1994), 15–29. For the quoted passages, see 29.

satory. In one of the greatest stories of what Kate Murphy calls O'Connor's "unnatural world"[6] (a setting generally remote from urban middle-class Ireland), "The Bridal Night," an old woman laments to a stranger that her son is in the lunatic asylum in Cork because of his unrequited love for a new school-teacher who had come to the isolated area sometime before. The loneliness of the place is emphasized at the beginning of the story and the old woman tells the tale in a voice, says the narrator, that "was like the birds', hurrying high, immensely high, in the colored light, out to sea to the last island where their nests were" (20). O'Connor is not often praised for his natural descriptions but his use of them is shrewd and skillful. They are indeed rare but often comment, in a few deft strokes, illuminatingly on the theme of a story. The old woman says she realized from the beginning that Denis's love for Winnie Regan was hopeless—"'well I knew it from the first day I laid eyes on her, that her hand would never rock the cradle'"(21)—and the night before he is to be taken to Cork he is particularly disturbed. He asks that the teacher come into bed with him at night and, surprisingly, Winnie agrees; she and Denis spend a calm, chaste night together, the old woman and a neighbor nearby in the kitchen, and in the morning when the police come Denis goes with them "'without commotion or handcuffs or anything that would shame him'" (25). It is a powerful story which in a very brief space contains a large number of moving and strange elements: the isolated setting, the old woman sorrowing for her child (a contemporary Shan Van Vocht weeping for her country), the capable and attractive schoolteacher whose "'hand would never rock the cradle,'" Denis, denied being either his mother's comfort in her old age or the husband of Winnie by a nature always gentle and considerate and therefore easily broken. Yet in the midst of this poignant bleakness there is that moment of illumination when Winnie quite against the odds takes pity on Denis and the old woman declares, "'for the time being I felt 'twas worth it all, all the troubles of his birth and rearing and all the lonesome years ahead'" (25). She also adds how strange it was that in all the sur-

---

[6]"Grappling with the World," *Twentieth Century Literature* 36 (Fall 1990): 310–43. Murphy says that "In contrast to contexts defined as normal and natural, the 'unnatural' worlds in O'Connor's stories are defined, not by an individual's stage of consciousness, but by the difference of these worlds from the majority world that surrounds and dominates them" (313).

rounding countryside, no one, "'the world as wicked as it is,'" would say the "'bad word'" about Winnie. It is true that the last line of the story is foreboding: "Darkness had fallen over the Atlantic, blank gray to its furthest reaches" (25). But isolation and loneliness in this story are not oppressive elements that diminish the human actors but rather the stage upon which are illuminated their gratuitous acts of human kindness: the gentleness of Denis in the grip of passionate forces he cannot understand, the sympathy of Winnie, the bravery of Mrs. Sullivan in defying what the neighbors might think in letting Winnie sleep with Denis, the unexpected silence of those same neighbors. O'Connor's stories, no less than Joyce's, contain epiphanies but they are epiphanies with a heart.

"Uprooted" is a story which takes place half in the "unnatural world," half in the middle class world of Dublin. Most of the action takes place in Kerry where its hero, Ned Keating, had been raised, but counterbalancing this is the fact that Ned's mind had belonged mostly to the city. When the story opens, though, Ned, a schoolteacher in Dublin, is unexpectedly despondent: "The city was what he had always wanted. And now the city had failed him" (82). His timid nature has not taken advantage of what opportunities he has had and his few pleasures have been drained of gaiety by their routine. He seems indeed to have become, in a remarkably short time, one of Joyce's Dubliners: "his nature would continue to contract about him, every ideal, every generous impulse another mesh to draw his head down tighter to his knees till in ten years' time it would tie him hand and foot" (83). Then he returns home on Easter weekend with his brother Tom, a priest, where their father has arranged to go out to some islands where his wife's relatives live. While they are there, arrangements are made to pair Ned off with the beauty of the islands, Cait Deignan, who shelters him under her "turf-reeking shawl" when a rainstorm breaks out (95). It is a heady experience for the returning native Ned, of whom the narrator says that "Something seemed to have descended on him that filled him with passion and loneliness. He could scarcely take his eyes off Cait" (95). His brother Tom, who had apparently had a close relationship with Cait the year before, advises Ned to marry her and start a local school. Ned replies "gravely": "'No'.... 'We made our choice a long time ago. We can't go back on it now'" (98). The temptation to stay is a real one, as Cait is presented most winningly and Ned clearly has little to return to in Dublin. But again, it is the sensation of "loneliness," of being alone in the midst of frivolity (which in his father's case derives from drunkenness), that makes possible what is perhaps the first truly free decision of his life. It sets him off from life both in the city and in the country, forces decision upon him, and gives him the sense, as related in the last sentence of the story, that when he returned to Dublin this time, it would be "as if only now for the first time was he leaving home; for the first time and forever saying good-bye to it all" (98). Earlier in the story, while still in Dublin, Ned had reflected that he would like to "leave it all and go to Glasgow or New York as a labourer" because he felt that if he could "work with his hands for a living and was no longer sure of his bed" he could find out "what all his ideals and emotions meant" (83). The likelihood of his doing at least something like this is perhaps greater by the end. Self-knowledge is the prerequisite to freedom and is something which O'Connor's characters achieve surprisingly often.

One of his recurring clerical characters, for example, Father Fogarty, discovers in "The Frying Pan" that he and the wife of his best friend, Tom Whitton, are in love. Una Whitton tells Father Fogarty that her husband is more in love with the idea of the priesthood, for which he had once studied, than he is with her, and that he blames her for having caused his abandonment of his vocation: "'He wants to say Mass and hear confessions, and be God Almighty for seven days of the week,'" she tells the priest (156). In the midst of sharing these confidences Una turned to Father Fogarty in "an excess of emotion and threw her arms about him" and they kissed. "'Darling!' she said in an agony of passion, and it was as if their loneliness enveloped them like a cloud" (157). This occurs at the end of the story and, again, the discovery of loneliness is the occasion for self-knowledge. After this embrace Father Fogarty goes to meet Tom, who has just come into the house, and he is "thoughtful," for he realizes, says the narrator in the story's last line, that "the three of them, Tom, Una, and himself, would die as they had lived, their desires unsatisfied" (157). This kind of awareness could cause great shock to many people but it does not devastate or cripple Father Fogarty—as his subsequent life demonstrates (see especially "The Mass Island").

O'Connor has excelled in stories about children but in general his characters are grown-ups, maturely willing to accept the world even after it has stripped them of their romantic illusions. Roger Chatalic, in an article that contains often positive and insightful remarks about O'Connor, says that "He could not refrain from idealizing, or sometimes even sentimentalizing, whatever in his eyes could belie the ultimate possible emptiness of the world."[7] But this begs the question of whether the world is in fact ultimately empty. O'Connor did not think that it was. As Kate Murphy says very well about "The Frying Pan": "Father Fogarty's acceptance of his world, which completes the story, again suggests O'Connor's vision of the individual as a soul rather than a sensibility; for in such a vision the satisfaction of desires is not an end but a means."[8]

Indeed, it is not too much to say that O'Connor's characters frequently undergo a conversion, a turning of their lives in a different direction which, it is true, may be accompanied by pain and must be borne with stoicism, but which at least always involves self-understanding. This shock of recognition, what John Hildebidle calls "double vision"[9] and which is O'Connor's version of Aristotle's *peripeteia*, is one of the most characteristic effects of his stories. He describes his own experience of the phenomenon in his essay "The Conversion," helpfully reprinted by Michael Steinman in his *A Frank O'Connor Reader*, in which he found himself unexpectedly caught up in a Good Friday liturgy in a nondescript French church because of the almost rapturous state of the (otherwise) ordinary priest who was celebrating it: "He was not celebrating a service for three reluctant women and two small girls who had merely been dragged in to see members of their family perform in a countryside where God was dead. He was celebrating it in a crowded church in some cathedral town of the Middle Ages."[10] O'Connor goes on to say that this is an experience which was frequent for him: "It is the sudden reversal of situation which is familiar in dreams and which sooner or later happens to all of us and to the civilizations to which we belong. Bethlehem itself was merely an interesting object which the Roman Empire had studied with amusement, till suddenly it opened its eyes and the Roman Empire was no more" (374). This kind of transformation occurs

---

[7]"Frank O'Connor and the Desolation of Reality," in *The Irish Short Story*, ed. Patrick Rafroidi and Terence Brown (Atlantic Highlands, NJ: Humanities Press, 1979), 201.

[8]"Grappling with the World," 341.

[9]*Five Irish Writers: The Errand of Keeping Alive* (Cambridge: Harvard University Press, 1989), 204.

[10](Syracuse: Syracuse University Press, 1994), 373.

most famously in O'Connor's fiction at the end of "Guests of the Nation," when the narrator Bonaparte has been forced to help execute two English prisoners of war with whom he had become friendly. He describes his feelings after this act almost as though he then sees the world through the wrong end of a telescope, everything small and remote, with himself also a tiny and lonely piece of that landscape, and he makes the oft-quoted remark: "And anything that ever happened me after I never felt the same about again" (12). It occurs also in O'Connor's story "The Mad Lomasneys" in which the capricious and whimsical girl Rita Lomasney decides to marry the first man who comes to her house on a particular afternoon, who happens not to be the man she really admires, Ned Lowry. Ned, a generous but rather diffident young man, finds this out at the end of the story and the shock produces (for him) quite an outburst of emotion, as he "lashed his cigarette savagely into the fire" (120). He, who had been accustomed to observe rather detachedly the chaotic goings-on of the Lomasney clan, now found himself under observation and "a month later," says the narrator in the story's last line, married another woman (120).

We do not know the consequences of Ned's sudden turnabout, although "The Mad Lomasneys" could hardly better demonstrate the disastrous way in which Rita misused her freedom (she had chosen to marry the wrong man and her sister Nellie "was sorry for her" [120]), but another story of romantic entanglement states the man's point of view in a clearer fashion. In "The Masculine Principle" a solid and steady young man, Jim Piper, loves another capricious woman, Evelyn Reilly, and is made to suffer both the shame of her irresponsible actions and, in the eyes of her family, the unspectacular nature of his own virtues. Jim methodically tells Evelyn he wants to marry her but only after he has saved two hundred pounds so they can start off life properly together. Her two romantic sisters scoff at this lack of daring and one Christmas Evelyn decides that they are right and takes the money Jim had saved (he had given it to her for "safe keeping") and runs away to England. After spending all the money there as well as indulging in a love affair, she returns home ruined. Jim, though, is entirely willing to forgive her, all too willing in the eyes of Evelyn's sisters, and Evelyn, too, is frustrated by his easy forgiveness. They start "walking out" together again, though, and Evelyn becomes pregnant by Jim. He is adamant that still they cannot marry, as he has started to save another two hundred pounds, but says he will pay for the baby and help her go to London to have it delivered. The stolidity of Jim's response maddens Evelyn but she reflects: "There was no doubt about it, he was a worm, but at any rate he was her worm" (236). The baby is sent to the country to be nursed, and sometime later Jim comes to the Reilly house, drunk, throws two hundred pounds down on the table, and asks Evelyn to marry him—as long as she will withdraw earlier statements that she would not do so if he were "the last living thing in the world" and that he was a "worm" (239). Evelyn responds, "'You never know,'" but it is clear that she will marry him, and Jim says, "'You can go down the country now, tomorrow if you like, and bring Ownie [the baby] back, and tell the whole bloody town to kiss your ass'" (239).

This is one of O'Connor's great stories about freedom, conversion, and self-knowledge. At one time or another Jim is criticized by everyone of the Reilly household. Mr. Reilly, a contractor given to self-delusion, starts off liking him but plays the conventional role of the outraged father when Evelyn becomes pregnant. Jim's lack of romanticism enrages all the Reilly girls and the town is scandalized that he would pick up with a girl who had jilted him so humiliatingly—and then is scandalized again when he causes her to bear an out-of-wedlock child. True, his boss won't fire him for this because he is a good worker, and his mother blames Evelyn for his situation, but basically Jim's world is turned upside down for the simple fact that he loved one girl from beginning to end and had one rather sound idea about how such a love was to be conducted. If we do not see him literally spending the night in his room alone, as does Pascal's virtuous man, it is because his whole life had been turned into something like this, his course of action understood by no one who knew him. He is lonely and misunderstood, but this becomes the backdrop for his virtues to become clear. Evelyn is converted in the story, from seeing Jim as everyone else had seen him to understanding that her worm had turned into something much more beautiful (his drunkenness mysteriously aiding this process), and she reflects at the end "how much of Jim's life she had wasted along with her own" (239).

It is true that freedom and the changes it brings do not always have as conclusive a result as they do in this story, but the point is that change is possible and the results are quite often positive. "The Face of Evil," for example, presents a typical young O'Connor hero who is a victim of his own innocence: "I was a saint for quite a bit of my life and I never saw anything hard in it."[11] For this lad (not named) the principle of sanity was this: "Not to become involved, to remain detached—that was the great thing; to care for things and for people, yet not to care for them so much that your happiness became dependent on them" (159). He goes frequently to Mass and to Confession, but without anything grand to confess, and his whole attitude to church-going is changed when he becomes friendly with another boy, Charlie Dalton, "a fellow any kid on the road would go a long way to avoid." The basis of the saint's attraction to Charlie was that he was "a fellow who had done all the things I would never do" (162). The story is about the mysterious intersection between good and evil, the saint and the sinner, and the young hero's perception of the connection between the two is fortified when he talks to Charlie at an intersection in Cork called the "Cross" which "had become a place of mystery" where "everything about you melted and fused and became one with a central mystery" (164). This is the prelude to the change which overcomes the boy in church where, after he had persuaded Charlie to go to confession, he became resentful at the severe penance the priest had prescribed for his friend: "What right had Father O'Regan or anyone to treat him like that? Because he was down, people couldn't help wanting to crush him further" (166). This sympathy with the sinner, which the narrator calls "one of the major decisions of my life" (166), is indeed the "central mystery" of the cross in Christianity, and Charlie is one of those "outlawed figures wandering about the fringes of society" that a true saint always takes a great interest in. The change in the boy narrator could not be more profound: from self-satisfied "saint" to one who identified with an outcast of society, and the transformation made him realize, he says at the story's end (O'Connor is not shy about moralizing at the end of stories, but his morals arise naturally from the story's events), that the "life before me would have complexities of emotion which I couldn't even imagine" (166). The story's very last sentence is an epilogue and relates that Charlie was subsequently arrested for stealing and sent back to reformatory, and William Tomory says "the young protagonist learns how delicately an individual's fate hangs in the balance at times—and how

---

[11]This story is in Michael Steinman, ed., *A Frank O'Connor Reader*, 157–66; the quoted passage occurs on 157.

inexorable that fate eventually becomes."[12] But this is not a story about fate; it is a story of a young man, the narrator, who discovers that real saints must learn how to seek out sinners, again a piece of valuable self-knowledge. "Again and again," as John Hildebidle says, "O'Connor allows his characters to *choose*."[13]

O'Connor's concern with freedom is never more vividly and paradoxically presented than in the story "Freedom." Based on his experiences in the Irish Civil War, the story is instead set in the war for independence against England a few years earlier. The narrator says that "When I was interned during the war with the British I dreamed endlessly of escape," and he looks out from his prison camp on the "brilliantly green" landscape of County Kildare and imagines himself traveling across it "maybe for years, maybe till I died" (302). The story concerns one of his friends, Mick Stewart, refusing to carry out one of the menial tasks his Irish hut leader had assigned him to do. In order to have the absolute minimum contact with their British captors, the Irish had established their own prison hierarchy to conduct their affairs. Mick persists in his stubbornness and is punished for it, the theme of the story being that the Irish were subverting the ideals of freedom for which they were fighting by this tyranny against one of their own mates. Mick eventually goes on hunger strike and the narrator comments that the Irish had "allowed themselves to become more tyrannical than the British themselves.... If Mick were to die on hunger strike ... no one would ever take the staff seriously again as suffering Irish patriots" (310). A compromise solution is found and Mick and those who sympathized with him are transferred to another camp. At the end of the story the narrator is depressed because he can no longer think of an adequate definition of liberty, and remarks that now "even the wide fields of Ireland were not wide enough" to ensure his sense of freedom. "Choice," he concludes, "was an illusion. Seeing that a man can never really get out of jail, the great thing is to ensure that he gets into the biggest possible one with the largest possible range of modern amenities" (312–13).

While such a conclusion would seem to deny the existence of freedom, it denies in fact only the romantic idea of freedom of endless possibility and accomplishment that O'Connor always ar-

---

[12]*Frank O'Connor* (Boston: Twayne, 1980), 128. This is generally, though, a helpful overall view of O'Connor's work.

[13]*Five Irish Writers*, 198.

gued against. And it is entirely consistent with the conclusions of some other prison narratives: Socrates in the *Crito* telling his students who tried to rescue him from jail that, given the principles by which he lived his life, there was really nowhere for him to go; Thomas More in the *Dialogue of Comfort Against Tribulation* showing that he was more free after his imprisonment by Henry VIII, that is, that he was more content than those who came to comfort him; Solzhenitsyn in the *Gulag Archipelago* expressing a humor entirely out of keeping with his circumstances. All would agree with O'Connor's narrator that a man never does really get out of jail, a piece of self-knowledge necessary to live in the world as it is. And to live in such a world with the "largest possible range of modern amenities" is to put that knowledge into constructive practice.

Loneliness, then, is the condition of freedom and it is the use of that freedom which determines whether its fruit will be bitter or satisfying. In either case O'Connor always affords his characters the dignity of human beings, and the result is usually happier than is sometimes acknowledged. "Happiness" in the conventional sense, that is, as merely the satisfying of initial desires or impulses (which may be misdirected) or of having only emotions of well-being, O'Connor was not concerned with, as these are quite likely delusory, a point also made in Mary Lavin's great story "Happiness." But to see that one's life presents a number of alternatives and to be conscious of having chosen one of them is the dignity that O'Connor finds appropriate to human beings. Not for him is the oppressive and inexorable constriction of life that Joyce displays with great artistry but also with great inhumanity in *Dubliners*. The early story "There is a Lone House" is typical in this respect. Again there is portrayed the isolated human figure, in this case a country woman abused in early life by her uncle whom she has risen up and killed; she has been permitted to live out her life by her neighbors as long as she stays isolated from them. A young wanderer passes her cottage and stays with her and they start a love affair accompanied by all the expected fluctuations as they discover each other's experiences in life. This is not the "sweet Annie Bradie, the rose of Dunmoyle" of whom the vagabond sang when he first arrived at the woman's cottage (659), but he does find in her an almost bewitching spirit and she finds in him a man who for the first time in her life she can trust. They decide to marry, and when the young man goes to the priest to ask permission, the priest asks the young man if he knows the woman's past and if he is "'satisfied to marry her, knowing that?'" "'I'm satis-fied,'" is his reply (672).

For O'Connor it is this sort of "satisfaction" that an individual might expect to find in the world, known to this couple and to others such as Jim Piper and Evelyn Reilly in "The Masculine Protest." One may miss it, of course, as do Ned Lowry and Rita Lomasney, or may see that its realization still lies ahead of him, as does Ned Keating in "The Uprooted," but it is always present. In-deed, one may run from it, as does Gussie Leonard in "Don Juan's Temptation"—the temptation in this ironic title being that Gussie will give in to the temptation to seek love from a woman rather than only sex—but always there is the knowledge of what one is doing and the possibility that it could be otherwise.

There is of course a certain pathos to a modern sensibility and undoubtedly to O'Connor himself in a character such as Nan Ryan in "The Ugly Duckling," a woman who was ugly as a girl but turned suddenly as a young woman into a great beauty. She rejects her suitor Mick Cortney because he is insufficiently ambitious but also rejects another apparently more suitable man in order to enter a convent. After many years have passed Mick thinks he knows why Nan has acted in this unexpected way: "Because of some in-adequacy in themselves—poverty or physical weakness in men, poverty or ugliness in women—those with the gift of creation built for themselves a rich interior world; and when the inadequacy dis-appeared and the real world was spread before them with all its wealth and beauty, they could not give their whole heart to it" (457). Nan tells Mick that she, too, is somewhat amazed that she is in the convent but adds: "'And it's not that I'm not happy here,'" an assessment with which Mick agrees. He concludes that Nan's "interior world" had called her back and that for her, as for others of the type, "it was a case of having to return there or die" (458). Mick, an agnostic, asks Nan to pray for him, and she, with a "mocking laugh," says, "'Do you think I ever stopped?'" But Mick, too, shows that he has an interior world, as he reflects in the sto-ry's final words that their "old love affair went on unbroken in a world where disgust or despair would never touch it" and would continue to do so till "both of them were dead" (458). There is a poignancy in Mick's saying that Nan had rejected the world with "all its wealth and beauty" but such a world for most O'Connor characters is a false lure—usually one must be a child or childlike to traverse it safely ("The Drunkard," "The Man of the House")— and one's "rich interior world" is a good stay against confusion.

Satisfaction, then, and not frustration, is what O'Connor's characters can expect from the world, a satisfaction based on a knowledge of their freedom, limited but real, and an ability to confront and examine the consequences of their choices—an ability, that is, in Pascal's terms, to quiet the terror of infinite spaces by spending a night alone in their room. But is there anything beyond this? In "The Long Road to Ummera" Abby Driscoll certainly thought so, as death for her meant meeting again her husband. This story, reportedly, helped at least one reader to prepare for death.[14] By almost universal testimony O'Connor himself was an agnostic through most of his life, although published sources do not speak with the same assurance of his last years. He does seem in his writing to be a real agnostic, that is, one who did have an open mind about ultimate questions and did hope to know more. He is more the Thomas Hardy of "The Darkling Thrush," who at least hears the melody of the bird's "happy goodnight air" and its promise of "some blessed hope" than he is the J. Alfred Prufrock who, though the mermaids may be singing, does not think that they will sing to him. O'Connor recognized the transcendence of the Good Friday liturgy on his visit to the lonely French church and its capacity to "convert," although he candidly noted that it had not converted him. Civilization will improve, he also said, when there is a "restoration of the concept of God," which he made clear was not just a theory but a concept, the concept of completeness, of the absolute opposed to the relative, of "a dark sun towards which all life turns."[15] And a concept, as O'Connor would have known very well from Aristotle, is something abstract but nonetheless real, the thing that makes thought possible. He concludes his account of his mother's death in his autobiography by saying, "And I await the resurrection from the dead and eternal life to come" (74), although he has characteristically said just two pages before that he suspected that the Last Judgment will "be rather less than just." At the end of that superb book he says that it is our "vanity that desires eternity," and that for his own soul he could foresee only "nothingness," an example of the humility found throughout *An Only Child*. Yet he allows that some souls are immortal, such as his mother's, and those "even God, if He wished to, could not diminish or destroy," and the last line of the book,

---

[14]See Chatalic, "Frank O'Connor and the Desolation of Reality," 201.

[15]"The Writer and the Welfare State," in Michael Steinman, ed., *A Frank O'Connor Reader*, 290.

where so often he placed the moral of his stories, is a verse from the Psalms: "And when I wake I shall be satisfied with Thy likeness." Or, as Browning's Abt Vogler said in a poem O'Connor knew and quoted[16] and which might be still another appropriate epigraph for his work, "On earth the broken arcs, in heaven the perfect round."

16"The Writer and the Welfare State," 291.

Off-Stage Narrators:
The Evocative Narrative Voice in Frank O'Connor's Stories

Michael Neary

When Richard Rorty dramatizes the "Pragmatist's Progress"—a journey he ruefully attributes to philosophers, novelists, literary critics, and other disillusioned intellectuals—he might well be describing the progression of a character out of Frank O'Connor's short stories. "The final stage of the Pragmatist's Progress," Rorty writes, "comes when one begins to see one's previous peripeties not as stages in the ascent toward Enlightenment, but simply as the contingent results of encounters with various books which fall into one's hands."[1] Time and again we see O'Connor's characters disillusioned in such a way: we see them abandon any notions of teleology and accept what a Sean O'Casey character might term "chassis."[2] It is as if these characters have finally learned to read their lives properly; they have finally seen the ordinary and often sordid details for what they are, recoiling from them (as Larry Delaney does in "Christmas Morning") or embracing them (as Gussie Leonard does in "Don Juan's Temptation").

O'Connor's mode of telling, though, re-opens the sense of possibility so many of his characters learn to scorn. Though his narrative in one way generates intimacy by capturing the sound of a speaking voice, it simultaneously—and for the same reason—cre-

---

[1]Richard Rorty, "The Pragmatist's Progress," in *Interpretation and Overinterpretation*, ed. Stefan Collini (Cambridge: Cambridge University Press, 1992), 89–108, esp. 92.

[2]Jack Boyle ends *Juno and the Paycock* with a declaration of "chassis" (73). See Sean O'Casey, *Three Plays by Sean O'Casey* (New York: St. Martin's, 1957), 1–73.

ates distance. If we seem close to the teller in a folksy, fireside sort of way, we seem equally distant from the told, whose lives are given to us in such a consciously crafted second-hand fashion that we cannot help but question the accounts. We may even be led to conceptualize another story outside of the text, outside of a tale infused with the peculiar, idiosyncratic skepticism engendered by the narrator. Often O'Connor's short fiction slams the door on romanticism, reminding us all the while that it has only depicted one door.

In early stories, O'Connor tends to make this radical uncertainty, this sense of possibility, overt. At the end of "Guests of the Nation," for instance, the narrator does not become skeptical; he grows confused and terrified. He gains consciousness of his own smallness and loses confidence in his previous modes of perception: "... the old woman and the birds and the bloody stars were all far away, and I was somehow very small and very lonely. And anything that ever happened me after I never felt the same about again."[3] In a story from the same volume, "The Procession of Life," young Larry Delaney also confronts sheer mystery, sheer impenetrability, when he encounters a watchman after being locked out of his house:

> He [the watchman] sat in his little sentry-box, smoking his pipe, and looked, thought Larry, for all the world like a priest in the confessional. But he was swathed in coats and scarves, and a second glance made Larry think not of a priest but of some heathen idol; his face was so bronzed above the grey beard and glowed so majestically in the flickering light of the brasier. (*Guests* 264)[4]

The rhythm of movement from familiar to unfamiliar—from the trappings of Larry's own culture, the Catholic Church, to the alien world of the "heathen idol"—repeats itself in the conversation the two have. At first, the man chastises Larry for not standing up to his father: "'And there's a big fella' like you now, and you'd let your father bate you, and never rise a hand in your own self-defence?'" (266). Then, finding that Larry "'took a couple of pulls out of me father's pipe once'" (266), the man's response shifts diamet-

---

[3]Frank O'Connor, *Guests of the Nation* (London: Macmillan, 1931), 19.

[4]Both of these stories come from *Guests of the Nation* (1931), O'Connor's first volume of stories. Since I make a point about the placement of these stories, I quote them from the original volume. Hereafter quotations will come from the latest versions of the stories.

rically: "'No wonder you're locked out!... No wonder at all! I think if I'd a son like you 'twould give me all I could do to keep me hands off him. Get out of me sight!'" (266) The horror of these responses to a young child lies in their inconsistency, an inconsistency Larry absorbs by the end of the encounter: "Terrified at this extraordinary conclusion, Larry retreated to the edge of the circle of light. He dared not go farther" (266).

In a sense, these are the most profound realizations characters can achieve in O'Connor's fiction—or at least the ones most commensurate with O'Connor's own notion of the experience a short story can penetrate. He begins *The Lonely Voice*, his critical work on the modern short story, with this statement from Pascal: "The silence of those infinite spaces terrifies me."[5] His sense of the short story, as he describes it in this work, is that of a genre intimately concerned with loneliness and smallness—a genre, in short, where confidently over-reaching assertions about the world must continually be overturned. In stories after the ones appearing in *Guests of the Nation*, however, this presentation of uncertainty increasingly enters O'Connor's fiction not through direct revelation but through narrative technique. In many later stories we see characters reaching not a sense of mystery but a sense of confident disillusionment. The limited narrative voices, however, undercut our own sense (as readers) of confident disillusionment and rekindle, indirectly, the kind of mysterious appreciation the earlier characters achieve.

Jacques Lacan's discussion of causality illuminates O'Connor's rhythm of back-door revelation, or revelation through opposition. "Whenever we speak of cause," Lacan writes, "... there is always something anti-conceptual, something indefinite."[6] To say that the "phases of the moon are the cause of tides" or that "miasmas are the cause of fever," he continues, is inadequate, for "there is a hole, and something that oscillates in the interval. In short, there is cause only as something that doesn't work" (22). I want to focus here on Lacan's insistence—building on Freud—that a cause works by creating a gap that must be filled, that a cause's power flows from its limitation. The application to O'Connor's narrative voices is clear: his strikingly personalized, finite narrative voices

[5]Frank O'Connor, *The Lonely Voice: A Study of the Short Story* (Cleveland, OH: World, 1963), n.p.

[6]Jacques Lacan, *The Four Fundamental Concepts of Psycho-Analysis*, ed. Jacques-Alain Miller; trans. Alan Sheridan (New York: Norton, 1978), 22.

alert us as readers to the possibility of other voices. These human, alluring, but ultimately inadequate voices carve the "hole[s]" that produce the oscillations of our own imaginations. These voices elicit dissent. Lacan's later characterization of the synchrony between the unconscious, or unspoken, and the conscious, or spoken, continues to dramatize the effect of O'Connor's highly personalized narrative voices: "Rupture, split, the stroke of the opening makes absence emerge—just as the cry does not stand out against a background of silence, but on the contrary makes the silence emerge as silence" (26). The pen-stroke, the brush-stroke, the voice-stroke—any such finite "cry" marks the silence by etching a contrasting particularity, a mental vantage point from which we can apprehend the existence of an Other whose form remains unrealized. My contention with regard to O'Connor is that his lucidly idiosyncratic voices evoke (through contrast) this other, this silence, with unusual acuity. It is a silence whose infinity contradicts the skeptical realization of limitation so many of his characters reach.

A story that seems to assert skepticism with certainty—a certainty granted apparent solidity by the simplicity of the subject—is "Christmas Morning." In this story young Larry Delaney discovers there is no Santa Claus. He also discovers, in the bargain, that his parents are poor and not particularly fond of one another:

> I understood it all, and it was almost more than I could bear; that there was no Santa Claus, as the Dohertys said, only Mother trying to scrape together a few coppers from the housekeeping; that Father was mean and common and a drunkard, and that she had been relying on me to raise her out of the misery of the life she was leading. And I knew that the look in her eyes was the fear that, like my father, I should turn out to be mean and common and a drunkard.[7]

That the solidity of this skepticism is only *apparent* becomes more and more evident as the passage progresses. The first two assertions, that there is no Santa Claus and that Mother is not wealthy, do seem solid; the next, though probably somewhat accurate, may be a bit narrow. The final two lack credibility altogether. Larry's mother had been relying on him "to raise her out of the misery of the life she was leading...."? Not a shred of evidence supporting this conclusion arises in the story. And whether or not "the look in

---

[7]Frank O'Connor, *The Collected Stories of Frank O'Connor*, ed. Richard Ellmann (New York: Knopf, 1981), 206.

her eyes," whatever that look may be, indicates the prophecy young Larry perceives is also unsubstantiated. My point with regard to this story is not that the situation is any brighter than Larry imagines it to be; my point is that the situation remains radically other, radically separate from Larry. He is just as ignorant of the truth by the end of the narrative as he is at the beginning, when he believes in Santa Claus. Skepticism and faith prove equally unhelpful, equally unenlightening. This double-failure illuminates a gap, in readers' minds, in which regeneration—or even further degeneration—can occur. Eavan Boland speaks of this potential in O'Connor's stories as a kind of innocence, a deep innocence pervading the disillusionments O'Connor's characters undergo. She recalls a scene in "My Oedipus Complex" in which young Larry likens himself to the sun, "ready to illumine and rejoice" (in Larry's words) each morning. Boland tellingly describes the way the story progresses:

> With irony as bitter as a lemon "My Oedipus Complex" tells a droll, tough story about how this joy was shattered into a joyless cunning. But even when this process is complete, when the reversal of innocence has been accomplished, the image of a boy beginning his day in imitation of the sun rises out of the action like a flare over a shipwreck.[8]

What I find most revealing about Boland's comment is her last image: a flare that begins another story, a story of what takes place in the massive space outside of the ship, or outside of the arena carved by one of O'Connor's narrators.

The third-person narrators in O'Connor also suggest, indirectly, alternative stories. By mimicking the oral fireside tale, O'Connor continually calls attention to the limitation of the narrator's consciousness, reinforcing the limitation with a clear personality often at odds with the other characters. Calling a character "an uncouth and irritable bastard" (*Collected Stories* 154), as in the story "The Frying Pan," is not unusual for an O'Connor narrator. A paradox is at work in this structure. On one hand this kind of consciousness limits the sense of possibility within a story: a character called an "irritable bastard" has few avenues of development opened to him. On the other hand, though, this limited consciousness accentuates the illusion of existence outside of narrative lines.

---

[8]Eavan Boland, "The Innocence of Frank O'Connor," *Michael/Frank: Studies on Frank O'Connor*, ed. Maurice Sheehy (London: Gill and Macmillan, 1969), 77–85; the quoted passage is from 79.

By making the narrator so fallibly human, O'Connor calls into question his portraits, reminding us that the narrator is presenting details according to his own biases. This act of choice implies other details not chosen. It opens up in a reader's mind a range that would not be suggested with a more reliable-sounding narrator. Quirky narrators who do not inspire our faith create a hermetically sealed narrative-universe with an extremely low ceiling, and a staggering space of secret beyond it.

"Don Juan's Temptation" hints alluringly at such a space. Originally O'Connor created this story with an elaborate frame and a first-person narrator.[9] In his revisions O'Connor eliminated the names and created a third-person perspective. The result is narrative distance: a story-teller with limited knowledge and clear biases. He begins:

> Against the Gussie Leonards of the world, we poor whores have no defenses. Sons of bitches to a man, we can't like them, we can't even believe them, and still we must listen to them because deep down in every man jack of us there is the feeling that our own experience of life is insufficient. (*Collected Stories* 167)

Certainly this narrator cannot be trusted to tell the whole story. O'Connor has consequently drawn our attention to the possibility of a portion *left out.*

The consequence of this nagging suspicion of an extra-textual presence undercuts the possibility of firm disillusionment. This undercutting is crucial to this story since it, like "Christmas Morning," seems to be about disillusionment. Gussie Leonard spends much of the story trying to disabuse Helen of romantic attitudes. "'Being romantic,'" he says, "'is thinking you're very fond of someone you really don't give a damn about, and imagining on that account that you're never going to care for anyone else. It goes with your age'" (171). The most dramatic disillusionment, though, occurs within Gussie himself. As he wanders around the streets after leaving Helen at her doorstep, he thinks of Joan, "a girl who had crossed for a moment his lonely boyhood" before she died (174). When he reaches his own door he sees "a figure by the door, leaning back against the railings" and immediately his skepticism is overturned: "'It's Joan,' was his first thought, and then: 'She's coming back,' and finally, with a growing feeling of incredulity:

---

[9]See Frank O'Connor, *The Common Chord* (New York: Knopf, 1948), 266–78.

'So it does last'" (175). When he realizes the figure is Helen's, and that she has abandoned her idealism and agreed to sleep with him, the intrusion of mystery recedes from his consciousness. "It was all over now, but he felt he had been through a really terrible temptation, the temptation of a lifetime" (175).

Such a conclusion may bring us back to a kind of disappointed comfort, a settling into an ordinary world devoid of spirits. If James Joyce had written the story, though, the comfort would be solider: we would experience the recesses of Gussie's consciousness through the precision and coolness of an artistic surgeon, following language that seems to echo every tremor of consciousness. But O'Connor's narrator unabashedly shuns such intimacy. The story closes, "Sons of bitches! That's what they are, to a man" (175). Gussie stays outside, stays other: the solidity of his skepticism remains thoroughly in question. Has this narrator wrapped up the story neatly and coldly, to fit Gussie into his Don Juan mold?

It is necessary, of course, to recall that O'Connor is writing fiction: the only Gussie that exists is the Gussie delivered by this narrative voice, however hostile that voice may be. "The ultimate basis of our knowing," writes Bernard Lonergan, "is not necessity but contingent fact, and the fact is established, not prior to our engagement in knowing, but simultaneously with it."[10] Lonergan makes this claim about historical knowledge; the claim is even harder to dispute in the realm of fiction. There is no *a priori* Gussie; there is no one in existence whom this narrator can treat unfairly. My claim, then, has to do with the illusion O'Connor creates as part of the fiction. "He saw," writes Richard Ellmann, "that his own art must radiate out from a single nucleus, must not attempt detachment or alien centers-of-consciousness in the manner of James or Joyce."[11] Part of the story, in O'Connor's fiction, entails flaunting narrative limitation—the "single nucleus"—rather than, as Joyce does trying to combat it; in the process his fiction implies the potential for a multiplicity the text itself does not contain.

---

[10]Quoted in Andrew Beards, "Reversing Historical Skepticism: Bernard Lonergan on the Writing of History," *History and Theory* 33.2 (1994): 198–220, esp. 203.

[11]See Richard Ellmann, "Michael/Frank" in *Michael/Frank: Studies on Frank O'Connor*, ed. Maurice Sheehy (London: Gill and Macmillan, 1969), 23–27, esp. 26.

This pattern is not confined to his short stories: even in his letters and essays O'Connor experimented (perhaps inadvertently) with voices of striking limitation—and striking suggestiveness. Ruth Sherry observes the "absoluteness" that characterizes some of O'Connor's letters to Dublin newspapers, noting in particular his suggestion to young Irish writers: "'Read modern books only, and read every book by a modern Irish writer.... Education is a preparation for life, and the only suitable preparation for Irish life is Irish literature.'"[12] Sherry comments: "The advice, whatever prompted it, invites instant dissent. Certainly it sounds unconvincing coming from a writer whose own education came largely from Turgenev, Chekhov, and Goethe" (297). In a few lines Sherry has summed up the reaction I contend O'Connor's short story voices elicit—"dissent"—and confirmed the validity of imagining other realities (in this case consisting of non-Irish readings) outside the strict and often skeptical narrative confines O'Connor generates.

* * *

This suggestion of multiplicity, however, while refusing to assert a definitive skepticism, does refute the kind of romanticism advocated by Yeats and other Irish Revivalists of the early twentieth century and scorned, in this passage, by Seamus Deane:

> ... the desire to see Ireland as "a country of the imagination" led to a conclusion that was identical with its premise. And that was the old Romantic premise that the world could be seen, falsely, in a bleak Newtonian light or, truly, in a pre-Newtonian aura. The destruction of aura, the argument runs, has been brought about by the development of modern science and its evolution into philosophies such as dialectical materialism which Yeats, in an astonishing and garbled paragraph, claims "works all the mischief Berkeley foretold."[13]

That O'Connor disagrees with notions of "Romantic Ireland" certainly becomes evident in the irony of "Guests of the Nation." His impatience with the myth of a pre-Newtonian pastoral (and aristocratic) utopia, furthermore, surfaces in his thorny caricatures of

---

[12]Quoted in Ruth Sherry, "Fathers and Sons: O'Connor Among the Irish Writers: Corkery, AE, Yeats," *Twentieth Century Literature* 35.3 (1990): 275–302, esp. 297.

[13]Seamus Deane, *Celtic Revivals: Essays in Modern Irish Literature: 1880–1980* (London: Faber and Faber, 1985), 33.

figures who hold such views. The Canon in "The Miracle," for instance, receives this kind of barbed, mocking portrait. He is described as a man who "ate his delicate meals with the right wines, brewed coffee and drank green chartreuse" and "liked to read about days when the clergy were really well off" (*Collected Stories* 158). He also yearns for an aristocratic utopia akin to that of the Revivalists:

> It was distasteful to the Canon the way the lower classes were creeping into the Church and gaining high office in it, but it was a real heartbreak that its functions and privileges were being usurped by new men and methods, and that miracles were now being performed out of bottles and syringes. He thought that a very undignified way of performing miracles himself.... (*Collected Stories* 158)

But aside from these caricatured portraits, which come from narrators who as we have seen are themselves suspect, O'Connor disrupts Revivalist notions in a more basic way. By revealing his narrators' blatant biases—a revelation that may alert readers to other narrators' less blatant biases—O'Connor neutralizes the force necessary to transmit a myth as history: un-critical belief in the messenger. In essence O'Connor scoffs at the English Romantic philosophy (so important to Yeats and the Irish Revival) that dubs, in Shelley's words, the poet as "legislator of the world." O'Connor's "poet," or narrator, is too busy fighting his own preoccupations to rule the world. And so, by implication, is everyone else, though some may be less forthcoming in revealing their preoccupations.

My point in this discussion is not, however, that O'Connor's stories contain no complexity within themselves; they do. Frequently, intrinsic complexity and a narrative voice that acknowledges greater, unstated complexity exist within the same story. We see this combination in "Darcy in the Land of Youth," though it takes some time for it to emerge. For much of the story, the tale of Oisin, who spends three hundred earthly years in fairy land with his goddess-wife Niamh only to become trapped on earth during an ill-fated visit, hovers heavily over O'Connor's narrative. For Darcy, England is fairy land, where he befriends Janet (Niamh), who unveils for him a life without Irish inhibitions. Initially the story is appropriately clichéd, a simple plot that meshes neatly with the drama of Oisin: it looks to be a modern re-telling with humor, local color, but also loyalty to the essence of the myth's presentation of a radical dichotomy, an irreconcilable separation of

two worlds. The narrator's language re-enforces the applicability
of the tale:

> Suddenly he remembered the story of Oisin that the monks had
> told him, and it began to have meaning for him. He wondered
> wildly if he would ever get back or if, like Oisin in the story, he
> would suddenly collapse and spend the rest of his days walking
> up and down the Western Road with people as old and feeble as
> himself, and never see Niamh or the land of Youth. You never
> knew what powerful morals the old legends had till they came
> home to you. (*Collected Stories* 276)

The passage so far suggests a kind of latent "Irishness" haunting a
character, lurking below consciousness but animating movement.
One could search hard before finding a more succinct fictional expression of the Revivalists' essentialist philosophy. The next sentence and the rest of the story, though, would quickly send a budding Revivalist back to the library: "On the other hand, their
heroes hadn't the advantages of the telephone." At this point the
dichotomy begins to collapse: Darcy un-mythically returns to the
land of youth (England) and finds the earthly (Irish) qualities he
has tried to escape thriving in fairy land. Janet, whom he had
imagined to be free from sexual scruples, says to him, "'Don't you
see that I wanted to prove to myself that I could be a decent girl for
you, and that I wasn't just one of the factory janes who'll sleep
with anything?'" (281). The story annihilates the boundary which
is the very essence of the Oisin myth. Its narrator, furthermore,
seals the erasure in readers' minds through an absurdly, obviously
unconvincing effort to create a new dichotomy: "That was the
worst of dealing with the English, for the Irish, who had to be serious whether they liked it or not, only wanted to be frivolous, while
the one thing in the world that the English seemed to demand was
the chance of showing themselves serious" (281–82). Given the
fallacy of the first dichotomy, this one has little chance of surviving. But by this time we are buried in the consciousness of a fickle
narrator, as the other characters recede into secret and vast space,
containing a multiplicity of possibility, beyond the tight restraints
of an Irish essentialism, and far away from narrative view: "Later,
he became more reconciled to the idea, and when last heard of was
looking for a house ..." (283).

What is unusual in O'Connor's stories, at least after his first
volume, is a narrative that not only contains complexity, but refuses to call attention to its own limitation. "In the Train" diverges
from O'Connor's other stories in this way. Its narrator is restrained

and, for the most part, nonjudgmental. No hint of a frame, of a communal sharing, appears in the telling. This narrator comes as close as any in O'Connor to a dexterous, self-effacing voice presenting its material from within characters' consciousnesses. In so doing it makes explicit the rhythm I have been discussing as implicit in other stories: it actually depicts rather than suggests a multiplicity of voices. Even the physical description in the story speaks plurals, multiples. As four men converse in one of the carriages we see images reproducing themselves until the hint of any original is lost:

> And while they talked the train dragged across a dark plain, the heart of Ireland, and in the moonless night tiny cottage windows blew past like sparks from a fire, and a pale simulacrum of the lighted carriages leaped and frolicked over hedges and fields. Magner shut the window; and the compartment began to fill with smoke.[14]

In the most basic way this image reminds us of numerous perspectives because we are aware, at least upon second reading, that in the various cars of this train there are separate conversations, separate versions of a trial. The language itself accentuates this notion of multiple perspectives: the train reproduces itself in the form of "a pale simulacrum" on the hedges—a simulacrum that seems to take on life, to "frolic." The scene also explodes into an indiscernible mass of windows and metaphorical sparks until finally, and appropriately, our vision is obscured altogether by smoke. Absent from the description is the characteristic O'Connor narrator summing up the details into a clearly biased, idiosyncratic opinion: this one lets the chaos remain, acknowledging a mystery we are left to intuit in many of the other stories.

The action of this story develops the obscurity latent in this early image. Though presumably a woman has been acquitted for a murder she actually committed, the details remain out of view, offered up only in mocking, sardonic fashion. We instead move from car to car eavesdropping, escorted suggestively by a drunken man looking for his proper car, but never finding it. Our frustration increases when we find that if we had been privy to the trial, we would be no further along in discerning the truth. One juror sums up the situation succinctly: "'We told our story, the lot of us,'

---

[14]See *A Frank O'Connor Reader*, ed. Michael Steinman (Syracuse, NY: Syracuse University Press, 1994), 19.

he said, 'and we told it well'" (24). In a sense reading this story is like reading a host of O'Connor stories simultaneously: it is a story of narrators presenting and distorting reality with clearly biased, clearly self-interested motives, leading us into our own speculations as we observe the gaps these narratives begin to frame.

The presence of this story in O'Connor's opus can serve almost as a focal point: as a reminder of how conscious O'Connor is of the power of perspectives, and as a sign of how reluctant he is to privilege the authority of any single perspective, including his own. But pervading such suspicion, of course, is a deep affection for idiosyncratic perspectives or, more specifically, for voices. O'Connor insisted that he possessed an ear for voices more acute than any other of his senses, an observation noticed by his biographer[15] and confirmed by his stories—stories that carve out narrative voices of peculiarly human distinction and stories that, sometimes, acknowledge the passion directly. The narrator of "Music When Soft Voices Die," for instance, attributes the affection he receives from one of the characters to the fact that "like me, she hears those voices 'vibrate in the memory' and wonders over them."[16]

Harriet O'Donovan Sheehy, widow to O'Connor, acknowledges O'Connor's awareness of a story's latent voices when she describes O'Connor's seemingly endless stream of revisions, his constant re-articulation of stories: "The basic design never changed, but in each new version light would be thrown in a different way on a different place" (*Variations*, Introduction). The existence of these re-writings, as keenly as any observation about O'Connor's stories, hints at the well of possibility lurking within one of his narratives—a well that, in lieu of a truly endless stream of O'Connor revisions, leaves the reader to ponder, or to wonder over, the many voices that may still emerge.

---

[15]James Matthews called the biography *Voices: A Life of Frank O'Connor* (New York: Atheneum, 1983). He discusses O'Connor's quest to replicate the sound of the speaking voice in, among other places, his discussions of O'Connor and Yeats (see esp. 100).

[16]Frank O'Connor, *A Set of Variations on a Borrowed Theme* (New York: Knopf, 1969), 152.

The Making of Sensibility: Loneliness, Shame, and the Narrative Voice of Frank O'Connor

Julianne White

"Certain men, born into haphazard and incoherent surroundings, do not acquiesce to them, but grow isolated. For a while, they search dispiritedly for a contrast, until one day they stumble on a clue in the paperchase. In their attempt to follow it out, to reconcile it with the blind alleys of their previous experience, a huge and tragic innocence is involved."

Eavan Boland

I. Introduction

Loneliness and its cousin shame figure prominently in the work of Irish short story writer Frank O'Connor. They are key ingredients in the creation of O'Connor's "submerged population groups,"[1] and they are tempered by the warmth and humor of O'-Connor's narrative voice. Monica, in "The Grand Vizier's Daughters," and Larry Delaney, in "The Duke's Children," are indeed members of O'Connor's submerged population groups, whose struggle toward understanding (of themselves and others)—painted in compassionate and humorous colors by the narrative technique perfected over the course of O'Connor's career—will be the focus of this essay.

O'Connor's stories are very often narrated by or centered around children or adolescents. These characters therefore have a unique (and very often skewed) view of the events going on around them, or even of the events they themselves set into motion. In "The Grand Vizier's Daughters," Willie (the narrator) be-

---

[1]See Frank O'Connor, *The Lonely Voice: A Study of the Short Story* (Cleveland, OH: World, 1963), 18.

comes the detached observer, chronicling the father's awareness of his daughter's shame of him. The act of storytelling itself—here mirrored by the father's drunken storytelling—becomes "a communion, a sharing of experience"[2] which creates a paradox: while it brings the father closer to his daughter, it also creates a rift between them, exposing, as it does, Monica's sense of isolation and shame. While the outer story of Monica's grappling with her own emotions (and her father's potentially abusive behavior) could have made for a bleak, grim story of a dysfunctional family, O'-Connor's narrative skill makes the story-within-a-story laughably silly. The result is that the funny aspects of the father's story work, like the proverbial spoonful of sugar helping the medicine go down, to buffer the seriousness of his message without sacrificing any of its impact.

Larry Delaney, the teenaged narrator of "The Duke's Children," is convinced of one thing in his life: these coarse, uncouth creatures could not possibly be his parents. Surely, a mistake was made somewhere, and he is actually the long-lost son of a duke or earl or some other personage of "quality." "The Duke's Children," according to Eavan Boland, "describes the resentment and isolation which must precede the making of any sensibility."[3] This process, of Larry inventing "a larger meaning for himself" (Boland 83), arises from and is intensified by the loneliness of isolation, of living in "an imaginative kingdom" (Boland 82). Larry Delaney isolates himself in his own "imaginative kingdom" partly because of his shame of having working-class parents. His narration of that isolation is funny, though, in its very preposterousness. This story, coming nearly twenty years *after* "The Grand Vizier's Daughters," shows the mature O'Connor at the height of his narrative skill: the element of the abusive father/dysfunctional family is only suggested, and the focus instead is on Larry Delaney's interior pretensions, making his revelation at the end of the story even more effective and satisfying for the reader.

Both of these stories represent a departure from O'Connor's usual habit of placing the mother/son relationship center-stage,

---

[2]Deborah Averill, "Human Contact in the Short Stories," in *Michael/ Frank: Studies on Frank O'Connor*, ed. Maurice Sheehy (New York: Knopf, 1969), 28–37, esp. 29.

[3]Eavan Boland, "The Innocence of Frank O'Connor," in *Michael/Frank: Studies on Frank O'Connor*, ed. Maurice Sheehy (New York: Knopf, 1969), 77–85, esp. 82.

featuring instead relationships between *fathers* and their off-spring. In "The Grand Vizier's Daughters," the reader's attention is completely commanded by the troubled relationship between a father and a daughter; in "The Duke's Children," Larry Delaney must reconcile himself to the reality of his father's working-class status, as well as to the reality that Nancy Harding's relationship with her father is just as troubled as Larry's is with his. In these two stories, fathers and their children join mothers and their sons in that category of submerged population groups for which O'Connor is so famous.

The literary depiction of these submerged population groups by O'Connor reflects his preoccupation with and "intense awareness of human loneliness" (Averill 30). O'Connor's theories concerning the nature of literature in general and the short story in particular are put into practice in his own writing in a narrative voice that is rich with his belief in the inherent dignity of human beings and full of compassion for human tragedy. The tandem themes of loneliness and shame appear in both "The Grand Vizier's Daughters" and "The Duke's Children" as deliberate constructs created by an author concerned with both their deleterious effects and their ability to "precede the making of any sensibility" necessary for living a human life.

II. "The Grand Vizier's Daughters"

In "The Grand Vizier's Daughters," O'Connor layers the narratives like three levels of an inner-city housing tenement. The story is being told by Willie, nephew of the father and cousin to the girls, Monica and Josie. Willie, however, is a biased narrator, as he admits his hero-worship early on in the story, even while reporting the sounds of his uncle's drunken behavior on the street and his groping of the maid before he comes upstairs to say good night to the children. When the children demand a story from their father, Willie then dutifully narrates the father's story as well; by the end of the father's story, however, Willie's presence has become relegated to the background, giving the Uncle's story full prominence. Willie's narration is the far outer story, surrounding the story of the relationship between Uncle and his adolescent daughter Monica, which further surrounds the inner story which is narrated by Uncle.

The reader does not learn until the final four paragraphs the source of the implied friction between Monica and her father: Monica, interested in a shopkeeper's son, will not invite him home because her father's drunkenness and lecherous reputation embarrass her. The shopkeeper influences his son to give up on the young woman, who then has to endure the gossip of the women in the village. Yet the drunken, blasphemous old man—both the "Grand Vizier" of the father's tale and the father of O'Connor's story—is revealed as not so out of touch after all. He knows how his daughter feels, both about the boy from town and about his own reputation. He knows how gossipy women can affect his daughter's views. But he also believes that family loyalty is more important than any of these other considerations, and he wants to remind Monica of that belief.

Uncle tells a silly story of a "Grand Vizier" in Turkey who has a dispute with a "Grand Mufti" over an umbrella and some suspiciously English/Irish-sounding manners, and who also conveniently has a daughter who is ashamed of him. Uncle tells this far-fetched tale in order to hold a corrective lens up to his daughter's eyes, to force her to face her shame and hold her accountable for it, firmly, but allowing the blow to be softened by the humor of his story. His action is not mean-spirited. It serves, rather, a greater purpose: "The storyteller in O'Connor's stories assumes the universal relevance of human action and its consequences and the analogy of the hearer's values to his own."[4] Monica's shame of her father, in O'Connor's vision, is a universal experience, one from which she learns about herself, about her father, and about family. Monica's vehement denial rings quite hollow against the truth of her father's "'God help us,' he said bitterly, 'she was ashamed of her father.'"[5] Uncle, after all, is only telling the truth, and Monica will be strengthened in the future because she has come to terms with her own failings and makes a sincere promise not to repeat them.

The storytelling-after-a-night-of-drinking motif provides the "communion, a sharing of experience expressed in the concrete acts of speaking and touching" (Averill 29) necessary for reinte-

---

[4]Kate Murphy, "Grappling with the World," *Twentieth Century Literature* 36.3 (Fall 1990): 310–43, esp. 312.

[5]Frank O'Connor, "The Grand Vizier's Daughters," in *Crab-Apple Jelly* (New York: Knopf, 1945), 33. All subsequent parenthetical citations refer to this publication.

grating Monica back into the family fold. Monica's task is to reconcile social expectations with the human failings apparent within the family structure. This is a difficult task for adults, much less for adolescents. But in this moment of contact, in the act of storytelling and listening, the reader can see O'Connor's belief that "contact with others draws them [his characters] out of themselves; the imperfect struggling animal in them impels them to overcome barriers to communication" (Averill 32).

Monica's problem is not just that she remains closed off, from herself and from the family. Monica's problem is also one of

> loyalty.... [All of O'Connor's characters] will be successful human beings when they choose in personal action to be loyal to the demands of the individual soul, and unsuccessful when, by adherence to a lesser loyalty, usually a group loyalty, they betray those demands. (Murphy 319)

The lesser, "group" loyalty Monica mistakenly chose consisted of the social expectations created by the class distinctions of her community. The loyalty she betrayed was to her family, and her father in particular. Her denial of her shame and her promise at the very end of the story—"'I'll never do it again!'"—illustrate her awareness of that betrayal and its consequences, as well as her desire to make amends. Her "final position is one of a fully human aloneness, unmitigated by false assumptions of commonality with groups" (Murphy 321). It is only from this position that she can broach reintegration into the family.

III. "The Duke's Children"

"The Duke's Children"—because of its gentle humor, the universality of human experience at its core, and the character of Larry Delaney—is perhaps the finest achievement of Frank O'-Connor's storytelling art. In this story, O'Connor tones down his usually acerbic humor, choosing instead to allow the humor to arise from Larry Delaney's dreamy delusions. This change indicates, perhaps, a more mature storyteller who is far more interested in Larry's self-discovery than in one character forcing another character's confession.

Kate Murphy explains that "The Duke's Children" focuses on "the relationship of a narrator to a father who fails his inborn responsibility as a father-ideal.... The young narrator rejects his laborer father, who is unfitting to the falsely superior self-image the narrator has assumed" (317). Larry Delaney rejects the father who works in a manure factory, who becomes impatient if his evening paper is the least bit late in arriving, and who fashions his own "slippers" from "boots cut into something that resembled sandals."[6] He prefers instead Nancy Harding's father, who works in a bank and is described as "a small man with a face like a clenched fist, always very neatly dressed, ... [who] usually carried his newspaper rolled up like a baton and sometimes hit his thigh with it as he strode briskly home" (97).

The contrast between these two men is striking. The reader, from the vantage point of objectivity, sees Mr. Delaney at first as a simple if perhaps stubborn man lacking his son's grand pretensions. Mr. Harding, in contrast, is a man whose face like a "clenched fist" and whose rolled up newspaper-baton/weapon suggest a barely contained violence, a man who wields considerable power, both at home and at work. But Larry Delaney, absorbed in his own isolation, sees his father as a slob and Mr. Harding as a paragon of manly virtue. Mr. Delaney, in his son Larry's eyes, fails as an ideal father just by being down-to-earth and completely without the social graces that Larry so highly esteems.

Eavan Boland attributes Larry's misguided preference for the genteel directly to Frank O'Connor's Irishness: "Across years of humiliation no people can hold their possessions intact and least of all their chief possession of identity. Sooner or later they begin to lose it by seeing themselves through the eyes of their oppressors, and to measure worth by that measure until pride becomes shame, self-knowledge self-denial" (81). Larry Delaney's denial of his father's worth illustrates this very process in microcosm. Unfortunately, he sees his father "through the eyes of his oppressors," measuring his worth by false standards, the standards of the "ducal scorn" (O'Connor 96) to which Larry aspires. This theory finds further support in Larry's description of his father's irritation with him when he would rather read than talk with his father and his father's "comrades" (a very pretentious word, when "mates" would have suited). Larry reports that his father "seemed to think it a matter of pride" (O'Connor 96) that he was born in their

---

[6]Frank O'Connor, "The Duke's Children," in *Adventures in Appreciation*, ed. Laurence Perrine, et al. (New York: Harcourt, 1979), 93–102, esp. 93. Subsequent parenthetical citations will refer to this text.

neighborhood, an attitude that leaves Larry bewildered and more convinced than ever of his "true identity."

Larry's notions of "breeding" and gentility come from his exposure to the literature of England (mostly Dickens), Ireland's oppressor for centuries. He rejects the boisterous talk and story-swapping of his father and his father's friends, preferring instead to read. Larry, isolated in his fantasy world, tells ridiculous tales to Nancy Harding of his accomplished learning. His misguided attempts to impress her with his acquired knowledge (which, in his fantasy-world, is proof-positive of his real patrimony) actually backfire on him. The much-longed-for invitation to visit the Harding household never materializes, but not because Nancy's family see him as the son of a laborer (which is what he assumes), but rather because Nancy actually believed Larry's preposterous stories and assumed that her own home would not live up to his standards. This paradox is what Michael Neary calls the "inside-out world" so prevalent in O'Connor's stories:

> The inside is not, in its "commonness," relying on an outside to nourish it. The outside, so horrible and chaotic, has left the inside to its own resources—and the inside, now disillusioned, enters a process of profound change. This is aloneness: a receding from the outside world, an annihilation of old modes of perception.[7]

This definition of "aloneness" elevates the concept of loneliness from the banal to the sublime: O'Connor's characters' loneliness is more than just isolation from others or from the environment, although it is also both of those things as well. This concept of loneliness is alienation from self, from one's very identity.

Kate Murphy delineates the duality of Frank O'Connor's world: "Man's challenge, then, is to accomplish the objective ... by discovering and correcting errors within himself, and by discovering and avoiding the errors in his world. His primary method for correction is dissociation from error within and without" (313–14). This method very nearly fails Larry Delaney, however, when he applies it to his father (without) and himself (within). He is "saved," though, by Nancy Harding's similar mistake. "By discovering an individual who gives evidence of a vision identical to his own, the child finds his own loneliness suddenly relieved" (Murphy 315). As soon as Larry discovers that the real reason he

---

[7]Michael Neary, "The Inside-Out World in Frank O'Connor's Stories," *Studies in Short Fiction* 30 (1993): 327–36, esp. 332.

was never invited to the Harding house was Nancy's shame of her father, her sisters, and her house, he realizes that "the reason I had cared so much for Nancy was that she, like myself, was one of the duke's children, one of those outcasts of a lost fatherland who go through life living above and beyond themselves like some image of man's original aspiration" (O'Connor 101).

As Neary puts it, "The vision that ultimately brings solace to O'Connor's characters is a shared vision, though one that emerges from isolation" (332). Larry, faced with an image of his own warped perceptions in the person of Nancy Harding, can finally see himself—and, by extension, his father, his neighborhood, and his own, real heritage—for who and what he really is, an Irish boy of working-class Irish parents. He sees without by looking within. Larry's loneliness, then, functions as a corrective lens, which Larry places on his own face (as opposed to Uncle's placing that same lens on Monica's). He can finally see his own loneliness only when it is reflected through someone else's identical alienation, projected onto someone else's matching canvas.

Larry Delaney experiences a "radiant intuition" (Boland 81) about his own identity when faced with his mirror image in the person of Nancy Harding. Monica's experience may be less radiant, perhaps, but no less intuitive, when she is faced with the truth of her shame. For both of these characters, the moments of illumination in their own souls come from human contact, which reflects an image of their own loneliness. It is within the context of this paradox that they find—and come to terms with—themselves.

IV. O'Connor's Narrative Voice

None of the narrators in these two stories is particularly reliable: Larry's perceptions are distorted by his fantasy life; Willie confesses his bias (he worships his uncle); and the unnamed Uncle, besides being a drunken, blasphemous lecher, has an agenda, which is to make his daughter admit to her shame of him. Larry's internal dialogue, Willie's biased observations, and Uncle's plan all work toward muddying the narrative waters considerably.

Like Conrad's *Heart of Darkness*, "The Grand Vizier's Daughters" is a tale told by a narrator who is witness to a tale told by another narrator. Willie, the narrator of the outer story, confesses immediately that he is not impartial:

> He was a tall, gaunt, melancholy-looking man. I worshiped him
> and he never saw it, the old idiot. Often when we met in town he
> went by without noticing me, lost in his own thoughts, his hands
> behind his back, his head bowed into the collar of his overcoat,
> while his lips moved as if he were talking to himself.... It wasn't
> wishing to me to break in on him. (26)

This is not a flattering or sympathetic description. The reader is
not invited to join in Willie's hero-worship. In fact, we are left
wondering what in the world Willie sees in this man that is fit to
worship. Quite a distance exists between narrator and narratee at
this point in the story. The reader has neither an intellectual appreciation of nor an emotional commitment to either Willie or his
uncle yet. Uncle is never named in the story but instead is referred
to only as "my uncle" or "the Boss"; yet the inner story the uncle
narrates dominates the outer story. So the reader is left to examine
and identify with the emotions of the listeners of the inner tale,
Uncle's daughters Monica and Josie, particularly Monica.

The relationship between Uncle and Monica is not an easy one.
O'Connor skillfully foreshadows the end and paints the picture of
their estrangement by noting Monica's constant interruptions of
her father's story and his irritated and short-tempered responses.
However, there are also instances during the storytelling when
Uncle praises Monica as well. "'Exactly!'" my uncle exclaimed ex-
citedly, punching his left palm with his fist.' 'Pon my word, Mon,
you have it!'" (27) is followed by "'But, God Almighty, when ye
won't listen to me! How the blazes can I tell the story at all if ye
keep on interrupting me?'" (29). This is a tempestuous, difficult fa-
ther-daughter relationship.

The fact that the daughters have to drag the climax and the *real*
point of Uncle's story from him only increases its emotional impact, especially for Monica. Although Monica, with the self-recog-
nition of the guilty, realizes immediately that the father and
daughter in her father's made-up story are really herself and her
own father, her vehement denial and equally vehement promise
never to repeat her mistake take the reader aback for a bit. These
layers of characterization are complex and fraught with a family
dynamic of which the reader has no prior knowledge. Even Willie
has removed himself and his hero worship from the story by the
end. All that is left is Uncle's pronouncement of his daughter's
shame and her denial and promise.

The reader's slow realization of Uncle's wisdom forces us to
take a step back and come to understand that Uncle is, indeed,

aware of the life happening around him and not stuck in his own melancholy, as the picture of him provided for us by the biased Willie first implies. Moreover, although his use of storytelling as a way to force his daughter into accountability seems cruel and harsh at first, we are left with a begrudging awe for the skill with which he wields that storytelling power, just as we appreciate O'-Connor's equally powerful storytelling skill. This narrative technique has results that require the reader's reflection and thought; the surprise of the ending does not happen instantaneously, as it does in "The Duke's Children." Rather, realization dawns slowly, unfolding after the fact, leaving the reader pondering. The full impact of such reflection penetrates by degrees and lingers long after.

Larry Delaney's warped notions are crucial to creating the effective ending of "The Duke's Children." In order for Larry to be shocked by Nancy Harding's mirror-image shame of her own father, he has to be completely enmeshed in his own version of his life. O'Connor achieves this narrow focus by telling the story through Larry's first-person retrospective narration—an adult's memories. James Kilroy refers to this as "a *purportedly* naive perspective" (emphasis added).[8] Larry's utter conviction that his parents could not possibly be his parents is a fantasy that most adolescents entertain at some point, so the reader immediately shares a point of reference with Larry. Even though there are hints throughout the narration that Larry is indeed wrong, his romantic notions are so commonplace among adolescents that the reader at first easily overlooks those hints. The technique of using a grown narrator who looks fondly back on childhood or adolescent experiences is, in fact, a hallmark of O'Connor's narratology.

It is the absolute reality of Larry Delaney's world that he most vigorously denies: he is a common Irish lad of hard-working parents who wants badly to believe that he is not. This hard reality is softened by being recalled by the adult narrator's memory, so much so that the humor and warmth of the narrative voice fool the reader, just as Larry fools himself. For example, from the very beginning we are told that Larry was "at work as a messenger boy on the railway" (93), a fact placing him squarely in working-class commonness rather than in the aristocratic nobility he claims. He confesses to "having always been Mother's pet" and to being

---

[8]James F. Kilroy, "Setting the Standards: Writers of the 1920s and 1930s," in Kilroy, ed., *The Irish Short Story* (Boston: Twayne, 1984), 95–144, esp. 117.

"comparatively grown-up" (the qualifier "comparatively" speaks volumes about how far from "grown-up" he really is [93]). He describes his habit of creating a fantasy inner-life, one which seems so plausible, even though both Larry and the reader recognize it as fantasy, when

> by some sort of instinct I knew who I really was, [and I] could stand aside and watch myself come up the road after my day's work with relaxed and measured steps, turning my head slowly to greet some neighbor and raising my cap with a grace and charm that came from centuries of breeding.... I could hear an interior voice that preceded and dictated each movement, as though it were a fragment of a storybook: "He raised his cap gracefully while his face broke into a thoughtful smile." (93)

These passages provide the gentle comic relief of this story, and they also charm the reader into sharing Larry's fantasies right alongside him, clues to the "truth" be damned. In fact, Larry is the veritable opposite of the objective third-person narrator. His fantasies control the story to such an extent that the reader over-identifies with him, thus making the distance between narrator and narratee negligible.

This lack of distance is vital for the ending of the story to work. The reader must be as shocked as Larry to discover Nancy's "real identity" as "one of the duke's children." Although on some level the reader can and does laugh at the preposterousness of Larry's pretensions, that is only because we see so much of ourselves in Larry. The humor in this story is so gentle, so couched in Larry's desire for a better life than his parents', that it is difficult even to blame him for creating a world where his social-climbing is the only appropriate response to his working-class circumstances.

Gerald Prince explains that the "intrusiveness of a given narrator, his degree of self-consciousness, his distance from the narrated or the narratee not only help characterize him but also affect our interpretation of and response to the narrative."[9] Larry does not just intrude himself into this narrative; he also controls it and manipulates the reader's emotional commitment to him, so that *his* surprise revelation and self-knowledge at the end of the story become the reader's surprise and self-knowledge as well. O'Connor's narrative control is at its most effective in this story. Larry Delaney's inner life of genteel good breeding is contrasted

---

[9]Gerald Prince, *Narratology: The Form and Functioning of Narrative* (New York: Mouton, 1982), 13.

with the humor, insight, compassion, and real life represented by his parents. It is in the contrast itself that both Larry and the reader find understanding.

V. Conclusion

While most scholars generally agree that Frank O'Connor is a master of the short story, I would argue that his most specific strength lies in his stories about children, who constitute their own "submerged population group," a specialized group within a specialized group. O'Connor not only seems to know and understand the terrors and joys of children's experiences, he also seems to love such experiences for the truth they contain, not only about children's lives, but about the adults those children will soon grow into. The characters in O'Connor's stories are very much like the people we know and the people we are; the "distinctive voice" (Kilroy 105) which tells us those stories is warm with compassion and regard for the characters it describes.

This is a narrative voice that concerns itself with the everyday successes and failures of the common person, not the exploits of heroes. This is a voice that cannot accept a world devoid of meaning, and so instead finds meaning in—and even romanticizes—everyday life, especially the everyday life of children. This is a voice that wants to believe. This voice tells us stories that make us laugh at ourselves, finds order amid chaos, and finds beauty and meaning in what only *seems* ugly and meaningless. This voice, the voice of Frank O'Connor, expresses on our behalf the loneliness inherent in the human condition. Yet it thereby encourages a communal sensibility toward which we aspire and which we sometimes achieve.

Frank O'Connor's *New Yorker* Stories: The Serious Side

James D. Alexander

By the time Frank O'Connor was ten years into publishing in the American magazine *The New Yorker*, he had assumed a reputation as a teller of humorous stories, light anecdotes, and first-person whimsical narratives. Readers tend to recall him as a consummate storyteller, but withal a literary light-weight who is not to be taken seriously. As a result of this *New Yorker* connection, his stories are seen as having, in the words of Richard J. Thompson, a "puckish charm, mannered humor, quaint local color, predictable warmth, and a general blandness." The author is too "gentle," at times too "slapstick."[1] This is one of the grandiose misconceptions of the American reading world; the Irish would never have recognized the O'Connor envisioned by Americans. In Ireland O'-Connor had already achieved a name for annoying compatriots with his comments on the abysmal state of the country,[2] for saying things about his native land that the Irish did not want to hear,[3] and for making himself, in general, a curmudgeon.[4]

---

[1]"A Kingdom of Commoners: The Moral Art of Frank O'Connor," *Eire–Ireland* 13.4 (1978): 65–80; see 67.

[2]See John V. Kelleher, "Frank O'Connor," *Harper's Bazaar* (Oct. 1952): 162.

[3]See James H. Matthews, *Voices: A Life of Frank O'Connor* (New York: Atheneum, 1983), 198.

[4]See The Bellman, "Meet Frank O'Connor," *The Bell* 16:6 (March 1951): 41–46.

By 1950 Irishman Benedict Kiely was writing that O'Connor in his current works was indulging in pointless defiance and irreverence; see Kiely's *Modern Irish Fiction—A Critique* (Dublin: Golden Eagle Books, 1950). Also, O'Connor's 1950 article for *Holiday* magazine on Ireland ac-

The profile of O'Connor among Americans is largely based on his *New Yorker* stories, to be sure,[5] and the stories that are remembered tend to be those like "The Drunkard" (first published 7/3/48), which have been dazzlingly successful and have appeared in numerous anthologies in the United States. In fact, merely mentioning O'Connor among Americans at scholarly conferences is enough to bring smiles, chuckles, and guffaws from the audience.

As we become more familiar with the O'Connor *New Yorker* canon, however, we find that even the funniest stories confront some social taboos. "The Drunkard," for instance, includes a lengthy scene of child drunkenness, against a background of periodic alcoholism on the part of the father. "Fish for Friday" (6/18/55) presents an amusing pub crawl by a man who has gone out to get a doctor for his wife, gets diverted, forgets what he went for, and returns with fish. Meanwhile his wife is in the pangs of childbirth. "The Man of the House" brings smiles by virtue of the innocent complacency of the narrator, a boy who on his trip to get medicine for his mother is seduced by a slum girl and ends up bawling like a baby. But while the child's behavior is humorous, he does have Oedipal yearnings,[6] becomes intoxicated on the medicine, and leaves his mother in the throes of tubercular coughing.

It turns out, in other examples of his *New Yorker* fiction, that humor is part of O'Connor's way of giving light treatment to serious subjects. Without such humor, the stories would be dealing with material that might otherwise appear too seamy. "News for the Church" (9/22/45) seems to invade the confidentiality of the confessional, but much of the story is lightened by the satire of Father Ring, who is scandalized not by what he hears, but by the aplomb with which the girl tells it. "My Da" (10/25/47: 30–34) presents a masochistic and alcoholic mother who tends to squeeze money out of her child to support her habit, and a generally absent father who, when home, is a wife-beater. The one "caretaker" child

---

tually was not a tourist piece but focused instead on the country's social problems; see the anonymous article entitled "Master of the Short Story," *The Irish Times* (11 March 1966): 4.

[5]See James H. Matthews, "Frank O'Connor's Stories: The Contending Voice," *Sewanee Review* 84.1 (Winter 1976): 56–75, esp. 70.

[6]See Edward C. McAleer, "Frank O'Connor's Oedipus Trilogy," *Hunter College Studies II* (1964): 33–40.

has to deal with them, and his clumsiness and pusillanimity are the only source of humor. Ironically this Stevie Leary turns out to be a priest in the end, thus winning his mother's pride, if not her sobriety. More ironically, the mother has been saying of the boy that he would never be the man his father is.[7] Indeed, it seems that in O'Connor's fictional world, as Benedict Kiely would have it, serious ideas are booby-trapped with laughter (9–14).

If the Frank O'Connor of the *New Yorker* stories seems funny, half of the explanation is that the magazine by the early fifties was taking on the cast of a humorous publication when there was a dearth of humorists on the New York literary scene. No one felt this dearth more than chief editor and founder Harold Ross, whose career extended to 1952, some seven years after O'Connor began to write for the magazine.[8] Ross had already influenced the writing in the magazine departments—such as the Profile, the "Talk of the Town," and the "letter" from abroad—so that it was "light-handed."[9] Moreover, many readers' impression of *The New Yorker* may rest upon pieces by James Thurber, dialogues by Frank Sullivan ("The Cliché Expert"), or the squibs (which were always good for a laugh). Rightly or wrongly, readers perceive *The New Yorker* as being a medium for—at most—sophisticated, though not necessarily serious, writing.

The other half of the explanation is that O'Connor, on the American side of the Atlantic, projects certain qualities in his fiction which are allied to humor. One is a speaking voice with warmth,[10] a quality that pervades such stories as "The Drunkard," of course. But similar warmth leaps out at us early in others like "The Pretender" (12/2/50: 40–43), a story that is otherwise acrid: "But Mother was like that, with an ear for any story and ready to give things away to everyone in the city of Cork" (40). This warm tone is a function of O'Connor's use of the child's point of view for

---

[7]"My Da" was selected as the writer's best *New Yorker* story up to 1949, and was included, along with those from the magazine's other writers, in a collection titled *55 Stories from The New Yorker* (New York: Simon and Schuster, 1949).

[8]Dale Kramer, *Ross and The New Yorker* (Garden City, NY: Doubleday, 1951), 279–80.

[9]Brendan Gill, *Here at The New Yorker* (New York: Random House, 1975), 388.

[10]See Thomas Molyneux, "The Affirming Balance of Voice," *Shenandoah* 25.2 (Winter 1974): 27–43.

many of his narrators. Another typical trait of some of his *New Yorker* stories is what Michael G. Cooke identifies as the quality of "artlessness" in the telling and construction of the tales.[11] This quality can easily be misread as implying humor.

However, most of O'Connor's forty-five *New Yorker* stories are not humorous. At most they contain ironic outcomes or reversals that are not even risible. A group of these stories deal with characters passing up suitable marital choices or making *mesalliances* ("Expectation of Life" [8/13/55]; "The Duke's Children" [6/16/56]; "A Torrent Damned" [9/13/52]; "Unapproved Route" [9/27/52]; and "The Pariah" [9/18/56]). For instance, in "The Duke's Children" the narrator discovers years afterward that while he thought he was being snubbed by his girlfriend's affluent family, it was really his former girlfriend who thought he was snubbing her.

If we look at the whole of the O'Connor canon in *The New Yorker*, we find that the fictional materials, together and without the overlay of humor, present a sordid picture of Ireland. It is a country rife with alcoholism, voyeurism, family violence, poverty, slums, prostitution, and other social dysfunctions that Americans do not associate with a romanticized society. The average American would find O'Connor's Ireland disquieting: it bears little resemblance to any picture of a green land of innocent sturdy people living in white thatched cottages framed by shamrocks and graced with lines from the Melodies of Moore. The sophisticated reader of *The New Yorker* would be harder to shock by O'Connor's Cork portraits; after all, the magazine was founded on the premise that it would make no concessions to "'the little old lady from Dubuque.'"[12] But even so, O'Connor often lightens his literary naturalism with humor.

The charm of "The Face of Evil" (4/3/54: 24–28), for example, is in its beginning, in which the boy narrator takes his heroic virtue for granted: "I could never understand all the old talk about how hard it is to be a saint. I never saw anything hard in it, and I was a saint for quite a bit of my life ..." (24). This opening leads to the expectation that a humorous story will follow—an expectation fulfilled for a page or so as the narrator talks about his way of living

---

[11]"Frank O'Connor and the Fiction of Artlessness," *University Review* 5 (1968): 87–102.

[12]Ross quoted in Philip Stevick, *The American Short Story, 1900–1945* (Boston: Twayne, 1984), 9.

as a saint in the real world of slums and corner boys. But things change soon enough. The narrator is shown to be surprisingly articulate when he explains to Charlie, the neighborhood tough, the benefits of confession. And after Charlie accompanies him to church, the narrator discovers that Charlie, like Shakespeare's Claudius, can do no more than bend his knees; soon he reverts to his old life. There is a lesson here if the narrator could only tease it out. The influence of example is a powerful one, and in setting an example the narrator at least gets Charlie into the confessional. But beatings from his father are another powerful determinant in Charlie's life, and the rage they trigger in him cannot be offset by the narrator's sanctity. Thus Charlie will soon lapse back among the unredeemable. The story ends on an ominous note, but the insight it confers on the reader makes it worth reading. It implies that although more good can be achieved by example than by brute force, brute force may undo the good.

The more "serious" stories are to be found among others than the ones told by small boys. A subset of these has to do with priests, or with the conditions of the priesthood. The majority revolve around Father Fogarty, a good-natured, rather worldly, strongly sympathetic churchman. And while some stories, like "Requiem" (6/29/57), in which the curate strains himself to convince a parishioner that her deceased dog will go to heaven without benefit of clergy, are hilarious, most of the stories are devoid of humor. For this they substitute a quality of warmth. They consistently portray the humaneness of Father Fogarty, a man possessing (in the words of the narrator) "a heart as big as a house," a man characterized by his "profound humanity." Three of the stories are towering ones in O'Connor's creative output: "An Act of Charity," "The Mass Island," and "The Teacher's Mass."

In "An Act of Charity" (5/6/67: 48–51) Fogarty, from whose viewpoint the story is told, is involved in the cover-up of Father Galvin's suicide, but his redeeming quality is that he is more sensitive to the ethics of the situation than are Father Maginnis, Fitzgerald the undertaker, and the new curate. A number of themes are brought out powerfully by O'Connor in this story, which rivals his pre-*New Yorker* "Guests of the Nation" for its depiction of an ethical choice. One theme is the element of professionalism. Father Maginnis, "'the Old Pro'" according to Fogarty, instinctively knows how to behave and to rationalize his response when the body of Father Galvin is discovered. The experienced Fitzgerald falls right into line. These are men who have become seasoned in their professions. In Fogarty's admiring eyes, being a professional entails knowing how to handle a catastrophe with composure, and not agonizing over a decision. But being a professional has another side, and it is represented by Doctor Carmody's desire to be true to the ethics of his profession and put his name only to an honest death certificate. Fogarty can see how Carmody's "professionalism" clashes with Maginnis's, but it is Maginnis's that wins out, and Maginnis whom Fogarty admires.

Allied to this theme is the one of differences between youth and age. Father Galvin does not fit in with the other priests partly because he is a social misfit, but partly also because he is young. He is scrupulous enough to look away when a dirty joke is told among the priests. Carmody, the doctor, is shown as scrupulous also (about signing the death certificate), and this is a consequence of his own youth. As we get older, more experienced, and more wizened in our craft (O'Connor suggests), we are more willing to cut corners, to make compromises. Youth, on the other hand, is intolerant of compromise.

Beyond this are intertwined the themes of loneliness and the special status of the priest. Now of notable authors who have written about priests, perhaps only the American Edwin O'Connor, in his *Edge of Sadness*, has included a suicide, and that only peripherally. In nations where they are held to rigorous spiritual standards and act as authority figures, priests live lives of social isolation. This is more true in Ireland because of their celibate status, and so priests may seek out other priests for companionship. (When they seek out others, as in O'Connor's other stories and in O'Faolain's stories, they drift from their moorings.) Father Galvin, like Father Fogarty, has only the small circle of the clergy at the parish house as his society. But whereas Fogarty fits in and says the right things, Galvin is totally maladjusted. Rejected by Maginnis and smirked at by the others, Galvin appears to see no other redress but the ultimate disavowal of life. To see this as inadequate motivation for suicide is to overlook the significance of "belonging to a group" (48), which Fogarty prizes; identification with a community is a powerful yearning among isolated people in O'Connor's fiction.

O'Connor characterizes the short story as a dramatic art that manifests, as Richard F. Peterson expresses it, an "intense awareness of human loneliness."[13] It has been observed that O'Connor

---

[13]"Frank O'Connor and the Modern Irish Short Story," *Modern Fiction Studies* 28.1 (Spring 1982): 53–67, esp. 54–55.

wrote about priests because they exemplify loneliness, which is the human heritage.[14] Fogarty himself realizes that priests have no one to confide in. In this respect, therefore, he is like Galvin, and he must keep his misgivings to himself and take them to the grave. The final lines of the story have him thinking sadly, "What lonely lives we live" (51). Although the "we" applies to priests, on a more extended level it refers to all humans, who must make moral decisions alone, who must die essentially alone. But Fogarty may have been able to help Galvin when the man was alive. If he were not so preoccupied with the role of the professional, if he were more of what a priest should be (that is, a minister), he may have been able to respond to Galvin's emotional pain. The fact that Fogarty is cast into moody introspection by the gravity of this dilemma underscores the humaneness that is a constant in the way O'Connor characterizes him throughout all the four stories in which he appears.

Allied to the focus on loneliness is the theme of the coverup. Father Maginnis, the senior member of the curacy, like many entrenched officers of organizations, is more concerned about the survival of his institution than about abstract notions of truth; he is clearly most faithful to the good reputation of the clergy in his diocese. He translates this zeal into his sympathy for the feelings of Galvin's family and into a desire to avoid scandal among his parishioners. In sum, his masking the true account of Galvin's death—like sealing the coffin for the funeral—is "an act of charity." He rationalizes this behavior by saying, "'There never was a time when we could do more for him'" (49). The story, then, shifts from Pilate's question ("What is truth?") toward another question: "How important is truth?" So a churchman's suicide is dissembled, with the collusion of other professionals, and life goes on: institutions keep their stability, keep their reputation intact. By extension the reader is invited to wonder how many more cases of priestly suicide, or how many instances of alcoholism, illicit love affairs, or pederasty, are concealed by a conspiracy of silence among sacred and secular authorities, all in the service of propping up the Church's good name.

---

[14]William M. Tomory, *Frank O'Connor* (Boston: Twayne, 1980), 133.

At the time of this story's composition, the Irish would have considered "An Act of Charity" anathema[15]; even Americans would have found it painful reading. But O'Connor is registering a social criticism against the dead hand of the church in Irish provincial life. This story is an outgrowth of O'Connor's fiction in the two decades before, both in and out of the *New Yorker*, and also of his journalism in the Irish *Sunday Independent*, in which he takes to task his homeland's institutions. More especially he was concerned with exposing what Roger Chatalic calls "the death-in-life of the Nationalist Catholic establishment" in a country whose communities are "ridden by an intolerant, obscurantist priesthood."[16]

Like "An Act of Charity" the Fogarty story "The Teacher's Mass" (4/30/55: 30–33) is about death, and it reads more like a work of literary fatalism than a good yarn. O'Connor offers this story as a testament to the "profound humanity" of Fogarty for allowing the slow, inflexible Considine to serve as acolyte for the early morning Mass right up until the time the man dies at the altar. His human feeling is underscored by the small-town tact he employs in repeatedly giving Considine the last rites and in hinting that the old man should not exert himself. Now Considine is something of a type character, a former school headmaster, who claims the youngsters are illiterate brutes, who makes himself a savant on obscure history, who writes letters to the local newspaper on fine points, and who shields his daughter from the attentions of the rough local swains.

But Fogarty's feelings have a striking ambivalence. In Considine's intensity about serving the Mass, he sees a quality that he lacks, a quality that would have fitted Considine to be a priest. At the same time he realizes that Considine is stuffed with pedantry that has no relation to life. What Fogarty does not realize is that while he himself is no scholar, and may lack enthusiasm for unvarying ritual, he is fully integrated into his community. He loves his parishioners, has an affection for the rough-cut country youths, and even indulges the young men who return from America prone

---

[15]In fact, much of O'Connor's fiction was at the time on the national list of censored readings, so that his sources of income were drying up in Ireland and he needed to look further afield for a readership.

[16]See "Frank O'Connor and the Desolation of Reality," in *The Irish Short Story*, ed. Patrick Rafroidi and Terence Brown (Atlantic Highlands, NJ: Humanities Press, 1979), 189–201, esp. 194.

to flaunt their small successes. Edwin O'Connor, in *Edge of Sadness*, has his main character, an urban cleric, come to the realization of a parallel thesis: all his scholarly exertions mean little if he cannot love his parishioners, cannot minister to their needs.

Like the two stories on Father Fogarty previously discussed, "The Mass Island" (1/10/59: 26–31) is essentially plotless and seems to consist of lengthy exposition incorporated within the conversations among the characters. At the outset the reader is unsure of where the story is going, because the only crucial question seems to be where Father Fogarty will be buried. A certain amount of suspense is generated in the ruse adopted by Jackson, Hamilton, and Keneally to thwart Fogarty's brother in his designs for a modest local burial. Then the remains of the priest can be carried inland 150 miles to the place he often said he wanted to be interred. The Mass Island holds an historic significance as the place where Mass was said in the Penal Days earlier, and it may be a symbol of Fogarty's romantic attachment to an Irish past.

As the cortege proceeds to the coast, the trickle of people coming out to pay their respects grows to an outpouring of crowds. "'He seems to have been fairly well known,'" says Fogarty's brother (31), understating the priest's popularity. And we follow Father Jackson to a realization that Jerry Fogarty, a little too worldly perhaps, a little too close to the people, is venerated in a way that is reserved for none of the other priests. "What they gave to the fat, unclerical young man who had served them with pints in the bar and egged them on to tell their old stories and bullied and ragged and even fought them was something infinitely greater" than mere respect (31). There is the sense at this point that the profound human loneliness that all priests suffer, which Jackson has commented upon earlier (27), and which they must suppress, has been assuaged for Fogarty by his membership in this wide community of rural folk. In the final scene, the Mass Island is flooded in light from the head-lamps of the many onlookers' cars, as the huge "mountainy" pallbearers carry Fogarty's coffin over the causeway to the island. The scene validates Fogarty's strange choice of the island for his burial and stifles his brother's objections against it.[17]

---

[17]There is some evidence that O'Connor was not wholly attentive to the plot strategy in the early section of the story. *New Yorker* editor William Maxwell wrote to O'Connor with several directions for substantive revisions for that section of the tale. Among them were to stipulate

O'Connor liked to hold that the short story concerns itself with "submerged populations," those members of society who attract little notice or about whom we do not wish to know.[18] In this subgroup may be found priests, in that they are religious functionaries expected to have no lives of their own; old women, especially the shawlies who are the furnishing of Irish roads; and children, the more so if they are foster children, a social embarrassment.

A subset of *New Yorker* stories, for instance, is based on the painful theme of the abandonment of children raised in foster homes. Matthews reports that O'Connor initiated this theme in his fiction with the story "The Babes in the Wood" (*Voices* 224). Others include "The Weeping Children," "The Pretender," and "A Set of Variations on a Borrowed Theme." These works have common features: the element of "story" about them is muted; instead, they emphasize emotion and characterization. O'Connor may have suspended his greatest gift—that of the raconteur—in favor of exposing the plight of abandoned children he may have known in Ireland.

O'Connor's stories of illegitimate children share a poignancy which saps their humor. In "The Babes in the Wood" (3/8/47: 31–36), Terry is being weaned on the expectation that his mother—whom he knows as Aunt Madge—will take him to live with her when she marries an Englishman. But then she abandons him in favor of children born during her marriage. "'Aren't we proper children?'" Terry asks his cohort, another foster child named Florrie Clancy (36). Florrie is a more wizened child, envious of Terry's flaunting his good fortune, and at the same time cynical of parents' intentions. The final scene has her comforting the hapless Terry in a situation which presents no resolution other than the prospect that these "babes in the wood" will, for a while, have each other.

In all of the foster children stories, the worst privation the children suffer, worse than social ostracism, worse than the poverty of their lives, is the sense that their real parents have re-

---

that Hanafey did not go to Mass Island if he did not, to make sure that the reader understands that the funeral was to take place the morning after the visit to the Keneallys', and to make it clear that Father Hamilton came along with Father Jackson. See Michael Steinman, ed., *The Happiness of Getting It Down Right: Letters of Frank O'Connor and William Maxwell 1945–1966* (New York: Alfred A. Knopf, 1996), 107–11.

[18]See his "Introduction" to *The Lonely Voice: A Study of the Short Story* (London: Macmillan, 1963).

jected them. In "The Weeping Children" (1/21/61: 38–44), for example, Joe Saunders, an English husband, goes back to Cork to retrieve his Irish wife's earlier illegitimate child. He perseveres until he can tactfully remove Marie from the foster cottage. As they leave, they see the other children quietly weeping, weeping for themselves. Their surroundings are straitened, though they appear to be well tended. They simply long for the security of a real family. The story seems to lack emotional unity: most of it focuses on the dramatic interplay between Joe and Brigid Saunders, in which Joe demonstrates his patience and generosity toward his sorely strained wife. It is only in its last third that the story charts Joe's progress toward the cottage in Cork. Here the focus of the work shifts to the mute state of privation of all the foster children at the cottage; now the story takes on a deadpan quality, different from O'Connor's lyric narrative style. It is as if the author wants nothing to divert his readers from the pathos of the final scene, and at the same time wants to avoid sentimentality.

Joe Saunders is one of that handful of O'Connor's young male heroes who, out of love for their women, attempt to legitimize their motherhood. ("Unapproved Route" [9/27/52] has another.) In this story, about half of the motivation seems to consist of Joe's concern for the child, a concern that expresses itself in the abstract even before he travels to Ireland. Says he to Brigid, "'A child is too helpless'" (41)—words that echo the author's own voice. The final scenes, though emotionally disjunctive with the earlier ones, show the center of gravity shifting in Joe's heart from concern for his wife to concern for the child. In this story, moreover, the sympathetic male is English, not Irish, and so it seems an attempt on O'-Connor's part to revise the common misconception of the English as inevitable exploiters of the Irish. Indeed, it is Brigid who has exploited Joe, by having married him without telling of her illegitimate child.

Whatever may be "gentle" and "bland" in O'Connor's *New Yorker* fiction does not show up in "The Pretender" (12/2/50: 40–43). This story offers an almost perfect integration of humor with a painful subject, a technique O'Connor mastered in his *New Yorker* stories. Denis Corby, a child from a foster home, is brought on Saturdays by the warm-hearted Mrs. Murphy to stay at her house. The boy's natural mother has gone off to make a new life for herself. Mrs. Murphy's children, Michael and Biddy, with their keen sense of social distinctions, reject the boy because of his poor dress and obtuseness; they finally badger him with questions about his real mother. The story's comedy resides in Michael's bravado and spurious sense of savvy (he is sure that Denis Corby is plotting against him), which is a technique of humor that O'Connor exploits in many of his little boy-narrated stories. While Mrs. Murphy dotes on the boy, the brother and sister grow jealous of his usurping the mother's affections, and they drive him out—in a climax that is far from comic.

The final scenes show Michael lashing out at Denis with his fists, and Biddy lashing out with her tongue. About the boy's foster family, the narrator finally says sourly, "You could see they were no class, and, as I said after to Biddy coming home, it was like his cheek to pretend that we were his brother and sister" (43). The story gains its impact from Michael's cruelty as he voices his contempt for the innocent outsider. On one level "The Pretender" shows the animus that children from conventional families tend to adopt toward the foster child, such that the foster child is pushed further out to the fringes of society. On a higher level, "The Pretender" works to reveal the right of possession that children want to establish toward their natural parents.

Relations between children and parents are also the subject of another of O'Connor's serious *New Yorker* stories. All over Ireland women are having illegitimate children and are leaving them to go off to England to find a proper life with a respectable husband and raise a conventional family. This, at least, is what a worldly-wise nurse tells Kate Mahoney when she sets about to take on a child in O'Connor's story "A Set of Variations on a Borrowed Theme" (4/30/60: 46–78). At first, old Kate undertakes to board some foster children because, her daughters having grown up on her and married, she needs to find a means of subsistence, and mothering is the only skill she knows. The borrowed theme, of course, is the one of abandonment of children, and O'Connor rings some changes on it by showing how a foster household may look from the inside. At the age of 60, Kate secures two infants whose mothers have left them and gone off to pursue their lives in England. The old woman, however, does more than function as a foster parent: she expresses herself in motherhood.

This story has a dramatic quality that breaks through in a number of dialogues. In one confrontation Kate's daughter Nora says, "'You love it, woman. And you care more about that little bastard than you ever did about Molly and me'" (47), which brings a cascade of invective from her mother, whose natural vocal intensity expresses itself in a shout. Likewise, in an outburst of envy, when her foster-child Jimmy is about to be united with his real mother, Kate cries, "'Go to the well-heeled ones! Go to the ones that can look after you!'" (56). Later, when Jimmy runs away from his mother to resume life with Kate, O'Connor presents an engaging scene in which the pursuing stepfather—who has attempted to legitimize Jimmy by having him come home with the family to live—charms Kate into an admiring silence: "'Mrs. Mahoney, what do we have them for?'" (62). O'Connor, who claims he knows how everything can be said in Ireland, here shows himself a master of Irish rhetorical sallies. By the end of the story the boys have metamorphosed into Kate's own children, and when she addresses them on her deathbed, she seems to hark back to her earlier married life: "'An yeer father is proud of ye, I'm sure'" (77). This comment leads to a rare moment of discovery for her daughter Molly: "They were her real children all the time, and we were only outsiders" (78).

"A Set of Variations," far longer than O'Connor's typical stories, takes on the length of a novella: its narrative line runs from the time of Kate's decision to become a foster mother to her death, while the boys are in adolescence. The narrative is held together by the personality of Kate, whose character shows wide range. She demonstrates archness, for example, as she parades her baby Jimmy in a pram before her skeptical neighbors and says proudly, "'My first!'" (46). Her ebullience comes through when she is out visiting and Jimmy comes looking for her: "'I suppose it was the way you couldn't get on without me?'" (47). Her character is built of her possessiveness toward the boys and her consequent desire to create dependence. She wants to shield her boys from the knowledge that they are bastards. She displays righteousness because she was always loyal to one man, but she also shows romantic indulgence for a girl who would have her fling. She is gentle in explaining to Jimmy how his younger brother has come to be a foster child. She has a mother's natural ability to detect how her two boys differ. She shows perception in explaining to Jimmy that he ran away from his mother because he was jealous of his stepfather, and also in explaining later to his stepfather that Jimmy's leaving school at fourteen is consistent with the values of his class. And withal, we are not allowed to forget that Kate, when roused, has a "dirty" tongue.

What transfigures Kate as a character is her indomitability. At an age when most people are willing to pack it in and resign themselves to a life of useless dependency, Kate refuses to become a member of a submerged population and begins the child-raising process anew. We see a woman in her 60's, gnarled with rheumatism, almost unskilled, hovering on the brink of poverty; but rather than live on the sufferance of her daughters, she resolves to exercise the one skill she has by expressing herself in motherhood. She takes the dregs of society and creates with them a family, not born of her womb but created of her heart. She does so in the face of the resentment of her neighbors and the hostility of her daughters, and she prevails. At the story's end, her crony Hanna Dinan sums up Kate's resolve to fashion her own life: "'Wisha, wasn't she a great little woman! She had them all against her and she bested them. They had everything, and she had nothing, and she bested them all in the end'" (78).[19]

O'Connor in a 1956 article entitled "A Good Short Story Must Be News" says that ideally a story must rouse the reader's attention like a person grabbing his lapels: it must be suitable for telling around a fire.[20] He also, when he was teaching creative writing at American universities, said that the plot should be the *raison d'être* of a short story.[21] Some of his *New Yorker* stories, such as "An Act of Charity," "Mass Island," and "A Set of Variations," lack that "story" element, but they in their own ways excite the reader's wonder. Moreover, O'Connor never said that a short story must have humor. His own greatness in his *New Yorker* fiction comes not because he used humor—he often did not—but because he makes, with humor, unpalatable truths go down more easily.

When O'Connor died, a friend of his, actor Michael Mac-Liammoir, paid a tribute to him that could only come from his friends among the Irish. He said O'Connor was a man of great sympathies, especially for the downtrodden.[22] This may be the common chord that resonates throughout his life as a writer. It is clearly a chord that finds its way into much of his *New Yorker* fiction.

---

[19]James Matthews gives an equally lengthy explication of "A Set of Variations" at the end of his article "Frank O'Connor's Stories: The Contending Voice" (73–75).

[20]See *The New York Times Literary Magazine* (10 June 1956): 1, 20.

[21]Richard T. Gill, "Frank O'Connor in Harvard," in *Michael/Frank: Studies in Frank O'Connor*, ed. Maurice Sheehy (Dublin: Gill and Macmillan, 1969), 36–49.

[22]See Terence De Vere White, "An Appreciation" [on the death of O'Connor], *Irish Times* (11 March 1966): 1, 4.

A Woman's Voice Speaking: Glimpses of Irish Womanhood in the Short Stories of Frank O'Connor

Owene Weber

Frank O'Connor was gifted with a resounding speaking voice and an intense appreciation for voice in literature and life. He also had an ardent interest in women and in improving their lot. Through his efforts to restore to the short story the narrative impulse and because of his sensitivity to the experience and politics of women, O'Connor gave a voice to women of mid-twentieth century Ireland which anticipates the outpouring of creative expression that Irish women writers of the 1990s are now enjoying. This is an unexplored aspect of O'Connor scholarship and one which should gain importance as the new interest in Irish women writers increases. O'Connor's stories featuring women can be divided into four groups according to the ages of the women presented: Irish Tomboys, Quicksilver Girls (young unmarried women), Hard Cases (married women), and Bold Crones.[1]

---

[1] As a primary resource, I read material in O'Connor's story files when they were located at the family home of his widow in Annapolis, Maryland. Later, when the University of Florida purchased the collection, I helped catalogue the holdings. Where I refer to stories from published collections, I have abbreviated titles (for example, *DR* refers to *Domestic Relations*, etc.). Where I use alphabetical references (such as A/33b), I refer to the code names under which one can locate the work at the O'Connor Collection at the University of Florida. The essay which follows is excerpted from my doctoral dissertation, which I am in the process of revising for publication.

O'Connor story collections will be abbreviated as follows: *BC = Bones of Contention* (New York: Macmillan, 1936); *C2 = Collection Two* (London: Macmillan, 1964); *C3 = Collection Three* (London: Macmillan, 1969); *CAJ =*

I. Irish Tomboys

O'Connor's tough little Tomboys first appeared in the 1930s, but (with one exception) these early works were included in no collection until Harriet Sheehy compiled *The Cornet Player Who Betrayed Ireland* (1981). As a character type, the Tomboy is an aggressive, sometimes violent little girl who fights like a warrior and is feared yet admired by her siblings and peers. As a group, the tomboys comprise the foundation for O'Connor's female characters, whose stories extend from childhood to old age.

The term "Tomboy" also distinguishes her from her male counterparts, whose stories are better known and who are often classified as *the* "Juveniles." Tomboys were not new to literature; they follow the canonical tradition of Stowe's Topsy and Faulkner's Caddie Compson. They also recall women from earlier Irish literature like Queen Medb and the members of the "Midnight Court." Most important, these little girls suggest O'Connor's awareness that a woman's search for autonomy was an integral part of her formative years and an experience one must understand to appreciate a woman.

In recent years, little girls have become an important academic and psychological topic. Thus Emily Hancock concludes that "woman's full development depends on circling back to the girl within and carrying her into womanhood."[2] Similarly, Lynn Mikel Brown and Carol Gilligan write that society needs to listen to little girls to understand why at adolescence they abandon the voices of

---

Crab Apple Jelly (London: Macmillan, 1934); *CC = The Common Chord* (London: Macmillan, 1947); *CP = The Cornet Player Who Betrayed Ireland* (Dublin: Poolbeg, 1981); *DR = Domestic Relations* (London: Hamish Hamilton, 1957); *CS = Collected Stories* (New York: Random House, 1981); *GN = Guests of the Nation* (London: Macmillan, 1931); *MS = More Stories by Frank O'Connor* (New York: Knopf, 1954); *SBFO = Stories by Frank O'Connor* (New York: Knopf, 1962); *SV = A Set of Variations* (New York: Knopf, 1969); *TS = Traveller's Samples* (New York: Knopf, 1951); *TT = Three Tales* (Dublin: Cuala, 1942). Other works by O'Connor will be abbreviated as follows: *BL = The Backward Look: A Survey of Irish Literature* (London: Macmillan, 1967); *OC = An Only Child* (New York: Knopf, 1961); *SMK = The Saint and Mary Kate* (London: Macmillan, 1932).

[2] See *The Girl Within* (New York: Ballantine, 1989), 260.

childhood and let "prescriptions of nicety" force them into uncertainty and conformity.[3]

Sixty years earlier, Frank O'Connor had already begun hearing a little girl's voice and experimenting with her motives in his novel *The Saint and Mary Kate* (1932), the story of the teenage daughter of a prostitute in love with a pious boy. Written before O'Connor was married and had children, this novel suggests that his interest in young lives may have come from the poverty he felt in his own life without siblings. Through imagination he could compensate for this privation. Over the years O'Connor remained drawn to the image of this early portrait, and he perfected the character until he rendered a younger girl from a more respectable family who would challenge the traditional submissive female part and play a supporting role to none.

In 1936 O'Connor presented his first Irish Tomboy in "The Flowering Trees": Josie Mangan, the acknowledged leader of a gang of girls and boys. The children of the Tomboy stories operate in their own milieu with their own rules, like peasants of the middle ages who lived apart from the official existence of the nobility. They even develop a kind of abusive language which adds to their freedom. Also belonging to their world is the element of the grotesque: thus from certain distortions and perverse behaviors which imply a degeneration comes a *regeneration* as the children begin leaving childhood and learning about adulthood.[4]

The plot of "The Flowering Trees" revolves around an itinerant Fiddler whom the gang finds one day in early spring in an old garden. Josie determines first to attract the Fiddler by dancing for him, and then to persuade him to play for the gang picnic. When her little brother balks, Josie goes after him with violence: "She smacked Jackie's hands … she smacked his face … she pummelled his stomach … she pinched his behind …" (*CP* 55). When the others cross her, she prays that "'God [will] strike them all dead'" (*CP* 60). An unexpected illness interrupts Josie's plan, and when she recovers, she finds the gang dispersed, the "leaves falling," and the Fiddler gone (*CP* 64).

Josie Mangan reappears as the same Tomboy with the same family in "The Climber" (1940). Leaving behind the gang and the

---

[3]On this general idea, see *Meeting at the Crossroads: Women's Psychology and Girls' Development* (Cambridge: Harvard University Press, 1992).

[4]See Mikhail Bakhtin, *Rabelais and His World*, trans. Helene Iswolsky (Cambridge, MA: MIT Press, 1968), 4–32.

Fiddler, O'Connor concentrates on his native Cork, where Josie and Jackie meet a pair of sissified brothers whom they lead on a series of misadventures. Fired by envy of the boys' respectability and shamed by the shabbiness of her own family, Josie urges her father to emulate her new friends' elegant mannerisms until she almost loses her father to the boys' refined mother.

To curb the attraction between the parents, Josie takes the unsuspecting boys on a walk and bundles them over a wall where they are apprehended by the terrible Mrs. Ryder-Flynn, the lady of the manor with "legs of a greyhound and arms of a prizefighter" (*CP* 96). As Josie stands watching the boys carried off in disgrace, she is filled with "remorse and pity," and she confesses that "whoever had said revenge was sweet didn't know what he was talking about" (*CP* 96).

Three other of O'Connor's little girl characters from this era express some of the independence and self-possession of Josie but little of her leadership or swagger. The gentle Afric of "The Storyteller" (1937) defies her mother and places her faith in her dying Grandfather's fairy stories. The haughty little girl of "Old Fellows" (1944) scorns the little boy narrator and manages to make an unhappy outing with their drunken fathers even more miserable. Only the wily Florrie Clancy in "Babes in the Wood" (1947) is presented as a dominant character, because as the older of a pair of illegitimate children she has already come to terms with being an "outcast."

The following year O'Connor returned to the Tomboy in "The Adventuress" (1948), in which Brenda Regan, the toughest of five children, threatens blackmail if the others do not help her buy their father a pen for Christmas. Because they cannot afford a good one, Brenda has to settle for a cheap copy and changes the price tag, only to have her father recognize the difference and ruin her gesture.

In this story O'Connor shifts from an omniscient narrator to an admiring little boy, probably because he had developed this highly successful voice in stories about his "Juveniles" such as "First Confession." It is an effective device to have Brenda's "faithful vassal" boast that his sister was "a natural aristocrat" with "the stoicism of a Red Indian," but it robs her of her own voice and the chance to prove herself (*CP* 140). As a result the more genteel, superior Brenda is somewhat removed from the belligerent, swearing Josie; nevertheless, "Lady Brenda" wields a fair portion of verbal power until the end, when her mother rescues and thus disempowers her by donating housekeeping money to fund the more expensive pen.

The last of the Tomboy stories, "The Ugly Duckling," appears in O'Connor's early files under a series of titles: "The Miracle," "Beauty," and "That Ryan Woman." The plot, however, remains essentially the same: an ugly child grows up beautiful and goes into a convent. As a young writer O'Connor began exploring the attraction of the church for a woman with his translation of "Liadain," an early Irish poem about a woman poet who enters a convent rather than marry her poet lover. His first attempt at a nun's story, "After Fourteen Years" (1929), depicts a young man who visits his former sweetheart in a convent and finds her life less than fulfilling. In "The Ugly Duckling," which first appeared in *The Saturday Evening Post* (1957) and later was included in several collections, O'Connor prefaces her convent decision with a Tomboy childhood experience which helps explain the conclusion.

Because of her ugliness, Nan Ryan has lost her mother's affection, but her spunk earns her the admiration of her four brothers. As their friend Mick (the narrator) notes, "she grew up a tomboy, fierce, tough and tearless, fighting Danny's gang ... a pocket-sized Valkyrie leaping from rock to rock, chucking stones in an awkward but effective way and screaming insults at the enemy" (*CS* 444). In time Nan abandons fighting for praying, and then, as in a fairy tale, she grows ill and recovers beautiful. Years later, after visiting her in the convent, Mick decides that people who grow up suffering from ugliness or poverty develop an interior life which they prefer to reality.

After Nan, O'Connor left his Tomboys. One might argue that he lost interest or feared the topic would always be too trivial to appeal to the general public. One might also argue that he fell in love with the Tomboy and chose to preserve her in childhood or a convent rather than share her with her many suitors.

II. Quicksilver Girls

In the introduction to *Collected Stories*, Richard Ellmann suggests that reading O'Connor gives one "the pleasure of catching Ireland as it was changing, and of enjoying it, flyspecks and all" (*CS* xiii). Readers will achieve the same momentary magic if they focus on O'Connor's unmarried Irish girls on the brink of womanhood. The term "Quicksilver" derives from James Matthews's description of O'Connor's first heroine, Mary Kate.[5] Like her, the girls in O'Connor's early stories are "unpredictable, bright-eyed, and witty" and often creatures of "instinct rather than intellect" (Matthews 80). Later, after O'Connor had lived and taught in America and married an American, he began to portray young women who could make choices more carefully and form more meaningful relationships. With all his unmarried women, however, one senses the fleeting moments of youth and inexperience turning into something more solid, and not without some sadness as in the passing of an era.

The stories about the Quicksilver Girls represent two lifestyles. The first is lived by a small, disparate group who remain single by choice and have limited options. The second reflects the experience of a larger, more homogeneous set who are socially active and looking for husbands, although they risk uncomfortable consequences if they have premarital sex, and a lifetime of unhappiness if they rush into an unsuitable marriage. Thus as the Tomboys leave the land of childhood, they find that adolescence dwells in "dangerous worlds."[6]

O'Connor wrote only three stories about girls who choose to enter convents, although surveys suggest that over eighty per cent of girls leaving school considered being a nun. The first two tales, "After Fourteen Years" and "The Ugly Duckling," have been mentioned earlier; the third is the tale of a girl who enters a convent not out of piety but to emulate a very religious family. In time she is disillusioned, and after leaving the convent, she decides to marry the religious family's youngest son, now free to have his own life because his heretofore dependent mother has entered the convent at age fifty. Thus for the mother of "The Corkerys" (*SV*) the choice represents security and a benevolent gesture, but for youth it appears confusing, disillusioning, and restricting.

Another choice for the single woman was emigration, about which O'Connor wrote only one story, although the census shows that by the mid-1920s nearly forty-three per cent of all Irish-born women were living abroad.[7] In "The Awakening" Eileen is being sent to America to an uncle she has never seen because her older

---

[5]See *Voices: A Life of Frank O'Connor* (New York: Atheneum, 1987), 80.

[6]132See Joan O'Donovan, *Dangerous Worlds* (New York: William Morrow, 1985).

[7]See Terence Brown, *Ireland: A Social and Cultural History, 1922 to the Present* (Ithaca: Cornell University Press, 1985), 18.

sister has returned home from a broken marriage and displaced her.[8] Eileen's awakening comes when she realizes, despite the pain of her dilemma, that she has the power to try for a new life away from her ailing mother and the young man she had briefly considered marrying.

Although career opportunities for women were few in mid-century Ireland, O'Connor seemed to admire the working woman, perhaps because his mother had provided for her family as a "char" when his father squandered his meager pay. One of O'-Connor's strongest career women is Winnie Regan, a teacher in "The Bridal Night" (TT) who moves into a remote area and befriends a young man plagued with madness. Denis Sullivan has fallen in love with Winnie, and with a display of great compassion and courage, she risks social censure and consents to lie in bed with him all night to calm his troubled spirit until the men from the asylum come for him.

Yet another career woman exhibits individuality and courage in "A Life of One's Own." Jane Harty, modeled after O'Connor's first love (Nancy McCarthy), is a small-town chemist who has endeared herself to the community through service, but who has also raised eyebrows by daring behavior. When a mentally deranged man breaks into her house and steals her underwear, she feels her security invaded until she realizes that she has come up against a "loneliness deeper than her own" (SV 162).

Only one of O'Connor's career women seems safe in the professional world: Dr. O'Brien, who appears briefly in "The House That Johnny Built" and "Deirdre of the Sagas." She is described as "a handsome woman in a white coat" and "a bitch for beer" (SBFO 247), but compared with those who face serious challenges, Dr. O'Brien seems too comfortable to be of much interest to the spokesman for a submerged population.

One group on the margin did need a spokesman: girls in trouble. In writing about them O'Connor repeatedly deplores the sanctions and ignorance which a narrow-minded church and state imposed on young women, leaving them to resort to gossip and experimentation, and denying them the chance to make satisfactory choices and terminate unsatisfactory situations. Thus he used his fiction to plead for the rights of Irish women by criticizing the practices which, under the guise of protection, actually punished them.

---

[8]Published in *Dublin Magazine* (July 1928): 31–38.

In "News for the Church" (1945), O'Connor portrays a light-hearted school teacher who has her first sexual experience with her sister's former beau because she is curious to find out what married women "whisper, whisper, whisper" about (*SBFO* 114). With a childish boastfulness she confesses to an irate priest who tells her it is her duty to marry the man, not for the sake of her soul but because no one will hire her. Although O'Connor makes us laugh at the naivete of the young woman, he begs our sympathy, and he also calls attention to the church, which seems more prone to saving faces than souls.

In one of his last stories, "A Mother's Warning" (1967; *C3*), O'Connor examines the plight of a young woman confessing to a priest that she has been lured into a relationship with her boss, a married man. This time the priest, rather than prescribing penance, finds himself falling in love with the girl and as sympathetic to her situation as the author himself.

In "The Weeping Children" (1964), O'Connor points to the tragedy of the illegitimate child and the fear and guilt which erode the native goodness of the mother. When Brigid Saunders, "a wild girl with a vivacious temperament" (*SV* 74), has a child out of wedlock, she commits her baby to a foster home and later is almost paralyzed when she reveals her deed to her husband. Once again O'Connor finds himself sympathizing with the consequences of being a woman in Ireland.

Among other customs of the country which O'Connor deplored was the young Irish woman's tendency to approach marriage unadvisedly. In "The Mad Lomasneys" (1942; *CAJ*), Rita, one of three wild sisters, decides to marry the next suitor who comes through the door, only to discover too late that she is in love with another man. Harriet Sheehy claims that O'Connor modeled many of these characters after girls he knew in Cork who approached courtship like a parlor game: "I'll trade you my fella' for your new umbrella."[9]

Not all of O'Connor's stories address social wrongs. Some point to a sort of zany irrationality to which young women cling while their solid male counterparts gaze on them with dismay. In "Lady of the Sagas," Deirdre finds living with the name of a mythic heroine has led her to fantasize about men's pasts to the extent that she decides that her beau is "hopelessly undignified" (*MS* 16), and she leaves him in search of a bona fide hero. In a

---

[9]Personal interview, January 1987.

tough world, O'Connor suggests that modern women who appreciate myth like story-tellers of yore will find life a little better. By contrast O'Connor occasionally reverses his stand, as with the impatient Evelyn in "The Masculine Principle" (*TS*) who is bested by a practical fiancé, who refuses to marry her until he has enough money to support her—despite her pregnancy.

The last stories in the Quicksilver group continue to show O'-Connor's empathy for women, which he tends to slide beneath a gentle mockery of their feminine logic or illogic. At the same time O'Connor comes to realize some of what goes on *among* women, and he honors the valuable advice they give to each other. In "The Sorcerer's Apprentice" (*MS*) Una is about to become an old maid because she cannot make up her mind to marry an old beau. It is only after she spends a lot of quality time conversing with a married friend that she realizes she loves another man. In both "The Pariah" (*DR*) and "Sue" (*SV*), Jack the narrator berates his sister and her friends because they interfere with his peaceful homelife after work. Although Jack often dismisses the girls' attitudes as irrational, he claims to be fascinated by them and he admits their worth in society, if reluctantly.

Looking at O'Connor's unmarried women overall, one can see in their stories the record of the progress of the rights of women and the advances in information which he saw them acquiring. In "Music When Soft Voices Die," a young office boy sits at his desk, eating lunch and listening to three secretaries discuss some of the major sexual issues of their day. This story, which is often dramatized, consists of a frank dialogue orchestrated among three opinionated young women as they explore the alternatives and consequences of illegitimate children, unfaithful husbands, and surrogate motherhood. The discussions produce a variety of suggestions—some angry, some practical, and some laughable. As in other stories, O'Connor sometimes disguises real feelings in buffoonery, such as when Marie asks Larry (the narrator) if he will be glad to get a girl and settle down, to which he replies, "'Begod, I will not.... I'd sooner a horse'" (A/52–a 10). We know, however, that he really values their conversations since he has taken the time to recount them. Like the narrator, O'Connor shows increasing awareness of women's issues and seems to delight in the capacity of women to talk about those issues and to be accountable for their choices.

III. Hard Cases

In O'Connor's "The Landlady," two Irishmen discuss the difficulties of married life and conclude it is a difficult prospect.
"'There's nothing else only hard cases,'" they decide. "'There's no
such thing as a happy marriage.... All you can do is make the best
of what you have'" (CP 151).

O'Connor wrote repeatedly about hard cases in marriage. His
early stories reflect the lives of abused women who are pathetic
voiceless peasants living narrow lives with neither friends nor
family to help them. Later stories consist of a set of sketches of
painful liaisons in which women, although more educated than
the first group, nevertheless find themselves bound to the wrong
men, burdened by parents, or inadvertently acting unwisely in
their own self-interest. The third group is a collection of light, often
witty stories which present O'Connor's image of the liberated
woman and recall the Quicksilver Girl now beyond adolescence
and wrestling to regain her Tomboy spirit.

O'Connor first addressed the married woman in "The Ring,"
published in *The Irish Statesman* (28 July 1928) but to date uncollected. It is the story of a nameless woman who has been locked
out of the house by her drunken husband and is assisted by a
young "man about town" named Philip. At first Philip curses his
luck at running into the woman, but gradually he begins to play
the "knight errant" (409) and takes his silver-headed cane to break
the window and help the woman back into her own house. While
they are outside, the woman tells Philip about the ring by which
she was lured to marry her "brutish" husband, but once Philip has
departed, she wraps her face in the cowl of her shawl, and with the
loss of an audience she also loses her voice.

Two years later, in *Guests of the Nation*, O'Connor presented
another brutalized woman known only as "Jumbo's Wife." Set
during the "troubles," this is the story of a nameless, illiterate
woman who unknowingly reveals her husband's activities as a
traitor to his enemies. Although Jumbo repeatedly has beaten and
abused his wife, she is drawn by a pathetic loyalty to help him
when he is in jeopardy, but she is powerless to divert his enemies.
Horrified, she finds him dead in hospital with the sign "SPY"
crudely pinned to his bloody flannel nightshirt (*GN* 45).

Unlike Jumbo's wife, Helen McGuire of "In the Train" (*BC*)
takes steps to defend herself by poisoning her abusive husband,
but she is confronted by the community, who perjure themselves

at her trial to obtain her release so they can take the law into their own hands. While O'Connor seems to favor the woman in this version of a true story, he is also aware that women had little hope of revenge or release even in hard cases.

In another version of a true story, "Michael's Wife" (*BC*), O'-Connor presents Annie Shea, who emigrates to America with her husband and returns alone to visit his parents. During her stay in Ireland, she never admits to her husband's death, although the narrator implies it and her father-in-law senses it from her talking in her sleep. Communication throughout the story proceeds awkwardly, and O'Connor ultimately allows her the refuge of silence as she departs, without explanation or censure.

Just as the old man wonders about Annie's reticence, O'Connor puzzled about the refusal of his first love, Nancy McCarthy, to marry him. To explain her motive, he wrote "Goldfish," which is the only Quicksilver story to use the persona of an adult woman.[10] The story is structured as a monologue spoken by a woman, addressed to her former love, and written years after he has left to pursue his career and she is married and the mother of an unruly bunch of children. Over the years Nancy McCarthy, who did marry and remain in touch with O'Connor, would read in public this piece about their youthful dreams and their rambles around "Michael's Cork."[11] Her last performance was in the late 1980s on Radio Eireann at the 20th anniversary commemoration of O'Connor's death, just months before her own death.

As Nancy hoped, O'Connor married a woman in the arts, the actress Evelyn Bowen, but the marriage failed, and even after his successful marriage to Harriet Rich, bitterness would break through to darken his portraits of married life. "The Frying Pan" is the story of a priest who comes to realize that he and the wife of his friend are in love, while her husband resents his wife, claiming she lured him from the priesthood to marry her. One night when Una Whitton and Father Foley are alone, she confesses to him and he kisses her, but afterwards he realizes that she, her husband, and he "would die as they had lived, their desires unsatisfied" (A24a11). Una brings a new image to O'Connor's depiction of women, since he allows her to verbalize her desire for a man's love. Like those before her, however, she cannot take steps to achieve it.

---

[10]Published in *Harper's Bazaar* (February 1939?), 81+.

[11]Nancy McCarthy, personal letter to the author, 23 November 1986.

Nellie Lynam, by contrast, is suing her husband for divorce, claiming adultery and cruelty; however, O'Connor makes his account a comic tale in which the attorney tries to prove the little woman a villain until the injured husband ironically comes to his wife's defense. "Counsel for Oedipus" (*MS*), written about the time of O'Connor's own divorce, presents a humorous picture of a shrewish wife, in contrast to her gallant but erring husband, who cannot stand to see his wife maligned. Here, as in some of the Quicksilver Girls' stories, O'Connor tends to serve women a harsh blow, departing from his usual defense of their plights.

"The Unapproved Route" (*MS*) presents something of the same picture, although O'Connor finishes by suggesting that even gallant gestures go awry. Frankie Daly, a magnanimous Irishman, volunteers to marry Rosalind, a pregnant woman deserted by her Irish lover, Jim Hourigan. Reiterating the concept of curious female logic, O'Connor depicts Rosalind as grateful to her rescuer but also as so in love with the father of her child that she runs off with him after the birth of their son. In the end, however, O'Connor serves Frankie the blow for taking the unapproved route in marrying to save a woman rather than to love her.

Eileen Clery and Jim Graham in "The Impossible Marriage" (*SV*) follow another unapproved route, but O'Connor allows them a moment of happiness before Jim's early death separates them. They are a pair of adult only children who refuse to leave their widowed mothers, and even after their marriage they live with their respective mothers. Despite Eileen's claim of happiness and O'Connor's clear delight in a whimsical situation, he imposed a negative judgment when he changed the title from the original "Only Children" to "The Impossible Marriage." Their plight might have been relieved had they followed the advice in O'Connor's "A Sense of Responsibility": "'Marriage is a secret between two people. 'Tis at an end when outsiders join in'" (A/69–a 8), a joining which produces many of O'Connor's hard cases.

Yet another impossible situation appears in "The Rebel," the only complete story O'Connor never published. Don McNamara, a popular Irishman who frequents an English pub, falls in love with Carrie, the shy wife of Jim Wright, the publican. Carrie suddenly comes to life and plans a series of romantic idylls with Don. Later when her husband is away, Carrie decides that it will be less deceiving if she and Don "play" married and make love at home, and she even sets out Jim's pajamas for Don. Don's reason for refusing Carrie suggests a mindset uncharacteristic of O'Connor's attitude toward women: "There are certain things no woman ever understands in love, and one is the determination of a man like Don to pay for his girl as he would pay for anything else he regarded as his own." In the margin of the typescript of "The Rebel" in the O'Connor papers is the following message: "Bill Maxwell read June 1982, Too didactic. Should not be published. Harriet Sheehy" (A/67 1). One might argue that the real problem with the story is not the moralizing but the patronizing attitude of a man's owning a woman like "anything else." Had O'Connor rewritten this story he might have found more valid reasons for Don's refusal to play the game.

Offbeat ideas always appealed to O'Connor, as in the story (entitled "Orphans") about a girl who felt obliged to marry her deceased beau's brother because "like all earnest people Hilda went through life looking for a cause, and now he was her cause, and she would serve him as best she knew" (*DR* 9). As in other impossible marriages, Hilda seems trapped by a quirky notion which denies her the fulfillment of a rewarding relationship.

Probably the darkest of O'Connor's married women's stories, "The Cheat," was written when he was an older man and undoubtedly concerned with his own mortality. It is the story of a Protestant girl who marries a Catholic-born atheist and wrecks the marriage by converting to Catholicism without telling him. In the end the narrator claims that "only a wife can destroy a man for only a wife can know what his essential loneliness is and hold it up to ridicule" (A8–a4). After Barbara Gordon has suspected her husband's lack of religion and is facing his early death, she is shamed by a priest's revelation: "'I wish I were as sure of my own salvation as I am of Dick's'" (A/8–a 9).

The last of O'Connor's married women stories were not all dark, although they, too, offer hard cases, most of which suggest women who make choices and even rise above compromise. In "The Landlady" (*CP*) a group of lodgers cast lots to see who will marry their landlady so they can prevent her closing down their boarding house, but she is a chancer like the Tomboys and falls in love with the lodger who won the lottery and determines to make him a good wife. In "Expectations of Life" (*DR*) Sheila Hennessey sets her cap for an older man and then plagues him with worries about his health until she herself dies unexpectedly. The story is a spoof on Harriet Sheehy's constant concern for O'Connor's health; the tale enacts his gentle claim to revenge by "killing her off in a story" (Interview, 1987) so she will stop nagging him. Nevertheless, Sheila represents a strong woman who married for love and of her own choice rather than to better her lot like the woman in "The Ring."

O'Connor creates another spoof on his wife Harriet in "The American Wife" when he writes the story of a woman who marries a spoiled Irish male but finds reckoning with him less trouble than dealing with the "weaknesses in Ireland" and the "willingness to accept them as irremediable" (A3 10). In time Elsie becomes too idealistic for the realism of Ireland, and she returns to the safety of America. Nevertheless, O'Connor presents the end as a draw: each partner too set to relent.

"The School for Wives" makes a strong conclusion for the picture of married women because O'Connor gives Rosin Mooney the strength and integrity which none of the previous wives can claim. Originally entitled "Don Juan Married," the story depicts Jack Maguire, "a charmer" and "as crooked as they come" (A68, 4–b 1), who marries a saintly girl and tries to isolate her from all his old friends. In the end Rosin moves into the real world, makes new friends, and, although married to an unreasonable man, develops a rewarding life for herself.

Thus the hard case marriages range from ones involving the women of the lanes, hampered by inadequacies, to ones involving empowered new women able to reach beyond the confines of home and be accepted as participating members of society. Overall the picture shows women doing the best they can, and they address a certain progress, if small, as women gain skills with which to operate and chances improve for Irish women to live better lives.

IV. Bold Crones

The old women among O'Connor's females are true eccentrics who have outlived the confines of their earlier lives. They are ugly, unwanted, or impoverished old women who devise brilliant schemes to stave off poverty, achieve lifetime goals, or cope with life's inequities. I have named them the "Bold Crones" because of their age and energy. Maiden, mad, or maddening, they represent women who fascinated O'Connor, and he collected and cherished their stories throughout his life. The first Crone appeared in the 1920s; the last a month after O'Connor's death.

Like the Tomboys they have a literary heritage in early Irish poetry with the Hag of Beare and in modern fiction with Yeats' Crazy Jane and Synge's Widow Quinn. Most have had some kind of relationship with a man; many have comfortable associations with other women; but none are burdened by Irish legislation. The early ones (1929–1936) are usually bizarre, reclusive characters with a legendary quality. Most are lower class, live by their own laws, and are prone to violent language. The later creations tend to be more capricious than shocking and belong to a higher social and economic class—but they all exit in grandeur.

The earliest Bold Crone story is "The Picture," published in 1929 and never collected.[12] It is a simple story about a visual marvel named Julie Casey with "a crop of red hair that she neither washed nor combed" and "the longest tongue and the loudest voice in Coal Quay" (87). For her living she keeps a junk shop where she almost loses a five-hundred-pound sale because she is suspicious of a barracks officer who wants to buy a small picture. The tale is recounted by an old man to his aged listener, who marvels over how close Julie came to missing her fortune. In the end the Bold Crone saves herself, responding to the officer's offer in a loud voice before he withdraws it.

The next two Bold Crones appear in "The Sisters," published only once (in *Guests of the Nation*). It is one of the few mystery stories O'Connor created, and one might see a resemblance to Poe's plots in this tale of a pair of sisters with a "strain [of insanity] in the family" (*GN* 184). When they move into town, Miss Kate tells villagers she must keep "her poor mad sister," Miss Ellen, locked in the back, but when Miss Kate dies, Miss Ellen proves to have been the sane one all along.

From the beginning it is a woman's story, told to the narrator by another Bold Crone, who had "more queer stories than anyone in Cork" (184). The women form a sisterhood of rescuers who first suspect then welcome the newcomers and later discover the dead Miss Kate and the surviving Miss Ellen. In the end the narrator is completely in awe over the women's ability to figure out the intricacies of the mix-up.

In 1936 O'Connor published another Bold Crone story, "Grandeur," which appeared in *Ireland Today* and, like others, remains uncollected.[13] It opens with a shocking statement by the old

---

[12]See *The Irish Statesman* (6 April 1929): 87–88.

[13]See *Ireland Today* (August 1936): 43–50.

story-teller: "'the only difference between one woman and another is how often and how hard she should be beat'" (43). Jane Dwyer has come down in the world socially, and after she is widowed she alienates her children and neighbors. When she has sold or pawned everything, and dressed in "'a hat like a hearse,'" she departs for the workhouse, but they put her in the asylum and in a year she is dead. The narrator cannot understand such madness and suggests that Jane should have been beaten, but one suspects O'Connor could smile and distinguish a brave spirit masquerading as insanity.

The best known of the Bold Crones is Aby Bat Heige, a "shapeless lump of an old woman" (CS 48) who in "The Long Road to Ummera" (1940) wants to be buried in the town from which she came forty years earlier and completes the plan through scheming and determination. Abby is modeled after O'Connor's "huge, shiftless, and dirty" (OC 19) paternal grandmother, who promised to come back and haunt her son if he did not take her home for burial. Perhaps because his father failed to comply, O'Connor gave her a literary burial which lives on in words.

It was fourteen years before O'Connor created another Bold Crone in "The Lonely Rock" (MS), also based on a family member. The rock is O'Connor's mother, living with her son and wife. When the son has a child by another woman, he and his wife decide to invite the woman and child to stay with them, and they tell his mother it is the child of a pilot killed in the war. The Lonely Rock recognizes her grandson immediately and delights in his company, but O'Connor paints a sad picture of her isolation as the son, wife, and visitor keep up the lie which they do not know she has already guessed, and she keeps praying that the imaginary deceased husband will never know the child is not his. Brendan Kennelly, in his graveside tribute to O'Connor, stated that "negative things formed no part of his life or outlook; his emphasis was always on the positive and the possible."[14] No characters exemplify Kennelly's words better than the Crones.

Shortly after finishing "The Lonely Rock," O'Connor wrote a story based on his friend Nancy McCarthy in her old age. "Requiem" presents an old woman who asks the priest to say mass for her dead dog Timmy. Appalled, the priest argues that animals do not have souls, but like the Bold Crones before her, the old

---

[14]See *Michael/Frank*, ed. Maurice Sheehy (New York: Knopf, 1969), 166.

woman is unmoved and retorts, "'They have souls, and people are only deluding themselves about it'" (*CS* 634). Although she does not get the mass, she gets the last word—a better bargain from a story-teller's viewpoint—when she tells the priest that she will pray for him and that she *hopes* to see him in heaven.

Four years later O'Connor created another Bold Crone who was equally vocal and much more successful. Nellie Conneely, the Bishop's housekeeper in "Achilles' Heel" (*C2*), is a schemer and an incomparable manipulator. In addition, as the title suggests, she is the point of weakness of a great man. Nellie is running a smuggling business by which she keeps the Bishop in chops and chicken, and she and the Bishop must resort to subterfuge to avoid her arrest and his gastronomic privation. She marks a change in O'Connor's depiction of old women in that she uses every device from lies to intercepted letters and ends unscathed, with the gloomy Bishop acknowledging her triumph and his dependency.

Yet another Bold Crone appeared in 1960 in "A Set of Variations on a Borrowed Theme," the story of an old woman who is too arthritic to work and decides to take in a pair of illegitimate foster children to obtain income and thus independence. O'Connor reaches back to his early grotesqueries in describing Kate, who had "a battered, inexpressive country woman's face, like a butcher's block" and who "shouted enough for a regimental sergeant-major" (*CS* 470). Although her own daughters and the neighbors oppose her venture, O'Connor allows her oldest friend to pay her high tribute at her death: "'Wisha wasn't she a great little woman. She had them all against her ... and she bested them all in the end'" (*CS* 469).

The last Bold Crone, Josephine Corkery in "The Corkerys," has already been discussed in the section on the Quicksilver Girls, yet she deserves a postscript. Although the act of entering a convent seems like a magnanimous gesture, O'Connor's old women were not prone to work out their last days in self-sacrificing deeds. Thus it is revealed at the end that as a girl Josephine had abandoned her wish to be a nun because her family was unable to finance her entrance to a convent. In old age she was able to voice her wish and provide herself security as well.

O'Connor grew up listening to the sound of older women's voices, his mother's and later those of her cronies. Although he never planned a separate collection for their stories as his journals suggest he did for children, priests, and villagers, he devotes a full chapter of his autobiography to three of his mother's old friends.

The chapter is entitled "I Know Where I'm Going," and there probably was little O'Connor admired more in women than that kind of direction.

The Child In, Around, and Of Father Fogarty

Megan L. Denio

Gordon Bordewyk groups Frank O'Connor's short stories into four major clusters: stories of war, of religion, of youth, and of marriage.[1] Two of these four clusters, religion and youth, are prominent in the stories of one of O'Connor's recurring characters, Father Jerry Fogarty. Father Fogarty is by profession a priest, a "father," but he is by nature both a lover of children and very childlike himself. O'Connor, of course, had good warrant for juxtaposing these qualities in such a character, for it was Fogarty's exemplar, Jesus Christ, who told his disciples that "unless you change and become like children, you will never enter the kingdom of heaven."[2]

As Fogarty's character unfolds in the several stories in which he appears, it is clear that he embodies many attributes of a child and that he also has a passion for the children of his flock. For along with being their shepherd, their pastor, he is also their father and friend. Like a child, he has "not yet lost [the] naturalness and innocence"[3] that O'Connor habitually associated with children. Fogarty is one of "O'Connor's adult characters, [who] like his children, are lonely innocents who determine their identity through contact" with those he encounters in his profession and life

---

[1]Gordon Bordewyk, "Quest for Meaning: The Stories of Frank O'-Connor," *Illinois Quarterly* 41 (1978): 37–47.

[2]Matthew 18:3–5, New Revised Standard Version.

[3]Deborah Averill, "Human Contact in the Short Stories," in *Michael/Frank: Studies on Frank O'Connor*, ed. Maurice Sheehy (New York: Alfred A. Knopf, 1969), 31.

(Averill 32). He is a father in his job and childlike in his actions, a combination of qualities which makes him very attractive.

Father Fogarty first appears in the story "The Frying Pan."[4] This story offers the greatest insight into the person of Father Fogarty as a child and into his love for children. As he dines with his friends Tom and Una Whitton, he confronts his own mortal passions and his own human desires. He loves Una. He loves being with her children. After the Whittons visit his house one night, he realizes that "with all the things he bought to fill his home, he was merely trying desperately to stuff the yawning holes in his own big, empty heart" (152). Like a child, he fills his life with his latest little toys: "his lumber-room was piled high with every possible sort of junk from chest-developers to field glasses.... He passed from craze to craze, each the key to the universe" (149). His newest craze is films:

> Una ... watched [Jerry and Tom] with amusement. Whenever they came to the priest's house, the same sort of thing happened. Once it had been a microscope, and the pair of them had amused themselves with it for hours. Now they were kidding themselves that their real interest in the cinema was educational. She knew that within a month the cinema, like the microscope, would be lying in the lumber-room with the rest of the junk. (152)

Fogarty shows the Whittons his most recent film and ends with childish enthusiasm: "'But wasn't it good?' Fogarty asked innocently as he switched on the lights again. 'Now wasn't it very interesting?' He was exactly like a small boy who had performed a conjuring trick" (152). His eagerness and desire to please are like a young child's attempts to win the favor of peers or parents. Like a child, he always looks for the next best toy to make life more fun and to draw others in. And just like a child (or at least some children), he, "in the warmth of his heart, was always wanting to give his treasures away" (150), like the "eight bob a bottle" (150) Burgundy he offers the Whittons. But the man, Jerry Fogarty, realizes that these toys, which entertain him only for a short time, are not enough. He wonders "what his own life would have been like

---

[4]In the original publication of "The Frying Pan" (*The Common Chord* [London: Macmillan, 1947]), the character's name is Father Foley. O'Connor changed this to Fogarty in a later revision (*More Stories by Frank O'-Connor* [New York: Knopf, 1954]); this is the version included in *Collected Stories* (New York: Knopf, 1981). Unless otherwise noted, the O'Connor stories cited in the present essay are from this collection.

with a girl like [Una], all furs and scent and laughter, and two bawling, irrepressible brats upstairs" (152). In fact, it is the children he misses most in his life, as he realizes when he later visits the Whitton home: "He was in a wistful frame of mind when he came downstairs again. Children would always be a worse temptation to him than women" (153). He realizes this after the Whitton children, Brendan and Ita, "[refuse] to sleep till he [says] goodnight to them" (152–53). They want "'Father Fogey.'" His wistful mood reminds him of the week before, when "he tiptoed up to his bedroom [and] he remembered that there would never be children there to wake" (152). He abandons his desires for children and his love for Una, however, to continue with his priesthood, to be Father Fogarty, to continue to help lead the children in his parish to further devotion to God.

Although Fogarty is not the central character in another story, "The Old Faith," that work nonetheless shows his humility, his childlike qualities, and how this virtue strengthens his vocation. Father Fogarty, along with Bishop Gallogly, Father Whelan and Canon Lanigan, imbibes a little too much of Bishop Gallogly's poteen with dinner. The dinner discussion then centers around the fairies of the Bishop's youth, a topic which leads to a discussion of Father Fogarty's aunt who came to stay with him when, as a child, he "got fever very bad" (409).

> "And you got better?" said the Bishop, with a quelling glance at the Canon.
> "I did, my lord," said Father Fogarty. "But that wasn't the strangest part of it." He leaned across the table, scowling, and dropped his eager, boyish voice to a whisper. "I got better, but her two sons, my first cousins, two of the finest-looking lads you ever laid eyes on, died inside a year." Then he sat back, took out a cigar, and scowled again. "Now," he asked, "wasn't that extraordinary? I say, wasn't it extraordinary?" (409)

As the evening ends, the priestly men walk toward Father Fogarty's car, which is parked "outside the seminary" (410). Along the way, both Father Whelan and Canon Lanigan fall: Father Whelan "fell in an ungraceful parody of a ballet dancer's final curtsy" and Father Devine and Paddy, the Bishop's boy, "were just in time to see the collapse of the Canon" (411) after they had returned from delivering Father Whelan back to the palace. Father Fogarty is the next to fall: "Next moment Father Fogarty was lying flat at the foot of the wall, roaring with laughter" (411). This laughing abandonment resembles laughter from innocent children—the joyous laughter of the free, unbounded spirit, which does not know that such raucous noise is not "good."

In this instance, too, Father Fogarty resembles young Larry in "The Drunkard." Both have surrendered to drink that they have apparently unwittingly imbibed. Just as Larry shouts in drunken abandonment at the women on the street (198), so Father Fogarty is "in a paroxysm of chuckles" (411). The Bishop, the last to fall, falls on the other side of the wall on which Fogarty leans. They were attempting to climb the wall, a feat of the sort youngsters attempt. Fogarty feels that "'the fairies have [him]'" (411)—the very same fairies the Bishop had been discussing at dinner. Such fairies usually are seen only by children in their "naturalness and innocence." Fogarty's hearty delight shows the abandonment of spirit of which he is capable. And he also, of course, has experienced the poteen his parishioners know so well, thereby allowing him to understand the common deeds of both the young and the old children that he leads.

The naturalness and innocence of Father Fogarty are further displayed in "A Mother's Warning."[5] As he learns about Sheila Moriarty's predicament, he reveals his simplicity, especially concerning women. He sees and responds like a boy. Sheila confesses the theft of a brooch she has stolen from Carden's Stores, an act that violates her mother's first warning. When Fogarty examines the stolen jewelry, "it [looks] to him as silly as any other brooch" (55). He sees no merit in "the silly little trinket" (56). He asks her to leave it with him; he plans to call Mr. Joyce, the assistant manager, who encouraged her to steal it. (Sheila, transgressing her mother's second warning, had taken up with Joyce.) When Fogarty leaves the brooch out for Joyce, the latter "[smiles] gaily when he [sees] it" (56) and says "'That's a nice little ornament, Father'" (56). Fogarty, again like a young boy, wants to hit Joyce for "trying to brazen it out" (56): "He knew he should have hit the man.... It was clearly a public duty on somebody's part" (56). But, like most children, the "next morning he woke up in a more cheerful mood" (56), now realizing that because "he was a man who, largely because of his circumstances, had to live a great deal in his own imagination" (56), he "was far too unworldly to deal with slickers like [Joyce]" (56). And it turns out that he is far too unworldly to deal with "a woman and her infinite vagaries" (57), a lesson he has learned from Sheila, who has ignored her mother's final warning: "'And

---

[5]*Saturday Evening Post* 20 (7 October 1967): 55–57.

lastly, don't throw temptation in a priest's way because they're not so well protected as other men'" (57). His innocence regarding the ways of women and ways to defend against them is like that of a younger brother coming to the rescue of his slightly older sister, or of a young older brother trying to reconcile a younger sister and her adversary.

Father Fogarty's child-like emotion and love for children are further revealed upon the death of Father Devine in "The Wreath." Here, as he reveals his affection for Devine, we can see Fogarty's simple nature:

> and now the warm and genuine love for Devine which was natural to him welled up, and realizing that never again in this world would he be able to express it, he began to weep. He was as simple as a child in his emotions. (603)

As he weeps, Fogarty begins to "[blame] himself cruelly and unjustly for his own shortcomings" (603), but the narrator lets us in on a secret of which Fogarty is unaware: "He would have been astonished to learn that ... his understanding had continued to develop through the years, when that of clever men had dried up, and that he was a better and wiser priest at forty than he had been twenty years before" (603–4). Throughout the day of the funeral, when the coffin is being transported to Devine and Fogarty's hometown, Fogarty and Father Jackson try to guess the identity of the woman who sent a wreath of red roses to Devine's grave. As they ponder the improbability of Devine having known anything about the woman, they confront their own loneliness in the priesthood.

> "God!" [Fogarty] burst out. "Don't we lead lonely lives. We probably knew Devine better than anyone else in the world, and there's that damn thing in front of us, and neither of us has a notion what it means."
> ... Jackson [questioned,] "Isn't that the one thing we all really want from life?"
> "Would you say so?" Fogarty asked in astonishment. (608)

This conversation reveals how Fogarty could have lived outside the loneliness of the priesthood if he had married Una Whitton.

> "You think I might have made her a good husband?" Fogarty asked, flushing with pleasure, for this was what he had always thought himself when he permitted his imagination to rest on Una Whitton.
> "Probably. You'd have made a good father at any rate."

> "God knows you might be right," said Fogarty. "It's easier to
> do without a woman than it is to do without kids." (609)

Again, Father Fogarty shows how he values children; even Jackson
can see that Fogarty would have made a good parent. But this ability to have been a good father carries over into his profession,
where Fogarty is indeed "a good father" for the parish.

Father Fogarty again questions his decision to be a priest in
"The Teacher's Mass." The narrator remarks that there were times
when Fogarty "had periods of terrible gloom when he felt he had
mistaken his vocation. Or, rather, the vocation was all right, but
the conditions under which he exercised it were all wrong, and
those conditions, for him, were well represented by the factitious
scholarship of old Considine" (614), an elderly schoolteacher and
acolyte. Considine disapproves of Father Fogarty's "active instinc-
tual life" (614). He cannot "understand how any educated man
could make so little of the cloth as to sit drinking with 'illiterate
peasants' instead of talking to a fine, well-informed man like himself" (615). Considine resembles the disciples who want to keep
the children away from Jesus. But Jesus, like Father Fogarty, welcomes them:

> People were bringing little children to him in order that he might
> touch them; and the disciples spoke sternly to them. But when
> Jesus saw this, he was indignant and said to them, "Let the little
> children come to me; do not stop them; for it is to such as these
> that the kingdom of God belongs."[6]

As in "The Frying Pan" and "The Old Faith," Fogarty is depicted
as "an energetic and emotional man who in other circumstances
would probably have become a successful businessman" (614). But
his circumstances were such that he is now a curate, a man devoted to leading and blessing God's children. However, they are
more than just God's children; they are the people he cares for:

> These were his own people, the people he loved and admired,
> and it was principally the feeling that he could do little or noth-
> ing for them that plunged him into those suicidal fits of gloom in
> which he took to the bottle. (614–15)

Nevertheless, although his actions were not always endorsed
by the "church," he was always meeting the people and serving
them. "The country people knew that from him they would either
get a regular blasting in a language they understood or the loan of

---

[6]Mark 10:13–14, NRSV.

a few pounds to send a girl to hospital in England so that the neighbors wouldn't know" (615). He behaves as a father with the children he loves—despairing over not being able to help, providing for their well-being when able, and disciplining when necessary. Father Fogarty, despite the occasional whisper against his actions and comments, is a priest who loves the people he serves. He "[likes] the wild, barefooted, inarticulate brats from the mountainy farms" (613). He meets them where they are in their lives and gives them either a blasting or succor, just as the unnamed priest in "First Confession" encourages young Jackie. Shocked to find Jackie on the elbowrest in the confessional, he asks the boy to wait until he is "finished with these old ones [who,] by the looks of them ... haven't much to tell" (180)—as opposed to Jackie and his "crimes of a lifetime" (180). The priest, who understands young boys, imposes three Hail Marys as Jackie's penance since the boy's confession included admission of plans to kill his grandmother and reports of attacking his sister Nora with a bread-knife. The priest understands that Jackie needs someone to help him through his terror of "[making] a bad confession and then [dying] in the night and ... continually coming back and burning people's furniture" (178).

Father Fogarty is like Jackie's priest: he knows his parishioners' needs and meets them. And just as the priest in "First Confession" is able to tolerate the boy's sister, Nora, so Fogarty even comes to love old Considine, who, because of his scorn for the illiterate peasants, had "always roused a bit of the devil in [him]" (613). Fogarty's heart is with the people, who are his "children."

Even when circumstances exceed his ability as a curate to help, as in "Requiem," Father Fogarty still proves loving and merciful. When an old woman asks him to say Mass for Timmy, Fogarty is consumed with sorrow. "He was a man who took death hard, for himself and for others" (629). But the woman has come to him not because she knows that he takes death hard, but because "there was something about him that invited more confidences than a normal man could respect" (629). It turns out that the woman can come only to Father Fogarty because only he is known to step across the line on occasion to meet his parishioners' spiritual needs. But when she explains that the proposed Mass is for Timmy, her French poodle, Fogarty is outraged and feels unable to "'commit [such] sacrilege'" (631). Although he can sympathize with her and seems to understand her plight, he explains that "'this is something that, as a priest, [he] can't do'" (634). He softens

his manner and wishes her well while also asking for her forgiveness and prayers because he cannot help her. In other words, he
loves her as a father without compromising the "rules" that govern a Father. Even though circumstances prevent him from helping her, he does not abandon her in spirit. She is still the same
woman he welcomed when she arrived: "he had a heart like a
house, and almost before the door closed behind her, he was
squeezing the old woman's hand in his own two fat ones" (628).
She is still one of his parishioners, one of the children God has
placed in his care.

"The Mass Island" is the final story of Father Fogarty's life, the
one describing his death and burial.[7] This is, however, one of the
most powerful stories in which he appears, partly because it
makes clear how many lives he has touched as a man and as a
priest, how many "children" he has fostered during his life. When
his brother, who had wanted him to be buried at Asragh, finally
agrees to let the funeral take place at the Mass Island, people come
from all around in the cold of winter to show their affection. They
come to give Fogarty their parting tribute, their thanks for his care
and friendship.

> [Jackson] had thought when he was here with Fogarty that those
> people had not respected Fogarty as they respected him and the
> local parish priest, but he knew that for him, or even for their
> own parish priest, they would never turn out in midwinter,
> across the treacherous mountain bogs and wicked rocks. He and
> the parish priest would never earn more from the people of the
> mountains than respect; what they gave to the fat, unclerical
> young man who had served them with pints in the bar and
> egged them on to tell their old stories and bullied and ragged
> and even fought them was something infinitely greater. (653)

Father Fogarty has involved himself in the lives of those he has
been leading. He has spent time with them. He has gotten to know
them and has shown them that he values their company. In fact, he

> liked to stand in his shirtsleeves behind the bar, taking turns
> with the proprietor, who was one of his many friends, serving
> big pints of porter to rough mountainy men, or to sit in their cot-

---

[7]"An Act of Charity" (*New Yorker*, 6 May 1967) and "A Mother's
Warning" (*Saturday Evening Post*, 7 October 1967) were printed almost ten
years after the publication of the account of Fr. Fogarty's death in "The
Mass Island" (*New Yorker*, 10 January 1959).

tages, shaking in all his fat whenever they told broad stories or
sang risky folk songs. (646)

In these instances he is being more than "Father" Fogarty. He is respecting these people, joining with them in life and sharing his
joviality. He is being both father and friend. And they have noticed
this. As Fogarty's funeral procession advances toward the Mass
Island, Father Jackson observes cars falling "into line behind
them" (652) and also "other lanterns and flashlights, coming down
the mountain or crossing the stream" (653). He realizes "that they
[represent] people, young men and girls and an occasional sturdy
old man, all moving in the direction of the Mass Island" (653).
They thus pay homage to the man who devoted time to them. This
is their tribute to his love. He treated them as individuals, as his
own children. He encouraged them and disciplined them. And he
thereby left a legacy as strong as any genealogical line.

Fogarty is only one of multitudes of characters O'Connor created. And there is much more to him than just his child-like behavior and his love for children. He is also known, for example, for
being Bishop Gallogly's "fiery Republican curate" (405) and "a
good nationalist" (407); he was also "witty and waspish and said
whatever came into his head about his colleagues who had nothing like his gifts" (603); and he was a man "who loved giving people nicknames" (635). But given the fact that O'Connor wrote
many stories about children and many other stories concerning
clerical life, it is refreshing to see how he combined the two aspects
in the character of Father Jerry Fogarty.

Irony and Paradox
in Frank O'Connor's Style

Robert C. Evans and Katie Magaw

A creative writer's worth depends less on his topics than on his style, less on the "content" he examines than on his way with words. Almost anyone can write a decent essay on conflicts between duty and conscience; only an artist as skilled as Frank O'-Connor could have written "Guests of the Nation." Almost any psychologist or sociologist can offer a useful discussion of human loneliness, but only a writer as talented as O'Connor could produce a work as richly haunting as "The Bridal Night." Yet these stories represent only one aspect of O'Connor's talent, only one facet of his creativity. They are lyrical, poetic, and full of imagery; their language is often striking and memorably evocative. Many of O'Connor's other stories, however, seem more obviously plain, simple, and unadorned. This is especially true of the comic works, but it is true as well of much of his writing from the 1940s, 50s, and 60s. His studies of courtship, childhood, religion, family life, and Irish society often lack the obviously rich language or complex structure that help make works such as "Guests," "The Bridal Night," or "The Long Road to Ummera" so instantly appealing.

O'Connor's less lyrical works, however, frequently possess stylistic attractions of their own. Often, for instance, they wonderfully capture the give-and-take of real human dialogue and the colloquial tone and diction that sometimes turn conversation into music. Two neglected stories—"Sue" and "Lady Brenda"—are full of such vivid dialogue, and the same is true of such better-known works as "First Confession," "The Procession of Life," and "In the Train." In addition, another aspect of O'Connor's style that often makes his stories so vigorous is their energetic use of dialect, slang, and vernacular idioms. Just as one reads Flannery O'Connor partly to hear the authentic diction of the American south, so one reads Frank O'Connor to hear the unexpected twists and turns of the mid-century Irish tongue. A random sampling of such phrases might include "'that's where the ferryboat left ye'" (to describe someone as old-fashioned [72]), "'tis no use taking it to the fair'" (i.e., going to an extreme [72]), "'bags of tin'" (i.e., lots of money [254]), "got into a wax" (i.e., became angry [285]), or "Signs on it" (i.e., certainly [320]).[1] Such highly metaphorical expressions help enliven even O'Connor's plainest, most straightforward writing.

Another technique O'Connor frequently employs deserves even fuller examination, especially because (like any worthwhile stylistic trait) it also contributes richly to his stories' meanings. This technique might be called his penchant for ironic or paradoxical juxtapositions—his tendency to switch, suddenly and unexpectedly, from one tone or implication to its opposite. Such twists not only contribute immeasurably to the interest and complexity of his works but also suggest some typical aspects of his whole way of perceiving and interpreting experience.

A simple sentence from "Unapproved Route" provides a useful example. When describing two central characters, the narrator remarks, "Rosalind and Kate could have been sisters, they had so little in common" (412). The phrase after the comma comes as a witty shock, but the twist is more than simply clever. Instead, it typifies how O'Connor often uses abrupt juxtapositions to achieve various effects: to disrupt stale, conventional ways of thinking; to implicitly characterize his narrators (making them almost characters rather than mere reporters); to imply the complexity, ambiguity, and ambivalence of human experience; to create narrative suspense (since, when we have been tricked once, we can never be sure when we will be tricked again); to imply that life cannot be easily or routinely explained or predicted; to demonstrate authorial wit; and to state insights that seem surprising at first but correct on reflection. In the apparently simple twist already quoted, for instance, O'Connor captures part of the complicated essence of being siblings.

O'Connor uses such paradoxical turns in a rich variety of ways. A sentence in "Expectation of Life," for instance, begins by stating, "According to Shiela's own story, which was as likely as not to be true ..." (432). Here the twist at the comma economically characterizes Shiela as simultaneously complex, devious, imagina-

---

[1]All citations are from Frank O'Connor, *Collected Stories* (New York: Knopf, 1981). Hereafter page numbers will be cited parenthetically.

tive, yet sometimes also genuinely honest, and all these possibilities are effectively implied rather than being lamely stated. A similarly forceful twist occurs a bit later when the narrator first quotes and then assesses Shiela (who is speaking of two rivals for her affection):

> "Matt, I don't care what it ends in. That's my look-out [i.e., my concern]. All I want is for you and Jim to be friends."
> It wasn't so much that Shiela wanted them to be friends as that she wanted to preserve her claim on Matt. (433)

Here the sudden alteration in perspectives not only implies that Shiela may be partly insincere and have a hidden agenda but also that this agenda is perhaps hidden even from herself. O'Connor often employs such abrupt turns in point-of-view to make the narrator the reader's partner, the one who gives us the fuller truth, which the characters themselves either suppress or don't fully recognize. Here as elsewhere, the narrator undercuts a character's claim, implying a contrast between stated and real intention, but he does so with subtle equivocation, complicating his own complication through the simple words "so much." If his general tone seems cynical, the phrase "so much" partly undermines that impression: delete those words and the comment seems far more bitterly sarcastic. The two words thus demonstrate the narrator's concern to do justice both to his readers and to his characters.

Inevitably, in fact, O'Connor's juxtapositions imply as much about the narrator as about the characters. The opening paragraph of "The Ugly Duckling," for example, is full of unexpected twists (here represented by bold-faced slash marks):

> ... she had practically lost her mother's regard / by inheriting her father's looks. / Her ugliness indeed / was quite endearing. She had a stocky, sturdy figure and masculine features / all crammed into a feminine container till it bulged. / None of her features was really bad, / and her big, brown, twinkling eyes were delightful, / but they made a group that was almost comic. (444)

Reading this paragraph is like watching a tennis match: the evaluations shuttle back-and-forth, back-and-forth, but we can never quite predict where, exactly, the ball will land. The narrator's blunt honesty (one might even say his crudeness) ironically increases our trust: he is willing to say what shouldn't be said, but he says it without obvious malice. His unexpected comment about the mother rings true as an accurate assessment of human motives, while his balanced comments on the girl's appearance seem simultaneously engaging, witty, biting, spontaneous, and ultimately sympathetic. This is not a simplistic portrait, nor is this a simplistic narrator. The opening paragraph leads us to expect that he will tell us truly what he thinks, no matter how momentarily shocking his comments may prove.

A brief paragraph from later in the same story once again illustrates O'Connor's penchant for paradox. Here the narrator describes how a woman reacts angrily when a man reacts calmly to another's woman's ill-treatment of the man:

> But if Mick didn't resent it, / Mrs. Ryan resented it on his behalf, / though she resented his complaisance even more. / She was sufficiently feminine to know / she might have done the same herself, and to feel that if she had, / she would need correction. No man is ever as anti-feminist / as a really feminine woman. (451–52)

Because Mick is unconcerned, Mrs. Ryan is selflessly concerned "on his behalf"; yet she is also angry at his own unconcern. She bristles at the other woman's behavior, although she might well behave the same way herself. However, if she did act badly she would expect to be punished, for as a true woman she can't bear to see *this* woman escape uncensured. In three brief sentences O'Connor sketches the strange complexities of typically human motives, repeatedly forcing us to second-guess the character, the narrator, and our own reactions to both. Mrs. Ryan can seem both flighty and rigid, both cynical and sincere, a woman who knows a lot but who perhaps doesn't completely know herself. Is she a hypocrite? The narrator doesn't say: he seems less interested in judging his characters than in presenting them fully.

Pardoxically, if O'Connor used such twists *too* frequently they might become predictable. They might then seem overdone, overbearing, smug, and even arrogant. The narrator might seem to be abusing rather than describing the characters, and his attitude toward the reader might seem calculating or manipulative. Usually, though, O'Connor strikes just the right balance, employing the twists sporadically and thus to great effect. Sometimes the twists not only emphasize the complexity of motives but also bring us suddenly down to earth, as in the following passage (from "The Expectation of Life"), which describes the relations between a wife and her contractor-husband, who is fascinated by modern plumbing:

> At times like these he even shouted at Shiela, and she promised
> in the future to wait for him, / but she didn't. She was a born
> fidget, and when he left her somewhere to go to one of his
> beloved / urinals, she drifted on.... (434)

With the word "urinals" we are suddenly back in a very real
world of things (rather than of abstract feelings or emotions),
while the brevity of "but she didn't" is all the more forceful because of the long phrases that precede it. Another use of juxtaposi-
tion (from "The Ugly Duckling") suddenly switches us from outside to inside—from what a character says to what he really feels
when a friend tells him that the woman he loves is not "the marrying kind": "'I dare say not,' said Mick, / but he did not believe it
for an instant" (455). What are Mick's motives for assenting when
he doesn't truly agree? Is the white lie a way of protecting himself
from shame, or is he trying to shield himself from a deeper kind of
pain? Here as elsewhere, the sudden contrast suggests how subtly
O'Connor perceives human character.

Elsewhere, however, the effect of his switches is more darkly
humorous, as in this bit of black comedy describing a character
who is always careful to exercise: "Mr. Corkery, a mild, inarticulate solicitor, whom May remembered going for lonely walks for
the good of his health, / had died and left his family with very limited means ..." (548). The switch here is more than ironically
macabre; it implies how, in real experience, even the best intentions often come to naught and also how ineluctably mortal we
mortals are. In a good O'Connor story, life is unpredictable, but so
is death. A similar, more obviously tragic twist occurs (for instance) in "The Luceys," where the narrator ends one paragraph
by describing how a son, to escape prosecution for theft, changes
his name and joins the air force. To his father (we are told), "This
was already a sort of death." Here the focus is on the self-centered
father's personal shame and familial pride. Then the other shoe
immediately drops: "The other death didn't take long in coming"
(74). Now the focus shifts—but only briefly—to the son's accidental demise. Father and son have missed their chance to reconcile,
and suddenly the first "death" seems wholly unimportant. O'-
Connor doesn't need to *say* that the old man has been foolish for
ostracizing his son; the jolting twist does the job for him, even as it
contributes to one of the story's larger themes. In a well written
O'Connor story, neither characters nor reader can afford to be

complacent. Abrupt turns emphasize our human fallibility and vulnerability—as persons and as interpreters of narrative.[2]

Sometimes, as in the example from "The Luceys" just quoted, O'Connor will deliver a single jolt; at other times the jolts will come in waves, like a series of seismic shocks. A good instance of the first technique occurs in the following sentence (also from "The Luceys"): "All conversations with his uncle tended to stick in Charlie's mind, / for the simple but alarming reason that he never understood what the hell they were about ..." (68). However, a nice example of the second technique is evident in these sentences from "The Corkerys," which describe the interactions of an Irish priest, his relatives, and their young female visitor:

> They really were an extraordinary family, and the Dean was as queer as any of them. The Sunday following the ceremony May was at dinner there, and he put his hand firmly on her shoulder / as though he was about to yank off her dress, and gave her a crooked smile that would have convinced any reasonable observer that he was a sex maniac, / and yet May knew that almost every waking moment his thoughts were concentrated / on outwitting the Bishop, who seemed to him the greatest enemy of the Church since Nero....
>
> "The man's a bully!" he said, with an astonishment and grief that would have moved any audience / but his own family. (549)

Here again O'Connor plays with shifting impressions, with the contrasts between appearance and reality. At first the Dean seems almost fatherly in his touch, then almost perverted. Yet just when we think that this impression of worldliness will be corrected (since the narrator seems about to tell us that the Dean's "thoughts were concentrated" on spiritual matters), we discover that his thoughts are worldly in another way: he is obsessed with ecclesiastical politics. Then, just when we are invited to see him not as a politico but as an impassioned defender of the powerless against a "bully," we are told that even his own family rejects that assessment. Is the Dean, then, a hypocrite? O'Connor doesn't say, and in fact he leaves open the possibility that the Dean is entirely sincere in his own self-perception. The switches, once more, are

---

[2]For a classic discussion of the ways a talented author can exploit a reader's pride and vulnerabilty, see Stanley Fish's famous book on Milton, *Surprised by Sin: The Reader in* Paradise Lost (Berkeley: University of California Press, 1971).

not simply clever or witty; rather, they inevitably complicate our response to the characters and to the entire story.

O'Connor's penchant for paradox, then, is not merely a stylistic tic. Instead, it seems to reflect his whole view of human life. Here, after all, was a man who attacked the church but admired many priests; who was a professed agnostic but knew the attractions of religion; who fought on one side of the Civil War and then later celebrated his faction's greatest opponent (in his biography *Michael Collins*). Here was a man who didn't hesitate to oppose his own comrades when he thought them wrong, even though he and they were all imprisoned by a mutual enemy; a man who always displayed a strong streak of fierce independence; a man who seems to have been as free-thinking in his politics as in his religion; a man who could see both the attractions and the shortcomings of Irish life; a man who always insisted on doing things his own way. O'Connor's attraction to paradox, then, seems neither surprising nor incidental. It seems instead a direct result of his attempt to look at the world accurately and to see it whole, with all its mess and complexities, all its mixed, hidden, or unsuspected motives, all its examples of virtue, vice, and everything in-between. Paradoxical twists are one way that O'Connor honors the richness of experience and displays both his skill and humility as a writer.

Comparisons and Contrasts

"The Procession of Life":
The Writer as Son and Father

Michael Steinman

The evidence Frank O'Connor left us—more than two hundred published stories and more than a hundred manila folders of rewritten stories in multiple versions—shows that his commitment to revision was an essential stimulus to creativity, and the two published versions of "The Procession of Life," separated by thirty years, prove it was worthwhile.[1] He said that he rewrote "... end-

---

[1] All Frank O'Connor texts are reprinted through the courtesy of his widow, Mrs. Harriet Sheehy. I am grateful to Carmen Russell Hurff of the University of Florida Libraries for making "A Night Out" available to me, as noted below. (The greater part of O'Connor's papers are in the Gainesville, Florida, archives, including many unpublished versions of stories.)

Because some termed O'Connor's artistic method self-indulgent, his comments in the 1963 introduction to *Collection Two* are pertinent. Sean O'Faolain was the skeptical writer, William Shawn of *The New Yorker* the editor:

> "Forgery" is how an eminent Irish writer has described this method of editing one's own work, but "forgery" is not a term of literary criticism, and is, I think, an unnecessarily harsh one to describe what at worst is a harmless eccentricity. Literature is not an aspect of banking. It is true that a number of my stories have been rewritten a score of times—some as many as fifty times—and rewritten again and again after publication. My wife has collected copies of "The Little Mother" she found in the wastepaper basket, but has lost count of the total, which is distributed over three countries and ten years. This is a great annoyance to some of my friends, particularly my publishers and editors, who would prefer me to write new stories instead; I am afraid it shows a certain lack of respect for one's own public image ("after all, old man, you are a professional or you aren't"); but simply as a forger I must be the

lessly. And keep on rewriting, and after it's published, and then after it's published in book form, I usually rewrite it again. I've rewritten versions of most of my early stories and one of these days, God help, I'll publish these as well."[2] His widow, Harriet Sheehy, corroborated this: "When there were enough stories to form a new collection he didn't start trying to choose between the

---

greatest failure who ever lived because I forge only cheques that have already been cashed and spent.

The only criticism of this eccentricity, if I may so call it, that ever shook me was that of the editor of *The New Yorker* in which so many of these stories have appeared. He asked, "But can you remember the story you set out to write?" and it is a question I still cannot answer. I believe I can remember. I believe the essence of any story can be expressed in four or five lines, but I cannot prove it. All I could possibly do would be to refer the reader to a textbook of the short story in which the earliest and latest versions of one of my stories are printed together. But this would mean taking myself a great deal too seriously, which, from my point of view, would be hardly less objectionable than not taking myself seriously enough. (See *Collection Two* [London: Macmillan, 1964], iii.)

The texts of "The Procession of Life" defy precise dating. O'Connor had first dramatized this story as "A Night Out" in 1928 or 1929 (see Ruth Sherry, "The Manuscript of 'Rodney's Glory,' by Frank O'Connor," *Irish University Review* 22.2 [Autumn–Winter 1992]: 219–24, esp. 219–20), and the stories in *Guests of the Nation* were completed in mid-1930 (see James Matthews, *Voices: A Life of Frank O'Connor* [New York: Atheneum, 1983], 64–65). However, O'Connor may have finished the collection that contained this story even earlier; in an October 1925 letter to Geoffrey Phibbs, he wrote, "My book to McMillan but no answer yet." (No details of the book's contents appear in his correspondence.) The second published version is harder to date; unlike other stories from this period, it was not sent to or published in an American magazine. Also, his description of *Collection Two* as a book resulting from his unhappiness with the 1954 *More Stories* offers no precise evidence; O'Connor might have rewritten the story any time during that decade. (Had it been written for *More Stories* and put aside, his eldest son, Myles, would have been in his teens, which might have deepened O'Connor's empathy with Mr. Coleman.) The Florida archives contain two drafts of the second version, titled "A Night Out," which resemble the published text. These are in the Harriet Sheehy Collection, University of Florida Libraries at Gainesville.

[2]See Anthony Whittier, "Frank O'Connor," in *Writers at Work: The Paris Review Interviews*, ed. Malcolm Cowley (New York: Viking, 1959), 161–82, esp. 168.

many extant versions of them—he simply sat down and prepared to rewrite every story...."[3]

Significantly, "The Procession of Life" appears both early and late in O'Connor's bibliography: as the closing story of *Guests of the Nation*, his first collection, published in 1931, and, revised, in the 1964 *Collection Two*, the last book of stories he assembled. Of his early work, only it and "Guests of the Nation," also rewritten, were republished in *Collection Two*. Given his dismissal of his youthful work, this indicates that "The Procession of Life" had remained essentially true. Yet these two texts are more than evidence of fruitful "tinkering," for they reflect two writers: one, a young man deriving inspiration from literary ancestors, balancing stereotypes, autobiography, and realism; the other, a mature, experienced artist, dissatisfied with his earlier perceptions.

In the light of his biography, the title "The Procession of Life" also reflects on a writer's life. When O'Connor first attempted the story in 1928 or 1929, he was not yet thirty, an unmarried only child with both parents—Mick O'Donovan, the alcoholic, threatening "Father" of many stories, and his beloved mother Minnie— very much part of his life. When he rewrote it, he had officially become an adult; he had become a father several times and he had outlived his parents.

His first version of this theme grew out of his painful experiences as a child in his parents' house in Cork. At sixteen, the age of his protagonist, he, too, had been locked out of the house by his father when he returned home late from the Gaelic League Hall with Daniel Corkery (Matthews, *Voices* 71). Mick O'Donovan was a terrifying man: "brooding, melancholy, violent," "enormously powerful," plunging his wife and son into despair and poverty:

> [When he had exhausted his credit for drink] ... he would grow vicious. "Jesus Christ, I'll put an end to this!" he would mutter, and take down his razor. His threats were never empty, as I well knew since the night when I was an infant and he flung the two of us into Blarney Lane in our night clothes, and we shivered there in the roadway till some neighbours took us in and let us lie in blankets before the fire. Whenever he brandished the razor at Mother, I went into hysterics, and a couple of times I threw myself on him, beating him with my fists. This drove her into

---

[3]See her "Foreword" to O'Connor's *Collection Three* (London: Macmillan, 1969), vii–viii, esp. vii.

hysterics, too, because she knew that at times like that he would
as soon have slashed me as well.[4]

The fictional father of "The Procession of Life," unyielding and
stern, draws on these memories. Although Larry's father is cold
rather than violent, choosing silence and a locked door rather than
a razor, his power to threaten and exclude is undiminished. The
plot is simple: an adolescent only child comes home late to find
himself locked out. With no hope of softening his father's obsti-
nacy, the boy goes to the riverbank, meets night-dwellers, and returns home, changed. In the spare exposition, his father is a de-
humanized force, unable or unwilling to communicate, while Larry's deceased mother is an unalterable fact:

> At last his father had fulfilled his threat. He was locked out.
> Since his mother died, a year ago, it had been a cause of dire
> penalties and direr threats, this question of hours. "Early to
> bed," his father quoted, insisting that he should be home by ten
> o'clock. He, a grown boy of sixteen to be home at ten o'clock like
> any kid of twelve! He had risked being late a dozen times before,
> but to-night had cooked it properly. There was the door locked
> against him, not a light in the house, and a stony ear to all his
> knockings and whisperings.[5]

Disinherited, an ineffectual rebel tentatively seeking hospitality, Larry encounters another forbidding male who offers scant
welcome to his strange environment. "Squinty," the watchman,
"an oldish, bearded man with a sour and repulsive face" (264), a
nocturnal fool-king, is not shocked or impressed by Larry's disobedience but thinks him contemptibly effeminate. Because Larry
has no girl, does not drink or smoke, and will not "bate the door
and kick up hell's delights," being locked out is the fate he deserves. Squinty's code of manhood is based on primitive rites of
passage; when he was Larry's age and his father asserted himself,
"'I up with a poker, and hit him such a clout over the poll that they
had to put six stitches in him in the Infirmary after.'" Where have
we heard this apocryphal boast before? Its source is "... I hit him a
blow on the ridge of the skull, laid him stretched out, and he split
to the knob of his gullet," Christy Mahon's tale of murdering his

---

[4]See Frank O'Connor, *An Only Child* (New York: Knopf, 1961), 5, 7–
13, 31–37, and esp. 35.

[5]Frank O'Connor, *Guests of the Nation* (New York: Macmillan, 1931),
263.

Da in John Synge's *The Playboy of the Western World*.[6] In this saga of a son who would free himself from an overbearing father, O'Connor's echoing his literary forefather so closely is surprising.

The conflict between Larry and Squinty is interrupted by Molly, a "mysterious woman" the timid boy idealizes, mishearing her "caressing" voice as "a peal of bells": "'Are you really sore because I let you down the other night? I was sorry, Squinty, honest to God I was, but he was a real nice fella' with tons of dough, and he wanted me so bad!'" Hardly celestial, she deftly guides "'the poor kid'" into the role she has written for him:

> And with amazing coolness she put him sitting on an improvised bench beside the fire, sat close beside him, and drew his hand comfortably about her slender waist. Larry held it shyly; for the moment he wasn't even certain that he might lawfully hold it at all. He looked at this magical creature in the same shy way. She had a diminutive face, coloured a ghostly white, and crimson lips that looked fine in the firelight. She was perfumed, too, with a scent that he found overwhelming and sweet. There was something magical and compelling about her. (*Guests* 267–70)

Living in a house devoid of femininity, except as defined in the void left by his mother's death, Larry interprets Molly's erotic forwardness as romance, although the reader knows her as a genuinely Painted Woman, her affections negotiable commodities: "Her voice dropped to a thrilling whisper, and her hand fondled Larry's knee in a way that sent a shiver of pleasure through him. 'Will you come home with me, darling?' she asked ..." (271). The fantasy she sells is that of the sexually experienced woman who gives herself freely, without mockery or risk, to a male virgin. When translated into gesture, Molly's allure collapses into pornographic cliché: her whisper thrills; her hand fondles; Larry, author, and reader shiver with pleasure. The encounter recalls *A Portrait of the Artist as a Young Man*, a book O'Connor first read, appropriately, at sixteen, finding in it "echoes of my own tormented youth in Cork."[7] Although Larry is less introspective and less articulate than Stephen Dedalus, Larry shares Stephen's dream of sexual initiation, a magical "tryst" in a "secret place": "They would be alone, surrounded by darkness and silence: and in that moment of

---

[6]See John M. Synge, *Complete Plays* (New York: Vintage, 1960), 37.

[7]See O'Connor's "Introduction" to James Joyce, *A Portrait of the Artist as a Young Man* (New York: Time Reading Program, 1964), xviii.

supreme tenderness he would be transfigured.... Weakness and
timidity and inexperience would fall from him in that magic moment" (Joyce 68).[8] Casting Larry not as Handsome Young Suitor or
as Chivalric Rescuer but as generic Customer, Molly leads him off
to the loss of virginity needed for a twentieth-century rite of passage, the equivalent of Squinty's entrance into manhood. Their
journey is blocked by a policeman, the text's third father-king, who
captures a reluctant Molly for himself (*Guests* 274, 275–76).

Alone with Squinty, Larry decides abruptly to return home
and "contemptuously" tries out his new power, imitating Squinty's coarse bravado and diction, discarding his polite middle-class
attitudes:

> "Ah, my boy," said the watchman with fierce satisfaction
> "your old fella' will hammer hell out of you when he gets you
> inside the door!"
>
> "Will he?" asked Larry. "Will he now? I'd bloody well like to
> see him try it."
>
> And, whistling jauntily, he went off in the direction of the city.
> (278)

The transformation into swaggering man is gratifying yet
startling, even implausible, for Larry has been a passive recipient
of others's actions.[9] Because the text gives no specific reason for his
defiance of his father's curfew, even his first act lacks clear purpose. True, Molly's solicitation, momentarily defining him as an
adult male, gave him "startling new courage," enabling him to
disdain his father as "'me ould fella,'" and to curse, "'Bad luck to
him'" (271–72). He has choked down a mouthful of the policeman's whiskey and lit a cigarette (276, 277), but these are only gestures the pose of bravery demands. Although he may assume the
mask of a braver man, he is still inexperienced and virginal. To
him, the night-world would have been intimidating rather than inspiring, for in it appearances mutate into their opposites—Squin-

---

[8]In fairness to O'Connor, *The Playboy of the Western World* was not the
only source for a son's fantasy of revenge, nor was *A Portrait of the Artist*
the sole model for erotic imaginings. Although he had read Synge and
had met Joyce in Paris, O'Connor's inspirations may well have been personal.

[9]Except for the temporary courage Molly supplies, Larry is consistently fearful: he sees the landscape as "frightening" (twice); is "terrified"
(twice), "frightened" (twice), "startled," "afraid," "in despair"; his voice
rises "on a note of fear"; he gasps, is hysterical, runs away from Squinty.

ty's protection into ridicule, Molly's affection into sex-for-sale, the policeman's law into amorality. As Larry instinctively turns submissive when faced by older, more powerful males, his brief experiences hardly prepare him to defeat an opponent. Yet this meek son leaves to inherit the earth, to recapture his birthright by force.

Although the story's situation, landscape, and diction mimic realism, its characters are fanciful: a child reborn a warrior without performing heroic deeds; Madonna and whore; adversaries whose menace is easily quieted, combined into a noisy yet toothless Cerberus. Although Squinty is no wizard, Molly no seductive fairy godmother, the policeman no sage, Larry's quest ends in wish-fulfillment, as if he, not Jack, had bought the magic beans. The happy ending might signify that O'Connor found the awful realism of "Guests of the Nation" difficult to sustain in domestic fictions, just as the echoes of Christy Mahon and Stephen Dedalus, literary sons who recreate themselves, make Larry appear derivative, only half-created. Having been Larry, O'Connor put little emotional distance between recollected experience and his fictional recreation of it. The text's perceptions are narrowed by a child's egocentric perspective, where adult characters exist only as flat embodiments of their power to menace or enthrall. Still, the story's charm remains, and flat characters are appropriate to comedy. Readers may at first not even notice how little information they are given. Larry's naive myopia is amusing, he is likeable, and we hope that the night's experiences will have been instructive.

The first version of "The Procession of Life" is significant evidence of O'Connor's need to create a fiction to deflect the terrors of his childhood—neutralizing old fears by recording and thus resolving them or making narrative into a weapon to defeat his tormentor. He dramatized his frustrated rage at his father doubly, as if a supernaturally powerful Mick would only die when killed twice—by Squinty's violence and through Larry's new manhood, a shield against further injustices. Although O'Connor no longer lived under his father's roof when he wrote the story, it is an attempt to exorcise Mick's terrifying presence. Notably, the final confrontation between son and father is unwritten, just as Larry never has to prove himself with Molly. We cannot tell if O'Connor thought these scenes would be better imagined offstage, or if he did not share Larry's new confidence in himself.

Although O'Connor was an unabashed "Mother's Boy" in life, Minnie O'Donovan is absent (although mourned), as if the story was only about elemental male conflict. But her influence is present, for being denied a home had been her nightmare also. She had told her young son how she had been left at an orphanage by her mother: "... she rushed after my grandmother, clinging to her skirts and screaming to be taken home. My grandmother's whispered reply is one of the phrases that haunted my childhood—indeed, it haunts me still. 'But, my store, I have no home now.' For me, there has always been in my imagination a stage beyond death—a stage where one says 'I have no home now'" (*An Only Child* 46–47). As it vanquishes the oppressor, "The Procession of Life" also calms this primal fear by writing a landscape where exile is at worst temporary and always reversible.

When O'Connor returned to this story, he had first become a father in 1939; Mick had died in 1942; Minnie, ten years later. Tracing the empirical evidence that reveals O'Connor as a father is not as simple as analyzing Mick's effects on him. O'Connor's eldest children, Myles and Liadain, characterized him as a difficult parent, a paradox considering the sympathetic understanding he brought to a fictional sixteen-year old.[10] The years between the first and second versions were emotionally turbulent for him, and his relations with children, step-children, wives, and lovers are too complex to summarize.[11] Yet his increased awareness of behavior and motivation is obvious in this version, distinguished by expansiveness, as characters engage one another in leisurely, revealing, humorous conversations. More than an accretion of detail, this reflects O'Connor's mature choice to imbue all his characters with emotional depth, to grant them subtler motives. The simplest acts have shadings of ambiguity, as the dark, silent house of the first version is now full of hostile energy:

---

[10]In 1990, Harriet Sheehy said that her husband "was wonderful with babies and small children, but he found adolescents difficult, and the exaggerated responses of teenagers probably reminded him too much of the trauma of his father's rages and the dramatic scenes of his marriage. He often didn't understand what they were about.... But he loved them and worried endlessly about them and they knew it." See Michael Steinman, "The Perils of Biography: A Talk with Harriet Sheehy," *Twentieth Century Literature* 36.3 (Fall 1990): 243–58, esp. 247.

[11]The testimony we possess makes balanced evaluation difficult. James Matthews's *Voices* details O'Connor's family relations but with the apparent purpose of proving him a selfish man, an abusive husband, a callous father.

One night Andy Coleman came home and found the front door locked against him. It was not the first time it had happened. Ever since his mother died six months before Andy's father had made a dead set at him. It was an extraordinary thing, just as though his mother's death had released in his father a flood of malice and jealousy that until then had been dammed up. Jealousy was the only way Andy could describe it to himself, though when he tried to think what his father had to be jealous about he couldn't put his finger on it. He had a miserable little job on the railway, few friends and no girl, but that was how things were. Watching Andy put on a tie, light a cigarette, or even brush his hair before going for his evening walk, his father seemed like a man distracted with envy. Andy knocked again, a little bit louder.

"Who's that?" his father asked from upstairs—as if he didn't know, the old bastard!

"It's me, father," Andy repled in a low, appealing voice.

"This house is locked at ten o'clock," his father snarled.

"Ah, for God's sake, let us in, can't you?" Andy begged.

"This house is locked at ten, I say."

Despairingly Andy began to knock again. It was easily seen that his mother was dead. She wouldn't have lain there and left him outside, not for twenty men like his father. Now, they were both of them out. Andy was a finely-strung young fellow with a long, keen face, quick to mirth and quick to misery. Suddenly he put his hands before his eyes and began to sob, as much for his mother as himself—all her years of misery and toil, and nothing to show for it but this. (*Collection Two* 22)

This scene quickly attains an intensity usually found only at a story's conclusion. Its new density results from O'Connor's shift from narration to dramatization; originally, we were told that Larry knocks and whispers without success; Andy's knocking and whispering are infused with feeling through an interplay of gestures. Larry was conscious only of himself; Andy feels the shifting dynamics of his family, and he identifies with his dead mother as another of his father's victims. Even the appalling behavior of Mr. Coleman has motive; malice is his reaction to bereavement. Andy's disobedience of parental law is less an affront than his being young and alive.[12] The text also amplifies Andy's internal conflict:

---

[12]In 1957, O'Connor had explored paternal jealousy in "The Party." Johnny, another watchman, sympathizes with Mr. Hardy, a widower bitterly observing his children having a party, oblivious of his absence: "I used to feel the same myself, after the wife died. I'd look at the son

attempting a good son's subservience, he defiantly envisions his father as an "old bastard," potentially deadly to his mother and himself.

In both versions, O'Connor avoided making his adult males too similar: after Larry's father was "stony," Squinty was loquacious; after Mr. Coleman snarls, "Mac," the watchman, proffers homilies: "'It would be wiser for you to obey your father. He knows what is good for you, better than you do. But things are made too easy for young people nowadays,'" which leads to tedious didacticism about twelve-hour workdays for sixpence a week and a lecture on the evils of temptation (24–25). Mac's monologue, "one long moan, like a Good Friday service," gives Andy no consolation (26). However, even Mac, a moralist lacking a pulpit, later reveals himself as having been a son victimized by "'a severe man,'" now a father whose sons have turned on him (28). Painful parent-child relations are general all over Ireland.

Molly, a one-dimensional adolescent male's sexual fantasy, is now fully realized as the womanly Lena, "with the remains of her good looks still about her, and something pleasant and musical in her loud, hoarse, scolding voice." Although she shares Molly's profession, Lena's intimacy is sympathetic, not sexual commerce:

> "Sit down and tell us about yourself," she said, making room for Andy.
>
> "Ah, there isn't much to tell," Andy said. "I came home at half ten, and my old fellow had the house locked up and wouldn't let me in."
>
> "And wasn't there anyone to open the door for you?"
>
> "Ah, no, I'm an only child."
>
> "And what about your mother?"
>
> "She died a few months ago. I had to leave school, and 'tis since then all the trouble started."
>
> "I suppose he can do what he likes now," she said bitterly.

---

putting grease on his hair in front of the mirror, and I'd say to myself, 'That's my grease and that's my mirror, and he's going out to amuse himself with some little piece from the lanes, not caring whether I'm alive or dead!'" See Frank O'Connor, *A Set of Variations* (New York: Knopf, 1969), 244. Another pairing of bereaved father and disobedient son animates the 1953 "The Face of Evil." The narrator describes Mr. Dalton: "Everyone was sorry for his loss in his wife, but you knew that if it hadn't been that it would have been something else — maybe the fact that he hadn't lost her." See *More Stories by Frank O'Connor* (New York: Knopf, 1954), 54.

"He might have his reasons," the watchman said, addressing nobody in particular.

"Ah, 'tis easy the talk comes to you," she said shrilly. "'Tis a hard day for a child when he leaves his mother in the graveyard and comes back to live with his father. Bloody misfortunate brutes! I seen too much of them."

"You know nothing about it," the watchman said violently.

"Don't I? I suppose I don't know what happened to the houseful of us after we left my poor mother up in the Botanics? It wasn't long before she had company either."

"I say it's not fair to judge a man you do not know," said the watchman. "Men have great responsibilities that women know nothing about."

"They have, I hear!" she retorted mockingly. "Like my old fellow. The only responsibility he ever had was to see that his kids wouldn't have enough to eat for fear the publicans wouldn't go short, and he done that like a right true Christian. Bloody old brute! God forgive me!" (28–29).

Daughter, sister, and surrogate mother, Lena recognizes Andy as another orphan, spiritual kin. The crescendo of her speech, from conversational beginning to impassioned climax, shows that O'-Connor had taught himself much about capturing voices on the page. No male character would have communicated with Andy so personally; Lena eschews lecture or threat. Her suggestion that he come home with her for "'a few hours' sleep before he goes to work'" is maternal and compassionate: "'Come on, child,' she said, giving Andy her hand. 'I may as well get you back to the old doss or you'll be on my hands tomorrow.'" When a jealous Mac declaims tearfully, in melodramatic cliché, "'Go! But don't ever come back here again! Don't come to me for anything again, the longest day you live!'" Lena is torn between loyalties. Made bold by a "new feeling of confidence and excitement," Andy imagines himself mythic Youth triumphantly defeating Age and tries to lead Lena, his female prize, off, but she hesitates, sensitive to Mac's distress: "'Can't you see the poor divil is lonely?'" (30). In the first version, when Molly deserted Squinty, her parting words were crude ("'Now, now, don't be snotty!' ... 'It's not becoming to your years'"), then coy ("'And if you're good maybe I'll come round and see you to-morrow night'" [*Guests* 273]). Lena instinctively reaches out to those deprived of love.

She never has to choose between suitors, however, with the arrival of the policeman she had hoped to avoid. Entirely recreated in this version, Guard Dunphy is the night-world's only cheerful inhabitant, perhaps because he is free from family troubles. Lena explains that he is both sexually insatiable and pious: "'Biggest old ram in Cork, and he's never out of churches and chapels'" (*Collection Two* 29). Dunphy is more than a buffoon, although his homegrown mixture of Eros and Agape annoys Lena, who is compelled to join him in a "'little walk'":

> "And what would the holy fathers say about that?" the woman asked with ill-concealed acerbity. It was lost on the policeman though.
>
> "Ah, the holy fathers are men like ourselves," he replied complacently. "'Sins against Faith are serious, sins against morals, sure we all commit them.' Some great Corkman said that, if only if I could remember his name. Don't you agree with me, Mac?"
>
> "I knew that fellow's father well," said the watchman. (31–32)

As before, Andy decides to return home, but his choice is no longer a child's truculence: "'I think I might as well be making for home'" expresses quiet acceptance that he belongs there and cannot evade discord:

> ... Andy set off slowly in the direction of the city. The dawn was breaking over the cliffs to his right across the river, and buildings and ships began to emerge from the shadows. Soon a single spot of light reached out and struck the sleeping city, and in a curious way Andy's heart felt lighter. He knew he wasn't as good a boy as he had been when he came down but he felt better prepared to deal with his father and the rest that life might have in store for him. His life had been too sheltered, too much under the wing of a woman who was now under the ground. Now, the world stretched ahead of him, different from what he had imagined it, different from what it seemed by daylight, lit up with the spectral intensity of the night. (32–33)

Because Andy, unlike Larry, is constrained by adult responsibilities—he must be at work the next morning—he acknowledges that the riverbank has been only a temporary solution. Larry remained a child; Andy's maturity, although latent, was evident in the first scene, when he makes himself stop crying, "... shaking off the boy in him. But he could not reach for a man quickly enough" (22). Having passed through a dreamscape, he returns to the familiar world transformed by his experience. His place in the world is not fully clear, but he is animated by an awareness beyond self-pity or belligerence, as he returns home "better prepared to deal with his father and the rest." Surviving conflict, O'Connor implies, requires vision, not aggression.

Recreating "The Procession of Life" as a man nearing sixty, a father and husband, O'Connor envisioned his characters from a generous perspective, more forgiving than a young man's distrust of all male authority, and Andy's increased sensitivity colors the story. Although the second version's characters are still unpredictable, they are united by loneliness, however they express it or react to it. O'Connor affirms his faith that the most odd behavior is emotionally comprehensible, that the most perverse behavior is worth celebrating. Our sympathy is greater because of his unsentimental but deep feeling for his creations, even the oppressive (Mr. Coleman, Mac) or comic (Dunphy), whose behavior is rooted in motives we recognize even when Andy cannot.

The second version is also colored by Mick Donovan's death, which would have diminished O'Connor's need to give the emotions of his childhood an outlet. When Andy returns home, his awareness mirrors the sensibilities O'Connor brought to a late reading of his own relations with Mick. In the second volume of his autobiography, tellingly titled *My Father's Son*, he described meeting Mick, drunk and uncontrollable, for what would be the last time, his father's behavior evoking "childish terror and hatred." But O'Connor also wrote with an adult's sadness of his decision to send his father away because Mick terrified his stepson: "My heart was torn with pity and remorse because I knew that was no way to behave to a dog, let alone to someone you loved."[13] O'Connor did not identify with Mr. Coleman, but he could now better understand him as victimized by loss.

Were the story of "The Procession of Life" to end here, its history would be uncharacteristically tidy, given O'Connor's struggles to perfect his work. There is, appropriately, a coda: after his sudden death in 1966, his widow reread the stories he had been working on for *The New Yorker* or a new collection, but did not recognize the story he had been rewriting when he died. She asked his long-time editor and friend, the American novelist and short story writer William Maxwell, to help her determine if it was a new story. After reading it, he wrote Harriet that his wife, Emily, had found it in *Guests of the Nation*; it was "The Procession of Life." This last version, characterized by Maxwell as "the skeleton of a wonderful story," no longer exists, so we do not know what direc-

---

[13]Frank O'Connor, *My Father's Son* (New York: Knopf, 1969), 166–67.

tions it would have taken.[14] However, rewriting it yet again speaks of O'Connor's lasting connection to the subject and his feeling that no story was ever entirely finished.

In *The Lonely Voice*, he had said of Maupassant, "... like every other writer, either when he has got tired and begun repeating himself or when he is at the top of his power and can only repeat himself, Maupassant is writing the same story again and again."[15] Rewriting "The Procession of Life" was not the busywork of a weary artist, for O'Connor revealed himself as most willing to improvise when his self-chosen materials were most familiar. Perhaps, in rereading his early work with dissatisfaction, he knew that the young writer he was once, his experience and perceptions limited, had oversimplified his subject. Given another opportunity, he hoped to make it more true. Whatever moral the versions of "The Procession of Life" offer, he himself has the last word, indefatigable, proud, and amused: "... if you work hard at a story over a period of twenty-five or thirty years, there is a reasonable chance that at last you will get it right."[16]

---

[14]Unpublished letter from William Maxwell to Harriet O'Donovan Sheehy. Undated [1967?], private collection.

[15]Frank O'Connor, *The Lonely Voice: A Study of the Short Story* (Cleveland, OH: World, 1962), 68.

[16]See Frank O'Connor, "Writing a Story—One Man's Way," *The Listener* (23 July 1959): 139–40, esp. 140. This essay, along with O'Connor's introduction to Joyce's *Portrait*, is reprinted in *A Frank O'Connor Reader*, ed. Michael Steinman (Syracuse, NY: Syracuse University Press, 1994).

The Quest of Joyce and O'Connor in "Araby" and "The Man of the House"

Robert Fuhrel

A young man narrates a tale about a time when, as a boy, old enough to leave the house and travel some distance by himself but innocent in matters of the heart, he had created an imaginary world in which he was a hero. Focusing on everyday matters is a continual problem for the boy. Desiring to please an older female, he recalls having traveled in quest of something for this lady. He reaches his destination and meets another woman, but he is sadly disappointed. Nothing turns out as he had imagined; as a result, his views of the world and himself significantly change. Though he fails to bring back anything for the woman, he has taken an important step toward maturity.

A reader familiar with the work of James Joyce immediately recognizes this summary of "Araby," a story in *Dubliners*. Yet the motif of the quest, an important, recurring element in world literature, also underlies another important Irish short story, "The Man of the House" by Frank O'Connor, although the similarity ends with the plots. Like the unnamed narrator in "Araby," Gus in "The Man of the House" is a young boy who goes on an errand for a loved one. On his travels he meets someone, and the experience, seen in retrospect, changes his ideas of himself and his world. However, given the authors' different ideas of their own roles as writers and of the sound and function of stories, the differences in setting, tone, point of view, and theme are both significant and understandable.

Joyce's story reflects his urban upbringing, his education, and the purposes he expressed in letters he wrote attempting to get *Dubliners* published. "Araby" is set in the Dublin of Joyce's youth, and the setting and plot are based on his experiences. The location of O'Connor's story is never specified, and, for all we know, the events could be entirely imaginary.

Joyce didn't consider himself imaginative, preferring to take notes on what he saw and heard around him, later arranging and transforming those notes into fiction, departing from fact when it suited him. Besides, his intention in *Dubliners* "was to write a chapter of the moral history of [his] country and [he] chose Dublin for the scene because that city seemed ... the centre of paralysis...."[1] Joyce believed that a person must be "a very bold man who dares to alter in the presentment, still more to deform, whatever he has seen and heard" (Scholes and Litz 267). A number of facts testify to Joyce's fidelity to his experience in writing "Araby."

First, the setting is entirely urban, essentially unrelieved by nature. The only exceptions are ruined remains, gardens described as either "wild" with "a few straggling bushes" and a "rusty bicycle pump" or "dark" and "dripping ... where odours arose from the ashpits...."[2] Ellmann's biography, *James Joyce*, reproduces the cover of the program for a real "Araby in Dublin," a "Grand Oriental Fete," which Joyce presumably attended in mid-May of 1894, when he was twelve, about the age of the protagonist.[3] Further, the Joyce family once lived on North Richmond Street, only a year later than the period when Joyce attended the Christian Brothers' School there, between two periods with the Jesuits. Given Joyce's praise of the Jesuits for instilling in him the rigorous habits of organization he demonstrated, and given his father's well-known preference for Jesuit education, it is entirely appropriate that this interim with the less worldly Christian Brothers, during his adolescence, is the setting for "Araby." For this is indeed, in the life of the protagonist, a dark, confused time, full of illusions and misunderstood emotions. Not surprisingly, all that is mentioned of the school is in terms of escape: the "blind street" was "quiet ... except at the hour when the Christian Brothers School set the boys free" (29). "I chafed against the work of the school" (32). One notable

---

[1]This is from a letter Joyce wrote to Grant Richards on May 5, 1906, quoted in James Joyce, *Dubliners*, ed. Robert Scholes and A. Walton Litz (New York: The Viking Press, 1969), 269.

[2]All references to "Araby" are to the Viking Critical Edition mentioned above. For these particular quotations, see 29–30. References hereafter will be cited in the text.

[3]Richard Ellmann, *James Joyce* (New York: Oxford University Press, 1959), Plate III, following page 80.

departure from fact, though not from spirit, is that the boy in the story lives with an aunt and uncle rather than with his parents, but if we view the narrator as a portrayal of the youthful author, the behavior of Joyce's often drunken father helps to explain the boy's being an orphan in the story. For that matter, even the uncle in the story comes home late and at least slightly inebriated, causing a crucial delay in the boy's departure for the bazaar.

Frank O'Connor, very familiar with Joyce's work, approached the short story differently. According to William Tomory, "O'Connor often commented on Joyce's fiction—not just because Joyce was Irish and such a towering literary influence, but because he had come to be at odds with what Joyce's fiction represented."[4] While Joyce's story is narrated relatively straightforwardly in comparison to his later work, it is full of his typical allusions to obscure books such as *The Devout Communicant* and *The Memoirs of Vidocq* (29) and poems like "The Arab's Farewell to His Steed" (34). In contrast, Tomory points out that one "would search O'Connor's fiction in vain for stream of consciousness, interior monologue, or phantasmagorical dream sequences" because, as O'Connor says in *Towards an Appreciation of Literature*: "The nineteenth century novel still seems to me incomparably the greatest of the modern arts, the art in which the modern world has expressed itself most completely."[5]

Richard Ellmann greatly admired O'Connor as well as Joyce, and he, too, comments on O'Connor's lack of the experimentation that so characterizes Joyce, especially in the later work: "He saw that his own art must radiate out from a single nucleus, must not attempt detachment or alien centers of consciousness in the manner of James or Joyce."[6] In the same article, Ellmann discusses O'Connor's noted penchant for revision, one aspect of writing he shared with Joyce. However, Ellmann makes clear that even in this shared habit, O'Connor had a different purpose: "When he repeatedly revised his work ... he did so not only to make it more

---

[4]William M. Tomory, *Frank O'Connor* (Boston: G.K. Hall and Co., 1980), 58.

[5]Ibid., 57.

[6]Quoted in "Michael-Frank" in *Michael/Frank*, ed. Maurice Sheehy (New York: Alfred A. Knopf, 1969), 26.

wrought, but more free; for all that he had learned with desperate acquisitiveness stood in the way of primary apprehension."[7]

The reader's primary apprehension does not seem to have been a priority of Joyce, despite his efforts at self-promotion. Though he supplied charts and schemes to help a few selected critics understand his work and wrote detailed letters of explanation to his publishers and patrons, one suspects to help them more effectively publicize his writing, much of Joyce's technique is involved with puzzles and references obscure to the common reader, something O'Connor shunned. For example, in "The Man of the House," as opposed to Joyce's method in "Araby," O'Connor tells in plain language a tale devoid of allusions to other works of literature. Also unlike the Dublin of "Araby" is the setting of O'Connor's story, which cannot be precisely determined. It seems to be far more rural, perhaps a small village or the outskirts of a city as it takes the boy no time to get out into the countryside. A similarity between the two stories involves the protagonists' attitudes toward school. Gus, in "The Man of the House," reflects that he "had always known a fellow could have his troubles, but if he faced them manfully, he could get advantages out of them as well. There was the school for instance...." Gus doesn't go to school this day because of his mother's illness, but he walks by it while journeying to get medicine for her and notices "the chorus of poor sufferers through the open windows, and a glimpse of Danny Delaney's bald pate as he did sentry before the front door with his cane wriggling like a tail behind his back."[8] Neither boy seems particularly concerned with success in school, although the boy in "Araby" does comment on the concern of his teacher about the boy's daydreaming.

The urban setting of "Araby" is particularly grim, appropriate to Joyce's view of the city. One house is "uninhabited" and "detached from its neighbors." The other houses have "brown imperturbable faces." The boys play in "dark, muddy lanes" (29) and must run "the gauntlet of the rough tribes from the cottages," probably like the cottages where O'Connor's Gus lives.[9] Physi-

---

[7]Ibid., 27.

[8]All references to "The Man of the House" are to Frank O'Connor, *Collected Stories* (New York: Random House, 1981). This quote is from page 184.

[9]That Joyce, like his protagonist in "Araby," was distinct from the "rough tribes" was emphasized by O'Connor in a projected broadcast

cally, in "Araby" the surroundings are bleak, but the boy's imagination transfigures all, however briefly, as it does in O'Connor's story as well. The insistent dreariness of the setting makes the reader wonder how any degree of imagination on the part of the boy can for long hold out against his surroundings, and in fact, the week is not out before the transfiguration, along with the boy's youthful naiveté, is shattered.

The boy in "Araby" thinks he is in love, and he goes on a quest in search of something for the lady he thinks he loves. Because of his attraction to his friend Mangan's[10] older sister, to whom he has never spoken "except for a few casual words," the boy is able to interject into "places the most hostile to romance" an element of magic. When he shops with his aunt, walking "through the flaring streets, jostled by drunken men and bargaining women, amid the curses of labourers" and "the shrill litanies of shop-boys" (30–31), he imagines, "I bore my chalice safely through a throng of foes" (31). The young boy in "The Man of the House," on the other hand, doesn't allow his imagination to rule him for long: for a brief moment only the world around him is transformed, and he feels

---

scheduled for July 16, 1937, for Radio Eireann, a broadcast never made because of last-minute censorship. The transcript for the talk was published five days later in *The Irish Times*. In it, O'Connor says that the real tragedy of the Parnell split "was the desolation of the spirit it produced among the people, of whom Joyce is the very pattern.... This despair produced a violent overweening individualism" and "the desire to break forever with the tribe." This is discussed in Alan Cohn and Richard F. Peterson, "Frank O'Connor on Joyce and Lawrence: An Uncollected Text," *Journal of Modern Literature* 12 (1985): 211–20.

[10]Most of *Dubliners* was written while Joyce was living in Trieste, when he was also writing overtly political newspaper articles for the Italian press. During this time, he also wrote in praise of James Clarence Mangan, author of "Dark Rosaleen," one of the better known personifications of Ireland. Perhaps naming the object of his young protagonist's infatuation "Mangan's sister" in some way identified her for Joyce with what many young men of the time desired, a more traditional Ireland, a desire the more mature Joyce did not share. Joyce at this time was also lecturing on Irish history and teaching conversational English; his teaching methods included much discussion of politics, as attested to by his former students in the documentary entitled *Is There One Who Understands Me?: The World of James Joyce* (Producer and Director Sean O'Mordha). Dublin: Radio Telefis 1982. Dist. Princeton: Films for the Humanities and Sciences, FFH 897. Videocassette. 120 mm.

"exalted, a voyager, a heroic figure" (187), but primarily he remains conscientious about sticking to his duty and finishing the errand for his mother. Nevertheless, he will also be distracted by a young lady, if only temporarily.

In "Araby" the boy is very confused, and he doesn't know whether he "would ever speak to [Mangan's sister] or not" or how he "could tell her of [his] confused adoration." His feelings are permeated with religious images, and in the chivalric image so similar to that in "The Man of the House," the boy blends his attraction for the girl with the thought of the divine. O'Connor's young protagonist has heard his mother describe him to her friend Mrs. Ryan as "'the best anyone ever reared.'" Mrs. Ryan responds by remarking, "'Why then, there aren't many like him.... The most of the children that's going now are more like savages than Christians'" (185). He wishes to please his mother and realizes that if he isn't careful, he will disappoint her. "One slip and I should be among those children that Minnie Ryan disapproved of, who were more like savages than Christians" (185). He, too, sees himself as the lone bearer of the sacred in a profane world.[11]

When the boy in "Araby" finally speaks to Mangan's sister, he promises rashly to bring her a gift from Araby, a "splendid

---

[11]This image of bearing a chalice among enemies, more explicit in Joyce than in O'Connor, as one would expect, derives from stories of early Christian martyrs in Rome, particularly the story of Tarsicius, killed by a group of pagan boys as he tried to take the Blessed Sacrament to converts hiding in catacombs. See H. George Hahn, "Tarsicius: A Hagiographical Allusion in Joyce's 'Araby,'" *Papers on Language and Literature* 27 (1991): 381–85. According to Hahn, Joyce would have known about Tarsicius from a popular novel entitled *Fabiola: or, the Church of the Catacombs*, written by an Irish cardinal. Further, under the tutelage of the Jesuits, Joyce would have written narratives on the lives of the saints, and he certainly knew Butler's *Lives of the Saints*, where Tarsicius is linked with St. Stephen, the first martyr, about whom Joyce knew a great deal and to whom he alluded in a concurrent project, *A Portrait of the Artist as a Young Man*, going so far as to name the protagonist of that book Stephen. The story of Tarsicius also appeared in *Our Weekly Messenger*, a parochial elementary school publication, in the early 1950s, testimony to the staying power of the tale. My first reading of "Araby" made such an impression on me in part because I had read of Tarsicius in Philadelphia as a boy and identified with him. The legend would naturally have appealed to Joyce, who seems to have considered himself superior to his comrades in most respects.

bazaar," to which she off-handedly replies she would "love" to go, though she cannot because "there would be a retreat that week in her convent" (32). She has always been inaccessible, and he has watched her either from the street below, gazing up to where she has stood at the top of stairs in the doorway, or from across the street, peering voyeuristically at her through blinds. Always railings or walls have stood between them. But now Araby itself takes over his mind. "The syllables of the word 'Araby' were called to me through the silence in which my soul luxuriated and cast an Eastern enchantment over me" (32). Reaching Araby and winning this girl's love become his confused quest. In stark contrast, the young boy in "The Man of the House" has never before met the girl who momentarily leads him astray, and the quest he is on is for his mother. But this young lady is enticing. She urges him, after helping him to drink the bottle of cough medicine, to fill it up with water, and he cannot refuse her. "Mother was far away, and I was swept from anchorage into an unfamiliar world of spires, towers, trees, steps, and little girls who liked cough bottles. I worshiped that girl" (189). However, it takes but a moment and the empty bottle to bring him to his senses, and he "remembered my mother sick and the Blessed Virgin slighted, and my heart sank" (189).

Numerous critics have commented on the myth of the quest undertaken by "one who has been stirred by chivalric love in the tradition of the Arthurian romances."[12] Concepcion Dadaufalza points out that the quest itself was "meant to bring fertility to a blighted land."[13] This accurately describes Joyce's view of Dublin. The sterility of the Dublin setting, Dadaufalza explains, is reflected partly in the barrenness of the boy's relationships. Though he has playmates, they remain unnamed. His love is known only by her relationship to her brother. The boy himself lacks parents and lives in the home of an apparently childless aunt and uncle, surrounded by a "dead priest, an apparently unmarried sister, and a pawnbroker's widow." No wonder he seeks a Grail.

The boy in Joyce's tale does finally get to Araby after what seems to him an interminable delay caused by his uncle. He pays more than he had planned to get into the bazaar, which is about to close, and he "recognize[s] a silence like that which pervades a

---

[12]Robert P. apRoberts, "'Araby' and the Palimpsest of Criticism or, Through a Glass Darkly," *Antioch Review* 26 (Winter 1966–67): 468–69.

[13]Concepcion D. Dadaufalza, "The Quest of the Chalice-Bearer in James Joyce's 'Araby,'" *Dilman Review* 7 (1959): 317–25.

church after a service." He remembers only "with difficulty" why he had come and realizes he cannot buy anything. As he hears the English accents of a young woman and two men engaged in a most banal conversation, the boy's dream bursts. All his illusions about his maturity, about Mangan's sister and what he thought was her interest in him, about the exotic Araby, and, most significantly, about himself are destroyed, and the story concludes: "Gazing up into the darkness I saw myself as a creature driven and derided by vanity: and my eyes burned with anguish and anger" (35).

In order to understand Joyce's choice of setting, style, and theme, one must recall, again, that Joyce wrote this story as part of the whole of *Dubliners* "to betray the soul of that hemiplegia or paralysis which many consider a city," as he wrote in a letter to Constantine Curran reprinted in Scholes and Litz's volume (259). In other words, his purpose was moral in addition to artistic. Only by careful examination of conscience, such examination to be conducted by him, did Joyce believe the Irish could free themselves of the physical, intellectual, and spiritual paralysis he felt they were suffering. Had he remained in the home of his youth, as portrayed in "Araby" and the other *Dubliners* tales, he, too, would have fallen victim to Dublin's paralyzing influences: as self-exiled artist, it fell to him to aid in the cure of his countrymen.

None of this need to awaken his fellow Irishmen seems to have bothered Frank O'Connor. On the contrary, he is on record as having said about himself that "the thing this man likes best in the story is the story itself.... I like feeling that the story-teller has something to communicate, and if he doesn't communicate it he'll bust."[14]

Another aspect of "Araby," its style, is a matter of debate. Joyce himself called it "for the most part a style of scrupulous meanness."[15] Joyce agreed only most begrudgingly to alter or omit certain phrases to which the printers had objected, but he was determined to change nothing else. Again, to his prospective publisher, Richards, Joyce wrote, "These details may now seem to you unimportant but if I took them away *Dubliners* would seem to me

---

[14]Frank O'Connor, "Writing a Story—One Man's Way," *The Listener* (23 July 1959): 139–40. Reprinted in *A Frank O'Connor Reader*, ed. Michael Steinman (Syracuse: Syracuse University Press, 1994), 312.

[15]Quoted in Scholes and Litz, 269.

like an egg without salt."[16] Further, he argued, "'You say that it is a small thing I am asked to do, to efface a word here and there. But do you not see clearly that in a short story above all such effacement may be fatal.'"[17]

While Joyce here certainly refers to particular words and phrases, his insistence by implication is that every word was deliberate and important, something O'Connor also demonstrated. In fact, O'Connor went further, revising his stories incessantly, both before and after publication. By "'scrupulous meanness,'" Joyce was not referring to a sparsity of detail, for the stories are thick with references to popular and classical culture, the history and rituals of Catholicism, and the history and culture of Ireland. A perhaps not entirely undeserved criticism of Joyce is directed at his display of erudition, an integral part of his method. If his writing relied on plot and character alone, his stories would be nowhere near as rich as they are, but then again, they wouldn't be his stories. As it is, the language is appropriate as the voice of an imaginative narrator, perhaps himself an artist, reflecting on his youth, but it is hardly ordinary life described in "Araby."

Frank O'Connor's "The Man of the House" is another story told in the first person by a narrator recalling his youth, but here we have the youth of an imaginative but plain-speaking person. He is younger at the time the story takes place than the twelve-year-old in "Araby," for he tells us that when he reads the police court news to his mother, "I wasn't very quick about it because I was only at words of one syllable" (185). This boy, too, is fatherless, but in O'Connor's tale this detail is directly functional; it is the lack of an adult male in the family that motivates the boy to try to act maturely. On the other hand, the mother is more than present; she, not a peer, is the object of the boy's affection, for whom he ventures out into the potentially dangerous world. As in "Araby," the boy's imagination transforms what he sees there. A "wooded gorge" becomes "the Rockies, Himalayas, or Highlands ..." (185). The city below, seen from a hilltop, appears "more like the backcloth of a theatre than a real town," causing the boy to feel "exalted" (187). On his quest to bring back a bottle of medicine for his mother, he notices a "murmuring honeycomb of factory chimneys and houses" and a "gently rounded hilltop with a limestone spire and a purple sandstone tower rising out of it and piercing the

---

[16]Ibid., 270.

[17]Ibid., 273.

clouds. It was so wide and bewildering a view that it was never all lit up at the same time" (187). The details described here are much more grounded in the boy's physical surroundings than are the descriptions in "Araby," which much more often reflect the boy's emotional state.

At home, Gus sees himself as more manly, more useful, than he really is, but this self-perception is based on the desire to provide for and please his mother. He tells her he won't go to school but will care for her instead. He has a very practical imagination when focused on his duties. He notices her illness right away, orders her to bed, builds the fire properly, and makes her breakfast, though he is less than successful with the tea. He informs his mother's employer that he isn't sure if he will allow her to come to work, and he is elated when the boss agrees with his assessment of the situation. He successfully journeys to a nearby pub to get some whisky for his mother; in the pub he faces adults who threaten him, as the boy in "Araby" feels threatened by the crowds in the street. Gus sees a drunk in the pub, "grinning at me diabolically," who mistakes him for his "'old flower'" and calls him "'a thundering ruffian'" and "'the most notorious boozer in Capetown'" (186). As in "Araby," here again youth is threatened by an inebriated adult.

When Gus gets home, with his mother is Minnie Ryan, "gossipy and pious" (185). She corresponds to Mrs. Mercer in "Araby," who is described as "an old garrulous woman ... who collected used stamps for some pious purpose. I had to endure the gossip of the tea table" (33). And when Gus goes out to play, he deliberately stays close to home, so as not to lose his concentration and be counted among the savages. Like the boy in "Araby," Gus views himself as the saved one among the heathens.

Common to the two stories also is the theme of economic frustration. The boy in "Araby" cannot buy what he would like for his beloved, even if he could find something suitable, because he has spent too much on the special train to get to the bazaar and must still get home. In O'Connor's tale, the boy cannot both light a votive candle and buy candy. Before he can even go to the dispensary, he must visit the Poor Law guardian for the humiliating purpose of proving the family cannot pay for the doctor's visit. When the doctor arrives, apparently drunk, like the man in the pub, he does nothing but needlessly advise the boy to "'Look after your mother while you can,'" and then he writes a prescription. Presumably, more money would have provided a better physician, but Gus thinks little still of a doctor who "never washed his hands" (187).

So far, the details, including a poor, fatherless family with a sick mother and a boy who clearly dislikes school, another gossipy old lady, a man blindly drunk in a bar, and a doctor "like all the drunks of the medical profession" (186) seem to be as dismal as those in "Araby." But the sordidness of the description is undercut by the boy's acceptance of his world and his determination not to escape from it but to manage it maturely. Waiting for the bazaar, the boy in "Araby" is wont to wallow in self-pity and confusion, expressed in phrases like "I was thankful that I could see so little. All my senses seemed to desire to veil themselves.... I wished to annihilate the tedious intervening days.... I had hardly any patience with the serious work of life" (31–32). Gus, on the other hand, although aware of his shortcomings, still welcomes the challenges of the real world. He reads to his mother and successfully ventures to the pub, but both incidents are affected by his youth and inexperience. Even though, as he admits, he has begun "to feel the strain of my responsibilities," he knows that "Concentration ... was what I had to practice" (185).

Later, he is sent to the dispensary for the cough-bottle. This trip is directly reminiscent of the quest of the boy in "Araby." Gus must go "through a thickly populated poor locality," down a "stoney pathway flanked on the one side by red-brick corporation houses and on the other by a wide common with an astounding view of the city" (187). The boy balances the poverty of state housing with the "astounding" view; he sees both the bad and good at once. Here, however, he starts to lose his concentration. The view is "bewildering." His thoughts turn to religion, as do the boy's in "Araby," but this boy is far more practical if just as naive. Seeing a cathedral's spire and deciding to spend his penny on a candle to the Blessed Virgin, for his mother's recovery, he is "sure I'd get more value in a great church like that so close to heaven" than in an ordinary one down in the town (187).

Arriving at the dispensary, he meets the young lady who is destined to dispel his illusions. In "Araby" she was the banal shopkeeper flirting with two men, totally disregarding the boy, who brought him to his senses; in "The Man of the House," Gus is certainly paid attention to by the more experienced girl, but it becomes apparent to him that she only wants his cough-bottle. At first, he is attracted to her "pleasant, talkative" manner, her worldliness—"She obviously knew her way around"—and her green eyes (188). Gus is seduced from his mission and dismisses any need to light a candle. "In a queer way the little girl restored my confidence," he explains—a result quite different from the effect of the girl in "Araby" on that boy.

After they finish off the sweets he buys with the money he had intended to use to light "a candle to the Blessed Virgin in the cathedral on the hilltop for [his] mother's speedy recovery," the girl asks to try his mother's cough-bottle: "She took a long drink out of it, which alarmed me" (189). She then shares the rest with him and convinces him to "'Finish it and say the cork fell out.'" At this point, he realizes, "I had sacrificed both to a girl and she didn't even care for me" (189). But he can still hope for a miracle, and he goes into the nearest church, conveniently the cathedral with a shrine to the Blessed Virgin, and promises to buy a candle with his next penny. He returns home, broken in pocket and spirit (he, too, has wasted his substance on frivolities), thinking that his weakness, his failure to concentrate, has conquered him once more. But he phrases it quite differently than the boy in "Araby"; all Gus says is, "All the light had gone out of the day, and the echoing hillside had become a vast, alien, cruel world" (190).

When he arrives, he finds his mother still sick, and he breaks down in tears. She consoles him and says she was only concerned for his safety. This elicits from him the truth about the medicine; as a result, she mothers him even more. His lack of concentration, far from being the problem he has considered it, has forced her to resume her role as mother and protector. Although Gus is sure he is a failure, he has accomplished his mission in spite of himself. His return from his illusion of himself as a man to the realization that he is still a boy, in need of a mother, cures her, the very miracle he had sought.

We have what appears to be the same story told in two very different ways. The plot elements are remarkably alike though the characters differ, as do the writers' techniques. Joyce characteristically loads his tale with references to obscure books, popular ballads, and poems, but he undermines the references by having the narrator tell us the boy liked the books because they were old and yellow, putting the ballads in the mouths of nasal street singers, and having the boy leave while his uncle is just beginning to recite the poetry. "The Man of the House" is empty of such allusions, with the result that the boy comes across as a normal child instead of a budding artist. Joyce's tale is unrelievedly dark, from the blindness of the street at the beginning, through the short days of winter dusk, to the darkness of the empty hall at the conclusion; O'Connor's story begins on "a lovely summer morning" (184), and the boy has visions of himself as a knight on a hillside where "sunlight wandered across it as across a prairie" (187). These differences are significant, but more striking are the differences in the language of the two stories, differences that make "Araby" sound like the work of a writer and "The Man of the House" the work of a storyteller.

For example, consider this portion of the description of his surroundings given by the boy in "Araby": "When we met in the street the houses had grown more somber. The space of sky above us was the colour of ever-changing violet and towards it the lamps of the street lifted their feeble lanterns" (30). O'Connor, in contrast, rejects almost all figurative language as he has his narrator say: "At the end of the lane was the limestone spire of Shandon; all along it young trees overhung the high, hot walls, and the sun, when it came out in hot, golden blasts behind us, threw our linked shadows onto the road" (189). Both boys are confused about their emotions, but the boy in "Araby" expresses himself in phrases such as: "Her name sprang to my lips at moments in strange prayers and praises which I myself did not understand. My eyes were often full of tears (I could not tell why) and at times a flood from my heart seemed to pour itself out into my bosom" (31). Gus is more likely to say things like "I worshiped that girl" (189). As opposed to Gus, who on more than one occasion "loses his concentration," the boy in "Araby" puts it differently: "What innumerable follies laid waste my waking and sleeping thoughts after that evening!" (32). When Gus realizes, very quickly, that he has been tricked by the young lady, he says, "I saw her guile and began to weep" (189). This is certainly more directly stated than the words of the boy in "Araby" at his awakening: "Gazing up into the darkness I saw myself as a creature driven and derided by vanity; and my eyes burned with anguish and anger" (35).

Here are two writers intensely interested in the word, but one seems more interested in the magical properties of it, the other in the functional. O'Connor relates one famous anecdote, often repeated, that illustrates the two authors' different attitudes. He says he had visited Joyce in Paris, and states, "I had admired an old print of Cork in the hallway and wondered what the frame was made of. 'That's cork,' said Joyce. I said, 'I know it's Cork, but what's the frame made of?' 'That's cork,' Joyce repeated, and it was."[18] Hugh Kenner comments: "Being an old fashioned story teller for whom words have chiefly instrumental interest, O'Connor thought Joyce was going out of his mind."[19]

In any case, one of O'Connor's main interests was getting the voices right, as he made clear on many occasions. O'Connor, as he himself said, could not "pass a story as finished unless I know how everybody in it spoke.... If I use the right phrase and the reader hears the phrase in his head, he sees the individual."[20]

Different goals and attitudes about stories led Joyce and O'-Connor to two very different treatments of essentially the same situation. While Joyce was primarily an experimenter interested in "Europeanizing" Irish literature, O'Connor seems more in the tradition of the Irish storyteller, the *shanachie*, though with the crucial difference that his art was certainly not one of improvisation. James D. Alexander discusses O'Connor's attitude about fiction and his differences with Joyce's methods. Regarding O'Connor's narrators, Alexander points out that they "may not be reliable—often ... partly reliable—but his voice, even when ironic, confers the 'warmth' on the literary creation."[21] A perfect example is Gus in "The Man of the House." When he is giving and getting instructions from his mother at the start of the story, he suggests to her that eggs would be a good choice for dinner. Then, in one of his frequent asides to the reader, he informs us: "That was really only a bit of swank, because eggs were the one thing I could cook, but the mother told me to get sausages as well in case she was able to get up" (184). Also, according to Alexander, O'Connor used "the word 'cold' for Joyce's technique in *Dubliners* and *Ulysses*, to describe the quality of detachment he finds in Joyce.... Anything that gets in the way of the account, any reportage for its own sake, word play, allusion or symbol, struck O'Connor as sterile exhibitionism and was to be avoided."[22]

---

[18]In Frank O'Connor, *A Short History of Irish Literature: A Backward Glance* (New York: Putnam, 1967), 211.

[19] Hugh Kenner, *A Colder Eye: The Modern Irish Writers* (Baltimore: Johns Hopkins, 1983), 219.

[20]"Frank O'Connor," *Writers at Work: The* Paris Review *Interviews*, ed. Malcolm Cowley (New York: The Viking Press, 1969), 169.

[21]James D. Alexander, "Frank O'Connor's Joyce Criticism," *Journal of Irish Literature* 21 (1992): 40–53.

[22]Ibid., 50.

While no doubt an accurate assessment of O'Connor's feelings about Joyce's methods, this ignores the fact that Joyce was deliberately "cold" to many of his characters, whom he had not so much created as found in Dublin and in himself and whom he did not wish to portray sympathetically. Given such different ideas about the story and its purpose, it seems even more remarkable that the two writers would use the same quest motif in stories so similar in plot. One explanation of the similarity lies in O'Connor's undoubted respect for Joyce despite whatever criticism he might have leveled at him. In Eric Solomon's memoir of being O'Connor's student, he recalls that of O'Connor's many qualities, his lectures were exceptional, and Solomon states emphatically, "Frank O'Connor's classroom concert is what I recall best. He would read from Joyce's 'Araby.'"[23]

---

[23]Eric Solomon, "Frank O'Connor as Teacher," *Twentieth Century Literature* 36 (1990): 239–41.

"Fact" and "Fiction" in Frank O'Connor's "Guests of the Nation" and *An Only Child*

Robert C. Evans and Michael Probst

Frank O'Connor's most famous story, "Guests of the Nation," has also proven to be one of his most influential compositions. So far it has inspired a silent film, a play by Brendan Behan, a dramatic adaptation, and a highly popular movie (*The Crying Game*) written and directed by Neil Jordan, one of Ireland's most important contemporary artists.[1] Apparently the story also inspired, almost from the start, further fiction. In his autobiography *My Father's Son*, for instance, O'Connor himself reports that even W.B. Yeats was aware of the story's powerful impact. According to O'Connor, Yeats one night said to him, "'I see the Censorship Board has banned the book by So-and-So—the fellow who stole your story.'" O'Connor continues: "I didn't know that anyone had stolen that particular story; it has been stolen so often since that even the newspapers comment on it, but Yeats was the very first to notice the plagiarism."[2]

---

[1]For information about the film and play, see James Matthews, *Voices: A Life of Frank O'Connor* (New York: Atheneum, 1987), 104, 325–26. In the years since the success of *The Crying Game*, Neil Jordan has based another film on a work by O'Connor, in this case O'Connor's biography of Michael Collins. For details, see Neil Jordan, *Michael Collins: Screenplay and Film Diary* (New York: Plume, 1996), 4–6.

[2]We quote from the Pan Books edition of *My Father's Son*, which also includes the earlier volume of O'Connor's autobiography, *An Only Child*. For the specific citation, see *An Only Child and My Father's Son: An Autobiography* (London: Pan Books, 1988), 216. All subsequent citations here from these autobiographical works will refer to this edition.

"Plagiarism," in this case, is obviously the sincerest form of flattery: the fact that O'Connor's story has been so often imitated testifies to its deep and enduring power. In "Guests of the Nation" O'Connor had created a tale of such profound resonance that few readers can help being permanently moved and affected by it. Once read, it is not an easy story to forget; it has an almost elemental, archetypal force, partly because it deals with matters of the most basic and permanent importance. It is one of the most morally haunting tales composed in the twentieth century and is likely to remain one of our era's most influential works of short fiction. Small wonder, then, that a standard reference work calls "Guests" "in a sense the seminal story of modern Irish literature."[3]

O'Connor himself seems to have been unable to forget the tale, for although it was one of his very earliest fictional works (first published in 1931), echoes of its phrasing appear frequently in the opening volume of his masterful autobiography, *An Only Child* (first published in 1961). Tracing and pondering the echoes between the published story and the written life seems worthwhile, for such echoes raise a number of interesting issues. To what degree, for instance, was the story influenced by the events the autobiography recounts? To what degree, alternatively, was the autobiography influenced by O'Connor's own recollection of his most famous fictional tale? In what senses (in other words) is "fiction," in this case, connected with "fact"? To what degree can clear boundaries be drawn? Exploring the links between "Guests of the Nation" and *An Only Child* can perhaps help us better understand the genesis of each as well as the complicated relations between "reality" and "imagination."

***

O'Connor himself ascribed the origins of "Guests" to a variety of influences, including childhood recollections of English dialect, rumors he had heard while incarcerated during the civil war, his reading of prison journals, and his exposure to the short stories of Isaac Babel (Matthews, *Voices* 71–72; 392). Whatever the precise genesis of "Guests," however, the story became instantly famous when it was first published in *The Atlantic Monthly* in 1931, and it has remained a standard anthology piece ever since. The subse-

---

[3]See Brian Cleeve in *A Dictionary of Irish Writers* (Cork: Mercier Press, 1967), 1:101.

quent impact of the tale is complicated, though, by the fact that in the 1950s O'Connor issued a substantially revised version. His habit, notoriously, was to revise even his most accomplished works, and it is the revised version of "Guests" that is most often printed in contemporary college anthologies.[4] Most students, therefore, tend to read the work in the updated form (which is indeed arguably superior to the original). As if all this were not complicated enough, however, the version printed in the 1981 *Collected Stories* (introduced by Richard Ellmann) is the earlier rendition, with its heavy emphasis on dialect.[5] All this variation makes any discussion of the connections between "Guests of the Nation" and *An Only Child* potentially quite confusing.

Nevertheless, many echoes of the story can be traced in the autobiography—a fact that suggests that O'Connor himself could never quite forget his own most famous tale. To anyone familiar with "Guests," the echoes leap off the pages of *An Only Child*, especially (as one might expect) off the pages in which O'Connor discusses his personal experience of war. Some of the echoed phrases, of course, may simply have been part of O'Connor's habitual ways of writing; others, though, seem more intriguing. In either case the parallels in phrasing between the work of fiction and the work of "fact" imply interesting connections between two of O'Connor's best pieces of prose.

At one point in the autobiography, for instance, O'Connor mentions a "Divisional Commander" named Liam Deasy, whom he describes as "the kindest man I'd met in my short military experience" (151). Instantly one recalls the similar phrasing used by Bonaparte in "Guests of the Nation" when he describes his first exposure to Hawkins and Belcher, his new English friends: "I never in my short experience seen two men take to the country as

---

[4]This revised version is the lead story, for instance, in the widely available collection entitled *Stories by Frank O'Connor* (New York: Vintage Books, 1956), 3–16. In citing the work here, we will refer parenthetically to this edition, mentioning year of publication and appropriate page number(s).

[5]See Frank O'Connor, *Collected Stories* (New York: Knopf, 1981), 3–12; in citing from this edition we will use the abbreviation "*CS*." Oddly enough, the version printed in the recent reprint of O'Connor's first collection of stories, entitled *Guests of the Nation* (Dublin: Poolbeg, 1985) is the 1954 revised text! This fact, however, is nowhere noted in the edition.

they did" (1956; 3).[6] In both cases O'Connor emphasizes the youth of his narrators, and one can't help but think that the story's phrasing influenced the words chosen for the autobiography. Similarly, the autobiography later describes a war-time "dance at the village hall," where "the men stacked their rifles and danced 'The Walls of Limerick' and 'The Waves of Tory' before leaving for the battle" (162). Again one hears an echo from "Guests": "Hawkins learned to dance 'The Walls of Limerick,' 'The Siege of Ennis,' and 'The Waves of Tory' as well as any of [the Irish soldiers]" (1956; 4).[7] Similarly, O'Connor's repeated reference in the story to the friendly nightly routine of the two Irish guards and their two English prisoners (a routine which involves drinking tea, playing cards, and engaging in playful argument) seems to anticipate phrasing O'Connor later used in the autobiography to describe his own war-time imprisonment: "Every night we met in their big room and brewed our tea and cocoa, and I got them to sing, and they dragged me into arguments" (181).

An even more obvious echo of the story occurs, however, when the autobiography describes a pair of Britons who were being hunted throughout the Irish countryside. O'Connor remarks that "the two damned Englishmen had become the most unwelcome guests in Ireland" (165). Moreover, another obvious similarity between the work of "fact" and the work of "fiction" occurs when the autobiography depicts a "North Corkman, small and thin" whom O'Connor met while imprisoned: "he had a capacity for swearing and bad language that beat anything I ever heard" (179). Surely O'Connnor, when he wrote this sentence, was at some level recalling his own earlier description of the feisty little Hawkins in "Guests": "I never in all my career met a man who could mix such a variety of cursing and bad language into an argument" (1956; 5).[8] Was the description of Hawkins influenced by O'Connor's war-time encounter with the small North Corkman? Or was his account of the small North Corkman influenced by his

---

[6]In the 1931 version, the sentence reads as follows: "I never seen in my short experience two men that took to the country as they did" (*CS* 3).

[7]In the 1931 version, the relevant phrasing reads as follows: "'Awkins told me he learned to dance 'The Walls of Limerick' and 'The Siege of Ennis' and 'The Waves of Tory' in a night or two ..." (*CS* 4).

[8]The 1931 version reads as follows: "I never in all my career struck across a man who could mix such a variety of cursing and bad language into the simplest topic" (*CS* 5).

description of the fictional Hawkins? In this case as in others, the boundary between "fact" and "fiction" seems porous at best.

The links between O'Connor's autobiography and his most famous story, however, seem to involve more than echoes of isolated phrases. The links seem also to involve significant incidents and characters. These possible connections raise, once again, intriguing questions: did the autobiographical events influence the composition of the story, or did O'Connor's most famous published story influence the composition of his autobiography? Or, alternatively, are the connections between the two works even more complicated, messy, and entangled than these opposed options might suggest?

One thinks, for instance, of O'Connor's description, in *An Only Child*, of the execution of Erskine Childers, an Englishman who fought for the Irish republic. O'Connor clearly admired Childers, and in the account of his death one can't help but hear echoes of the execution of Belcher, the big, quiet, stoic, mature, and appealing Englishman in "Guests." Contrasting his immature younger self with the dignified Childers, O'Connor might just as easily be describing the contrast between the immature Bonaparte and the wiser, more experienced Belcher:

> ... there is nothing in nature more removed from the imaginative boy than the grown man who has cut himself apart from life, seems to move entirely by his own light, and to face his doom almost with equanimity. And yet again and again in my own imagination, I have had to go through those last terrible moments with him almost as though I were there: see the slight figure of the little grey-haired Englishman emerge for the last time into the Irish daylight, apparently cheerful and confident but incapable of grandiose gestures, concerned only lest inadvertently he might do or say something that would distress some poor fool of an Irish boy who was about to level an English rifle at his heart. (166)

Obviously differences exist between this "factual" narrative and O'Connor's fictional story: Childers was small, Belcher is big; Childers was shot in the heart by a rifle, Belcher is gunned down with a pistol from behind; Childers was shot in daylight, Belcher at night. Yet the similarities between the two deaths are nonetheless striking, and surely O'Connor saw in Childers an embodiment of the same brave, thoughtful spirit he had already immortalized in Belcher. One thinks especially of Belcher's concern lest he distress the Irish lads who are about to shoot him: "'I'm ready, and you boys want to get it over'" (1956; 15).[9] Was the real Childers a model for the fictional Belcher? Or did the "death" of the fictional Belcher influence O'Connor's account of the "real" execution of Erskine Childers? Once again the line between "fact" and "fiction" cannot be easily drawn.

The same seems true of another striking incident recounted in *An Only Child*—an incident that seems to have helped inspire (or to have been inspired by) the final paragraphs of "Guests." The autobiography describes the fate of a captured boy who was beaten to a pulp before being executed by O'Connor's comrades. The beating and the killing were justified by an officer who bears a striking resemblance (even in the language he uses) to the malignant Donovan in O'Connor's story:

> The officer, who in private life was probably a milkman, began some muttered *rigmarole* about the prisoner's having tried to burn a widow's home and poured petrol over the sleeping children.... A few days later the boy was shot. That scene haunted me for years—partly, I suppose, because it was still uncertain whether or not I should be next, a matter that gives one a personal interest in any execution; partly because of the over-developed sense of pity that had made me always take the part of kids younger or weaker than myself; mainly because I was beginning to think that this was all our romanticism came to—a miserable attempt to burn a widow's house, the rifle butts and bayonets of hysterical soldiers, *a poor woman of the lanes kneeling* in some city church and appealing to a God who could not listen, and then— a barrack with some smug humbug of a priest *muttering prayers*. (169; emphasis added)

Reading this, one thinks of Donovan's own "rigmarole" as he attempts to justify the killings in "Guests" (1956; 10), or of the story's final vision of the old woman who "fell on her knees and began praying" (1956; 16) after the brutal executions, or of the sound of the old woman and Noble "mumbling" prayers while Bonaparte stands in an open doorway, staring at the black night sky (1956; 16).[10] Even more striking, however, are the parallels—in phrasing,

---

[9]The 1931 version reads as follows: "'I'm ready if you want to get it over'" (*CS* 11).

[10]The word "rigmarole" is also used in the 1931 version (*CS* 9). In that version, the old woman is described as follows: "she fell on her two knees by the door, and began telling her beads ..." (*CS* 12). The word "mumbling" is also used in the 1931 version (*CS* 12).

rhythm, and meaning—between the final sentences of both accounts. In the autobiography, O'Connor concludes his description
of the boy's death as follows:

> I had been able to think of the Killmallock skirmish as though it
> was something I had read of in a book, and even ten years later,
> when I was sitting reading in my flat in Dublin, the door would
> suddenly open and he would walk in and the book would fall
> from my hands. Certainly, that night changed something forever
> in me. (169)

Here the repeated "ands," combined with the sense of a memory
that cannot be erased, clearly recall the famous final sentences of
"Guests" ("and even Noble and the old woman, mumbling behind
me, and the birds and the bloody stars were all far away, and I was
somehow very lost and lonely ..."), especially the story's very last
words: "And anything that happened me afterwards, I never felt
the same about again" (1956; 16).[11] Did the Killmallock incident
help inspire "Guests"? Or did O'Connor's memory of "Guests"
help color his account of the Killmallock incident? Here as before,
"fact" and "fiction" seem to blur, merge, and combine.

The evidence suggests, then, that O'Connor's many readers
and the numerous other writers who "plagiarized" from "Guests"
were not the only persons on whom the story had made a powerful impact. Another person who seems to have been unable to forget the tale, it would seem, was Frank O'Connor himself. No one
else, certainly, had better reason to recollect a work so memorable
in every sense.

---

[11]In the 1931 version, the passage reads as follows: "... and even Noble mumbling just behind me and the old woman and the birds and the
bloody stars were all far away, and I was somehow very small and very
lonely. And anything that ever happened me after I never felt the same
about again" (*CS* 12).

"Guests of the Nation": Story and Play

Katie Magaw and Robert C. Evans

"Guests of the Nation" is not only one of Frank O'Connor's best stories but is also one of his best-known and most influential works. It helped beget two films, many other stories, a radio script, and at least two plays. One of these dramas, Brendan Behan's *The Hostage*, has only an indirect connection to O'Connor's work; the other, mainly prepared by Neil McKenzie, is a direct adaptation.[1] Comparing and contrasting the original story with McKenzie's dramatic adaptation can help highlight the unique features of each and thus help us better appreciate O'Connor's masterwork.

The original version of O'Connor's story, first published in 1931, is apparently the version McKenzie used in preparing his play.[2] Much of the dialogue of the drama is taken directly from the

---

[1]Behan's debt to O'Connor was at first (and has been since) so widely noted that one student of Behan has taken pains to deemphasize it. See Ted E. Boyle, *Brendan Behan* (New York: Twayne, 1969), 88–89. O'Connor's story inspired a black-and-white film produced in the 1930s (see James Matthews, *Voices: A Life of Frank O'Connor* [New York: Atheneum, 1987], 104) and was a major influence on Neil Jordan's acclaimed 1992 film, *The Crying Game*. The story was adapted for radio in 1959 (see pages 363–383 of this book) and was read by the author on television in 1964; for details, see John C. Kerrigan's bibliography (in this volume).

McKenzie's adaptation was staged in New York in June 1959 (Matthews, *Voices* 325). Although Matthews reports that O'Connor himself "was delighted with the performance," he unfortunately cites no source (325). Incidentally, the index of Matthews' book mistakenly implies that this was a filmed rather than a staged presentation (442).

[2]The 1931 version is reprinted in O'Connor's *Collected Stories* (New York: Knopf, 1981), 3–12. References to this text will hereafter be cited parenthetically by page number(s), preceded by the abbreviation "*CS.*"

story, as is most of the plot. McKenzie does, however, depart from the original in a number of significant respects. The changes, however, help spotlight the details of the story's original design. Knowing the play can help us better perceive the story.

The plot of the original 1931 tale is well known. Told from the perspective of Bonaparte, a young soldier in the Irish Republican Army, it recounts what happens when he and his partner, Noble, are assigned to guard two English prisoners, Hawkins and Belcher. The story opens after the men have already spent enough time together to develop comfortable nightly routines. Each evening they relax by drinking tea and playing cards while Noble and Hawkins engage in spirited debates about politics and religion. Isolated from the war and from other people while living in the remote rural home of an old Irish woman, they have been temporarily able to forget the burdens of military duty and thus have cultivated an unusual intimacy. Despite their political, religious, and cultural differences, they have developed a camaraderie rooted in fundamental and shared human experiences. The harmony of their relationship suddenly collapses, however, when Jeremiah Donovan, an Irish officer, announces that the Englishmen are hostages who must be shot to retaliate for executions by the British army of Irish prisoners. Although Bonaparte and Noble feel torn between the demands of duty and the call of conscience, ultimately they do help kill their new friends. At the end of O'Connor's story, both men feel empty and forever scarred; in the famous final line, Bonaparte comments, "And anything that ever happened me after I never felt the same about again" (CS 12).

A summary of the drama's plot immediately suggests both its similarities to and differences from the plot of the story. Perhaps the most striking contrasts are McKenzie's more detailed portrayals of all the main figures, as well as his addition of incidents and characters not present in O'Connor's tale. Whereas the story begins by describing the already established intimacy among the men, the play ominously does not. Its brief prologue differs dramatically from the relatively peaceful and inviting opening of the story, for it immediately creates a depressing sense of despair. Barney Callahan (whose nickname, we later discover, is "Bona-

---

McKenzie's text was published as *Guests of the Nation: Play in One Act* (New York: Dramatists Play Service, 1960). Page numbers of this text, preceded by the abbreviation "*GN*," will be cited parenthetically. The text is apparently flawed in several places.

parte") speaks in soliloquy directly to the audience and announces that "There are things you do in life, and things you see, that stay with you forever, no matter what you may do to forget them" (*GN* 5). McKenzie thus announces at once a theme O'Connor saves for the end, and this change immediately darkens the tone of the play. Whereas in the story Bonaparte first seems a disinterested observer, in the play we know right away that he has been personally involved in some misfortune. In the story the news that the Englishmen must be executed comes as a complete shock, both to Bonaparte and Noble and to O'Connor's readers; in the play, however, we are led from the start to expect something bad.

This opening sense of tension is reinforced as soon as the first scene of the drama begins. Here McKenzie (probably echoing the opening of Shakespeare's *Hamlet*) depicts Barney and Noble as guards who challenge two approaching characters (Doody and Cooney) to stop and identify themselves. McKenzie uses these added figures in two main ways: first, to introduce and characterize the Englishmen before we actually meet them (since Doody and Cooney already know and like them and describe them in highly positive terms [*GN* 6–7]); and, second, to establish how strongly Noble and particularly Barney seem initially committed to following strict military procedure—especially how vigilant they are not to become too friendly with the prisoners they are presently guarding. This vigilance, of course, makes their later friendship with the Englishmen all the more ironic and implies how easily natural human bonds can form despite our best efforts to resist them. Moreover, by adding Doody and Cooney, McKenzie presents characters who can directly speak many feelings that Bonaparte (in the story) simply narrates. They openly articulate what O'Connor's Bonaparte silently thinks, and through these added characters the audience immediately senses the inherent decency of the two Englishmen. The need for Cooney and Doody is especially crucial since McKenzie's Barney is (at first and throughout) quite different from O'Connor's Bonaparte: he is more assertive, more outspoken, more argumentative, more cynical and skeptical, and far more obviously committed to his military duty. He is also more competitive than O'Connor's Bonaparte and seems determined at first not to be outdone by any accomplishments of the Englishmen. He even seems threatened by their values, habits, and actions (*GN* 6–9). In O'Connor's story, Bonaparte seems attracted to the Englishmen from the very beginning; in the play, his attraction develops only slowly and despite his strong initial resistance.

Bonaparte, however, is hardly the only O'Connor character who is transformed in McKenzie's play, for the dramatist also develops much more explicitly the character of the old woman, whose house the four men eventually occupy. In O'Connor's story, the men inhabit the house from the start; in the play, however, they are transferred there only during the third scene (*GN* 12–13). The transfer allows McKenzie to emphasize their interactions with the old woman. In the story, she is anonymous and intriguingly mysterious; she speaks little, implies much, and seems more a servant than the owner of a home (*CS* 4). In the play, however, she is given a definite name (Kate O'Connell), many more words and actions, and a more obviously domineering and assertive personality. A widow clearly committed to Irish nationalism and to her Catholic faith (*GN* 10; 17; 24–25), she takes command, gives orders, spouts clichés, and quickly intimidates all four men (12–13). McKenzie transforms the old woman, then, much as he transformed Bonaparte: she is literally more outspoken, literally more a presence in the play than she is in the story.

Another difference between O'Connor's tale and McKenzie's drama involves the presentation of the two Englishmen. Whereas O'Connor depicts these characters as seen through the eyes of the unassuming Bonaparte, McKenzie presents them on stage in more explicit and assertive roles. Belcher, for instance, is quietly dignified and thoughtful in the story but is assertive and even argumentative in the play. O'Connor emphasizes Belcher's placid benevolence, but McKenzie makes him seem far more prominent, active, and competitive, as when he shows his skill at bird-calling (*GN* 8) or when he vigorously disputes the names (and demonstrates the techniques) of various Irish dances (*GN* 14). Belcher, in short, is a less distinctive character in the play than in the story; like the old woman, he is changed in ways that make him seem more forceful but less mysteriously intriguing, and in general he resembles the other men more than he does in O'Connor's tale. In the story, Bonaparte the Irishman and Belcher the Englishman share similarly reserved and calm personalities despite their different national origins, just as the English Hawkins and Irish Noble share similar temperaments despite their obvious religious and political conflicts. In the play, however, all four men are very much alike. Thus Belcher and Bonaparte both seem more religious in the drama than in the tale (*GN* 21–22), and all the men seem more connected to families (in the play, Hawkins is even married [*GN* 21]). Most of McKenzie's added scenes give the Englishmen far more prominent roles in the drama than they play in the story. In one of these added vignettes, for example, Hawkins expresses the same kinds of feelings about duty as Barney had expressed in the play's beginning, while Belcher seems much more openly articulate in McKenzie's work than in O'Connor's (*GN* 22).

A further major difference between the drama and the story involves the presentation of Jeremiah Donovan, the superior Irish officer. In the story, Donovan appears at once, and O'Connor stresses his importance by almost immediately describing him in detail, in the process emphasizing his personal awkwardness and social inadequacies. He seems a weak man trying to appear strong, and he has private reasons to resent the friendship the other four have developed, especially since he seems excluded from it (*CS* 3). In the play, however, he appears much later, and when he does he seems immediately more self-assured and in command (*GN* 10–11). The story conveys Bonaparte's strong distaste for Donovan, but the play presents him much more objectively. Only when he comes to lead the Englishmen to their deaths does he seem obviously unattractive (*GN* 23–25), and even then the play presents him far more neutrally than does the story (in which his lack of love for the Englishmen is mentioned [*CS* 5]), in which 'Awkins accuses him of "'plying at soldiers'" shortly before Bonaparte dismisses his arguments as "the usual rigmarole" [*CS* 9], and in which he is described as speaking in "a cold and excited voice" [*CS* 10]). In the play, Donovan behaves as any superior officer might be expected to act; in the story, his motives seem far more personal, tangled, and insidious.

Finally, another major difference between the story and the play concerns their depictions of the killings and their aftermaths. In the story the moments leading up to the shootings are almost unbearably agonizing, not only for the four friends but also for the reader. In the play, though, the whole scene is rather hastily handled. O'Connor presents the scene in tormenting slow-motion: Bonaparte, trying to pray, closes his eyes, only to open them at the sound of a shot, thereby witnessing 'Awkins' death:

> … I saw him stagger at the knees and lie out flat at Noble's feet, slowly, and as quiet as a child, with the lantern light falling sadly upon his lean legs and bright farmer's boots. We all stood very still for a while watching him settle out in the last agony. (*CS* 10)

The play depicts none of this. Instead, in McKenzie's work, 'Awkins conveniently staggers off stage and quickly dies, out of sight. Oddly enough, McKenzie also omits one of the most powerful events of the entire story: the moment when Belcher notices that 'Awkins is "'not quite dead'" and that his knee is beginning to rise (*CS* 11). Seeing this, Bonaparte kneels down to put the Englishman out of his misery, then quickly rises when it occurs to him that Belcher may not want to wait any longer to be shot. The ever-thoughtful Belcher, though, shows more concern for 'Awkins than for himself, and urges Bonaparte, "'Give 'im 'is, first.... I don't mind'" (*CS* 11). None of this appears in the play, and in general the conclusion of the drama seems much more compressed than the conclusion of the story.

Whatever one's attitude toward McKenzie's adaptation, comparing and contrasting story and play can help highlight not only some basic differences between drama and fiction as genres but also the specific artistic choices each artist made in writing his work. Certainly the most significant contrast between the drama and the tale involves the development and presentation of the characters. O'Connor effectively filters the other figures through the consciousness of Bonaparte, so that we come to know *them* by coming to know *him*. McKenzie, on the other hand, must present characters who can affect us through dramatic presentation alone. All the characters in the play, therefore, tend to be more forceful, more fully developed, but perhaps less clearly differentiated than they are in the story. Subtleties and nuances are sometimes lost in the transition from page to stage.

As an adaptation, the play is simultaneously faithful and inventive. Sometimes, for instance, McKenzie clearly borrows devices from O'Connor: thus Barney's soliloquies are taken almost verbatim from Bonaparte's meditative reflections, while the raising and lowering of lights on stage mimic the patterns of light and darkness in O'Connor's imagery. At other times, however, McKenzie invents dramatic devices of his own (such as the play's various performances of music, which cumulatively suggest the harmony and vitality later destroyed by the killings). In all these ways and others, juxtaposing the imitation with the original not only can help us better perceive McKenzie's talent but can also help us better appreciate O'Connor's genius. Story and play illuminate each other, reminding us that even works sharing the same title, characters, and the same basic plot can differ fundamentally when seen as works of careful and deliberate art.

Critical Kaleidoscope

O'Connor the Critic:
A Sampling of His Views
on Writers and Writing

prepared by John M. Burdett, Michael Probst (MP);
Claudia Wilsch (CW), *and Carolyn T. Young* (CTY)

Sean O'Faolain famously compared Frank O'Connor the critic
to a man who hauls a machine-gun to a shooting-gallery: everyone
hits the floor as he blasts away, but when they stand they discover
that he's scored several perfect bulls-eyes.[1] We have kept that
comparison in mind while preparing this section of the present
volume. It provides quick paraphrases and thumb-nail summaries
of some of O'Connor's most provocative views about writers and
writing. These views, always lively and sometimes apparently
contradictory, were expressed over a number of years in a variety
of essays, books, and interviews, some of which are either out of
print or no longer easily available. The following paraphrases are
meant to help kindle interest in O'Connor's criticism, which is obviously relevant to his own fiction. Comparing and contrasting his
critical principles with his creative writing would clearly be a
fruitful avenue for students of O'Connor to explore. In any case,
we hope that this quick survey will encourage readers to seek out
O'Connor's exact phrasing in its original contexts. Perhaps these
snapshots of his critical mind in action will even help encourage a
publisher to collect and reprint all the relevant texts themselves.

O'Connor, of course, was not a professional critic; he was
(alas) merely a highly gifted author. We hope that this brief survey
of his critical views will be useful not only to his own readers but
to other writers as well. Most of the paraphrased comments deal
with broad issues rather than with specific figures. The boldfaced

---

[1]*Vive Moi!* (Boston: Little, Brown, and Co., 1964), 369.

summary comments have been added to make the topics easier to spot.—RCE

***

O'Connor, Frank. *Towards an Appreciation of Literature.* **Dublin: Metropolitan Publishing, 1945.**

Purposes of Literature: The first purpose of literature is to entertain.... Nevertheless, readers can enjoy true recreation only when they choose works which not merely divert them but which also arouse their intellects. Thus, imaginative literature begins when reading functions as genuine recreation rather than as a mere pastime. (*TAL* 7–8; CW)

Authorial Commentary: An author who not only gives an account of a story but who also comments on the events he relates usually succeeds in engaging the reader. Such an author-commentator seems an actual person conveying true experience and seems almost a friend.... However, such commentary may at times be so subtly embedded in a story that it may require more than one reading to be detected. (*TAL* 9–11; CW)

Literature and Life: With its abstract meanings, literature complements and illuminates our practical life experience. Although less intense than real experience, it can seem more profound. Thus, readers faced with real-life problems sometimes consult certain writers who communicate exemplary moral standards, such as Jane Austen. (*TAL* 13; CW)

Literature and Languages: Knowing several languages is a prerequisite for truly understanding such international forms as literature. (*TAL* 16; CW)

Holding a Reader's Interest: Ideally a writer should so craft his book that even after its plot is known, the reader will still be sufficiently interested in it to re-examine it and contemplate its details. (*TAL* 21; CW)

Sentimental Nostalgia: Sentimental nostalgia in a work of literature can blur characterization and diminish the significance of the narrative's events. Nostalgia may work for poets, but fiction writers must illuminate the long-term significance of seemingly trivial events. (*TAL* 22; CW)

Details, Pace, and Feelings: Carefully chosen details and incongruities make a story come to life.... Too quick a pace prevents a story from conveying emotion. (*TAL* 23–24; CW)

The Appeal of Realism: An understated realism, focusing on the richness of common life and conveying a basic moral message, seems most likely to survive re-reading; books full of narrative suspense or complex philosophical dilemmas age quickly. (*TAL* 29; CW)

Old Books and New Times: Attempting to create a work in the style of earlier writers is useless, since it is their relevance to their contemporary society which makes literary works of a certain style appealing to their original audience.... Thus, the closer a piece of literature is to our own time, the easier it is for us to appreciate it.... Literature tends to be ephemeral because the shared meanings, values, and language of which it is composed date quickly. Although less true of lyric poetry, this is especially true of drama. (*TAL* 32–33; CW)

The Bible and the Classics: Just as the Bible is the basis of Christianity, so the classics constitute the foundation of Western culture. (*TAL* 37; CW)

Literature, Yesterday and Today: In order to appreciate literature, one must see it from both past and present perspectives.... To appreciate it fully, one should read both old and new books. A person who reads only old books is really more interested in history than in literature itself. (*TAL* 49–50; CW)

Modernism: By the early twentieth century, the increasing influence of the middle class and of scientific discovery had promoted the evolution of an urban, uprooted, alienated society. The options for writers were now to turn either to an almost scientific objectivity or to introspective autobiography.... Some authors, in their quest for answers to modern problems, have turned to either religious or political dogma. (*TAL* 58; CW)

Literature as Human Contact: Literature involves a sharing of thoughts; it penetrates our isolation and allows us to know the joys and aspirations, but also the concerns and worries, of other people. (*TAL* 58; CW)

***

O'Connor, Frank. *The Mirror in the Roadway: A Study of the Modern Novel.* **New York: Knopf, 1956.**

Nineteenth-Century Novels: These works are by far the best examples of modern art—even better than the symphonies they so resemble, and possibly better than any other kind of popular art since Greek drama.... As with the plays of the ancient Greeks and the Elizabethans, the whole society took an interest in these novels, in a manner incomprehensible in either the century before or the century after. (*MR* 3–4; CTY)

Chronology and the Novel: The only appropriate way of classifying the writing of Europe is by eras: any novelist in England probably shared more with a novelist in France from his own era than with a novelist in England from some different era.... [Because] the conditions that affected the novelists bound them together, ... the nineteenth-century novel is an art form of its own century and is a European art. All of its diversifications are simply regional and comparatively incidental. (*MR* 5; CTY)

The Comic and Tragic in Novels: Unfortunately, because the novel speaks to the intelligence rather than to the imagination, it blurs the ancient categories of comedy and tragedy, and since comedy is so definitely the art of the intelligence, the novel favors the comic writer.... A gifted poet or playwright may be improved by having no sense of humor, but a novelist with none (e.g., Lawrence or Tolstoy) starts with a disadvantage. (*MR* 12; CTY)

Novels and Middle-Class Ethics: The novel, when it arrived, dealt mainly with home, family, and community affairs. It focused on the examination of society and the individual's position in it, and on the organization of socio-economic groups rather than on the traditional tales of gods and heroes or on the written record of the past.... The novel is limited both in subject matter and in point of view.... Its code of right and wrong is mainly that of the tradesman classes, who were concerned with profits instead of status, character instead of good manners, and trustworthiness instead of glory.... Yet such ethics endow the nineteenth-century novel with its distinctive quality of deep human emotions, as satisfying to an unsullied moral sense as the sheen of tiles in a Dutch painting is to an unsullied aesthetic sense. (*MR* 12–14; CTY)

Art and Politics: O is both a nineteenth-century realist and a nineteenth-century liberal. Whether or not realism or liberalism are intrinsically good beliefs, they are two sides of the same outlook, just as conservatism and romanticism may be different aspects of an identical outlook. Perhaps symbolism and naturalism in literature resemble fascism and communism in politics. (*MR* 15–16; CTY)

Austen vs. Romanticism: [Jane] Austen's early work is as much literary criticism as creative writing. It ridicules specific kinds of literature (especially fiction) that she faulted, especially the kinds that were overly fantastical and sentimental.... The real novelist always rejects romanticism in fiction. (*MR* 18; CTY)

Transportation and Truth: Jane Austen criticizes her heroines' lack of judgment based on what she herself knew to be true. The available knowledge expanded greatly during her lifetime, even if it seems quite narrow to us. In fact, improvement in transportation has played a larger role in the history of the novel than critics realize. (*MR* 18–19; CTY)

Emotion vs. Morality in Jane Austen: Austen, fearing her own strong emotions, sometimes restrained them too much.... This fear made her a moralist and thus often weakened her fiction.... Her work often produces an effect different from her intent because morality and art, reason and feelings, battled within her. She never separates esteem (the aim of the moralist) from emotion (the aim of the artist). For in art, we can only learn through the emotions.... This characteristic can especially be seen in the portrayal of her heroes. When Austen wanted to portray a hero, she used her own masculine side, the one she herself admired. Therefore, her heroes are too burdened in judgment, with no light side, no feelings and fantasies to fight.... A reader who enjoys *Mansfield Park* all the way through values it for reasons different from the moralism Austen intended. (*MR* 25–30; CTY)

Jane Austen as Precursor of Freud and Joyce: In *Emma*, Austen discovered and explored the unconscious long before Freud.... As in certain passages in James Joyce, she attempts to reveal information that has not yet risen to the consciousness; thus she must express it symbolically. (*MR* 34–36; CTY)

Amateur vs. Professional Novelists: When we leave Austen and Stendhal and confront Dickens, Balzac and Gogol, we encounter a new world of thought and technique—the world of the professional. Whereas amateurs such as Austen had a select readership, the professionals had a large but poorly educated one; the amateurs explored issues of individual integrity, but the professionals were interested in great civic causes. The amateurs passionately sought true knowledge, while the professionals pursued a type of mass delusion. (*MR* 61; CTY)

Local Color in the Novel: [By the time of Dickens], the novel had to discover a medium that was the same as poetry was to the Elizabethan tragedy, and this medium was local color ... [from which the] later novels gain a sensual force, a material presence absent in the novels of Jane Austen and Stendhal. (*MR* 61–66; CTY)

Showing vs. Telling: Excessive narration, as in some of Stendhal's novels, is tedious and boring.... Excessive dramatization can be unendurable because undramatic, becoming a tormenting blend of exposition and development.... Drama belongs to the unfolding of the plot, not to the interpretation of ideas. (*MR* 77–78; CTY)

Pleasing and Teaching in French and English Novels: While the English saw novels as entertaining, the French saw them as instructive. Thus the finest English novel is more artistic than a French one because it simply tries to please. (*MR* 83–84; CTY)

Self-Conflict in Writers: [Like Thackeray], every outstanding writer harbors opposite beliefs; even if he depicts real life, his characters and plots will inevitably reveal contradictions that finally disclose the entire tendency of his own personality. (*MR* 119; CTY)

The Immaturity of Writers: Most writers have a youthful, immature side that never develops, even though their development in other ways may seem extraordinary. (*MR* 124; CTY)

Novels and Novelty: Any novel that piques interest in the unknown is less interesting when read again; when a novel *simply* creates such interest in novelty, it can hardly be read again at all. (*MR* 129; CTY)

Politics vs. Artistic Instinct: Although Turgenev initially valued art for its artistry and considered politics deadly to a creative writer, his later weakness as a novelist was caused by deep-seated conflict between his political liberalism and his instinctive traditionalism.... By skewing his novels toward politics he was acting against his own nature. He interpreted his personal dilemmas politically, thus creating neither an honest personal disclosure nor a thoughtful objective analysis.... Whereas Jane Austen feared poetry (even though she was greatly drawn to it) because she thought it would undermine reason, Turgenev feared poetry because he feared it would sap the will. Although steeped in poetry, Turgenev thought his excessive yielding to it caused all his frailties of character, and his one idea of a hero was a man too focused in will for such a waste of his energy. (*MR* 134–38)

Flaubert and the Rise of Naturalism: *Madame Bovary* may be the most exquisitely written book ever created; without a doubt it is the most exquisitely written novel.... It was the most significant novel of the century, because the new style, naturalism, coalesced about it.... The relation between naturalism and realism paralleled the relation between symbolism and romanticism: each overstated and extended a trend.... Both naturalism and symbolism involved a detachment from life. (*MR* 189; CTY)

Literature, Mutability, and Morality: Literature is a terribly mixed skill. Language evolves over time; thought always changes; and from its very genesis writing has been bound up with philosophy and morals.... An artist may paint a portrait of a Borgia without giving a thought to whether he sanctions poisoning, but a writer who tries this kind of amorality breaks his contract with his readers. (*MR* 194; CTY)

Literary Style and Political Ideology: At the beginning of the nineteenth century there were only two viable political positions that were feasible, conservative and liberal, and only two literary positions, romantic and realistic.... There is much too close a connection between the excessive realists, who are the naturalists, and the excessive radicals, who are the communists, on the one side, and between the excessive romantics, who are symbolists, and the excessive conservatives, who develop into fascists, on the other side, for us to fail to recognize the conceivability that they are exactly alike at the core. Communism throws everything into the outside world, shrinking the individual to a mere shade, and this is extraordinarily close to the literary theory of naturalism. Contrarily, fascism is inclined to see the outside world as only a representation of an individual point of view.... (*MR* 196; CTY)

Art for the Sake of Art: [Writers such as Jonson, James, Flaubert, and Joyce] cared more for the form of literature than for its substance and worshipped it as do old maids, reduced to poverty, when they inherit old family residences.... But their worship was so strong that it abused a human quality. None of these writers could portray ordinary human love because literature itself was their one true love. (*MR* 224–25; CTY)

Poets vs. Novelists: Poets are rarely great novelists, because, in the first place, a poet's world is an inner one.... A novelist's world is an outer one that he strives to make resemble an inner world.... Poets are more often affected by broad concepts than novelists are, whose ideas must be transmitted through human routes not noted for their ability to hold onto ideas. (*MR* 237–38; CTY)

Novels vs. Short Stories: The essential quality of a novel is that it takes for granted a collection of people, an orderly social arrangement that can swallow up the solitary individual.... The short story, however, is the art form that is concerned with the individual when there is finally no collection of people to take him in, and when he is forced to persist, in effect, by his own inner vision. (*MR* 253; CTY)

Free Will and Its Absence in Victorian and Modern Fiction: While Victorian fiction undoubtedly overstates the freedom of the individual, there is a much graver overstatement in modern fiction of man's lack of freedom.... The people in the works of Joyce, Proust, and Faulkner are completely overpowered by situations; they are too weak in strength of character to be able to extricate themselves from their own quagmires. (*MR* 267; CTY)

Freud's Influence on Modern Novels: Maybe the most important effect of the Freudian theory is that since it deals with the imagination and excludes nearly everything else, the theory has caused the modern novelist to become uncertain that there actually is an objective reality supporting what he writes. (*MR* 269; CTY)

Homosexuality in Modern Writing: In modern literature there is no sexuality that is true homosexuality; there are only depraved sexual practices that combine voyeurism and exhibitionism, sadism and masochism with other practices similar to homosexuality.... This style of sex is just physical and excludes human love, as in Gide's unusual marriage, in which emotion was limited to the virgin wife and physical gratification to streetboys. (*MR* 284; CTY)

Joyce and Subjectivity: Joyce's style of repeating certain key words, possibly one set to provide a framework for the story and another set for sensory significance, is new in literature. It defines the mark which Flaubert expected, in which style is no longer a connection between author and reader but becomes a mystical kind of connection between author and object.... The right word is no longer right for the reader, but for the object.... The writer is not trying to explain an incident or a feeling to the reader.... The reader is supposed to be present only on sufferance; the writer is trying to make his prose equal with the incident or feeling (304).

In fact, one could say that the writer intends to substitute the words for the actual happening. (*MR* 302–4; CTY)

Joyce: Writing as an End in Itself: When one reads Joyce one is reading Literature with a capital L. The tide washes over the island and covers the little people marooned there, and slowly they sink beneath the water until nothing is left but broad, blank Literature reflecting the blank countenance of the sky.... The problem with Joyce's novel *Ulysses* is that it dilutes man himself to a metaphor, with no personal experience, a progression that is frankly accomplished in *Finnegans Wake*, so that the Aristotelian empirical philosophy with which O started has flown.... Like using the atom bomb, this can only end in annihilating mankind, and mankind has no alternative but to go back to the beginning and learn the work of living all over. (*MR* 312; CTY)

***

"Frank O'Connor." An interview conducted by Anthony Whittier; first published in *Paris Review* 17 (Autumn–Winter 1957): 42–64. Reprinted in *Discussions of the Short Story*, ed. Hollis Summers (Boston: D.C. Heath, 1963), 100–9.

Short Stories, Novels, and Poems: O writes short stories because they are closest to his original medium, the lyric poem.... The short story, like the lyric, is much less constrained than the novel by a demand for logic and understanding of circumstances. (*PR* 100; MP)

Time in Novels and Stories: O disagrees with the view that the novel is the easiest form of writing, the short story being more difficult and poetry most.... Novels demand the creation of a sense of life's continuity, which short stories need only imply.... A novel must portray the effects of time on characters and events. If a lengthy work fails to do this, it is merely an extended short story—such as Faulkner's *As I Lay Dying*. (*PR* 100–1; MP)

Chekhov's Structured Stories: O admires Chekhov but believes that to mimic the Russian without employing his techniques is a folly destined to end in incoherence.... Those presuming to imitate Chekhov's style (e.g., Katherine Mansfield) write as though the essential unity of plot is unnecessary. They fail to perceive that, while skillfully concealed, a structural skeleton of this sort does underlie Chekhov's work. (*PR* 101; MP)

Babel's Impact: O's greatest influence was Isaak Babel. At least three stories in O's *Guests of the Nation* volume are imitations of stories in Babel's *The Red Cavalry*. (*PR* 101; MP)

Plot and Development in Stories: When writing a story, O's first concern is to get a rough outline on paper, since he considers the blueprint of a tale its most significant aspect. He is especially concerned with spotting and plugging holes in the plot. Polishing the work and filling in the details comes second. (*PR* 102; MP)

Four-Line Outlines: When planning stories, O restricts himself to four-line themes or plot summaries. Anything much longer is already too developed and rigid. Notes longer than four lines over-construct the details, thereby restricting the theme's development.... If the theme cannot be stated in around four lines, the essence of the story has not been captured. (*PR* 102; MP)

Physical Description vs. Mood and Sound: O acknowledges that his stories lack descriptions of landscape details and characters' physical features (which are typically present in other authors' works, e.g. those of A.E. Coppard). Instead, he begins by focusing on his characters' thoughts.... When O meets someone, he responds to that person's aura. He tends to distinguish people by their voices, manners of speech, and use of particular phrases. He is acutely sensitive and responsive to voices. (*PR* 102; MP)

The Writer's Autonomy: O enjoys writing short stories because the process is free from the creative strictures imposed by other media, particularly theater and television.... Attempts to reach a mass audience inevitably corrupt an art form by making it commercial and by encouraging self-censorship.... Art can only succeed when an artist intimately knows his audience. (*PR* 104; MP)

Novels and Human Beings: For O, the novel is essentially about real persons. As soon as a novel becomes an academic exercise and loses sight of the real people who should constitute its characters and audience, O loses interest in it. (*PR* 104; MP).

Why We Read and Write: People do not create or read literature with a view to some high-minded morality; rather, they do so for pure enjoyment. Faulkner's technical innovations and attempts to seem profound (for example) are far less interesting than his more basic, more powerful gift for humor. (104)

Artificial Technique in the Modern Novel: O believes technique is not nearly as important as having a story to tell about people and telling it in chronological order. The problem with the modern novel is its attempt to concentrate a story within a specific time frame, omitting everything that happened before that period.... The concentration on "the unities" present in the twenty-four-hour novels (e.g., *Ulysses* and writings by Virginia Woolf) is entirely unnecessary. These novels miss the vital, matter-of-fact feeling of real life.... The goal of a good novel is to capture a character's thoughts. Concentrating on unities inhibits this process. (*PR* 105–6; MP)

Form and Character in Detective Fiction: O is fascinated with detective stories, because their form often seems genuine rather than contrived. He appreciates the logic, passion, and mystery of such stories and the convincing characterization in the best of them. (*PR* 106; MP)

Individualism and Middle-Class Fiction: Although academic novelists seem most interested in technique, O laments the loss of character in stories. People (not abstract or ideological stereotypes) are the most worthy subjects of literature.... He wonders why writers from America (the only remaining middle-class nation) have not been able to overcome modern skepticism about individualism. (*PR* 106; MP)

Humanism vs. Psychologism: O eschews the psychological approach to writing in favor of traditional humanism. This humanism, derived from the Romans and Greeks, takes a man at face value, judging his obvious behavior without attempting to discover its hidden motives. (*PR* 107; MP)

Time in the Novel: Modern novels (such as those of Hemingway) are too compressed in time; a novel ought to cover an extended period so the characters can be measured against a variety of events. In this sense, Joyce's *Ulysses* is an inflated short story that lacks progression. (*PR* 108; MP)

American Writing and New England: O ascribes all that is good in American literature to New England; even the writings of Katherine Anne Porter and Willa Cather show that region's influence, if only by implication. (*PR* 108; MP)

Theme as the Essence of Fiction: The fundamental element of a good story is theme.... A good theme is more than a tale about some personal experience. It is a story that has merit in and of itself, something that will immediately intrigue everybody (not just the person telling the story). (*PR* 108–9; MP)

The Purpose of Writing: A writer must be n. than an observer. He must be a reformer in the sense of one who honors a great person or idea. (*PR* 109; MP)

***

O'Connor, Frank. *The Lonely Voice: A Study of the Short Story.* **Cleveland, OH: World Publishing, 1963.**

Stories vs. Short Stories: Stories, like plays and poems, once addressed broad audiences, although stories were less technically sophisticated than dramas or lyrics. Yet both the short story and the novel are specifically *modern* kinds of art; in other words, they best convey our contemporary attitudes. (*LV* 13; JMB)

Plausibility in Modern Fiction: The technical devices of modern novels and short stories derive from an era of science and analysis, and we tend to judge the success of both forms by how plausible they seem—by how believably they present an abstract plot. (*LV* 13; JMB)

The Lone Reader: Modern short stories and novels, unlike older tales created for masses who were freely willing to believe, are private forms of art which must meet the demands of the specific, isolated, analytical reader. (*LV* 14; JMB)

Gogol and the Origins of Short Fiction: Like many short stories influenced by it, Gogol's story "The Overcoat" focuses on a seemingly insignificant character whose view of life is suddenly and significantly transformed. (*LV* 14–16; JMB)

Heroes and Norms in Novels and Stories: Novels tend to focus on the relations between "normal" society and a character who in some way represents an aspect of the reader, but a reader cannot identify with the main character of a short story or see the society depicted there as providing a norm. Short stories lack heroes. (*LV* 17–18; JMB)

Short Stories and Outcasts: Short fiction usually depicts marginal populations—exiles loitering at the edges of society who often resemble such symbolic outcasts as Christ, Socrates, or Moses. For this reason, short stories emphasize a theme that novels tend to neglect: the theme of human isolation. Novels can provide companionship, whereas short stories stress alienation. (*LV* 18–19; JMB)

Isolation in Short Fiction: Novels depict communities, but short stories present characters who tend to be sensitive, private, and stubborn. These can include hobos, artists, isolated romantics, visionaries, and ruined clergy. (*LV* 20–21; JMB)

Selecting a Meaningful Episode: Because the short story writer can never describe a character's entire life, he must choose one significant moment. This choice gives each story its special form but can also lead to disaster if the wrong choice is made.... The moment chosen must simultaneously imply the past, represent the present, and foreshadow the future.... In this sense the short story writer must be more of a craftsman and dramatist than the novelist needs to be. (*LV* 21–23; JMB)

Artistry and Short Fiction: Almost by definition the best short story writers must be fine *writers* with a skill for drama. Yet the craftsmanship demanded by short fiction can itself lead to excess and artificiality; a single moment can be overloaded with significance. (*LV* 23; JMB)

Emotion in Novels and Stories: The length of a novel sometimes allows a novelist to vent his emotions, but in short fiction such venting is usually impossible. (*LV* 25; JMB)

Facts and Values: The short story writer must provide just the right amount of detail to stimulate the reader's ethical response. (*LV* 25; JMB)

Three Elements of Good Fiction: A successful story must consist of three components: explanation, change, and interaction.... Unlike a short story writer, a novelist can provide unlimited exposition. (*LV* 26; JMB)

Size and Shape in Novels and Stories: In the novel, form is determined by duration; in short fiction, duration is determined by form. A story's plot will define a story's length. (*LV* 27; JMB)

Brevity and Craft in Short Fiction: The best short stories need not be brief; the short story writer need not specialize in tiny fictions. A story is distinguished from a novel less by its length than by its concentrated craftsmanship.... Stories tend to be more pure and more self-contained than novels. (*LV* 27–28; JMB)

Laryngitis in Short Fiction: Modern short stories are often so artful that they lack the sound of a credible speaking voice. (*LV* 29; JMB)

The Origins and Excellence of American Short Fiction: Recent American short fiction grew out of Sherwood Anderson's *Winesburg, Ohio*, and Americans have written so many good stories that the form almost seems a national art. The supremacy of American short fiction probably results in part from the fact that so many inhabitants are members of marginal groups. (*LV* 41; JMB)

Enduring Fiction: Because novels and short stories are modern versions of primal arts, they are unlikely to die so long as modern culture isn't overtaken by the crowd. (*LV* 45; JMB)

Art vs. Propaganda: Fiction differs from persuasion: the latter seeks to resolve problems confronted by society, the former to resolve problems confronted by the artist. (*LV* 46; JMB)

The Story as Sponge: A richly textured story swells with many impressions that are not crucial to its most basic plot. (*LV* 69; JMB)

Sex in Fiction: As a subject for fiction, sex can boomerang; stories written to condemn sexual manipulation can themselves seem sexually manipulative. (*LV* 71; JMB)

Chekhov's Effectiveness: Chekhov's "Misery" and "The Dependents" are two of literature's most powerful treatments of human isolation.... In the former story, the characters who behave badly implicate us all, because they behave as anyone might.... Chekhov shows how small sins can be the most corrupting. (*LV* 83–84, 87–88; JMB)

Unity in Diversity: A worthy collection of stories, like a worthy collection of poems, epitomizes a particular period of an author's life. For this reason, stories from collections should not be read in isolation from one another. James Joyce's *Dubliners* is a case in point. (*LV* 113; JMB)

Facts vs. Feelings: Descriptions of things should be plain and simple; evocations of emotion should pack a punch. (*LV* 119; JMB)

Sentimentality: Literary sentimentality always seems bogus and deceptive. (*LV* 131; JMB)

Showing and Telling: The best fiction combines and balances subjective telling (implication) and objective showing (proof). Hemingway often loses this balance; the two components often seem indistinct.... Moreover, his technical expertise often lacks a worthy subject. (*LV* 163–65; JMB)

The Range of Subjects in Novels and Stories: Novel-writing is more difficult to teach than story-telling or play-writing because novels are less restricted in potential subject matter than dramas or short stories. (*LV* 216; JMB)

How to Write a Story: Faced with a possible subject, O asks himself whether the exposition and development can be combined or whether they must be separated; dialogue should not explain but should illustrate explanation. (*LV* 218–19; JMB)

A Thing of Beauty: Although impermanent, the beauty of art is the closest mortals come to the permanent pleasure the gods enjoy. (*LV* 220; JMB)

Theories and Practice: "Guests of the Nation" and "The Bridal Night" from Diverse Critical Perspectives

Kathleen B. Durrer, Scott Johnson, Katie Magaw, and Claire Skowronski

Although Frank O'Connor is generally regarded as a master of the modern short story, his fiction has not received as much critical attention as might have been expected. Perhaps because much of his work seems relatively uncomplicated and straightforward, it has been discussed (when discussed at all) mainly in thematic terms. In other words, critics tend to have been as interested in what O'Connor writes *about* (such as the theme of loneliness) as in *how* he writes. O'Connor, therefore, is an author ripe for critical re-evaluation, and his work invites attention from a wide variety of interpretive perspectives. Among the ancient and modern theories that might prove useful in reading his writings are the following: Platonic, Aristotelian, Horatian, and Longinian criticism; thematic, historical, formalist, and archetypal criticism; psychoanalytic, Marxist, feminist, and structuralist criticism; and (to name just a few more examples) dialogical, deconstructive, postmodern, reader-response, multicultural, and new historicist criticism.

Readers unfamiliar with these various theories will have an easier time making sense of them if they recall M.H. Abrams' famous argument that any literary theory that tries to be complete must account for four basic aspects of literature: the author, the text, the audience, and the universe (or "reality").[1] Abrams' list can

---

[1]For a fuller explanation of Abrams' views and of the theories already mentioned, see the lengthy introduction to *Short Fiction: A Critical Companion*, ed. Robert C. Evans, Anne C. Little, and Barbara Wiedemann (West

be usefully supplemented by adding a fifth category: the role or function of the critic herself. Any reasonably well developed theory, in other words, will be a theory about all these factors and the relations among them. The assumptions a theorist makes about the author, for example, will inevitably affect (and be affected by) the assumptions he makes about the text, the audience, "reality," and the purposes of criticism. Indeed, Abrams argues that each theory will tend to emphasize *one* of these aspects as crucial or most important. Plato, for instance, tends to emphasize the importance of accurately understanding reality, and his entire theory of literature seems affected by this central emphasis. He thus assumes that because neither the author nor the literary text can help us understand reality, and because most members of the audience do not seek such understanding, literature has little value. Plato's views of the critic derive directly from this conclusion: for him the critic functions as a kind of philosophical traffic cop, admitting certain "useful" kinds of literature to the republic but banishing the rest.

In attempting to suggest some ways in which two of Frank O'Connor's best stories ("The Bridal Night" and "Guests of the Nation") might be approached from a variety of theoretical perspectives, it may be worthwhile to review quickly the basic assumptions these theories make concerning the categories just mentioned. These assumptions are summarized (by Robert Evans) in the barest terms in the following list, and then some brief possible applications of the approaches to the two stories are immediately provided.—RCE

Platonic Criticism

Because Plato prizes an accurate, objective understanding of "reality," he sees "creative" writers and "literary" texts as potential distractions: they may lead the already-emotional audience to neglect the proper pursuit of philosophical truth, which the critic should seek, explain, and defend by using logic and reason.

"The Bridal Night": Plato probably would view this story (as he viewed most literature) as trivial and potentially dangerous, if only because the repeated references to loneliness and wildness obviously appeal to the

---

Cornwall, CT: Locust Hill Press, 1997), xv–lxxvi. The word "reality" will be placed within quotation remarks to emphasize that it is a fundamentally contested concept.

reader's emotions. The passion-driven action of the story seems to encourage irrationality. Plato might feel vindicated by the fact that Denis ends up in an asylum, safely purged from society. Nevertheless, because Denis is presented sympathetically, the reader may finally empathize with a character who has abandoned all reason. Plato might therefore ultimately attack the story for contributing almost nothing to the reasonable pursuit of truth.—**Scott Johnson**

Although the old woman obviously feels sympathy when she describes her son crying (21–23),[2] Plato would condemn such an emotional outburst (especially in an adult human male, who has a particular obligation to be rational) because such behavior both expresses and reinforces enslavement to the passions.—**Katie Magaw**

"Guests of the Nation": Since Plato prizes a person's ability and willingness to subjugate any sense of individuality in favor of the good of the "whole," a Platonic critic might fault the Irish soldiers for allowing their private emotions to conflict with the dictates of their public responsibilities. Such a critic might similarly blame Hawkins for his willingness to abandon loyalty to his country in order to save his own life. On the other hand, a Platonic critic might also conceivably argue that the Irishmen, by participating in killings they consider unreasonable and unjust, fail in their responsibilities to a higher truth. In either case, Plato would most probably be interested in whether the story encourages or discourages reasonable conduct and a proper appreciation of transcendent truths. The story would be praised if it promoted reason and morality and condemned if it did not.—**Claire Skowronski**

Aristotelian Criticism

Because Aristotle values the text as a highly crafted complex unity, he tends to see the author as a craftsman, the audience as capable of appreciating such craftsmanship, the text as a potentially valuable means of understanding the complexity of "reality," and the critic as a specialist conversant with all aspects of the poetic craft.

"The Bridal Night": Aristotle would probably praise "The Bridal Night" since every aspect of the story contributes to its overall effect. He might

---

[2]The text of "The Bridal Night" used throughout this section is the version published in O'Connor's *Collected Stories* (New York: Knopf, 1981), 19–25. Citations will be given parenthetically, preceded by the abbreviation "*CS*." The text of "Guests" used here will be the revised version, available (for instance) in *Stories by Frank O'Connor* (New York: Vintage Books, 1956), 3–16, and reprinted in most recent anthologies.

especially note, for example, the ways the end of the story mirrors its beginning. Moreover, O'Connor's subtle, unobtrusive repetition of words and images not only unifies the work but also helps propel it toward its logical and inevitable conclusion. Aristotle valued this sense of inevitability because it implied that every part of a work was tightly linked to every other part. In the story's first paragraph, for instance, the narrator mentions seeing "one light only"—a phrase that anticipates the old woman's reference, a few sentences later, to her "'one son only'" (*CS* 19). Such echoes help unify the work, in part by underscoring its basic mood and theme of human loneliness. Throughout the story, O'Connor uses similar techniques to ensure that the story achieves a complex unity.—**Scott Johnson**

"Guests of the Nation": Aristotle considered skill in the use of genres (i.e., different forms of writing) crucial to the writer's craft. In the genre of the short story, for instance, Aristotle's insistence on complex unity can seem especially crucial, since the short story form is so restricted in length. "Guests," however, may be viewed not only as an exemplary model of the short story form but also as a perfect illustration of Aristotle's criterion of complex unity. By repeating various activities, settings, and phrases (the significant word "chum," for instance, recurs more than twenty times), O'Connor gives his story a highly unified structure. Yet he also gives the story (as Aristotle recommended for tragedy) a clear beginning, middle, and end, while the story's conclusion provides both the "reversal" (of fortune) and the "recognition" (sudden new insight) Aristotle prized in an effective tragic work. In addition, like a good Aristotelian tragedy, "Guests" evokes both pity and fear, particularly since it involves good but flawed men harming persons close to them. Finally, the reversal and recognition nearly coincide (as Aristotle recommended). In all these ways, then, O'Connor has created a work that is both highly complex and tightly unified.—**Kathleen B. Durrer**

Horatian Criticism

Because Horace emphasizes the need to satisfy a diverse audience, he tends to see the author as attempting to please and/or teach them, the text as embodying principles of custom and moderation (so as to please the widest possible audience), "reality" as understood in traditional or conventional terms, and the critic as a fatherly advisor who tries to prevent the author from making a fool of himself.

"The Bridal Night": Horace might have admired both the effectiveness and the restraint and moderation of O'Connor's story. Certainly he would have admired its unity—a unity that is neither too complex nor too obvious but rather one that conforms to the moral and artistic expectations of a broad-based audience. For example, the language of the characters conforms to such expectations, for the woman, in her own lonesome cadence, uses the kind of colloquial diction one would imagine an old Irish woman using to convey her heartfelt emotions. Moreover, Horace probably would have admired O'Connor's ability to create a story that is both pleasing and implicitly enlightening since it depicts the beauty and necessity of human attachment and compassion. Although Denis's madness might easily have seemed inexplicable or ridiculous if depicted by a less talented writer, O'Connor manages to create characters and situations that are both credible and affecting.—**Katie Magaw**

"Guests of the Nation": O'Connor's use of language in this story exemplifies Horace's criteria of moderation and decorum. The four men speak as one would expect simple soldiers to do, and O'Connor avoids any extreme use of language, even when using such language might have seemed appropriate. Hawkins' "deplorable tongue" (5), for instance, is never allowed to interrupt the narrative flow. Even at the end of the story (when, shortly before the killings, profanity might have seemed justifiable), Bonaparte simply reports that Hawkins "let out a cold-blooded remark that even shocked me" (13). O'Connor also practices moderation in describing the Englishmen's deaths. No blood or violent images are mentioned; instead, Hawkins falls to his knees and lies "flat at Noble's feet, slowly and as quiet as a kid falling asleep" (13). Belcher falls over "like a sack of meal" (15)—a powerful image, but not one that might cause an audience to reject the work as too violent. While the reader's mind imagines the horror, the actual narration is a model of Horatian moderation. O'Connor, however, does not sacrifice his artistic or ethical principles to satisfy his audience. His story challenges conventional views of war as heroic and just, but he does so by implication and thus again exercises moderation.—**Kathleen B. Durrer**

Longinian Criticism

Because "Longinus" (whose real identity is unknown) stresses the ideally elevated nature of the sublime author, he tends to view the text as an expression of the author's power, the audience as desiring the ecstasy a great author can induce, social "reality" as rooted in a basic human nature that everywhere and always has a yearning for elevation, and the critic as (among other things) a moral and spiritual advisor who encourages the highest aspirations of readers and writers alike.

"The Bridal Night": Longinus might have admired O'Connor's ability to create a work that appeals to one of the loftiest capacities of humanity by portraying the beauty and dignity of human love and attachment. Indeed, Longinus might emphasize how Miss Regan's final act of selfless, genuine

kindness exemplifies the human potential for moral and spiritual elevation. Her selfless act suggests how humans can counteract the despair of
loneliness and behave nobly and generously in an often brutal world.—
Katie Magaw

"Guests of the Nation": Although O'Connor's generally plain, straightforward style of writing may seem remote from the "sublimity" or elevation Longinus endorses, the story's evocative final paragraph—with its intense imagery, haunting rhythms, and deeply serious content—deliberately transcends the more colloquial tone of the rest of the work. By memorably expressing and eliciting powerful emotions that all people can
share, the final paragraph strikes the reader with what Longinus might
characteristically term the force of a lightning bolt. If any part of the story
qualifies as "sublime," this is it.—**Kathleen B. Durrer**

Traditional Historical Criticism

*Because traditional historical critics tend to emphasize the ways social
"realities" influence the writer, the writer's creation of a text, and audiences' reactions to it, they stress the critic's obligation to study the past
as thoroughly and objectively as possible to determine how the text
might have been understood by its original readers.*

"The Bridal Night": Near the beginning of the story the narrator asks the
old woman about her son and then explains his own question: "'Is it in
America he is?' I asked. (It is to America all the boys of the locality go
when they leave home. [*CS* 19])" A traditional historical critic would
probably contend that this brief passage tacitly reflects the social and economic conditions of Ireland during the period in which the story takes
place. Such a critic might emphasize the tumultuous social and economic
displacement that resulted in the mass emigration of many members of
the lower classes to America. Indeed, a historical critic might contend that
Denis's mental depression can be explained, at least in part, by the general
depression (the economic hardship and despair) common during this period of Ireland's history.—**Katie Magaw**

"Guests of the Nation": A traditional historical critic would obviously
want to explore the actual details of typical relations between English and
Irish soldiers during this particular conflict. Such a critic might want to
examine the plausibility of O'Connor's depiction of the men's friendship
and might be especially interested in knowing whether the story reflected
any specific facts or genuine incidents (as apparently it did). A historical
critic might also want to know how O'Connor's own experiences with
war may have affected his writing of this tale.—**Claire Skowronski**

Thematic Criticism

Because thematic critics stress the importance of ideas in shaping social and psychological "reality," they generally look for the ways those ideas are expressed by (and affect) the texts that writers create. They assume that audiences turn to texts for enlightenment as well as entertainment and that writers either express the same basic ideas repeatedly or that the evolution of their thinking can be traced in different works.

"The Bridal Night": A thematic critic might assert that the basic theme of this work is human loneliness, and that life's greatest moments occur when a person penetrates another's insularity, however briefly. Everyone in this story seems isolated to some extent. Mrs. Sullivan has "'the one son only'" (*CS* 19), and her husband is absent for one reason or another. Denis goes mad from loneliness after he is unable to win the woman he loves. Winnie is always either alone or with her students and thus seems disconnected from the rest of the village. The language of the story reinforces the theme of loneliness, partly through the repetition of such words as "lonesome" and "stranger." In fact, the characters are basically strangers to one another. Although they occasionally alleviate each other's loneliness, none of these instances suggests a permanent union. When Winnie lies down with Denis, he is soothed (but only temporarily) by her presence. Even the narrator is lonely, as his first spoken words ("'Tis a lonesome place'" [*CS* 19]) make clear.—**Scott Johnson**

"Guests of the Nation": A thematic critic might emphasize how this story blends such themes as intellect versus emotion, duty versus friendship, and isolation versus communion. Donovan, for instance, expects his fellow soldiers, Bonaparte and Noble, to respond intellectually and carry out the executions without emotions. The old woman, on the other hand, seems to embody a more intuitively emotional response to life. Bonaparte and Noble are thus torn between the expectation that they should listen to "reason" and the temptation to follow their hearts. Similarly, Bonaparte and Noble also feel torn between duty to their cause and friendship for the English soldiers, a friendship Donovan does not share. As the story proceeds, the early feelings of communion are lost and all the men become increasingly isolated from each other and, eventually, from themselves. At the end, one wonders whether Noble is praying for the dead British soldiers or for his own soul. In any case, Bonaparte leaves him and goes outside to face his own demons—alone. A thematic critic, then, would show how the story wrestles with some of the most important ideas and problems any human can confront.—**Claire Skowronski**

Formalism

Because formalists value the text as a complex unity in which all the parts contribute to a rich and resonant effect, they usually offer highly detailed ("close") readings intended to show how the work achieves a powerful, compelling artistic form. Formalist critics help audiences appreciate how a work's subtle nuances contribute to its total effect.

"The Bridal Night": A formalist critic might approach this story by emphasizing how the patterns of imagery succinctly contribute to the harmonious and unified complexity of the work. For example, such a critic might note how the story begins and ends with patterns of imagery associated with light and darkness. In fact, a formalist critic might argue that such images—including the single light in the beginning and the blanket of darkness at the end—underscore the themes of loneliness and despair that help unify this text. A formalist might note how other aspects of the work (including the old woman's lonesome voice and the pining cries of the wild birds) also contribute to the work's artistic unity.—**Scott Johnson**

"Guests of the Nation": A formalist critic might choose to focus on the pattern of repetition and subtle variation apparent in the first three sections of the story, culminating in an abrupt shift of tone at the opening of section four. Initially, the soldiers settle into a pleasant, predictable routine. The first paragraph in each of the first three sections opens "at dusk." The work day is over, and the soldiers—both Irish and English—play cards to relax and while away the hours before retiring for the evening. Each time, Donovan joins them. In the first section, however, Donovan "supervises" the game, and the reader knows that he is both "above" and "outside" the camaraderie shared by the other men. In the similar opening paragraph in section two, the reader learns that the four friendly soldiers enjoy "tea" together before Donovan comes in, a fact that further emphasizes their "civil" relations—relations not shared by Donovan. In fact, at this point Bonaparte senses that Donovan feels "no great love" for the English soldiers. At the start of section three the routine begins to repeat itself, but this time Donovan is literally associated with a "dark presentiment." As darkness inevitably follows dusk, the opening paragraph of section four cycles into a night rather than another routine and predictable day. The men—and the reader—all know the terrible act ahead of them, and nothing remains *but* Donovan's darkness—a darkness that swallows the faint "light" of possibility that someone can prevent the deaths.—**Claire Skowronski**

Psychoanalytic Criticism

Freudian or psychoanalytic critics emphasize the key role of the human mind in perceiving and shaping "reality" and believe that the minds of writers, audiences, and critics are highly complex and often highly conflicted (especially in sexual terms, and particularly in terms of the rational ego and the irrational "id"). They therefore argue that such complexity inevitably affects the ways texts are written and read. The critic, therefore, should analyze the psychological patterns that affect the ways texts are created and received.

"The Bridal Night": A Freudian psychoanalytic critic might approach "The Bridal Night" by focusing on how the complex psychological manifestations of such latent impulses as sexuality and desire resonate throughout the story. Perhaps such a critic would begin by juxtaposing the ways in which Denis and Miss Regan respond to these latent sexual impulses, particularly the ways in which their actions reflect the three fundamental realms of the psyche—the id, the ego, and the superego. For example, such a critic might conjecture that Denis's imploring request to have Miss Regan spend the night with him is significantly motivated by the instincts of the id (the primal component of the human psyche that is dominated by bodily impulses and desires). Perhaps a Freudian critic would suggest that because Denis' mental incapacity enables him to exist apart (or at least detached) from the oppressive precepts of society, he is not constricted by the mandates of either the super-ego (the realm of the psyche that strives for perfect social conformity and obedience) or the ego (the component of the mind that mediates between the desires of the id and the demands of the superego). Miss Regan, however, does operate within society and therefore acknowledges societal expectations. Her awareness is reflected in her "worried" but determined desire to fulfill Denis's earnest wish (*CS* 24). Indeed, a Freudian critic might contend that the very fact that she is concerned about the social consequences of her actions represents the influence of the superego. Conversely, her determination to fulfill Denis's request might reflect the inevitable emergence of the ego, for perhaps her complex conduct is motivated both by her own primal desires and by her attempts to repress these desires and thereby conform to societal conventions.—**Katie Magaw**

"Guests of the Nation": A psychoanalytic critic, focusing on the story's setting, might contrast the associations of the bright interior of the house with the exterior darkness. The cottage, with its comforting fires and the domestic influence of the motherly old woman, might be seen as representing social and moral order and might therefore be interpreted as symbolizing the tempering influence of civilization on the uncivilized impulses of the unconscious. When inside the house, the men treat each other as equals, and disagreements (such as the ideological differences of

Hawkins and Noble) are settled through discourse rather than through physical aggression. In contrast, the exterior darkness might be seen as representing the untamed unconscious. Only under the cover of darkness is the full extent of human aggression revealed. Furthermore, a psychoanalytic critic might have many interesting things to say about the ostensibly rational Jeremiah Donovan, who ironically seems unable to control his emotions. He blushes when addressed, rocks back and forth when speaking, quickly loses his temper with the old woman, and shakes with excitement when anticipating the killings. Perhaps he feels a desperate need to assert power. Although Bonaparte and Noble eventually return to the house and re-light the lamp, Donovan remains literally and figuratively in the outer darkness.—**Kathleen B. Durrer**

Archetypal or "Myth" Criticism

Because archetypal critics believe that humans experience "reality" in terms of certain basic fears, desires, images (symbols), and stories (myths), they assume that writers will inevitably employ such patterns; that audiences will react to them forcefully and almost automatically; and that critics should therefore study the ways such patterns affect writers, texts, and readers.

"The Bridal Night": An archetypal critic influenced by the theories of Carl Jung might claim that in this story, Denis journeys into his unconscious. The first part of this journey ends in madness, just as Oedipus' similar journey in Sophocles' *Oedipus Rex* ends in blindness and exile. An important part of Denis' journey involves initiation into femininity—an initiation completed when Winnie, his "anima" or female aspect, lies down beside him. The two halves of his psyche are temporarily reconciled in this brief "bridal" union. By ending with the same imagery with which it began, the story appropriately achieves an almost circular structure, since circles often function as archetypal symbols suggesting completion and unity.—**Scott Johnson**

"Guests of the Nation": An archetypal critic might comment on the heavy use of the symbolism of darkness in this work. The story opens with the words "at dusk"—immediately suggesting the setting sun and the end of life. Such imagery then continues throughout the work. Each of the first three sections opens at dusk, and the entire story takes place in the evening, with only candles, lanterns, and firelight available to hold off the darkness (thereby suggesting the uncertainty of life, which is easily extinguished). As death draws nearer, the significance of darkness intensifies. Bonaparte, for example, extinguishes the candle before he reveals to Noble that they may have to kill their English friends (8). Later, when the Irishmen enter the cottage to remove the Englishmen, the house is "pitch-dark," but at first no one even thinks of lighting a lamp (15). Earlier, although the men walk toward the lantern light in the dark bog (12), this light will bring only death (not life or hope). At the site of the killings, Noble holds the lantern between his legs, as if to hide in the darkness. Finally, when Noble returns to the cottage after the killings and attempts to light the lamp, the old woman's question ("'What did ye do with them?'" [16]) startles him so that the match dies in his hand. By using such strong symbolic imagery (an archetypal critic might claim), O'Connor evokes some of our most basic human fears and thus helps give his story an almost automatic power.—**Kathleen B. Durrer**

Marxist Criticism

Because Marxist critics assume that conflicts between economic classes inevitably shape social "reality," they emphasize the ways these struggles affect writers, audiences, and texts. They assume that literature will either reflect, reinforce, or undermine (or some combination of these) the dominant ideologies (or patterns of thought) that help structure social relations. Marxist critics study the relations between literature and society, ideally seeking to promote social progress.

"The Bridal Night": A Marxist critic might argue that Denis's madness is linked directly to his poverty. Although he lacks even "'the price of an ounce of 'baccy,'" he is obsessed with a woman who has "'money to her name in the bank'" (*CS* 21). Indeed, the text implies that she is considerably wealthy. The references to Denis's and Winnie's contrasting economic classes appear, in fact, in the same paragraph that first mentions Denis's madness. Moreover, although at the end of the story Winnie is no worse off than before and is not even subject to public criticism (facts explicable in terms of her superior social status), the impoverished Denis ends up in an asylum—a fate a richer person might have escaped.—**Scott Johnson**

"Guests of the Nation": A Marxist critic might emphasize how this story illustrates the artificial divisions nationalism can create between men who are not only friends but who also are members of the same social class.—**Kathleen B. Durrer**

A Marxist critic might respond to the story by arguing that Hawkins is right: war is a tool that capitalists manipulate in order to protect their own selfish interests. Soldiers in the field are simply pawns, willingly sacrificed by higher-ranking officers in order to protect the men who make decisions in relative safety and comfort at a distance from the fighting. In the end, the Irish soldiers epitomize the operations of the capitalist system. Unable to bring about their own small "revolution" to save their British friends, Bonaparte and Noble symbolize the oppressed lower class, forced to carry out blindly the orders of their superiors, while Donovan willingly embraces the status quo and, without conflict or hesitation, shoots the British soldiers. A Marxist critic might argue, however, that Donovan is also a victim of a capitalistic war machine since he did not personally make the decision to murder the soldiers but was simply following a superior's orders. Another Marxist critic might suggest that the story fails as a political statement because, in the end, the system seems inevitably to "win," and no social progress occurs. Still another Marxist critic might argue, though, that the story succeeds as a political statement because Bonaparte and Noble refuse to shoot the soldiers themselves, even though Donovan might easily have ordered them to do it. The reader thus sees, at least to some extent, that solidarity and listening to one's conscience can supersede blind obedience to duty.—**Claire Skowronski**

Structuralist Criticism

Because structuralist critics assume that humans structure (or make sense of) "reality" by imposing patterns of meaning on it, and because they assume that these structures can only be interpreted in terms of the codes the structures embody, they believe that writers will inevitably rely on such codes to create meaning, that texts will inevitably embody such codes, and that audiences will inevitably use such codes to interpret texts. To understand a text, the critic must be familiar with the systematic codes that shape it; he must master the system(s) inherent in the text.

"The Bridal Night": A structuralist might note that this story is organized by a series of paired opposites such as youth/age, light/dark, land/sea, and isolation/community. Land, for instance, symbolizes safety, sanity, and nurturing, whereas the sea symbolizes the unknown, instability, and madness. Thus when Denis's madness begins to worsen, Mrs. Sullivan says that "'he could hardly sleep'" and could be heard "'groaning as loud as the sea on the rocks'" (*CS* 21). This dichotomy between land and sea is often very important to the structure of human narratives. In myth, a return to land is almost always joyous, while travels at sea are conventionally filled with peril. This land/sea pairing, then, is one of the codes by which this story achieves its meaning.—**Scott Johnson**

"Guests of the Nation": A structuralist critic might focus on the many patterns of oppositions within this text and might then examine the ways they contribute to the story's meanings. In fact, the story itself is a study in oppositions—not only between nations but between religion and atheism, war and peace, life and death, rural and urban, light and dark, warmth and cold, noise and silence, male and female, joy and guilt, and many other paired opposites. By studying how O'Connor employs such patterns, a structuralist critic would help map the "codes" by which the story achieves and conveys significance.—**Kathleen B. Durrer**

Feminist Criticism

Because feminist critics assume that our experience of "reality" is inevitably affected by categories of sex and gender (such as divisions between male and female, heterosexual and homosexual, etc.), and because they assume that (heterosexual) males have long enjoyed dominant social power, they tend to assume that writers, texts, and audiences will all be affected (usually negatively) by "patriarchal" forces. The critic's job will be to study (and even attempt to counter-act) the impact of patriarchy.

"The Bridal Night": Near the beginning of the story, the narrator asks the old woman, "'Your own flock are gone from you, I suppose?'" (*CS* 19). A feminist critic might note how explicitly this question implies a fundamental, perhaps even rigid, definition of a woman as a mother. Indeed, such a critic might stress how O'Connor's use of the word "flock" emphasizes this prescribed role, for it accentuates the primitive perception of a woman as a breeder who is defined by her capacity to nurture, sustain, and fulfill the needs of her children. Certainly a feminist critic would reject this implication, since it fails to value the woman's full individuality. Such a critic might also note how the question anticipates the elderly woman's enveloping sense of barrenness, for after tragically losing her only son to a mental illness, she seems to lack any substantial purpose and thus succumbs to a sense of aimless despair and emptiness.—**Katie Magaw**

"Guests of the Nation": A feminist critic might see O'Connor's story as typifying the male-dominated literary and social worlds of the early 1920s. The story has only one female character, "the old woman of the house where we [the male soldiers and prisoners] were staying." Although the house presumably belongs to her, her ownership does not alter her subservient position. She labors to keep the household running—chopping sticks, carrying water, or hauling turf for the fire. Her resignation to her solitary labor is so strong that Belcher's offer of assistance renders her literally speechless. In addition to playing a subservient role, she is also portrayed as mentally inferior to the male characters. When the argumentative Hawkins tries to get her to complain of the drought she responds with confused pagan folklore, and when she rebukes Hawkins for blaming the capitalists for starting World War I, she is portrayed as a woman with only a vague, confused, inaccurate idea of world events. Nowhere is her insignificance in the male-dominated events of the story more vividly portrayed than when Donovan silences her protests when the prisoners are being removed. Obviously (a feminist might contend) this is a society in which men make the rules and women serve without question.—**Kathleen B. Durrer**

Deconstruction

Because deconstructive critics assume that "reality" cannot be experienced except through language, and because they believe that language is inevitably full of contradictions, gaps, and dead-ends, they believe that no writer, text, audience, or critic can ever escape from the insoluble paradoxes language embodies. Deconstruction therefore undercuts the hierarchical assumptions of any other critical system (such as structuralism, formalism, Marxism, etc.) that seeks to offer an "objective," "neutral," or "scientific" perspective on literature.

"The Bridal Night": A deconstructor might approach this story by noting the inherent instability and inconsistency embedded in the male/female pairing, in which the male is usually privileged over the female. Such a critic might begin the process of subverting this hierarchical arrangement by illustrating how the text (which is itself intrinsically unstable) contradicts the supposed stability of this pairing. Perhaps a deconstructor would begin by noting, for instance, that Miss Regan fills a more elevated and privileged social role than Denis despite the fact that he is male, while Denis himself, incapacitated by his mental illness, plays a less important role. Furthermore, such a critic might contend that Denis, in his fervent longing for Miss Regan, ultimately relinquishes himself to her control and power. Nevertheless, while seemingly at a disadvantage, Denis, as an embodiment of a male-dominated society, is still able to exert influence over Miss Regan by convincing her to submit to his impulsive demands. Indeed, a deconstructor might also emphasize the freedom that is paradoxically inherent in Denis's insanity, for he is no longer bound by severe societal dictates that mandate proper behavior, and therefore his excessive request is attributed merely to his "madness." Miss Regan, on the other hand, is constrained by these social values, for she ultimately risks losing her reputation by fulfilling Denis's desires. A deconstructor might show, therefore, that in this story the standard male/female hierarchy is highly unstable and full of contradictions.—**Katie Magaw**

"Guests of the Nation": A deconstructive critic might note that a trained soldier's duty requires demonstrating loyalty to the state and subjugating his will and his private morality to the appropriate chain of command. A soldier's duty, then, implies a hierarchy of the state over the individual. A deconstructor might subvert this assumed hierarchy, however, and suggest that a soldier is first a member of a moral society that condemns cold-blooded murder; therefore, his duty as a human being conflicts with his military training and inevitably leads to an unstable tension. The story shows how difficult it can be to follow one's duty (*which* duty?) and how tightly entangled "public" and "private" morality can be. Further, a deconstructor might argue that war inevitably establishes a binary opposition of "us" versus "them" in which whoever is "us" is superior to "them." Yet O'Connor shows how difficult it can be to preserve this distinction, as well as how easily such other opposites as "winner/loser," "victory/defeat," "life/death," and "free/imprisoned" can collapse. By the end of the story, the nominal victors feel defeated: although technically free, they are now imprisoned in a kind of perpetual living death. Similarly, the nominal losers have in a sense triumphed: they now enjoy a sort of freedom from the pain of life while still living quite intensely in the minds of the men who helped kill them.—**Claire Skowronski**

Reader-Response Criticism

Because reader-response critics assume that literary texts are inevitably interpreted by individual members of the audience and that these individuals react to texts in ways that are sometimes shared, sometimes highly personal, and sometimes both at once, they believe that writers exert much less control over texts than we sometimes suppose, and that critics must never ignore the crucial role of audience response(s).

"**The Bridal Night**": Early in the story the old mother responds to a question from the narrator, who then comments on her response: "'I never had but the one,' she replied, 'the one son only,' and I knew because she did not add a prayer for his soul that he was still alive" (*CS* 19). One type of reader-response critic might approach this passage by focusing on how O'Connor uses it to encourage a particular experience or interpretation in the minds of diverse readers. Such a critic might focus on the underlying pathos embedded in such phrases as "'but the one'" and "'the one son only.'" A reader-response critic might contend that these phrases powerfully evoke sympathy for the old woman and therefore elicit a positive response to O'Connor's underlying theme of the despair of human loneliness. However, another reader-response critic might argue that various interpretations of this passage are inevitable since ultimately the individual experiences of particular readers dictate the "meanings" of texts. For instance, readers who have endured the traumatic loss of a child might be especially inclined to empathize with the old woman and perhaps even be able to find a consoling expression of their own sorrow in the woman's despairing words. Conversely, it may be difficult for a reader who has never been a parent and experienced intense attachment to a child to be strongly affected by the woman's resounding grief as she mourns the loss of her only son.—**Katie Magaw**

"Guests of the Nation": A reader-response critic would probably be interested in the diverse interpretations the story has elicited from different kinds of readers. Readers with personal experience of the long-standing Irish/English conflict, for example, might react indignantly at the portrayal of certain characters. Thus a patriotic Englishman (or a committed leftist) might find Hawkins unsympathetic since he seems to have little loyalty either to his country or to his ideology. Similarly, a committed Irish nationalist might respond negatively to Bonaparte and Noble (who find it difficult to justify retaliating against the English army's murder of Irish soldiers). On the other hand, to a Christian reader Hawkins' atheism might intensify the tragedy of his death because he dies with no hope of redemption. Readers with military experience might empathize with the responses of Bonaparte and Noble to the requirements of duty, while pacifists might use the story to illustrate the senseless results of war. Clearly, the list of such possible responses could easily be extended.—**Kathleen B. Durrer**

Dialogical Criticism

Because dialogical critics assume that the (worthy) text almost inevitably embodies divergent points of view, they believe that elements within a text engage in a constant dialogue or give-and-take with other elements, both within and outside the text itself. The writer, too, is almost inevitably engaged in a complex dialogue, through the text, with his potential audience(s), and the sensitive critic must be alert to the multitude of voices a text expresses or implies.

"The Bridal Night": A dialogical critic might emphasize the differences in the voices of the narrator and Mrs. Sullivan. The narrator's more sophisticated voice seems consciously literary. Mrs. Sullivan speaks in the vernacular, and her telling of the story has a conversational feel. The narrator, apparently an outsider, refers to Mrs. Sullivan as one of "[t]hese lonesome people in the wild places" (*CS* 20), suggesting that he is from a more civilized place. The text therefore includes voices representing two distinct social classes. Interestingly, Mrs. Sullivan does most of the talking: O'-Connor allows the lower-class character to express herself freely, rather than have the narrator impose a monological view. The narrator, in fact, is part of the audience, a fact that further detaches him from the text and allows the different voices in the story free rein to express their varied perspectives.—**Scott Johnson**

"Guests of the Nation": A dialogical critic might first choose to focus on the "voice" (Bonaparte) telling the story, because he speaks for everyone. Through both Bonaparte's conversations with the other characters and his dialogue with the reader as the story's narrator, the reader hears (perhaps more clearly than Bonaparte himself) the conflicting voices he articulates. Another dialogical critic might suggest that Bonaparte unfairly colors Donovan's personal character, since the reader perceives Donovan only from Bonaparte's point of view, which is not sympathetic to the possibility that Donovan is acting honorably in his role as a soldier. A reader looking at events from Donovan's perspective might even suggest that Bonaparte and Noble, not Donovan, act inappropriately by befriending enemy soldiers during a war. Finally, still another dialogical critic might choose to focus on the colloquial speech that moves the men (and invites the reader to come along) through the comfortable routine of their days together, particularly since the casual speech changes abruptly in the fourth section of the story. At that point, there is suddenly no conversation among all four friends. In fact, Bonaparte and Noble fail to speak at all until the British soldiers are dead and buried. The seemingly emotionless Donovan now speaks for the Irish soldiers, and his suddenly animated but "cold" and "excited" tone is anything but conversational. The previously silent Belcher suddenly speaks up, while Donovan shoots down the always-loquacious Hawkins in mid-speech. The silence of Bonaparte and Noble speaks of the inevitable grave even as Belcher and Hawkins attempt to affirm their lives through their frantic—but abruptly silenced—speech. Fittingly, the closing passage of the story contains no conversation at all except Bonaparte's dialogue with himself. His lyrical thoughts contrast sharply with the friendly, colloquial conversations heard earlier, but the terrible beauty the reader sees through his eyes makes the reality of the murders an even greater horror. In the end, Bonaparte's cold, snowy isolation is complete, even from the reader.—**Claire Skowronski**

New Historicism

Because new historicist critics assume that our experience of "reality" is inevitably social, and because they emphasize the way systems of power and domination both provoke and seek to control social conflicts, they tend to see a culture not as a single coherent entity but as a site of struggle, negotiation, or the constant exchange of energy. New historicists contend that no text, audience, or critic can stand apart from contemporary (i.e., both past and present) dynamics of power.

"The Bridal Night": A new historicist critic might approach this work by emphasizing how the lives of the characters are shaped by the fundamental (and all too often irreconcilable) ideological assumptions that compose the social forces of a community. Because new historicists are especially concerned with uses and abuses of power, they might particularly note how quickly (and lengthily) Denis is confined for mental illness once he refuses to conform to prescribed codes of social behavior. Alternatively, a new historicist might note how Miss Regan's selfless act of compassion for Denis also reveals a brave willingness to defy the rigid social conventions which, in her day, defined the "proper" relations between men and women. Indeed, almost the last comment of the story emphasizes how unusual it was to violate those conventions without suffering any punishment or criticism. The power of the community is paradoxically confirmed by its decision not to exercise that power in this one instance.— **Katie Magaw**

"Guests of the Nation": A new historicist might emphasize the myriad of power relations—and the inevitability of experiencing such power-struggles in any society—evident in this story. First of all, the Irish hold British soldiers as prisoners of war, but the British forces have the Irish soldiers on the run, forcing the Irish to stay on the move (in their own homeland) in order to avoid capture themselves. Secondly, Donovan is a superior officer, but his men don't take him very seriously. Bonaparte, for example, "didn't like the tone" (7) Donovan took with him over the issue of guarding the prisoners, as if such a reason justifies a subordinate questioning a superior officer. On another level, a new historicist might choose to address the power-struggle going on in Bonaparte's mind as he wrestles with the question of friendship versus duty. A new historicist might suggest that Bonaparte is weak in both respects: he neither tries actively to save his friends in the end nor takes a definitive role in their murders. A new historicist might suggest that his indecision and lack of any strong convictions reflect the spirit of the Irish nation, tearing itself apart, caught between two religious faiths, both condemning and condoning killing, etc.—**Claire Skowronski**

Multicultural Criticism

Because multicultural critics emphasize the numerous differences that both shape and divide social "reality," they tend to see all people (including writers, readers, and critics) as members of sometimes divergent, sometimes overlapping groups. These groups, whether relatively fluid or relatively stable, can include such categories as races, sexes, genders, ages, and classes, and the critic should explore how such differences affect the ways in which literature is both written and read.

"The Bridal Night": A multiculturalist critic might argue that Winnie could conceivably be a lesbian or at least asexual. Numerous clues suggest this possibility. Mrs. Sullivan says, for instance, that Winnie's "'hand would never rock the cradle,'" and she jokes that Denis should tell Winnie that he is "'her intended'" (*CS* 21), as if the very notion is absurd. Also, although Winnie lacks any sexual interest in Denis, this is apparently not because she is involved with another man. She is almost always alone, perhaps because (if she has sexual relations at all) her partner must remain secret in such a small rural community. Nevertheless, others in the village may suspect her possible secret; certainly such suspicions would explain why, even after she spends the night in bed with Denis, "'no one would speak a bad word about what she did'" (*CS* 25). Perhaps they recognized, in the words of Mrs. Sullivan, that while "'another [woman might] … take pity on [Denis], knowing he would make her a fine steady husband,'" Winnie "'was not the sort, and well I knew it from the first days I laid eyes on her, that her hand would never rock the cradle'" (*CS* 21).—**Scott Johnson**

"Guests of the Nation": A multiculturalist critic might suggest that the friendships among Bonaparte, Noble, Belcher, and Hawkins represent a utopian ideal of enemy cultures coming together in harmony. However, a multiculturalist might also point out that although the reader gets a sense of genuine camaraderie among the soldiers, especially through their casual conversations and common language, the fact remains that Bonaparte first describes Belcher and Hawkins in terms of "their accents," which were so thick "you could cut [them] with a knife" (4). By emphasizing this difference in their speech, Bonaparte separates the soldiers, perhaps unconsciously, into groups of "us" and "them," an unfortunate division that inevitably paves the way for one group to oppress the other. A multiculturalist might note that the Irish have a history of rejecting the English language and speaking Gaelic in an effort to reject British rule, so Bonaparte's emphasis on the soldiers' accents may not be as innocuous as it first appears.—**Claire Skowronski**

Postmodernism

Postmodernists are highly skeptical of large-scale claims to objective "truths" and doubt the validity of grand explanations. They see such claims as attempts to impose order on a "reality" that is, almost by definition, too shifting or fluid to be pinned down. Postmodernists assume that if writers, readers, and audiences abandoned their yearning for such order, they would more easily accept and enjoy the inevitable paradoxes and contradictions of life and art. The postmodern critic will look for (and value) any indications of a text's unstable heterogeneity.

"The Bridal Night": A postmodernist might respond to this story by celebrating the freedom implicit in Miss Regan's defiant gesture of genuine kindness. By acting as she does, she rejects the blindly repeated and all-embracing system of broad, often abstract social values that unambiguously dictate a prescribed form of behavior. Such a critic might argue that simplistic, unequivocal systems of values fail to do justice to the indeterminate complexities of human experience. For this reason, a postmodern critic might also admire the community's willingness to accept, and even embrace, the "strange and wonderful" ambiguity of Miss Regan's selfless act of compassion for Denis (*CS* 25). By passively and openly accepting Miss Regan's actions, they illustrate their recognition that it is futile to adhere to rigid codes of conduct when dealing with the complexities (and inevitable moral contradictions) created by life's dilemmas.—**Katie Magaw**

"**Guests of the Nation**": A postmodern critic might suggest that the struggle Bonaparte and Noble feel between duty and morality reflects the other struggles we all face when confronted with conflicting systems of value. Especially today, the traditional standards of value provided by religion, ideologies, or cultural mores may no longer seem to provide clear or unequivocal guides to conduct. Thus Hawkins's (admittedly superficial) commitments to communism and atheism are of little use or comfort to him in his moment of crisis. Significantly, however, neither are the much stronger, more traditional beliefs of Noble. Although in the end Noble is left praying, the reader is left with the impression that neither his sense of military duty nor his religion can completely reconcile him to his role in the killing. No single grand explanation can help him accept what has happened.—**Kathleen B. Durrer**

Ways of Reading:
Frank O'Connor's "Lady Brenda"
and the Possibilities of Criticism

*Patricia Angley, Kathleen B. Durrer, Timothy Francisco,
Ashley Gordon, Karen Worley Pirnie, Michael Probst, Claire
Skowronski, Ondra Thomas-Krouse, Claudia Wilsch,
Jonathan Wright*

Frank O'Connor's short story "Lady Brenda," originally published in December 1958, has not received much attention and has not been reprinted in major collections of its author's fiction. However, "The Adventuress," an earlier and strikingly different version of the story (first published in 1948) *was* reprinted in a 1981 collection of O'Connor's works. "Lady Brenda," though, has not been easily accessible and thus has not attracted the attention it seems to merit.

The contrasts between the two versions are immediately apparent. "The Adventuress," for instance, begins as follows:

> My brothers and sisters didn't really like Brenda at all but I did. She was a couple of years older than I was and I was devoted to her. She had a long, grave, bony face and a power of concealing her real feelings about everything, even about me. I knew she liked me but she wasn't exactly what you'd call demonstrative about it. In fact there were times you might even say she was vindictive.
>
> That was part of her toughness. She was tough to the point of foolhardiness. She would do anything a boy would do and a lot of things that few boys would do. It was never safe to dare her to anything....

The difference between this and the opening of "Lady Brenda" could hardly be more striking:

Joe Regan's sister Brenda was several years older than himself, and by long chalks she was the toughest of the family, though none of them was exactly what you would call a sissy. A sissy would have had very little chance with Joe's father. He was tall and gaunt and angular, a monk who had strayed into workaday clothes and grown a big mustache. In Mr. Regan's considered view of the universe, the whole town was in a conspiracy against him, and that included every one of his own family from the baby up—always excepting his wife whom he regarded as a friendly neutral. As long as Joe had known it, life at home was one long battle, with his father, in an imperialist frame of mind, trying to get at them, and his mother, acting as protecting power, trying to keep him off....

They had to be tough, there was no other way; but Brenda, whose principal task was looking after Joe, was tough by disposition. She was tall and gaunt and handsome like their father, and she would do anything a boy would do and a lot of things that most boys in their senses would not do. It was never safe to dare Brenda to anything. She scared Joe a great deal more than his father did.

In the revision, O'Connor shifts from first-person to third-person narration; from an immediate emphasis on Brenda to a diversionary (but thematically significant) emphasis on the colorful father; from straightforward and explicit statement to language full of metaphor and vivid phrasing; and from a sober tone to humorous diction that also immediately implies the potential for intriguing comic conflict. These, however, are just a few of the many differences the two versions reveal. The experience of teaching the two stories suggests that "Lady Brenda" works far better in class and appeals far more immediately to most readers than does "The Adventuress."

As it happens, "Lady Brenda" was much discussed during a special seminar in pluralistic critical theory sponsored by the Andrew W. Mellon Foundation in the summer of 1997, when the present book was in its final stages. Participants in the seminar included graduate students working on theses or dissertations, teachers with years of classroom experience, and even a few advanced undergraduates. "Lady Brenda" was used, to some extent, as a test case, and the fact that the story had hitherto received almost no critical attention made it, in some respects, a perfect litmus test for a variety of ways of reading. Nearly all the seminar's participants expressed real enthusiasm for O'Connor's story as well as a definite preference for the revised version.

It seems worthwhile, in fact, to append a few of these readers' reactions to the following reprint of the story itself. Their responses raise issues that may prove interesting to other readers, especially since many of the seminarians' comments suggest the usefulness of various current literary theories as ways of approaching O'Connor's works in general. (In this respect their comments are relevant to, and build on, the survey of critical theories offered in the preceding chapter of this book.) The students' comments are offered, then, to help stimulate thought (and perhaps even to help generate disagreement), not only about this particular story but about a variety of current approaches to literary interpretation.

In addition, the appended comments are also designed to suggest the usefulness of previous commentary dealing with O'Connor's fiction in particular. By applying to a single story some of the numerous insights reported in the "Selected Stories ... and Quick Critiques" section of this book, we hope to illustrate how that section, too, can be used to provoke thought about many of O'Connor's other works.

First, however, "Lady Brenda."

***

LADY BRENDA

by Frank O'Connor

Joe Regan's sister Brenda was several years older than himself, and by long chalks she was the toughest of the family, though none of them was exactly what you would call a sissy. A sissy would have had very little chance with Joe's father. He was tall and gaunt and angular, a monk who had strayed into workaday clothes and grown a big mustache. In Mr. Regan's considered view of the universe, the whole town was in a conspiracy against him, and that included every one of his own family from the baby up—always excepting his wife whom he regarded as a friendly neutral. As long as Joe had known it, life at home was one long battle, with his father, in an imperialist frame of mind, trying to get at them, and his mother, acting as protecting power, trying to keep him off.

That didn't mean that life wasn't sufficiently exciting. Protect her flanks as she might, Joe's mother never could keep one or another of the children from showing a light in some position covered by his father, or his father from discovering a new firing point from which for days on end he could decimate the children. But his mother's defenses were superb. No reconnaissance of his father's ever brought back prisoners or information; his intelligence system was blown to bits—and Joe's mother rationalized it all to herself as "not worrying poor Dad." When there really came to be things to worry about, the suspicion of all that was concealed from him nearly drove Jim Regan to his grave.

They had to be tough, there was no other way; but Brenda, whose principal task was looking after Joe, was tough by disposition. She was tall and gaunt and handsome like their father, and she would do anything a boy would do and a lot of things that most boys in their senses would not do. It was never safe to dare Brenda to anything. She scared Joe a great deal more than his father did.

For instance, the two of them would be sitting by the tram-stop in the evening when some corner-boy would start to jeer at her, and then anything might happen. One evening a fellow named Wright accused her of swanking—people were always accusing her of that—and Brenda began to boast more and more of her grand acquaintances. Everyone in the big houses by the tram-stop were friends of her family. Joe began trying to get her away, but you couldn't detach Brenda from a row.

"Go on!" bawled Wright. "Prove it! Go up to Lacy's house and prove it."

"Come on, Joe," Brenda said lightly.

"Don't, Brenda, don't!" sniveled Joe.

"Why wouldn't I?" snapped Brenda, angrier with him than with Wright. "Don't be a blooming baby!"

"They might send for the bobbies," said Joe. Everything about Brenda suggested policemen to Joe.

"Well, let them send for the bobbies," Brenda replied contemptuously.

Away she went up the steps to the house while Joe in terror watched from the gate. He knew if it was only the maid answered, she could get away by pretending she had come to the wrong house, but instead a lady came out. Brenda spoke to her a few minutes and then the two of them came down the steps together. Joe was astonished at the way Brenda spoke, just like a grownup.

"You turn down here by the church," said the lady. "Then take the turn to the right when you reach the old bridge, and you're almost opposite the station. Is this your little brother?"

"Yes," Brenda said with a sad smile at Joe. "I have to look after him. My mother died last year, and my father is thinking of putting him in an orphanage."

"You should really hurry and get home before dark," said the lady. "Here's something for you, sonny," she added, giving Joe sixpence.

They walked off in silence, Brenda looking mockingly at Wright who was sitting on the wall, a picture of mortification.

"Keep the tanner," she said good-naturedly to Joe. "It was only that I didn't want to give that fellow the satisfaction."

It was like Brenda to give sixpence away in that lordly way of hers, but all the same it wasn't wishing to Joe. For weeks he went round in dread the lady might see him with his mother and find out that he wasn't an orphan. He felt it was fated that one of those days Brenda would get him into the hands of the bobbies.

One year Brenda took it into her head that they should give their father a proper Christmas present, not the miserable pincushions and things the girls had made him previously.

"Why should we give him a Christmas box?" snapped Colum. Colum was the eldest of the family and very conscious of his superiority, particularly with the girls.

"What does he do for us?" asked Maeve who always supported Colum.

"Doesn't he keep us, woman?" asked Brenda. "Sure only for him we wouldn't be here at all."

"That's no good reason for giving him a Christmas box," growled Colum. "What could we give him?"

"He wants a fountain pen," said Brenda, who, as usual, had it all worked out.

"Pity about him!" said Colum.

"Ye needn't be so blooming mean," said Brenda, beginning to get into a wax. "Rooney's have very nice pens for ten and six. What is it only two bob a man? Ye'll get more than that out of the aunts."

The aunts were the O'Regan sisters from Kanturk who always stayed with their brother during the Christmas shopping, and, on the strength of their half crowns, it was decided to give Mr. Regan the fountain pen. Brenda collected the subscriptions and Joe paid up like a man. He knew that with Brenda you had always to pretend generosity even when you didn't feel it, and he was shrewd enough to realize that, since he was her favorite, he never really lost by it. It was the same about the pen. She not only allowed him to go to town with her to buy it, as well as that, she took him to a toyshop and out of her own money bought him an air gun. That was another peculiar thing about Brenda. Not even the other girls ever knew how much money she really had, and if anyone asked questions she always replied with lies. But Joe liked her just the same. It would be a long day before ever he got anything out of Colum or Maeve.

After that they went back up Patrick Street in the twilight, and into Rooney's, which was a combined stationery and bookshop. Brenda made straight for an assistant called Coakley who lived near them and who was friendly with her father; a tall chap with pince-nez, black curly hair and a pencil behind his ear. He leaned across the counter, laughing at Brenda, and Joe could see that he liked her.

"And what can I do for you, Miss Regan?" he asked, and Joe nearly died with pride to hear her so addressed.

"You can show us a few fountain pens," she said with a queenly air as if she had never been called anything else.

"Well," Coakley said eagerly, producing a tray from under the counter, "to make a long story short, you can't do better than the best." Then he produced another tray. "Of course, we have the cheaper ones as well, but they're not a patch on those."

"How much is this?" asked Brenda frowning, taking one from the first tray.

"Thirty bob," Coakley said, leaning his elbows on the counter.

"'Tis too dear," said Brenda, putting it back.

"That's a Standard," said Coakley. "'Tis a lot of money, of course, but 'tis worth it. That other stuff, I wouldn't waste your time recommending it to you."

"They all look much alike to me," said Brenda, taking up one of the cheaper pens.

"Ah, Miss Regan," Coakley said bitterly, "they're only got up like that to please the mugs. 'Tisn't the appearance that counts at all, but the nib." Then he took a fountain pen from his breast pocket and unscrewed the cap. It looked as if it would hold a half pint. "See that pen?" he asked, holding it out to Brenda. "Go on! Look at it! Guess how long I have that!"

"How long?" she asked curiously.

"Fifteen years," Coakley replied dramatically. "Fifteen blooming years. I bought that pen out of the first week's money I ever earned, and I give you my word there wasn't much of it left when I bought it. They were cheaper then, of course. That's so old that they're not even making them any more. They mend it for me as a personal favor, because I'm in the business. I had that through the war, in gaol and everything. I did every blessed thing with that pen only stop a bullet with it, and, I declare to God, I believe if I did that itself, I could have written home afterward with it to tell the story. I'm not telling you a word of a lie, Miss Regan. If you offered me the full price of that pen at this minute I wouldn't sell it to you. That's a Standard for you! There isn't another pen on the market you could say the same about."

He took it back from her, looked at it lovingly, screwed back the cap and returned it to his breast pocket. Joe could see he was really fond of the pen and that Brenda was impressed in spite of herself.

"Give it to us for a quid and I'll take it," she said coolly.

"A quid?" he replied, taken aback by her tone. "You might as well ask me to give it to you for nothing. Thirty bob is the price of those pens, and God knows I wouldn't tell you a lie."

"Don't be so blooming mean," said Brenda, a bit put out at her failure in her first attempt at bargaining. "What's ten bob one way or the other to ye?"

"What's ten bob to us?" he echoed blankly. Then he raised his hand to his mouth, reached a bit farther across the counter and indicated a small fat man serving at the far end of the shop. "Do you know Mr. Rooney?" he whispered.

"No," replied Brenda. "Why?"

"You ought to go up and ask him that question," Coakley said, and went into a stifled guffaw that shook every bit of him. "Just ask him what's ten bob to him, one way or the other. I'd love to see his face!"

"Anyway," said Brenda, seeing that this line was a complete wash-out, "you can split the difference. I'd give you the thirty bob, honest to God, but I'm after buying an air gun for the kid."

"Listen, Miss Regan," Coakley said with genuine earnestness, throwing himself over the counter again and speaking in a confidential whisper. "I'd do it like a shot, only 'twould be as much as my blooming job is worth. Your father will tell you. He knows the way I'm situated. I wouldn't tell you a lie."

Joe thought that Brenda would still take the good pen even if it meant throwing in his air gun to make up the price. By that time he would not have minded. He was fond of Brenda, and he could see that she was having a terrible time with her pride. It went through her to offer their father anything that was not the very best. It was as though she wasn't quite the thing herself. Then she gave a shrug.

"Ah, I'll take the ten and a tanner one so," she said. "It looks all right anyway."

"Oh, it is, it is," Coakley said, shaking his head and trying to put things in the best light. "I wouldn't give it to you at all if it wasn't. As a matter of fact, 'tis quite a decent little pen considering the price. We're selling them by the hundred."

Even Joe could see that this was a most unfortunate remark because in his sister's eyes nobody valued what everyone had. She was a natural aristocrat. It was dark when they came out and stood on the edge of the footpath with the lights reflected in the wet streets all round them. Brenda set her jaw and shook her head.

"I was an idiot to go to Coakley," she said with finality and turned to go.

"But why, Brenda?" asked Joe.

"He knows us too well," she said shortly. "If we might have gone to a stranger I could have fecked one of the good pens."

The panic Joe knew so well was beginning to rise in him again. They had still a good bit of Patrick Street to walk, and he knew his extraordinary sister so well that he realized there was every possibility of her staging a smash and grab raid on some other shop, with policemen chasing after them through town. The very thought of it made him sick.

"We'd get caught," he said sagaciously.

"Ah, you never think of anything only getting caught," Brenda said and gave him a savage dig. "Old baby!"

"Anyway," he said, trying to assert himself, "'twould be wrong."

"What'd be wrong about it?" she retorted. "As if they were going to miss one pen out of all they have! Robbers!"

He saw that was the wrong approach too. It was never much use talking to Brenda about right or wrong. He summed up all his cunning.

"I think the pen we got is better," he said.

"It is not better, you idiot!" said Brenda viciously. "Only for you and your blooming old air gun I'd have had enough for it, too. Not," she added in bitter meditation, "that *I'd* get any thanks for it. That crowd at home think I'm going to offer Daddy any old thing as if that was all we thought of him. Then they blame him if he gives one of us a clout. Is it any wonder the man would give us a clout and the little we make of him? God, it makes me sick!"

On Christmas morning Mr. Regan came downstairs in what for him was a very benevolent mood. Christmas was always a trying time for him. Between the universal claims for Christmas boxes, his sisters, and his children home from school, he could not help feeling put-upon. His wife had worked hard on him that morning, and he had almost been persuaded into promising not to do anything to upset the occasion for the children. He looked at the little parcel on his own plate and studied it for a moment.

"Hullo," he said with a pleasant grin. "What's this?"

"Something Santa brought for you," said Brenda. Then he sat down, undid the wrapping, opened the little box and saw the pen.

"Oh, now, that's very nice," he said with real glee, just like a kid. "That's the very thing I want. Which of ye thought of that?"

"Brenda did," Joe said quickly to make sure that no one robbed his sister of the credit.

"That was very thoughtful of her," said Mr. Regan, making a really gracious bow. "Very thoughtful of all of you," he added, giving each of them a grin in turn. "How much was it?" he asked briskly. That was more like him.

"Really, Jim," said Mrs. Regan with a laugh. "Such a thing to ask!"

"Why wouldn't I?" he asked, beginning to frown.

"The price is on the box," Brenda said quietly.

"Oh, begor, so it is," said Mr. Regan, glancing at it.

"Thirty bob!" he added, impressed in spite of himself. His patrols had never brought back information about the economic state of the enemy's troops, and most of the time he seemed to think they lived off the country. Joe looked at Colum, Maeve and Brigid, and he saw that they were impressed too, only in a different way. They were looking at Brenda to see what she was up to now. She didn't look as if she was ever up to anything. She just sat there with a radiant look that would have suggested sanctity except to someone that knew her.

"Where did you get it?" her father asked with a trace of suspicion.

"Rooney's," Brenda replied lightly.

"Rooney's?" her father echoed as he unscrewed the cap of the pen and looked at the nib. "Rooney's have Standard pens for that."

"I know," Brenda said composedly. "Joe and myself looked at them but we didn't like them. The assistant didn't like them much either. Isn't that right, Joe?"

"That's right," Joe said loyally. "Them were the best, Daddy."

"*They* were the best, dear," his mother said comfortably. "Wisha, Jim," she added. "I don't know is that school any good at all. The monks don't seem to teach them anything."

The children knew that their mother was sketching a diversion on her flank, but their father did not follow it up. Monks were another of his phobias. Any other time he'd have had quite a lot to say on the subject of monks, but not just then. He lived in a state of suspicion about life in general and shopkeepers in particular. He sucked in his cheeks, breathed through his nose and looked at that pen as though it could tell him what dirty trick the world was trying to play on him now. He rubbed his forehead briskly and turned on Brenda again.

"Which assistant was that?" he asked. "Coakley?"

"No," said Brenda. "A fellow we didn't know."

"Hah!" exclaimed her father, nodding as he began to see deeper into the plot. "I thought as much. I'd be surprised if Coakley had anything to do with that. Isn't that Rooney all out?" he said to his wife. "He saw the unfortunate children coming and knew he could impose on them."

"Wisha, nonsense!" she replied lightly. "He couldn't stand over a thing like that."

"But you don't mean to tell me that—that thing is worth thirty shillings?" he snarled, handing her the pen.

"Wisha, really, Jim," his wife said indignantly, "what way is that to talk about the children's present?"

"Now, I'm not complaining about the children at all," he said vindictively. "I know the intention was good. What I'm complaining of is Willie Rooney and his sanctimonious air, and I'm going to show him that he can't treat me like that."

"Sure, if you don't like it, they'll change it," said his wife.

"I'll do it after the holidays," Brenda said quickly.

"You'll only let yourself be fooled again," said her father.

"She's no fool at all," her mother said with a touch of asperity.

"Oh, all right, all right," said Mr. Regan, as cross as two cats at being deprived of such a neat excuse for a row. "Here, Brenda," he added, replacing the pen in the box, "put that away carefully till Thursday, and then take it back. Mind, now, and don't use it. Go to Coakley. You know Coakley? Pay attention to what I'm telling you. Have nothing to say to the other assistants. Go to Coakley and say I sent you, and that he's to give you a Standard pen instead of that one. He'll see you're not codded again."

Then Mr. Regan was perfectly happy, having ruined the whole day on the family.

"That's the last Christmas present that old show is going to get from me," said Maeve.

"Never mind him," snapped Colum. "What do you say to this one, changing the price on the box?"

"Ah," said Maeve contemptuously, "we might have known what she'd do with it. Always swanking."

Brenda was laughing at them. At least, she seemed to be laughing, but she frightened Joe.

"Anyway," she said. "I want another four bob now from each of ye."

"Try and get it." said Colum.

"Oh, I'm going to get it all right," said Brenda, tossing her head. "If ye don't give it to me I'll go and tell my father that ye put me up to it."

"I wouldn't put it past you," said Maeve with a sneer.

"I suppose you think I wouldn't?" asked Brenda.

They had gone too far, and they knew it. It was in the highest degree unsafe to challenge Brenda to do anything, because there was nothing you could positively say she would not do, and what was worse, nothing you could positively say her father would not believe. As Colum said once, they were lick alike. Joe knew it was wrong, and he was sorry that Brenda made the rest of them feel that way about her, but he could not help admiring her spirit.

They paid up and walked out on her. Joe emptied his pockets and offered her everything he had. It was his way of showing that he didn't really mind.

"Keep it," she said sharply. "I had it all the time, and I'd have paid it too if only they had the decency to stick by me." Then she smiled, a bitter sort of smile, and Joe thought with interest that she was probably going to cry. "The trouble with our family," she went on, "is that they have all small minds. You're the only one that hasn't, but you're only a baby, and I suppose you'll grow up like the rest."

Joe thought that unkind, but he could see she was upset.

***

In responding to O'Connor's "Lady Brenda," participants in the 1997 Mellon Seminar on Critical Pluralism were particularly interested in testing the usefulness of current literary theories as ways of reading and interpreting creative writing. **Patricia Angley**, for instance, adopted a *feminist* perspective when she suggested that

> Brenda is described as having masculine traits.... Attributing such traits or behavior to female characters is a method male writers often use to create "strong" female characters.... By constructing Brenda as he does, O'Connor creates a character who refuses to fit neatly into the boundaries imposed by her culture and who thus poses a critique of those boundaries. Must a girl always be timid, placating, and/or manipulative (like Brenda's mother, for instance)?... Joe sees his mother as a miracle worker because she protects her children; he idealizes her. What he is idealizing, however, is a woman who cannot express herself freely for fear of what her husband, the ultimate family "authority," might do. Joe idealizes the woman in his life who stays clearly within cultural boundaries. Yet Joe also loves Brenda, even though her predictably unpredictable behavior frightens him.

Similar opinions were also expressed by **Claire Skowronski**, who contended that

> a feminist critic might applaud O'Connor's characterization of Brenda, since she represents a strong female role model, in spite of her less savory actions (such as stealing). She is strong-willed and manipulative, demonstrating her ability to take command of a situation and use it to her advantage. She is resourceful, cunning, alert, and in tune with the personalities (particularly the flaws and weaknesses) of the people around her, giving her command of many situations. A feminist critic might note that, both historically and in contemporary society, these characteristics are generally considered desirable and are encouraged in males in order to give them an "edge" in the business world. In creating a female character with these attributes, O'Connor demonstrates that women, too, reap the rewards—and experience the drawbacks—of possessing such a personality.

Karen Worley Pirnie also used a feminist approach to argue that

> many readers would be troubled by Brenda's intractable position, beginning with O'Connor's sarcastic title. Like all women in patriarchal societies, Brenda is in a "no win" situation: she is damned as "swanking" or frighteningly "tough" for her aspirations and assertive efforts to escape the "wisha" weakness of her mother (which seems manipulative and likely to drive Jim Regan "to his grave"). If we see the main plot conflict as involving Joe's

view of his sister, his growth comes from seeing her less as "tough" and more as vulnerable, "going to cry," and "upset." Thus Joe matures by perceiving his sister's traditionally female weakness. The male character advances at the cost of the female.

Timothy Francisco, on the other hand, used a *Marxist* perspective to present a reading of the story that both resembles and significantly departs from feminist interpretations. According to Francisco,

> At the heart of "Lady Brenda" lie deeply entrenched class and ideological stratifications, which the action of the story (indeed, the very title) interrogate and finally lament. Thus the title apparently encourages a response evocative of tales of chivalry, adventure, and romance—all powerfully classist genres which reestablish the status quo and conventional hierarchies under the guises of liberation and exploration.... [In O'Connor's story, both] Brenda and her father adhere to classic bourgeois notions of class and power. The latter asserts a blatant paranoia, which actually seems somewhat justified given the story's setting (in an Ireland still affected by imperialist colonialism) as well as the family's awkward dynamics. Brenda, meanwhile, by "swanking" and apparently seeking to subvert dominant class paradigms, actually reinforces them, as her successful charade in retaliation against the corner boy forces her to assume a stereotypical mantle of poverty and submissiveness to gain momentary access to the rich woman's domain. Class and market issues also surface through Brenda's virulent consumerism. She is a heroine to her brother, partly because she is generous with gifts and money, and, more important, she is shrewdly aware that money buys her a temporary reprieve from her lower-class status, as Coakley addresses her as "'Miss Regan.'"
>
> ... Brenda's pen-swank at the end of the story recapitulates the narrative's opening concerns with class and status as she tries, again through deception, to purchase a marker of status to which she feels she is entitled. But again, her attempt at subversion serves only to re-entrench the status quo, as she and Joe learn that no amount of "swanking" can change the nib of a cheap fountain pen.

Another participant who experimented with Marxist analysis to help explain the story was **Claudia Wilsch,** who likened the conflicts within the Regan family to the larger struggle between economic classes. From this perspective,

Mr. Regan's children, an economically weak group symbolizing the proletariat, not only lack the solidarity necessary to confront representatives of the strong capitalist class but also succumb to the very values a Marxist might wish to see them oppose. Complaining that her sister does not "stick by" her, Brenda points out the disloyalty of her siblings. A Marxist critic might see the reason for this split in the "proletariat" in the children's adherence to capitalist values. Colum's and Maeve's questions— "'Why should we give him a Christmas box?'" and "'What does he do for us?'"—show that they appraise the worth of a human being by gauging the quality of the services the person renders, which in turn determines the "salary" he or she merits.... Brenda, on the other hand, appears to appreciate her father more. However, her attempt at procuring an expensive present ("the very best")—or at least one that *seems* expensive—reveals the capitalist in her.... [Similarly], by making money his primary concern and by expressing his dissatisfaction at the "dishonest" shopkeeper, Brenda's father not only manifests his own capitalist thinking but also shows that he thoroughly understands the capitalist class system in place. O'Connor's description of Mr. Regan as living "in a state of suspicion about life in general and shopkeepers in particular" and the father's question "'Isn't that Rooney all out?'" demonstrate that it comes as no surprise to him that his children have apparently been fooled by a businessman. In this manner, Mr. Regan implicitly communicates his acceptance of the notion that it is natural for capitalists to exploit others economically.

Furthermore, a Marxist critic might suggest that, by complaining about the poor quality of his children's present, Mr. Regan alienates these "workers" from the product of their collective efforts. Not only does he fail to compensate the children emotionally for their "labor," thus exploiting them, but he also takes advantage of his superiority as the recipient and judge of the product of their work to weaken the children's unity as a group opposing him.

This Marxist or materialist approach was also adopted by **Pirnie**, who argued that

each of the three incidents [in the story] includes currency, from the sixpence given to Joe to the thirty shillings Brenda will finally pay for the pen. Reading the story as one of class conflict and economic determinism would therefore unify it. The title could be seen as ambiguous, perhaps expressing sympathy with Brenda's futile efforts to cross economic class lines. Focusing on the economic conflicts within the story makes the family's internal conflicts seem less personal and more tragic. This materialist analysis thus helps explain the flashes of sympathy we get for the bellicose Mr. Regan, as when we learn that "suspicion ... nearly drove Jim Regan to his grave." He, like Brenda, seems to seek upward mobility, as is suggested by his change of name from the original O'Regan (still used by his sisters at home in Kanturk). Brenda's efforts to rally her siblings, although by trickery, might seem to express this same craving for economic advancement (symbolized by the ironically named "Standard" pen, available only to the "non-standard" bourgeoisie).... Regardless of Frank O'Connor's personal politics, his story "Lady Brenda" supports a materialist reading better than any other.

Jonathan Wright, however, also seeking to explain Brenda's trickery or deceit, suggested that a *psychoanalytic* critic might argue that

> Brenda does not tell the truth because she is unable to cope with reality. Since reality is uncomfortable, she essentially escapes into a fantasy world that is far removed from the truth. She seems to be completely in control of herself (and of others such as Joe) when she dictates her own reality. Nevertheless, at the end of the story Brenda comes close to breaking down emotionally because she is forced to face the reality of rejection by her father and her siblings.

Wright himself, meanwhile, found significance in the fact that the story's central event occurs on Christmas day—a fact that ironically highlights the story's emphasis on materialism, pride, and combativeness and its absence of emphasis on genuine love and generosity. In this connection, Wright noted that, "in an odd role reversal, Mr. Regan stares gleefully at the gift on his plate 'like a kid' while his children watch him closely for signs of approval."

Michael Probst, conversely, expressed a *formalist*'s admiration for O'Connor's subtle and complex characterization of the Regan family:

> The father, Jim, is stern and difficult to please. His paranoid attitude toward the world, his family, and shopkeepers in particular evoke images of the typical father who is harried by the never-ending pressures of providing for his family. Constantly aware of the demands imposed by his responsibilities, he is unable to find relief from his free-floating anxiety. Jim's wife, like her son Joe, is also something of a diplomat (though "double agent" might be a more accurate term). She too is in a conflicted role,

torn between her husband's expectation of loyalty to him and her desire to protect her children from their father's subtle aggression. Finally, there are the relationships between the children and each other, and between them and their parents. We see the children struggling with the frequently discordant demands for conformity and acceptance—the desire to placate other siblings, curry the favor of parents, and avoid trouble with the outside world.

Ashley Gordon also praised the story from a *formalist* perspective. According to Gordon, one strength of the work is

the narrator's voice, which engages the reader from the beginning. By using highly specific language, O'Connor helps establish a camaraderie between narrator and reader, creating a likable and human personality for the narrator, as if to imply that we are being *told* the story orally rather than reading it. Slang words and phrases such as "long chalks," "sissy," and "swanking" make us feel as if we are the characters' neighbors. Such diction implies a tacit understanding that the reader and narrator share the same background and a common vocabulary.

The narrator's conversational tone, colloquial phrasing, and occasional use of asides help make the story dramatic rather than didactic. O'Connor consistently *shows* his readers the characters' motives rather than merely *telling* them. Even when the narrator does resort to telling rather than showing, the use of qualifiers keeps the tone conversational and provides clues to unspoken feelings (particularly Joe's), as the following examples demonstrate:

… none of them was *exactly* what you would call a sissy....

***

When there *really* came to be things to worry about, the suspicion of all that was concealed from him *nearly* drove Jim Regan to his grave.

***

He knew that with Brenda you had always to pretend generosity even when you didn't feel it, and he was shrewd enough to realize that, since he was her favorite, he never *really* lost by it.

Such phrasing not only makes the reader feel more closely involved with the story by continuing the casual diction but also implies that the narrator is himself (or herself?) a complicated observer of fundamentally complex characters and events.

Kathleen B. Durrer also used a *formalist* approach, this time to help explain the effectiveness of O'Connor's use of military language in the first paragraph:

> Although this terminology already suggests the father's battle with the family and particularly with Brenda, as the story unfolds we see that far more serious battles are being fought, and that few, if any, are being won. Brenda is introduced in the opening sentence as the "toughest of the family," phrasing that immediately suggests the competition among the family members. However, Brenda's battles are not limited to the long-standing conflict with her father; they extend to her siblings, friends, and the surrounding community. Ironically, her battles closely resemble the ones her father constantly fights. She is described as looking like her father, and, like him, she also seems to view the world as a force to be dominated. Joe's insightful observations about his sister reveal that Brenda is not struggling to achieve acceptance from others but to be recognized as somehow better. Her perception of the shopkeepers as "'robbers,'" her dismissal of any threat from the "bobbies," and her refusal to acknowledge any concept of right and wrong suggest that her battle extends beyond the boundaries of her own family and out into society in general. Her attitudes seem to parallel closely her father's own animosity to shopkeepers, monks (perhaps symbols of a moral authority), and "life in general." Ultimately, Brenda's efforts are also just as ineffectual as her father's. Although she extorts the money from her siblings to buy the more expensive pen, the gesture has lost any meaning. She wins neither the love of her father nor the support or respect of her siblings and is left with only Joe as a "friendly neutral" to accompany her in future campaigns. As Colum would say, Brenda and her father are sadly "lick alike."

Furthermore, **Claire Skowronski** contended that

> a formalist critic might note that O'Connor's choice of title effectively conveys the complex unity of his short story. "Lady," of course, is ironic; the reader quickly learns that Brenda is a member of the lower working class, so the title "lady" speaks both to her disdain for her station in life and to her desire to taste something more. Her name itself supports the assertion that Brenda is both willing and able to take a bigger bite out of life: "Brenda" means "flame." Her personality is heated, passionate, and dangerous to those who get in her way; yet she draws people in, like moths to a candle flame. Joe, for instance, is both drawn to and repelled by his older sister's compelling personality.

Yet **Skowronski** also observed that a new historicist critic, deeply interested in questions of literary and social power,

> would perhaps suggest that O'Connor, widely published in commercial periodicals considered "women's magazines," deliberately set out to create a powerful female character to appeal to an influential audience, since he needed to attract such an audience to make his fiction marketable.

Finally, **Skowronski**—this time adopting the perspective of a *traditional historical* critic—proposed that such a critic might note that Joe's relationship with Brenda is consistent with O'Connor's own experiences growing up with a mother rather than a father as the strongest role model in his own life.

The varied responses to "Lady Brenda" by Angley, Durrer, Francisco, Gordon, Pirnie, Probst, Skowronski, Wilsch, and Wright seem useful not only as readings of this particular story but also as examples of how O'Connor's fiction might generally lend itself to a variety of interpretive approaches. The choice by several of these readers to pursue feminist approaches is perhaps not surprising in a story so obviously featuring a prominent female character. Nor is the decision of others to adopt a formalist perspective a matter of surprise, since the close analysis of artistic craftsmanship favored by formalist critics works well with the writings of most serious authors. Both feminist and formalist approaches might be fruitfully applied to many of O'Connor's other stories. Meanwhile, Wright's psychoanalytic speculations about Brenda's motives certainly seem worth pursuing, and indeed psychological approaches to O'Connor's whole *œuvre* seem promising, especially in view of O'Connor's own demonstrably strong interest in Freudian thought.

The fact that Francisco, Pirnie, and Wilsch all found Marxist or materialist perspectives useful in responding to "Lady Brenda" might at first seem surprising, especially given O'Connor's own publicly expressed lack of sympathy with Marxist politics. Much of his fiction, however, does seem to lend itself to materialist readings, since so many of his writings deal either explicitly or implicitly with economic tensions and relations between economic classes. Similarly, one can easily imagine how *new historicist* perspectives, such as Skowronski's, could easily be applied to O'Connor's stories in general and to "Lady Brenda" in particular. This story, after all, explores the complicated power relations within a single family, thereby suggesting that politics are not confined to the public sphere. In addition, a *traditional historical* approach (of the sort touched upon by Skowronski) would also work well with this story and with O'Connor's writings at large. As the Ireland of the first half of the twentieth century recedes in time, O'Connor's fiction is likely to need (and benefit from) the kind of contextual interpretation that historical research can best provide.

To say this is hardly to suggest, however, that either "Lady Brenda" or O'Connor's writings fail to resonate beyond their specific time or place. Probst's comments in particular (and the other formalist responses in general) suggest that one need not be a denizen of twentieth-century Ireland to appreciate the force of O'-Connor's fiction, and the same argument might be made by *archetypal* (or "myth") critics. Any story (such as "Lady Brenda") that so prominently features protective mothers, aggressive fathers, adventurous quests, and imagery of battle is likely to have archetypal resonance, just as the story's emphasis on the complex relations of siblings is likely to seem relevant to persons in all cultures. Similarly, a *thematic* approach is almost always likely to prove useful in dealing with O'Connor's works, since he so often explores the same basic themes. Thus his favorite topic, human loneliness, obviously seems relevant to "Lady Brenda," especially to its bittersweet conclusion. However, *dialogical* readings can also work well with O'Connor's writings, especially in view of his well-known efforts to capture the real sounds of distinct human voices. The encounter between Brenda and Coakley in the stationery shop wonderfully exemplifies these efforts, while the different modulations or tones of Coakley's voice alone suggest the potential usefulness of dialogical theory.

Multicultural theory might apparently have little to say about a story such as "Lady Brenda," which seems to focus so totally on one segment of one distinct culture. Yet it is precisely such a limited focus that multicultural criticism can help illuminate, partly by reminding us of the groups or identities that O'Connor here ignores. Even this story, however, suggests the specific relevance of a multicultural perspective, especially if one notices (as Pirnie does) the subtle detail of Brenda's father's decision to Anglicize his name by changing it from "O'Regan" to "Regan." Details like these imply conflicting cultures, and even the opening emphasis on the need to be tough (and to avoid seeming a "sissy") suggests much about the notions of gender embedded within the story. For similar reasons, *structuralism* would prove a useful approach to a tale so obviously structured in terms of such binary oppositions as masculine/feminine, rich/poor, war/peace, strength/weakness, etc. And wherever structuralism seems applicable, *deconstruction* cannot be far behind, showing how apparently neutral descriptive categories that seem natural and inevitable are actually imposed, unstable hierarchies. Thus Brenda can be seen as a walking, talking contradiction of the oppositions just mentioned: she is a masculinized female who commands wealth (but not enough) and whose peace offering ignites another family conflict, to which she then reacts with both "weakness" and "strength." Clear and simple opposites, therefore, seem continually deconstructed or destabilized by O'Connor's story, and at the end Brenda seems, once again, both victorious and defeated. These and the story's other complexities, along with the diversity of interpretive perspectives to which it lends itself, thus help suggest the fruitfulness of a *reader-response* approach to O'Connor's fiction. How one interprets this work (and his others) is likely to depend greatly on the expectations one tacitly assumes when reading.

Even a story as apparently straightforward as "Lady Brenda," then, can be illuminated by viewing it from diverse theoretical perspectives. However, another way to approach this and other insufficiently examined works by O'Connor is to draw on the insights already offered by previous O'Connor critics who have discussed his other works. This approach was adopted by another Mellon seminarian, **Ondra Thomas-Krouse**, who used the summarized critical comments reported elsewhere in this book as points of departure for analyzing "Lady Brenda."[1]

According to Thomas-Krouse, for instance, James Matthews's claim that O'Connor sometimes depicts love as "a matter of wary diplomacy" (277) obviously applies to "Lady Brenda," especially to its descriptions of the uneasy relations between the father, mother, and siblings, whose interactions also illustrate Matthews's argument that O'Connor sometimes focuses on confrontations within families (275). Loneliness and alienation, two other common themes of O'Connor's writings (Tomory 120; Averill 297), also can be found in "Lady Brenda," according to Thomas-Krouse, who argued that these themes are not only implied in the presentation of the isolated mother but also become explicit in the final

---

[1]See the section entitled "Selected Stories of Frank O'Connor: Synopses and Quick Critiques." Full bibliographical details concerning the authors cited here are given there.

glimpse of a tearful Brenda. The conclusion, indeed, illustrates the claim that O'Connor often ends his works by focusing on a character's sudden realization of being alienated (Kilroy 110). In this connection, Thomas-Krouse additionally claimed that the story illustrates the assertion that O'Connor frequently depicts characters who search for meaning and love (Bordewyk 42). In her opinion, Brenda continually seeks her father's affection, while Joe seeks not only love from Brenda but also some sense of the larger meaning of her experiences. In fact, Thomas-Krouse also noted that O'Connor's frequent concern with surrogate parenthood (Matthews 234) is relevant here, since Brenda acts almost as a parent to Joe, who looks to her (more than to his mother) for guidance and affirmation. Furthermore, Thomas-Krouse observed that another common theme of O'Connor's fiction—the contrast between innocence and experience (Tomory 109)—seems relevant to the presentation of Joe, who at first appears naive but whose eyes are opened (during the course of the tale) to a more mature, if perhaps more jaundiced, vision of life. Here as in other stories (Thomas-Krouse claimed), O'Connor suggests that maturity is acquired through loss of innocence (Bordewyk 44): Brenda has "matured" by becoming increasingly like her father, and, with Brenda as a role model, Joe is also likely to mature by losing his youthful innocence.

Thomas-Krouse also noted that the story exemplifies O'Connor's occasional tendency to focus on eccentrics (Thompson 77), such as both Brenda and her father; his habit of presenting self-centered fathers (Wohl 91–92) who perhaps reflect O'Connor's ambivalent feelings toward his own father (Matthews 230–31); and his frequent efforts to treat the depressing aspects of his own childhood in a light-hearted way (Matthews 109; 259). In the view of Thomas-Krouse, Brenda's father is so used to trying to function as the head of his family that he has become unaccustomed to receiving love, so that his instinctive reaction, when presented with the Christmas gift, is to ask pointed questions and try to take charge. His behavior thus illustrates the claim that in O'Connor's fiction, foolish pride often prevents a desired communion (Tomory 95). As always (according to Thomas-Krouse), Brenda tries to make the best of a bad situation, and Joe obviously admires his strong-willed sibling. Indeed, Brenda exemplifies O'Connor's frequent interest in (and respect for) "mercurial, quick-witted, impulsive" girls (Matthews 298). His focus on such a character here helps absolve this story from charges occasionally levelled at some of O'Connor's other tales, such as the claim that his writing can be excessively maudlin (Matthews 266) or damagingly sentimental (Tomory 96). In this story, meanings are *not* too openly stated (Averill 303), nor is the tone here too preachy (Matthews 312). Instead (according to Thomas-Krouse), O'Connor creates an ending that leaves plenty of room for interpretation while still concluding with his characteristic emphasis on a final revelation (Kilroy 110).

Thomas-Krouse's ability to mine the comments other O'Connor critics have made about other O'Connor stories in her own effort to interpret "Lady Brenda" thus illustrates a method that might be fruitfully applied to many works by O'Connor—works that have not yet been examined in the detail they deserve. Here again the basic intellectual procedure of comparison and contrasts yields useful results. Whether measuring a particular story against the insights previous critics have offered about other works, or whether measuring such a story against the claims or suggestions of current literary theories, potential critics of O'Connor's fiction have a wealth of material (both primary and secondary) with which to work.—RCE

"Guests of the Nation":
A Close Reading

Robert C. Evans

"Guests of the Nation" is perhaps the single story by Frank O'Connor that has been most widely praised, published, and studied—and deservedly so. One of his earliest works of short fiction, it remains one of his best. Few stories by few authors are so simultaneously simple and complex, comic and tragic, parochial and universal, lucid and profound. Few other stories make such a powerful impact when read for the first time, yet few other stories remain as powerful on re-reading. Each return to "Guests" reveals subtleties of style and structure overlooked before; each re-visit deepens one's sense of the work's rich significance. In this story perhaps more than in any other, O'Connor comes close to artistic perfection. In this work, nearly everything fits and functions: almost every detail resonates.

What follows is an attempt to justify the claims just made. It is an effort, born of fifteen years of teaching the story at least three times per annum, to comprehend why the work seems just as powerful now as it did on first reading and why it seems, if anything, even more meaningful each time it is read. Each discussion of this story with students has taught their instructor something new—has illuminated some previously unregarded aspect of the work. Similarly, each exposure to published commentary on the story has encouraged both reflection and response.[1] The "close

---

[1] I have offered fairly full annotations of some of the most important critical studies in a book co-edited with my colleagues Anne C. Little and Barbara Wiedemann: *Short Fiction: A Critical Companion* (West Cornwall, CT: Locust Hill Press, 1997). Inevitably my familiarity with these studies has influenced my own thinking about the story, and I wish to express my

reading" that follows, however, basically elaborates reactions first felt (and hastily jotted down on note cards for later classroom use) on my first acquaintance with this story. These comments are offered as a kind of homage to the work and to the artist who crafted it. Although lengthy, they inevitably fall short of the fascinating complexity of "Guests of the Nation" itself.

Much critical work remains to be done on this story, as indeed on O'Connor's fiction in general. In particular, "Guests of the Nation" would reward examination from a wide variety of theoretical perspectives, including archetypal, Aristotelian, deconstructive, dialogical, feminist, Marxist, new historicist, reader-response, and structuralist points of view. The following commentary, which is offered mainly from a formalist perspective, only begins to touch on the manifold complexities of O'Connor's masterpiece.

***

As numerous scholars have noted, Frank O'Connor was a habitual reviser of his own work, often tinkering with stories again and again for years after they were first published. Thus the version of "Guests of the Nation" that is most widely printed in anthologies today is not the version O'Connor first submitted to *The Atlantic Monthly* in 1930. Instead, it is a significantly altered version first printed in 1954. In the revision, O'Connor radically eliminated the original version's heavy emphasis on the narrator's Irish dialect. For example, whereas the feisty British soldier had been called "'Awkins" in the first version, he becomes the plainer "Hawkins" in the revision.

Each reader will have his or her own opinions about the success of O'Connor's revision. (Certainly this has been true of the students with whom I have discussed the matter.) My own view is that the revised story is an improvement. I find the emphasis on dialect in the original version somewhat heavy-handed and a bit distracting. By removing it (I think), O'Connor made his story more obviously universal in its implications.[2] In any case, it is the

---

thanks here to anyone from whom I may have borrowed an idea or whose reading of the story parallels my own.

For references to some other studies of "Guests of the Nation," see John C. Kerrigan's annotated bibliography printed in this collection.

[2]For a different view see, for example, William M. Tomory, *Frank O'-Connor* (Boston: Twayne, 1980), 80–81.

widely reprinted revised text to which I refer in the following commentary.[3]

***

O'Connor's story falls into four distinct, numbered sections. As I try to demonstrate in detail below, these divisions are hardly arbitrary. Instead, they are part of the sophisticated cyclical pattern that contributes both to the design and to the meaning(s) of "Guests of the Nation." The ensuing analysis of the story is organized by the numbers of each section, followed by numbers referring to my comments on that section. Thus the abbreviation "4:5" refers to the fifth comment dealing with the fourth section. Using this numbering system also allows for easy cross-referencing, so that the connections between different parts of the story can be indicated with a minimum of explanation. Such cross-references are printed in square brackets.

To make it even easier to link the following analysis to the appropriate parts of the story, I have also reprinted, in large bold-faced type, key words from each phrase or paragraph analyzed. Doing so has permitted me to keep quotation and exposition to a minimum and has thus allowed me to focus, as tightly as possible, on the work itself.

***

Part One

1:1. DUSK. Appropriately, dusk is a time when light and darkness blend and seem difficult to distinguish, just as good and evil, right and wrong, duty and conscience will be similarly entangled in this story.[4] As a time of

---

[3]The revised version is widely available in *Stories by Frank O'Connor* (New York: Vintage Books, 1956), 3–16 and in many college anthologies.

[4]For a similar assessment, see Deborah M. Averill, *The Irish Short Story from George Moore to Frank O'Connor* (Washington, DC: University Press of America, 1982), 249–53, esp. 252: "The setting is an unnamed, almost metaphorical place. There is only an isolated cottage with a warm hearth inside and a desolate bog outside. Images of light and dark, warmth and coldness, contribute to the symbolic pattern that enlarges the theme. Most

relaxation, of cessation from work, dusk suggests peacefulness and thus helps create the opening mood of serenity and calm—a mood later shattered. At dusk, daily routines cease and new ones commence. O will use routines and cycles of all sorts to help organize the story.

1:2. BIG ENGLISHMAN. Belcher's physical size might at first suggest self-assertion or dominance. Instead he is polite, thoughtful, and sensitive. Already O begins to imply that superficial traits or impressions cannot do justice to complex realities (a theme important to the whole story; [see, for example, 4:16]). The opening emphasis on Belcher's physical dimensions helps highlight the later emphasis on his spiritual depth and psychological complexity. By stressing Belcher's physique, O prepares for the end of the story, when he will suddenly reveal the depths of this man's mind.

1:3. BELCHER. Ironically, the name suggests someone loud, crude, or discourteous—traits just the opposite of the ones Belcher exhibits.

1:4. ASHES. This repeated detail [e.g., 2:7, 26] associates Belcher with a desire for peace, warmth, and relaxation (a desire that seems especially understandable when we later learn about his past [4:12]). Yet the references to ashes also imply his later death and the larger mortality and transitoriness of all human life (an important theme of the entire story).

1:5. "WELL CHUMS ...?" This is the first use of the key word "chums" [e.g., 1:35, 2:7; 3:1, 8; 4:2, 11, 14], which suggests already the relaxed nature of the relationship. Interestingly, the word "chums" probably originated as an abbreviation for "chamber-mate" or "chamber-fellow" (i.e., a college roommate [see the *Oxford English Dictionary*]). The word thus seems especially appropriate, not only because the men are young and room together but also because all learn important (if tragic) lessons by the end of the work. Later, of course, the word becomes increasingly ironic as their friendship is torn apart. Meanwhile, Belcher's ambiguous reference to "it" suggests already the history the men have shared and their easy expectation that their routines will continue. Belcher speaks with the full expectation that his reference to "it" will immediately be understood by the others. Appropriately, Belcher (the embodiment of fellowship) introduces the first communal activity O describes.

1:6. NOBLE. Each character is appropriately named. Noble, of course, will defend conventional moral and religious ideas; ultimately, however, he will feel the opposite of "noble." The as-yet unnamed narrator's reference to the "curious expressions" of the Englishmen already implies the difference in nationalities (an important theme), even as it also calls attention to the use of dialect (both Irish and English) in the story as a whole.

---

of the action takes place at dusk or in the dark, when everything takes on a greater sense of mystery and obscurity."

1:7. HAWKINS. The name, with its diminutive ending, aptly suggests a small, feisty bird of prey. Both traits fit the pugnacious Hawkins.

1:8. LAMP. This is one of the details O uses to create the opening mood of serenity, calm, and security. Near the end of the story, however, the lamp is used much more ironically [2:1; 3:5; 4:1, 18].

1:9. CARDS. Card-playing is an apt opening activity; it involves friendly competition, with small victories and defeats but with no permanent winners and losers (unlike the war, the deadly competition between nations, that will soon engulf all these men).[5]

1:10. JEREMIAH DONOVAN. Appropriately, O (who was christened Michael O'Donovan) gives nearly his own last name to the least attractive character—as if he does not wish to distance himself from Donovan's ugliness. Even "Jeremiah" perhaps suggests the Old Testament prophet famous for his denunciations and complaints ("jeremiads").[6]

1:11. SUPERVISE. Appropriately, even here Donovan is a literal overseer rather than an active participant in the game-playing; he always stands somewhat apart and usually acts as an observer. "Supervise" already implies his superior rank. Ironically, this opening moment is the closest he comes to full involvement with the others; from this point on he will seem increasingly distant, both figuratively and literally. Here Donovan becomes excited over the cards; later he will become excited for far more ominous reasons [3:7; 4:5].

1:12. ALWAYS PLAYED BADLY. The fact that Hawkins is not adept at playing cards already foreshadows his later bad luck and nicely contrasts with his very vocal self-confidence. Later he will seem unlucky in more ominous ways.

1:13. AS IF HE WAS ONE OF OUR OWN. The phrase seems ironic, since Donovan himself is less a part of the group than any of the others. This phrase, too, already suggests the distinctions between groups that will later become so important—distinctions that constitute an important theme of the entire work.

---

[5]On the card-playing as symbolizing the theme of chance, see Stanley Renner, "The Theme of Hidden Powers: Fate vs. Human Responsibility in 'Guests of the Nation,'" *Studies in Short Fiction* 27 (1990): 371–77, esp. 371.

[6]For more on name symbolism in the story, see esp. Earl F. Briden, "'Guests of the Nation': A Final Irony," *Studies in Short Fiction* 13 (1976): 79–81. Briden suggests in particular that Donovan's name may have been inspired by "the historic Jeremiah O'Donovan (1831–1915), a notorious Irish nationalist" (80).

1:14. "AH, YOU DIVIL ..." Ironically, this first joking comment is the closest Donovan comes to seeming attractive, to seeming part of the group. "Divil," ironically, is the most affectionate word he ever speaks. (Later, he himself will seem almost demonic in his coldness [4:5].) Even at this point, however, his participation characteristically takes the form of a complaint. Even here he engages in fault-finding and accusation.

1:15. SOBER AND CONTENTED POOR DEVIL. Later, of course, Donovan will be anything but sober: he will shake with excitement at the prospect of killing the Englishmen [3:7]. His apparent contentment seems to mask his essential discomfort and sense of inadequacy. Even the phrase "poor devil" suggests that the others feel pity or contempt for him rather than the respect his higher rank would seem to demand. The word "devil," too, may carry darker connotations in light of Donovan's later behavior and attitudes. This is the second time within a few sentences that the word has been used by or about Donovan [1:14].

1:16. LIKE THE BIG ENGLISHMAN. Ironically, by the end of the story Belcher and Donovan will seem nearly opposite in their personalities, values, and conduct. Their physical resemblances are only superficial and will later help highlight their important differences of ethics and character. Likewise, in this story generally, superficial differences (such as nationality) often mask deeper similarities.

1:17. FAIR HAND ... EVEN WITH THEM. Donovan's status as a paper-pusher may help explain his later interest in proving himself a real soldier, capable of giving and carrying out fatal orders. He seems more adept at dealing with paper than with people, although even as a paper-pusher he is inadequate. The fact that he receives (and feels) little respect may help explain his later self-assertive exertions [e.g., 3:9].

1:18. HE WORE ... FARMER'S FEET. Again, Donovan's discomfort in dealing with other people may help explain his later need to prove or assert himself. Here his blushing seems to express his essential uneasiness; later, however, his redness will symbolize his anger and his need to impose control [e.g., 3:2]. His inability to look his comrades in the eyes already implies his distance from them.

1:19. NOBLE AND MYSELF ... TOWN. Typically, O provides a nice touch of comic irony at the expense of the narrator, who himself uses dialect. This very sentence, for example, is grammatically incorrect. The fact that the narrator could not "at the time" see the point of guarding the Englishmen already creates some suspense by implying that the reasons will eventually be revealed.

1:20. PLANTED THAT PAIR ... NATIVE WEED. This is merely the first of many significant references to nature and the natural [1:24, 27, 29, 30; 4:10, 16, 18]. This story shows "natural" processes disrupted and destroyed and natural cycles broken. The imagery of taking root and growth, of course, prepares ironically for the later emphasis on death. "Native" already suggests the crucial question of what it means to be at home in a particular place, to belong to a particular soil or nation.

1:21. MY SHORT EXPERIENCE. The story's tragedy is emphasized by the soldiers' youth. The survivors will suffer with their memories for the rest of their lives [4:23]. The story is partly a tale of initiation into the harshness of mature reality, and the fact that the men are young and relatively inexperienced not only helps explain their conduct (first in befriending "enemies," then in killing "friends") but also emphasizes the loss of innocence the survivors will feel at the end. At this point the narrator's experience is "short"; in no time, however, it will be forever transformed.

1:22. TAKE TO THE COUNTRY. The fact that the Englishmen feel at home in a land not theirs is, of course, part of the story's great irony. O's emphasis on a pastoral, rural setting (associated with peace, calm, and life) only highlights the later brutal tragedy. The men's rural existence is at first almost Edenic; they are literally and figuratively remote from war. Later, war will disrupt their pastoral existence. The quick reference to the "search for them" already implies that the opening peace and calm are inherently unstable and may be disrupted. Ironically, the very attempt of their fellow-countrymen to rescue them from captivity will be one of the reasons that they will later be shot.

1:23. BEING YOUNG. Again O emphasizes the relative innocence of the Irish guards, thus making their later loss of innocence seem all the more devastating and their later conduct more excusable by readers (if not by themselves).[7]

1:24. A NATURAL FEELING OF RESPONSIBILITY. This is the first of several significant references to the word "natural" or its variants [e.g., 1:29; 4:10]. Already O suggests that although certain feelings are "natural," larger external forces sometimes compel us to choose to violate or transgress our natural feelings. By the end, of course, the survivors will be feeling a much heavier, darker sense of "responsibility" than they feel here [e.g., 3:11]. Hawkins demonstrates a sense of mastery here, just as he will throughout the story—even, ironically, at the end, when he, the prospective victim, is being led to his execution but, in his typically self-assertive way, keeps "call[ing] a halt" to the proceedings [3:11].

1:25. BONAPARTE. Only now do we learn the narrator's (ironic) name. Napoleon Bonaparte was, of course, one of the most famous of all military leaders—a soldier through and through. O's Bonaparte, however, is the

---

[7]For a less sympathetic assessment of Bonaparte and Noble, see Renner, "The Theme of Hidden Powers," 373–75 (cited in note 5 above).

most reluctant and inexperienced of soldiers. Although he thinks he wants to engage in combat [2:10], by the end of the story he will feel disgusted with the militarism his name suggests, just as Noble will also feel ignoble.[8]

1:26. SOCKS. This reference provides a typically nice touch of domestic comedy. Clearly this is not the sort of conversation we would normally expect between ostensible combatants. It is almost as if the war, at this point, is not real. Later, however, it will intrude unforgivingly and unforgettably, as when Belcher must himself borrow Bonaparte's handkerchief to cover his eyes before he is shot [4:8].

1:27. LITTLE EVENINGS. These parties seem not unlike the socially relaxed evenings the soldiers now enjoy with each other. Again O emphasizes a sociability or natural friendliness that seems at odds with his war-time setting. This conflict between "natural" and "unnatural" behavior is also implied by the fact that the Irish soldiers felt that they *"could not* leave the two Englishmen out" (emphasis added). The entire story explores such contrasts between feelings that seem innate and behavior that seems unnatural, artificial, or imposed.[9]

1:28. DID NOT DANCE FOREIGN DANCES. Again O offers a nice touch of comic incongruity. Later the felt need to adhere to principles and duty will take on a much grimmer tone [3:7; 4:4, 15]. The commitment to principles here seems a bit silly or ridiculous and therefore unthreatening and inconsequential.

1:29. THEY JUST NATURALLY TOOK WITH US. Variations of this term (such as "nature" and "natural") will become increasingly important as the story proceeds [1:30; 4:10, 16, 18]. The conflict between what seems "natural" and what seems "unnatural" is, indeed, one of the story's central themes.

1:30. OLD WOMAN. Her age suggests that she is wise, experienced, and mature—unlike the young soldiers. Her sex allows her to play an almost motherly role in her dealings with the men. Associated with natural, instinctive reactions, she also seems entirely comfortable with herself. In both senses she is unlike the rigid but insecure Donovan. Indeed, he and

---

[8]The possibility that "Bonaparte" is a nick-name is supported by Neil McKenzie's one-act dramatization of the story, *Guests of the Nation* (New York: Dramatists Play Service, 1960). The play was co-copyrighted by McKenzie and O'Connor. In the play, Bonaparte's "real" name is "Barney" (11).

[9]On this point see also (for instance) J.R. Crider, "Jupiter Pluvius in 'Guests of the Nation,'" *Studies in Short Fiction* 23 (1987): 407–11, esp. 410.

she seem to represent two extremes: she is linked with nature and the instincts, he with inflexible rationality.

1:31. HOUSE. The word implies domesticity, peace, and human control of nature (which will all eventually be disrupted). Later, after the tragedy, the house will be thrown open to the elements [4:21].

1:32. SHE WAS A GREAT WARRANT TO SCOLD. This information not only anticipates her later sparring with Hawkins [1:49] and Donovan [3:4] but also ironically foreshadows her powerfully *understated* reproach of the Irishmen after they return from the killings [4:20].

1:33. GUESTS. This word helps emphasize the sense of violation and unnatural transgression the story will stress, since one is normally under special obligations to treat guests with kindness and hospitality.[10]

1:34. BELCHER HAD MADE HER HIS FRIEND FOR LIFE. The phrasing seems ironic in view of Belcher's subsequent fate; but it also seems appropriate, since she will probably never forget him while she lives. The phrase helps make the ending more surprising, since it ironically suggests that Belcher will enjoy a long life.

1:35. "ALLOW ME, MADAM." It's utterly typical of Belcher to ask permission to do a kindness for another person; later he repeatedly demonstrates similar thoughtfulness and concern (especially, and ironically, when he is about to be killed [3:6; 4:14]). Because he treats the old country woman with such respect, both she and we respect him all the more. Apparently he treats all persons respectfully, regardless of their appearance, status, or nationality. Later, of course, we discover additional reasons for his solicitous and thoughtful behavior, especially for his particular kindness toward the old woman [4:12].

1:36. QUEER LITTLE SMILE. This is one of many phrases suggesting that Belcher is more complex than he might at first seem; there is more to him than first meets the eye.[11] The fact that his smile is "queer" suggests that he is intriguing; the fact that it is "little" suggests his quiet, reserved nature. Later the old woman will herself be characterized as "queer" [1:50], and the word is also strongly linked to Belcher [4:11, 13]. Belcher's grasping of the "bloody hatchet" might in another context seem a threatening gesture; here, of course, it is just the opposite.

---

[10]On this point, see esp. J.R. Crider's previously cited article.

[11]On the effectively slow unfolding of Belcher's character, see esp. the discussion of this story by Caroline Gordon and Allen Tate in *The House of Fiction: An Anthology of the Short Story with Commentary* (New York: Scribner's, 1950), 441–44, esp. 443.

1:37. SHE WAS STRUCK TOO PARALYTIC TO SPEAK. In a story that will soon become tragic, O here provides a nice touch of comedy, and indeed he uses comedy throughout the first half to intensify our sense of the tragedy at the end. Apparently the old woman is not used to such considerate treatment from the Irishmen (presumably her natural allies) who have been staying with her, let alone from someone who is technically an "enemy." Perhaps this phrase functions, too, as a bit of ironic foreshadowing, since at the end of the story the old woman will once again be stunned into near silence [4:18–19]. Nearly all the surviving characters will feel paralyzed by the end of the tale.

1:38. FOR SUCH A HUGE MAN. O provides another touch of comic irony; the narrator fancies himself a "big man" because he is five-foot-ten. This detail echoes his earlier pride in his city origins and in his lack of a country accent [1:19]. Appropriately, the pride or self-centeredness expressed in this first section of the story seems relatively benign. By the end of the story the survivors will feel anything but proud; indeed they will feel morally small [4:23].

1:39. I HAD TO LOOK UP AT HIM. At this point Bonaparte feels physically compelled to look up at Belcher; later he (and we) will "look up at" Belcher more meaningfully—when he reveals his full spiritual dimensions, showing himself as the most decent of men.

1:40. UNCOMMON SHORTNESS—OR SHOULD I SAY LACK?—OF SPEECH. This phrase prepares, obviously, for Belcher's sudden loquaciousness later [4:13]. His silence here makes his later talk all the more memorable and striking. The interjected question (like the interpolated parenthetical phrase that preceded it) helps give the story its sense of spontaneity, its sense of being told rather than written, of being remembered rather than composed, of being heard rather than read. This oral/aural quality was a trait for which O deliberately strove in much of his writing.

1:41. LIKE A GHOST. The phrase ironically foreshadows Belcher's later fate, just as the reiterated reference to his silence again ironically foreshadows his later burst of speech [4:13].

1:42. HIS ONE AND ONLY PASSION. Later, of course, we discover that Belcher all along has been a man of deep and complex feeling [4:11–15].

1:43. WHATEVER WE LOST TO HIM. O describes a nicely circular movement of money around the table. Circular imagery and structures are in fact important to the whole story. O deliberately establishes routines, for example, only to break or disrupt them [e.g., 2:1; 3:1]. By the end of the story the circle the men had formed will be forever shattered. Their card games lack real winners or losers. In contrast, by the end of the story there will be nominal winners (the survivors) and nominal losers (the dead); in another sense, though, all will have lost. The fact that Belcher had the ability to take advantage of the Irishmen but doesn't seems ironic, of course, in light of their later treatment of him.

1:44. TOO MUCH OLD GAB. The emphasis on lively conversation at the beginning of the story only stresses the deafening silences at the end.

1:45. SPIT AT ONE ANOTHER ABOUT RELIGION. The emphatic, unexpected verb is typical of O's style at its best. Ironically, the "chums" spend much time arguing explicitly about matters of right and wrong, good and evil, mortality and immortality. At present the arguments are mere intellectual exercises; later, however, these matters will impinge directly on their own lives, and at that point there will seem no simple, easy, definitive answers [e.g., 4:15].

1:46. HAWKINS WORRIED THE SOUL OUT OF NOBLE. This seems ironic phrasing in light of later events, not only because Hawkins is the one who will be killed through Noble's acquiescence but also because the killing will subsequently torment Noble for the rest of his life. The arguing, like the card-playing, symbolizes *friendly* competition, without real winners or losers; it thus contrasts with the later killings. One great paradox in this highly paradoxical story is that the arguments between Hawkins and Noble help solidify their friendship. They would not argue repeatedly if they did not enjoy their mental combat.

1:47. NOBLE, WHOSE BROTHER WAS A PRIEST. Noble's religious background makes his participation in the killings all the more ironic and painful [e.g., 3:11]. Paradoxically, in some ways it is Hawkins who becomes Noble's true brother by the end of this story.

1:48. HE NEVER DID A STROKE OF WORK. This is simply one of many contrasts between Hawkins and his quiet countryman, Belcher. O suggests that Hawkins and Noble, despite superficial differences, have much more in common temperamentally than either has with his fellow compatriot; the same is true of Belcher and Bonaparte. "Natural" divisions of temperament, however, are later broken by artificial divisions of nationality. Hawkins's arguments here about capitalists anticipate, with great irony, his very last words [4:6].

1:49. HEATHEN DIVINITY ... HIDDEN POWERS. O associates the old woman with mysterious, intuitive, instinctive knowledge. She implies that there are natural (even supernatural) laws that should not be broken or violated.[12] Such a violation, of course, is precisely what this story will describe. By the end the survivors will feel that they have in fact disturbed hidden powers—a feeling O will reinforce by describing the birds dis-

---

[12]This point, and indeed this whole episode, is well discussed in Crider's previously cited article.

turbed by the sounds of their guns [4:16, 21]. O effectively ends the first section on a highly ominous, mysterious, and provocative note; he thus encourages our desire to read further, to discover the meaning of the old woman's words.

1:50. QUEER OLD GIRL. O here provides an extremely effective final sentence; its brevity stands in nice contrast to the old woman's long and mysterious explanation of the origins of the war. Belcher had earlier been described as "queer" (inscrutable [1:36]), and later his "queer" laugh will be mentioned [4:13]. Indeed, it is Belcher with whom the old woman has the most in common. She is, paradoxically, an "old girl"—a phrase that suggests wisdom as well as vitality, experience as well as freshness. Although in some ways the opening section of the story seems deliberately very plain, ordinary, and prosaic, it ends on a note of uncertainty, mystery, and foreboding that helps create suspense [see also, e.g., 1:19]. There is even a touch of humor in this final assessment of the old woman. The humor of the first part of the story enhances our sense of its later tragedy.

Part Two

2:1. TEA ... CARDS. O repeats many details of the story's opening paragraph to emphasize the differences that are beginning to develop. His reference to "tea" again suggests the unusual domesticity of the men's relationship. The lit lamp suggests both their comfort and their mastery of the environment; meanwhile, their sitting implies relaxation. Cards, again, suggest friendly competition, soon to be superseded by deadly conflict.

2:2. JEREMIAH DONOVAN. As at the beginning, Donovan is mentioned only after the bond between the others is emphasized. When Donovan earlier entered the story, he had joked with the other men [1:14]; here he enters, watches, but says nothing. His distance has grown, both physically and psychologically; the word "all" does not include him, which may help explain his bitterness. As usual, he is an onlooker, a supervisor [1:11]. Later he will become a more active (and deadly) figure. The fact that Donovan receives so little attention and respect from the others may help explain his later need to assert his authority. Ironically, of course, his attempt to assert such power will only further undermine the respect the others feel for him.

2:3. A REALLY TERRIBLE ARGUMENT. Ironically, the arguments between Hawkins and Noble help cement their connection; their friendship is paradoxically rooted in their intellectual sparring, which itself functions as a kind of friendly competition, like the card-playing. This "terrible" argument will later seem minor when true terror and horror enter the story.

2:4. PEOPLE BELIEVED IN THE NEXT WORLD. This is an obviously ironic subject of discussion considering the story's eventual outcome. O is here preparing for later references to the same topic in part four [4:11].

2:5. HAWKINS ... SERMON. This is a nice touch of irony considering Hawkins's atheism. O will use similar irony later [3:8].

2:6. EVE AND EDEN AND THE APPLE. The men engage in an ironically appropriate topic of discussion: the loss of paradise through sin and death. At this point Hawkins views the topic as a "silly old fairy tale," but the relevance of such themes to the lives of him and his friends will soon become clear. In a sense the story reenacts the loss of paradise, the fall from innocence into tragic knowledge.

2:7. "YOU'RE RIGHT, CHUM." Belcher's comment typifies his amused indifference. His silence makes his later talkativeness, as he faces death, all the more powerful. Belcher seems to distrust mere talk and abstract theorizing; his knowledge (like the old woman's) seems more intuitive, more rooted in actual experience than in abstract concepts. Yet his indifference to the arguments suggests no lack of intelligence; rather, it suggests his profounder wisdom. Once again Belcher is associated with ashes—a pattern in the story that eventually takes on quite ominous significance [1:4; 2:26].

2:8. STROLLED DOWN TO THE VILLAGE. This nice detail suggests relaxation and remoteness from fighting. The verb suggests a leisurely pace; the noun suggests a rural setting. "Village" implies a small, tight-knit, isolated community, thus mirroring the relationship these men enjoy. The placement of this phrase is especially effective since such relaxation and remoteness are about to be shattered.

2:9. HE STOPPED ... THE PRISONERS. Again O emphasizes Donovan's awkwardness, his insecurity, his need to assert his authority, his tendency to view the Englishmen as military regulations require. Bonaparte's confession of boredom will soon seem extremely ironic.

2:10. WE'D BOTH RATHER BE OUT WITH A FIGHTING COLUMN. This desire is, of course, very ironic, since their wish to take a more active part in the war will soon be granted in a way they neither anticipated nor sought. O again emphasizes the inexperience of these young men, who at this point are ignorant of war but who will taste its realities all too soon. The word "column" suggests a shared, communal experience of combat, whereas Bonaparte and Noble, at the end of this story, will feel utterly isolated and alone.

2:11. HOSTAGES. O effectively places this word at the very end of Donovan's sentence. The whole tone of the story suddenly darkens when this word emerges from his lips. The word catches both Bonaparte and the reader off guard; we experience the latter's own surprise and shock. Appropriately, Bonaparte's stunned response ("Hostages?") is the only one-word statement in the whole story.

2:12. "WE'LL SHOOT THEIRS." O effectively contrasts Donovan's long, unemotional sentences and Bonaparte's clipped, astonished replies. Donovan doesn't hesitate to use the blunt verb "shoot"; later the other soldiers, both Irish and English, cannot bring themselves to use the word, employing euphemisms instead [2:23; 3:10].

2:13. "WASN'T IT VERY UNFORESEEN OF YOU ...?" Like "natural" and its variants, "unforeseen" is a crucial word in the story; from this point O will use it repeatedly [2:24, 27; 4:3].[13] Here it seems to mean "thoughtless, inconsiderate, insensitive." Later it will take on still other connotations.

2:14. "YOU MIGHT HAVE KNOWN IT." Here as later, Donovan characteristically accepts no personal responsibility [3:7; 4:4, 15]. His comments about others usually reveal much about himself, especially about his own ways of thinking.

2:15. "WHAT DIFFERENCE IS THERE?" The possibility that this question is actually sincere only emphasizes the huge mental gulf between Donovan and the others. He tends to think abstractly rather than in personal terms. In this sense he partly resembles Hawkins and Noble (both abstract thinkers who are nonetheless capable of making real human contact in spite of their abstract differences), and he is the opposite of Belcher and the old woman, for whom knowledge and conduct are rooted in experience, intuition, and personal relationships.

2:16. AN OLD DOG ... GOING TO THE VET'S. O ironically uses a standard symbol of fidelity and loyalty—both important themes of this story [4:3–6]. The fact that the imagined dog is old implies greater dependence and attachment. The remark also anticipates Bonaparte's own act, later, of putting Hawkins out of his misery [4:10].

2:17. "YOU'LL BE FREE SOON ENOUGH." This is one of the most ironic comments in the entire story, since by the end of this experience Bonaparte and Noble will feel anything but free.

2:18. MAINTAINING THAT THERE WAS NO NEXT WORLD. Suddenly the topic of argument seems considerably more ironic and sardonic. Hawkins will soon know whether or not there is a "next world." The ensuing comic references to "the next world" only heighten the irony. Noble's confidence

---

[13]This point is explored in detail by Michael Lieberman in "Unforeseen Duty in Frank O'Connor's 'Guests of the Nation,'" *Studies in Short Fiction* 24 (1988): 438–41.

in a providential explanation of the universe will also soon be shaken. Hawkins has "had the best" of the argument, but he will soon be the obvious loser.

2:19. WITH A SAUCY SMILE. Hawkins's confidence here makes his later desperation all the more ironic. Hawkins's claim that Noble lacks knowledge directly foreshadows one of the very last comments made about Hawkins himself [4:11].

2:20. "DO THEY WEAR WINGS?" The comedy of the question heightens the countervailing sense of impending tragedy. The fact that the debate has degenerated into speculation about the equipment of angels makes it seem both funny and unreal, thereby emphasizing the inescapably real dilemma that is fast approaching. Although Hawkins is cantankerous and assertive, his sense of humor makes him attractive. His lively passion contrasts with the dry, unemotional tone of Donovan, who gives lip service to larger beliefs without seeming to have any real beliefs of his own. Perhaps the debate between Hawkins and Noble implies the pointlessness of such abstract sparring, especially when contrasted with the far deeper, more serious questions and problems raised by the story itself [e.g., 4:6].

2:21. LOCKED UP AND WENT TO BED. These are ironic details, since they suggest relaxation and security—just the opposite of what Bonaparte (and soon Noble) is feeling.

2:22. BLEW OUT THE CANDLE. It seems appropriate that this revelation occurs in literal darkness. This moment is part of a larger pattern of imagery in which light and darkness are juxtaposed [e.g., 2:1; 4:1–2, 16, 18]. If the reference to being "in bed" implies that Bonaparte and Noble share the very same bed, then their relationship seems even closer than had already been suggested. Such sleeping arrangements would make them seem even more like brothers.

2:23. TO WANT THEM PLUGGED. When Bonaparte considers the possibility of the English army executing its prisoners, he is able to echo Donovan's blunt verb, "shoot" [2:12]. However, when he considers the possibility that he and Noble may have to kill their friends, he resorts to the euphemism "plugged," and Noble similarly uses the euphemism "put the wind up them." Although they try to use words suggesting an indifference to killing, those very words imply the opposite. Later, Hawkins will use the very same euphemism when faced with the prospect of his own death [3:10].

2:24. "UNFORESEEN OF JEREMIAH DONOVAN." This is another repetition of a key adjective [2:13, 24; 4:3]. The fact that Bonaparte tends to use Donovan's full name when speaking of him already suggests the distance between them.

2:25. BELCHER DIDN'T SEEM TO NOTICE. "Seem" is the crucial word; it already suggests that he may indeed notice. As we later learn, Belcher is far more thoughtful and perceptive than his quietness might otherwise suggest. The emphasis on quietness here is part of an image pattern important throughout the story, especially near the end [e.g., 4:7, 11, 19].

2:26. STRETCHED INTO THE ASHES. O provides another repetition of a key detail [1:4; 2:7]. Earlier this image had implied Belcher's desire for warmth and relaxation; now the reference to "ashes" (associated with death) takes on a far darker connotation.

2:27. WAITING IN QUIETNESS FOR SOMETHING UNFORESEEN. "Unforeseen" here implies "unexpected." Paradoxically, Belcher expects the unexpected. Later we learn why he is not completely shocked by the betrayal he suffers [4:12]. In the meantime, his expectant attitude makes him a bit mysterious and intriguing, providing another element of suspense [see also 1:19, 50]. This mystery makes us desire the self-disclosure he later provides. Hawkins's outspokenness makes him seem less mysterious, although we later learn unexpected details even about him [4:11].

2:28. HAWKINS NOTICED. Although Hawkins seems the more perceptive, in fact he shows less real insight. Typically, he interprets events from his own limited (often narrowly ideological) perspective; he is usually the center of his own attention [e.g., 3:6].

2:29. NOBLE BEING BEATEN. This assumption is obviously ironic in light of Hawkins's eventual fate. In a sense, though, Noble does in fact emerge from the story as a loser, a beaten man.

2:30. HE SAYS SEVERELY. Throughout the story, Bonaparte as narrator alternates between the past tense and the historical present. The latter tense makes his account more vivid, more immediate—as if he is reliving the events rather than simply describing them.

2:31. "PICKING BLEEDING APPLES." As before, O ends a section of the story with significant and ominous words. The tone here is richly complex. It blends comedy and exasperation with much darker connotations of sin, loss of innocence, and loss of paradise. At the end of the first section, the old woman had warned about the consequences of "disturbing the hidden powers" [1:49]. The reference here to picking apples has similar resonance. The technique typifies O's tendency to structure this story through repetitions and cyclical organization: just as parts one and two begin similarly, so they conclude similarly. "Bleeding," Hawkins's favorite curse word, has by now obviously acquired very ironic connotations.

Part Three

3:1. I DON'T KNOW HOW WE GOT THROUGH THAT DAY. Once again, the evening routine begins; O opens this section, as he opened sections one and two, by describing the preparations for a relaxing game of cards. Once again, too, Donovan enters, but this time his entrance is even more ominous than it had been at the beginning of section two. By using this cyclical structure, in which important routines are repeated, O can also emphasize subtle changes in the story. The fact that Belcher speaks in a "peaceful" way now seems especially ironic, not only because the four men are technically at war with one another but also because that war is about to be literally brought home to them; their peace will very soon be disrupted. The fact that Belcher can be understood even though he doesn't state his meaning clearly is typical of the almost intuitive relations that have developed between the prisoners and the guards [see, e.g., 1:5]. This emphasis on unspoken understandings will continue throughout the story and will be especially important at the time of the shootings. Significantly, O describes them sitting "round the table," thus providing another example of the circular patterning that is so important in this story (especially to its cyclical structure) while also reminding us of the circle of friendship that is now about to be destroyed. Interestingly, Donovan is not even allowed to intrude on the circle at this point (as he had twice earlier); Bonaparte prevents him from even entering the house. Significantly, here the card game never even has a chance to begin. Instead, a far more deadly game of chance is about to commence.

3:2. "THOSE TWO SOLDIER FRIENDS OF YOURS." Donovan's phrasing seems significant, as does his physical reaction as he speaks the words. By calling the Englishmen "friends of yours," he already begins to emphasize his own psychological distance from the two hostages. However, even as he separates himself from them, he also implicitly acknowledges that he has never really been a part of the circle of friendship. From the start he has been an outsider, both literally and figuratively. His turning red as he speaks can simultaneously imply various emotions, including anger and resentment at the special friendship the others have developed and also embarrassment, insecurity, shame, and awkwardness. This, after all, is one of his few experiences (perhaps even his first) as a real "soldier" himself. The shooting of the sixteen-year-old boy is indeed "bad," but Hawkins and Belcher bear no personal responsibility for this act, and the act that will now follow the killing of the boy will seem even worse, at least to Bonaparte and Noble, who will feel personal responsibility for their conduct. After all, the boy's killing is carried out impersonally, by the British army; the killing of the Englishmen is carried out by their own friends. For the moment Bonaparte tries to distance himself from such responsibility by asking what Donovan intends to do in response to the boy's death. Donovan, however, deflects the responsibility by emphasizing what he wants Noble and Bonaparte to do. Noble apparently believes that participating in the execution will be bad enough; he does not want the extra burden on his conscience of having to look the Englishmen in the face and tell them a lie.

3:3. "A HOLE BY THE FAR END OF THE BOG." The fact that the killings will take place in a bog will come to seem highly significant. For the moment, it merely seems worth mentioning two practical reasons for killing the Englishmen there: digging the grave will be easier in the soggy soil, and the bodies will decay more rapidly in such conditions. Although Donovan wants the killings to occur as far away physically as possible ("the far end"), it will soon prove impossible for Bonaparte and Noble to distance themselves psychologically from their complicity in the murders. Donovan's concern that the Irishmen not be "seen" with tools will subsequently seem ironic; at the end of the story, the old woman will not need sight to know what the Irishmen have done or even that they have used tools [4:20]. Donovan's concern that knowledge of the killings should not go beyond themselves seems ironic for several reasons. In the first place, his precautions are immediately defeated when we later discover that the old woman has intuitively guessed the whole thing. Secondly, it will prove part of the special pain of this act that knowledge of it will be so much contained within (and felt by) Bonaparte and Noble. Furthermore, by telling the story and by quoting Donovan's words, Bonaparte implicitly violates Donovan's wishes. In a sense the story amounts to a confession.

3:4. THE OLD WOMAN WAS FOR HAVING THEM STAY. The old woman seems to symbolize the "natural feelings" which are at conflict, in this work, with duties or external obligations. The fact that she is old makes her seem experienced in life, a bearer of intuitive (rather than purely rational or intellectual) knowledge, and therefore in some sense a voice of wisdom. The typical wit, efficiency, and richness of O's diction is exemplified by the simple verb "advising": although the word superficially suggests calm, patient counsel, clearly it is a euphemism here for strenuous, emotional argument. Thus by using this one, apparently simple word, O manages implicitly to characterize not only the cantankerous old woman but also the amused, ironic narrator (who carefully chooses this word) as well as the tension of the situation. Donovan's loss of temper with the old woman is simply one of many forthcoming instances in which he will reveal a bitter anger. As a master of prose rhythm, O effectively follows the long sentence describing the conflict between Donovan and the old woman with the very brief sentence describing Bonaparte's observation of Donovan's nastiness.

3:5. IT WAS PITCH-DARK IN THE COTTAGE. Both literally and symbolically the story has now shifted to darkness, and both darkness and coldness will be emphasized (appropriately enough) from this point on [3.11; 4:1, 5, 16, 18, 21, 23]. No one presently thinks of lighting the lamp, and when, after the murders, Noble initially attempts to light it, he will at first fail [4:18]. Once again O is using light and its absence as one of the major patterns of imagery in this story—a pattern crucial to the story's tone and impact.

3:6. SAID GOOD-BYE TO THE OLD WOMAN. The Englishmen are, of course, saying "good-bye" in a far more permanent sense than they realize. The differences in their leave-takings are completely typical: Hawkins is characteristically profane and expresses mainly his own anger and discomfort (his shaking of the old woman's hand seems almost an afterthought), whereas Belcher, ever the gentleman (and gentle man) focuses totally and sincerely on his hostess, addressing her with emphatic dignity. He offers her a "thousand thanks ... as though he'd made it up." "A thousand thanks" is an old Gaelic expression of gratitude, but Belcher the Englishman speaks the words with utter sincerity—almost as if he were the first person ever to use the phrase.[14]

3:7. WENT DOWN TOWARDS THE BOG. Both the direction and the destination are significant: they are descending both literally and morally, and the wet and spongy marsh will prove both a literal and figurative morass, which will leave them physically and ethnically stained. The quick, clipped sentences describing how Donovan informs them that they are to be shot seem highly appropriate to this tense moment, even if they also seem socially inept. Perhaps Donovan is shaking with excitement for several reasons: he is nervous, he knows that Bonaparte now despises him; he anticipates the anger of Hawkins; and he is full of anticipation of the kind of military "action" in which he has probably never before participated. Earlier he had been excited when advising Hawkins how to play his cards [1:11]; now he is excited (in an obviously more ominous way) when he tells Hawkins that the latter must die. In his excitement, Donovan thoughtlessly makes no effort to break the news gently to the Englishmen: he simply announces it, in an extremely simple, tit-for-tat fashion. The social awkwardness he had exhibited from the beginning [1:18] manifests itself here again. Hawkins's reaction combines equal doses of contempt, anger, dismissal, and disbelief, and the verb "mucked about" will in some ways prove both perfectly literal and symbolically apt when the men reach the bog. Donovan's belated attempt to soften the blow exhibits both his awkwardness and his insincerity, and in the disparaging reference to people who talk about "duty," O introduces a note that will be repeated later, just before Belcher is killed [4:15].[15]

---

[14]I wish to thank a number of persons (including Katie Conrad, Richard Harp, Ruth Sherry, and Bruce Stewart) who answered a query posted on the internet about this phrase.

[15]Lieberman, in the article previously cited, mentions that O'Connor added references to "duty" to the revised version of the story (439).

3:8. "ASK BONAPARTE." The fact that Hawkins fails to take Donovan seriously typifies the similar reactions of most of the other men, especially the two Irishmen. Donovan's status as an outsider (a status both imposed and chosen) helps explain his hostility toward the Englishmen (they, after all, are the ones who should be treated as outsiders) and toward his Irish compatriots (who have rejected him in favor of their English "chums"). Two simple words from Bonaparte are enough to convince Hawkins that he and Belcher will be killed. Hawkins's reaction typifies O's artistry; the words and reaction hit us with the kind of abrupt impact that we must imagine the characters themselves to have felt. Faced with the certainty of death, Hawkins the atheist instinctively (and ironically) invokes Christ. This reaction contributes to one of the larger patterns of O's story: the contrast between instinctive and learned behavior, between what seems "natural" at the moment and what seems fitting from a "rational" point of view. Just as it is ironic that the atheist invokes Christ, so it is ironic (in the first place) that "enemies" have become friends and then that two of these friends kill their comrades.

3:9. DONOVAN, WORKING HIMSELF UP. This effort already implies Donovan's weakness, his lack of a strong, consistent personality [1:18]. He seems to be trying to play a role rather than behaving "naturally" [1:24, 29]. Hawkins's question about what Donovan personally has against him may at first seem pointless or naive, since Donovan in one sense is simply following orders. In another sense, however, Donovan does seem to feel personal resentment against the two Englishmen, and this fact undermines his disinterested pose. On the other hand, Donovan's retort to Hawkins—in which he asks Hawkins why the British army executed its Irish captives—seems particularly nonsensical, especially since Hawkins and Belcher bear no personal responsibility for the army's decision. Donovan's tendency to think in terms of simple polarities (implied by his words "your people") is a habit of mind the story implicitly opposes.

3:10. IF THEY DID RUN FOR IT. Although the Englishmen's attempted escape or resistance would give Bonaparte some legal (and perhaps even moral) justification for shooting at them (thus relieving him of the guilt he now anticipates), he expects that even if they did run he would not fire at them. (If they fought, he would presumably have no choice.) Significantly, at this point he finds himself "wishing to God" that they would either run or fight. Later, after the killings, he seems unable to acknowledge at all the possibility of God's existence or concern [4:21]. Does his participation in the shootings push him over the edge into non-belief? Hawkins wonders why Noble wants to "plug" him, thus unknowingly echoing the euphemism used earlier by the Irishmen as they lay in bed [2:23]. Just as they earlier did not want to face reality by using the more common words "shoot," "kill," or "execute," so Hawkins now also resorts to language that seems "tough" but is actually evasive. The string of questions

Hawkins utters, like all his talk in this scene, implicitly emphasizes by contrast the quiet acceptance displayed by Belcher. Belcher's silence contributes to O's subtle characterization of him. Similarly, Bonaparte's decision to substitute the phrase "so-and-so" for the profanity Hawkins actually speaks helps characterize Bonaparte himself, implying that his sensibility is not hardened (and thus helping to explain why the killings are so difficult for him to commit). Typically, Hawkins sees the shootings as the result of class conflict, as one between officers and common soldiers. Here as later, however, the story seems to imply that this analysis is too simplistic, and that even a truly classless society could not prevent the kinds of agonizing moral dilemmas O here explores.

3:11. BY THIS TIME WE'D REACHED THE BOG. The "bog" continues to acquire symbolic significance each time O mentions it; here it becomes increasingly associated with death, especially when O describes how the men "walked along the edge of it in darkness" (phrasing that also contributes to the pattern of light/dark imagery so prominent in this story). To enter the bog is not only to enter the territory of death but also to enter a moral wasteland; to cross over the "edge" is to make a fundamental ethical transition. Ironically, although Hawkins is about to be shot, at times he seems the person most alive and in control: it is he who "every now and then ... would call a halt," almost as if he, not Donovan, were the officer in charge. This paragraph quickly and effectively cross-cuts from Bonaparte's reaction to Hawkins's reactions to Bonaparte's reaction again, finally ending with Bonaparte's musings about Noble's reaction. With understandable selfishness, Bonaparte initially wishes that "Noble would take over the responsibility from me." Then, in a selfless thought that again makes Bonaparte resemble Belcher (as he already does in so many other ways), Bonaparte states simply, "I had the feeling that it was worse on Noble than on me." Noble, after all, has become far more closely involved with Hawkins than Bonaparte has become connected to either of the Englishmen. Despite (but also in part because of) their constant arguing, Noble and Hawkins have indeed become "chums." Whereas the first two sections of the story had ended with final comments suggesting touches of humor, this section ends with a sentence that seems grimly foreboding.

Part Four

4:1. AT LAST WE SAW THE LANTERN IN THE DISTANCE. Although a glimpse of light in darkness would normally be a hopeful sign, here it serves an ironic purpose: the closer they come to the literal light, the closer they also come to metaphorical darkness. The fact that Noble (the committed Christian) bears the lantern seems both significant and ironic, while the fact that Feeney stands in the shadows helps keep the focus literally on the original characters. Feeney plays almost no role in the ensuing scene; responsibility for the killings therefore cannot be shifted to him, however much Bonaparte and Noble might wish that it could. By emphasizing the still silence of the bogland in the beginning of this section, O artfully prepares for the disruption of that silence at the time of the killings and even later [4:16, 23], when the birds hoot and screech at the sounds of the gunfire. The "and ..., and ..., and ..." structure of these opening sentences anticipates the similar structure of the story's powerful final paragraph [4:23].

4:2. BELCHER, ON RECOGNIZING NOBLE. Typically, even at this point Belcher is friendly, using (apparently without sarcasm) the key word "chum" [1:5, 35; 2:7; 3:1, 8; 4:11, 14], which by this point carries an irony Belcher himself does not intend. Belcher may in fact say these words precisely to help put Noble at ease. Hawkins's frantic reaction, by contrast, is equally typical. Although he is technically the more intellectual of the two Englishmen, his understanding of the real complexities of life seems poorer than Belcher's, and his response also seems more emotional. Is the posture of Noble (head down, with the lantern between his legs) in any way meant to suggest the image of a faithful dog, conscious that it has done wrong (with its tail between its legs)?

4:3. AS THOUGH IT WAS HAUNTING HIS MIND. The verb here, referring to Hawkins's thinking, is ironically apt since he will soon (in a sense) be a ghost who will himself be haunting the minds of Bonaparte and Noble. (Perhaps this phrasing also subtly recalls the earlier reference to Belcher "walking in and out, like a ghost" [1:41]). Donovan's confident claim that Hawkins would shoot Noble for fear of being shot himself tells us more about Donovan's character and motives than about those of Hawkins. Characteristically, Belcher stands aloof from the argument, but the reference to his having now experienced whatever "unforeseen" thing he'd always anticipated highlights again a significant word already emphasized earlier [2:13, 24, 27]. Specifically, the phrasing here looks back to the end of section two, and here as well as there the reference to Belcher's expectation of something "unforeseen" raises our curiosity about him, makes us wonder why he reacts in this somewhat mysterious way, and thus prepares for O's later heavy emphasis on Belcher—an emphasis that finally answers the questions generated by ambiguous moments such as this one. Belcher's quietness throughout the first three quarters of the story helps arouse our curiosity about him and also helps give him a depth lacking in Hawkins (who undoubtedly considers himself a deep thinker). The sudden switch to Belcher's talk just before he is killed therefore does not seem extraneous or gratuitous; rather, it satisfies a yearning O has carefully built up in his readers.

4:4. "IS THERE ANY MESSAGE YOU WANT TO SEND?" Typically, Donovan goes by the book, asking the routine questions (even when, as will shortly be the case, they seem highly inappropriate). He proceeds in a mechanical fashion, not only because he lacks much personal feeling for the Englishmen but also, probably, because he has never participated in an execution before.[16] Probably he has read about the proper procedures, and now he mechanically acts his role. His lack of tact becomes obvious when he asks the atheist Hawkins whether the latter wishes to say his prayers. In a touch of comedy during a highly charged moment, the embarrassed Bonaparte refuses to repeat Hawkins's profane response. Just as Donovan speaks of duty without really pondering what the concept truly means, so he also trivializes prayer.

4:5. "LISTEN TO ME, NOBLE." Hawkins's flood of brief assertions is nicely balanced by the equally clipped (but much briefer) comment by Bonaparte: "Nobody answered him. We knew that was no way out." The last phrase, in fact, epitomizes one of the main themes of the story—the theme of fate, of being placed in a situation from which there seems no real escape [4:11, 21].[17] Hawkins, typically, thinks that problems can easily be solved; the story as a whole, however, implies that some dilemmas may be insoluble. It is the sense of having "no way out" that makes the story precisely tragic. The fact that Donovan speaks in a voice that is both "cold" and "excited" seems almost a contradiction, but in fact the paired adjectives sum up the essence of his character. Probably he is now excited because he realizes that control of the situation is beginning to slip from his hands—that Hawkins, ostensibly the prisoner, is beginning to steal Donovan's authority. Thus the killing, when it comes, is not merely an official act but is also motivated by a need for personal revenge. This motivation sullies the execution, despite all of Donovan's efforts to go by the book and make the execution seem purely legalistic.

4:6. "SHUT UP, DONOVAN!" Hawkins's repeated reference to Noble and Bonaparte as "lads" subtly emphasizes one of the most tragic aspects of the story—the youth of both the slayers and the slain. Once again Hawkins's analysis of the situation (although perfectly understandable given the circumstances) seems insufficiently complex: the Irishmen are not acting (indeed, cannot act) simply as "pals." Similarly, Hawkins's very last words indicate another insufficiently complex explanation of the killings: to imply that Donovan is acting as a tool of capitalists does not even begin to explain his extraordinarily complicated motives and situa-

---

[16]On this point see, for instance, Murray Prosky, "The Pattern of Diminishing Certitude in the Stories of Frank O'Connor," *Colby Library Quarterly* 9 (1971): 311–21, esp. 312–13.

[17]Stanley Renner, in "The Theme of Hidden Powers," sees such emphasis on fate as a "cop-out" by Bonaparte and Noble (375–76). I am inclined to see their situation as more tragic and sympathetic.

tion.[18] The fact that Hawkins's last words amount to little more than an ideological cliché is in some respects grimly humorous, making him seem fixated, even at the end, on his ideological obsessions. At the same time, however, the smile his comment momentarily provokes is instantly snuffed out by the tragedy of his death. The inadequacy of his analysis does not diminish our pain when his life is finally sacrificed.

4:7. I ALONE OF THE CROWD SAW DONOVAN RAISE HIS WEBLEY. The fact that only Bonaparte witnesses the actual shooting implies that the others are looking down or away, reluctant to face the painful spectacle. The emphasis on Bonaparte's aloneness here anticipates the story's final words [4:23]. The fact that Hawkins is shot in the back of the neck by Donovan makes the execution seem somehow even uglier and more reprehensible; it seems the darkly logical outcome of Donovan's reluctance (described earlier) to face people, to look them in the eyes [1:18]. It seems highly appropriate to the character of the talkative Hawkins that he dies, literally, in mid-sentence, just as he begins to speak once more. His speech, so strongly associated with his vitality, now becomes one of the main causes of his death. By noting that he shut his eyes and "tried to pray," Bonaparte prepares us for the very end of the story, when he will find it impossible to pray [4:21]. Similarly, the fact that Hawkins (after being shot) at first falls to his knees anticipates two later moments in the tale: the moment when Bonaparte himself will kneel down to put the suffering Hawkins out of his misery [4:10] and also the moment, near the end, when the old woman and Noble will both drop to their knees in prayer [4:20]. Hawkins's final position—literally at the feet of his close friend Noble—is almost unbearably ironic.[19] One can easily imagine Noble's pained response. The imagery of Hawkins dying "slowly and as quiet as a kid falling asleep" anticipates the extremely powerful imagery of the story's very last sentences [4:23], while the emphasis on slowness here contrasts with (and thereby reinforces) the suddenness of the shooting itself. Ironically, of course, Hawkins is not truly experiencing his "*last* agony" (emphasis added): soon his leg will begin to rise—a testimony not only to his vibrancy but also to Donovan's sloppy, amateurish shooting.

4:8. THEN BELCHER TOOK OUT A HANDKERCHIEF. Although Belcher's gesture here might at first suggest that he has been overcome with emotion, in fact the opposite is true: he stoically prepares for his own execution, perhaps assuming that he (unlike Hawkins) will be shot face-to-face

---

[18]Once again I find myself in disagreement with Stanley Renner's view in "The Theme of Hidden Powers," esp. 372.

[19]In fact, Patrick Kavanagh considered O'Connor's depiction of the Englishmen sentimental and designed to provoke "maudlin pity"; see his essay "Colored Balloons: A Study of Frank O'Connor," *Journal of Irish Literature* 6.1 (January 1977): 40–49, esp. 44. Obviously I disagree.

and, for that reason, taking care that neither he nor his killer will have to stare into one another's eyes. In this sense his act typically shows concern for another's feelings—even the feelings of Donovan (of all people). The excitement of the Irishmen, which has caused them to neglect to cover Hawkins's eyes (despite Donovan's obsessive preoccupation with following proper procedures) emphasizes again the unprofessionalism of the executions. Here as always, Belcher is mentally a step ahead of the others, and, just as typically, he is courteous and thoughtful in "ask[ing] for the loan" of Bonaparte's handkerchief. (The word "loan," in particular, seems subtly ironic, since Bonaparte, surely, will never again want to use this handkerchief.) Belcher's understated observation that Hawkins is "not quite dead" not only typifies his calm nature but also presents the alarming news in the least alarming, least disturbing, most considerate way. His matter-of-fact statement catches us, as readers, off-guard just as much as it surprises the other characters.

4:9. SURE ENOUGH, HAWKINS'S LEFT KNEE IS BEGINNING TO RISE. Although Bonaparte often shuttles back and forth between past and present tense when describing (and thus reliving) these events, the use of present tense seems especially powerful here. The entire paragraph, indeed, is written in present tense, whereas Bonaparte normally uses only past tense when speaking of his own actions. Obviously he is re-experiencing his actions as he describes them, thus already illustrating the story's final claim that these events have forever changed his perspective on the world. Bonaparte's action of bending down, along with his immediate counteraction of standing again, both demonstrate his concern for others—first for Hawkins, then for Belcher. The fact that he and Belcher understand one another without the need for speech suggests the depth of their silent bond, just as Noble and Hawkins were bound together by their common flood of talk. Belcher understands what Noble is thinking even before we, as readers, do; the fact that we understand belatedly (only after Belcher speaks) confirms the close link between the two men. In an irony that typifies the method and meaning of the entire story, Belcher expresses both his concern for Hawkins and his own lack of self-concern by urging that Hawkins be "give[n]" (an unintentionally ironic verb) his shot first. Significantly, Belcher takes a term used before only in anger by Hawkins ("bastard" [2:3; 3:6]) and transmutes it, turning it into a term of gentle affection and pity.

4:10. I KNELT AND FIRED. Surely this is one of the most powerful sentences in the entire story. Like the tale itself, it abruptly juxtaposes gentleness and violence. Its power is enhanced by its brevity and by its monosyllabic simplicity. Its power is also enhanced by the paradox the sentence epitomizes (a killing committed as an act of mercy) and by the paradox embedded in the very gesture itself: kneeling is usually associated with prayer. Later, in fact, Bonaparte will feel unable to kneel in prayer alongside Noble and the old woman [4:21]. Ironically, the only shot Bonaparte himself fires results from his compassion; one recalls that earlier he had swaggeringly expressed a wish to be a fighting soldier [2:10], but here he discovers how difficult it is to kill even with the best of motives. Belcher's laugh when he hears the shot is as shocking to us as to Bonaparte; since we are confident that the laugh cannot express sadistic pleasure, we are immediately curious about the feelings it might in fact convey. (Once again O catches us, as readers, off-guard, just as he catches the characters [4:8].) When Bonaparte notes that the laugh sounded "unnatural," he uses a word that has by now acquired enormous resonance in this story [1:24, 27, 29, 30].

4:11. "POOR BUGGER!" HE SAID QUIETLY. Belcher's paradoxically quiet exclamation describes not only Hawkins specifically but also the general human condition. Every human being, in a sense, shares Hawkins's predicament of enduring a curiosity that can be answered only when that answer can no longer be shared. Indeed, Belcher is characteristically generous in describing Hawkins as "curious," since Hawkins might more accurately be described as dogmatically certain. Hawkins, after all, was confident that he knew the truth, but Belcher generously attributes his friend's strong opinions to curiosity. Belcher's comment that now Hawkins "knows as much about it as they'll ever let him know" typifies (especially in its reference to an unspecified "they") Belcher's own sense that human beings are partly the playthings of fate [see 4:5, 21]—that each of us has little personal control over what happens to us or over the larger forces that help mold our lives. When Belcher thanks Donovan (now the killer of Belcher's friend) for helping him with the handkerchiefs, he behaves with an unselfconscious generosity and charity central to his nature. The word "chum," used repeatedly here, seems almost unbearably ironic, although the irony is hardly intended by Belcher. Once again, Donovan goes by the book in asking whether Belcher wants any messages sent. The posthumous revelation that Hawkins was "great chums" with his mother adds a whole new dimension to Hawkins's character now that he is dead. We suddenly discover his tender side, his capacity (and need) for affection, his almost sentimental attachment to his mother. We thought we had known Hawkins fairly well, especially since he had apparently revealed himself so fully through his voluminous talk, but here we unexpectedly glimpse an entirely fresh and unsuspected aspect of his life. In the same way, we will soon discover an unexpected (or at least unknown) dimension of Belcher's own character. Here as elsewhere O implies that human character is too complicated to be reduced to simple abstractions or slogans.

4:12. "BUT MY MISSUS LEFT ME EIGHT YEARS AGO." Suddenly Belcher's previously somewhat-mysterious behavior makes sense. Having been betrayed once, he is not surprised at being betrayed again; having once trusted another person and been disappointed, he almost expects such disappointment to happen again. His silence, we now realize, has not resulted from simple-mindedness, awkwardness, or lack of personality; rather, it has been due at least in part to a cautiousness, a wariness, and perhaps also a sadness born of his previous disappointment. Superficially, Hawkins had earlier seemed the Englishman most full of thoughts, but Belcher (particularly now) seems the most genuinely thoughtful. His capacity for kindness, ironically, has probably been intensified by the hurt he himself experienced. We suddenly realize, too, that Belcher's death will be even more tragic than that of Hawkins, since Belcher will leave behind an orphan (whom he calls, with exquisite restraint, merely "'the kid'"). Suddenly, in retrospect, Belcher's kindness toward the old woman makes sense in a whole new way: she had been, for him, a substitute for the wife and family he had earlier lost. His selfless concern for her had been motivated, at least in part, by an understandable personal desire to recapture the lost feeling of a "'home.'" Also, having been betrayed himself, he could recognize the ways in which the other soldiers were unthinkingly taking advantage of the old woman. Just as Belcher has all along been more observant than his quiet conduct may have led us to assume, so he generously attributes the same perceptiveness to others ("'I like the feeling of a home, as you may have noticed'").

4:13. IN THOSE FEW MINUTES BELCHER SAID MORE THAN IN ALL THE WEEKS BEFORE. Just as the sounds of the shots will later stir up the shrieking of the birds [4:16], so they now unleash Belcher's flood of talk. This is, of course, another highly paradoxical moment in a powerfully paradoxical story: suddenly Belcher becomes loquacious; suddenly the man who previously had called no attention to himself now makes himself the focus of attention. In part his talkativeness can be explained as motivated by a subconscious desire to explain his life, to make it make sense to others while he still has the chance. Partly, too, he is probably motivated by an understandable fear and by a sheer desire to live: as long as he talks, his life will continue. Although Belcher at this point is literally blind, he ironically also seems the character with the greatest insight, the greatest depth of perception. Ironically, at this moment of injustice, he is blindfolded (just as Justice is in conventional representations). How should we interpret the moment when Noble shakes his head at Donovan? Is he expressing disgust, frustration, or impatience (or all of these), or is he emphatically rejecting an implied offer to serve as an executioner himself? The description of Donovan raising his Webley immediately reminds us of the similar phrasing just before Hawkins was shot [4:7] and thus ratchets up our dread and sense of suspense. Here as earlier in the story, O takes advantage of cycles of repeated action. Also, here again O implies that Bonaparte and Belcher understand one another almost telepathically, without needing to speak.

4:14. "EXCUSE ME, CHUMS." Belcher's apology and his ensuing request for forgiveness are both, of course, richly ironic given the situation; without intending to do so, he probably makes Bonaparte and Noble feel even guiltier than they do already. Donovan's routine, by-the-book question about saying a prayer emphasizes once more how mechanical the whole procedure is for him. At the same time, it reminds us again of Hawkins's death [4:4] while also anticipating the final scene, when Noble and the old woman will pray but Bonaparte will find doing so impossible [4:20–21]. For the last time, the key word "chum" is used—by Belcher, appropriately enough, who was also the first to use it (in the story's opening words). Belcher's approach to religion, as to most things, seems level-headed and practical: he doesn't think it will help to pray, just as Bonaparte will later feel the same way [4:21]. Once again, then, O implies the deep connection between these two quiet, thoughtful men. Presumably both Belcher and Bonaparte are agnostics (rather than atheists), or perhaps events have made them one-time believers who now have lost their faith. If Belcher has indeed lost an earlier faith, his comment here about prayer would be just another reflection of the string of losses he has suffered in his life. Significantly, though, he speaks about prayer as he speaks about most things—matter-of-factly, without bitterness. His reference to the Irishmen as "boys" once again reminds us of the tragic youthfulness of these executioners, who will be forced to remember and relive this event for years and years. At the same time, the word suggests Belcher's inherent tenderness, thoughtfulness, and compassion. Paradoxically, of course, although these "boys want to get it over," for Noble and Bonaparte Belcher's killing will be only the beginning of a whole new agony, one that cannot be easily overcome [4:23]. Belcher's temporary blindness (soon to become permanent) is emphasized just before he utters one of the most insightful sentences in the entire story.

4:15. "I NEVER COULD MAKE OUT WHAT DUTY WAS MYSELF." This statement, of course, strongly echoes Bonaparte's own earlier thought [3:7]—although Belcher's phrasing, typically, lacks the anger felt by Bonaparte. Bonaparte's thought had served as an implicit indictment of Donovan; Belcher's comment, instead, expresses his own sense of puzzlement. Again O suggests that these two men are on the same wave-length, that they share many of the same values, instincts, and assumptions. Once more Belcher uses a term ("'lads'") that reminds us of the tragic youth of his executioners. Appropriately, Belcher dies in silence, having finished his sentence (Hawkins, appropriately, had died in mid-sentence [4:7]). Appropriately, too, Belcher's last words sum up his entire attitude toward life: "'I'm not complaining.'" His lack of self-pity, paradoxically, makes his death seem all the more lamentable and sad.

4:16. NOBLE, JUST AS IF HE COULDN'T BEAR ANY MORE OF IT, RAISED HIS FIST. Earlier, just before Hawkins was shot, Noble had raised his head as if to speak but then had lowered it again [4:5]. Here he communicates without speaking, his gesture perhaps indicating both anger and pain. The description of Belcher's death (the "big man went over like a sack of meal") is extremely powerful. It reminds us, of course, of Belcher's imposing size, but it thereby also emphasizes the contrast between his bulky body and his delicate soul—between his large physique and his fine and subtle character. O's simile might seem to imply an undignified, almost grotesquely comical death, but in fact the phrasing underscores the difference between Belcher as a physical body and Belcher as a human being, whose complexities of personality we have just glimpsed. The emphasis on the victims as physical bodies then continues as Bonaparte describes the awful task of actually having to touch and carry the corpses. Apparently Belcher and Hawkins are buried together (appropriately enough) in a single grave—joined forever in death as they had briefly been joined in life. (Could this image possibly look back to Bonaparte and Noble apparently sharing the same bed [2:22]?) By describing the atmosphere after the killings as "all mad lonely," O not only uses idiomatic phrasing very effectively (the jumbled syntax reflects Bonaparte's mental confusion) but also, of course, makes explicit one of the central themes of the story and one of the central themes of all his fiction: the essential loneliness of the human condition, the fundamental solitariness of each human soul [2:10; 4:7]. The phrase also anticipates the very closing sentences of the entire story [4:23]. O's reference to the "patch of lantern life between ourselves and the dark" looks back to the image with which this section of the story began [4:1], and the phrasing is also obviously symbolic and metaphorical: Bonaparte and Noble are about to enter, literally and figuratively, into a newly dark period of their lives. The image of the birds "hooting and screeching all round" makes powerfully literal one of the main themes of the story: the violation and disruption of the natural order, the disturbance of what the old woman had long ago termed the "hidden powers" [1:49]. Conventionally, birds symbolize the spirit or soul, and so the disturbance of these birds suggests a far more fundamental disturbance. It is almost as if nature cries out against the killings, and, as the last paragraph of the story suggests, the disturbance lasts for a good while, since the birds are still shrieking after the Irishmen return to the cottage [4:23].

4:17. NOBLE WENT THROUGH HAWKINS'S BELONGINGS. It seems fitting that Noble should be the last person to attend to Hawkins, with whom he had developed such a close friendship. The reference to the letter to Hawkins's mother reminds us again of that feisty man's tender side and thus of his complex character [4:11]. The fact that Noble joins together the hands of Hawkins, the atheist, is richly ironic. This is probably not the way Hawkins would have preferred to be buried, but Noble's gesture indicates his own sincere concern and respect for his friend as well as his tendency to rely on conventional gestures for consolation [4:20]. As will soon become apparent, Bonaparte will feel unable to take any comfort in such conventional piety [4:21]. Throughout the story we had seen Jeremiah Donovan make entrances [1:10; 2:2; 3:1]; now, near the end, we see him leave. O dismisses him in a single short sentence, subtly underlining his essential unimportance both as a character and as a human being, and also effectively suggesting that for Donovan this event will have no long-term psychological consequences. For him the killings are over; for Bonaparte and Noble, the killings will never cease to prey upon their consciences and consciousness. The placing of the tools back in the shed is a common, mundane image that thereby emphasizes, by contrast, the horrible uniqueness of the event just ended. Bonaparte and Noble will be unable to shut away their thoughts as easily as they have shut away their tools. Their silence here reminds us of the last time they really talked with one another—on the night when they learned that they might have to participate in the execution they now have just concluded.

4:18. THE KITCHEN WAS DARK AND COLD AS WE'D LEFT IT. This detail is just one of many ways in which O uses change in the story's setting to emphasize the more important changes in tone and meaning. Whereas the cottage was once warm, bright, enclosed, and filled with activity and the sounds of laughter and talk, now it is cold, dark, still, silent, and exposed to the elements. Here again the darkness and cold are more than literal; they figuratively symbolize the Irishmen's changed feelings and perceptions. The fact that the warm-hearted old woman sits over the now-cold hearth (of all places) seems significant: literally the fire has gone out of the story; her presence there emphasizes the cold that has now descended on the cottage. The fact that she is "saying her beads" instantly implies what soon becomes apparent: that she already knows about the killings (despite Donovan's concern to keep them quiet [3:2, 3]), and that she regards the executions as an affront not only to nature (as the disturbed birds have implied) but to God. The fact that the executed men were, quite literally, "guests" in her house probably exacerbates her pain. By walking past her, Bonaparte and Noble try at first to pretend as if nothing has changed, as if they can literally put the matter behind them. Here as earlier, however, she functions as a voice (and symbol) of conscience [1:50; 3:4]. Noble's initially unsuccessful attempt to light the lamp seems highly symbolic; he will never again experience the consistent brightness O had sketched so effectively in the opening scene.

4:19. "WHAT DID YE DO WITH THEM?" SHE ASKED IN A WHISPER. Paradoxically, the quietness of the question makes it all the more powerful; her subdued tone suggests that she already knows the answer, and her whispered expression makes the question far more (unintentionally) cutting than if she had asked it in a louder, angrier tone. Both the tone and the question obviously disturb Noble, and the fact that the light literally goes out when he hears it is obviously symbolic. Significantly, the religious old woman addresses her question to the equally religious Noble:

they share the same values and beliefs, and she probably finds it especially difficult to believe (as he probably does himself) that he has participated in this act, especially since the old woman has heard him repeatedly defend his Christian views against the challenges of an atheist. He must thus feel doubly hypocritical—as if he has betrayed not only a friend but also his loudly professed faith. At first Noble pretends not to have heard the question, but the pretense is effectively undercut by the old woman's simple statement that she has heard him putting the tools away. Her repetition of the simple, three-word phrase "I heard ye" is devastatingly effective in a way that longer, more involved phrasing could never have been. Noble thinks of himself as a thoughtful, educated man, but her plain words cut him to the quick, even though her tone is subdued and not emphatically accusatory. He feels accused more by his own conscience than by the old woman. Noble's successful lighting of the lamp on the second try now seems powerfully ironic, since in a moment he will be plunged into a dark night of the soul of the sort he has never before known.

4:20. "WAS THAT WHAT YE DID WITH THEM?" SHE ASKED. The very vagueness of her phrasing ("'that'") gives the question force, not only implying that she cannot bring herself to speak of the specific act but also suggesting that she *need* not speak of it, that they understand her only too well. This sentence, like so much in the final scene, perfectly illustrates O's talent for understatement, restraint, and subtle implication. Her question implies both her knowledge and her disbelief. The next sentence is very carefully constructed, so that the crucial act (her falling to her knees) is delayed, being preceded by several brief intervening clauses that lend the sentence both suspense and irony. The interjection "by God" exemplifies O's verbal skill: in one way the phrase functions as merely a conventional, idiomatic expression of surprise; in another way it is perfectly appropriate to the old woman's behavior; in another way still it sounds ironic, issuing as it does from the agnostic Bonaparte, whose inability to accept or embrace the consolation of Christian prayer will soon become apparent [4:21]. The old woman literally collapses, as all of them must at this point feel like doing, but her literal fall symbolizes her spiritual strength, the sincerity of her devotion to the "hidden powers" she had invoked earlier in the story [1:49]. (However, her reference to those "powers" makes her behavior here seem more complex, less dogmatic and less limited, than a mere Christian reflex. Once again she seems to embody a deep wisdom that transcends any particular creed.) Noble's delay in imitating the old woman can be explained in several ways: perhaps he feels unworthy to imitate her; perhaps his faith has been shaken so that he feels at first unable to imitate her; perhaps he feels at first too sophisticated to engage in such a simple response to the event. Perhaps all these explanations apply. In any case, he does eventually join her in prayer—although it is significant that even the prayers are solitary and isolated (once again reinforcing O's theme of loneliness). The effect would have been totally different if he had (say) knelt down beside her and joined hands with her. Each of them appeals to God alone (in both senses of "alone"). When the story opened, the activities of the characters had been communal, loud, and literally playful; now the activities of the survivors are isolated, silent, and extremely solemn.

4:21. I PUSHED MY WAY OUT PAST HER AND LEFT THEM AT IT. The first verb here suggests Bonaparte's anger and impatience—perhaps as much with himself as with the old woman and Noble. Perhaps he finds it impossible to pray, not only because he finds the act strangely ironic at this point but also because he feels particularly and personally unfit for prayer at this time. The phrase "left them at it" is a wonderful example of O's plain, unadorned style: the very simplicity and vagueness of the words (especially "it") imply Bonaparte's dismissive, resigned, perhaps even contemptuous reaction. Literally but also symbolically, Bonaparte stands at a threshold—neither totally inside nor totally out, neither totally distanced from Noble and the old woman nor closely involved with them. The imagery of the stars reinforces the earlier imagery (in section three and at the beginning of section four) of light engulfed by darkness, even as it also looks forward to Bonaparte's ensuing emphasis on the immensity of the universe and man's comparative smallness. The stars may be taken to suggest fate (an important theme in the story [4:5, 11]), or perhaps they symbolize the beauty and order of the larger universe—a universe from which Bonaparte now feels estranged. The fact that the birds are still "shrieking" underscores the depth of the disturbance they (and the Irishmen) have experienced, although the fact that the birds' shrieks are now "dying out" not only reminds us again of the executions but also highlights an important difference between the birds and the survivors: for the former the killings will be only a temporary disturbance, but for Bonaparte and Noble the disturbance will, in a sense, never completely die out.

4:22. IT IS SO STRANGE WHAT YOU FEEL AT TIMES LIKE THAT THAT YOU CAN'T DESCRIBE IT. Ironically, of course, this statement introduces one of the most powerfully descriptive and affecting pieces of prose O ever composed. Although Bonaparte apparently distances himself from his ensuing statement by twice using the word "you," this paragraph is perhaps the most intensely personal in the entire story. Just as O had in this last section transformed the setting and activities first described in the opening section, so he now transforms the language. When the story began, the language had been colloquial, ordinary, and often light-hearted; now the language becomes poetic, uncommon, and deadly serious. In this final paragraph O uses many standard devices of poetry: striking imagery, powerful similes, insistent, rhythmic repetitions, and even alliteration. The power of such language is enhanced, paradoxically, by the fact that such a style has been relatively absent before this point. Yet the shift to a more poetic style is not an arbitrary choice; instead, it perfectly mirrors the transformation that has taken place within Bonaparte's mind and soul. Just as he no longer feels as he once felt, so his language itself must change. Moreover, just as the events he has just experienced have been strangely unfamiliar and quite literally unique, so his language must be transformed as he attempts to put that experience into words. Like Belcher, who had suddenly (before dying) lost his silence and had become loquacious, so the normally quiet and prosaic Bonaparte here becomes extraordinarily eloquent.

4:23. NOBLE SAYS HE SAW EVERYTHING TEN TIMES THE SIZE. O provides one last indication that Bonaparte and Noble have talked about the experience. The last time we saw them share their feelings in such a way had been, ironically, when they had discussed the mere possibility of the killings [2:23]. Now we intuit that they also have talked in the aftermath of the executions. This later sharing of thoughts, however, has ironically only emphasized once more how isolated each man feels, since each describes his reaction using radically different imagery. For Noble the bog seems overwhelmingly huge; for Bonaparte it seems tiny and remote. In an example of O's stylistic mastery, Bonaparte's description of Noble's perception already is filtered through Bonaparte's own perspective: Noble is said to feel as if "there were nothing in the whole world but that *little patch* of bog" (with the italicized phrase smuggling Bonaparte's view of the matter into his description of Noble's view). O's skill as a stylist is exemplified again by the powerful image of the bodies of the two Englishmen "stiffening into" the bog. The verb suggests the process of rigor mortis, but it also provides one last reminder of the finality of the act, of the ugliness of the killings, of the fact that the Englishmen are now mere bodies, and of the paradox of such stiffening taking place in the spongy soil of a bog. In the long, seemingly endless sentence in which Bonaparte describes his own perception, O pulls out every stylistic stop. Perhaps the most notable stylistic device here is the use of anaphora (the constant repetition of the word "and"), so that the sentence functions almost literally as an example of the stream-of-consciousness technique: the words spill forth onto the page in an apparently unstructured (but actually highly organized) fashion. The language is simultaneously vague ("million miles ... far away ... very small ... very lost") and precise ("mumbling ... birds ... stars ... child ... snow"), thereby allowing us to share the complexity of Bonaparte's feelings, which are simultaneously painful and unfocused. The heavy emphasis on "l" and "s" sounds as the sentence closes emphasizes its status as poetry, while the image of Bonaparte feeling like a "child" ironically symbolizes the newly mature outlook on life into which he has now been initiated. His view of life will never again be as innocent or child-like as it once was, and indeed the long and highly poetic sentence just ended helps emphasize, by contrast, the blunt, prosaic brevity of the story's final statement: "And anything that happened to me afterwards, I never felt the same about again." As a summary sentence, this is masterful, especially in its awkward syntax and its emphasis on the lonely, solitary ego; its stress on being subject to events that seem simply to happen to oneself; the finality of "never" (which again reminds us of Bonaparte's youth at the time of the killings); and the ironic final word "again" (which suggests, significantly enough, a cycle forever broken).[20]

---

[20]For a less sympathetic view of Bonaparte, see Stanley Renner, "The Theme of Hidden Powers," 373.

Selected Stories of Frank O'Connor:
Synopses and Quick Critiques

prepared by

*Curtis Bowden (CB), John M. Burdett (JMB), Robert C.
Evans (RCE), Tasheka Gipson (TG), Ashley Gordon (AG),
Katie Magaw (KM), Karey Oakley (KO), Lane Powell (LP),
Denean Rivera (DR), Dianne Russell (DGR), Claire
Skowronski (CS), Gwendolyn Warde (GW),
and Carolyn T. Young (CTY)*

and by
*Kelly J. Beyer (KJB), Clint Darby (CD), Heather Edwards (HE),
Earl Eidem (EI), Jennifer Henderson (JH), Michael Probst (MP),
Cheri Norwood (CN), Douglas Scarborough (DS),
Angela Soulé (AS), Kalicia K. Spigner (KKS), Clinton
Van Der Pool, Jr. (CV), and Claudia Wilsch (CW)*

Frank O'Connor famously claimed that the essence of a story could be reduced to a few lines, and when composing a tale he would begin with a brief "theme" or plot and proceed from there. The following synopses, in a sense, reverse this process. By offering the barest overviews of many of O'Connor's stories, we hope to achieve several objectives. First, we hope to stimulate further interest in (and enjoyment of) O'Connor's works by making it as easy as possible for potential readers to find the stories that may most intrigue them. Second, by bringing all these synopses together in one convenient place, we hope to offer a quick panorama of O'Connor's career. Third, we hope to indicate concisely the kinds of critical reactions the stories have evoked. We thus offer brisk summaries (mainly paraphrased) of the reactions the stories have generated from some of the most prominent students of O'-Connor's writing. By presenting these summaries we hope to indicate the main concerns of O'Connor's best critics, including their agreements, disagreements, likes, and dislikes. We thereby hope to stimulate further study of O'Connor's works: a reader may, for instance, want to apply the insight offered by one critic about one story to a totally different work; or a reader may want to compare and/or contrast the techniques or themes of two (or more) distinct stories; or a reader may want to dispute or confirm a critic's assessment of some particular work. In offering these synopses and summaries, then, we hope not merely to report information but to provoke further thought and study.

The sources from which critical reactions have been drawn are the following:

Averill, Deborah M. *The Irish Short Story from George Moore to Frank O'Connor*. Washington, DC: University Press of America, 1982.

Hildebidle, John. *Five Irish Writers: The Errand of Keeping Alive*. Cambridge, MA: Harvard University Press, 1989.

Kilroy, James F. "Setting the Standards: Writers of the 1920s and 1930s." In James F. Kilroy, ed., *The Irish Short Story: A Critical History*. Boston: Twayne, 1984. 95–144.

Matthews, James F. *Voices: A Life of Frank O'Connor*. New York: Atheneum, 1987.

Tomory, William M. *Frank O'Connor*. Boston: Twayne, 1980.

Wohlgelernter, Maurice. *Frank O'Connor: An Introduction*. New York: Columbia University Press, 1977.

These basic sources have been supplemented by the following few others:

Bordewyk, Gordon. "Quest for Meaning: The Stories of Frank O'Connor." *Illinois Quarterly* 41 (1978): 37–47.

Chatalic, Roger. "Frank O'Connor and the Desolation of Reality." In Patrick Rafroidi and Terence Brown, ed., *The Irish Short Story*. Atlantic Highlands, NJ: Humanities, 1979. 189–204.

Fallis, Richard. *The Irish Renaissance*. Syracuse, NY: Syracuse University Press, 1977.

Steinman, Michael. *Frank O'Connor at Work*. Syracuse, NY: Syracuse University Press, 1990.

Thompson, Richard. "A Kingdom of Commoners: The Moral Art of Frank O'Connor." *Eire/Ireland* 13 (1978): 65–80.

Warner, Alan. *A Guide to Anglo-Irish Literature*. Dublin: Gill and
   Macmillan, 1981.

Many other valuable critiques of O'Connor's writing are summarized in John C. Kerrigan's detailed bibliography printed elsewhere in this volume. All the critical summaries that follow have
been prepared by Robert Evans (RCE). Synopses of stories have
been prepared by the person(s) whose initials are given in parentheses.

   By scanning the following synopses of stories and summaries
of critics, readers (especially new ones) can gain a good quick
sense of O'Connor's characteristic themes and techniques, particularly during the different phases of his life. For this reason, we
have provided (after the title of each story) two dates in brackets:
first the year of initial publication, then the year of publication *of
the version synopsized here*.[1] Because O'Connor constantly revised
his stories (some as many as fifty times), it seemed to us particularly important to indicate *which* version any particular synopsis
covers. In choosing published volumes with which to work, we
have been deliberately eclectic and have tried to draw on a sampling of volumes, including the following, which are indicated by
italicized abbreviations:

BC = *Bones of Contention* (New York: Macmillan, 1936).

CP = *The Cornet-Player Who Betrayed Ireland* (Dublin: Poolbeg,
   1981).

CS = *Collected Stories* (New York: Random House, 1981).

C3 = *Collection Three* (London: Macmillan, 1969).

CC = *The Common Chord* (London: Macmillan, 1947).

DR = *Domestic Relations* (New York: Knopf, 1957).

GN = *Guests of the Nation* (Dublin: Poolbeg, 1985).

ML = *The Mad Lomasneys and Other Stories from Collection Two*
   (London: Pan, 1970).

MS = *More Stories by Frank O'Connor* (New York: Knopf, 1954).

---

[1]Information about dates has been drawn largely from the bibliography appended to *Michael/Frank: Studies on Frank O'Connor*, ed. Maurice
Sheehy (New York: Knopf, 1969). In the case of some stories not widely
(or not at all) reprinted, we cite the original publication information in
brackets directly after the story's title.

SBFO = *Stories by Frank O'Connor* (New York: Vintage, 1956).

SFO = *The Stories of Frank O'Connor* (New York: Knopf, 1952).

SV = *A Set of Variations* (New York: Knopf, 1969).

TS = *Traveller's Samples* (New York: Knopf, 1951).

V2 = *Collected Stories: Volume Two* (London: Pan, 1990).

Some of O'Connor's stories remain unpublished or un-reprinted. For information about these, as well as for much other helpful data about O'Connor, see the bibliography in *Michael/Frank: Studies on Frank O'Connor*, ed. Maurice Sheehy (New York: Knopf, 1969). When unreprinted stories are synopsized, details of the original publication are provided with the summary. We have not been able to include summaries of *all* the unreprinted or un-published stories.— RCE

ACHILLES' HEEL [1958/1981; *CS*] Celibate priests can be controlled by their female housekeepers, as the elderly Bishop of Moyle was by Nellie Conneely, who prepared him excellent meals. When a local customs offi-cer alleged that Nellie might be involved in smuggling, she slyly manipu-lated the Bishop into suppressing further investigation. Although the Bishop was finally convinced of the charges and Nellie seemed likely to be fined and jailed, the cleric arranged to handle matters more quietly. Even-tually he and Nellie had returned to their old routine. **(RCE) Wohlgelern-ter:** O shows how loneliness makes priests vulnerable to exploitation (58–59).

AN ACT OF CHARITY [1967/1981; *CS*] An unnamed narrator tells how an awkward young priest, persecuted by Father Maginnis (his suave, profes-sional superior) and Father Fogarty (Maginnis's partner), eventually committed suicide. The two priests worked to make the suicide seem a natural death and thus prevent a scandal. Maginnis, who saw the cover-up as an "act of charity," pressured the local doctor into signing an inac-curate death certificate, and when the undertaker arrived, he reacted without emotion, as if he had handled such cases before. Although Foga-rty grew increasingly disturbed, the only person he could speak with honestly was the doctor. In the end, Fogarty mused on life's loneliness. **(AS) Averill:** In one of his darkest tales, O shows Fogarty moving from comfortable membership in a group to lonely isolation (291). **Hildebidle:** The story deals with conflicting responsibilities (197). Ironically, Fogarty's sense of personal guilt encourages his posthumous concern for the young priest's reputation (197). **Matthews:** The story is based on a true incident (363). **Tomory:** One of a series of Fogarty stories, this work addresses a forbidden subject (121). **Wohlgelernter:** The final "act of charity" is espe-cially ironic in light of the priests' initial lack of charity (55).

ADVENTURE [*Atlantic Monthly* (January 1953): 47–51] Mick recalls how, when he was twenty, he witnessed the courtship of Doris Beirne by two rivals, the local Irish shopkeeper Tom Diamond and the English businessman Martin Holmes. Craving excitement, Mick himself felt simultaneously drawn to and repelled by the boisterous, extroverted Holmes while dismissing the quiet, unassuming Diamond. As the events surrounding Doris's engagement to Holmes culminated in tragedy, Mick learned not only the true depths of Diamond's steady character and Holmes's unstable nature, but a new meaning of "adventure" as well. **(CS)**

THE ADVENTURESS [a 1948 version of "Lady Brenda"]

AFTER FOURTEEN YEARS [1929/1985; *GN*] When Nicholas Coleman visited a woman with whom he had once been close but who had long since joined a convent, the two reminisced about family, friends, and old times. Both had settled into predictable routines, but on the ride home Nicholas could not help recalling, with sadness, his memories of a more vivid past. **(RCE) Bordewyk:** Theme: the need to take risks and live fully (46). **Tomory:** too didactic, the story suffers from simplistic characters (35). **Wohlgelernter:** Theme: the disappointments of withdrawal from life (78).

ALEC [1931/1985; *GN*] The narrator remembers Alec Gorman as a spirited lad who befriended old women, fiercely protected his reputation, argued with his parents, and led daring sabotage raids during the insurrection. However, after Gorman and his comrades were captured, Alec suffered from repeated beatings and sickness in prison. When he was suddenly released, his fellow prisoners suspected that he had turned informer, but later they learned the details of his dramatic escape and successful revenge. **(RCE) Averill:** The narrator has mixed feelings about Alec (249). **Matthews:** As in other early stories, the presentation is idealized and undisciplined (69). **Tomory:** Theme: the dark tragedy of war (33).

THE AMERICAN WIFE [1961/1969; *SV*] An unnamed narrator describes a trip by a first-generation American girl, Elsie Colleary, to her father's Irish homeland. While there, she meets and marries Tom Barry. Although she had admired Irish men when she was in America, after her marriage she becomes dissatisfied with Irish life. Returning to America to give birth, she hopes that Tom will also come. When he stays, she comes back with the baby. Elsie goes back to America again for the birth of their second child. Although the same pattern is repeated during her second pregnancy, during the third she makes a different decision. **(TG) Averill:** Once more O depicts a neurotic, masochistic woman whose morbid idealism leads her to reject reality (301). **Hildebidle:** The story illustrates how badly foreigners tend to adapt to Ireland in O's fiction (176). The wife considers the Irish son's focus on his mother unnatural, unhealthy, and self-destructive (181–82). To Elsie, Ireland seems middle-aged (186). **Kil-**

roy: Despite a negative environment, the husband develops attractive qualities. Like similar stories, this one progresses toward a clear, unsurprising statement of theme (119).

ANCHORS [1952/1990; C2] An unnamed young man, disgusted with his mother and her religion, eventually abandons his faith altogether. Yet his father, rather than becoming upset, seems to understand and offers him religious books to study. Consequently he becomes almost a religious fanatic: he challenges his mother's beliefs—especially about whether her dead child is in heaven or in limbo. Then, again deciding that he has lost his faith, he thinks that he is free. But after talking with his father, he realizes that his father expects that when he marries, the young man's wife will resemble his mother while he will resemble his father. The young man feels concerned: he cannot believe that his own wife could be so irrational or that he could prove so weak. **(DGR) Matthews:** In this "atheist club" story, the father encourages his son not to confuse lack of faith in clerics with lack of faith in God (274).

AND WE IN HERDS THY GAME [a version of "The Shepherds"]

ANDROCLES AND THE ARMY [1958/1981; CS] When John Cloone (a lion tamer for a small traveling circus) decided to join the army, his boss, Ned Healy, was distressed. Cloone nevertheless went off for training and soon became a corporal, but when the circus showed up near his camp, he could not resist paying an unexpectedly tumultuous visit to the lions he loved. **(CV) Wohlgelernter:** This funny story emphasizes the power of affection and compassion (37–38).

ATTACK [1931/1985; GN] Owen tells how he and Lomasney, planning to help attack a nearby police station, stayed overnight in the house of Mike Kieran, a cantankerous old man whose son, Paddy (wanted for an accidental killing), had fled to America years ago and had not been heard from since. After the men slept awhile they awoke, only to catch Mike in a loft, caring for the feeble, emaciated Paddy while the boy's old mother cried. Mike now endorsed the killing of the police, while Lomasney contemplated Mike's future usefulness to the cause. **(RCE) Tomory:** The conclusion is forced and unpersuasive (31).

THE AWAKENING [*Dublin Magazine* 3.3 (July 1928): 31–38] Shortly before having to depart from Cork for America, Eileen began to reflect on her relations with her community, her mother, her suitor (a shy man named Jim), and Madge, her older sister. Just as she had begun to see them freshly, she realized that she would have to leave them. She felt sure that even if she someday returned she would not be the same person, and that in dating Jim she had been motivated by a desire to hold on to a part of her past. **(RCE)**

THE BABES IN THE WOOD [1947/1981; *CS*] Five-year-old Terry always looked forward to his aunt's Sunday visits. During one visit, she secretly told him that a generous Englishman wanted to marry her and give Terry a home and presents. Later, Terry's friend Florrie said that his aunt was really his mother. Eventually the aunt arrived with kindly Mr. Walker. Because Terry greatly liked him, he asked if Mr. Walker were planning to marry the aunt, whom Terry revealed was really his mother. After that, his aunt did not come again, although Terry watched and waited. Florrie finally revealed that the planned marriage had been broken off at the insistence of the aunt's mother, because Mr. Walker was a Protestant and was in any case already married. The aunt subsequently married her employer, who wanted proper children rather than Terry. Florrie explained that she and Terry were not proper children, but she promised to be his girl again if he would swear to be always constant. **(CTY) Averill:** O often attacked the poor treatment of illegitimate children and unmarried mothers; this is one of his most poignant works (277). The third-person narration makes the implied criticisms all the more effective, and the remote setting (particularly the woods) enhances the motif of isolation (277). The mother is irresponsible, while Florrie is possessive and jealous (278). The narrative perspective effectively widens as the story ends (279). **Hildebidle:** Here again O emphasizes family (179). **Matthews:** *The New Yorker* welcomed this story, O's first about illegitimate children (224). Although sentimental, it typifies O's focus on the need for love (234).

A BACHELOR'S STORY [1955/1957; *DR*] Larry describes how Archie Boland, an opinionated bachelor, developed an absolute distrust and disdain for the "abominable" nature of women. When Archie met Madge Hale, a young school teacher, he became convinced that she suitably matched his old-fashioned ideals: she was not only intelligent but also conscientious, virtuous, and simple. When he proposed to her, she (after some unexplained hesitation) accepted. He soon discovered, however, that she was already engaged. Unable to accept Madge's desperate and perhaps even compassionate explanations of her deception, Archie abandoned her. **(KM) Matthews:** Some characters reflect aspects of O and his friends (306). **Tomory:** Archie's self-centeredness and lack of passion condemn him to isolation (107).

BAPTISMAL [*American Mercury* (March 1951): 319–27] Mick Mahoney recalls how, when he was eighteen, he and Peter Daly (an experienced Brigade Commander in the Irish Republican Army) exchanged gunfire with English soldiers. The skirmish set off a chain of deadly events throughout the rest of the pleasant March day. Mick's rite of passage ultimately culminated in three fatalities, including the death of a child; collectively, these sealed his "baptism by fire" into the IRA way of life (and death). **(CS)**

THE BLACK DROP [Untraced]

BONES OF CONTENTION [1932/1936; *BC*] An unnamed narrator describes an old lady, a friend of his feisty grandmother. Having lost all three sons to war and been left with a long-distant daughter, she approached death almost alone. When the old woman died, the bed-ridden grandmother insisted on escorting the body to the grave. During the journey, irate and drunken relatives of the old woman ambushed the hearse, claiming that her body was being stolen. A gathering crowd, at first sympathetic to the relatives, were soon won over by the spirited grandmother. Nevertheless, the relatives made off with the body. Although the whole scene acutely embarrassed her son, her grandson valued the adventure. Three weeks later, the family made another trip to the cemetery. **(DR) Matthews:** Based on a real anecdote, the story reflects O's own grandmother; the ironic title emphasizes the trivial events described (110).

THE BOOK OF KINGS [read on Radio Eireann, 15 November 1940]

THE BRIDAL NIGHT [1939/1981; *CS*] Recalled by an unnamed narrator, an elderly Irish mother in a remote coastal village describes the tragic fate of her son Denis, now committed to a mental asylum in Cork. When a friendly and somewhat wealthy schoolteacher, Winnie Regan, came to the village, Denis would often talk with her. Although his mother and Miss Regan teased about Denis being the young woman's "beau," the relationship at first seemed simple. However, when both women realized that Denis was falling in love with Miss Regan, she began to keep her distance and the mother tried to distract her increasingly agitated son. One night, however, Denis suffered a violent breakdown. After being subdued and restrained, Denis asked that the ropes be undone, and his mother agreed despite the neighbors' misgivings. When he began to cry out for Winnie, she was sent for. After Denis implored her to climb into bed next to him, she willingly did so, and he slept the rest of the night peacefully. The next morning he was taken calmly away. No one in the village ever criticized her decision. **(RCE) Averill:** This simple, poignant tale (which echoes Daniel Corkery's "Storm-Struck") focuses on a transforming moment (270). O effectively uses local color, idealized characters, natural imagery (especially birds), lyrical diction, and final darkness (271). The story's technique resembles oral legend (271). **Matthews:** O later rejected such emotional stories (155), preferring technique over feeling (176). The emotion seems appropriate, however, and the story is cathartic. Telling the tale comforts the old woman (202). **Thompson:** This work is "a brief, major effort, a gem" (75). **Tomory:** The narrator is organically linked to the tale (77). Sentimentality is avoided; emotions are presented with objective control (96).

BRIEF FOR OEDIPUS [version of "Counsel for Oedipus"]

THE CALL [1971/1981; *CP*] Paddy Verchoyle watched as his reclusive, religious brother-in-law, Declan, developed a close friendship with the assertive Mick Ring. When Mick announced his plans to join the Cistercians, Declan soon followed suit. Stopping for drinks on the drive to the monastery, the three men argued about life, then Paddy left the drunken novitiates in the care of a kindly monk. Although the lives of Declan and Mick eventually took unexpected turns, all three men seemed to have been affected by their discussion. **(LP)**

A CASE FOR THE ROARER [version of "Legal Aid"]

A CASE OF CONSCIENCE [1970/1981; *CP*] Dan Marlow, a milkman, delivered to a convent school in London. After two years of visiting there, he became acquainted with Sister Agatha, a young Irish nun who had recently arrived. She had begun to feel terribly alienated from her English sisters as well as from her faith. Marlow, an atheist, found himself supporting Sister Agatha's principles and ultimately urging and aiding her to escape. Sister Agatha assured him that God would not forget his gracious act. **(CD)**

THE CHEAPJACK [1942/1981; *CS*] Everyone pitied the blunt headmaster, Sam Higgins. When a new teacher was appointed without his being told, Sam suspected that Carmody had been sent to spy on him by the parish priest. Carmody, who constantly wrote in a diary, even supplanted Sam in courting Nancy McCann, a widowed teacher. Angry and despairing, Sam accidentally discovered Carmody's diary, which revealed how the other man sought to exploit Nancy. In dictation class, Sam read aloud from the diary of the "cheapjack," and when Carmody heard him, a fight ensued. After breaking up the scuffle, the women teachers left Sam alone. Gathering his things, he dropped off his keys, went home, took an early train the next morning, and never returned. The community pitied a man who was so decent but too honest. **(CTY) Averill:** The story typifies O's focus on failed love (271).

THE CHEAT [1965/1981; *CS*] An unnamed narrator tells of the marriage of Dick Gordon and Barbara Hough. Dick had been a principled atheist since age eighteen, but Barbara's atheism was more vague. After their marriage and the birth of their son, Barbara began to feel a need for religious belief and secretly converted to Catholicism. Although Dick felt betrayed, he held his tongue and even allowed his son to be sent to a religious school. A few years later, when he became terminally ill with cancer, Dick became the object of various efforts to convert him. He was even visited by a priest who informed him of his impending death and warned him to convert, but Dick refused. Barbara was shocked when she learned of the priest's bluntness, so when another priest, a friend, stopped by for a drink with Dick, she worried about his intentions. The priest, assuring her that he had come for a drink only, expressed confidence in Dick's salvation. He suspected that Barbara's view of her conversion had now changed. **(EI) Kilroy:** In one of O's last stories, "complementary themes—love, regret at past mistakes, responsibility to others and to self—are integrated and resolved" (119–20). **Matthews:** O sympathized with Dick, perhaps because he also found himself surrounded by the religious (362). When the story was rejected, O lost confidence (364). **Wohlgelernter:** Like other stories by O, this one explores the unfortunate influence of the church on love. O depicts the conversion as involving a loss of paradise. The cheating wife in turn feels cheated in the end (67).

CHRISTMAS MORNING [1946/1981; *CS*] Larry describes his childhood disdain for his younger brother, Sonny, whom he considered a know-it-all, show-off, and mother's pet. Certain that he could persuade Santa Claus of his own merit if he could just stay awake long enough to intercept the old man, Larry unfortunately fell asleep, only to discover on Christmas morning a book in his own stocking and a pop-gun in Sonny's. Reasoning that Sonny would make better use of the book, Larry switched the presents, but when their mother recognized the deceit, Larry suddenly and painfully realized how much he had disappointed her, since she probably feared he would resemble his selfish, untrustworthy father. **(RCE) Bordewyk:** Theme: overcoming negative legacies as a way to maturation (44). **Matthews:** The story is based on a real incident (224).

THE CLIMBER [*Harper's Bazaar* (April 1940): 91; 131; 134] Cultures clashed when Josie Mangan and her little brother Jackie met the Donoghue brothers outside one day. Coveting their "respectability," Josie coerced Jackie into acting like the proper little Donoghues. When her widowed father pursued Mrs. Donoghue's hand in marriage, however, Josie decided that the price of "respectability" was too high, and she plotted against the poor Donoghue boys to break up her father's romance with their mother. By the end of the tale her old man had returned to his old self. **(CS)**

THE CONVERSION [*Harper's Bazaar* (March 1951): 161; 367–68] A middle-aged Irish Catholic narrator recounts a bicycle trip he made through the French countryside on Holy Thursday accompanied by his older Irish Protestant friend Géronte. Churches dotting the landscape remained empty even during the Christian holy days for want of permanent parish priests. Joined on their trip by a young French organist, who proclaimed himself an atheist, the men happened across a church where a lone, nondescript priest celebrated a service attended by a few disinterested parishioners. The priest's faith in his service to God affected each of the three travelers in profoundly different ways. **(CS) Matthews:** The story reveals the rarely seen humble side of O's personality; he appreciates the priest as another lone artist (262).

THE CORKERYS [1966/1981; *CS*] May, the only child of Jack and Margaret MacMahon, was an intelligent girl who enjoyed reading books on psychology. She became friendly with the Corkery family. The elder Corkerys were involved in vocations in the Church. Over the years, May watched as all of the sisters and brothers except Peter (now responsible for caring for the family) entered the convents or monasteries. Feeling that she would never attract Peter's attention because she thought him homosexual, May also joined a convent. After some thinking, she began to feel depressed. She was transferred to a sanitarium and, upon recovery, was released from the order. Although her life becomes commonplace, ironic twists of fate present her with a happier ending. **(KJB)**

THE CORNET PLAYER WHO BETRAYED IRELAND [1947/1981; *CS*] A nameless son recounts how Mick Twomey, a cornet player in an Irishtown band, attempted to ignore the growing and divisive political unrest by pretending that "music is above politics." Because Twomey's phlegmatic attitude was causing him to lose his son's admiration, when the man was asked to play for a political foe, he had to choose between upholding his political convictions (and thus regaining his son's respect) or being known as a traitor to Ireland. **(KKS)**

COUNSEL FOR OEDIPUS [1954/1981; *CS*] An unnamed male narrator opines that men don't stand a chance in divorce court, especially since judges automatically sympathize with women. When Ted Lynam's wife testified about her husband's physical abuse and adultery, the case seemed lost. Then his normally hapless lawyer, Mickey Joe Dougherty, methodically managed to depict the woman as a controlling shrew. Just when the case seemed won, though, the couple reconciled—further proof that men can't win. **(RCE) Averill:** A humorous, slightly satiric portrait of love (298). **Hildebidle:** This unappealing, vituperative, anti-feminine story shows O's dark, even mean side; the treatment of Mrs. Lynam ironically resembles the abuse of O's mother by O's father (192). Typically, O begins by stating a moral (198). **Wohlgelernter:** O shows that law courts cannot impose order on complex human emotions (105–6).

CROSSROADS [version of "First Love"]

THE CUSTOM OF THE COUNTRY [1947/1976; *ML*] When Anna Martin, a young Irish Catholic, fell in love with an older English Protestant, Ernest Thompson (who desired her sexually), she thought they would never be able to marry, and indeed Anna's ironic and socially conscious mother insisted that Ernest had to convert. Although the opinionated Ernest failed to be persuaded by a local nun, he was eventually won over by a young priest. Just when marriage seemed likely, however, Anna discovered that Ernest was already married and had two children. Pregnant and alone, Anna returned home, where she felt mocked by her mother and neighbors. Finally, however, she decided to reject social and religious restraints, follow her heart, and reestablish contact with Ernest. **(KO) Averill:** O satirizes the pettiness and malice of small-town Irish life; the objective narrator implicitly sides with Ernest's liberal views (283). The revised version presents a stronger narrator, a clearer story-line, and greater humor and satire (283–84). Eventually Anna frees herself from the narrow attitudes of her mother and town (285). **Bordewyk:** Anna succeeds by transcending restrictions (46). **Matthews:** The story deals explicitly with sexuality (224). **Thompson:** Theme: warring Irish customs—inhibition vs. flight from mother (78). **Wohlgelernter:** Even here O is not interested in religious dogma for its own sake (46).

DARCY IN THE LAND OF YOUTH [1949/1981; *CS*] During World War II Mick Darcy worked in England, where he felt lonely until he met Janet, an experienced girl, and her "inhibited" friend, Fanny. Shocked by Janet's casual view of sex, Mick argued on behalf of more traditional values. After a return to Ireland, though, he found himself attracted to more liberated views, and he convinced a friend to come back with him and meet Fanny. On a vacation the two men bedded their girls, but just when Mick was feeling like a man of the world, he heard Janet crying: she now regretted falling short of Mick's earlier ideals, and in the end they began to consider marriage. **(RCE) Tomory:** This humorous tale emphasizes the loss (and value) of innocence while exploring Irish ideas of affection, decorum, and manhood (110). **Matthews:** O originally wrote such works for an English market but later tired of writing "dirty" stories (234).

A DAY AT THE SEASIDE [a version of "Old Fellows"]

DAYDREAMS [1957/1957; *DR*] When Larry Delaney, an unemployed young man absorbed in the reverie of his youthful idealism, unknowingly became involved in a dispute over money between a defenseless prostitute and her dishonest procurer, he was surprised by his valiant efforts to retrieve the woman's hard-earned money. Indeed, he felt elated at having fulfilled his heroic self-expectations. However when, after much hesitation, he accepted payment for his chivalry, he lost much of his earlier self-respect. **(KM) Averill:** An autobiographical story (295). **Matthews:** The work reflects O's interest in, but distrust of, dreams and dreaming (314). **Tomory:** The story seems forced and unpersuasive (108).

DON JUAN (RETIRED) [1947/1981; *CS*] Joe French visited his neighborhood tavern one night where, as usual, middle-aged Spike Ward was regaling patrons with his intimate knowledge of women. The bartender demanded proof, and Joe wagered that Spike could not entice even one decent woman in the town. His pride hurt, Spike left, followed by Joe. As they walked, Spike spotted an attractive young woman, left Joe behind, engaged her in conversation, went behind a wall with her, and emerged an hour later. Joe paid off the bet, his general view of women greatly lowered. **(RCE) Averill:** One of only a few stories by O in which sex does not lead to a lasting link (282). **MATTHEW:** O's first effort at depicting an Irish tomcat (224). The sexual views here seem blunt but immature (233). **Wohlgelernter:** The story does not endorse Spike's cynicism (106–7).

DON JUAN'S APPRENTICE (version of "The Sorcerer's Apprentice")

DON JUAN'S TEMPTATION [1947/1981; *CS*] An exasperated narrator describes how Gussie Leonard, a confident and successful ladies' man, took a liking to a natural, innocent girl named Helen. After he made his sexual interest clear, the two traded gibes—Helen defending romance, Gussie preferring sensuality (including adultery). After they parted, Gussie began to feel real affection for the principled Helen, who reminded him of a girl he loved when he was younger. Reaching his door, however, he found Helen waiting, ready to spend the night. He almost thanked his "guardian angel" for protecting him from the temptation of love. **(RCE)** **Averill:** This story violates O's usual preference for community and marriage (282). **Kilroy:** By including the provincial narrator, O allows for irony and ambivalence (112). **Matthews:** Based partly on a true anecdote and on O's own affairs, the story's cynicism is balanced by "grim faith in the ability of love to ease ... radical loneliness" (233). **Hildebidle:** Here sex seems routine and lonely and provides no real escape (187). **Tomory:** Revisions made the story more vigorous and immediate yet also less swiftly compelling; the over-elaborate revision states its theme too openly (81–82). The story exemplifies O's usual concerns with loneliness, romanticism vs. realism, and innocence vs. experience (111). It implies that humans are attracted to ideals that may seem unrealistic but that help give life some meaning (112).

THE DRUNKARD [1948/1981; *CS*] Larry Delaney recalls his father, Mick, a working man who was kind to his family and neighbors until he drank. After the funeral of a friend, Mick (accompanied by Larry, who had been sent along as a preventative measure) met a drinking buddy and settled into a binge. Although bribed with lemonade, Larry soon grew bored and decided to sample his father's porter. After downing a pint he was drunk, sick, unsteady, and being pulled toward home by his father. Then, bawling out a few choice tunes and words (to the amusement of the neighbors), he was put to bed. Although his mother was initially upset, the event turned out to be the perfect end to a nearly disastrous day. **(HE)** **Kilroy:** The viewpoint of the boy (who occupies the father's role) complicates and enriches the treatment of alcoholism (114–15). **Matthews:** O claimed the story was autobiographical (230); perhaps it exorcises O's own fear of disappointing his mother (266). **Tomory:** Although this is one of O's best humorous stories, the walk home is over-done. Yet the sentimentality is countered by the engaging narrative voice (126–27).

THE DUKE'S CHILDREN [1956/1957; *DR*] Larry Delaney recalls how, as a boy, he considered himself superior to his parents, even thinking he had been switched with another child at birth. He dreamed that one day he would discover his true lofty family. Larry's disdain for his parents (particularly his father) affected his courtships with neighborhood girls. Only when his smugness was matched by that of a sweetheart did he realize the vanity of his vanity. **(GW) Averill:** This work seems more obviously autobiographical than some earlier Delaney stories, and it may also be less subtle, less objective, and less satisfactory in its less-than-healthy resolution; Larry seems more self-forgiving in this tale (295). **Kilroy:** O balances the boyish narrative tone by ending with serious, considered commentary (117). **Matthews:** The story was inspired by an incident in which O's adolescent son seemed embarrassed by his father's appearance (307–8). In this splendid tale, which emphasizes guilt, self-forgiveness, and the need for love, O uses the Larry persona to be both personal and distanced (310–11).

THE ENGLISH SOLDIER [1934/1936; *BC*] Cissie Dorgan, seeking to hoodwink her English soldier (who wanted to meet a real Irish mother), pretended that Mrs. Donegan was her mother. Mrs. Donegan initially agreed to the deceit but later regretted it and was embarrassed in the Englishman's company. Unfortunately for Mrs. Donegan, the English soldier took a liking to her family and continued to visit, even when Cissie no longer interested him. Gradually the Donegan family came to care for the soldier. Later, when they learned that he had died in war, they discovered that he knew of the deceit and apparently thought no less of them for it. **(DR) Matthews:** The story reflects O's war-time imprisonment and relations with his father (109). **Tomory:** The story is clearly weak (76).

ETERNAL TRIANGLE [1951/1981; *CS*] An unnamed watchman recalls how, during a period of political violence, he was ordered to keep an eye on a disabled tram in the center of the city, where a disorderly gun battle had broken out between two factions. Determined to do his job, he hunkered down on the bus and was eventually joined by a prostitute and an incoherent drunk. Surrounded by gunfire and the burning city, they spent the night in oddly inconsequential talk. **(RCE) Wohlgelernter:** In this exuberantly funny tale, O expresses his disgust with human pettiness, meanness, and violence (39–40).

EXPECTATION OF LIFE [1955/1981; *CS*] Although Shiela Hennessey loved Matt Sheridan, she long dallied with other men. When she announced her intent to marry Jim Gaffney, a contractor twenty years her senior, Matt angrily moved away. Jim and Shiela enjoyed a happy marriage, and when Matt returned, Shiela encouraged him to marry Kitty O'Malley, a young friend of Jim. When Kitty unexpectedly died, Shiela assumed that she and Matt would marry when the aging Jim passed on. Jim and Matt reacted differently, however, to an unexpected event. **(RCE) Averill:** Here again O focuses on a woman whose idealism is masochistic (301). **Hildebidle:** Theme: the power of routines (191). **Kilroy:** Using an assured narrative tone and ending with conflicting points of view, O explores the theme of sacrificing the present for an imagined future (117–18). **Matthews:** The story may reflect O's relations with his young second wife (306–7).

Wohlgelernter: Shiela makes herself unhappy by failing to be satisfied with the limits and uncertainties of life (107–8).

THE FACE OF EVIL [1954/1990; *V2*] An unnamed "saint" and altar boy recounts his apparently contradictory admiration for Charlie Dalton, the local bully. One night, on the way to confession, the narrator saw Charlie and stopped to talk. Noticing all the "ticks" in the narrator's notebook of wrong-doings, Charlie realized the traits they shared and decided to go along to confession. Ultimately the story reveals the reason for the narrator's admiration and further traits the boys shared. **(JMB) Tomory:** Theme: innocence versus experience (128).

FAITH MOVED HIS DICTIONARIES [*Everyman*, 10 May 1935] A man named Dillon describes his friend Tom Harvey, a salesman of dictionaries whose faith in his product explained his success. He recounts Harvey's exasperated tales about the difficulty of selling the books to pub owners, including one old woman whose daughter could have used one. **(RCE)**

FATHER AND SON [1954; *MS*] When Min, Dan's former wife, expressed an interest in visiting their children during the holidays, Dan's new wife, Mildred, volunteered to spend the time elsewhere, even though Dan felt uncomfortable being alone with his ex-spouse. When Min arrived, she was greeted warmly by her daughter, Bawn, but cooly by her son, Tim. Eventually, after Dan and Tim talked frankly one night, Tim's whole attitude changed. **(RCE) Averill:** This is one of several stories about families that emphasizes an adult viewpoint and a personal (rather than social) perspective (197). **Matthews:** The story reflects O's conversations with his own son after O's divorce (298). **Wohlgelernter:** O here depicts a positive relationship between father and son (90–91).

FATHER FOGARTY'S ISLAND [a version of "The Mass Island]

FIRST CONFESSION [1935/1981; *CS*] Jackie recalls how, when he was a young boy, his hated grandmother, the cause of all his sins, made him fear his first confession. The terror was exacerbated by his religion instructor, who threatened that one bad confession could lead to a burning eternity in hell. When the inept Jackie finally entered the confessional, he admitted to thinking of killing his grandmother and his annoying sister, Nora. The indulgent young priest listened intently, warned Jackie that hanging is a horrible death, but then absolved him and even gave him candy, causing Nora to marvel indignantly at the rewards of sin. **(DGR) Averill:** Only after switching from third to first person did O feel satisfied with this story (280). **Matthews:** Based on a real anecdote. Guilt is a frequent theme of O's writing (266). **Tomory:** This work, one of O's most popular, focuses on two of his favorite kinds of characters: priests and children (114). **Wohlgelernter:** If only more priests behaved like this one! (59).

FIRST LOVE [1952/1952; *SFO*] Peter Dwyer was younger and less popular than self-assured Mick Dowling, who eventually accepted Peter into his group. Peter was jealous of Mick's girlfriend Babiche, but when Mick left town to take a job, she and Peter would talk about their mutual friend. Eventually Peter became involved with Babiche, and although he realized he had grown up, he felt disloyal and diminished and knew that even if Babiche were forgiven, he could not forgive himself. **(RCE)**

FISH FOR FRIDAY [1955/1981; *CS*] Ned McCarthy, a village teacher, was awakened by his sister-in-law, who told him that because his wife was about to deliver their latest child, the doctor should be fetched. Meeting several friends who persuaded him to drink and talk, Ned mused about the disappointments of middle age and reminisced about the freedom of his youth, but he also became less and less sober. Unable to remember the purpose of his trip, he convinced himself that he had been sent to buy fish. When he and a friend arrived at Ned's home, they heard a baby crying, and the friend indicated that he would eat lunch elsewhere. **(RCE) Aver-ill:** Theme: fatherhood (297). **Matthews:** Based on a true anecdote, this "is a poignant story delicately balanced on the edge of humor" (306).

THE FLOWERING TREES [1936/1981; *CP*] Young Josie Mangan led a gang of girls and boys who befriended an itinerant and entertaining Fiddler. After an illness prevented Josie (and thus the others) from attending a picnic they had planned, the gang dispersed and the Fiddler disappeared as summer drew to an end. **(RCE) Matthews:** Like many of O's early stories, this one reflects the influence of Maupassant (201).

FRANCIS [early version of "Pity"]

FREEDOM [1952/1981; *CS*] The narrator yearned for freedom while interned in a British prison camp, where he became friendly with Mick Stewart. When Mick disobeyed an Irish superior, he was tried, convicted, and eventually jailed by his fellow Irish prisoners. In response, Mick declared a potentially embarrassing hunger strike. As the Irish debated their next move, the narrator (disgusted with rigidity) tried to advocate freedom. Realizing, however, that he could not define the term, he concluded that since all the world's a jail, being imprisoned as comfortably as possible is most important. **(RCE) Hildebidle:** The story reflects O's own experiences during The Troubles (180n).

FRIENDS OF THE FAMILY [1946/1947; *CC*] Kate, the sister of John Joe Humphreys, had a friend named Gretta who, unhappily married to Sonny Dorgan, became involved with Ned Campion. Shocked to hear that Gretta might leave Sonny, John Joe encouraged Dorgan to give her more attention. After eventually leaving Sonny, Gretta discovered that she was pregnant with their third child. They reconciled, but when John Joe and his sister visited the hospital shortly after the birth, both seemed stunned by the baby's appearance. **(RCE) Averill:** The story is undisciplined and unsuccessful (288). **Matthews:** The story may reflect O's personal ambivalence about family ties (233).

THE FRYING PAN [1947/1981; *CS*] Father Jerry Fogarty's best friends in his small town were Tom and Una. The men had studied for the priesthood together until Tom met and married Una and became a schoolteacher. Fogarty often sensed a tension with Tom but also felt attracted to Una. One night, after arguing with Tom, Una confessed her own attraction to Fogarty, and the two even kissed. Una then revealed the real cause of their mutual tension—a cause likely to leave them all unfulfilled. **(RCE) Averill:** In two brief episodes O manages to suggest the entire history and future of the characters (275). The ending disappoints because the characters seem too resigned (276). **Hildebidle:** Theme: loneliness as both the source of human connections and the symptom of their failures (182–83). **Kilroy:** Plot: typically, a sudden final awareness of alienation (110); O balances irony, humor, and serious analysis (112). "The theme of loneliness ... dictates [the story's] narrative structure, rapid exposition, limited plot and character development, leading to a realization of isolation" (112). **Matthews:** This was one of many stories that grew out of O's friendship and talks with Father Tim Traynor (90); by writing the tale, O was able to explore his own feelings about marriage (233). **Tomory:** Theme: the pain of choosing (60). O damaged the revision by cutting dialect (81). As elsewhere, O rarely focuses on sex *per se* (105). O uses irony to examine social codes; after writing this story, O increasingly wrote about other young priests (117–18). **Wohlgelernter:** O here seems to endorse marriage for priests, who would profit from having families (62–63).

THE GENIUS [1955/1957; *DR*] Larry describes himself as having been a bookish boy whose studiousness, encouraged by his mother, disappointed his father. The mother supported Larry's isolation from the neighborhood boys. Although Larry's father viewed their fighting and love of outdoor sports as normal masculine traits that he wished Larry would exhibit, Larry remained a loner, absorbed in art and literature. These interests were interrupted when he was befriended by Una, an older schoolgirl with whom he developed an innocent adolescent friendship bordering on romance. Larry assumed that one day he would marry Una, but their relationship suffered when Una began to court a schoolmate her own age. Ultimately Larry brought a new perspective to his artistic and literary activities. **(GW) Kilroy:** O undercuts the smug, optimistic young narrator (117). **Matthews:** Larry embodies O's own youthful snobbery (14). Adopting the persona of Larry allows O to write distanced autobiography (310). Theme: tensions between idealism and reality (315). **Tomory:** The adult Larry sympathizes with his father (130).

GHOSTS [1972/1981; *CS*] Tim Clancy, who ran a small store with his wife, Nan, describes the Sullivans, a family of "peasants" from remote Oorawn, who were expecting a visit from an American cousin they had never met. When the cousin, "Jer," arrived with his wife and two children, they seemed much more wealthy and sophisticated than their Irish kin. Yet Jer was genuinely moved by his visit to the property from which his beloved grandparents were long ago evicted by unfeeling landlords. While driving back into town, Nan insisted that the group stop at the imposing home of a wealthy family so that the Americans would see a more impressive side of Irish life. Irritated with his wife's condescending attitude toward the "peasants" and by the Americans' pleasure in touring the house, Tim revealed that its owners descended from the landlords who evicted the Sullivan grandparents. Although the rest of the family merely marvelled at the coincidence, Jer Sullivan, a sensitive man, seemed haunted by thoughts of the "ghosts" who inhabited his memory. **(RCE) Hildebidle:** In stories by O, foreign visitors often seem disoriented (176). **Matthews:** The story draws on the life of John Kelleher, an American friend of O (260).

THE GOLDFISH [untraced]

THE GRAND VIZIER'S DAUGHTERS [1941/1981; *CS*] An anonymous narrator recalls his elderly, eccentric uncle, who loved to drink and tell stories. After regaling his nephew and his two daughters, Josie and Monica, with an exotic farce set in Turkey, he told another tale implying that one of his daughters was ashamed of him. Both girls protested their innocence. **(RCE) Hildebidle:** Theme: the force of story-telling, especially its ability both to overcome and emphasize isolation and to provoke self-judgment (206). **Matthews:** This moving story was based on a family O knew (154); it masterfully illustrates O's adept handling of implication, voice, and point of view (204). **Tomory:** O effectively links story to story-teller, implying how alcohol damages the family (78). **Wohlgelernter:** Theme: alcohol can make children ashamed of their parents (90).

GRANDEUR [*Ireland Today* (August 1936): 43–50] An old man tells an acquaintance about Jane Dwyer, a proud, controlling widow whose children deserted her one by one as they left adolescence. Each time she responded with anger. Finally only Tess remained, and although she was dying and wanted to see her siblings again, she feared angering her mother by summoning them. When she did die they were summoned by a friend, who had to cajole the mother into allowing them to view the body. When the unforgiving Jane herself died later, she died poor, insane, and alone. **(RCE)**

A GREAT MAN [1958/1981; *CS*] An anonymous narrator recounts Dr. Dermot O'Malley's fond recollections of Jim Fitzgerald, an old doctor who supervised (and energized) a remote hospital where his feisty daughter, Margaret, was a nurse. O'Malley greatly respected the old man, but when Fitzgerald, confronting mortality, encouraged O'Malley to consider marrying Margaret, the younger doctor faced an agonizing dilemma. **(RCE)**

Hildebidle: The story typifies O's focus on the pettiness, oppressiveness, and nosiness of small towns (184; 198; 200).

THE GRIP OF THE GERAGHTYS [1981; *CP*] Over many years, Tony Dowse watched how his friend Timmy McGovern, a smooth-talking ladies' man, complicated his life and marriage through involvements with other women. Even as the wife lay ill, attended by her sister Kate, Timmy was having an affair with her nurse. When his wife finally died, Timmy felt so haunted by her that he eventually married her sister, who seemingly had taken things in hand. **(LP)**

GUESTS OF THE NATION [1931/1956; *SBFO*] Bonaparte, an Irish soldier, recounts the unusual friendship that developed between him and his comrade, Noble (on the one hand) and two English prisoners, Belcher and Hawkins (on the other). All were housed in the remote cottage of a friendly old Irish woman and were often visited by Jeremiah Donovan, a rigid and distant Irish officer. The four friends would spend their evenings drinking tea and playing cards; Hawkins and Noble, more boisterous than the other two, would engage in friendly, spirited arguments about politics and religion. When Donovan announced that the Englishmen had to be killed to retaliate for executions of two Irish prisoners held by the British army, Bonaparte and Noble faced an excruciating moral dilemma. At the end of the story they felt forever changed. **(RCE) Averill:** O effectively uses first-person narration in the only early story he valued enough to revise and republish (249). The point of view is more universal than in his other stories about war (250). The characters, victims of events, must choose between instinct and intellect; abstract values are made to seem meaningless when brought down to an intensely personal level (250). O shows sympathy for Bonaparte and Noble and refuses to judge them; both the English and Irish soldiers suffer a kind of death (251). Everything in the story contributes to its impact; O effectively uses foreshadowing, irony, balance of characters, a metaphorical setting, symbolism, and the single narrative perspective (251–52). The revision subtly minimized differences between narrator and reader by de-emphasizing idiomatic phrasing (252). Unlike most of O's narrators, Bonaparte is completely caught up in the events he describes; such a heavy emphasis on first-person point of view is usually confined to the stories about children (252). The story shifts from comedy to terror (253). **Hildebidle:** Like many of O's stories, this one focuses on a kind of family and home, with the old woman as the inevitable mother (179–80). Bonaparte, though skillful at telling a story, seems intellectually and verbally awkward (181). The story concludes with a sense of the mother's disappointment (always a powerful theme in O's fiction [181]). **Kilroy:** O effectively uses gestures, diction, and tone to characterize the men (106). Caught between the conflicting claims of abstract values and personal feelings, Bonaparte clearly is (and feels) guilty (106). Strong narrative momentum, shifts in tense, and a sense

of inevitability all strengthen the tale (107). **Matthews:** The story emphasizes the tragic futility of violence (71). "Although there is nothing quite
like it in the rest of O'Connor's writing, [it] contains those qualities that
are unmistakably O'Connor: simplicity, tight narrative design, and lively
drama carrying sparse revelations in language that is direct and alive"
(71). The story was inspired by anecdotes and historical events (72). Unlike most of O's early writings, this one seems artistically sure and uncon-
trived (72). **Thompson:** Right away, "the natural, congenial narrative
voice that was to become O's chief triumph is at work" (70). Donovan is a
multiple outsider (70). The reader's perceptions begin to deepen simultaneously with those of Bonaparte and Noble (71). From this tragedy Bonaparte "will attain the widening and isolated consciousness of moral vision" (71). Strengths are lost in the revision (72). **Tomory:** The "poignancy
and understatement" of the march to the bog are impressive (30). "The
story's starkness and lucidity beggar critical commentary; it is quite simply one of the most eloquent commentaries on the inhumanity of war"
(30). O economically creates six highly distinct characters (30). The narrative seems flowing but relentless; the theme is left implied; even the final
sentence seems wholly in character (31). O achieves the sound of real
speech; 108 lines were altered in the revision, but the cutting of dialect is
excessive. The revised story thus seems flatter than the first version (31).
The revision is less colorful but also less literary; cutting back the Cockney
dialect made sense, but in pruning the Irish idioms O went too far (81).
Wohlgelernter: Through Belcher's final comments, O condemns dishonor
and unfairness (35). The story explores inhumanity in universal terms,
showing how "duty" can mask evil. The reader ultimately shares Bonaparte's sense of being lost (36).

THE HOLY DOOR [1947/1981; *CS*] Although Polly Donegan and Nora
Lawlor were teen-aged girls who attended church together, Polly lacked
Nora's curiosity about sex. When Charlie Cashman proposed to Nora, she
refused him, so he courted and married Polly instead. Since Charlie's
business would be inherited by his brother's children if Charlie produced
no heir, the childless couple journeyed to the Holy Door in Rome (which
was supposed to promote fertility), and Nora advised Polly that thinking
of handsome men during sex might also help. Charlie, doubting his viril-
ity, had an affair with the family maid, who soon became pregnant. When
Polly found out, she threatened to leave but was dissuaded by the local
priest. In time, Polly died, and Charlie began to feel attracted once again
to Nora. Ultimately they married, and Nora soon gave birth. **(RCE) Averill:** One of several stories featuring Father Ring (285). Theme: tensions in
Ireland between sex and religion (285–86). Although the first version was
flawed, the revised text exemplifies O's mature satiric style, especially in
its distanced narrative tone (286). O shows human instincts conflicting
with social rules; imagery is spare yet effective (287). The happy ending is
rooted in a realistic vision of human needs (287). **Hildebidle:** The story

shows O's disdain for enforced sexual inhibitions (187). **Kilroy:** Shifts in point of view make all three major characters seem sympathetic; like many of O's works, this one ends in revelation and self-awareness (113). Themes: repression (113–14) and how abandoning egotism can lead to mutual fulfillment (114). **Matthews:** Based on a true anecdote and on local legends (215), the story became longer and less focused as O revised it (more than twenty times [215]) and increasingly showed the influence of Jane Austen (232). **Thompson:** O uses multiple door images (79). Charlie's mother "is one of O's last great eccentric creations" (79). O avoids farce; Charlie matures slowly (79). **Tomory:** O's longest story, this work contains moments of great humor (105); Charlie is the rare romantic in O's fiction who finally attains joy (106). **Wohlgelernter:** O shows how piety can conflict with natural instincts and needs (81).

THE HOUSE THAT JOHNNY BUILT [1944/1952; *SFO*] Johnny Desmond, a fiftyish but vigorous and prosperous store-owner, immediately fancied the town's new spirited and young female doctor. In his direct and good-humored way, he bantered with her and then suddenly proposed marriage. Although tempted, she refused because of the gap in their ages. Frustrated, Johnny decided to build a lavish new house connected to a new drug store. He hired a young female druggist to run it, but when she discovered that Johnny was unmarried, she felt awkward about the living arrangements. When the doctor explained the girl's discomfort, Johnny honestly declared that the bad appearance had never occurred to him. When he bluntly proposed marriage, she also refused. When Johnny died less than a year later, the doctor believed she knew why. **(RCE) Averill:** The work emphasizes irony, dialogue, characters, compressions of time, and a steady, primarily external narrative perspective (272). Although almost comic, Johnny evokes sympathy and compassion by sincerely seeking love (273). In depicting Johnny, O combines social satire and real respect (273). **Matthews:** In this story and others, love seems an unromantic prelude to marriage (231). **Wohlgelernter:** The druggist's refusal to marry symbolizes the self-destructive Irish obsession with celibacy (100–1).

HUGHIE [1941/1981; *CP*] The unnamed narrator, apparently a neighbor, tells of the odd friendship between Hugh Daly (an amateur, idealistic philosopher) and Phil (a proper and humorously cynical solicitor). The capable Phil advised Hughie (who was less equipped to deal with daily life) on his ties, on choosing medicine as a profession, on what fork to use, and even on his pursuit of a wife. Hughie typically followed the advice of his trusted friend with predictable success. After trying his own hand at love with lamentable results, he finally succumbed to Phil's pressure to marry Dr. Delany. The new Mrs. Daly, however, took her role with more enthusiasm than even Phil bargained for. **(AG)**

THE IDEALIST [1950/1952; *SFO*] Larry Delaney recounts how, as a youth, he was strongly influenced by reading about English schoolboys who never lied, never betrayed one another, and never flinched when being punished. Larry's attempt to imitate this lofty code of conduct at his own school, however, earned him the ire and violence of his teacher ("the Murderer") and the ridicule of his immature mates, who considered him mad. Finally, having suffered once too often for his principles, Larry decided that the role of gangster might be preferable to that of idealist. **(RCE) Averill:** An autobiographical Larry Delaney tale emphasizing painful maturation (276–77). Larry eventually abandons romantic idealism for a compromising realism (281). **Bordewyk:** The boy grows by shrinking, learning that ideals are impractical (44). **Matthews:** The story, one of O's best and most delightful (247; 250), reflects O's sense of guilt and fear of disappointing his mother (266).

THE IMPOSSIBLE MARRIAGE [1957/1981; *CS*] Although young Jim Grahame and Eileen Clery fell in love, they faced a major obstacle: both were only children who had to care for widowed mothers. Eileen's mother fretted that Eileen would forsake her. The townspeople scorned the couple's unusual marriage, calling it a "mockery." Still, Jim and Eileen spent time together whenever they could, and they eagerly dreamed of someday sharing a home. Despite the scorn of friends and family, they cherished their marriage—until unexpected events caused everyone to respect and admire their bond. **(CN) Averill:** Despite their "improvised" marriage, Jim and Eileen achieve a kind of happiness (298–99). **Hildebidle:** Themes: the complicated relations between mothers and children (especially sons) and the apparent vagaries of Irish courtship (174). The "rather wry, conversational" narrator, close but distant, sympathetic but judgmental, is also typical of O's fiction (174). Like O himself, such narrators are fond of establishing categories and making generalizations (175). O shows here how fear of loneliness often motivates intense if unlikely relationships, yet he also shows how familiar comforts can inhibit change (175). Although constricting duty is strongly emphasized in the story's final pages, the narrator's final tone mixes empathy and understanding (176–77). **Wohlgelernter:** In this "hauntingly moving" tale, O laments selfish "maternal possessiveness" and the sad relationships so prevalent in Ireland (70). Such tragedy makes us tremble, yet Eileen finally seems happy with the small satisfactions life has offered (71).

IN THE TRAIN [1935/1936; *BC*] An unnamed narrator tells how assorted villagers and police officers from rural Farranchreesht traveled home after testifying in the city at the trial of a village woman acquitted of killing her husband. As they discussed miscellaneous subjects, a drunk moved from car to car, finally arriving where the woman sat alone. Although the woman was clearly guilty, some villagers lied for her, but they would punish her in their own way. The woman was left contemplating her bleak future. **(RCE) Averill:** Prominent symbolism and a nearly dramatic style make the story singular among O's works. The train's compartments reflect the village's social order. Adapted for the theater, the tale has an unfocused, objective point of view; different groups discuss the same topics differently. The introduction of the woman is effectively delayed (258). The villagers object less to murder than to the woman's motives (259); the story, influenced by James Joyce's use of metaphor, is one of O's most complicated (259–60). Images of light, darkness, movement, irrationality, and time predominate (260–61). **Chatalic:** O later rejected the bleak Joycean formalism evident in this story (193). **Kilroy:** The theme of isolation is emphasized through repeated and paralleled episodes (108). **Matthews:** A real event inspired one of O's best, most famous, and most morally complex tales, which gains pace as it moves along (112–13). **Thompson:** The clever setting at once divides, unites, and imprisons the characters (73). This is one of O's "most haunting stories" (74). **Tomory:** Influenced by Turgenev, O here makes the most significant event occur before the story starts (75). Although much praised, the unfocused narrative can seem tedious (76–77). **Warner:** This may be O's best story (87). O is less interested here in narrative than in "moods and feelings" (87). "The confusion and mystery of life find an analogue in the moving train," with a few illuminations (87).

JEROME [1951/1954; *MS*] An unnamed narrator describes the relationship between two young Irishmen (Jerome Kiely and Flurrie Donoghue) and two young Englishwomen (Hilda Kenyon and Rosie). When the four vacationed at a seaside resort, Jerome, who was considering marrying Hilda, took her to a phrenologist who had earlier assessed Jerome's own personality. The results of the second reading, however, were not what the cautious Jerome expected. **(RCE) Bordewyk:** Theme: instinctive vs. planned behavior (47). **Wohlgelernter:** Theme: the importance of self-reform (106).

JO [1931/1985; *GN*] The narrator describes two other revolutionaries, Jo Kiely and a young man called the Marshal. Although Jo and the Marshal were friends at first, when the Marshal switched to the enemy's side, Jo readily killed him during a battle. Later, the narrator encountered Jo paying his respects to the Marshal's old father, who did not know the precise circumstances of his son's death. **(RCE) Averill:** The narrator's view of Jo is mixed (249). **Tomory:** An inconclusive, unaffecting study of war's grimness (33–34). **Bordewyk:** Theme: only allies can be friends (40). **Wohlgelernter:** Theme: O's rejection of wanton violence (38).

JUDAS [1947/1981; *CS*] Jerry, a young man living with his elderly widowed mother, tells his friend Michael John about an evening when he had promised the old woman that he would not stay out late. Jerry had long been attracted by a nurse named Kitty, whom he pursued with fumbling self-consciousness. That evening, they finally conversed intimately and she encouraged him to kiss her. When Jerry returned home late, his worried mother was waiting up. Annoyed by her questions, he responded sarcastically, then went to his room. Finally, wracked with guilt and unable to sleep, he went to apologize and found his mother also sleepless. The old woman comforted him as if he were still her small boy. **(RCE) Kilroy:** O complicates the narrative by including Michael John (113). "A crippled product of maternal possessiveness, Jerry repeatedly refers to self-destruction and violence in what seem to be flippant figures of speech, but that reveal his near desperation and even suggest a degree of masochism ..." (113). Even his decision to tell the tale suggests a masochistic impulse, although other motives may also be involved (113). **Matthews:** The story is autobiographical in its idealized view of sex and sense of guilt (25). The tale implies how even a good mother can cause conflict for a conscientious son (231). **Steinman:** Seven versions of the story exist, and changes in the character of Kitty (who had to be alluring but not threatening) are particularly interesting (37). She became increasingly strong and complex as O revised (43). **Tomory:** O blends comedy and pathos (124) in a story he revised and improved by making the narrator more appealing and the narrative more focused (125–26). **Wohlgelernter:** In this oft-reprinted tale, O shows how a possessive mother keeps her son a hopeless, helpless infant (93–94).

JUMBO'S WIFE [1931/1985; *GN*] When Jumbo (an old, abusive ex-soldier) beat his wife, she turned for help to Pa Kenefick, a young militant whose brother, Michael, had been betrayed to (and killed by) the police. Thus when a letter from the government arrived for Jumbo, his illiterate wife took it to Kenefick to decipher, not realizing that it revealed Jumbo as the betrayer of Pa's brother. Although the woman subsequently did her best to protect Jumbo, eventually Kenefick traced the ill, disguised man to a local hospital. **(RCE) Averill:** This story was an unsuccessful, one-time trial of a "sordid, naturalistic" style (246–47). **Kilroy:** Theme: the woman's natural instincts and the horror of violence (107–8). **Matthews:** A failed, excessive story (69). **Tomory:** One of the more skilled and effective of the early war stories (32). **Wohlgelernter:** Theme: love vs. hatred (37).

LADIES OF THE HOUSE [version of "Lonely Rock"]

LADY BRENDA [*Harper's Bazaar* (December 1958): 92–93; 129; 132–33] Joe, the youngest son of the Regan family, was the favorite of his older and very assertive sister, Brenda. Over the protests of their other siblings, she insisted on collecting funds to purchase a fountain pen to present to their combative father at Christmas. Joe, admiring Brenda's feisty behavior yet fearing her forceful personality, watched as she maneuvered to purchase the best pen she could afford. Her father, pleased at first, soon found cause to complain, but once again Brenda improvised a solution. In the end, however, Joe sensed that Brenda's victory had left her feeling isolated and pained rather than triumphant. **(CS)**

LADY IN DUBLIN [version of "Lady of the Sagas"]

LADY OF THE SAGAS [1951/1981; *CS*] Although she shared a first name with a legendary heroine, Deirdre Costello had few hopes of finding a hero with whom she could spend her life. The closest candidate (at least in looks) was Tommy Dodd, but he seemed dull and unromantic. During a series of feisty talks, Tommy admitted that he had once had an affair. After mentioning this intriguing fact to a gossipy friend, Deirdre feared that she might have destroyed Tommy's reputation in their moralistic, provincial town. She also feared that she had ruined his chances of courting a wealthy local doctor. In the end, however, Tommy admitted that he had been joking about the affair, that he had no interest in the doctor, and that he wanted to marry Deirdre. Yet Deirdre, who at one time would have welcomed the offer, now had different ideas. **(RCE) Averill:** Excessive emotion renders the story unsuccessful (288). **Hildebidle:** O here complexly explores the potential for change (189); the ending can be read either as an indictment or an endorsement of Deirdre (190). **Tomory:** As in other works, O here uses a friendly, familiar voice (78). Deirdre, a romantic, cannot accept the ordinary (106–7).

THE LANDLADY [*Penguin New Writing* 37 (1949): 21–33] Jerry, a young Irishman working at a factory in England during World War II, had three Irish friends who were boarding in the home of a free-thinking English-woman. When her romance with a chemist ended and she announced her intent to stop taking boarders, Jerry's friends tossed coins to determine which would try to marry her so she would continue to rent to the others. Although the least likely of them won both the bet and her hand, when unexpected problems arose she did not desert him. **(RCE)**

THE LAST POST [1941/1981; *CS*] Three old men, among the few remaining survivors of an experienced Irish regiment, gathered for the funeral of Sully, one of their elderly comrades. Mrs. Dunn, a neighbor whose own boy had never returned from service, often attended such funerals, hoping to hear news of her long-missing son. When "Broke" (an old, one-legged beggar) appeared, he soon began bumming money for drinks. As he reminisced he began to recall, relive, and reenact an enemy attack in which he had vainly tried to save the life of a young comrade named Jackie. The event never left his mind, although Mrs. Dunn, whose "missing" son had been named "Jackie," apparently had not heard the tale before. As she mourned for her "little boy," the gathered men seemed to hear the sound of a distant bugler. **(RCE)**

THE LATE HENRY CONRAN [1931/1981; *CS*] Elderly Larry Costello tells of a friend from his youth, Henry Conran, whose love of liquor often caused trouble with employers and with his nagging wife, Nellie, who eventually persuaded him to go to America, leaving her and six children behind. Twenty-five years later, their prosperous son Aloysius became engaged to a girl Nellie disliked. When the newspaper announcement mentioned only Nellie, she insisted that Aloysius instead describe himself as the son "of the late Henry Conran." Shortly thereafter, Larry was unexpectedly greeted by an angry Henry, back from America and outraged that his wife had proclaimed his death. When Nellie eventually persuaded the drunken Henry to go to bed, he protested that she should not let him sleep alone. **(CTY) Tomory:** Anecdotal, comic, and reliant on dialect, the story lacks a central theme, and Henry is not credibly presented (35). The prologue seems clumsy and artificial, and the tone is inconsistent (74). Yet the story typifies O's interest in first-person narrators (74–75).

LAUGHTER [1931/1985; *GN*] Young militants, having staked out a pub they planned to bomb, waited in the rainy night to attack. After their plans fizzled, they traded wit with a feisty old woman they encountered on their way home. **(RCE) Averill:** The story adopts an odd tone of black humor (249). **Matthews:** The tale offers a successfully absurd blend of tragedy and comedy (69). **Tomory:** The ending fails to fit (34).

LEGAL AID [1946/1952; *SFO*] Delia Carty, a young maid for the wealthier O'Gradys, became involved with Tom Flynn, an uncouth farmer's son whom she entertained in the O'Grady's home when they were absent. When she became pregnant, Tom refused to marry beneath him. As the case made its way to court, charges of seduction, entrapment, and false paternity flew, and Tom even testified that Delia had seen other men. Tom's family had hired Dan Cooper, a notoriously vociferous lawyer, but he and Michael Ivers, the Cartys' counsel, worked out not only a financial settlement but another arrangement from which Cooper's reputation suffered. **(RCE) Averill:** O here effectively shows that materialism can sometimes have positive results (288). **Kilroy:** The story ends with multiple ironies (115).

A LIFE OF YOUR OWN [1965/1969; *C3*] Jane Harty, a druggist, valued her independence and lived alone in a small town near a few friends. Mysterious and threatening break-ins, however, made her feel uncomfortable in her small bungalow. Although she felt increasingly attracted to Ned Sullivan, a friend's husband who also seemed attracted to her, she ultimately realized the wisdom of his advice to leave the small town. He, she, and the stalker all seemed lonely in different ways. **(RCE) Averill:** O here explores neuroses and mental abnormalities without romanticizing them, as he had in the more innocent "Bridal Night" (301). **Tomory:** Like many of O's characters, Jane is isolated and unable to make connections (64). **Wohlgelernter:** This convincing story is perhaps the most effective of O's explorations of loneliness, which Jane must overcome (98–99).

THE LITTLE MOTHER [1953/1981; *CS*] The Twomeys, from Cork, included three lively teenage girls (May, Kitty, and Joan), their indulgent father, and their kindly mother. When the mother suddenly died, Joan, the eldest daughter, felt obliged to supervise her younger siblings. When she broke off her long relationship with her own suitor, whom she now considered insufficiently respectable, he became involved with Kitty. Joan, however, soon put a stop to the relationship, and in general she tried to manage her younger sisters' lives, thus earning their resentment. She broke up May's relationship with a married man and forced Kitty to marry a poor student by whom she was pregnant. Meanwhile, Joan suddenly decided to marry Chris Dwyer, an old beau. She and Chris moved to Dublin, where they supposedly spent quiet evenings listening to Beethoven recordings. However, when Kitty and her husband visited unexpectedly, they discovered that Joan and Chris had become parents and that Joan's pregnancy had caused the hasty marriage. Joan's sisters were amused and frustrated by the apparent hypocrisy of their substitute mother. **(RCE) Averill:** Lengthy and greatly revised, the story focuses on typical O themes: conflicts between love and family, instinct and intellect, personal desires and social reputation, femininity and responsibility, freedom and religion (299). Natural instincts eventually triumph over social conventions (300). **Hildebidle:** Joan is not transformed; rather, innate pride and external events emphasize her always-latent desire for control (193–94). Ultimately she seems diminished and tamed (194). Yet we cannot entirely condemn her; she achieves a kind of stable happiness in an unstable world (195). **Kilroy:** Joan moves from dependence to dominance to dependence again (118). **Matthews:** Here again O explores complex relations between children and surrogate parents (319–20).

THE LODGERS [Untraced; read by O on BBC radio, 15 September 1938]

LOFTY [1936/1936; *BC*] Egocentric Lofty Flanagan did well in an Irish community that seemed to accept fools gladly. Although unable to pass a mirror without admiring himself, he married well and took over his father-in-law's plumbing company. Finding himself well set, he decided to become involved in politics but was a poor speaker and an inept politician. When his real traits were finally acknowledged by the community, the foolish braggart was ultimately rejected by both his countrymen and his family. Unable to resist a final act of vanity, he fell from grace. **(DR) Davenport:** This is perhaps O's "most ambitious treatment of the [Irish] Revolution" (111). **Matthews:** The story reflects O's relations with his own father (109). **Tomory:** This story, the longest in *Bones of Contention*, suggests that Lofty's romanticism is deeply ingrained rather than (as in other works) externally influenced (92).

LONELY ROCK [1954/1954; *MS*] An Irishman named Phil tells of his wartime friendship with another Irishman, the philandering Jack Courtenay; with Sylvia (Jack's liberated wife); with Mrs. Courtenay (Jack's lovable old mother); with Margaret (Jack's mistress); and with Teddy (Jack's illegitimate son). All except Phil lived together in a complex arrangement that finally revealed the loneliness of each. **(RCE) Averill:** Theme: relations between widowed parents and adult children (297). **Matthews:** The story, based on O's own life, was suppressed at first in Britain by his first wife's lawyers (298).

THE LONG ROAD TO UMMERA [1940/1981; *CS*] When Abby Driscoll, the primitive, elderly mother of Pat Driscoll, a city businessman, talked of her future death, she insisted on being buried in Ummera, her old home village. Pat resisted, so one night, after "seeing" her late husband, she convinced two friends to drive her to Ummera. Becoming ill, she had to be hospitalized. Later, on a spring day, she did indeed arrive in Ummera, accompanied by her mournful son. **(RCE) Averill:** In one of O's most affecting tales about peasant ways, he wonderfully transmutes his own memories of his unappealing grandmother while illustrating his recurrent interest in the importance of a home (263). O may have been indebted to Faulkner's *As I Lay Dying*, a work he revered (263). O's work achieves a "haunting transcendence" (264). **Chatalic:** Touches of comedy enhance Abby's dignity (197). **Hildebidle:** The story treats the themes of habit and duty (190). **Kilroy:** As a tale of an inevitably triumphant quest, the story resembles Eudora Welty's "A Worn Path"; it stresses order, tradition, and personal relationships (109). **Matthews:** O "admitted that the voices of the story are those of his townee father and peasant granny" (13). One man claimed that hearing O's story on the radio helped his own mother die an easier death (203). **Thompson:** Theme: return to the womb/tomb (66). The story "opens with one of the loveliest paragraphs in O's work" (76). **Tomory:** The text magnificently depicts the old woman's strength (98). **Wohlgelernter:** O's "serious regard for tradition" is nowhere "more apparent than in [this] hauntingly sad and moving tale" (51). Like Ireland, Abby feels the tug of the past (52).

LOST FATHERLANDS [1954/1990; *V2*] An unnamed narrator recounts the humbling of a main character. After Spike Ward, essentially a taxi driver, brought an unknown man from the monastery to the train station, he persuaded him to have a drink at Hanagan's lounge to pass the time until the train arrived. Spike left, and three days later he saw Mick Hurley, the stationmaster. When Mick told Spike that the unnamed man had left his bags, Spike, Hanagan, and Linehan, a policeman, went back to the monastery to inquire about him. Discovering that he was a monk and was hiding out on the mountain, they went to find him. Later events led to a humbling awakening for one of them. **(JMB) Averill:** The story effectively uses irony, symbolic settings and actions, parallel characters (Hanagan and the monk), alternating perspectives, and such themes as intolerance, disillusionment, alienation, and impossible escape (292–93). Both Hanagan and the monk are left in a kind of disappointing, uncertain limbo (293). **Matthews:** Based on a real incident, the story emphasizes loneliness and loss (299). The tale derived from a sketch O wrote in the 1930s (305).

THE LUCEYS [1944/1981; *CS*] Although their fathers had long stubbornly quarreled, Peter and Charlie Lucey were best friends. When the prosperous Peter eventually got into trouble, neither Charlie's father (Ben) nor Peter's (Tom) would get involved. Ironically angry at Ben's indifference, Tom thereafter never spoke to him. Yet when Peter later died, Charlie broke the news to his uncle, and Ben offered his condolences. Nevertheless, Tom refused to shake Ben's hand because the old man had previously spoken against Peter, and nothing would soften Tom's heart. Years later, as Ben lay dying, Tom adamantly refused Charlie's pleas that he go to Ben, who wanted to see him. When Tom asked to be forgiven, Charlie replied, "'Tis yourself you'll have to forgive." In despair, Charlie trudged home, praying that the blinds would already be drawn when he arrived. **(CTY) Averill:** This powerful work, narrated mostly from Charlie's perspective (268), explores both the influence of public opinion on personal conduct and the conflict between rigid principles and instinctive affection (269). The final scene is one of O's most pathetic, since Tom realizes that he is trapped by his principles but still refuses to bend (269). The greatly revised version is less episodic and has a stronger narrative voice, although sometimes the commentary is insufficiently subtle (269). Although such lack of subtlety became increasingly apparent in O's writing, "The Luceys" is still powerful (269). **Hildebidle:** The story typically stresses family (178), stubborn loneliness (184), and provinciality (185). **Matthews:** Theme: how provinciality can reinforce self-destructive conduct (205). O long considered this his favorite story and remarked that he had tried "'to keep the issues small but the men big'" (205) and that the voice of each main character had been modeled on someone he had met (206). The story is indeed difficult and did not prove instantly appealing (206), but Eamon Kelly, an actor, considered it quite moving (350). **Thompson:** Tom "is probably O's chiefest eccentric," an out-dated, bitter "capitalist who must now live in an egalitarian society he detests" (77). **Tomory:** Foolish pride prevents desired communion (95).

MAC'S MASTERPIECE [*Best British Short Stories* (1939): 191–203] MacCarthy, an aging teacher at a religious school, suffered periodic bouts of depression but seemed to gain a purpose when he decided to write a novel expressing the philosophical ideas he often defended in arguments with his long-time friends. However, when his friends and employers began to suspect that he might attack them in the book, he defied both them and their expectations. **(RCE) Matthews:** The story probably reflects O's own moods, ideas, and experience with Daniel Corkery (150–51).

MACHINE GUN CORPS IN ACTION [1931/1985; *GN*] The narrator describes the various encounters he and his comrade, Sean Nelson, had with an erratic machine-gunner who caused general havoc wherever he went. Ordered to track him down and bring him back dead or alive, they found him at a widow's farmhouse and were about to haul him off when a far more imposing figure arrived and took command. Nelson, unable to drive, elected to stay with the widow while the narrator reported back to headquarters. **(RCE) Averill:** The most comic of the early war stories (249). **Matthews:** An unsuccessful example of "romanticized violence" (69). **Tomory:** Weak in theme and structure, the story nonetheless shows touches of O's later comic talent (34).

THE MAD LOMASNEYS [1944/1981; *CS*] Ned Lowry and Rita Lomasney had long been in love, but Rita eventually fell for a young man studying to be a priest. Although he wanted to get married, his mother prevented the match. Nellie and Kitty, Rita's sisters, were preoccupied with courting and thus found her unhappy secretiveness hard to understand. Although Ned told the eighteen-year-old Rita that he'd always been keen on her and would marry her whenever she liked, Rita felt that he didn't know what true love was. Another suitor, an older lawyer named Justin Sullivan, also proposed to Rita, who eventually announced their engagement. After the marriage, Ned became engaged to a Spanish-looking girl. Months later, when Rita's expected baby was due, she jealously explained to Ned that her marriage to Justin had been impulsive. After Nellie commented that Rita had married the wrong man, Rita replied, "'If I did marry the wrong man, it wouldn't be likely I'd tell you.'" Ned married the Spanish-looking girl a month later. **(CTY) Averill:** O commented that this story and others like it "'describe[d] for the first time the Irish middle-class Catholic way of life with its virtues and faults without any of the picturesqueness of earlier Irish writing which concentrated on colour and extravagance'" (268). Here as in other works, O explores "inhibitions" and "misunderstandings" that prevent happy love (271). Rita, like some other women in O's fiction, is neurotic, unhappy, and masochistic (301). **Chatalic:** Theme: the need to balance instinct and intellect (196). **Hildebidle:** The Lomasneys typify O's presentation of chaotic, conflicted families (178–79). Sex proves an illusory escape for Rita (186). O often presents sensible if dull men and passionate, energetic women (191). **Kilroy:** Like many of O's stories, this one ends with a final revelation, and at the end Ned remains as inarticulate (and gentle) as ever (110). The narrative finally seems illogical and episodic (111). **Matthews:** One of O's best stories about love in Ireland, the tale uses cigarettes in a symbolic way not usual in O's fiction, especially in Ned's final gesture (204–5). **Tomory:** Rita, one of O's most interesting creations, seems excessive, but O still prefers her to her conventional counterparts (102). In one year, she moves from romanticism to angry realism; unable to control her life, she punishes herself by submitting to chance (104). Ultimately Rita must accept the blame for rejecting the steady if unromantic Ned (104).

THE MAJESTY OF THE LAW [1935/1981; *CS*] An unnamed narrator describes old Dan Bride and his guest, the sergeant. After drinking illegally, the two men discussed how people had lost the art of making good liquor. After Dan poured them some tea, they discussed the lost art of home medicine. Afterwards, the sergeant left but soon returned to ask Dan if he planned to pay a fine for assaulting another man. Dan's reply reflected his simple life and values. **(JMB) Averill:** The story pays homage to traditional life and rituals, showing how they undercut modern concepts of justice (257). **Kilroy:** The theme is stated in the title but not made part of the story until the very end (108). The story celebrates traditional communal rituals that preserve individual dignity (109). **Tomory:** By withholding important facts until the end, O deepens the story's impact (90). Dan is presented convincingly; small details give the story a rich texture and make the lack of a forceful narrative seem unimportant (91). O shows impressive control, especially in the understated comedy; the theme of loneliness is implied rather than emphasized; the convincing dialect never descends into self-parody (91).

THE MAN OF THE HOUSE [1949/1981; *CS*] Gus recalls how, when he was ten and his mother became sick, he ordered her to bed, took the day off from school, took care of her errands, visited a bar to get her some whiskey, then walked across town to fetch her some cough syrup. At the druggist's he met a girl who talked him into sharing all the sweet syrup with her. Feeling guilty when he returned home, he tearfully confessed, after which his forgiving mother helped him get ready for bed. **(RCE) Matthews:** This "brilliant" tale is autobiographical (250).

THE MAN OF THE WORLD [1956/1957; *DR*] Larry Delaney recalls how, when young and innocent, he sought worldly knowledge from a sophisticated friend, Jimmy Leary. Jimmy offered to appease Larry's curiosity about relations between "fellows and girls" by arranging to spy on a newly married couple. The late-night vigil, however, made Larry feel ashamed for having deceptively witnessed the couple's solemn and dignified intimacy. **(KM) Averill:** Although less powerful than O's best works, such stories are biographically intriguing (295). **Bordewyk:** Theme: Maturity acquired through loss of innocence (44). **Matthews:** Larry shifts from watching to feeling watched (310). **Tomory:** Theme: innocence vs. experience (128).

THE MAN THAT STOPPED [1934/1936; *BC*] An old man tells a curious tale about a melancholy bachelor named John Cronin. Cronin became fed up with the monotony of life and took to stopping in the middle of public streets—apparently unconsciously removing himself from life's activity. His strange behavior eventually attracted the attention of the community. People were frightened by his actions, viewing them as part of a larger conspiracy. Cronin was eventually taken in hand by an equally queer person, Julia, who sought to save him from incarceration. She was able to keep Cronin from stopping by staying with him at all times. They eventually married, but ironically others in the community began to stop. Perhaps Cronin had started an unstoppable trend. **(DR) Matthews:** The story may reflect O's belief that his old friend Sean Hendrick was wasting his abilities (109). **Tomory:** Here as in other works, O includes the narrator in the narrative (75).

THE MARTYR [1951/1981; *CS*] Told by an officer ("Mick") who commanded a barracks operated by the army of the Irish Free State during the Civil War, the story describes the precise circumstances behind the martyrdom of Myles Hartnett, who died (according to a monument) "For the glory of God and the honor of Ireland." Hartnett had been captured and brutalized by Captain Morrisey, who blamed him for leading an ambush in which MacDunphy, the narrator's good friend, had been killed. Although Hartnett denied the charge (and although the narrator doubted its truth), Hartnett was inevitably convicted and scheduled for execution. He accepted his fate stoically, but as the execution neared he offered to tell the narrator the name of the man really responsible for MacDunphy's death. To save his life, he accused Mickey Morgan. Morgan was then arrested and brought to the camp, where he and Hartnett ironically became friends. When the narrator was informed that Hartnett might be organizing an escape, he privately threatened to reveal Hartnett's role in the capture of Morgan. Such news would have ensured Hartnett's death at the hands of his own comrades. Meanwhile, Captain Morrisey, who felt intense personal dislike for Hartnett, was frustrated that the man he had captured had not been executed. While the narrator was away from camp one day, Hartnett was shot by Morrisey, supposedly for trying to escape. In fact, however, he was a victim of personal hatred—a factor perhaps more important than lofty principles during civil wars. **(RCE) Kilroy:** Like many of O's best stories, this one ends with a sudden realization of being alienated (110). **Matthews:** Here as in other stories, romanticism surrenders to realism (260).

THE MASCULINE PRINCIPLE [1950/1981; *CS*] Evelyn Reiley squirms in her relationship with Jim Piper, who delays their marriage until he saves sufficient funds. Disillusioned with Jim, Evelyn takes his savings and goes to London. Having had an affair and spent the money, she returns home to her family and Jim. After becoming pregnant, she manages to have the baby in London. When she returns a second time, she continues to see Jim and later puts the baby boy up for adoption. Then one night Jim, drunk, comes to the Reileys' home and announces that he has enough money to marry Evelyn and build their house. **(CB) Averill:** O here shows an unusual bias toward rational rather than instinctive conduct and an untypical lack of concern for illegitimate children (288). **Kilroy:** O undercuts the narrator and sympathizes with the unconventional couple (115–16). **Matthews:** Although somewhat superficial, this satirical tale may reflect O's guilt about his own involvement with another woman, with whom he had had a son (256).

MASCULINE PROTEST [1952/1981; *CS*] Dennis Halligan recounts how, as a boy, he was especially close to his mother, antagonistic to his sister, and relatively indifferent to his father. A quarrel with his mother, however, made him decide to run away. After biking twenty miles he changed his mind and called his father. Because the father, too, had run away when a boy, he kept news of the event from the mother and sister, thus winning a new respect from his son. **(RCE) Bordewyk:** Theme: male bonding (45). **Tomory:** Theme: altered relations between parents and children (131).

THE MASS ISLAND [1959/1981; *CS*] When Father Jackson visited Father Hamilton shortly after their friend Father Fogarty died, both wondered whether he had written down his long-expressed wish to be buried on the remote Mass Island, where for years he had shared the plain, common ways of the local folk. Although his brother, a businessman, was reluctant to bother with such an impractical, expensive burial, the two old priests felt bound to honor their old friend's desires. Thus they contrived to convince the brother that Fogarty had indeed put his wishes in writing. Father Jackson assumed that the country folk would long ago have lost interest in the once-popular priest. At the funeral, however, people came from miles around, despite darkness and bad weather, to show their love for the man who had once shown them such fellowship and affection. **(RCE) Averill:** Possibly O's admiration for Fogarty suggests his own desire, in old age, to make peace with the church (294). **Hildebidle:** Although lonely himself, Fogarty inspires affection (198). **Tomory:** The final mood is deeply religious, with death as relief from lonely suffering (122).

MAY NIGHT [*Life and Letters* (April 1935): 45–50] As two tramps, long-time companions, drunkenly argued one night, they were approached by a country lad despairing over his harsh mother's response to his inability to find work. While one tramp tried anxiously to encourage the youth, the other's conduct was more cynical. When the boy disappeared, the tramps' conflict escalated. **(RCE)**

MICHAEL'S WIFE [1935/1936; *BC*] When Tom Shea met his son's wife, Kate, at the station, she was a strange and sickly American girl who inspired tenderness. As she began to recuperate during her time with Tom and his wife, Marie, they worried that something was amiss in her relationship with their son. Marie suspected a disagreement resulting in a planned two-year separation, with Michael in America and Kate in Ireland. Tom, optimistic, initially refused to believe that Kate was being less than candid, yet he was eventually convinced that a problem did exist. However, by the time Kate was ready to leave, Tom understood the soulful relationship between Michael and his wife—a link greater than their distance and loftier than Tom could once envision. **(DR) Averill:** Exile, landscape, and intense revelations are important traits of this tale (264). **Matthews:** This is the "most evocative" story of *Bones of Contention* (113). Its irony is subdued, and it conveys a strong sense of place and achieves both lyricism and drama (114). It shows how people communicate without speaking, and it conveys emotions deeply felt by O himself (114). This was the favorite story of O's first wife, although O himself later considered it too emotional (176). **Tomory:** As in other works, by not reporting crucial facts until the end, O deepens the story's drama (90). Although based on fact, the story risks seeming improbable, but its theme of loneliness is powerfully implied (91).

A MINORITY [1957/1969; *SV*] Denis Halligan, a Protestant student at a Catholic school, felt friendship and admiration for the tough Willy Stein, another Protestant who remained dedicated to the faith of his dead parents. Although Denis eventually decided to convert to Catholicism so that he would no longer suffer the strain of being an outsider, Willy refused. Denis later learned that Willy's parents were not Protestants but Jews (a fact that even Willy did not know). After discovering that conversion had repercussions he had never considered, Denis admired Willy even more for clinging to the supposed faith of his deceased parents. **(TG) Kilroy:** O here deals with religion in unusually direct ways. "In its admission of heroism and in the unrelieved intensity of the conclusion," the work echoes some of O's earliest stories, "but by the end of his career mature acceptance has replaced disillusionment as the usual response" (119).

THE MIRACLE [*Life and Letters* (May 1934): 210–13] When a couple and their young son insisted on visiting a shrine during a rainstorm to pray for a miracle, the nuns could not refuse. When the miracle seemed to have occurred, however, the eldest nun reacted differently than the others. **(RCE)**

THE MIRACLE [1947/1981; *CS*] The canon, a prosperous cleric, disliked the new ways and new men (such as Bobby Healy, a doctor) who seemed to threaten his privileges. Even more, however, he disliked Bill Enright. After he ordered Bill to stop living in sin with his housekeeper, Nellie, Bill rejected the church and won the community's sympathy. When Bill became sick, Nellie sent for Bobby Healy, who, although finding that the case was not serious, recommended that Bill take confession from a Jesuit the canon disliked. The Jesuit thus won credit for Bill's miraculous recovery of his health and faith, and Healy triumphed over the canon. **(CTY) Averill:** Such stories imply O's regard for religion (283).

THE MISER [1944/1952; *SFO*] Although Tom Devereux came from a once-prominent family, in his old age he was as grimy and unkempt as his run-down shop. His only companion, a decaying old soldier named Faxy, begged credit from merchants on the strength of Devereux's rumored wealth. After the feisty Devereux was confined to bed, Father Ring convinced him to allow some nuns to take care of him. The two women set the annoyed Faxy to work cleaning the place, while they groomed and fed old Devereux. As Devereux decayed, Father Ring persuaded him to compose a will and leave large sums to the church. When Faxy became outraged by the old man's stinginess to him, the priest did his best to change Devereux's mind. After Devereux died, the chests containing his wealth were opened, to everyone's surprise. **(RCE) Matthews:** This is one of several tales featuring the unappealing Ring (203). **Tomory:** Devereux hilariously turns the tables on the priest (99). **Wohlgelernter:** The greedy priest seems the true miser (54–55).

A MOTHER'S WARNING [1967/1969; C3] Father Fogarty was visited by Sheila Moriarty, a clerk who confessed that a married assistant manager (with whom she was involved at the store where they both worked) had encouraged her to steal a brooch. She wanted to return it but feared being blackmailed. When Fogarty confronted the man, he brazenly denied involvement and threatened to report Fogarty for persecuting him. Still, Fogarty realized that the man would now probably leave Sheila alone, but when she and the priest discussed the matter, Fogarty inadvertently said something that caused her to exit in quick distress. **(RCE) Matthews:** The story derived from a real event (363). **Tomory:** Ultimately Fogarty questions his own motives and realizes the loneliness of his job (120).

THE MURDERER [version of "First Confession"]

MUSIC WHEN SOFT VOICES DIE [1958/1969; C3] Larry recalls how, as a boy, he worked at an office and would overhear the random conversations of three young women. In his memory their voices resound like music, and although he and they are now much older and much different than before, he realizes that their voices will survive as pleasant reminders of youth. **(RCE) Wohlgelernter:** The women waste time in fruitless talk and thus never lead fulfilling lives (99–100).

MY DA [1947/1952; SFO] A grown boy recalls Stevie, a young friend, and the results of his parents' separation. Stevie lived with his mother because his father had left for America. Although Stevie took on many jobs, his mother used his income to buy alcohol. When Stevie's father returned from America, the boy began to refuse money for his work in order to emphasize that he had a father. When the father left again, Stevie focused on going to school and joining the library. Ultimately his studies led him to a surprising choice. **(JMB) Matthews:** Rewritten fifty times, the story may have touched too closely on O's ambivalent relations with his own father (230–31).

MY FIRST PROTESTANT [1951/1981; CS] Dan Hogan tells of his involvement with Maire Daly and her boisterous Catholic family (including her brother Joe) and with Winifred Jackson, Maire's Protestant friend. When Joe began to court Winifred, his mother hoped to win not only a daughter-in-law but also a convert. When their religious differences finally came between them, Dan was mystified, since he felt that *all* marriages were mixed. After Dan expressed his views too insistently, Maire eventually dropped him, and he began to spend his Sunday mornings at the docks with other agnostics and atheists. Winifred, meanwhile, had married a

Protestant. Ten years later, after the husband's death, Dan was surprised to see Winifred leaving a Catholic Mass with her children. He reflected that a woman always tries to give her children what she feels she has missed, although "the kids never value it, of course. They have never really known the loss of it." **(RCE) Bordewyk:** This may be O's "most sensitive and ambiguous story about religion" (42). Themes: human rather than religious communion (42); the search for meaning and love (43). **Matthews:** Dan represents O's ideal self (253). **Wohlgelernter:** Even here, O is uninterested in religious dogma *per se* (46).

MY OEDIPUS COMPLEX [1950/1981; *CS*] Larry recalls how, as a young boy, he dealt with feelings of jealousy and neglect after his father returned from the war. While his father was away for the first five years of his life, Larry became accustomed to his mother's undivided attention. After his father returned, however, Larry felt cast aside and unimportant. Instead of enjoying the usual morning ritual of climbing into his mother's bed and talking about the coming day, Larry now had to keep quiet for fear of angering his father. He now wished that his father would go off to war again, whereas before he had prayed with his mother for his father's safe return. To further complicate matters, the arrival of his baby brother— whose company he had desired before his father's return—served only to increase his feelings of abandonment. Yet "Sonny's" birth also changed Larry's relationship with his father. **(DS) Averill:** "The gap between the child's and the adult's perspective provides detachment and humor" (281). The ending is typical of O's middle period in its focus on a re-establishment of normality (282). **Bordewyk:** The subtlety and gentle comedy are appropriate to the theme of fluid family roles (45). **Fallis:** The story is a masterpiece, especially in being so credible, lucid, and complex (223–24). **Kilroy:** O is less antagonistic to fathers here than in some other stories; Larry is viewed with some irony, although he assumes some power over his father by the end (117). **Tomory:** In O's stories, children often shift allegiance from one parent to another (130). **Wohlgelernter:** O mocks the over-emphasis on boys' ties to mothers in Irish culture. Boys are emotionally stunted by this over-powering relationship (70).

THE NEW TEACHER [version of "The Cheapjack"]

NEWS FOR THE CHURCH [1945/1981; *CS*] Father Cassidy was surprised in the confessional by an unfamiliar girl who confessed various sins, including casual sex with a man she did not intend to marry. Realizing that she was confiding rather than confessing, Cassidy demanded intimate details until she cried, "'You're making it sound so beastly!'" Later, after assigning penance, he saw her, small and dejected, leaving the church. Passing a statue of the patron saint of marriageable girls, he nearly winked. **(CTY) Averill:** Cassidy is presented without sympathy (274). **Bordewyk:** Cassidy, denied physical love, lives vicariously (42). **Hildebidle:** As in other works by O, here sex seems unfulfilling (186). This is O's most obvious effort to show how priestly pride can conflict with human kindness; the final glimpse of the ignorant Cassidy is ironic (201–2). **Kilroy:** The smug, repressive Cassidy, confronted by a spirited girl, takes vengeance when she implicitly challenges his knowledge and authority, yet the story's tone is humorous (111). Both characters are changed and troubled, although Cassidy remains self-satisfied (111). **Tomory:** O typically focuses less on sex itself than on its social consequences (105). O's attitude toward Cassidy is difficult to determine; the priest dislikes the girl's sin less than her romanticism (116).

NIGHT OF STARS [version of "Judas"]

NIGHTPIECE WITH FIGURES [1931/1985; *GN*] When a group of young revolutionaries took refuge in a barn one night, they bantered with an old man and a feisty old nun. The appearance and words of an inspiring young nun, however, cheered the men's spirits unforgettably. **(RCE) Bordewyk:** Theme: ideals beautifully embodied (39). **Averill:** A "lyrical sketch" (249). **Matthews:** Heavy use of light/dark imagery (161). **Tomory:** A fragmentary work that is too self-consciously artful to be convincing (33).

OLD AGE PENSIONERS [1951/1951; *TS*] Rivalries between two communities often came to a head when the elderly residents of the outlying village came into town to retrieve their monthly pensions. When an old townee defeated a younger villager in a rowing contest, the villager's ancient father demanded a rematch, which he narrowly won. Flushed with victory, he reminisced about his hard life. **(RCE) Matthews:** The style is excessively maudlin (266).

THE OLD FAITH [1954/1981; *CS*] After celebrating mass, the bishop noticed a local peasant hiding illegal liquor. Later he shared the confiscated bottle with some other priests. Talk turned to past customs and superstitions. Later, while the group crossed a field, the younger men began to pass out, but the spry old bishop was able to climb a wall. **(RCE) Averill:** One of O's most appealing later stories, it ends hilariously (290). **Bordewyk:** A light account of alternative sources of meaning (41). **Tomory:** The story, one of O's best late works about priests, would have been too controversial to publish in a magazine (118–19).

OLD FELLOWS [1941/1952; *SFO*] A man recalls how his "Father," at the request of "Mother," reluctantly took him as a boy on an excursion down the river. After mass, the boy, Father, and J.J., Father's old friend, began their journey. Along the way, Father stopped at his true destination, a tavern, gave the boy a penny, and told him to behave. Between Father's first two visits to taverns, the boy met a girl whose father was a sailor. They met again later on the river boat, where Father, contemptuous of sailing, argued in a tavern with the girl's old man. After much arguing and drinking, the two men peaceably separated because the sailor had to get his daughter home to bed. As the boy, Father, and J.J. walked home, Father noticed the sailor's daughter and went inside her house to argue some more with the sailor. Thus the boy was left alone with the girl, and a dare resulted in a stroke of genius by the boy. **(JMB) Averill:** The story is an unusual early work since it is told from a child's perspective (262). **Matthews:** Here as elsewhere, O transmutes the horror of his early relations with his own father into comedy (259). **Tomory:** Here as in other stories probably based on O's own father, the character is depicted with objectivity, balance, and even sympathy (17). In the revised version, too much of the Irish dialect is deleted (81).

ORPHANS [1956/1957; *DR*] When Hilda Cramer, a reserved and overly conscientious young girl seeking to define herself through a noble cause, unwittingly became involved with Jim Redmond, a young soldier with a casual, impulsive, and overbearing manner, she was overwhelmed by his ability to impose himself inoffensively on her and her family. In fact, Jim, who grew up with his younger brother Larry in an orphanage, eagerly embraced them all. Thus when Jim was killed in the war, Hilda felt guilty: by not having heeded her parents' advice to accept his proposal, she felt that she had denied him his chance to fulfill his earnest desire to have a family and a home. Within a few months, however, Hilda became engaged to Jack Giltinan, a young mechanic who was steady, cautious, and sincere. Her marriage plans altered dramatically, though, when Larry, who shared many of his brother's free-wheeling traits, unexpectedly arrived. **(KM) Averill:** Theme: uncommon but successful pairings (298). **Matthews:** Based on a true anecdote, the story also reflects O's life and heritage in complicated ways (305–6). **Wohlgelernter:** The link between Hilda and Larry is unsound (104–5).

ORPHEUS AND HIS LUTE [1936/1936; *BC*] The musical charms of Orpheus were apparently possessed by an odd little Irish band whose members were more inclined to drinking than to playing music. This competition between "porter and music" (two things for which people willingly give body and soul) is described by the narrator as "God's holy will." Members of the inebriated, motley little band would pawn their very instruments to get money to drink and then turn around and buy back their instruments at a higher price in order to march in the St. Patrick's parade. Their exertions fell short of success when they brawled with another band. Ironically, though, the brawl seemed to release their energies, causing them to render, with stolen instruments, an inspirational performance of their best tunes. The band retained its soul, even as its members were on the way to jail. **(DR) Averill:** The first version included a listener, later cut (271). **Matthews:** Here and in other stories, O tries to treat his depressing childhood in a humorous way (109). Although autobiographical, the story is told objectively (113). **Tomory:** The revision omits the awkward prologue and epilogue, focusing instead on the elderly narrator (80).

AN OUT-AND-OUT FREE GIFT [1957/1981; *CS*] Although Ned Callanan had always enjoyed a close bond with his son Jimmy, by the time the boy was sixteen he was distant, secretive, and insubordinate. After catching Jimmy in a lie, Ned contemplated punishment but instead did nothing. To his and his wife's surprise, the youth's behavior suddenly improved. **(RCE)**

THE PARAGON [1957/1957; *DR*] Larry Delaney recounts how Jimmy Garvin, sheltered but ambitious, became entangled in the moral conflict that had divided his pious and embittered mother from his unscrupulous father. The conflict arose when Jimmy's Aunt Mary shrewdly persuaded him to visit his father in England despite his mother's warnings. Indeed, when Jimmy returned, his mother was not surprised by his changed behavior, especially his new interest in visiting pubs and pursuing women. Jimmy, torn between his father's lack of principles and his mother's badgering claims that the father was deliberately trying to sabotage her good influence, lost his scholarship and was forced to take a menial job to support himself—and soon his wife and child. However, because of his ardent determination—a determination distinctly his own and not shaped by the antagonism of his parents—he did succeed in getting his degree. **(KM) Matthews:** The story was emphatically declined by *The New Yorker*, whose editors considered it too preachy (312). **Wohlgelernter:** Theme: the need for young males to establish independent identities (96–98).

THE PARIAH [1956/1957; *DR*] When Jack met Terry Connolly, an intelligent, handsome, and amiable young man who was dating his sister Sue, he was immediately impressed by Terry's benevolence and, above all, by his steady character. However, when Sue rejected Terry, Jack had to struggle to understand why she (like many other single and "brainless" women in Cork) was not enamored by Terry's decency and stability. When Jack finally learned the reasons for Sue's rejection of Terry, which he considered evidence of her instability and flightiness, he felt only intensified cynicism and contempt for women. Jack's cynicism was only confirmed when Terry returned from Dublin with Martha, his stunning fiancée, for it was then that Sue (and many other women in Cork) began to lament the loss of such a decent man—a man she had wantonly rejected. **(KM) Matthews:** Jack resembles the "atheists" depicted in some of O's earlier stories; in this work O achieves more objectivity than he had in some other recent writings (312).

THE PARTY [1957/1981; *CP*] When old Johnny, a night watchman, took up his post across the street from an elite home where a party was being held, he enjoyed imagining the lives of the arriving guests. Eventually an obviously wealthy man left the house and offered the watchman money if the man could assume Johnny's place for a few hours. Only later, after much confusion, did Johnny discover the man's identity and the reason for his strange request. **(RCE) Averill:** Theme: alienation within families (297).

Wohlgelernter: O suggests that self-centered fathers sometimes hold their children to unrealistic standards of conduct (91–92).

THE PATRIARCH [1931/1985; *GN*] Jeremiah Coakley recalls his long acquaintance with old Michael Callanan, an Irish nationalist who encouraged the boy's interest in Gaelic and later in revolutionary politics. Jeremiah's link with Callanan (and with his feisty housekeeper Ellen) endured through many important personal and political events until the old man, broken by age and sickness, died in Coakley's presence while Ellen prayed. **(RCE) Averill:** A domestic tale set against the background of war (253). **Fallis:** An "exceedingly fine story" about innocence and experience (226). **Tomory:** A vivid, lyrical sketch, largely from a child's perspective (34–35). **Wohlgelernter:** A lovely work that contrasts ideals with reality (34).

PEASANTS [1922/1981; *CS*] When a local youth stole funds from the community athletic league, his conduct only confirmed the town's worst opinions of his whole family and their ancestors. The locals anticipated that the youth would be exiled to America, but Father Crowley, the rigid parish priest, demanded criminal prosecution. The parish committee resisted, thinking the punishment too harsh for the youth and his family; they even took up a collection to replace the stolen money. Yet the priest still insisted on prosecution, refusing to write a letter of reference for the young man even if he agreed to depart for America with a ticket the neighbors were willing to purchase. Alleging bribery, Father Crowley even rejected a proposed contribution to the church fund. The youth was indeed jailed, but afterwards, with the help of the community's contributions, he went into business and eventually became a prosperous businessman. When he later exploited his position to take advantage of his neighbors, they blamed Father Crowley for having prevented them from shipping the unscrupulous boy, from the unscrupulous family, off to America, where he could have done the community no harm. **(RCE) Averill:** Theme: the strength of communal traditions (256). Although the narrator speaks from the community's perspective, author and reader sympathize with Crowley (256) because the peasants' sense of justice seems perverse and unfair (257). O "exposes a closed, sterile society which expels the agent of constructive change and embraces the agent of corruption" (257). The story works on two levels, offering humor but inviting reflection (257). **Hildebidle:** Crowley discovers the provincials' distrust of "foreigners" (185). **Tomory:** The inflexible Crowley is O's first major priest (114); the first version of the story was written when O was nineteen (114). O sympathizes more with the thief than the priest (114). **Wohlgelernter:** O considers the hard, uncompassionate priest worse than the thief; the rigid failure to be charitable lowers both priest and peasants (53).

THE PEDDLER [*Irish Statesman* (26 November 1926); untraced]

THE PICTURE [*The Irish Statesman* (6 April 1929): 87–88] Subtitled "An Old Man's Story." An old man tells about Julie Casey, her elderly aunt, and their boarder, Gabriel Quinlan. The aunt, who owned a small shop selling old books and pictures, closely supervised the haughty Julie, who assumed that the scholarly boarder was an Irish patriot. When a British officer wanted to buy an old painting, Julie misunderstood his interest and unwittingly bid up the price, inadvertently earning a tidy sum through a mistaken sense of allegiance. **(RCE)**

PITY [1954/1957; *DR*] When Francis Cummins, a virtuous young boy destined for the priesthood, arrived at an unruly and remote boarding school, he immediately attached himself to Denis Haligan, a wayward boy from a dysfunctional family. Denis did not mind Francis's sudden attachment, for Francis, in his unfailing generosity, was always willing to share the precious wares he received each week from his affectionate parents. Denis, impressed by such parental generosity, described it to his own indifferent mother in the hope of altering her behavior. Soon he did in fact receive a parcel loaded with niceties. Elated by the possibility of his mother's unprecedented display of love, he did not at first ponder its actual source. **(KM) Matthews:** The story reflected an incident in the life of O's son. In revising the work and changing its original title ("Francis"), O shifted focus from character to concept. "In both versions the story is a small gem" (298).

THE PRETENDER [1950/1981; *CS*] Michael Murphy recounts how, as a child, he and his sister Susie were bothered by their mother's interest in poor, parentless Denis Corby. Denis was invited to visit so often that Michael grew jealous. After a highly public confrontation, the Murphy children felt less threatened by the pathetic Denis. **(RCE) Matthews:** The story, typical of O's interest in illegitimate children, was based on real events (258), including O's links to his own mother (259). **Wohlgelernter:** Theme: the often intense focus of Irish children on their mothers (95–96).

PRIVATE PROPERTY [1950/1957; *DR*] An unnamed young man describes his struggle to maintain his lofty, ideal beliefs about the necessity of change in the midst of a tumultuous revolution. As a newly promoted officer in the Irish Republican Army, he was full of revolutionary fervor and adamantly dedicated to the organization and its cause. He became disillusioned, however, by the betrayal and disunity resulting from a petty argument between two other soldiers. **(KM) Davenport:** This is perhaps O's most noteworthy late war story (115). **Matthews:** At the time it was written, the story was an unusual return by O to earlier subjects (260).

THE PROCESSION OF LIFE [1931/1970; *ML*] After his mother's death, Andy Coleman discovered that his life would never be the same. Because he missed his curfew, his father locked him out, so Andy wandered the streets. Down by the river he encountered an argumentative night watchman, a friendly prostitute, and a conniving policeman. They all sat and talked awhile, and eventually the woman left with the officer. Although the watchman finally told Andy that he could stay for the night, the young man, newly confident, decided to go home. **(KO) Averill:** This is O's earliest story about growing pains (254). **Matthews:** Like many stories in O's first collection, this one focuses on the transition from romanticism to realism (71). **Tomory:** Even the first version of this story of initiation was convincingly real (36). **Wohlgelernter:** Theme: the inevitable conflict between fathers and sons (89).

PUBLIC OPINION [1957/1981; *CS*] Doctor Ryan comically warns a writer from Dublin not to romanticize small Irish towns, which are rife with judgmental gossips. At first the doctor tried to ignore them, even hiring a young unmarried housekeeper, but his hapless experiences as he secretly tried one night to dump a rotting side of beef changed his mind about the power of small-town rumors. **(JH) Hildebidle:** Sometimes, as here, O's characters blame their behavior on their environment (184). **Matthews:** The story derived from O's experiences in England (224). **Tomory:** As in other stories, O here uses a friendly, first-person voice (78–79).

A RAINY DAY [*John O'London's Weekly*, August 1938; untraced]

REPENTANCE [version of "First Confession"]

THE REBEL [1994; *A Frank O'Connor Reader*, ed. Michael Steinman] Don MacNamara, an Irishman who frequently visited a small English pub, became involved with Carrie Wright, the pub owner's wife. Although they went off on secret vacations together, Don felt uncomfortable doing anything in Carrie's house. Ironically, when Jim Wright, Carrie's husband, also befriended Don, the development not only changed the relationship of Don and Carrie but also made each of them realize something new about Don. **(RCE)**

REQUIEM [1957/1981; *CS*] When an elderly lady visited Father Fogarty, the town curate, she asked him to say a mass for "Timmy" (recently deceased). Fogarty, knowing that she had no children of her own, assumed that Timmy was a stepchild. When he learned that Timmy was the lady's dog, he was dismayed and refused to commit sacrilege by saying a mass, since animals lack souls. The woman, mournfully disappointed, argued reproachfully that "Anything that can love has a soul." **(MP) Matthews:** Although Fogarty responds rigidly at first, his compassion and sensitivity correct his first reaction (203). **Tomory:** Again O deals with loneliness (119), yet the tone here is more light-hearted than is usual in the stories about Fogarty, who seems out of place (120). Does the woman deserve pity or laughter? Usually when O writes comically about priests, he focuses on an older man (120). **Wohlgelernter:** O regrets that Fogarty fails to respond with a love as deep as the old woman's (54).

THE RING [*The Irish Statesman* (28 July 1928): 409] When Philip, a "man about town," inadvertently came across a woman locked out of her house one night, he cursed his luck for putting him in such an embarrassing situation. Since the woman's drunken husband could not hear him rapping on the door, Philip broke a window to let her enter her home. She then told him how she had been courted simultaneously by a respectful postman and by her future husband, whom she feared even then. When the latter suddenly thrust a gaudy ring on her finger, she perversely wore it in front of the postman, who dropped her despite her belated apologies. She had glimpsed him only once in the two years since her marriage to the impoverished, abusive drunk. **(RCE)**

THE RISING [version of "Eternal Triangle"]

THE RIVALS [version of "Judas"]

A ROMANTIC [1936/1936; *BC*] Noel, at age seventeen, fell in love with a girl named Anne who was somewhat above his own station in life. Noel initially perceived Anne as beyond his reach, yet, when he gained her promise of marriage, he suddenly lost interest in her and became attracted to a series of other girls: Joan, Helen, Anne again, Helen again, Joan again. In the end he pined once more for Anne. **(DR) Hildebidle:** O here illustrates the power of fantasy (186). **Matthews:** The story "builds on a string of quick, almost cinematic movements unveiling the shifting moods of a young dreamer in love" (115). Anne typifies O's ideal female (115). Externally confident but internally uncertain, Noel resembles O himself (115). The final scene juxtaposes attractive but ephemeral fantasy and stark reality (115). **Tomory:** O completely revised the story after it first appeared in *Bones of Contention*, even renaming the main character Miah and making his idle fantasies revolve around France (108). **Wohlgelernter:** Romantics are common in O's fiction; Noel resembles O in appearance, jobs, and relations with his father (92). Like other early works by O, this one denigrates unrealistic idealism (92); actual people fall short of Noel's fantasies (93). By being casually involved with so many women, he avoids deep attachment to any (93). The story, weakened by an episodic plot and sketchy characters, does convincingly portray the romantic mindset (94).

THE SAINT [*Mademoiselle* (June 1952): 91; 104–5; 107] As a young boy, the unnamed Catholic narrator learned from his father that the candles the child bought in church for a penny each (to show his devotion to the Virgin Mary) really only cost "a penny for eight." Outraged at the exploitation of himself and the Virgin, the boy lit five candles for every penny, considering the deal a bargain to all concerned. Caught by Mickie Mac, the church sacristan, the boy confessed to the priest, paid for the used candles, learned the difference between "price" and "value," and changed his devotion to Saint Francis. **(CS)**

A SALESMAN'S ROMANCE [1956/1957; *DR*] An unnamed narrator recounts the obsession that a salesman-friend of his, Charlie Ford, had with selling. While on a drive with his girl, Celia, he had a minor run-in with a carriage whose shrewd driver pretended to be injured. At the trial Charlie nearly sold the jury on his version of events, but then the less diplomatic Celia took the stand. Although Charlie won the verdict, he lost the girl—although the whole incident gave him another fine story to tell prospective customers. **(RCE) Averill:** O offers a gently mocking treatment of love (298).

THE SCHOOL FOR WIVES [1966/1969; *SV*] Jimmy Maguire had been a ladies' man whose romantic exploits had impressed his friends, but when he married Roisin Mooney, who worshipped him, he began to move in new circles, abandoned his old friends, and lied about them to Roisin to discourage her from making any inquiries about his past. Having known many unfaithful wives in his time, he did not want to give Roisin any ideas. When she contacted his old friends nonetheless, he warned that any further contact might trigger the tendency to mental illness he claimed to have inherited. From that point on, his relations with Roisin changed quite ironically. **(RCE) Matthews:** O was dissatisfied with this late story's first version (361).

SEAGULLS [Boston University; untraced]

A SENSE OF RESPONSIBILITY [1952/1981; *CS*] An unnamed narrator tells about Mick and Jack Cantillon; Jack's friend Pat Farren; Jack's involvement with Susie Dwyer; and Mick's marriage to Madge Hunt. When Mick died, Jack supplemented his widowed sister-in-law's income, even though Susie's family disapproved. To make Mick jealous, Susie began to flirt with Pat; when Pat died, she even claimed he had been her lover. Nothing disturbed Jack, however, and eventually he and Susie married. When Jack's manipulative but impoverished mother had no place else to live, Jack offered her a room, despite the objections of Susie and her mother. Jack's mother succeeded in turning Susie against him, but when the old woman herself died, the marriage returned to normal. Finally, when Susie's own mother became too old to stay by herself, Jack offered her a room. Jack's high opinion of Susie's mother eventually became reciprocal, and in the end even Susie had to admit her husband's merits. **(RCE) Averill:** This is one of several stories about widowed parents (297). **Hildebidle:** Susie is victimized by her own and Jack's mothers (195–97); conflicting duties undercut Jack's and Susie's marriage (197). **Kilroy:** Jack consistently embodies the title phrase (118). **Matthews:** The story, which would be better if it had a stronger ending, typifies O's tendency during his period of marital instability to depict family life as confrontational, but the work is unusual in presenting mothers so unattractively (275).

THE SENTRY [1950/1981; *CS*] Father MacEnery and Sister Margaret were Irish Catholics serving a parish near an English military base during World War II. Sister Margaret distrusted the English and their ways, but the priest counseled charity. However, when he caught an English sentry apparently stealing from his garden, he angrily threatened to beat the man, who proclaimed his innocence. When an English officer later informed MacEnery that the soldier might be shot for deserting his post, the priest regretted the affair and did his best to exonerate the sentry. **(RCE) Averill:** This is a comic tale illustrating the development of social links (274). **Matthews:** Based on a true anecdote, the story shows O's ability to present attractive priests (196). The tale is too sentimental and abstract (267). **Wohlgelernter:** O here attacks Irish contempt for the English; the priest and nun are hypocrites (56).

SEPTEMBER DAWN [1929/1985; *GN*] After disbanding their troop, Hickey and Keown, two soldiers, made their dangerous way across the countryside, evading pursuers and gunfire. When they arrived at the house of Hickey's elderly aunt, the cocky Keown told his friend that he planned to woo a girl also staying there. That night, however, his sleep was sorely troubled. The more prosaic Hickey, rising early, found comfort in the girl's embrace. **(RCE) Averill:** Perhaps influenced by Sean O'Faolain's "Fugue," the story illustrates O's more subtle, objective style and his skilled use of contrasting characters and shifting perspectives (247–48). Powerful feelings are implied by the final actions (249). **Bordewyk:** Theme: human contact vs. wartime isolation (39). **Matthews:** The story juxtaposes conflicting tones and themes, prefiguring O's mature style (70). **Tomory:** One of the more effective early stories (31–32). **Wohlgelernter:** Theme: love vs. brutality (36–37).

A SET OF VARIATIONS ON A BORROWED THEME [1960/1981; *CS*] When the husband of sixty-year-old Kate Mahoney died, she decided to supplement her income by raising a foster child, Jimmy, rather than moving in with either of her married daughters, Nora and Molly. Jimmy grew up thinking of Kate as his "Mammy," although he was visited occasionally by his birth mother, "Aunt Nance." After Jimmy agitated for a brother, Kate took in James. Eventually Jimmy began to suspect that Kate was not his real mother, and when "Aunt Nance" married a kind man, the boy moved away with them. He soon returned, however, feeling that his mother resented his resemblance to his real father, whom he eventually sought out. Much later, as Kate lay on her deathbed, she expressed pride in her adopted sons, and although one of her daughters seemed jealous, her neighbors marvelled at the perfect family she had created so late in life. **(RCE) Averill:** This is one of O's best final tales (297); it affirms imagination and unconventional love (298). **Hildebidle:** In provincial towns, children suffer for their parents' failures (185). **Matthews:** This is O's "last *great* story" (334).

THE SHEPHERDS [1954/1981; *CS*] One night Father Whelan asked Father Divine to accompany him to a foreign ship where some local girls were reportedly consorting with the sailors. The frustrated captain, unable to speak English, assumed that Whelan was a jealous lover, and events ended in misunderstanding. **(CTY & KO) Hildebidle:** The story shows how priests sometimes feel forced to behave inappropriately (203). **Bordewyk:** Theme: nature vs. dogma (41). **Tomory:** The priests exemplify two types O often presented—one old and rigid, the other young and uncertain (115). Divine feels the contrast between his vocation, bound by rules, and the sensuality of life aboard ship, but Whelan (typically) never doubts himself or his dogmatism (116).

THE SINNER [*Argosy* (March 1946); untraced]

SION [*The Irish Tribune* (6 August 1926): 9–10] An anonymous narrator tells of his chance encounter in England with Sylvia, whom he had known when both were childhood neighbors in Cork. Her histrionic mother, married to a sailor, often seemed fascinated by the prospect of her husband's accidental death and the large pension she would enjoy as a widow. When the narrator, after remembering their early days, asked Sylvia about her father, he suddenly felt embarrassed by her brief reply. **(RCE)**

THE SISSY [version of "The Genius"]

THE SISTERS [1931/1985; *GN*] Norah Coveny told the narrator a story about two elderly sisters in Cork, Miss Ellen and Miss Kate. Although Kate owned a shop and spoke often of her mentally ill sister, Ellen was never seen. When Kate died, neighbors preparing her wake were startled by Ellen's appearance and conduct and by a shocking revelation. **(RCE) Matthews:** A treatment of death based on an anecdote O heard (70; 74). **Tomory:** One of the "most tightly plotted" early stories (35).

SOIRÉE CHEZ UNE JEUNE BELLE FILLE [1931/1985; *GN*] Young Helen Joyce, performing for the first time as an IRA courier, biked to a remote house where she met two contrasting militants, a female acquaintance from college, and a doctor accompanying a corpse. Her complex experiences gave her a less romantic perspective on her cause. **(RCE) Tomory:** The story's plotlessness may reflect the influence of Chekhov (63).

SOLDIERS ARE WE [version of "Jo"]

SOLO ON GABRIEL'S TRUMPET [*Irish Times* (28 March 1942); untraced]

SONG WITHOUT WORDS [1944/1981; *CS*] Brother Arnold and Brother Michael were both monks who had taken a vow of silence and thus communicated mostly by sign language. One day, after Arnold noticed Michael hiding something, Michael (an ex-jockey) eventually revealed a newspaper reporting racing results. The two men secretly began to share this interest, and Arnold even showed Michael where he had hidden some beer. However, after they later started to play cards, they suddenly felt guilty and in the end went off to confess their transgressions. **(RCE) Averill:** The ending is a bit disappointing, and O offers only a partial view of religious life (262). **Hildebidle:** In one of his best works, O shows a typical suspicion of fault-finding (189); the story is successful partly because the characters are more complex than the moral (198). **Kilroy:** The monks combat their own natures (rather than imposed rules) and eventually triumph (109). **Matthews:** This is O's gentlest story and is the first time he uses his mature technique of beginning with a generalization and then following with a tight, appealing narrative (203–4). **Tomory:** The oral quality emphasized here typifies O's later work (78); isolation leads to a desire for connection (95), but the story is damaged by its concluding sentimentalism (96).

THE SORCERER'S APPRENTICE [1954/1981; *CS*] Jimmy Foley and Una MacDermott had courted for many years and often seemed about to marry. Yet they also constantly fought, and after one such argument Una went to Dublin to stay with her friends, the Sheehys. While there she flirted and eventually had sex with their older friend, the divorced Denis O'Brien. Feeling newly matured, Una returned to Jimmy, but when they had sex while on holiday, the innocence seemed to drain from their relationship. Finally, while Jimmy was upstairs, Una phoned Denis. **(RCE) Hildebidle:** The tale ends with a "bitter if overdue loss of innocence" (187). **Kilroy:** The story typifies the works of O's last decade, which celebrate human variety and humanely refuse to criticize natural (if unconventional) behavior (118). **Matthews:** The work suggests that O's "ideal woman had always been the mercurial, quick-witted, impulsive girl, devoted, loyal, but greatly in need of the rational stability of a man" (298). **Tomory:** Originally entitled "Don Juan's Apprentice," the story typically focuses on innocence vs. experience (109). It effectively presents an aging Irish woman and the typical Irishman's hesitations about marriage (110).

THE STAR THAT BIDS THE SHEPHERDS FOLD [version of "The Shepherds"]

THE STEPMOTHER [1946/1947; *CC*] An anonymous narrator recalls his boyhood friend, Bob Desmond, whose mother died and whose father remarried. Although Bob fought frequently with his sister Sheela, when the well-intentioned step-mother once tried to punish Sheela, Bob kicked her. Questioned later by his father, Bob announced that because the step-mother was not the children's real mother, she had no right to punish them. As Bob's father angrily beat the boy, the step-mother pleaded on Bob's behalf. Afterwards the boy explained that his mother, before dying, had made him promise to resist any future wife. Both the stepmother and narrator seemed stunned at this news. **(RCE) Matthews:** Theme: deep bonds need not depend on blood connections (234). Perhaps reflecting O's own second marriage, the tale is one of several that focuses on isolated children and substitute parents (319–20). **Tomory:** Theme: the complex balancing in relations between adults and children (131). **Wohlgelernter:** Theme: the shocking influence of envious Irish mothers (94–95).

A STORY BY MAUPAUSSANT [1945/1981; CS] As youths, Ted Magner and Terry Coughlan were friends who traded opinions on many subjects, including the merits of various writers. Terry rejected Ted's regard for Maupassant, whom Terry considered crude and insufficiently noble. Later in life, though, Terry became addicted to alcohol and prostitutes, one of whom, in France, told him, "'It's only when you see what life can do to you that you realize what a great writer Maupassant is.'" (RCE)

THE STORYTELLER [1937/1981; CS] Young Afric's grandfather's impending death also symbolizes the end of her childhood. Having grown up with her grandfather's imaginative stories, she found it difficult to accept his sudden silence, as it shattered certain illusions. Her nightly journey to the top of a mountain in the symbolic presence of a "foolish" lamb, during which she conversed with her friend Nance and overheard her father and her uncle talking, served as a rite of initiation into adulthood. **(CW) Hildebidle:** Storytelling is presented as a means of overcoming isolation (207). **Matthews:** This is one of a number of stories from the 1940s that are "emotionally violent, enigmatic, stabbing" (201). **Tomory:** O never published this unusually mythic and magical tale in a book; it laments the death of oral storytelling (69).

THE STUDY OF HISTORY [1957/1957; DR] Larry Delaney explains how, when he was a boy, his curiosity about the past loves of his parents prompted him to visit one of his father's old flames. Larry's mother mentioned old sweethearts with little enthusiasm, but when Larry's father reminisced, he ceased to be a dry, stuffy businessman and recalled his past loves with a brazen enjoyment and vitality that annoyed Larry's mother. Larry's curiosity was assuaged when he visited the home of his father's old sweetheart, now married and known as Mrs. O'Brien. News of the visit worried Larry's mother in the same ways as his father's recollections had. Ultimately Larry matured as he compared and contrasted his own household with the O'Brien home. **(GW) Averill:** Theme: excessive imagination can sabotage real human contact (296). **Matthews:** Theme: lost identity and the meaning of dreams (314).

SUE [1958/1969; C3] Jack Horgan recalls his sister Sue and his exasperation with her various courters, who disrupted his life at home. One of them, Harry Ridgeway, seemed interested both in Sue and in Judy Holmes, about whom he constantly talked. Sue actually encouraged Harry to propose to Judy, but he proposed to Sue instead. Feeling inadequate, however, Sue turned him down. When he later did marry the flawed Judy, Sue and Jack's mother still expressed concern for him—thus displaying a generosity Jack admired. **(RCE)**

TEACHER'S MASS [1955/1981; *CS*] Father Fogarty's first mass each day involved an acolyte named John Considine, an elderly, irascible teacher contemptuous of illiterate peasants and proud of his own pedantic knowledge. Although Fogarty disliked Considine's involvement in the mass, when the old man became sick Fogarty began to realize how much the ceremony meant to him. One morning, when Considine was at death's door as he helped with the unattended mass, Fogarty realized that urging him to cease would be a greater source of pain. Even when Considine died during the mass, Fogarty continued with the ceremony, thereby showing his respect for the man's devotion. **(RCE) Averill:** Fogarty's humaneness appeals to O (294). **Hildebidle:** Fogarty's compassion triumphs over his initial disapproval (203). **Matthews:** The tale was rooted in fact (305). **Tomory:** This is O's most successful depiction of Fogarty and also perhaps his most orthodox tale (121). **Wohlgelernter:** Fogarty, at first deficient, is transformed into a more passionate priest by the end (60).

TEARS—IDLE TEARS [1936/1936; *BC*] An unnamed inspector describes his investigation of the disappearance, and perhaps murder, of a land agent called old Forester. His persistent attempts to solve the mystery were stymied by neighbors and police. His suspicions of conspiracy were supported when he found that the nearby pubs closed early and that none of the patrons saw anything on the night in question. His suspicions finally rested on the schoolmaster, who led him on a merry chase through the mountains in the dead of night. The chase turned out to have been conducted as a decoy so townsfolk could move Forester's body. Finally, when the inspector sent spies out, the community responded with contrived conversations that belied any guilt. For all of his efforts, the Irish inspector was ultimately defeated by the Irish themselves. **(DR) Averill:** Theme: comic conflict between old and new cultures (255).

THAT RYAN WOMAN [version of "The Ugly Duckling"]

THERE IS A LONE HOUSE [1933/1981; *CS*] An isolated woman, hearing a young man approach, offered him tea; he ended up doing chores and staying for months. Later, having learned that she killed her uncle, he drunkenly confronted her in fear and anger. As they confided in each other, their relationship deepened. When he returned home from drinking one night, she accused him of bragging about their non-existent sexual relationship. An ensuing fight led to sex and a new phase in their relationship. Shortly thereafter he left, promising to return after he supposedly visited relatives. Although not fooled, she somehow felt content. When he returned, she seemed pleased with his new maturity. Having molded him, she continued to control the relationship. Finally, incredulous villagers watched as the couple, requesting marriage, approached the local priest. Afterwards, the woman told the priest that she planned to start attending mass regularly. In the end she was examined by the pleased village doctor, who expected to see her again in a few months. **(CS) Hildebidle:** In this story (if not in others) reserved and lonely characters actually achieve happiness (198). **Kilroy:** The loose narrative allows O to articulate both the man's and woman's perspectives; detailed imagery and foreshadowing are used in this work about an evolving, conflictual relationship that finally ends in marriage (120). **Matthews:** First published in 1933, the story departs from O's previous style but foreshadows his recurrent theme of loneliness (103–4). O never reprinted the work, which perhaps reflects his own relationship with Molly Alexander and fantasies about his involvement with Nancy McCarthy (104).

THE THIEF [version of "Christmas Morning"]

A THING OF NOTHING [1946/1947; *CC*] After Ned Lynch (a merchant) married Katty, he began to receive friendly visits from his nephew and brother, from whom he had long been estranged. Although Ned was touched by the renewed contact, his attitude changed when Katty suggested that the relatives might be angling to inherit Ned's store after his death. This possibility made Ned even more anxious to have a son of his own, but Katty never became pregnant. Desperate, she secretly arranged to adopt a child. After pretending pregnancy, she journeyed to Dublin to fetch the baby. There she met the child's ambivalent mother. **(RCE) Averill:** The story does not entirely succeed (288). **Matthews:** Theme: surrogate parenthood (234). **Tomory:** Theme: the social complexities of sex (105).

THE TINKER [read on BBC radio, 17 March 1943; untraced]

THIS MORTAL COIL [1950/1970; *ML*] Michael John describes an atheist friend, Dan Turner, who was so outspoken and unyielding that he lost his true love to another man. After Dan retreated into solitude, Michael John vainly attempted to bring his friend out of despair and particularly opposed Dan's belief that he could end his troubles through death. Michael falsely believed that his friend was cured of his suicidal thoughts. However, after Dan unsuccessfully attempted to kill himself, he thought he had discovered the truth and decided to live. In the end, Michael John lost Dan's close friendship, but for reasons he would not have predicted. **(KO) Averill:** Here, religious conversion leads to happiness (283). **Bordewyk:** Themes: extremism vs. moderation; isolation as a penalty for atheism (42). **Matthews:** One of O's stories about atheists, the work may reflect a personal interest in suicide (253).

A TORRENT DAMMED [1952/1954; *MS*] Tom Looney, an unsuccessful chemist and a frustrated glutton, rushed through the lives of three women, searching for a fortune. Maudie was an old stand-by, comforting Tom even while he began to court the daughter of a rich Irish politician.

Hilda Doherty, on the verge of marriage to Tom, fell from a horse, severely injuring her pelvis and shoulder. As word spread that Hilda might never walk again, Tom drew close to Maudie's friend Kitty. She convinced Tom that his fortune awaited him in the much larger city of Dublin. By marrying Kitty (who also eagerly desired money), Tom lost his chance with the compassionate Maudie and a recovering Hilda. **(CB) Bordewyk:** Theme: economic pragmatism vs. inspiration (46).

THE TRAM [version of "Eternal Triangle"]

TWILIGHT [*Lovat Dickson's Magazine*; untraced]

THE UGLY DUCKLING [1957/1981; *CS*] Mick Courtney had been friends with Nan Ryan (an unattractive but pious tomboy) since childhood, but in late adolescence he noticed that she had suddenly become beautiful. Although courted by wealthier men, Nan had always loved Mick, but their plans to marry were disrupted by an argument. Mick moved to Dublin, where he married another woman; Nan, meanwhile, broke off an engagement to another man and eventually entered a convent. When Mick learned of her decision years later, he visited her, and suddenly her puzzling behavior began to make sense. As he left the convent, he realized, with joy, that their love would always remain undisturbed. **(RCE) Averill:** Theme: how early feelings shape later behavior (302). As in other late works by O, meanings are too openly stated, and both Mick and Nan are presented too sympathetically (303). **Kilroy:** This story reflects a movement toward sudden self-awareness typical of O's other best works (110), although here the moment of realization is subtly expressed by the narrator (118). **Matthews:** The story was rejected by *New Yorker* editors as too preachy, but O defended it as lyrical (312). **Tomory:** The final explanation seems unobtrusive (108).

UNAPPROVED ROUTE [1952/1981; *CS*] When Rosalind, an attractive and free-spirited English school mistress, became pregnant following a brief and scandalous affair with Jim Hourigan, a good-natured but insensible Irishman, she found herself feeling abandoned and disillusioned. She thus accepted an impetuous marriage proposal from Frankie Daly, a conscientious and benevolent Irishman. Although they were happy at first, as Rosalind neared the end of her pregnancy she wrote a derisive letter to Hourigan. Alleging that he was unaware of the pregnancy, Hourigan hastily returned. His return, however, inevitably undermined Rosalind's marriage with Frankie. Although hurt, Frankie accepted his loss stoically, regarding the marriage as an added bonus in his otherwise uneventful and simple existence. The narrator, however, is ambiguous about whether Hourigan and Rosalind ever did find lasting happiness, although he does not exclude that possibility, despite the "unapproved route" that brought them together. **(KM) Hildebidle:** O implies that happiness may be less important than not being unhappy; the narrator's summary comments are carefully qualified (199). **Matthews:** This is O's most revealing story about his own relationship with a mistress; O "considered love a matter of wary diplomacy" (277). **Wohlgelernter:** Frankie fails to understand Rosalind's vanity; magnanimity can never be a substitute for love (104).

UNCLE PAT (Unpublished; broadcast, probably early 1940s/1981; *CP*) Willie tells of his Uncle Pat and the uncle's cohort, Owney Mac, and a particularly memorable day at the races. Because of his superior intellect, Owney Mac was discouraged by the shortcomings of his native Ireland and mourned them each year with a week of drunken tomfoolery. Uncle Pat was the designated caretaker and commiserator during Mac's period of incapacitation. One year their antics landed them in jail, and it took some ingenious maneuvering by Willie and the local sergeant to get them out. **(AG)**

UPROOTED [1937/1981; *CS*] By spring, Ned Keating was tired of teaching and of Dublin, so he jumped at an invitation to go home to Kerry with his brother Tom, a priest. The shy, serious Ned admired the boisterous, sociable Tom. At a family gathering, Tom seemed in high spirits as he joked about matching Ned up with the beautiful Cait Deignan. Next morning, though, Tom revealed his painful isolation and despair. Ned began to realize that both he and his disappointed brother might never feel at home or achieve their dreams of youth. **(CTY) Averill:** The complex design, perhaps influenced by Joyce, contains "five sections linked by structural correspondences and parallels and by symbolic motifs" (264). Because Ned's present and future seem hopeless, his past seems initially attractive, and imagery of light and darkness is emphasized when O describes the return home (264–65). Theatrical imagery implies that Ned is now a spectator, while journey imagery implies change (265). Cait's lofty home suggests love's elevated perspective (266), but the brothers finally realize that they will be exiles anywhere (267). **Hildebidle:** Ned discovers that leaving home physically may not mean doing so mentally (188). The story illustrates O's narrative balance of closeness and detachment (204). **Kilroy:** The brothers' quest for peace at home leads to a sense of loss (109); Ned substitutes one dreamworld (his lost home) for another (the initially appealing city [110]). **Matthews:** Lyrical, poetic, and visual, this intriguing story depicts people caught between a lost past and an uncertain future (202–3). **Thompson:** Ned, full of pride, is an anachronism (78). **Tomory:** These typical O characters are presented in a lyrical, poetic style in the first of O's stories to describe a lonely priest (99–100).

VANITY [1953/1954; *MS*] When the elderly but proud Bishop of Moyle had an accident while visiting a distant city, he took care to ensure that he was hospitalized secretly, lest his young, annoying, and ambitious assistant find out. His secular disguise worked so well that visiting nurses spoke to him more frankly than he could have imagined. When he returned to Moyle, however, he was even more surprised. **(RCE) Wohlgel-**

ernter: The bishop's pride is heinously sinful; the story epitomizes O's view of the shortcomings of priests (57).

VARIATIONS ON A BORROWED THEME [version of "A Set of Variations on a Borrowed Theme"]

WAR [1926/1981; *CP*] An omniscient narrator describes an intense stand-off between a small contingent of Irish Army soldiers and some better-equipped rebels. The incident began with the Commandant easily taking a carload of rebels as prisoners, including their vociferous and wildly agitated driver. After the soldiers and prisoners stopped to eat at a farm-house, other rebels surrounded it and began attacking. The Commandant's control over his men wavered when they realized that surrender was inevitable. As the situation worsened, the soldiers, the prisoners, and especially the Commandant felt increasingly disjointed from each other and from reality. **(AG) Matthews:** Although O never reprinted or rewrote this early and relatively unsuccessful story (based on his own capture), it already reveals some of the typical stylistic and thematic traits of his later writing (63–64).

THE WEEPING CHILDREN [1961/1969; *SV*] Joe Saunders believed his young wife (a devout Catholic) to be honest and true and was ecstatic when their first child was born. However, his wife Brigid reacted very differently and began to behave oddly. When Joe questioned her, she confessed to having borne another man's child before she met him. Shocked and disappointed that she had not trusted him enough to tell him the truth before they were married, Joe nevertheless put aside his own hurt feelings in order to concentrate on ensuring the welfare of his wife's illegitimate child. He travelled to Ireland, where he met the young girl, who was staying with a group of other children. His final view of them was one he could never forget. **(TG) Hildebidle:** Theme: the darker aspects of small towns (184). The story illustrates O's "double vision"—his ability to examine yet also empathize with individuals and their circumstances (204).

WHAT GIRLS ARE FOR [*Collier's* (17 March 1951): 21; 68–69] Michael Murphy recalls his rivalry with his younger sister Biddy when they were children. When their baby brother Paddy became very ill, Michael promised God that he would give up such pleasures as his position as "Chief Gang Leader" and the "Viking Raids" conducted by his neighborhood gang if only Paddy would get well. Biddy, on the other hand, took immediate and very practical action. She nurtured the child back to health. Michael, proud of his sister's abilities, learned "what girls are for." **(CS)**

WHAT'S WRONG WITH THE COUNTRY [1936/1936; *BC*] An anonymous narrator relates Desmond's description of how Desmond and several friends intermittently debated Ireland's failings. Ferguson thought the

Irish were too lazy to accomplish anything. Joyce acknowledged the failures of society but blamed individuals who failed to complain about poor service. Desmond called Joyce's position "'moral cowardice.'" Nagel proposed that the entire country lived in a daydream. Essentially, the list of views of "what's wrong with the country" seemed as long as the list of Irishmen arguing. Desmond finally identified the problem as excessive talk. Ultimately the issue is left open for further debate. **(DR) Hildebidle:** Although O saw conversation as a way of defeating loneliness, here he depicts it as merely empty (215–16). **Matthews:** The story closely reflects an autobiographical incident (110).

THE WILD LOMASNEYS [version of "The Mad Lomasneys"]

THE WORLD OF ART AND REILLY [*Vogue* (July 1948): 74–75; 100] Tom Donovan recalls how he and his brother-in-law Jerry recently visited an antique shop ostensibly operated by a Mr. Cooney, a "friend" of an art speculator named Reilly. Donovan suspected a scam and watched, exasperated, as Jerry bought a ring to give to his wife on their wedding anniversary. On the train ride home, Jerry stunned Donovan by "scamming" an American jeweler, selling the ring for a respectable profit, only to find out that it was worth even more. Himself enamored of a "hand-carved" chess set in Cooney's shop, Donovan became quite put out when a friend he had tipped off bought the set for a lower price than Cooney had quoted Donovan. **(CS)**

THE WREATH [1955/1981; *CS*] When Father Devine died, his two friends, Father Fogarty and Father Jackson, drove to his funeral. The local priest objected that a wreath (a pagan symbol) had been sent by a woman (even worse). Fogarty and Jackson speculated about Devine's possible relationship with the woman and reflected about their own lives. Although members of Devine's family felt uneasy about displaying the wreath, the two priests, linked by their friendship for Devine and by a new friendship with each other, persuaded them to do so. **(RCE) Averill:** The wreath comes to symbolize the largeness of love (294). **Tomory:** This is one of O's best stories about young priests (119). **Wohlgelernter:** Here as in "The Frying Pan," O seems to endorse priestly marriage (61).

Some Final Words

O'Connor the Novelist:
Notes from a Conversation between Harriet Sheehy and Valentina Tenedini

In addition to writing short stories, plays, poems, criticism, and journalistic pieces, Frank O'Connor also composed two novels—*The Saint and Mary Kate* (1932) and *Dutch Interior* (1940). O'Connor believed that the abilities to write short fiction and novels were distinct talents, and his view of his own novels is suggested by his answer to a question posed by Walter Kerr during an unpublished interview:

> **WK:** Mr. O'Connor, I suppose there are still a great many people who think of the short story as a kind of test flight for an eventual novel. I gather that you don't.
>
> **FOC:** Not entirely, no.
>
> **WK:** You don't think of it as preparatory work or as experimentation toward a longer form?
>
> **FOC:** Well, if that had been the case I would have *done* something serious in the longer form by now, but I've already made two experiments with the novel and I didn't succeed.
>
> **WK:** Oh, you have tried novels?
>
> **FOC:** [in a tone of rueful mock chagrin]: I have, yes. [Kerr chuckles.] They disappeared![1]

---

[1]The full interview is available on a cassette tape entitled *Focus on Frank O'Connor: The Storyteller Talks with Walter Kerr about Literature* (West Hollywood, CA: Center for Cassette Studies, 1971).

Although many critics have concurred with O'Connor's opinion of his novels, these books surely deserve renewed examination. Evidence that they have not entirely "disappeared" and can indeed inspire enthusiastic reactions is available in many forms, including reprintings and translations into foreign languages. The most recent of these, Valentina Tenedini's forthcoming translation of *Dutch Interior* into Italian, was the subject of a recent discussion between Tenedini and Harriet O'Donovan Sheehy, Frank O'Connor's widow. Tenedini's remarks give some flavor of the nature and appeal of this particular effort by O'Connor in the "longer form."—RCE

***

HS: Valentina, when we first met you asked me a lot of questions. Now that you have finished translating *Dutch Interior*, I would like to ask you a few. To begin, I am very curious to know why you chose *Dutch Interior*. I would have expected it to present enormous problems because it is so strongly Irish (and specifically Cork) in both language and feeling.

VT: I very honestly must say I let my heart choose, so when it comes to accounting for this choice I am not sure I sensibly can. I suppose I somehow sensed it was a book that had not been paid much attention, or else too much, considering that it was banned for nearly twenty years. It stands out as a watershed within Frank O'Connor's work. I think anybody who studies his work and the evolution of his thought, art, style, and mind should read it. The language is absolutely beautiful and I had just to read a few lines to sense (no other term would be more appropriate to express the way I felt) it had to be translated, and if so, Italian had to be the language!

Each detail seemed to confirm my initial impression of an instinctive affinity between Irish-English and Italian (and, for that matter, between Ireland and Italy and between the Irish and Italian mentalities). Such an affinity I had never noticed in any English book I had read before. Consider the structure, for instance: the sentences and the paragraphs are very long, much longer in comparison with the English style. (As a matter of fact, one of the things we Italian students of English are reminded of, when writing in English, is to avoid the tendency to write long sentences as when writing in Italian.) Our sentences are long, I presume, because we are talkative people (most of us), and our written style is clearly affected by our spoken habits. And that is why the same feature in the structure of *Dutch Interior* was so impressive to me. Are not the Irish in fact famous for their talkative habits and eloquence too?

HS: Could you give me some specific examples of this "affinity," which (I must admit) I would never have imagined existed?

VT: The dialogues, for instance, witty and lively, sounded to my ears as if they had been spoken by Italians; they were, for a change, quite easy to translate since an Italian would have spoken in exactly the same way and tone, and often with even the same amount of words. Here's an example, when Eileen and Father Lynnot are talking:

> "Anyhow, I don't believe in religion any longer. I think it's just another swindle like all the others."
> "My goodness," he said with his maddening facetiousness, "that'll be a terrible blow to them in Rome. They might as well shut up shop." (Chapter 8, p. 145)

> "Comunque, non ho piú una religione. Penso che sia solo un imbroglio comme tutto il resto."
> "Dio mio," disse col suo irritante fare faceto, "Sará un colpo terribile per squelli lá a Roma. Tanto vale che chiudano bottega."

HS: Did the similarities extend beyond the phrasing—for example to expressions or attitudes?

VT: I also found the plot of the novel and its characters close to the Italian mentality. Family ties and reputation play an important role within Italian society, and in the 1930s (the time during which *Dutch Interior* is set) their influence would have been even stronger, so I guess the same events could have been set in Italy, too. The same speculation on the country made by some of the characters, at some stages in the book, could have been applied to Italy: the latter too used to be a nation of emigrants in those days. Many Italian emigrants would have been equally disappointed as [the character] Gus Devane was, going back to their native land, and would have escaped from it again.

HS: You've obviously studied the book very closely. What else did you find in it that particularly caught your attention?

VT: The style of the narration, so careful with the description of lights and shadows, people's movements, facial and physical features and attitudes, makes me think of a play script. Clearly Frank O'Connor was still close to his experience as a theater-lover and play writer and did not want, in my opinion, his readers to miss any detail of the situation he was describing. It seemed to me as if he were so dutiful and careful in order to avoid any possible misunderstanding.

Each chapter is a short story in itself, about a single character. (Many of them are recurrent in previous or later short stories.) All the chapters have poetic endings. This is, again, evidence of Frank O'Connor's previous interests and work: love and study of poetry. (Quotations from Irish and English poets are frequent in the text.)

The book is dominated by the idea of stillness: those who cannot adapt to it either escape or rebel and die (young). So the reader gets this feeling of a novel in which a lot of events take place yet nothing changes, and he/she is finally left with an "open ending," free to imagine which way the characters will turn: to surrender or rebellion.

HS: My husband loved translating Irish poetry, but he once told me that he thought the only thing more difficult than doing it well was breaking stones! What have been your goals in translating this book, and are you happy with the results?

VT: To me, translating is like penetrating within the structure of a building, a monument, to study what it is like, what it is made of, and then to try to re-build as close as possible to the original, only in a different color.... This image of mine may sound too literary or sophisticated, but it is, as a matter of fact, the best way I could find to "picture" the translation process and progress. Strangely enough, description has the lion's share in *Dutch Interior*, and references to portraits and paintings are frequent. Apparently figurative art is essential to any other form of artistic creation: do we not, in fact, see with our mind's eye what we are reading in a book?

As to my success: Translators, in my opinion, can only seize the moment, seize it with their heart and mind, and this is what I have honestly done. Whether I did a good job or a bad job is not my place to judge.

Postscript

Harriet O'Donovan Sheehy

I sometimes think that being a writer's widow is a career in it-self. Like all careers it has its highs and lows. The lows include dealing with tax authorities who deduct tax at source and then don't want to give it back, publishers who insist something is in the public domain when it isn't, other publishers who ask you to dig out a letter or a picture which they were sure they had but can't find, and graduate students who ask you questions which you don't understand. But the highs make up for everything. Best of all is getting a letter from someone who has read and loved something your husband wrote, and wants to tell you about it. Then there are editors and literary agents and other writers who become your lifelong friends; there is the endless fascination of talking about books; and there is also occasionally the opportunity of work with the editors (and contributors) to a book like this. Bob Evans, Richard Harp, and I have had a prolonged e-mail corre-spondence for the last year and a half. Bob and Richard have been endlessly patient and helpful, and everything they have asked for (or about) has been either interesting, challenging, and/or mem-ory- and thought-provoking. It was their suggestion that we might end the book with an "e-mail interview," but some of the ques-tions posed had been, I thought, better answered by critics and scholars (people with academic credentials). So I suggested a sort of postscript consisting of ideas, reflections, and partial answers to questions. (Perhaps I should say that I haven't read a single word of the book, so I am, as it were, writing in the dark, and this is more meditation than substantial contribution.)

There are three things I'd like to write about: Frank O'Con-nor's early work; his attitude to his own work and to criticism of it;

and the dramatic change in the Irish people's attitude to their own history, past and present, and how that might affect his reputation.

Because Valentina Tenedini is translating it into Italian and needed some help with Cork phrases and words, I recently reread *Dutch Interior*. I found it strange, or perhaps I should say "atypical" (unlike his other novel *The Saint and Mary Kate* which, though full of faults, is pure O'Connor). Then when the editors of this collection asked if I had copies of his early stories I began to read them as well. The last time I had read any of them was seventeen years ago when we were choosing stories for *The Cornet Player Who Betrayed Ireland*. One story, "The Awakening" (published in *Dublin Magazine* in 1928) struck me as being in the same mood as the novel, and interesting as a subject for analysis. We rejected it for *The Cornet Player* because it isn't (at least by his own definition) really a story. But what I found interesting about it is that it is an attempt by a young man of twenty-four to write about a confused and ambivalent young woman.

Eileen, the heroine, is describing her feelings as she goes through her customary routine on her last day in Cork. She is emigrating to America and all the usual sights and sounds have a special clarity and poignancy for her. We meet her sensible older sister, but more importantly, we meet her young man, Jim. It is in the conversations between Eileen and Jim that we find the theme of this story. It turns out to be a rather modern theme (though I suspect that O'Connor would not have phrased it this way) because Eileen wants to "find herself ... to find out who she really is." It is hard to know if that is what O'Connor thought he was writing about. There are no comments by the author (as there are in some later stories) and Eileen's remarks are far more inchoate than those of Jim (who is, on the whole, a better portrait). But the sense of frustration and impatience and desperate need to live—to get out of the claustrophobic atmosphere—are very similar to the mood of *Dutch Interior* (which was, in fact, written twelve years later). I wonder if one answer to the question "why did he reprint so few of his early stories?" can be found in the mood of this early work. Perhaps he felt that the tone was unduly pessimistic or sentimental or self-pitying, or too heavily influenced by the Russian writers or by Hardy and thus not his true voice. I don't know. But I think the question is pertinent and could make an interesting topic for further research.

As he has described it many times, O'Connor's attitude to his own work veered between exultation and despair. I could usually tell when he had hit a sticky patch because he became rather silent and spent a lot of time "staring" (as his son said) "at his sneakers." In his early letters to his writer friends Sean O'Faolain and Geoffrey Phibbs he would say things like, "... Sean agrees with you that I should have little difficulty in getting a publisher. There I part from you both. I'm in the dumps." Or "I'm working like a brute beast.... It's only in my stories I'm getting what I want though I slave more at poetry than anything else." Or "I'm sending you a copy of 'Sion.'... wretched, not worth the 12.6 I got for it, but still, a lovely story if only I can rewrite it properly." Or "I am experimenting with poetry again. It is curious how much I am attracted by it, although I am not a poet and am always just missing satisfaction in my own work." When he was in a cheerful mood he would say things like, "I suppose you missed my masterpiece in the Dublin Magazine?" And "I have just finished a story in a mood of exultation, and can only think 'poor Shakespeare.'"

He never talked about his own work to me in any abstract way, so I don't know what his strengths and weaknesses were. However, in his writing classes he did insist on certain rules and perhaps the following extract from a letter to John Kelleher gives some idea of what he demanded of himself: "I have at last convinced the students that there is such a thing as a good subject for a story.... Now I am hammering home the staggering fact that a treatment is not the same thing as either a theme or a completed short story." There is a specific reference to the way he saw his work in an interview which was published in the *Paris Review* in 1957. "'Get black on white' used to be Maupassant's advice.... that's what I always do.... I'm always looking at the design of a story, not the treatment."

He certainly said that his novels were honorable failures, but I never heard him say much about his books of literary criticism, so I was fascinated to find the following in a letter written to an English friend in the late 1940s: "I have just finished the little book on Shakespeare [*The Road to Stratford*] in a blaze of excitement and feel it is very good. I've been thinking of it for years, since the Blitz in fact, and it seems like a milestone passed." And about the same book he wrote to his literary agent: "My profoundest apologies for having written it instead of something practical, but like the servant's baby it came of its own accord." I think he thought of himself primarily as a short story writer for he used to say that his idea of a perfect Christmas was to have a ham sandwich, a glass of beer, a walk and then to be totally blessed by writing the perfect story. He also said that his idea of Hell was to be in a place where he had no work to do, which is probably why he would turn to criticism or to translating Irish poetry when he didn't feel well enough to try to tackle a story.

As to how he felt about criticism of his work, I am not really sure, but I have a few suspicions. He used to put a brave face on rejections, saying, "As I tell any aspiring young writer, you have to remember that an editor or critic is only another human being like yourself, who might have had a bad day. Don't be discouraged by rejection ... just send your work somewhere else." When one Irish critic wrote that "O'Connor's priests are all too fallible and human" he said, "I suppose what he would like is: 'God bless us all here,' said Father Fogarty, hanging his halo on the coat rack." William Maxwell, his editor at the *New Yorker*, wrote that "What he could praise honestly he praised. And he did not require you to praise him." I personally think that the only criticism which would really have hurt and annoyed him was the sort of thing which Francis Stuart is quoted as saying: "O'Connor is the soft centre of Irish writing." He despised sentimentality (often distinguishing it from sentiment) and would have been distressed if someone found his work sentimental. In the 1940s he wrote: "... if I were the sort of popular writer who could get into the *Saturday Evening Post* ... [it might be different] ... but I shall be content to compound for *New Yorker* rates for the rest of my natural existence." And later: "I haven't seen the *New Yorker* story, which is a pity because for the past week I have been in the mood AE described as a poor hen running around crying, 'Oh God, God! there'll be no more eggs!' I could have done with the lift." To the best of my knowledge, he never responded to criticism of his work, though he often took up the cudgels in defense of other writers who, he felt, had been unjustly criticized. And, of course, if he didn't like somebody's work (no matter how popular) he didn't hesitate to say so—and explain why.

The changing attitude in Ireland has been something I've watched with interest and, at times, incredulity. We were married in England in 1953 and first came here in the spring of 1954. Ireland, at that time, was very poor, the people were firmly conservative, pietistic, and moralistic and (to this American anyhow) seemed rather old-fashioned. I didn't much like the place, though I did like his few close friends. We used to visit every year, usually staying in Dublin and Cork—with side trips to Sligo, Kilkenny,

and Limerick. There were people who wouldn't speak to him because he had divorced his first wife and married me. There were
formal literary occasions to which he was not invited. After all, he
was a "lapsed" Catholic and an outspoken critic of the institutional
church. What's more, he wrote stories about Irish girls who had
babies when they weren't even married—and everybody knew
that such things happened in England (pagan place that it was) but
certainly not in Ireland. Many of his books were still banned; the
atmosphere was both repressive and depressing. To make matters
worse, he had written an article about Ireland in *Holiday* magazine
and had dared to say that the country was less than perfect—that
many of the people were poor and lived in squalor and had TB.
Bad enough to say these things in private, but to write in America
and expose the country to criticism by outsiders was unforgivable.
Needless to say the Irish Americans were as critical of him as the
Irish at home. They publicly objected to his stories. The *New Yorker*
told him with some amusement that the parish priest and all the
parishioners of a Catholic church in Brooklyn had informed them
that they were canceling their subscriptions to the magazine because it had published his "News for the Church," which, according to them, mocked the sacrament of confession. (He was rather
pleased when, a week later, he got a letter from a man who said he
had gone back to the practice of his religion after reading that
story.) Anyhow, the Irish of O'Connor's time were extremely defensive and there was just a faint hint of change in the atmosphere
when we came to live in Dublin in 1961.

Now, however, everything has changed utterly. Every scandal
is reported in detail and with relish by the papers, radio, and TV.
There are tribunals to investigate suspected wrongdoings (from
clerical abuse to government fraud). Recent statistics reveal the
rather surprising fact that almost a quarter of the children are born
to unwed mothers. The institutional Catholic Church has found itself having to adopt a defensive posture. The Constitution has
been amended to allow divorce. And, for the first time, there is so
much prosperity in the country that Ireland is referred to as The
Celtic Tiger and many former emigrants are coming back here to
work. When *An Only Child* was published in 1961 there was great
resentment about the fact that O'Connor told the truth about his
father's alcoholism and his mother's dreadful childhood. But today
[Frank McCourt's autobiography] *Angela's Ashes* is a runaway
bestseller. It is as though O'Connor were born and writing at just
the wrong time. He was ahead of his time, in writing about situa-

tions which would come to be almost taken for granted, and yet because he described attitudes which no longer exist, he has been described as old-fashioned.

Sometimes I think he was too gentle a writer ever to be wildly popular. He wrote so much about ordinary, decent people; their modest expectations; their misunderstandings and foolishnesses; their pride and stubbornness—people who make terrible mistakes and live in a world where they must suffer the consequences. On the whole his voice is low-key and affectionate, wry and compassionate, totally lacking in sensationalism and "marvels." I remember asking him once for whom he wrote. He thought a while and then said, "I think—no, I hope—I am writing for the lonely reader down the country somewhere who reads a story of mine and then says, 'Yes. That's how it is. He understands.'" Perhaps that is one of the reasons he has a devoted, loyal, intelligent but small following. I suspect he wouldn't want it any other way.

"Guests of the Nation":
A Radio Script

Frank O'Connor
(introduced by Robert C. Evans)

"Guests of the Nation," one of Frank O'Connor's earliest stories, is also by wide agreement one of his best. Indeed, it is considered one of the most powerful works of short fiction of the twentieth century. Little wonder, then, that O'Connor chose this story as one of three to dramatize for broadcast performance on Radio Eireann on 1 February 1959. (The other members of this trio of works were "The Martyr" and "Private Property.") Apparently the stories were broadcast under the collective title of *Fighting Men*, although a surviving text of all three scripts lists the title as "Three Plays of Civil War."[1]

I first had a chance to examine the radio version of "Guests of the Nation" just as the present book was in the final stages of preparation for the printer. When I contacted our publisher, Tom Bechtle, to ask if an already-long book might possibly be made just a bit longer, he readily agreed (as I suspected he would, since Tom is a generous and indulgent man). Similarly, when I contacted Mrs. Harriet O'Donovan Sheehy to ask if the radio script of "Guests" might be included in the present volume, she also in-

---

[1]See the bibliography in Maurice Sheehy, ed., *Michael/Frank: Studies on Frank O'Connor* (New York: Knopf, 1969), 175. The typed text of the three scripts is currently part of the O'Connor collection housed at the University of Florida. I am grateful to the librarians there for allowing me to copy these texts, and I am particularly thankful to Mrs. Harriet O'Donovan Sheehy (O'Connor's widow) for granting permission to reproduce here the script of "Guests of the Nation." *Please note that any permission to perform the script must be sought from the O'Connor estate by contacting the University of Florida Libraries Department of Special Collections.*

stantly granted permission. Such kindness has characterized her involvement with this book from start to finish, and, as the book now finally does near completion, it is a pleasure to acknowledge her splendid cooperation for one last time.

Students of O'Connor's great story should find much of interest in the following script. Here and now are neither the place nor time to discuss in any detail the many comparisons and contrasts that might be noted between the script and either the original or revised versions of the story.[2] Suffice it to say for the moment that in the radio version, both Bonaparte and Hawkins are given greatly expanded spoken roles; that Jeremiah Donovan seems a much less significant (and even somewhat more sympathetic) figure; that the role of the old woman (here named "Mrs. Leary") seems much diminished in the script; and, in general, that the two versions help highlight the important generic differences between short fiction and drama. The script contains much new writing as well as much that is taken over directly from the various versions of the prose tale, and these additions testify (if any more testimony were needed!) that for O'Connor, revision was rarely a mechanical process or merely a matter of self-repetition. Each time he went back to a story, O'Connor did more than tinker with it: he tried to see it as he had seen it at first—with fresh perception.

The typescript of the dramatized "Guests" inevitably contains a few typographical errors, including a handful of misspellings. In the version printed below, these have been silently corrected. Punctuation, particularly the use of quotation marks, has been made to conform to American usage. Annotations have been kept to a minimum. At one point near the very end of the play, someone (presumably O'Connor) has scored through an entire line of speech. The ensuing printed text graphically imitates this deletion rather than omitting the line altogether.

Apparently O'Connor himself introduced the three plays when they were broadcast on Radio Eireann. His comments (appropriately enough) fall into three sections, each preceding one of the stories. Part of the first and all of the third comments appear as follows (with manuscript additions and deletions reproduced):

---

[2]For discussion of the various versions of the story, including the 1959 dramatization by Neil McKenzie, see the essays co-written with Michael Probst and with Katie Magaw, which are printed on pages 189–202 of the present volume.

I

One of the stories that I've dramatized for tonight's performance was written in 1928, another in 1956. It's a long time to keep up your interest in a subject, but ~~violence~~ a war he's seen at close hand is a theme a writer never really tires of, because it shows characters and situations in such a vivid light. After all, ~~a man~~ you can spend ~~his~~ y[our] life in an Irish city or town without ever once meeting a real killer, but those of you whose age, like my own, verges on sixty, will remember having met real killers, and not only on the other side, [either]....

III

There's a professor in America[3] who has evolved an interesting theory that the third story, "Guests of the Nation[,]" reveals subconsciously my hatred of all Englishmen.[4] He points out ~~to his students~~ that the Englishmen are called Belcher and Hawkins, while the Irishmen are called Noble and Bonaparte. ~~Maybe he's right! Maybe I do hate Englishmen.~~ The little bit of dialogue that formed the core of the story I heard one summer day in Gormanstown Internment Camp when I ~~heard~~ listened to a couple of hefty country boys taking off the accents of two English prisoners. By the time I wrote it,[5] it had turned into a story about religion. That again is something people of my own age may remember—the way we had to ask ourselves what it was we really believed in. Maybe Belcher is Belcher only because I dislike belching, and Hawkins Hawkins because I dislike hawking, but ~~for me~~ my own guess [is that[6]] the four men in

---

[3]At this point O'Connor has scrawled a brief (presumably sarcastic) remark that is difficult to read. The main word seems to be "brilliant."

[4]O'Connor seems to have intended to add a five-word marginal comment here, although I have not been able to decipher it.

[5]O'Connor seems to have intended to insert a three- or four-word comment here, but I am unable to make it out. The second or third word seems to be "you."

[6]A phrase such as this seems demanded by the handwritten revision.

this story are all deeply religious men; all of them[,] to use a phrase I heard a good deal in childhood, living in the presence of God.[7]

***

BONAPARTE. I couldn't at the time see the point of myself and Noble guarding Belcher and Hawkins at all, seeing that you'd have recognized them for Englishmen anywhere. At the same time it's my belief that you could have planted them down anywhere from this to Claregalway and they'd have taken root like a native weed. I never in my life saw two men to take to the country the way they did.

They were handed on to us by the Second Battalion when the search for them became too hot, and Noble and myself took over with a natural feeling of responsibility, but Hawkins made us look like fools when he showed that he knew the country better than we did ourselves.

HAWKINS. Don't you worry, Bonaparte. We're not exactly keen on escaping, as you'll discover. You just be nice to us, and see that we're well-supplied with fags,[8] and you'll be sure to have a quiet life. That right, chum?

BELCHER (a heavy, comfortable voice). That's right, chum.

BONAPARTE. Who told you I was Bonaparte?

HAWKINS. That's easy, chum. We were told that Noble and you would be in charge, and that Noble had a brother a priest. One look at you is enough to show that if you've got a brother, he's much more likely to be doing time. And, speaking of that, Mary Brigid O'Connell told me to ask you what you did with the pair of her brother's socks you borrowed the last time you were there.

---

[7]Near the bottom of the page, O'Connor has scrawled a few other words, which seem to read as follows: "is because these belief & love are [illegible]."

[8]At the time O'Connor wrote, the main meaning of this word, of course, was "cigarettes."

BONAPARTE (a bit nonplussed). Ah, so you know Mary Brigid O'Connell too?

HAWKINS. I'm the first great love of Mary Brigid O'Connell's young life. I'm the man that taught Mary Brigid to dance. You silly coots won't dance proper dances on principle—though I'm damned if I know how a dance can have a principle.

NOBLE. If you lived here, you might soon find out.

HAWKINS. You forget, Noble. I do live here, whether I like it or not, and I can't find out. I don't mind dancing "The Walls of Limerick" do I? I suppose you think I can't? Well, what's wrong with this? (whistles and dances a few steps.) What is there in that that shows a lack of principle on my part? How do you deduce that I'm really saying "To Hell with the British Constitution and the Independent Labour Party?" You don't. You're nice boys, but you don't have your heads screwed on right.

NOBLE. You like arguing too, don't you?

HAWKINS. No, Noble, that's where you make your great mistake. I never argue. Never. I just like a rational basis for existence, that's all. You prove to me that something's scientifically correct, and I'll back you through thick and thin. But don't you come telling me that fox-trots have principles like those half-wits in Ballymorecrazy.

NOBLE. Ballymacasey.[9]

HAWKINS. I call it Ballymorecrazy. And in case you want to know the name of this place is[10] Ballymorelooney. All right. Now, let's have a nice patriotic game of cards. None of your foreign bridge or poker. Just straight Irish forty-five. That right, Belcher?

BELCHER. That's right, chum.

---

[9]An Irish place-name.

[10]Perhaps "is" was meant to read "it's."

MRS. LEARY. If ye're going to sit in here, I'll have to light the fire.

BELCHER. That's all right, madam. Allow me! (picks up bucket)

MRS. LEARY. Well, I never!

HAWKINS. Handy chap about the house, ain't he? Light the fire, fetch the water, clean the lamps, *and* bring the lady her morning tea in bed.

MRS. LEARY. Morning tea in bed? Oh, you blackguard, you!

HAWKINS. You're going to have it from this out, lady. All the comforts of the British workingman's home! That's us! Why is the British Army tearing the whole South of Ireland asunder, looking for us? Why is the Irish Republican Army trying to conceal us as if we were the Crown Jewels? To these two questions there is only one answer. Neither side can do without us. You'll see!

BONAPARTE. We saw all right. Any priveleges [sic] Belcher and Hawkins had with the Second Battalion they naturally took with us, and after a day or two we gave up all pretence of keeping an eye on them. We took it all as a joke, the way they seemed to take it. Coming on to dark, the big Englishman, Belcher, would shift his long legs out of the ashes and say "Well, chums, what about it?" and Noble or myself would say "All right, chum," and Hawkins would light the lamp and produce the cards. But even when we were playing cards, Hawkins would keep on arguing, and he worried the soul out of Noble, who had a brother a priest, with a string of questions that would have made a cardinal crazy. To make it worse, even in treating of holy subjects, Hawkins had a deplorable tongue. I never in all my career met a men who could mix such a variety of cursing and bad language into an argument.

BONAPARTE. Oh, for God's sake, don't get on religion again! Why the hell can't you mind the game?

HAWKINS. (angrily) How the hell can I mind the game when Noble keeps on making silly statements like that?

NOBLE. You're the one that makes the silly statements.

BONAPARTE. Never mind who makes the silly statements. Belcher can mind the game. Belcher can win every game because he's not always blathering like you.

HAWKINS. I resent that, Bonaparte. Belcher can win every game because Belcher has no social conscience. Belcher never gives a thought to the sufferings of the poor bloody mill-workers in Lancashire so long as he can win a tanner at forty-five. Isn't that right, Belcher?

BELCHER (peaceably). That's right, chum. (in the tone nearest to what counts with Belcher as anguish) No, Hawkins, you shouldn't have played the spade. Don't you have a diamond?

HAWKINS (viciously). Of course I've got diamonds. I'm a god-damn capitalist. I'm rolling in diamonds. There's a small one for yourself.

BELCHER. Not the ace, chum. You shouldn't play the ace. Stick to the rules. Highest in red and lowest in black. Bonaparte is right, you know. You really should concentrate.

HAWKINS. I ask you again, how the hell can I concentrate when those bastards keep on making silly remarks like that [?] Listen to Bonaparte, complaining that I'm talking about religion. I never mentioned religion. That silly cuckoo thinks I'm talking about religion when I'm just quoting simple economics.

BONAPARTE. You started attacking the priests. That's not economics.

HAWKINS. Of course it's economics. I said in passing that the capitalists pay the priests to talk to you about the next world so as you won't know what they're up to in this. You say that's not economics?

BONAPARTE. I say that's religion.

NOBLE. And I say it's neither economics nor religion. It's just damn nonsense, like everything else that Hawkins says. Before ever a capitalist was heard of, people believed in a life to come. Socrates believed in it.

HAWKINS. Oh, Socrates believed in it, did he? And I suppose you'll tell me next that Socrates believed that you'd lose your immortal soul if you danced foxtrots or played Rugby?

NOBLE. Oh, you're an impossible man to argue with.

BELCHER. Sit down, chum!

HAWKINS. (in a howl of protest) How can I sit down? I'm too upset. So far as Noble is concerned, progress might not exist.

NOBLE. Who said it exists?

HAWKINS. *I* say it exists, in spite of Socrates and the whole Irish Republican Army. That's just like you, Noble. You don't believe in progress. You don't believe in the evolution of man from mere protoplasm to higher forms.

NOBLE. Like you?

HAWKINS. Yes, like me. You believe in Eve and Eden and the Apple. Well, if you're entitled to a silly belief like that, I'm entitled to my own silly belief, which is that the first thing your God created was a bleeding capitalist with morality and Rolls-Royce complete. Am I right, chum?

BELCHER. You're right, chum.

BONAPARTE. (ruffled) Well, I'm going for a walk and let ye settle yeer blooming arguments.

HAWKINS. (sarcastically) That's right, Bonaparte, go for your walk and listen to your birds. They've got more intelligence than you have, I have no doubt. But before you do, give us a gasper.

BONAPARTE. I'd sooner listen to a bird than listen to you any day of the week.... There's three fags, and don't ask me for any more before tomorrow morning, because I haven't them. You seem to think I own a cigarette factory.

(A door bangs, but in the distance one can still hear Noble and Hawkins arguing. In the foreground are the noises of the bog; a bird crying and a dog barking faraway in the distance.)

NOBLE. Where you ought to be is in Hyde Park, Hawkins.

HAWKINS. All right, I ought. So what's wrong with Hyde Park? At least in Hyde Park you have freedom of discussion, whereas in this country....

BONAPARTE. Who's that? Put your hands up! I have you covered.

DONOVAN. All right, Bonaparte. It's only me. Put down the gun.

BONAPARTE. Jeremiah Donovan! What the hell are you doing, sitting out here like that?

DONOVAN. Ah, keeping an eye on things.

BONAPARTE. I know. You can't trust me and Noble.

DONOVAN. I didn't say that. What are your English pals up to now?

BONAPARTE. Oh, Hawkins is arguing with Noble about whether there's a next world or not.

DONOVAN. He might find that out sooner than he expects.

BONAPARTE. I wish he would, and let me get on with my own business.... What's that you said?

DONOVAN. Only that he might soon find out what the next world is like.

BONAPARTE. And what exactly does that mean?

DONOVAN. Well, the English are talking about shooting some of our prisoners.

BONAPARTE. But you don't mean we'd do the same to those fellows?

DONOVAN. Why wouldn't we? Isn't that what we're keeping them for—as hostages?

BONAPARTE. Hostages?

DONOVAN. What's wrong with it?

BONAPARTE. Oh, nothing, I suppose.

DONOVAN. Don't they take our fellows out in lorries as hostages, the way we won't fire at them?

BONAPARTE. I know, I know. But we have these fellows on our hands for so long.

DONOVAN. The English have our fellows longer.

BONAPARTE. 'Tis hardly alike.

DONOVAN. What difference is there?

BONAPARTE. They don't have to live with our lads the way we have to live with theirs.

DONOVAN. I told Noble and you already that it was a mistake to get too friendly with them.

BONAPARTE. You might as well have told us it was a mistake to be alive. How the hell do you prevent yourself getting friendly with a man? If 'twas even an old dog, you'd get friendly with him. When are you going to hear the result of this thing?

DONOVAN. We'll probably know tomorrow or the next day, so if it's hanging round here that's a trouble to you, you won't have much longer to wait.

BONAPARTE. It's not hanging round here that's a trouble to me at all, Jeremiah Donovan. I suppose I'd better tell Noble this. Good night.

DONOVAN. Goodnight, Bonaparte.

(Slow feet climb the hill, still among the lonely noises of the bog. The door opens and suddenly we are back in the middle of the argument between Hawkins and Noble.)

HAWKINS. Do you know what, Noble? I think you're just as big a bleeding unbeliever as I am. You say you believe in the next world, and you know just as much about the next world as I do, which is sweet damn-all. What's Heaven? You don't know. Where's Heaven? You don't know. Who's in Heaven, decent blokes like ourselves or members of the Conservative Party? You don't know. You know sweet damn-all! For the last time I ask you: do they or do they not wear wings?

NOBLE. Very well, then, they do. Is that enough for you? They do wear wings.

HAWKINS. Where do they get them then? Who makes them? Are the workers paid trade-union wages or is Heaven just another of your capitalist rackets? Have they a factory for wings? Have they a quartermaster's store where you hand in your chit and take your blooming wings?

BONAPARTE. Oh, for Christ's sake stop it!

HAWKINS. Naughty! Naughty! What's upset the Army of the Republic tonight?

NOBLE. What is it, Bonaparte?

BONAPARTE. I can't stand any more of this. Come here, Noble.

HAWKINS. My! My! Bad language, and then bad manners! Bonaparte, didn't your mother ever tell you not to whisper in company? Don't encourage him, Noble! (a door closes slowly.)

NOBLE. What is it, for God's sake?

BONAPARTE. (in a low quick voice) I saw Donovan. He says Belcher and Hawkins may be shot tomorrow or next day. It's a reprisal for some of our lads the English are threatening to shoot.

NOBLE. (after a pause) Where is Donovan?

BONAPARTE. Sitting down there by the hedge like an apparition. He doesn't trust us.

NOBLE. He never trusted anybody.

BONAPARTE. He says it was a mistake for us to get too friendly with them to begin with.

NOBLE. It's a mistake Donovan is never liable to make. Why didn't the fool tell us sooner?

BONAPARTE. He says he thought we understood all about it. You don't think we should warn the lads?

NOBLE. What's the good? If we did it now, and nothing was to happen, it would only be needless cruelty. All the lads in[11] the Second Battalion are friends of theirs, and 'tis most unlikely they'd want anything to happen them.

BONAPARTE. (after a pause) You don't think we should give them a chance?

NOBLE. What do you mean—a chance?

BONAPARTE. A chance to run for it? Show them how to get across country to the nearest barracks?

NOBLE. But how could we, Bonaparte? Isn't that exactly what Donovan expects of us?

---

[11]In the typescript, this word reads "on," which clearly seems a mistake.

BONAPARTE. One of these days I'd like to give Donovan exactly what he expects of me. It only came into my mind. We'll sleep on it before we do anything. Come on, or they'll be getting suspicious. (The door opens and closes again.)

HAWKINS. The Headquarters of the Irish Republican Army has now arranged its winter campaign. So now, what about a game of cards?

NOBLE. I can't play any more tonight. I'm going to bed.

HAWKINS. Now, now, Noble, don't you start getting sulky on me. If I can't argue with you, who can I argue with? Bonaparte means well but he doesn't have the brains, like Belcher. Isn't that right, chum?

BELCHER. (placidly) That's right, chum.

HAWKINS. You should learn to take a discussion in the proper spirit. You and your Adam and Eve! You just blame everything on poor old Adam and Eve because you're afraid to blame the capitalists. Isn't that right, Mrs. Leary?

MRS. LEARY. You can say what you like about who started the war, Mr. Hawkins, and think you'll deceive me because I'm only a poor ignorant country woman, but I know who started the war. It wasn't the capitalists, but the Italian count who stole the heathen divinity out of the temple in Japan.

HAWKINS. Perfectly correct, Mrs. Leary, or if not exactly correct, a praiseworthy use of independent judgment. But our friend, General Noble, still thinks it was Adam and Eve.... Adam and Eve! Adam and Eve! Nothing to do with their time but go picking bleeding apples.

BONAPARTE. I don't know how we got through the next day, but I was very glad when the tea-things were cleared away, and Belcher said in his peaceable tone "Well, chums, what about it?" We sat round the table, and Hawkins was shuffling the cards when I heard Jeremiah Donovan's footstep in the lane and a dark presentiment crossed my mind. I caught him before he reached the door.

BONAPARTE. (in a blustering tone) Well, Donovan, what the hell do you want now?

DONOVAN. (in a low, sinister voice) I want those two English friends of yours.

BONAPARTE. (dropping his voice) Is that the way it is?

DONOVAN. That's the way. Four of our lads were shot in Cork this morning.

BONAPARTE. Better tell Noble.... You know what we were talking about last night?

NOBLE. Yes, what about it?

BONAPARTE. It's happened, Donovan says.

NOBLE. And you're going to do what you said?

DONOVAN. Those are orders. You and Noble had better get them out. Tell them they're being shifted back to the Second Battalion or something. That'll be the quietest way.

NOBLE. That's one lie I won't have on my soul.

DONOVAN. I didn't know you felt that way about it, Noble.

NOBLE. You know now.

DONOVAN. Very well. In that case, you and Feeney had better get the tools and dig a hole somewhere by the end of the bog. He knows where. Bonaparte and myself will be after ye in a couple of minutes. Don't let anyone see the tools. I wouldn't like this to go beyond the four of ourselves. Come on, Bonaparte. (The door opens.)

HAWKINS. And here comes Jeremiah Donovan, looking even more sorry for himself than he usually does. Sit down and take a hand, and it'll make you feel better.

DONOVAN. I'm sorry, Hawkins, but I can't take a hand tonight. You fellows are going to have to move again. Word is just after coming through from headquarters.

HAWKINS. We have to move? Where is it this time?

DONOVAN. Back to the Second Battalion.

HAWKINS. Sorry, Donovan. I can't oblige. The fact is, Mary Brigid O'Connell has designs on me, and I'm already engaged to a nice girl in East Grimstead.

MRS. LEARY. Oye, what could they want to move the poor boys for? Aren't they better off where they are? I would never listen to people like that that can't make up their minds from one minute to the next. Let ye stop, Mr. Hawkins, and I'll talk to them if they come here for ye.

DONOVAN. They can't stop, Ellen.

HAWKINS. Of course we can stop. It's always the same bloody thing. Just as a man makes a home of a place, somebody at Headquarters thinks he's getting too cushy and wants to move him somewhere else.

BELCHER. Now, don't argue, chum. You know what orders are! Here's your topcoat.... A thousand thanks, madam. A thousand thanks for all your kindness.

MRS. LEARY. Kindness? What kindness did I ever show ye, only all the kindness I had from yourself, the good, thoughtful, kind-hearted man? Let ye come back at any hour of the day or night, Mr. Belcher, and I'll always have the bed and the cup of tea ready for ye.

HAWKINS. Thanks, Mrs. Leary, we will. We'll be back if we have to run away from those fellows. To tell the truth, I'm getting a bit tired of them. Good night.

(In a chorus of "goodnights" and "God bless yous" they leave the house.)

DONOVAN. (after a pause) I have bad news for ye, Hawkins. Ye won't be back. There were four of our lads shot in Cork this morning, and ye're to be shot, as a reprisal.

HAWKINS. (after another pause) I suppose this is your idea of a joke, Donovan?

DONOVAN. It's no joke to us. Ask Bonaparte.

HAWKINS. (after another pause) Well, Bonaparte? What's happened your tongue?

BONAPARTE. You heard what Donovan said.

HAWKINS. Now, Bonaparte.

BONAPARTE. I mean it.

HAWKINS. You don't sound as if you meant it.

DONOVAN. If he doesn't I do. It's our duty, and we have to do it. As a soldier you should know what duty means.

HAWKINS. I know what duty means—something dirty you're ashamed to do, and you have to invent an excuse for doing it. Don't you talk to me about duty, Donovan. You never liked me, and you know it. Why can't you say it, like a man?

DONOVAN. I never had anything against you. But why did your men take out four of our prisoners this morning and shoot them in cold blood?

HAWKINS. And what the hell have I to do with that? I didn't shoot them, did I? I never even laid eyes on the poor bloody bastards.

DONOVAN. No, but you'd shoot them quick enough, if it came to your turn.

HAWKINS. No, I wouldn't. Not if they were chums of mine.... Who's that over there with Feeney? Is that you, Noble? Why don't you come here and talk to this fellow?

DONOVAN. (dangerously) It's no use talking any more. You talked enough already.

HAWKINS. Me? I haven't begun to talk. How can I talk with a man like you who shifts his ground all the time? I'd sooner trust myself to this blasted bog than I'd trust myself to you. Are you suggesting that I'd shoot Noble?

DONOVAN. You would.

HAWKINS. I wouldn't.

DONOVAN. You would, if you were to be shot for not doing it.

HAWKINS. I wouldn't, if I was to be shot twenty times over. I wouldn't shoot a pal. Nor would Belcher. Isn't that right, Belcher?

BELCHER. That's right, chum.

HAWKINS. Anyway, who said Noble or Bonaparte would be shot it they didn't shoot me. Your blasted Brigade officers are a damn sight more frightened of them than they are of the British Army. And you're frightened as well Donovan. Aren't you? You know they're cleverer than you are, and you're afraid of what they might do to you?[12] What do you think I'd do if I was in Noble's place?

DONOVAN. (stung) You're not in Noble's place.

HAWKINS. (ignoring him) Go with him wherever he was going, of course. Share my last bob with him and stick by him through thick and thin. No one can ever say I let down a pal.

DONOVAN. We had enough of that sort of talk. Is there any messages you want sent?

---

[12]Perhaps O'Connor intended an exclamation point to end this sentence.

HAWKINS. (snarling) Yes, write to Auntie and tell her what good friends I made in Ireland.

DONOVAN. Do you want to say your prayers?

HAWKINS. Sorry, Donovan, I left my prayer-book in the Lagonda.[13] Better ask the butler to bring it.... Oh, Noble, you know I don't mean to be offensive to your religion. But you and me are chums. If you can't come over to my side I can go over to yours. I don't give a damn about your side, but it's no sillier than mine, and I can handle a gun as good as the next.

DONOVAN. For the last time have you any messages to send?

HAWKINS. Shut up, Donovan! Lenin was right. The peasant is only one degree removed from a pig, and you can't eat a peasant. You don't even understand what I'm trying to say, but these lads do. They're not just clods.

(A shot. Then a long silence, broken by the startled cries of the birds in the boglands.)

BELCHER. He's not quite dead. Better put him out of pain. (Silence) Go on! I don't mind. Poor old Hawkins! We don't know what's happening to him now.

(Another shot and Belcher laughs. For the rest of this scene he speaks in a tone that might almost be described as happy, as though he were pleased at discovering that all his worst anticipations about life were being precisely fulfilled. The whole speech should have a sort of eerie gaeity.)

BELCHER. Poor old Hawkins! And last night he was so curious about it all! It's very queer, chums, I always think. Now he knows as much about it as they'll ever let him know, and last night he was all in the dark.

---

[13]An expensive British automobile. I owe this suggestion to Mrs. Harriet O'Donovan Sheehy. Her guess was later confirmed by checking in *Brewer's Dictionary of Twentieth-Century Phrase and Fable* (Boston: Houghton Mifflin, 1992), 338.

DONOVAN. (in a subdued voice, all the hysteria gone from him) Is there anything we can do for you, Belcher? Any messages we can send?

BELCHER. No, chum, not for me, thanks all the same. If one of you likes to write to Hawkins' mother, you'll find a letter from her in his pocket. He and the old lady were always great chums. But my missus left me eight years ago—went away with another fellow and took the kid. I like the feeling of a home, as you may have noticed, but I couldn't start again after that.

(There is another frustrated silence.)

Of course, it wasn't the missus, really, with me—it was the kid. I always think it's not the woman that counts so much as the kids. Ours was a little girl, and we were great chums. When they took her away it was like losing something—a leg or an arm or something like that. You keep making movements, and then you remember that it's not there. But even if I could have found them, it wouldn't have been right to take the little girl. A man can never make a home for a child as a woman can.

(There is the same silence. Belcher laughs again.)

Excuse me, chums. I feel I'm talking the hell of a lot, and so silly, about being handy around the house and things like that. Noble and Bonaparte will tell you, I don't do it often. I suppose it was the shock. This thing came as a surprise to me. It always does, I suppose. You'll forgive me, I'm sure.

DONOVAN. You don't want to say a prayer?

BELCHER. No, chum, I don't think it would help, thanks all the same. A man dies as he lives is what I say. I'm ready, and I don't want to detain you boys.

DONOVAN. You understand that we're only doing our duty?

BELCHER. I never could make out what duty was myself. I thought about it a lot, but it never got any clearer. I think you're all good lads, if that's what you mean, and I'm very grateful.

(A shot. Then we hear a few sods being thrown into a hole.)

BONAPARTE. (quietly) Don't forget the letter.

NOBLE. What letter?

BONAPARTE. From Hawkins' mother.

DONOVAN. Get it so, but hurry!

BONAPARTE. What's the hurry? They won't come back.

(Again the shovelling goes on.)

BONAPARTE. Come on, Noble.

DONOVAN. Good night, lads.

(There is no reply. We hear them walking up the lane and opening the door.)

NOBLE. What are you doing, sitting there in the darkness? You gave me a start. (He strikes a match.)

MRS. LEARY. What did ye do to them?

NOBLE. This old wick needs to be cleaned.

MRS. LEARY. I heard ye.

NOBLE. What did you hear?

MRS. LEARY. I heard the shots. I heard ye putting the spade back in the shed. Was that what ye did to them? Never mind the lamp. Tell me what ye did to them.

NOBLE. 'And last night they were all in the dark.' That was what Belcher said.

MRS. LEARY. In the name of the Father, the Son and the Holy Ghost ...

NOBLE. ~~As it was in the beginning, now and ever shall be, world without end ...~~[14]

BONAPARTE. For God's sake let me out of this!

BONAPARTE. And anything that ever happened me after, I never felt the same about again.

THE END

---

[14]O'Connor himself seems to have crossed out this line in the type-script.

Facts and Figures

A Frank O'Connor Chronology

prepared by John M. Burdett and Robert C. Evans

The following chronology seeks to give a year-by-year sense of O'Connor's life and career, with special emphasis on his short stories. O'Connor constantly tinkered with many of his tales, sometimes revising them (and changing their titles) years after he first published them. Sometimes, too, the same story would be published in the same year but with different titles in England and America. (In this listing, the boldface years indicate the year of first publication; any titles in parentheses refer to alternative versions of the same story.) The chronology also attempts to place O'Connor's stories in the context of his other writings, including his poetry, plays, translations, and journalism; major historical events are mentioned as well.

This listing could not have been prepared without the prior work of several authors, including James Matthews, Ruth Sherry, William M. Tomory, and especially Maurice Sheehy.[1]

***

---

[1]See James Matthews, *Frank O'Connor* (Lewisburg: Bucknell University Press, 1976), 11–12; Ruth Sherry, ed., *Moses' Rock*, by Frank O'Connor and Hugh Hunt (Washington, DC: Catholic University of America Press, 1983), vii–xii; William M. Tomory, *Frank O'Connor* (Boston: Twayne, 1980), [11–13]; and especially Maurice Sheehy, "Towards a Bibliography of Frank O'Connor's Writing" in *Michael/Frank: Studies on Frank O'Connor*, ed. Maurice Sheehy (New York: Knopf, 1969), 168–99. Additional details have been taken from James Matthews' biography *Voices: A Life of Frank O'Connor* (New York: Athenaeum, 1987).

Professor Sherry is preparing a detailed analytical bibliography of O'Connor's writings which should clear up many uncertainties and will almost certainly add a number of previously unknown items to O'Connor's bibliography.

1903 Born on 17 September in Cork, the son of Michael O'Donovan and Mary (Minnie) O'Connor O'Donovan; named Michael Francis O'Donovan. Later uses his own middle name and his mother's maiden name to form his pen name, "Frank O'Connor."

1914 First meets his mentor Daniel Corkery while a student at St Patrick's National School in Cork. World War I breaks out.

1916 "Easter Rebellion" against British rule in Ireland violently suppressed; rebels later hanged.

1917 Formal schooling ends.

1918 End of World War I. Michael O'Donovan enlists in First Brigade of the Irish Republican Army. Parliamentary elections give the revolutionary party a majority of Irish seats.

1919 Illegal assembly of a revolutionary parliament in Dublin; formation of a secret government led by Eamon de Valera.

1919–21 Armed conflict between Irish Republican Army and British troops (the "Black and Tans").

1920 Britain agrees to establish an "Irish Free State" that will grant the Irish greater autonomy; six counties of Northern Ireland will remain part of Great Britain.

1921–22 Michael O'Donovan actively supports Irish Republican movement in opposing the Free State government.

1922 Civil War breaks out (in April) between opponents and defenders of the Free State treaty with Britain. Majority of Irish parliament accepts the treaty with Britain, and the Irish Free State is officially proclaimed (December). Michael O'Donovan publishes his first poems in a Republican newspaper in Cork. TOPIC[S] OF ARTICLES: Mozart; Solus. Publishes his first story, "Peasants."

1923 After being captured by Free State forces, detained at Gormanstown Prison Camp. Civil War ends (in April). Poem published.

1924-28 Released from Gormanstown Prison Camp. Teaches Irish in country schools; serves as librarian in Sligo (1924), Wicklow (1925), and Cork (1926). Adopts pseudonym to help protect his job. Publishes poems and essays (as "Frank O'Connor") in *The Irish Statesman*, beginning in 1925. While briefly visiting Paris (1927) meets with James Joyce.

1925 One poem and two poem translations published. ARTICLE TOPIC: poets.

1926 Four poems and two poem translations published. TOPIC[S] OF ARTICLES: Egan O'Rahilly; Spain; Irish love poetry; Irish anthology; emotions; Irish literature. STORIES: "The Peddler"; "Sion"; "War."

1927 Four poems and one poem translation published. TOPIC[S] OF ARTICLES: classic verse; fine arts.

1928 Six poems published. ARTICLE TOPIC: travel. STORIES: "The Awakening"; "The Ring."

1928–29 With Sean Hendrik, founds a drama league in Cork to begin producing plays by Chekhov and Ibsen. Relocates to Dublin to take over new position as a librarian at Pembroke Library.

1929 One poem and one poem translation published. TOPIC[S] OF ARTICLES: Heine; Proust. STORIES: "After Fourteen Years"; "The Picture"; "September Dawn."

1930 Two poems published. TOPIC[S] OF ARTICLES: Gaelic drama; Abbey Theatre; James Joyce. STORIES: "Soldiers Are We" ("Jo").

1931 As "Frank O'Connor," publishes first volume of stories, *Guests of the Nation*. AE (George Russell), an important literary figure, highly praises O'Connor's work. STORIES: "Alec"; "Attack"; "Guests of the Nation"; "Jo" ("Soldiers Are We"); "Jumbo's Wife"; "The Late Henry Conran"; "Laughter"; "Machine Gun Corps in Action"; "The Patriarch"; "Procession of Life"; "The Sisters"; "Soirée chez une jeune belle fille."

1932 Publishes his first novel, *The Saint and Mary Kate*, as well as his first volume of translations of Irish poetry, *The Wild Bird's Nest* (Cuala Press). Two poem translations published. STORY: "Bones of Contention."

1933 Amateur film of "Guests of the Nation." STORY: "There Is a Lone House."

1934 TOPIC[S] OF ARTICLES: life in prison; Gaelic. STORIES: "The English Soldier"; "The Man That Stopped"; "The Miracle."

1935 In October, appointed a member of the board of directors of Dublin's Abbey Theatre, which had long been dominated by the great Irish poet and dramatist, W.B. Yeats. STORIES: "Faith Moved His Dictionaries"; "In the Train"; "Repentance" ("First Confession"; "The Murderer"); "The

Majesty of the Law"; "May Night"; "Michael's Wife"; "Nightpiece with Figures."

1936 Publishes *Three Old Brothers and Other Poems* and *Bones of Contention* (a collection of stories). ARTICLE TOPIC: Gaelic literature. STORIES: "The Flowering Trees"; "Grandeur"; "Lofty"; "Orpheus and His Lute"; "Tears, Idle Tears"; "What's Wrong With the Country."

1937 Delivers first broadcast on Radio Eireann. Appointed Managing Director of the Abbey Theatre. In spring produces *In the Train*, a play based on one of his stories, at the Abbey. In the fall, in collaboration with Hugh Hunt, produces *The Invincibles*, also at the Abbey. Publishes *The Big Fellow* [American title: *Death in Dublin: Michael Collins and the Irish Revolution*], a sympathetic biography of the IRA leader who later helped negotiate the controversial treaty with Britain and sided with the Free State during the Civil War. STORIES: "The Storyteller"; "Uprooted."

1938 Produces *Moses' Rock* (another play) during winter at the Abbey. Resigns as librarian at Pembroke to devote full energies to writing; moves back to Wicklow. Publishes *Lords and Commons* (translations of old Irish poems). Produces another of his plays, *Time's Pocket*, at the Abbey Theatre near year's end. STORIES: "The Climber"; "The Lodgers"; "Mac's Masterpiece"; "A Rainy Day."

1939 On 11 February marries Evelyn Bowen Speaight, an actress. Publishes *Fountain of Magic* (translations of Irish poems). Forced to step down as member of the Board of Directors of the Abbey Theatre after the death of Yeats. On 12 May angrily resigns from National Theatre Society. His first son, Myles, born on 18 July. World War II begins in September; Ireland officially neutral. Radio broadcasts on Yeats and on AE. ARTICLE TOPIC: Yeats and AE; Synge. STORY: "The Bridal Night."

1940 Appointed poetry editor for new literary journal, *The Bell*, which publishes its first issue in October. Publishes *Lament for Art O'Leary* (translation of famous Irish poem). Also publishes his second novel, *Dutch Interior* (officially banned by the Irish Censorship Board on 10 July for being obscene and indecent). Radio broadcasts on Michael Davitt and on "Across St. George's Channel." ARTICLE TOPIC: AE. STORIES: "The Book of Kings"; "Long Road to Ummera."

1941 Moves to Dublin. Works in London for the British Ministry of Information and for the BBC. *The Statue's Daughter* staged by the Dublin Drama League at the Gate Theater. Radio broadcast on F.R. Higgins; W.B. Yeats. TOPIC[S] OF ARTICLES: advice to writers; Yeats; "The Midnight Court." STORIES: "A Day at the Seaside" ("Old Fellows"); "Hughie"; "The Last Post."

1942 Father dies on 20 March. Publishes *Three Tales* (story collection). Protests the banning of Eric Cross's book *The Tailor and Ansty*, which described a well-known elderly Irish story-teller whom O'Connor admired. The controversy leads to a larger debate about Irish censorship. TOPIC[S] OF ARTICLES: broadcasting; James Joyce; three churches; Galway, Kerry, and Clare. STORIES: "The Cheapjack" ("The New Teacher"); "The Grand Vizier's Daughters"; "Night of Stars" ("Judas"); "Solo on Gabriel's Trumpet"; "The Wild Lomasneys" ("The Mad Lomasneys").

1943 Publishes *A Picture Book* (describing his travels). Under the pseudonym of "Ben Mayo," begins publishing regular opinion pieces in the *Sunday Independent*; many of these criticize features of Irish life and politics. TOPIC[S] OF ARTICLES: poetry; Connemara; South Tipperary; Irish ruins; ministers; critics; great writers; "foreign" dance music; Clare people; Irish history; poverty and illness; peace; culture; Irish towns; education; prejudices; purposes in life; book industry; exiles; Irish people; government; politics; theaters; food vs. money; tourists; old politicians; Irish language; Irish legion of honor; memory; levelling communities; good citizens; toys for Christmas; letter to Santa; Ireland and Dublin. STORIES: "The House that Johnny Built"; "The Tinker."

1944 Continues war-time work for the British Ministry of Information. Publishes *Crab Apple Jelly* (short story collection). Radio broadcast on James Joyce. TOPIC[S] OF ARTICLES: Carlow; Kilkenny; Jim Larkin; idleness; Irish heroes; improving the countryside; bad buildings; art; history; second thoughts; practice; progress; turf; education; farmers; Dublin and Clare; partition; near future; politics; turning points; parents; profit; dreams; children; nationalism; Dublin; planning; Irish abroad; Irish failures; vocations; present and future; Irish laziness; citizenship; farmers; state control; hobby-horses; railways; foolish talk; Ireland and the world; farmer's wives; proportion; partition; Northern Ireland; peace on earth; Dublin and Belfast. STORIES: "The Luceys"; "The Mad Lomasneys" ("The Wild Lomasneys"); "The Miser"; "The New Teacher" ("The Cheapjack"); "Song Without Words"; "The Star That Bids the Shepherds Fold" ("And We in Herds Thy Game"; "The Shepherds").

1945 End of World War II. Publishes *Towards an Appreciation of Literature* (brief book of literary criticism) and *The Midnight Court* (translation of famous and bawdy old Irish poem). *The Midnight Court* sparks heated attacks because of its alleged indecency; O'Connor vigorously defends himself. *The New Yorker* publishes the first of nearly fifty O'Connor stories to appear in that magazine from 1945 to 1961. Ceases writing "Ben Mayo" articles in September. A son, Oliver, born in England from a liaison with Joan Knape. TOPIC[S] OF ARTICLES: architecture; Irish prigs; Jane Austen; Stendhal; Dickens; Flaubert; Trollope; Swift; Tolstoy and Turgenev; Hardy; Chekhov; Sommerville and Ross; theater writers, audience, actors;

political morality; newspapers; Dublin; Limerick; security; scientists and inventors; information; French women; the Ascendancy; St. Patrick's Day; Dublin's disgrace; exporting doctors, importing scientists; small nations; Britain; de Valera and Churchill; Ernest Bevin; British commonwealth; prime minister; ruin and loss in Ireland. STORIES: "Don Juan Retired"; "News for the Church"; "A Story by Maupassant"; "The Weeping Children."

1946 Censorship Board bans *The Midnight Court* (30 April). *Selected Stories* published. A second son, Owen, born to Evelyn, O'Connor's wife. STORIES: "A Case for the Roarer" ("Legal Aid"); "Christmas Morning" ("The Thief"); "Friends of the Family"; "Lady in Dublin" ("Lady of the Sagas"); "The Rivals" ("Judas"; "Night of Stars"); "The Sinner"; "The Stepmother"; "A Thing of Nothing."

1947 *The Common Chord* (collection of stories) published and then banned (on 12 December) because of its depiction of unsavory aspects of Irish life. The poet Patrick Kavanagh attacks O'Connor for writing superficial fiction. *Irish Miles* (travel book) and *Art of the Theatre* (drama criticism) published. Radio broadcast on W.B. Yeats. STORIES: "Babes in the Wood"; "The Cornet Player Who Betrayed Ireland"; "The Custom of the Country"; "Don Juan's Temptation"; "The Frying Pan"; "The Holy Door"; "Judas" ("The Rivals;" "Night of Stars"); "The Miracle"; "My Da."

1948 Publishes *The Road to Stratford* (on Shakespeare). Separates from Evelyn, his wife; moves to England. Radio broadcasts on theater, England, Irish sagas, Jonathan Swift, A.E. Coppard, and Irish writers. STORIES: "The Adventuress"; "The Drunkard"; "The Murderer" ("First Confession"); "The World of Art and Reilly."

1949 In December issue of *Holiday* magazine, publishes a highly controversial article emphasizing Ireland's poverty and other social ills. Radio broadcasts on Yeats and on Yeats and theater. STORIES: "Darcy in the Land of Youth"; "The Idealist"; "The Landlady"; "The Man of the House."

1950 Publishes *Leinster, Munster, and Connaught* (travel book on Irish counties). *When I Was a Child* (New York stage adaptation of "The Genius"). Radio broadcast on James Joyce. STORIES: "The Masculine Principle"; "My Oedipus Complex"; "This Mortal Coil"; "The Pretender"; "Private Property"; "The Sentry."

1951 Publishes *Traveller's Samples* (story collection; banned on 20 April). Leaves Ireland to lecture and teach at Northwestern University and Harvard. Radio broadcast on short stories. STORIES: "Baptismal" ("A Spring Day"); "The Conversion"; "Jerome"; "Lady of the Sagas" ("Lady in Dublin"); "The Martyr"; "My First Protestant"; "Old Age Pensioners";

"The Rising" ("Eternal Triangle"; "The Tram"); "A Romantic"; "The Thief" ("Christmas Morning"); "What Girls Are For."

1952 Divorced from Evelyn, his first wife. Resides in Brooklyn Heights and at Northwestern (spring) and Harvard (summer). Mother dies 10 November. Radio broadcast on George Moore. STORIES: "Anchors"; "Crossroads" ("First Love"); "Masculine Protest"; "The Saint"; "A Sense of Responsibility"; "A Spring Day" ("Baptismal"); "A Torrent Dammed"; "Unapproved Route."

1953 Publishes *The Stories of Frank O'Connor* (major and very successful collection of stories). In December marries Harriet Rich (of Annapolis, Maryland), who had taken one of his classes at Harvard. TOPIC[S] OF ARTICLES: novels; short stories; Yeats. STORIES: "Adventure"; "Freedom"; "The Little Mother"; "Vanity."

1954 Publishes *More Stories* (another large and successful collection). Now begins living in both Ireland and the United States. "The Martyr" adapted for television in New York. Radio broadcasts on Anthony Trollope, G.B. Shaw. ARTICLE TOPIC: novels. STORIES: "Brief for Oedipus" ("Counsel for Oedipus"); "Don Juan's Apprentice" ("The Sorcerer's Apprentice"); "Eternal Triangle"; "The Face of Evil"; "Father and Son"; "Francis" ("Pity"); "Ladies of the House" ("Lonely Rock"); "Lost Fatherlands"; "The Old Faith"; "The Shepherds" ("The Star That Bids the Shepherds Fold"; "And We in Herds Thy Game"); "The Tram" ("Eternal Triangle"; "The Rising").

1955 TOPIC[S] OF ARTICLES: Chekhov; Austen; short stories; Abbey theater. STORIES: "A Bachelor's Story"; "Expectation of Life"; "Fish for Friday"; "The Genius" ("The Sissy"); "The Teacher's Mass"; "The Wreath."

1956 Publishes *The Mirror in the Roadway* (study of the novel). Publishes *Stories by Frank O'Connor*. "Orphans" adapted for television in New York. TOPIC[S] OF ARTICLES: Mozart; Liam O'Flaherty; poetry anthology; Sean O'Casey; Arthur Miller; Jean Anouilh; comedy and comediennes. STORIES: "The Duke's Children"; "The Man of the World"; "Orphans"; "The Pariah"; "A Salesman's Romance."

1957 Publishes *Domestic Relations* (collection of stories). Writes introduction to Oxford University Press anthology of *Modern Irish Short Stories*. TOPIC[S] OF ARTICLES: Roger Casement; novelist as politician; England. STORIES: "The Majesty of the Law" adapted for film. "Daydreams"; "The Impossible Marriage"; "A Minority"; "An Out-and-Out Free Gift"; "The Paragon"; "The Party"; "Pity" ("Francis"); "Public Opinion"; "Requiem"; "That Ryan Woman" ("Ugly Duckling"); "The Study of History."

1958 Daughter, Harriet ("Hallie Og"), born. TOPIC[S] OF ARTICLES: his mother; satire; Joyce; Joyce and his brother; Joyce, Colum, Johnston, Meredith; New York. STORIES: "Achilles' Heel"; "Androcles and the Army"; "A Great Man"; "Lady Brenda"; "Music When Soft Voices Die"; "Sue."

1959 Publishes *A Book of Ireland* (anthology) and *Kings, Lords, and Commons* (translations of old Irish poems; banned in Ireland in 1961). Radio broadcast on short stories; radio broadcasts in Irish. Three stories dramatized for Irish radio. Three more stories dramatized for Irish radio. TOPIC[S] OF ARTICLES: autobiographical pieces. STORY: "Father Fogarty's Island" ("The Mass Island").

1960 Writes introduction to *Irish Street Ballads* by C.O. Lochlainn. Radio broadcasts in Irish. TOPIC[S] OF ARTICLES: in Irish; autobiography; Arthur Griffith; Chekhov; from Austen to Conrad. STORY: "A Set of Variations on a Borrowed Theme" ("Variations on a Theme").

1961 Publishes *An Only Child* (highly effective but controversial autobiography). Suffers stroke while teaching at Stanford University. Returns to Ireland. Interviewed by BBC television. Radio broadcast on Irish Civil War. Writes introduction to *Dead Souls* by Nikolai Gogol. TOPIC[S] OF ARTICLES: the Irish Civil War; English history; modesty of literature. STORY: "The American Wife."

1962 Receives honorary doctorate in letters from Trinity College, Dublin. Publishes *The Lonely Voice* (major volume of short story criticism). Radio broadcast of Irish Civil War and on translation. Participates in autobiographical television documentary. Translated poem: childhood of Jesus. TOPIC[S] OF ARTICLES: title(s) in Irish; censorship; an Ulsterman; the great famine; Dublin; Maupassant; poetry; Irish libraries, historical monuments, and provincialism; Roger Casement; Dublin theater festival; Thomas Kinsella; "lace curtain Irish"; remembering.

1963 Publishes *The Little Monasteries* (translations of Irish poems). Also publishes *My Oedipus Complex and Other Stories*. Interviewed by BBC television. Autobiographical radio broadcast. Two poem translations. TOPIC[S] OF ARTICLES: Mary Lavin; Chekhov; Irish holy places; Finn and Finnegan; Georgian Dublin; Irish verse; St. Patrick; Sean O'Casey; Daniel Binchy; Abbey Theatre; Dublin theater festival; Shakespeare; arts council; Irish monuments; John F. Kennedy; Sean T. O'Kelley.

1964 Lectures at Trinity College, Dublin. Publishes *Collection Two* (major collection of stories). Writes introduction to *A Portrait of the Artist as a Young Man* by James Joyce. Reads "Guests of the Nation" on Irish television. Radio broadcast on short stories. TOPIC[S] OF ARTICLES: Roger Casement; Chekhov; Oliver Gogarty; Patrick Kavanagh; Gogol; Yeats; John F. Kennedy; Irish monuments; famous (and neglected) Irish buildings; books on Ireland; New Grange Tombs; Dublin theater festival; Irish verse; unknown book.

1965 One radio broadcast on AE (George Russell) and two on W.B. Yeats. TOPIC[S] OF ARTICLES: James Stephens; Yeats; Osborn Bergin; Cork; Yeats; Irish monuments; literature in Irish; Roger Casement; Michael Collins; "literature and the lashers." STORIES: "The Cheat"; "A Life of Your Own"; "Variations on a Theme" ("A Set of Variations on a Borrowed Theme").

1966 Featured in two BBC television documentaries. Dies on 10 March in Dublin. Burial 12 March at Dean's Grange. *Three Hand Reel*, dramatic adaptation of three O'Connor stories, produced in New York. "Song Without Words" adapted for television by the BBC. TOPIC[S] OF ARTICLES: his mother; Synge, Gregory, and Yeats. STORIES: "The Corkerys"; "The School for Wives."

1967 *The Backward Look: A Survey of Irish Literature* published, as well as *A Golden Treasury of Irish Poetry A.D. 600–1200* (translations; co-edited with Professor David Greene). *The Invincibles* staged at the Abbey Theatre. TOPIC[S] OF ARTICLES: dreams; America; Joyce; Yeats; AE. STORIES: "An Act of Charity"; "A Mother's Warning."

1968 *My Father's Son* (second volume of autobiography) published. Dramatic adaptation of O'Connor's novel *The Saint and Mary Kate* produced at Dublin's Abbey Theatre. Recorded autobiographical radio broadcast in Irish.

1969 *A Set of Variations* and *Collection Three* (major story collections) published (in New York and London, respectively).

A Bibliography of Works by and about Frank O'Connor

John C. Kerrigan[1]

PRIMARY SOURCES

Short Story Collections

P1. *Guests of the Nation*. London/New York: Macmillan, 1931; Dublin: Poolbeg, 1979.

P2. *Bones of Contention*. London/New York: Macmillan, 1936.

P3. *Three Tales*. Dublin: Cuala Press, 1941. Limited edition.

P4. *Crab Apple Jelly*. London/New York: Macmillan/Knopf, 1944, 1945.

P5. *The Common Chord*. London/New York: Macmillan/Knopf, 1947, 1948.

P6. *Traveller's Samples*. London/New York: Macmillan/Knopf, 1951.

P7. *The Stories of Frank O'Connor*. New York: Knopf, 1952; London: Hamish Hamilton, 1953.

P8. *More Stories by Frank O'Connor*. New York: Knopf, 1954.

---

[1]I would like to extend thanks to all those who helped with this bibliography, most particularly to the staff at each of the libraries for which an entry appears below. As well, and most especially, I would like to thank the staff of the Interlibrary Loan Department at the Dickinson Library, University of Nevada, Las Vegas; Harriet O'Donovan Sheehy; Sibylle Gottschewski and Carol Baumann, my German translators; Dr. Ruth Sherry and Shawn O'Hare, who supplied information about as yet unpublished works; special collections librarians Lori N. Curtis of the University of Tulsa, Jeffrey A. Barr of the University of Florida, Stuart O Seanoir of Trinity College, and Chris Petter of the University of Victoria; and Kristin Kampschroeder and Donna Pattee for their assistance, support, and encouragement.

P9. *Stories by Frank O'Connor*. New York: Vintage, 1956. (paperback)

P10. *Domestic Relations*. New York: Knopf, 1957; London: Hamish Hamilton, 1957.

P11. *Collection Two*. London: Macmillan, 1964.

P12. *Collection Three*. London: Macmillan, 1969.

P13. *A Set of Variations*. New York: Knopf, 1969. (Similar, though not identical, to *Collection Three*)

P14. *My Oedipus Complex and Other Stories*. London: Penguin, 1969.

P15. *The Mad Lomasneys and Other Stories*. London: Pan Books, 1970.

P16. *Fish for Friday and Other Stories*. London: Pan Books, 1971.

P17. *A Life of Your Own and Other Stories from Collection Three*. London: Pan Books, 1972.

P18. *Masculine Protest and Other Stories*. London: Pan Books, 1972.

P19. *Day Dreams*. London: Pan Books, 1973.

P20. *The Holy Door*. London: Pan Books, 1973.

P21. *Collected Stories*. New York: Knopf; Random House/Vintage, 1980, 1981.

P22. *The Cornet Player Who Betrayed Ireland*. Dublin: Poolbeg, 1981.

P23. *Collected Stories* Vols. 1 and 2. London: Pan Books, 1990. (Contains previously published Pan stories)

P24. *The Collar: Stories of Irish Priests*. Belfast: Blackstaff Press, 1993.

P25. *Larry Delaney: Lonesome Genius*. Cork: Killeen Books, 1997.

Novels

P26. *The Saint and Mary Kate*. London: Macmillan, 1932, 1936; New York: Macmillan, 1932; Belfast: Blackstaff Press, 1990.

P27. *Dutch Interior*. London/New York: Macmillan/Knopf, 1940; Belfast: Blackstaff Press, 1990.

Poetry

P28. *Three Old Brothers and Other Poems*. London: Nelson, 1936.

Translations

P29. *The Wild Bird's Nest: Poems from the Irish by Frank O'Connor with an Essay on the Character in Irish Literature* by A.E. Dublin: Cuala, 1932. Limited ed.

P30. *Lords and Commons.* Dublin: Cuala, 1938. Limited ed.

P31. *The Fountain of Magic.* London: Macmillan, 1939.

P32. *Lament for Art O'Leary.* Dublin: Cuala, 1940. Limited ed.

P33. *The Midnight Court: A Rhythmical Bacchanalia from the Irish of Bryan Merriman.* Dublin: Fridberg, 1946; Dublin: O'Brien Press, 1989 (with new illustrations by Brian Bourke).

P34. *Kings, Lords, & Commons.* New York: Knopf, 1959; London: Macmillan, 1961; Van Nuys, CA: Ford & Bailie, 1989.

P35. *The Little Monasteries.* Dublin: Dolmen Press, 1963. Limited ed.

P36. *A Golden Treasury of Irish Poetry, AD 600–1200.* Ed. with David Greene. London: Macmillan, 1967. (Irish texts and prose translations.)

Plays

P37. *In the Train: A Play in One Act from the Short Story.* Written in collaboration with Hugh Hunt. First performed on May 31, 1937, at the Abbey Theatre. Revised text in *The Genius of Irish Theatre.* Ed. Sylvan Barnet, Morton Berman and William Burto. New York: New American Library, Mentor, 1960. 248–61.

P38. *The Invincibles: A Play in Seven Scenes.* Written in collaboration with Hugh Hunt. First performed Oct. 18, 1937 at the Abbey Theatre. [London]: Proscenium, 1980. Ed. Ruth Sherry.

P39. "The Lost Legion." Written in 1936? Unpublished. Acquired by the Trinity College, Dublin Library in 1996.

P40. *Moses' Rock.* Written in collaboration with Hugh Hunt. First performed Feb. 25, 1937, at the Abbey. Ed. Ruth Sherry. Washington, DC: Catholic University Press, 1983.

P41. "A Night Out." Written 1929? Dramatization of the short story "Procession of Life." Unpublished.

P42. "Rodney's Glory: A Play in One Act." Written 1929? Ed. Ruth Sherry. *Irish University Review* 22 (Autumn/Winter 1992): 225–41.

P43. *Time's Pocket.* Written in collaboration with Hugh Hunt. First performed December 26, 1938 at the Abbey. Unpublished. Versions held by the Mugar Library, Boston University, and the Abbey Theatre Papers in the National Library of Ireland (MS. 21426).

P44. *The Statue's Daughter: A Fantasy in a Prologue and Three Acts*. First performed December 8, 1941, at the Gate Theatre. Four-act version reprinted in *Journal of Irish Literature* 4.1 (January 1975): 59–117.

Stories/Poems Published in Isolation

P45. *First Confession*. Mankato, MN: Creative Education, 1990.

P46. "Kilcash." Illustrated broadside by John DePol. Omaha, NE: Buttonmaker Press, 1987.

P47. *My Oedipus Complex*. Mankato, MN: Creative Education, 1986.

Stories Not Published by O'Connor in Collections of His Work

P48. "Darcy I Dtir NA NOG." In *Nuascealaiocht 1940–50*. Ed. Tomas de Bhaldraithe. Dublin: Sairseal agus Dill, 1952. 24–32. (In Irish)

P49. "Darcy in Tir na nOg." Translated by Richard B. Walsh. *Twentieth Century Literature* 35 (Fall 1990): 375–80. Reprinted in Michael Steinman's *A Frank O'Connor Reader*, 1994 **[P226]**.

P50. "The Rebel." First published in Steinman's *A Frank O'Connor Reader*, 1994 **[P226]**.

Biography

P51. *The Big Fellow: A Life of Michael Collins*. London: Nelson, 1937. American edition, *Death in Dublin: Michael Collins and the Irish Revolution*. New York: Doubleday, Doran, 1937, 1966; Dublin: Poolbeg, 1986.

Autobiographies

P52. *An Only Child*. New York: Knopf, 1961; London: Macmillan, 1961, 1970; Belfast: Blackstaff Press, 1993.

P53. *An Only Child* and *My Father's Son*. London: Pan Books, 1988.

P54. *My Father's Son*. London: Macmillan, 1968; New York: Knopf, 1969; Belfast: Blackstaff Press, 1994.

Travel Books/Miscellaneous Non-Fiction

P55. *A Book of Ireland*. Ed. Frank O'Connor, with an introduction and translations by him. London: Fontana, 1959, 1971.

P56. *Irish Miles*. London: Macmillan, 1947; Hogarth Press, 1968 (with a new introduction by Brendan Kennelly).

P57. *A Picture Book*. Dublin: Cuala Press, 1943. Limited ed.

P58. *Leinster, Munster, and Connaught*. The Country Books Series. London: Robert Hale, 1950.

Anthologies

P59. *Modern Irish Short Stories*. Selected, with an introduction by Frank O'Connor. London: Oxford University Press, 1957. Issued in paperback as *Classic Irish Short Stories*, 1985.

P60. *A Book of Ireland*. Ed., introd. Frank O'Connor. London: Collins National Anthologies, 1959.

P61. *The Lonely Voice*. Special Anthology Edition. New York: Bantam, 1968. Contains "Guests" and stories by Babel, Chekhov, Coppard, Hemingway, Joyce, Kipling, Lavin, Lawrence, Mansfield, Maupassant, and Turgenev.

Literary Criticism and History

P62. *Towards an Appreciation of Literature*. Dublin: Metropolitan Publishing Co., 1945; New York: Haskell House Publishers, 1974.

P63. *The Art of the Theatre*. Dublin: Fridberg, 1947.

P64. *The Road to Stratford*. London: Methuen, 1948; revised as *Shakespeare's Progress*. Cleveland: World Publishing, 1960.

P65. *The Mirror in the Roadway*. New York: Knopf, 1956; London: Hamish Hamilton, 1956, 1964; Freeport, NY: Books for Libraries Press, 1970.

P66. *The Lonely Voice*. Cleveland: World Publishing, 1963; London: Macmillan, 1963; revised and enlarged paperback, New York: Bantam, 1968; New York: Harper & Row Books, 1985 (with a new introduction by Russell Banks).

P67. *The Backward Look: A Survey of Irish Literature*. London: Macmillan, 1967. Published in the U.S. as *A Short History of Irish Literature: A Backward Look*. New York: G.P. Putnam's Sons, 1967.

O'Connor on James Joyce

P68. "Joyce—The Third Period." *The Irish Statesman* (12 April 1930): 114–16.

P69. "James Joyce—A Postmortem." *The Bell* 5 (5 Feb 1943): 363–75.

P70. "Egotism in Irish Literature. (On James Joyce)." (18 May 1944, BBC broadcast.) *The Listener* (1 June 1944): 608.

P71. "Portrait of James Joyce." (13 February 1950, BBC broadcast.)

P72. James Joyce. Sound Recording. Folkway Records, 1958. O'Connor reading from and commenting on Joyce; especially valuable.

P73. "Joyce and His Brother." *Nation* (1 February 1958): 102–3.

P74. "Shadows on the Artist's Portrait." (On Joyce.) *New York Times Book Review* (24 August 1958): 1.

P75. "Introduction." *A Portrait of the Artist as a Young Man.* By James Joyce. New York: Time Reading Program, 1964. xv-xxi. Reprinted in *A Frank O'Connor Reader*, 1994 **[P226]**.

P76. "James Joyce—Thesis and Antithesis." *American Scholar* 36 (Summer 1967): 466+.

P77. "Frank O'Connor on Joyce and Lawrence: An Uncollected Text." Ed. Alan M. Cohn and Richard F. Peterson. *Journal of Modern Literature* 12 (July 1985): 211–20.

On William Butler Yeats

P78. "Literary Portraits: Yeats and AE." (1939–40 Radio Eireann broadcasts.)

P79. "Two Friends—Yeats and AE." *Yale Review* n.s. 29 (Sept. 1939): 60–88.

P80. "The Old Age of a Poet." *The Bell* (Feb. 1941).

P81. "The Plays and Poetry of W.B. Yeats." *The Listener* 25 (8 May 1941): 675.

P82. "W.B. Yeats: Reminiscence by a Friend." (4 May 1947, BBC broadcast.)

P83. "What Made Yeats a Great Poet." *The Listener* 37 (15 May 1947): 761.

P84. "Yeats and the Theatre." (6 June 1949, BBC broadcast.)

P85. "W.B. Yeats—a Dublin Portrait." (5 June 1949, BBC broadcast.)

P86. "W.B. Yeats." *Sunday Independent* (Dublin) (12 Sept. 1948): 4. Reprinted in *A Frank O'Connor Reader*, 1994 **[P226]**.

P87. "A Lyric Voice in the Irish Theatre." (On Yeats.) *New York Times Book Review* (31 May 1953).

P88. "Quarrelling with Yeats." *Esquire* (Dec. 1964): 157+.

P89. "Willie Is So Silly." *Vogue* (March 1965): 122+.

P90. "Yeats." *Sunday Independent* (Dublin) (13 June 1965).

P91. "W.B. Yeats." (11 and 13 June, 1965 BBC broadcast.)

P92. "The Yeats We Knew." (21 Feb. 1965, Radio Eireann broadcast.)

P93. *Horseman Pass By.* (23 Jan. 1966, BBC television documentary.)

P94. "A Gambler's Throw." *The Listener* (17 Feb. 1966). Published as mini-book, *A Gambler's Throw: Memories of W.B. Yeats.* Edinburgh: Tragara, 1975.

P95. "All the Olympians." (On Synge, Lady Gregory and Yeats.) *Saturday Review* (10 December 1966): 30–32+. Reprinted in *A Frank O'Connor Reader*, 1994 **[P226]**.

P96. "W.B. Yeats." *The Critic* (Dec. 1966–Jan. 1967).

Essays and Articles on Other Authors

P97. "A.E.—A Portrait." *The Bell* (Nov. 1940). Reprinted in *Great Irish Writing: The Best from The Bell.* Ed. Sean McMahon. Dublin: O'Brien Press, 1978.

P98. "Bring in the Whiskey Now Mary." *New Yorker* (12 Aug. 1967): 36–40.

P99. "An Author in Search of a Subject." *Critical Essays on Katherine Mansfield.* Ed. Rhoda B. Nathan. New York: G.K. Hall, 1993. 174–82. Reprinted from *The Lonely Voice.*

P100. "Shakespeare of the Drawing Room." (On Jane Austen.) *Irish Times* (11 Aug. 1945).

P101. "Stendhal." *Irish Times* (25 Aug. 1945).

P102. "Charles Dickens." *Irish Times* (8 Sept. 1945).

P103. "Flaubert." *Irish Times* (22 Sept. 1945).

P104. "Trollope." *Irish Times* (6 Oct. 1945).

P105. "The Extraordinary Story of Jonathan Swift." *Sunday Independent* (21 Oct. 1945).

P106. "Tolstoy and Turgenev." *Irish Times* (27 Oct. 1945).

P107. "Thomas Hardy." *Irish Times* (10 Nov. 1945).

P108. "Anton Chekhov." *Irish Times* (24 Nov. 1945).

P109. "Somerville and Ross." *Irish Times* (15 Dec. 1945).

P110. "The Last of the Liberals." (On Chekhov) *New York Times Book Review* (24 April 1955): 19.

P111. "Jane Austen and the Flight from Fancy." *Yale Review* 45.1 (Sept. 1955): 31–47.

P112. "A Good Short Story Must Be News." (On Liam O'Flaherty.) *New York Times Book Review* (10 June 1955).

P113. "A Writer Who Refused to Pretend." (On Chekhov.) *New York Times Book Review* (17 Jan. 1960): 1, and *New York Times Book Review: Opinions and Perspectives*. Ed. F. Brown. Boston: Houghton Mifflin, 1964. 126–32.

P114. Review of book entitled *From Jane Austen to Joseph Conrad*. *Victorian Studies* 3 (March 1960): 308–9.

P115. "Country Matters." (On Maupassant.) *Kenyon Review* 24 (Autumn 1962): 583–94.

P116. "The Slave's Son." (On Chekhov.) *Kenyon Review* 25 (Winter 1963): 40–54.

P117. "A Master's Mixture." (On Chekhov.) *New York Times Book Review* (1 March 1964): 4.

P118. "The Buck." (On Oliver St. John Gogarty.) *Spectator* (26 June 1964): 856.

P119. "Awkward but Alive." (On Patrick Kavanagh.) *Spectator* (31 July 1964).

P120. "But What of the Author?" (On Gogol.) *New York Times Book Review* (6 Sept. 1964): 10.

P121. "The Small Genius." (On James Stephens.) *Spectator* (7 May 1965).

P122. "Synge." In *The Irish Theatre: Lectures Delivered During the Abbey Theatre Festival Held in Dublin in August 1939*. Ed. Lennox Robinson. London: Macmillan, 1939.

Sound Recordings

P123. *The Irish Tradition*. Folkways Record 9825. 1958. O'Connor reads from and comments on selections from early Irish poetry, Mangan, Yeats, Synge, Lady Gregory, and Joyce.

P124. *James Joyce*. Folkways Record 9834. 1958.

P125. *Frank O'Connor Reads "My Oedipus Complex" and "The Drunkard."* Caedmon Records, TC 1036.

P126. *Ireland's Monuments*, Tapes—A.C.T., Dublin.

P127. *Leabharlanna agus me fein*, Tapes—A.C.T., Dublin.

P128. *Oiche Shamhraidh*, Tapes—A.C.T., Dublin.

P129. *Leabhar a theastuigh uaim*, Tapes—A.C.T., Dublin.

P130. *An Nodlaig i gCorcaigh*, Tapes—A.C.T., Dublin.

P131. *Nodlaig as Baile*, Tapes—A.C.T., Dublin.

Radio Broadcasts
a selection of Portraits and Talks,
and articles from *The Listener*

P132. "Literary Portraits: Yeats and AE," Radio Eireann, 1939–40.

P133. "Davitt—a Portrait." Radio Eireann, 1940.

P134. "Writer in the Witness Box. Classic or Best Seller." *The Listener* (7 Nov. 1940.)

P135. "Across St. George's Channel." BBC Radio, 27 Dec. 1940. *The Listener* (Jan. 1941)

P136. "An Irishman Looks at England." *The Listener* (2 Jan. 1941).

P137. "Curtain Up! What is Drama?" *The Listener* (23 Jan. 1941).

P138. "Curtain Up! In Defence of Realism." *The Listener* (30 Jan. 1941).

P139. "Curtain Up! The Actor Answers Back." *The Listener* (6 Feb. 1941).

P140. "Curtain Up! Verse & Prose in Drama." *The Listener* (13 Feb. 1941).

P141. "Curtain Up! Classical & Contemporary Theatre." *The Listener* (20 Feb. 1941).

P142. "Readings from F.R. Higgins." BBC Radio, 1 March 1941.

P143. "Curtain Up! Drama in the Air." *The Listener* (24 April 1941).

P144. "An Bothar go hEanach Dun." Radio Eireann, 16 Sept. 1941.

P145. "Plays and Poetry of W.B. Yeats." BBC Radio, 19 April 1941.

P146. "James Joyce." BBC Radio, 18 May 1944. "Egotism in Irish Literature (On James Joyce)." *The Listener* (1 June 1944).

P147. "W.B. Yeats: Reminiscence by a Friend." BBC Radio, 4 May 1947. "What Made Yeats a Great Poet," *The Listener* (15 May 1947).

P148. "The Art of the Theatre," BBC Radio, 5 March 1948.

P149. "John Bull and His Own Island," BBC Radio, 25 April 1948.

P150. "The Cu Chulainn Sagas," BBC Radio, 24 Sept. 1948.

P151. "The Riddle of Swift," BBC Radio, 2 Oct. 1948.

P152. "A.E. Coppard," BBC Radio, 27 Nov.1948

P153. "Irish Writers," BBC Radio, 2 Dec. 1948

P154. "Yeats and the Theatre," BBC Radio, 6 June 1949.

P155. "W.B. Yeats—A Dublin Portrait," BBC Radio, 5 June 1949.

P156. "Portrait of James Joyce," BBC Radio, 13 Feb. 1950.

P157. "My Art and Craft—the Short Story," BBC Radio, 19 October 1951.

P158. "George Moore," BBC Radio, 24 Feb. 1952.

P159. "Architect of His Own Reputation—Anthony Trollope," BBC Radio, 24 July 1954.

P160. "George Bernard Shaw—an Irish Portrait," BBC Radio, 20 Sept. 1954.

P161. "One Man's Way—the Short Story," BBC Radio, 24 June 1959. *The Listener* (23 July 1959).

P162. "Leabhar a theastuigh uaim," Radio Eireann, Nov. 1959.

P163. "An Nodlaig i gCorcaigh," Radio Eireann, Dec. 1959.

P164. "Nodlaign as Baile," Radio Eireann, Dec. 1960.

P165. "Scrapbook for 1921—Irish Civil War," BBC Radio, 2 Oct. 1961.

P166. "Adventures in Translation," BBC Radio, 17 Jan. 1962.

P167. "Interior Voices," BBC Radio, 13 Jan. 1963.

P168. "The Art of the Short Story," Radio Eireann, 26 Jan. 1964.

P169. "AE—George Russell," BBC Radio, 20 Jan. 1965.

P170. "W.B. Yeats," BBC Radio, 11 and 13 June 1965.

P171. "The Yeats We Knew," Radio Eireann, 21 Feb. 1965.

P172. "Leabharlanna agus m fine," Radio Eireann, 11 March 1968.

Literary Introductions/Prefaces

P173. *Selected Poems of Dafydd ap Gwilym.* Trans. by Nigel Heseltine, with a preface by O'Connor. Dublin: Cuala, 1944.

P174. "Introduction." *Irish Street Ballads.* Ed. Colm 0 Lochlainn. New York: Corinth, 1960.

P175a. "Introduction." *The Tailor and Ansty.* By Eric Cross. New York: Devin-Adair, 1942, 1964.

P175b. Gogol, Nikolas Vasilyevich. *Dead Souls.* Trans. by Andrew R. MacAndrew, with a foreword by O'Connor. New York: New American Library, 1961.

Selected Essays

P176. "A Boy in Prison." *Life and Letters* (August 1934): 525–35. Reprinted in *A Frank O'Connor Reader*, 1994 **[P226]**.

P177. "To Any Would-Be Writer." *The Bell* (March 1941).

P178. "The Future of Irish Literature." *Horizon* (Feb. 1942): 55–63.

P179. "At the Microphone." *The Bell* (March 1942): 415–19 [includes early manuscripts of "Night of Stars" and "Judas"].

P180. "Ireland." *Holiday* (Dec. 1949): 34–65. Reprinted in *A Frank O'Connor Reader*, 1994 **[P226]**.

P181. "The Conversion." *Harper's Bazaar* (March 1951): 160+. Reprinted in *A Frank O'Connor Reader*, 1994 **[P226]**.

P182. "And It's a Lonely, Personal Art." *New York Times Book Review* (April 12, 1953): 1, 34. Reprinted in *A Frank O'Connor Reader*, **[P226]**.

P183. "In Quest of Beer." *Holiday* (January 1957): 72, 156–58. Reprinted in *A Frank O'Connor Reader* **[P226]**.

P184. "Adventures in Translation." *Listener* (January 25, 1962): 175, 178. Also published in *Journal of Irish Literature* 4.1 (1975): 158–63.

P185. "Censorship." *Dubliner* (March 1962).

P186. "Why Don't You Write About America?" *Mademoiselle* (April 1967). Reprinted in *A Frank O'Connor Reader*, 1994 **[P226]**.

P187. "For a Two-Hundredth Birthday" [on W.A. Mozart]. *Harper's Bazaar* (January 1956): 94+. Reprinted as an eleven-page book by Tragara Press, Edinburgh, 1986. Also reprinted in *A Frank O'Connor Reader*, 1994 **[P226]**.

P188. "The Scholar" [on Osborn Bergin]. *Kenyon Review* 27 (Spring 1965): 336–43.

P189. "A Lyric Voice in the Irish Theatre." In *The Genius of the Irish Theater*. Ed. Sylvan Barnet, et al. New York: New American Library, 1960. 354–58.

Transcripts from Radio/Television/Lectures.

P190. "Adventures in Translation" [January 1962 BBC broadcast]. *Journal of Irish Literature* 4.1 (January 1975): 158–63.

P191. "Interior Voices" [1962 television broadcast]. Harriet Sheehy Collection, University of Florida Libraries at Gainesville.

P192. "Only Child" [11 Oct. 1950, Scottish Home Service (BBC) broadcast]. *Twentieth Century Literature* 36 (Fall 1990): 365–68. Reprinted in *A Frank O'Connor Reader*, 1994 **[P226]**.

P193. "The Writer and the Welfare State: The Welfare State and I" [Lecture at a Copenhagen Literary Conference, 8–14 Sept. 1960]. Printed in *A Frank O'Connor Reader* (1994), 283–91 [**P226**].

P194. "Writing a Story—One Man's Way" [24 June 1959, BBC broadcast]. *The Listener* (23 July 1959): 139–40. Reprinted in *A Frank O'Connor Reader*, 1994 [**P226**]. Also, longer text reprinted as "One Man's Way" in *Journal of Irish Literature* 4 (Jan. 1975): 151–57.

P195. "Across St. George's Channel" [27 Dec. 1940, BBC broadcast]. *The Listener* (Jan. 1941).

P196. "James Joyce" [18 May 1944, BBC broadcast]. *The Listener* (1 June 1944).

P197. "W.B. Yeats: Reminiscence by a Friend" [4 May 1947, BBC broadcast]. *The Listener* (May 1947).

P198. "One Man's Way—the Short Story" [24 June 1959, BBC broadcast]. *The Listener* (23 July 1959).

P199. "An Nollaig i gCorcaigh: Cuimhni ona Oige" [24 December 1967 Radio-Telefis Eireann T.V. broadcast]. *Comhar* 41 (1982): 116–17.

Translations of O'Connor's Work and Foreign Editions

P200. *al-Sawt al-munfarid: maqalat fi al-qassah al-qasirah.* Ta'lif Frank Ukunur; tarjamat Mahmud al-Rabi'i; muraja'at Muhammad Fathi. al-Qahirah: alHay'ah al-'Ammah lil-Ta'lif wa-al-Nashr: Dar al-Katib al-'Arabi, 1969. [Arabic translation of "The Lonely Voice."]

P201. *Ausgewahlte Erzahlungen.* Trans. by Elisabeth Schnack. Zurich: Verlag Diogenes, 1971.

P202. *Bitterer Whisky: Funf irische Erzahlungen.* Trans. by Elisabeth Schnack. Frankfurt: Insel-Bucherei, Insel-Verlag [1964].

P203. *Den hellige Dor.* Pa Dansk ved Harold Engberg. Kobenhavn: Gyldendal, 1954.

P204. *Der Trunkenbold: irische Geschichten.* Trans. by Elisabeth Schnack. Stuttgart: Philipp Reclam Jun., 1963.

P205. *Die lange Strasse nach Ummera: Elf Meistererzahlungen aus Irland.* Trans. by Elisabeth Schnack. Zurich: Verlag Diogenes, 1959.

P206. *Die Reise nach Dublin (The Saint and Mary Kate).* Trans. by Elisabeth Schnack. Zurich: Verlag Diogenes, 1961; Taschenbuch, 1964; Buchergilde, 1965.

P207. *Ein Mann Von Welt Geschichten.* Trans. by Elisabeth Schnack. N.p.: Deutscher Taschenbuch Verlag, 1969.

P208. *Einziges Kind (An Only Child).* Trans. by Elsabeth Schnack. Zurich: Verlag Diogenes, 1964.

P209. *Er hat die Hosen an.* Trans. by Elisabeth Schnack. Munich: Nymphenburger Verlagshandlung, 1957.

P210. *Geschichten von Frank O'Connor.* Zurich: Diogenes, 1967.

P211. *Grune Insel: Erzahlungen aus Irland von James Joyce bis James Plunkett.* Selected and trans. by Elisabeth Schnack. Zurich: Verlag Diogenes, 1961 [anthology with stories by O'Connor].

P212. *Hochzeit—Eine Liebesgeschichte.* Trans. by Elisabeth Schnack. Zurich: Verlag Diogenes, 1971. [*The Holy Door*]

P213. *Il Mio Complesso di Edipo e Altri Racconti.* Trans. by Barbara DiDodo and Carla Mantelli. Palermo: Selleno Editore, 1992.

P214. *Irische Erzahler der Gegenwart: Eine Anthologie.* Translated, edited, and introduced by Elisabeth Schnack. Stuttgart: Philipp Reclam Jun., 1965.

P215. *Irische Meister der Erzahlung.* Selected and translated by Elisabeth Schnack. Bremen: Walter Dorn, 1955. [anthology with stories by O'Connor]

P216. *Les Hôtes de la Nation.* Translated by Edith Soonckinot-Bieick. Paris: Marensell/Calman Levy, 1996.

P217. *Lob Der Grunen Insel Irische Erzahlungen.* Translated, with a foreword by Elisabeth Schnack. N.p.: St. Benno Verlag. 47–104. [five O'Connor stories in an anthology]

P218. *Mitt Odipus Kompleks og Andre Noveiler.* Foreward by Gordon Holmebakk. Norway: Glydendals Nouelleserie, 1979.

P219. *An Only Child.* Edited English text, with notes and preface in Japanese by Guchi Ouchi. Tokyo: Kaibunsha Ltd., 1971.

P220. "Rechtsbeistand." *Ewig Junges Irland.* Translated by Elizabeth Schnack. Bern: Gote Schriften, 1970. 57–70. [one story in an anthology]

P221. *Swiete Wrota.* Trans. by Maria Boduszzynska-Borowikowa. N.p.: Panstwowy Institut Wydawnioy, 1971.

P222. *Sue and Other Stories* by Frank O'Connor. Contains five stories, edited English text, with notes and an introduction in Japanese by Itatsu and Harakawa. Tokyo: Kenkyusha, 1973.

P223. *Und freitags Fisch: Sieben Geschichten von irischen Liebes- und Ehepaaren.* Translated by Elisabeth Schnack. Zurich: Verlag Diogenes, 1958; Taschenbuch 1963.

Miscellaneous

P224. "Frank O'Connor Issue." *Twentieth Century Literature* 36 (Fall 1990): 237–380.

P225. "A Frank O'Connor Miscellany." Ed. James H. Matthews. *Journal of Irish Literature* 4:1 (Jan. 1975). Poems, stories, a play, news articles, broadcast talks, letters, speeches.

P226. *A Frank O'Connor Reader*. Edited by Michael Steinman. Syracuse: Syracuse University Press, 1994.

Appearances in Anthologies and Other Collections

For information about reprintings of O'Connor's stories see Dorothy E. Cook and Isabel S. Monroe, eds., *Short Story Index: An Index to 60,000 Stories in 4,320 Collections* (New York: H.W. Wilson, 1953). Regular supplements published every few years have brought the number of stories covered to well over 100,000 and the number of collections covered to well over 10,000.

Unsystematic investigation suggests that "First Confession," "Guests of the Nation," and "My Oedipus Complex" have been, far and away, O'-Connor's most widely anthologized stories. "Guests," moreover, regularly appears in standard anthologies that are continuously revised and updated, such as *Fiction 100* and the *Norton Anthology of Short Fiction*.

"The Drunkard," "Judas," and "The Majesty of the Law" apparently have been the next most popular group of tales, followed by "Christmas Morning," "The Face of Evil," "Legal Aid," "Mac's Masterpiece," "The Man of the World," "Peasants," "The Storyteller," and "Uprooted." Next in apparent appeal (it would seem) have been "The American Wife," "The Bridal Night," "The Duke's Children," "The Eternal Triangle," "Freedom," "The Genius," "The Idealist," "In the Train," "The Long Road to Ummera," "The Mad Lomasneys," "The Man of the House," "Masculine Protest," "Michael's Wife," "Orpheus and His Lute," "A Set of Variations on a Borrowed Theme," and "Song Without Words."

Special Collections Materials

Among the several archives and libraries which hold special collections materials pertaining to Frank O'Connor, two specifically house "Frank O'Connor Papers": the libraries of Boston University and the University of Florida. The rest of the libraries and archives hold materials about O'Connor within some larger collection, usually associated with someone O'-Connor knew; among them, Sean O'Faolain and Richard Ellmann are the most notable. Several of the collections mentioned below have only been purchased within the last few years, and a few have not yet been adequately catalogued. This special collections information, then, is intended to aid those looking for rare O'Connor materials by providing an overview from which to proceed.

It should be noted that most of the letters Frank O'Connor wrote were undated, though in many cases reasonable speculation has been made about the dates from the content of the letters themselves.

Additionally, relevant materials which are not catalogued below may be found in the Cork Public Library, the University College Cork Library, the Dublin Writers Museum, and the Cork Writers Project.

Boston University, Mugar Memorial Library, Frank O'Connor Papers

Most of the holdings were purchased from O'Connor's first wife, Evelyn, in 1969. There are, additionally, eighteen letters and postcards from O'Connor (and two from his mother) to Molly Alexander, O'Connor's landlady while he was writing "Guests of the Nation"—these letters were purchased from Alexander's daughter in 1975. Also purchased in the early 1980s were four letters from W.B. Yeats (from the 1930s) and one from George Yeats.

The chief holdings include manuscripts, typescripts, galley proofs, notes and notebooks, business correspondences and records, personal letters to, from, and (a few) about O'Connor among his family, friends, and literary acquaintances. All are grouped in roughly chronological order, though in this description they are treated separately.

Among the O'Connor manuscripts are handwritten drafts of the short story "The Land of the Lamas"; typescripts and galley proofs, with handwritten corrections by O'Connor, for *The Saint and Mary Kate*, *The Big Fellow*, "Lady of the Sagas," a radio play, "Malachy," a play, *Time's Pocket*, several poems and articles, pages from *Irish Miles*, and the Cuala Press edition of "The Lament for Art O'Leary." Also included are publications by O'Connor such as "Seagulls" (a short story) and several articles, as well as notes on A.E. Coppard and Bernard Shaw, and two notebooks: (1) materials O'Connor and Evelyn gathered for *Irish Miles* and (2) fragments of plays, stories, and poems.

The business correspondence is generally separate, with files for the Abbey Theatre, the Cuala Press, and *The Bell* (within a Sean O'Faolain file). The business records are filed separately from letters to and from O'Connor, even if letters primarily concern business dealings.

The Abbey correspondence, mainly spanning the years O'Connor served as director, 1937–41, includes eighteen letters from O'Connor to others (a number regarding his resignation) and roughly thirty to O'Connor. In a separate file are business reports, contracts, and meeting notices and agendas for the Abbey.

The Cuala Press correspondence (1938–48) consists of fifty-six letters, the majority of them from Mrs. George Yeats, wife of W.B. and director of the press. Also, in a Cuala Press file are business papers pertaining to O'-Connor's Cuala Press books and to the time O'Connor served on the press's board of editors.

Regarding *The Bell*: within the O'Faolain file are letters to O'Connor, his wife Evelyn (who wrote drama reviews for the magazine), and O'Faolain.

The letters, which make up the largest part of the collection, are grouped chronologically into sections. The first consists of seventy-six letters from O'Connor to his wife Evelyn, before and during their marriage, in the period from 1937 to 1941, and about twenty letters from Evelyn to her husband. Within the second section are eleven letters from O'Connor to Evelyn from 1941–42. The third section is by far the largest and covers the longest span of time. It consists of 167 letters from O'Connor to Evelyn in the years 1944–58 (mostly 1944–48); fourteen letters (1944–48) to Evelyn from Joan, the mother of O'Connor's son Oliver; and seven letters between various family members, especially O'Connor's children. Lastly, there are forty-eight letters from 1953–55 regarding the terms of O'Connor's and Evelyn's divorce. In addition to these personal letters exchanged within O'Connor's family are various letters, including ones from publisher Harold Macmillan and writer Elizabeth Bowen; there are 147 letters from Sean O'Faolain from 1939–48 and five letters O'Connor sent to O'Faolain during this period. Also included are fourteen letters O'Connor sent to various Dublin associates from 1940 to 1947, among them letters to Elizabeth Bowen and Denis Johnston. Perhaps most interesting to Irish literature enthusiasts are the 433 letters contained in the Dublin file (1929–49), which holds correspondence from Osborn Bergin, Austin Clarke, Dermot Foley (25 letters), Hugh Hunt, Denis Johnston, Patrick Kavanagh, and L.A.G. Strong.

Other miscellaneous items include musical settings by Aloys Fleischman for O'Connor's poems "The Student," "The Lover," and "Autumn"; a play, "Still Waters," by John McGiffert (ca. 1945), based on "Song Without Words"; sixteen newspaper clippings about O'Connor from 1935–69; a typescript (with Yeats's corrections) of *Purgatory*, sent to O'Connor by Lennox Robinson; unpublished plays by Francis Stuart and Brendan Behan's father-in-law, Cecil Salkeld, among others; photographs of O'Connor, Evelyn, and their children, Liadain and Owen; and a copy of O'Connor's 1956 will.

The British Broadcasting Corporation, Written Archives Centre

The BBC archive contains files of scripts, contracts, and correspondence relating to O'Connor's broadcast talks and stories, primarily from 1936–48, but extending even to the last years of his life. Particularly of interest among the letters are the exchanges regarding the refusal of a visa for O'-Connor to come to England in 1942. The archive also holds articles from

The Listener, mostly from a 1941 series of talks called "Curtain Up." Further details on the O'Connor holdings are available through *The Register of 20th Century English Manuscripts* database.

Cork Public Museum

Among the items donated to the museum by O'Connor's friend Sean Hendrick are thirty-four of O'Connor's early poems, most of them copies; fifteen letters written by Michael O'Donovan, one of them from 1929, but almost all undated; three Cork Drama League play programs; and a few other miscellaneous items.

Harvard University Library, Pusey Library

Holds course descriptions for O'Connor's Summer 1953 courses at Harvard and a reading list for his 1953 course on the twentieth-century novel.

The Houghton Library, Harvard University

Contains a typescript version of "Guests of the Nation" (MS Eng 1309) and six undated letters (in bMS Am 1787), five of them in correspondence with Horace Reynolds, a critic who befriended O'Connor during his Harvard summers of 1952 and 1953.

The National Library of Ireland, Dublin

Holds one early letter to Earnan de Blaghd (Ernest Blythe) and the typescript of O'Connor's play *Time's Pocket*. Also holds, among uncatalogued materials acquired in 1984 from O'Connor's friend and one-time assistant at Pembroke, librarian Dermot Foley, typescripts of "Jumbo's Wife" and drafts of seven poetry translations; over one hundred letters from O'Connor, twenty-nine from his first wife, Evelyn, eight from Joan, the mother of O'Connor's son Oliver, and one from Harriet O'Donovan soon after O'Connor's death; the first draft of the first story Foley ever attempted, complete with comments from editor and critic O'Connor; and a twenty-three page diary Foley kept during the three days of O'Connor's wake and funeral, used (perhaps misused) by James Matthews in reconstructing O'Connor's last days in the biography *Voices*.

Northwestern University Library, University Archives

Within the Frederic E. Faverty Papers are two letters from O'Connor in March 1952 optimistically accepting Faverty's invitation and making arrangements for O'Connor's teaching engagement at Northwestern that spring. Also held are typescripts and handwritten drafts of Faverty's reviews of *The Mirror in the Roadway* and *The Lonely Voice*.

The Stanford University Libraries, Department of Special Collections

Contains typescript, galleys, and proofs of *An Only Child* and lecture notes from O'Connor's course at Stanford on the twentieth-century novel in the Frank O'Connor papers (M034); also contains one letter each from Michael O'Donovan and Harriet O'Donovan to Wallace Stegner in 1955 in the American authors collection (M122), and holds a number of rare editions of O'Connor's early work, among them the Cuala Press *Wild Bird's Nest* and *Lords and Commons*.

Trinity College Library, Dublin

Holdings include manuscript materials for O'Connor's *The Backward Look* (see Ruth Sherry's article, **P231**); an O'Connor play, *The Lost Legion*, written in 1936 and acquired by the library in 1996; twenty letters by Frank O'Connor, the majority to Seamus O'Sullivan and Denis Johnston; and two letters written to Frank O'Connor and one to his wife Harriet Sheehy.

University of California, Berkeley

The Bancroft Library holds the Sean O'Faolain Correspondence and Papers, 1927–76 (BANC MSS 74/11 lz), within which are thirty-three letters written by Frank O'Connor to Sean O'Faolain, circa 1932–54 (in Box I, folder 1:40).

University of Florida, Frank O'Connor Papers

Purchased from Harriet O'Donovan Sheehy, O'Connor's widow, in 1988, the Frank O'Connor papers at the University of Florida constitute not only the largest gathering of materials pertinent to O'Connor, but also by far the most abundant source of O'Connor manuscripts that would likely be of greatest use to scholars among the libraries and archives listed here. The materials are organized by genre. Among these are separate sections for short stories, books, introductions, newspaper/magazine articles, lectures, theatre, radio scripts, television scripts, secondary sources, notebooks and journals, business correspondence and records, and O'Connor's set of Shakespeare, with annotations.

Within the "short stories" section are multiple drafts of almost all of the 110 stories held, some in manuscript, but most in typescript form. The "books" section contains a few drafts of *The Lonely Voice*; mostly typescript chapters and sections for *The Mirror in the Roadway*, *Shakespeare's Progress*, and *An Only Child*; nearly complete typescripts or galleys for *Domestic Relations* and *Collection Two*; heavily annotated and corrected typescripts of the 1965 revised edition of *The Big Fellow* and *A Golden Treasury of Irish Poetry. A D. 600–1200*, with help from David Greene and Harriet Sheehy; the materials used by Maurice Sheehy to complete *My Father's Son* and by

Harriet Sheehy to prepare *Collection Three*; and materials pertaining to O'Connor's incomplete, unpublished dream book.

The "introductions" are typescripts which eventually appeared in C.O. Lochlainn's *Irish Street Ballads*, the 1961 NAL edition of Gogol's *Dead Souls*, the 1964 Time Reading Program edition of Joyce's *Portrait*, and the album notes to O'Connor's Folkways Records *The Irish Tradition* and *James Joyce*.

The "articles" section contains drafts of approximately fifty articles which appeared in print mostly from 1956 to 1966. In addition, there are approximately ten articles which were never published and a file of manuscripts and materials relating to the Roger Casement diaries.

The "lectures" section mainly consists of materials pertaining to O'-Connor's teaching engagement at Stanford: six letters, copies of a syllabus and an exam from his course, and notes for thirteen lectures on modern novelists, including Joyce Cary, Forster, Lawrence, Mansfield, Joyce, Ford Madox Ford, and Woolf.

The "theatre" section contains a rehearsal script for the Abbey's presentation of *Moses' Rock* and drafts and other materials from 1941 relating to *The Statue's Daughter*.

Twenty-two radio transcripts are held, mostly from Radio Eireann or the BBC, one in Irish, some autobiographical, some of them reminiscences of Yeats and A.E., and some radio adaptations of O'Connor's work. Five television transcripts by O'Connor are held as well.

Among a file of secondary sources on O'Connor's work are two adaptations: Mary Manning's *The Saint and Mary Kate* [**S229**] and Paul Avila Mayer's *Three Hand Reel* [**S228**]. Also held are Danish translations of a number of O'Connor stories, a file of materials pertaining to *Michael/Frank* [**S16**], and a file of clippings of articles and reviews of O'Connor's works.

Thirty-eight notebooks from periods throughout O'Connor's life (as early as 1927–1930) are held. The first of these is a diary, but the rest are mostly notes and drafts of stories, reviews, articles, lectures, books, translations, dreams, and travel sketches. Of special interest are a separate 125–page dream book which records dreams from the 1940s and 1950s and a 100–page book of 122 potential themes for stories. Michael Steinman has published his annotations of this theme book [**P233**], and Shawn O'Hare's Florida State University dissertation is on O'Connor's proposed dream book [**S107**]. The business correspondence and records involve O'Connor's various publishers, his agents (the Harold Matson Agency and A.D. Peters), the BBC, Caedmon and Folkways Records, and Radio Eireann, among others. Also, there are various invitations and correspondences from publishers and universities.

Above is a general descriptive overview for those who may be interested in delving more specifically into this abundant collection. For further information, see Carmen Russell Hurff's "Finding Guide" to this collection, listed below as item P227, now available on the Internet. For other general perspectives on the University of Florida papers, see the relevant articles by Owene Weber [**P235**] and Michael Steinman [**P232**] listed below in this bibliography .

University of Kansas Library, Department of Special Collections, Kenneth Spencer Research Library

The P.S. O'Hegarty collection and other special collections materials at the Spencer Library constitute one of the largest gatherings of special collections materials on the Irish Renaissance in the United States. Within these collections are three letters from O'Connor regarding O'Hegarty's assistance with *The Big Fellow* (the biography of Michael Collins). Also holds the rare publications of O'Connor's earliest poems and stories by The Cuala Press and others.

John Rylands University Library of Manchester

Within the Professor Hugh Hunt papers, acquired in 1980, are special collections manuscript materials pertaining to the O'Connor-Hunt dramatic collaborations *The Invincibles, In the Train,* and *Moses' Rock*. Regarding *The Invincibles* there are also two files of related correspondence, production notes, and press clippings. Also contains a book of press clippings from 1934–36.

University of Texas at Austin, Harry Ransom Humanities Research Center

Holds the papers of A.D. Peters, O'Connor's British literary agent, also the literary agent of AE (George Russell). Thus, the Research Center contains the correspondence between Peters and Michael O'Donovan, 1938 to 1963 (within boxes 58–61). Also holds a radio script of O'Connor's "The Midnight Court" translation from September 1947, manuscripts of two stories, and correspondence with various others, including a 1956 letter from O'Connor to A.E. Coppard and four letters to L.A.G. Strong.

University of Toronto, Thomas Fisher Rare Book Library

Built upon a gift of books from the estate of Dean Alfred De Lury in 1955, and expanded extensively since then, the Fisher Library holds one of the finest collections of Anglo-Irish literature in North America. This library houses one of the most complete collections of O'Connor's printed works: approximately fifty books by O'Connor, including first editions of *Guests of the Nation* and *An Only Child*, and both the American and British first editions of *Bones of Contention, Crab Apple Jelly, Stories, A Set of Variations/Collection Three, The Road to Stratford/Shakespeare's Progress, Kings, Lords, and Commons,* and *The Lonely Voice*; a complete set of O'Connor's short story volumes, novels, travel books, anthologies, picture books, and criticism; the Cuala Press editions of O'Connor's first books of short stories and poems; and the individual publications of *A Lament for Art*

O'Leary and *The Midnight Court*, in addition to a complete set of O'Connor's books of translations. The one genre lacking representation is the drama, which was largely unpublished until the 1980s.

The Fisher library also holds the German translations *Die lange Strasse nach Ummera, Die Reise nach Dublin*, and *Und freitags Fisch* by Elisabeth Schnack; Mary Manning's dramatic adaptation of *The Saint and Mary Kate*; editions complete with O'Connor's introductory remarks for Joyce's *Portrait*, Eric Cross's *The Tailor and Ansty* and Nigel Heseltine's translation of selected poems by 14th c. Welsh poet Dafydd ap Gwilym (Cuala, 1944); and a copy of the 1982 Tragara Press publication of O'Connor's *W.B. Yeats: A Reminiscence* and a clipping from *The Yale Review*'s O'Connor essay "Two Friends: Yeats and A.E." The one significant drawback for researchers is that the Fisher Library's books are non-circulating. Limited photocopying is available to scholars and persons with a genuine research need, while the library awaits new technology which will eventually enable it to offer copies of its books for interlibrary loan purposes.

University of Tulsa, McFarlin Library, Department of Special Collections

The University of Tulsa holds The Richard Ellmann Papers, an extensive collection of important personal and professional materials of the noted critic and biographer of Joyce, Yeats, and Wilde.

The papers contain a good deal of valuable and interesting information about O'Connor, for the two met while Ellmann was in Ireland researching the first of his books on Yeats, and their friendship carried on for years; it also led Ellmann to invite O'Connor to teach at Northwestern.

Shedding light on Yeats, O'Connor, and the Irish literary scene of the 1930s and 1940s are Ellmann's extensive 1946 notes from interviews with Mrs. Yeats, O'Connor, and others for his book on Yeats.

There are thirteen letters from Ellmann to O'Connor, sixteen letters from O'Connor to Ellmann, and one to Ellmann from Harriet O'Donovan—most from the 1950s. Included also are copies of Michael and Harriet's wedding invitation and announcement in *The New York Times*.

The collection contains a number of additional materials on O'Connor which Ellmann saved: copies of several reviews by O'Connor; O'Connor's article on Yeats, "Willie Is So Silly"; Ellmann's 1981 *New York Times Book Review* reprint of his introduction to O'Connor's *Collected Stories*; and articles on O'Connor's death from *Eire-Ireland, The National Catholic Reporter*, and *The Chicago Sun-Times*.

Further information about O'Connor may likely be found at Tulsa in files containing Ellmann's correspondence with other friends and colleagues, and in his notes and letters from his research on Joyce, Yeats, and Wilde.

University of Victoria B.C., McPherson Library, Special Collections Department

Within the Michael O'Donovan (Frank O'Connor) papers are manuscripts of "The Beauty"—an early draft of O'Connor's story "The Ugly Duckling"; "Fish for Friday"; "The Weeping Children," along with a clipping from *The New Yorker* of the story's publication; and an early draft of "The Weeping Children" titled "The Others." The University Library also holds a notebook which contains handwritten drafts of "The Lament for Art O'Leary" and an article titled "Modern Irish Literature." Also held are three draft versions of O'Connor's funeral oration for Yeats, two of them early drafts, the earliest a holograph in English, the later two typescripts containing an introductory passage in the Irish language. Also holds five holograph letters from O'Connor to John Betjeman from 1945 to 1950 within a separate Betjeman archive.

University of Virginia, Alderman Library, Special Collections Department

The Alida Monro (Klemantaski) correspondence with various writers regarding her anthology *Recent Poetry, 1922–33* contains letters to and from Michael O'Donovan, presumably from 1933.

Publications Regarding Special Collections, Letters, and Manuscripts

P227. Hurff, Carmen Russell. "Finding Guide." University of Florida Department of Special Collections, 1988. A well-indexed thirty-eight page catalog of the items purchased by the University from O'Connor's widow, this guide can be accessed on the World Wide Web (thanks to Jeffrey A. Barr) through the University of Florida Libraries' Rare Book and Manuscripts site at http://karamelik.eastlib.ufl.edu/bookill/OConnor/oconnor.html

P228. Lester, DeeGee. *Irish Research: A Guide to Collections in North America, Ireland, and Great Britain.* New York: Greenwood Press, 1987. Indexes special collections materials, listing six university libraries in the U.S. and Canada as holding some O'Connor materials, although detail and reliability of entries may vary due to the sheer breadth of the project.

P229. O'Donovan, Michael (Frank O'Connor). "Letters to Nancy McCarthy." *Twentieth Century Literature* 36 (Fall 1990): 369–74. Three letters to his first love, written in 1931.

P230. ———. Letters to Sean Hendrick. "A Frank O'Connor Miscellany." *Journal of Irish Literature* 4 (January 1975): 44–46.

P231. Sherry, Ruth. "Frank O'Connor: Manuscripts of *The Backward Look.*" *Long Room* 16/17 (1978): 37–38.

P232. Steinman, Michael. "The Frank O'Connor Papers." *Irish Literary Supplement: A Review of Irish Books* 9 (Fall 1990): 25. One-page encapsulation of the University of Florida papers, described in four sections: materials pertaining to O'Connor's short stories, books, and journalism, and notebooks.

P233. ———. "A Frank O'Connor Theme-Book." *Irish University Review* 22 (Autumn/Winter 1992): 242–60. Informs about O'Connor's creative method by printing and commmenting on over one-hundred of his four-line themes from his writing notebook.

P234. ———, ed. *The Happiness of Getting It Down Right: Letters of Frank O'Connor and William Maxwell, 1945–1966.* New York: Knopf, 1996.

P235. Weber, Owene H. "The Frank O'Connor Papers at the University of Florida." *Twentieth Century Literature* 36 (Fall 1990): 358–65. The scholar responsible for negotiating Mrs. Sheehy's sale of O'Connor's papers makes more accessible these twenty-eight manuscript boxes by breaking them into seventeen divisions by genre; proposes many significant ideas for utilizing these materials as the subject for further scholarly work.

Interviews

P236. Breit, Harvey. "Talk With Frank O'Connor." *New York Times Book Review* (14 June 1951): 14.

P237. Flynn, William. "Talk with the Author." *Newsweek* (13 March 1961): 98. Reprinted in *A Frank O'Connor Reader*, 1994 [**P226**].

P238. Lennon, Peter. "For Decency's Sake." *Manchester Guardian* (9 October 1963).

P239. Longley, Michael. "Frank O'Connor: An Interview." *Twentieth Century Literature* 36 (Fall 1990): 269–75.

P240. *Monitor.* Filmed interview in Cork. BBC TV, 19 Nov. 1961 and 12 Aug. 1963.

P241. Morrow, Larry ("The Bellman"). "Meet Frank O'Connor." *The Bell* (6 March 1951): 41–46. Reprinted in *A Frank O'Connor Reader*, 1994 [**P226**].

P242. *Self Portrait.* Radio-Telefis Eireann T.V., 2 and 9 Jan. 1962.

P243. Whittier, Anthony. *Writers at Work: The Paris Review Interviews.* Ed. Malcolm Cowley. New York: Viking, 1959. 61–82.

SECONDARY SOURCES

The following is a comprehensive review of materials pertaining to O'Connor and his work; this review chiefly cites books, articles, and dissertations which have critically examined and assessed O'-Connor's works and career, though included as well are selected book reviews of and about O'Connor and published personal remembrances of the man. The book reviews noted below are a selection of those which focus only on O'Connor's work (not those which review several books at once, for example) and which are of substantial length (over 500 words). The reviews do represent a variety of views; some may shed as much light on American stereotypes of the Irish or on moralistic attitudes as on the literary value of O'Connor's work.

All of the following cited sources are listed by subject and are reviewed through annotations which generally correspond to the length of the source (for example, a full-length critical study of O'-Connor receives more commentary than an article). If a work listed below is not annotated, it likely was regarded as too brief to require commentary, though in a few cases the original source was inaccessible.

Bibliographies

S1. Alexander, James. "An Annotated Bibliography of Works about Frank O'Connor." *Journal of Irish Literature* 16 (1987): 40–48. Provides one-sentence annotations of sources grouped into three categories: criticism, journalism, and dissertations.

S2. Brenner, Gerry. "Frank O'Connor 1903–1966, a Bibliography." *West Coast Review* 2 (Fall 1967): 55–64. This earliest bibliography usefully traces the appearances of each published O'Connor story, but otherwise it was superseded by Maurice Sheehy's bibliography of 1969.

S3. Tomory, William M. "Selected Bibliography." *Frank O'Connor*. Boston: Twayne, 1980. 188–94.

S4. Sheehy, Maurice. "Towards a Bibliography of Frank O'Connor's Writing." *Michael/Frank* [**S16**]. Ed. Maurice Sheehy. New York: Knopf, 1969. 168–99. Remains the best published bibliography of primary sources.

S5. Sherry, Ruth. (As yet) Unpublished annotated bibliography of works by Frank O'Connor. This thorough (ca. 400–page) bibliography will include variant texts and extensive coverage of O'Connor's broadcasts.

S6. Wohlgelernter, Maurice. "Selected Bibliography." *Frank O'Connor: An Introduction.* New York: Columbia University Press, 1977. 207–13.

Reference Materials on O'Connor's Life and Career

S7. Boylan, Henry, ed. *A Dictionary of Irish Biography.* 2nd ed. New York: St. Martin's, 1988.

S8. Brady, Anne, M., and Brian Cleeve, eds. *A Biographical Dictionary of Irish Writers.* New York: St. Martin's, 1985.

S9. Cleeve, Brian. *Dictionary of Irish Writers I: Fiction.* Cork: Mercier Press, 1967.

S10. Deane, Seamus, gen. ed. "Frank O'Connor." *Field Day Anthology of Irish Writing.* Vol. 111. Derry: Field Day, 1991. 127–28.

S11. Hogan, Robert, ed. *Dictionary of Irish Literature.* Westport, CT: Greenwood, 1980.

S12. Kunitz, Stanley, ed. *Twentieth-Century Authors. First Supplement.* New York: Wilson, 1955. 729–30.

S13. Pine. L.G., ed. *The Author's and Writer's Who's Who and Reference Guide.* London: Shaw, 1948.

S14. Welch, Robert. *The Oxford Companion to Irish Literature.* New York: Oxford University Press, 1996.

Books of Criticism on O'Connor's Works

S15. Matthews, James. *Frank O'Connor.* Lewisburg, PA: Bucknell University Press, 1976; London: Associated University Presses, 1976. A short critical study consisting of chapters which examine (1) O'Connor's career through autobiography and criticism; (2) his relationship to Ireland through translations, biography, novels, and the travel book *Irish Miles;* and (3) a selection of his stories by exploring one representative volume from each decade of his career.

S16. Sheehy, Maurice, ed. *Michael/Frank: Studies on Frank O'Connor.* New York: Alfred A. Knopf, 1969. A collection of reminiscences about and critical articles on O'Connor which paints a consistent portrait of the artist and the man. Each of the essays is treated separately in this bibliography.

S17. Steinman, Michael. *Frank O'Connor at Work.* Syracuse: Syracuse University Press, 1990. Textual criticism of variant drafts of seven O'Connor stories, including previously unexplored drafts of unpublished materials. Covered are "First Confession," "Judas," "The Genius," "Orpheus and his Lute," "The Cornet Player Who Betrayed Ireland," "The Little Mother," and "A Set of Variations." Particularly valuable is the first chapter, which explains the method and rationale for O'Connor's revision process. Each subsequent chapter deals with a particular story. A degree of familiarity with *Collected Stories* versions, at least, is assumed.

S18. Tomory, William M. *Frank O'Connor*. Boston: Twayne, 1980. Chapters two, six, and seven assess and explore the range of O'Connor's writing in various genres, and the first chapter is biographical, especially dealing with the early years. However, the focus for this study is chiefly on analyzing and assessing O'Connor's short fiction. Interesting and original are Tomory's treatment of the influences of Chekhov and Sherwood Anderson, among others, and his delineation of O'Connor's "submerged population" into romantics, priests, and juveniles. Tomory ultimately sees O'Connor as a quiet realist whose greatest achievement was in the development of narrative voice.

S19. Wohlgelernter, Maurice. *Frank O'Connor: An Introduction*. New York: Columbia University Press, 1977. A profile of O'Connor which relates his work and ideas to historical and intellectual events of his time. Each chapter deals with a different social context: (1) his formative personal influences; (2) his involvement in the Civil War; (3) his conception of religion and the role of the priest in Irish life; (4) Irish domestic life, the subject of most of his stories and the two novels; (5) his literary criticism; and (6) his ties to the Abbey Theatre.

Biography

S20. Matthews, James. *Voices: A Life of Frank O'Connor*. New York: Atheneum, 1983. The only full-length biography of O'Connor is thorough and honest, yet completely dispiriting. It aims at a psychological approach but ultimately fails in this attempt because Matthews seems unable, especially in the latter part of the book, to conjure O'Connor's warmth and sincerity, and often the happiness evident, for example, in the reminiscences in *Michael/Frank* (**S16**) or in the letters to William Maxwell (**P234**). Furthermore, Matthews seems to take a moral stand against O'Connor with gratuitous offhand remarks throughout the book. Though the biography is useful in many ways to O'Connor scholars because of its completeness, it is ironic that the life of an author known largely for his comic sensibility is represented by such a depressing book. In regard to this biography, see the following reviews: Thomas Flanagan, "Angry Son of Ireland," *New Republic* (25 April 1983): 32–34; William Maxwell, "The Duke's Child," *The New Yorker* 59 (27 June 1983): 96–99; Richard F. Peterson, *Studies in Short Fiction* 21 (Spring 1984): 167; Gregory A. Schirmer, *Eire-Ireland* 19 (Fall 1984): 152–53; Ruth Sherry, *Irish University Review* 14 (Autumn 1984): 290–99; Joseph L.

Schneider, *Modern Fiction Studies* 30 (Summer 1984): 359–61; and Michael Steinman, "An Olympian Portrait of an Olympian." *Irish Literary Supplement* 2 (1983): 23. See also:

S21. Steinman, Michael. "The Perils of Biography: A Talk with Harriet Sheehy." *Twentieth Century Literature* 36 (Fall 1990): 243–59. Reveals O'Connor's widow's assessment of the biography, chiefly her concern not with the facts Matthews presents, but with his abrasive tone and unbalanced presentation of subject matter.

On O'Connor's Career and Critical Reputation

S22. Alexander, James. "The Artist at Home." *Twentieth Century Literature* 36 (Fall 1990): 344–58. A survey of O'Connor's career shows he was a modern-day *seanchai* and that his writing in all genres attests to his vested interest in and consistent concern for his native land.

S23. Farrell, James T. *On Irish Themes*. Edited and introduced by Dennis Flynn. Philadelphia: University of Pennsylvania Press, 1982. A collection of essays and reviews by an Irish-American critic who regards O'Connor as the most talented of his generation of Irish writers, though Farrell discussses the difficulties of O'Connor's critical stances and perceived compromises in his later fiction.

S24. Finneran, Richard J. *Anglo-Irish Literature: A Review of Research*. New York: Modern Language Association, 1976. Evaluates O'Connor's scholarship and critical judgments, but this book, in focusing on the Irish Renaissance and on drama, largely ignores O'Connor's best work as a writer.

S25. Flanagan, Thomas. "Frank O'Connor 1903–66." *Kenyon Review* 28 (Sept. 1966): 439–55. Reprinted as "The Irish Writer" in *Michael/Frank* [**S16**]. Ed. M. Sheehy. 148–64. This reminiscence and review of O'Connor's work focuses on a number of levels while attempting to come to terms with O'Connor's complex relationship to Ireland and its people.

S26. Halton, Thomas. "In the Irish Blood." *Catholic World* 187 (July 1958): 252–56. Geared toward a 1950s Catholic American audience, this article takes exception to the morality of stories by O'Faolain and O'Connor, but it mainly criticizes O'Connor for not having varied his writing patterns since "First Confession."

S27. Kavanagh, Patrick. "Coloured Balloons: A Study of Frank O'Connor." *The Bell* (3 Dec. 1947): 11–21. Reviews the career (up to *Crab Apple Jelly*) of Ireland's "most exciting" writer, finding him a fine translator but as a short story writer mostly just an entertainer with no serious purpose or direction.

S28. Kerrigan, John C. "Rediscovering Frank O'Connor." M.A. Thesis. University of Nevada, Las Vegas, 1995. Attempts to challenge previous assessments of O'Connor's literary reputation by examining closely the supposed simplicity and humorousness of his stories of childhood; his turbulent relationship with Ireland and, in particular, Catholicism; his response to the modernist movement; and his place among the chief short fiction writers of his generation, O'Flaherty and O'Faolain. This thesis, in discussing a range of O'Connor's stories through the framework of his reputation, emphasizes his literary artistry through his construction of narrative voice, variety of characters, and extensive revision processes.

S29. Kilroy, James F. *The Irish Short Story: A Critical History*. Boston: Twayne, 1984. Containing a useful background chronology and introduction, this collection focuses most specifically on O'Connor in the chapter entitled "Setting the Standards: Writers of the 1920s and 1930s."

S30. Mac Aonghusa, Proinsias. "O'Connor, Fear an Mhisnigh." *Gaillimh agus Aisti Eile*. Dublin: Clochomhar, 1983. 62–63.

S31. Malloy, Ione. "Corkery, O'Connor, and O'Faolain: A Literary Relationship in the Emerging Irish Republic." Ph.D. Dissertation. University of Texas at Austin, 1979. Explores O'Connor's and O'Faolain's personal relationship to Corkery, and their critical and artistic ties to him through the frame of national and international identity.

S32. Matthews, James H. "Frank O'Connor: Improvising an Irish Writer." *Journal of Irish Literature* 4.1 (1975): 5–17. Traces O'Connor's self-education, particularly through the autobiographies, and O'Connor's improvised and often contradictory writing career.

S33. McKeon, Jim. "If He Was a Russian." *Cork Review* (1993): 31–32.

S34. McManus, Francis. "A Storyteller and His Craft." *RTE Guide* (Radio Telefis Eireann) (9 Feb. 1962): 5.

S35. O'Faolain, Sean. *Vive Moi!* New York: Little, Brown, 1964. These memoirs contain some reminiscences about his best friend from the early years and put forth the classic "shooting gallery" analogy for O'Connor's spontaneous, fumblingly intuitive approach.

S36. ———. "A World of Fitzies." Rev. of Maurice Wohlgelernter's *Frank O'Connor*. *Times Literary Supplement* (29 April 1977): 502–3. Provides some vivid glimpses at O'Connor's youth, and ultimately offers the assessment that even in spite of his occasional sentimentality O'Connor is probably the finest Irish short story craftsman and one of the finest in all of literature.

S37. Sherry, Ruth. "Fathers and Sons: O'Connor among the Irish Writers: Corkery, AE, Yeats." *Twentieth Century Literature* 36 (Fall 1990): 275–303. Examines the influence of these father-figures on O'Connor. Corkery helped to shape O'Connor's early work and broadened his horizons. AE had sparse literary influence but did contribute to his social and political outlook, in addition to establishing his recognition. Yeats's direct influence may be negligible; Yeats at least encouraged him to pursue translation and drama, and Yeats's own stances likely inspired O'Connor's public pontifications.

S38. Steinman, Michael. "Introduction to the Frank O'Connor Issue." *Twentieth Century Literature* 36 (Fall 1990): 237–38. Suggests possibilities for further critical study of O'Connor's work, which has previously been underestimated and has lacked serious analytical attention.

S39. Warner, Alan. *A Guide to Anglo-Irish Literature*. Dublin: Gill and Macmillan, 1981. Contains a ten-page biographical overview and brief approach to O'Connor's best work.

S40. Wohlgelernter, Maurice. Review of *Michael/Frank* [**S16**]. *Journal of Modern Literature* 1 (Spring 1971): 883–85.

Critical Studies of "Guests of the Nation"

S41. Bardotti, Marta. "'Guests of the Nation' di Frank O'Connor: Una proposta di lettura." *Studi dell'Istituto Linguistico* 7 (1984): 273–99.

S42. Briden, Earl F. "'Guests of the Nation': A Final Irony." *Studies in Short Fiction* 13 (Winter 1976): 79–81. Claims O'Donovan Rossa as a source for character Jeremiah Donovan.

S43. Cooke. M.G. "From Comedy to Terror: On *Dubliners* and the Development of Tone and Structure in the Modern Short Story." *Massachusetts Review* 9 (1968): 331–43. Discusses the transfer of emotion from laughter to terror in "Guests," as a conclusion to a wider discussion of the genre's evolution, particularly focusing on *Dubliners* as a turning point.

S44. Crider J.R. "Jupiter Pluvius in 'Guests of the Nation.'" *Studies in Short Fiction* 23 (Fall 1986): 407–12. O'Connor thematically emphasizes the tragic seriousness which engulfs his characters through allusion to the god who protects the sacred laws of hospitality.

S45. Evans, Robert C. "Frank O'Connor: 'Guests of the Nation.'" *Short Fiction: A Critical Companion*. Ed. Robert C. Evans, Anne C. Little, and Barbara Wiedemann. West Cornwall, CT: Locust Hill Press, 1987. 199–204. Detailed summaries of thirteen critical discussions of O'Connor's story.

S46. Lieberman, Michael. "Unforeseen Duty in Frank O'Connor's 'Guests of the Nation.'" *Studies in Short Fiction* 24 (1987): 438–41. O'Connor placed greater textual emphasis on the words "unforeseen" and "duty" in his 1954 revision of the original.

S47. Rafroidi, Patrick. "'Guests of the Nation': The Seminal Story of Modern Irish Literature?" *Journal of the Short Story in English* 8 (Spring 1987): 51–57. Points out the defects in O'Connor's critical reputation and in the story itself before cataloging the antithetical responses to modern Ireland that "Guests" initiated for many Irish writers.

S48. Renner, Stanley. "The Theme of Hidden Powers: Fate Versus Human Responsibility in 'Guests of the Nation.'" *Studies in Short Fiction* 27 (Summer 1990): 371–77. Identifies a moral judgment implicit within the story, since its narrative design shifts the responsibility for action from the actors themselves, Bonaparte and Noble, to "hidden powers" which supposedly govern their actions.

S49. Robinson, Patricia. "O'Connor's 'Guests of the Nation.'" *Explicator* 45 (1986): 58. The character Feeny, recalling the Fenians, serves to highlight the complex irony of a mindless, fanatical act of revenge.

S50. Rockett, Kevin, Luke Gibbons, and John Hill. *Cinema and Ireland*. Syracuse: Syracuse Univ. Press, 1988. 60–62. Glosses "Guests of the Nation" and, mainly, engages Denis Johnston's 1935 fifty-minute silent film version, which was hailed as "the best picture yet made in Ireland."

S51. Storey, Michael L. "The Guests of Frank O'Connor and Albert Camus." *Comparative Literature Studies* 23 (Fall 1986): 250–62. "Guests of the Nation" and "L'Hôte" share similarities of theme, setting, characterization, and tone inspired, likely, by similar colonial situations in Ireland and Algeria and a similar concern for the archetypal guest-host relationship.

Studies of Other Individual O'Connor Stories

S52. Allen, Walter. *The Short Story in English*. New York: Oxford, 1981. Terse discussion of O'Connor among Irish writers, with a significant treatment of "The Holy Door."

S53. Bartel, Roland. "'Judas,' Frank O'Connor." *Biblical Images in Literature*. Nashville: Abingdon Press, 1975. 183–84. Notes that the story's humor derives from allusion to the Biblical Judas's betrayal.

S54. Borgmeier, R. "Frank O'Connor, 'My Oedipus Complex.'" *Die englische Kurzgeschichte*. Ed. K.H. Goller and G. Hoffmann. Dusseldorf: n.p., 1973. 274–84.

S55. Coen, Frank. "Frank O'Connor's 'First Confession,' One and Two." *Studies in Short Fiction* 10 (1973): 419–21. Compares two of the published versions to show that the changes highlight the revised story's artistic integrity. (For a more complete and accurate discussion of the "First Confession" revisions, see Steinman's *Frank O'Connor at Work* [**S17**].)

S56. Finnegan, Barbara C. "An Analysis of Frank O'Connor's 'First Confession.'" *English Journal* 59 (Jan. 1970): 48–51. Attributes primary blame for Jackie's antipathy toward religion to the vividly characterized Mrs. Ryan and Nora; discusses possible strategies for teaching the story in the secondary school classroom.

S57. Fowler, Albert. "Challenge to Mood in Frank O'Connor." *Approach* 23 (Spring 1957): 24–27. Explicates "The Holy Door," praising O'Connor's variations of mood, attributable to his humorous sensibility even when presenting tragic circumstance. O'Connor refuses to give in to desolation, in contrast to French writers Sartre and Gide.

S58. Gerber, Helmut E. "O'Connor's 'Uprooted.'" *Explicator* 14 (October 1955). Item 7. This seemingly simple story is complex and carefully structured upon closer examination; it shows Ned and Tom's inner alienation and their external "uprootedness," since they have lost something to which they can never return.

S59. Havighurst, Walter. "Symbolism and the Student." *College English* 16 (April 1955): 429–34. Cites O'Connor's "Uprooted" as an example of realistic fiction to illustrate that literature always has wider significance beyond self-referentiality.

S60. Kramer, C.R. "Experimentation in Technique: Frank O'Connor's 'Judas.'" *The Dublin Magazine* 8 (1969): 31–38.

S61. May, Charles E. "Frank O'Connor's 'Judas.'" *Notes on Contemporary Literature* 2:5 (1972): 11–13.

S62. Steinman, Michael. "Frank O'Connor at Work: Creating Kitty Doherty." *Eire-Ireland* 19 (Fall 1984): 142–48. Traces the evolution of the "Judas" character as an example of O'Connor's diligence in rewriting.

S63. ———. "Frank O'Connor at Work: 'The Genius.'" *Eire-Ireland* 20 (1985): 23–42. Characters' portrayals and motivations shift through the ten drafts O'Connor used to polish his work.

S64. ———. "Frank O'Connor's 'The Man of the World' and the Betrayed Reader." *Colby Library Quarterly* 30 (Dec. 1994): 279–90. This seemingly simple O'Connor story defeats readers' expectations, implicating them in its voyeuristic cycle.

On Multiple O'Connor Short Stories or the Stories in General

S65. Alexander, James. "Frank O'Connor in *The New Yorker*, 1945–1967." *Eire-Ireland* 30 (Spring 1995): 130–44. O'Connor's twenty-year association with *The New Yorker* was a significant turning point in his career, as he manipulated his style of narration for an American audience.

S66. Averill, Deborah. "Human Contact in the Short Stories." *Michael/Frank* [**S16**]. Ed. Maurice Sheehy. 28–37. O'Connor's stories value human contact in their characterization and narrative technique, for when his characters are able to rise above their circumstances, it is due to their personal relationships.

S67. ———. *The Irish Short Story from George Moore to Frank O'Connor.* Washington: University Press of America, 1982. This introductory study judges O'Connor to be the greatest practitioner of the Irish short story. For each of the seven writers explored, Averill reviews biographical details and artistic influences before undertaking a chronological analysis of the stories, in O'Connor's case paying close attention to *The Lonely Voice* and to such stories as "Guests," "Uprooted," "The Babes in the Wood," and "The Holy Door."

S68. ———. "The Theme of Escape in the Short Stories of Liam O'Flaherty, Frank O'Connor and Sean O'Faolain." Ph.D. Dissertation. University of Rochester, 1976.

S69. Bloom, Diana. "The Storyteller's Voice in Frank O'Connor's Short Stories and Their Revisions." Ph.D. Dissertation. New York University, 1980. A linguistic study of O'Connor's aural style of narration through a personalized voice who converses with the reader as if physically present. O'Connor creates this voice by using a variety of linguistic and rhetorical techniques. Still, he avoided too overtly manipulating linguistic techniques, and his revisions reflect a less self-conscious narration and shifts between first and third persons.

S70. Bonaccorso, Richard. "Irish Elegies: Three Tales of Gougane Barra." *Studies in Short Fiction* 19 (Spring 1982): 163–67. O'Faolain's "The Man Who Invented Sin" and "The Silence of the Valley" and O'Connor's "The Mass Island" use settings from this ancient valley near Cork as elegiac symbols.

S71. Bordewyk, Gordon. "The Quest for Meaning: The Stories of Frank O'Connor," *Illinois Quarterly* 41 (1978): 37–47. Evident in the four major clusters (war, religion, youth, and marriage) of O'Connor stories is the idea that characters who seek meaning and happiness have the potential to find them through relationships. Those who do not bother to undertake the quest for meaning are alienated from life's vibrancy.

S72. Brenner, Gerry. "Frank O'Connor's Imprudent Hero." *Texas Studies in Language and Literature* 10 (Fall 1968): 457–69. The crucial point of O'Connor's early fiction lies in its celebration of individuality through the narrator's imprudence, though this gives way in the later fiction to a more serious approach toward individuality.

S73. ———. "A Study of Frank O'Connor's Short Stories." Ph.D. Dissertation. University of Washington, 1965. Devoting one chapter each to O'Connor's juvenile and lay priest characters, Brenner defines O'Connor as a storyteller and realist whose fiction shuns "modish" symbolist techniques. Also explores the theories set out in *The Lonely Voice*, drawing examples from O'Connor's stories for illustration. Ultimately claims that in O'Connor's fiction the "imprudent hero" is triumphant (see Brenner's 1968 article, [**S72**]). Contains the first complete bibliography of O'Connor's works, published in 1967 (see [**S2**]).

S74. Casey, Daniel J. "The Seanachie's Voice in Three Stories by Frank O'-Connor." *Anglo-Irish Studies* 3 (1977): 96–107. In "Peasants," "In the Train," and especially "The Majesty of the Law," O'Connor succeeded in developing his narrators into modern-day *seanachies* in a deceivingly complex manner.

S75. Casey, Paul F. "Studying Out of the Self-Educator: Frank O'Connor and German Literature." *Eire-Ireland* 11 (Spring 1976): 85–97. Traces O'-Connor's childhood fascination with Germany to a mature interest in its literature. A pattern of interest is reflected in O'Connor's German quotations, misquotations, and puns in his own writing.

S76. Chatalic, Rene. "Conte, Nouvelle et 'Short Story': Note sur la terminologie critique et la structure des nouvelles de Frank O'Connor." *Cahiers du Centre d'Etudes Irlandaises* 3 (1978): 75–87.

S77. Chatalic, Roger. "Frank O'Connor and the Desolation of Reality." *The Irish Short Story*. Ed. Patrick Rafroidi and Terence Brown. Atlantic Highlands, NJ: Humanities Press, 1979. 189–201. Argues that O'Connor's overriding concern is with human isolation and that O'Connor responded to the twentieth century with intimacy, emphasizing not existential angst but individual self-realization.

S78. Cooke, Michael G. "Frank O'Connor and the Fiction of Artlessness." *University Review* (Spring 1968): 87–102. Unique and complex treatment of the range of perception in the form and content of O'Connor's stories, demonstrating their sensitivity to language and their thematic variety, particularly focusing on driving impulses of tradition and freedom.

S79. Costello, Peter. *The Heart Grown Brutal*. Dublin: Gill and Macmillan, 1977. Offers an account of the relationship between literature and the Irish Revolution; this work even offers a historical source for "Guests of the Nation."

S80. Davenport, Gary T. "Four Irish Writers in Time of Civil War: Liam O'Flaherty, Frank O'Connor, Sean O'Faolain, and Elizabeth Bowen." Ph.D. Dissertation. University of South Carolina, 1971. Explores the effects of the Troubles during the formative years of these four writers' lives on their writing careers. Includes a long introduction on the effect of historic events from 1916 to 1923 and their background in the writing of Joyce, Yeats, Shaw, and O'Casey. A thirty-five page chapter on O'-Connor presents the context of his life up to and during the Troubles before submitting that O'Connor (in contrast to O'Flaherty's cynicism) responds with non-partisan humor and a comic sense of distance in the war stories from *Guests* and in "Lofty," "Freedom," "The Eternal Triangle," and "Private Property."

S81. ————. "Frank O'Connor and the Comedy of Revolution." *Eire-Ireland* 8 (Summer 1973): 108–16. Makes the general argument (expounded in Davenport's dissertation) that O'Connor's Irish war stories contain a comic sense of distance. Primarily, the comic tone is here explored through "Lofty."

S82. Dockrell-Grunberg, S. "Studien zur Struktur moderner anglo-irischer Short Stories." Ph.D. Dissertation. Tubingen, 1967.

S83. Erni, Felix. "Frank O'Connor und die Kurzgeschichte Konzept der Erzahlform und Realisierung in seinem Werk." Ph.D. Dissertation. University of Zurich, 1975.

S84. Fallis, Richard. *The Irish Renaissance*. Syracuse: Syracuse University Press, 1977. Examines "My Oedipus Complex," "Guests," *An Only Child*, and other "major" works, with emphasis on O'Connor's artistic reputation ten years after his death.

S85. Gatterer, C. "Frank O'Connor's Short Stories." Ph.D. Dissertation. Vienna, 1977. (German language?)

S86. Gross, Konrad. "Frank O'Connor's Short Stories." In *Gerd Einfuhrung in die zeitgenossische irische Literatur*. Ed. Joachim Kornelius and Erwin Otto. Heidelberg: Winter, 1980. 125–37. German language.

S87. Hanson, Claire. *Short Stories and Short Fictions 1880–1980*. New York: St. Martin's, 1985. Discusses O'Connor and O'Faolain as regional innovators; treats "Babes in the Woods," "Majesty," "My Da," "My Oedipus Complex," and "Uprooted."

S88. Hennig, John. "Frank O'Connor und Goethe." *Neue Folge des Jahrbuchs der Goethe Gesellschaft* 24 (1962): 296–99.

S89. Hildebidle, John. *Five Irish Writers: The Errand of Keeping Alive*. Cambridge: Harvard University Press, 1989. 173–216. Claims elegaically that O'Connor, O'Faolain, Liam O'Flaherty, Kate O'Brien, and Elizabeth Bowen are likely to be overlooked in terms of their critical significance, and thus examines the fiction of each of the five writers at length. As such, Hildebidle considers the range of O'Connor's fiction and autobiography, particularly outlining a frame of reference for the fiction: its obsessive themes, domestic, familial setting, and familiar narrative voice.

S90. Kaplan, Laurelynn Smith. "Images from Old Myths: An Analysis of Six Thematic Motifs in the Modern Irish Short Story." Ph. D. Dissertation. University of Miami, 1981. Mythic themes (the exile, the priest, animals, the sea, the Big House, and the dead) from the ancient myths have been reworked by modern short story writers who often seek to show the archetypal relevance of the Irish story-telling tradition. Stories in *Crab Apple Jelly* and *More Stories* are used to show that O'Connor's characters are often internal, spiritual exiles, that his priests are very much humanly flawed and sympathetic, and that he is much more concerned with the living than with the dead.

S91. Kiely, Benedict. *Modern Irish Fiction—A Critique.* Dublin: Golden Eagle Books, 1950. 9–14, 127–78, 143–45. Defends the author of *Guests of the Nation* from those who would say he is too superficial but criticizes *The Common Chord* for being too intentionally irreverent and "on the surface" thematically.

S92. Lamb, Melinda. "The Growth of a Design: Frank O'Connor's Story Cycles." Dissertation. University of North Carolina at Greensboro, 1979. Draws extensively from O'Connor's autobiography and criticism to frame a discussion of the traditional critical stances toward O'Connor—based on his realism, concern for style over form, contradictions, reactionary tendencies, and chiefly the moral values he espoused. Then, proceeds to argue that O'Connor's six volumes of original short stories each reflect their own "story cycle"—a term loosely defined as a group of stories with a similar thematic thrust, always of a moral nature for O'Connor. The story cycles are argued to be the grand design of O'-Connor's art, the embodiment of his imaginative vision of reality.

S93. Letruelle, Sophie. "Radio Eireann: Les Nouvelles, par Frank O'Connor." *Etudes Irlandaises* 26 (Dec. 1991): 43–53.

S94. Matthews, James. "Frank O'Connor's Stories: The Contending Voice." *The Sewanee Review* 84 (Winter 1976): 56–75. A study of O'Connor's story collections and an explication of a number of stories; unified in its tracing the progression of voice in range and tone.

S95. ———. "Magical Improvisation: Frank O'Connor's Revolution." *Eire-Ireland* 10 (July 1975): 3–13. Examines the bearing of the Irish Revolution on O'Connor's life and works, including *Guests of the Nation*, O'Connor's historical plays, and *The Big Fellow*; suggests that O'Connor's postwar fiction retreated further and further into a personal revolution.

S96. ———. "Women, War, and Words: Frank O'Connor's First Confessions." *Irish Renaissance Annual* 1 (1980): 73–112. Examines the circumstances behind O'Connor's early writings, *Guests of the Nation* and *The Saint and Mary Kate*, in addition to the works themselves; claims that O'Connor's relationships usually provided inspiration for his writing, though the writing itself required isolation (which in turn strained his relationships).

S97. Maxwell, William. "Frank O'Connor and the *New Yorker.*" *Michael/Frank* [**S16**]. Ed. Maurice. Sheehy. 140–47. Reprinted in *The Happiness of Getting It Down Right*. Ed. Michael Steinman. [**P234**]. 263–70. O'Connor's chief *New Yorker* editor constructs a pastiche of remembrances and provides both critical and personal insight into the creative process of O'Connor's revisions.

S98. McAleer, Edward C. "Frank O'Connor's Oedipus Trilogy." *Hunter College Studies* 2 (1964): 33–40. Explicates three O'Connor stories—"My Oedipus Complex," "The Man of the House," and "Judas"—which correspond to Jung's three stages of development. Finds both explicit and subtle strands of Freudian themes and motifs in each.

S99. McCrann, Anthony. "A Critical Study of Frank O'Connor's Short Stories." Ph. D. Dissertation. University of Oregon, 1975. Proposes the theory that O'Connor's overly-innocent narrators learn through experiencing defeat to balance the forces of imagination and reason; shows how O'Connor's life and his understanding of Irish history shaped this pattern in his fiction, and traces the pattern through O'Connor's stories, particularly those of *Domestic Relations*.

S100. ———. "Frank O'Connor and the Silence." *Irish Renaissance Annual* 1 (1980): 113–36. O'Connor battled repressive silence all his life, and the tools of his rebellion were his own outspokenness and his stories, which often derived from the vitality of ancient tradition, children, and the common people.

S101. McHugh, Roger, and Maurice Harmon. *Short History of Anglo-Irish Literature from Its Origins to the Present Day*. New York: Barnes and Noble, 1982. Distinguishes O'Connor's romantic treatment of rural life from his more bleak and satirical portrayal of townspeople, and from his oversentimental stories of children.

S102. Molyneux, Thomas. "The Affirming Balance of Voice." *Shenandoah* 25 (Winter 1974): 27–43. Recognizes O'Connor's crucial distinction in contemporary fiction between "explicit" and "felt" meaning. Uses comparisons between the "The Genius" and "Araby" and, primarily, Updike and Cheever as examples.

S103. Murphy, Kate. "Grappling with the World." *Twentieth Century Literature* 36 (Fall 1990): 310–44. Justifies O'Connor's comic vision, his realism, and other aspects of his fiction by arguing that it hinges on his inherent humanist belief that life's purpose is to validate one's significance by "grappling with the world." Delineates the worlds which O'Connor's fiction inhabits, with a significant treatment of O'Connor's female characters.

S104. Murphy, Katherine Alicia. "Imaginative Vision and Story Art in Three Irish Writers: Sean O'Faolain, Mary Lavin, Frank O'Connor." Ph.D. Dissertation. University of Dublin, 1967.

S105. Neary, Michael. "The Inside-Out World in Frank O'Connor's Stories." *Studies in Short Fiction* 30 (1993): 327–36. In O'Connor's stories one makes a psychological journey between the tiny world of self and the vast external world; it is a journey which makes isolation and communion occur simultaneously.

S106. ———. "The Paradox of the Solitary Child in Charles Dickens and Frank O'Connor." Ph. D. Dissertation. University of Massachusetts,

1992. The "little men," the often childlike narrators O'Connor says are key to the short story, are shown to exist in Dickens's novels, as well.

S107. O'Hare, Shawn. "Frank O'Connor's Repressed Modernity: An Examination of *Here Comes Everybody.*" Ph.D. Dissertation. Florida State University, 1996. Examines O'Connor's unpublished manuscript about the significance of dreams and argues that O'Connor is very much in the Modernist tradition because of his use of the subconscious and manifest and latent content in his short fiction.

S108. ———. "More Than the Collar: An Examination of Frank O'Connor's Priests." M.A. Thesis. University of South Alabama, 1989. O'Connor's stories of priests mix aspects of Catholicism with his own brand of humanism; they reflect a concern with morals, but they are not moralistic. O'Hare's study differentiates O'Connor's types of priests, discusses a key theme, the priest's struggle with loneliness, and deals with alcohol and its effects in the stories of priests.

S109. O'Malley, Jerome F. "The Broken Pattern of Ritual in the Stories of Frank O'Connor." *Eire-Ireland* 23 (Spring 1988): 45–59. Posits that O'Connor's fiction (exemplified by "The Luceys," "The Mass Island," "The Teacher's Mass," "First Confession," "Christmas Morning," and "Guests") operates on an assumption of universality driven by a loneliness resulting from unfulfilled patterns of ritual behavior.

S110. Owens, Colin. "Frank O'Connor." *Critical Survey of Short Fiction.* Ed. Frank Magill. Englewood Cliffs, NJ: Salem Press, 1981. 1988–95. Provides background on O'Connor's life and works and an analysis of his stories "Guests," "In the Train," "The Long Road to Ummera," and "First Confession," and discusses the theories espoused in *The Lonely Voice.*

S111. Peterson, Richard F. "Frank O'Connor and the Modern Irish Short Story." *Modern Fiction Studies* 28 (Spring 1982): 53–67. Uses O'Connor's theories on "the lonely voice" to weigh the value of Moore's *The Untilled Field*, Joyce's *Dubliners*, and several of O'Connor's own collections within the modern Irish short story canon.

S112. Prosky, Murray. "The Pattern of Diminishing Certitude in the Stories of Frank O'Connor." *Colby Library Quarterly* 9 (1971): 311–21. O'Connor's fiction operates on the notion that all is lost when human sympathy gives way to inhuman abstractions. This pattern is identified in a number of stories, among them "Guests of the Nation," "In the Train," "Uprooted," and a few of the Larry Delaney stories.

S113. Saul, George Brandon. "A Consideration of Frank O'Connor's Short Stories." *Colby Library Quarterly* 6 (December 1963): 329–42. Lists the stories which appear in O'Connor's collections, up to 1957's *Domestic Relations*; then reviews the volumes, highlighting the most noteworthy stories. Operates throughout on the assumption that O'Connor is a poet at his best in writing lyrical fiction.

S114. Sherry, Ruth. "The Working Class Fiction of Cork: Corkery and O'-Connor." *Threshold* 35 (1986): 4–10. A comparison of the Cork-related fiction of teacher (Corkery) and pupil, both working class writers from Cork. O'Connor's fiction exhibits a broader range of settings, themes, characters, and tones, particularly when contrasted to Corkery's consistently bleak tone.

S115. Thompson, Richard. "A Kingdom of Commoners: The Moral Art of Frank O'Connor." *Eire-Ireland* 13 (1978): 65–80. Reprinted in Thompson's *Everlasting Voices: Aspects of the Modern Irish Short Story*. Troy, NY: Whitston, 1989. O'Connor's stories reflect a trademark intense moralism seen in his desire for order, decency, and love.

S116. Throne, Marilyn. "Frank O'Connor's Lost Fatherlands: Displaced Identity." *Colby Quarterly* 28 (March 1992): 52–60. Examines variations on the theme of displaced identity in stories of men who leave Ireland and cannot return: "Lost Fatherlands," "Uprooted," "Darcy in the Land of Youth," "The Late Henry Conran," *Dutch Interior*, and "Ghosts."

S117. Tomory, William Michael. "A Man's Voice Speaking: A Study of the Fiction of Frank O'Connor." Ph. D. Dissertation. University of Denver, 1973. Contains analysis which formed the basis of Tomory's book *Frank O'Connor* [**S18**]. Examines the Irish literary tradition of 1800 to 1916 before proceeding to explore O'Connor's place among modern short story writers and his fictional concerns, including theme, character, and voice.

S118. Trautmann, Joanne Victoria Belfiori. "Counterparts: The Stories and Traditions of Frank O'Connor and Sean O'Faolain." Ph.D. Dissertation. Purdue University, 1967. Both writers are moralists who select similar subjects and tend to see life and literature in dichotomous terms. Two chapters on O'Connor stories are followed by two on O'Faolain. The first O'Connor chapter focuses on the stories of juveniles: their balance between humor and despair, romance and realism, and subjectivity (of autobiographical subject matter) and objectivity (of his storytelling techniques). The second questions the universality of O'Connor's stories by exploring their natural, political, religious, and social settings, as well as by examining themes involving love and family life. Lastly, the writers are placed within the context of the influential literary traditions of Ireland, Russia, and France, though implied throughout is that the pair's greatest literary inspiration came from each other.

S119. Weber, Owene Hall. "A Woman's Voice Speaking: Mid-Century Irish Womanhood in the Short Stories of Frank O'Connor." Ph.D. Dissertation. University of Florida, 1993. O'Connor's approach to images of women is shown through examinations of four groups: girls who are tomboys yet who retain sensuality; unmarried young women who must confront difficult choices; married women pursuing selfhood within relationships; and old women who are bold survivors. In all, the stories show the sensitivity of O'Connor's narratives in providing women with a significant voice.

S120. Weiss, Daniel. "Freudian Criticism: Frank O'Connor as Paradigm." *Northwest Review* 2 (Spring 1959): 5–14. Reprinted in *The Critic Agonistes: Psychology, Myth and the Art of Fiction*. Ed. Eric Solomon and S. Arkin. University of Washington Press, 1985. Evaluates "My Oedipus Complex" and, more thoroughly, "Judas" in light of Weiss's definition of psychological criticism as testing a literary work for psychologically valid material rather than as therapy.

S121. Zeiss, Cecelia. "Aspects of the Short Story: A Consideration of Selected Works of Frank O'Connor and Herman Charles Bosman." In *Literary Interrelations: Ireland. England and the World II: Comparison and Impact*. Ed. Wolfgang Zach and Heinz Kosok. Tubingen: G. Narr Verlag, 1987. 121–27.

Reviews of O'Connor's Writings

Reviews of O'Connor's books are indexed in such sources as the *Book Review Digest* (New York: H.W. Wilson, 1905–) and the *Index to Book Reviews in the Humanities* (Detroit, MI: Phillip Thomson, 1960–). See also *Book Review Index* (Detroit, MI: Gale Research, 1965–).

Regarding Posthumous Story Collections

For reviews, consult the sources cited in the preceding section. See also (for instance) Richard Ellmann's introduction to **P21**, Harriet Sheehy's introductions to **P13**, **P22**, and **P24**, and Michael Steinman's introduction to **P226**.

Aids in Teaching O'Connor's Stories

Stories by O'Connor that are discussed in instructors' manuals for textbooks and anthologies are listed in Warren S. Walker, comp., *Twentieth-Century Short Story Explication: Interpretations, 1900–1975, of Short Fiction Since 1800*, 3d ed. (Hamden, CT: Shoe String Press, 1975). Supplements, issued every few years (e.g., in 1980 and 1984), keep the listings fairly current.

On O'Connor's Poetry and Translations

S122. Binchy, D.A. "The Scholar-Gipsy." *Michael/Frank* **[S16]**. Ed. Maurice Sheehy. 16–22. The Irish-language scholar discusses O'Connor's own intuitive scholarship, founded on a passionate, unceasing interest in ancient Ireland. He concludes that O'Connor's artistry surpasses that of all previous renderings of Irish poetry.

S123. Clarke, Austin. Rev. of "The Midnight Court." *Dublin Magazine* 21 (January 1946): 53–56.

S124. Greene, David. "Poet of the People." *Michael/Frank* **[S16]**. Ed. M. Sheehy. 137–39. O'Connor brought to his extremely difficult, unfashionable, unprofitable hobby of translating poetry not just a great commitment, but (more important) a creative vitality and intuitive craftsmanship.

S125. "Irish Poetry and Life." *Times Literary Supplement* (30 June 1961).

S126. Kennelly, Brendan. "Little Monasteries." *Michael/Frank* **[S16]**. Ed. M. Sheehy. 103–13. The poet and Trinity College professor claims O'Connor is at his best as translator in "The Midnight Court" and in the love poems of *Kings, Lords, and Commons* and *The Little Monasteries*, where he developed a dramatic lyric.

S127. Mercier, Vivian. "Stories, Songs, and People." Rev. of *Kings, Lords, and Commons*. *Nation* (3 October 1959): 196–97.

S128. O'Faolain, Sean. "Poems from the Irish." Rev. of *The Fountain of Magic* and *Lords and Commons*. *Spectator* 162 (10 March 1939): 416.

S129. Partridge, A.C. *Language and Society in Anglo-Irish Literature*. Dublin: Gill and Macmillan, 1984. Brief but significant attention paid to O'Connor's contributions as translator; also suggests possibilities for linguistic analysis of the short stories.

S130. Reynolds, Horace. "Irish Verse from 600 A.D." Rev. of *Kings, Lords, and Commons*. *Christian Science Monitor* (28 April 1960): 11

S131. Scaly, Douglas. "Translations of Frank O'Connor." *The Dubliner* (Summer 1963): 76–84.

S132. Taylor, Geoffrey. "The Poetry of Frank O'Connor." *The Bell* (December 1945): 779–87. In commenting on *Three Old Brothers, The Fountain of Magic*, and *The Midnight Court*, Taylor posits that O'Connor's best poetic work is in his translations. As a translator, O'Connor constructed, from the foundation of early Irish poems, English-language poems which were largely his own, carefully and masterfully crafted.

S133. Tindall, William York. Rev. of *Kings, Lords, and Commons*. *New York Herald Tribune Book Review* (2 August 1959): 5.

On O'Connor's Drama and Relationship
with The Abbey Theatre

S134. Griffin, Christopher. "The Betrayal of Parnell." Rev. of *Moses' Rock.* *Irish Literary Supplement* 3 (Fall 1984): 40.

S135. Hunt, Hugh. *The Abbey: Ireland's National Theatre 1904–1979.* New York: Columbia University Press, 1979. O'Connor's collaborator for most of his dramatic works provides a full account of the Abbey, including a brief discussion of the collaboration and of O'Connor's tenure on the board.

S136. Kavanagh, Peter. *The Story of the Abbey Theatre.* New York: Devin-Adair, 1950. 171–83.

S137. Kenny, Herbert A. *Literary Dublin: A History.* Dublin: Gill and Macmillan, 1974. Contains a brief but insightful background perspective on O'Connor, especially in the Abbey Theatre years.

S138. McHugh, Roger. "Frank O'Connor and the Irish Theatre." *Eire-Ireland* 4 (Summer 1969): 52–63. Also in *Michael/Frank* [**S16**]. Ed. M. Sheehy. 64–76. Focuses on the themes and production of O'Connor's plays *The Invincibles, Moses' Rock,* and *The Statue's Daughter*; also notes that theatrical experience taught O'Connor the value of collaboration and the difference between the solitary art of poetry and the public art of drama.

S139. Mikhail, E.H., ed. *The Abbey Theatre: Interviews and Recollections.* Totowa, NJ: Barnes and Noble, 1988. Contains O'Faolain's comments on his and O'Connor's disputes with the national theater in the 1930s; also contains an extract from O'Connor's *Leinster, Munster, and Connaught* titled "Myself and the Abbey Theatre."

S140. Phillips, Gary James. "The Dublin Drama League: 1918–1942." Ph.D. Dissertation. Southern Illinois University at Carbondale, 1980. Traces the league chronologically from the founding of the Abbey to the lawsuit involving O'Connor's *The Statue's Daughter,* which caused the league's demise in 1942.

S141. Robinson, Lennox. *Ireland's Abbey Theatre: A History 1899–1951.* Includes full cast lists for the O'Connor plays performed at the Abbey.

S142. Sherry, Ruth, ed. "An Historical Note." Introduction to *The Invincibles.* [London]: Proscenium Press, 1980. 5–6.

S143. ———, ed. "Introduction." *Moses' Rock* by Frank O'Connor and Hugh Hunt. Washington, D.C.: Catholic University Press, 1983. 1–39. This introduction provides a background helpful for reading O'Connor's historical play by framing it within the historical circumstances of Charles Stuart Parnell's career and the Irish literary antecedents which have dealt with Parnell's mythic presence. Furthermore, discusses the play's wider historical references in the context of O'Connor's work on the whole. Also contains a six-page chronology which traces the careers of O'Connor and Hunt.

S144. ———. "The Manuscript of 'Rodney's Glory.'" *Irish University Review* 22 (Autumn/Winter 1992): 219–24. Introducing the first publication of this late 1920s one-act O'Connor play are Dr. Sherry's comments on the date and creative evolution of the play and on the play's value for students interested in O'Connor's development.

On O'Connor's Novels

S145. Cahalan, James. *The Irish Novel: A Critical History.* Boston: Twayne, 1988. Briefly analyzes O'Connor's two novels, in which innocent protagonists experience the frustration of adult realities in episodic narratives similar to short stories.

S146. Cronin, John. *The Anglo-Irish Novel. Volume 2: 1900–40.* Savage, MD: Barnes and Noble, 1990. 183–91. Contains a chapter on *Dutch Interior*; assesses O'Connor's two novels as derivative to a fault and points to the Cork setting, too thin for the scope of a novel, as the main weakness.

S147. Farrell, James T. Rev. of *The Saint and Mary Kate. New Republic* (26 Oct. 1932): 301.

S148. Kelleher, John V. "Irish Literature Today." *The Bell* 10 (July 1945): 337–53. Examines the historical turn of Irish literature after the death of such romantics as Yeats and Russell. This turn is seen in writers' penchant for biography in the early 1940s and for realism, particularly in the three most significant (though flawed) novels of the era: O'Flaherty's *Famine*, O'Faolain's *Come Back to Erin*, and O'Connor's *Dutch Interior*.

S149. Reynolds, Horace. "Frank O'Connor's *Dutch Interior* and Other Fiction." Rev. of *Dutch Interior. New York Times Book Review* (17 Nov. 1940): 6.

S150. Sherry, Ruth. "Frank O'Connor as Novelist." *Canadian Journal of Irish Studies* 9 (June 1983): 23–44.

S151. Stern, James. Rev. of *Dutch Interior. New Republic* 104 (20 Jan. 1941): 91.

S152. Strong, L.A.G. Rev. of *The Saint and Mary Kate. Spectator* (23 April 1932): 604.

On O'Connor's Autobiographies

S153. Boland, Eavan. "The Innocence of Frank O'Connor." *Michael/Frank* [**S16**]. Ed. M. Sheehy. 77–85. O'Connor, with irony and intense retrospection, exposes the loss of innocence throughout his writing, particularly in that "perfect chronicle" and continuous parable of innocence, *An Only Child*.

S154. Hicks, Granville. "Revolutions and Leprechauns." Rev. of *An Only Child*. *Saturday Review* (11 March 1961): 22.

S155. Hildebidle, John. "Clouded Patrimonies: A Glance at 'My Father's Son.'" *Twentieth Century Literature* 36 (Fall 1990): 303–10. Explores the implications of the book's title, arguing that the many fathers constructed in this autobiography, among them Yeats and Mick O'Donovan, illustrate oddity and stubbornness instead of being exemplary patrimonial figures.

S156. Kauffmann, Stanley. "O'Connor Seen by Himself and Others." Rev. of *My Father's Son* and *Michael/Frank* [**S16**]. *New Republic* (29 Nov. 1969): 21–24. The Knopf editor of *An Only Child* adds personal recollections of O'Connor's revising process to a review of two works about him.

S157. Mercier, Vivian. "The O'Connors of Cork." Rev. of *An Only Child*. *New York Times Book Review* (12 March 1961): 5.

S158. O'Donovan, Patrick. "The Hurt of the Irish." Rev. of *An Only Child*. *New Republic* 144 (13 March 1961): 22–23.

S159. Pritchett, V.S. "A Fighting Childhood." Rev. of *An Only Child*. *New Statesman* 61 (30 June 1961): 1048–50.

S160. ———. "A Memoir by, and Tribute to, an Irishman of Literary Genius." Rev. of *My Father's Son* and *Michael/Frank* [**S16**]. *New York Times Book Review* (16 Nov. 1969): 3.

S161. Reid, B.L. "The Teller's Own Tale: The Memoirs of Frank O'Connor." *Sewanee Review* 84 (Winter 1976): 76–97. Finds *An Only Child* a profound, authentically humorous self-portrait of an "inspired provincial" and his mother, drawing particular comparison to V.S. Pritchett's memoirs, and finds *My Father's Son* a competent companion which provides invaluable personal portraits of Yeats and AE, among others.

S162. Sullivan, Kevin. "Apostolic Succession." Rev. of *My Father's Son*. *Nation* (15 Dec. 1969): 668–70.

S163. ———. "The Son of Minnie O'Connor." Rev. of *An Only Child*. *Nation* (8 April 1961): 306–7.

S164. Trevor, William. "Irish Cloud." Rev. of *My Father's Son*. *New Statesman* 76 (29 Nov. 1969): 761–62.

S165. Wohlgelernter, Maurice. "Mother and Father and Son: Frank O'Connor's Portrait of the Artist as an Only Child." In *Modern Irish Litera-*

ture: *Essays in Honor of William York Tindall.* Ed. R.J. Porter and J.D. Brophy. New York: Twayne, 1972. 115–28. A discussion of O'Connor's early years, covering material from the autobiographies, shows his progression toward becoming a writer.

On O'Connor's Biography of Michael Collins, *The Big Fellow/Death in Dublin*

S166. Clarke, Austin. "Michael Collins." Review. *New Statesman and Nation* 13 (5 June 1937): 932–34.

S167. Reynolds, Horace. "Michael Collins, the Hero of the Irish Revolution." *New York Times Book Review* (12 Sept. 1937): 5.

S168. Sayers, Michael. "The Patriot." Review. *New Republic* 92 (22 Sept. 1937): 193–94.

S169. Williams, P.H. "Republic and Free State." Review. *Commonweal* 26 (8 October 1937): 555–56.

S170. "A View of Michael Collins." Review. *Times Literary Supplement* (12 June 1937): 437.

On O'Connor's Critical Writings

S171. Adams, Phoebe. Rev. of *Shakespeare's Progress. Atlantic* (November 1960): 159.

S172. Alexander, James. "Frank O'Connor's Joyce Criticism." *Journal of Irish Literature* 21 (May 1992): 40–53. Disputes O'Connor's claim of boredom with Joyce by reviewing the fifteen works in which he criticized Joyce; contends that O'Connor's commentary is often suspect, controversial, and contradictory; catalogues O'Connor's chief criticisms of Joyce; and concludes that while the Joyce criticism mainly illuminates O'Connor's literary philosophies, perhaps O'Connor was right in thinking Joyce's "art" stories an aberration in the art of fiction's evolution in the twentieth century.

S173. Allen, Walter. "In the Beginning Was Gogol." Rev. of *The Lonely Voice. New York Times Book Review* (5 May 1963): 14.

S174. Barnes, Sam G. Rev. of *The Lonely Voice. Studies in Short Fiction* 1 (Fall 1963): 83–84.

S175. "Celtic Highlights." Rev. of *The Backward Look* and *A Golden Treasury of Irish Literature. Times Literary Supplement* (20 July 1967): 640.

S176. Chatalic, Rene. "Conte, Nouvelle et 'Short Story': Note sur la terminologie critique et la structure des nouvelles de Frank O'Connor." *Cahiers de Centre d'Etudes Irlandaises* 3 (1978): 75–87.

S177. Cohn, Alan M., and Richard Peterson. "Frank O'Connor on Joyce and Lawrence: An Uncollected Text." *Journal of Modern Literature* 12 (July 1985): 211–20. In introducing a censored radio broadcast, Cohn and Peterson provide insight into O'Connor's evolving attitude toward Joyce and Lawrence; he ultimately concluded that they had "perverted their geniuses" by draining humanity from their art.

S178. Crutwell, Patrick. Rev. of *Shakespeare's Progress. Saturday Review* (18 Feb. 1961): 25.

S179. Ellmann, Richard. "Michael-Frank." *Michael/Frank* [S16]. Ed. Maurice Sheehy. 23–27. Discusses O'Connor's personal warmth as evidenced in his stories and, mainly, explores O'Connor's original, probing criticism and his relationship with Yeats.

S180. Faverty, F.E. Rev. of *The Mirror in the Roadway. Chicago Sunday Tribune* (23 Sept. 1956): 7.

S181. Kiely, Benedict. "Men Who Wrote Like Angels." Rev. of *The Backward Look. New York Times Book Review* (25 June 1967): 4.

S182. Lugo Filippa, Carmen. "Frank O'Connor y Sean O'Faolain y sus Respectivas Teorias sobre el Evento en los Cuentistas." *Los Cuentistas y el Cuento: Enuesta entre Cultivadores del Genero.* San Juan, PR: Division de Publicaciones y Grabaciones, Instituto de Cultura Puertorriquena, 1991.

S183. Maloff, Saul. "Some Thoughts on the Short Story—and Its Decline." Rev of *The Lonely Voice. Commonweal* 78 (10 May 1963): 200–1.

S184. Pritchett, V.S. "Great Day in the Novel." *New York Times Book Review* (23 Sept. 1956): 5, 22.

S185. Sullivan, Kevin. "A Labor of Love and Learning." Rev. of *The Backward Look. Nation* 205 (28 August 1967): 149–50.

S186. "Telling Tales." Rev. of *The Lonely Voice. Times Literary Supplement* (9 Jan. 1964), 28.

Applications of O'Connor's Theories

S187. Kelly, Mary Pat. "The Sovereign Woman: Her Image in Irish Literature from Medb to Anna Livia Plurabelle." Ph.D. Dissertation. City University of New York, 1982. An analysis of the roles of women in the Irish myths and literary tradition which draws significantly from O'Connor's *Short History of Irish Literature* and translations. This study to some extent seeks to revise previous Celtic scholarship to point out the long tradition of Irish heroines of independence, sensuality, generosity, and sovereignty through chapters on (1) *The Tain*, (2) Irish poetry from the sixth to the nineteenth centuries, and (3) Joyce's fiction.

S188. Melville, Clyde B., Jr. "Short Fiction on Film: The 'Little Man' in Cinematic Adaptation." Ph.D. Dissertation. University of Texas at Arlington, 1980. The narrative voice of a short story, which O'Connor has referred to as 'the little man,' is crucial to the success not only of the story but also of its cinematic adaptation.

S189. Mercier, Vivian. "The Irish Short Story and Oral Tradition." *The Celtic Cross: Studies in Irish Culture and Literature*. Ed. R. Browne, W. Roscelli, and R. Loftus. Lafayette, IN: Purdue University Studies, 1964. 98–116. Draws from O'Connor's conjectures on "a man's voice speaking" in arguing that the Irish mastery of the short story derives from the oral tradition, since the short story retains a close storyteller-audience relationship.

S190. Peterson, Richard F. "Frank O'Connor and the Modern Irish Short Story." *Modern Fiction Studies* 28 (Spring 1982): 53–67. Uses O'Connor's theories on "the lonely voice" to weigh the value of Moore's *The Untilled Field*, Joyce's *Dubliners*, and several of O'Connor's own collections within the modern Irish short story canon.

On O'Connor's Travel Literature

S191. Ziegler, John Henry. "The Travel Literature of Frank O'Connor, Sean O'Faolain, and Robert Gibbings." Ph.D. Dissertation. University of Connecticut, 1975. Treats the travel books of these three writers as literature in the Irish *imrama* tradition; the introduction explores this tradition through ancient tales such as "The Voyage of Bran." Each of the three main chapters focuses on the works of the modern writers themselves—showing how each uses the voyage as a metaphor. O'Connor is viewed as a writer struggling to free Ireland from repression, while simultaneously helping the country retain its sense of its past. O'Connor's view of Ireland in his three travel books is on the whole pessimistic, however: unlike the others, he sees for Ireland only a path toward decay.

Frank O'Connor as Teacher

S192. Edwards, Philip. "Frank O'Connor at Trinity." *Michael/Frank* [**S16**]. Ed. M. Sheehy. 129–36. Credits O'Connor for initiating important ideas about the teaching of the literature of Ireland during O'Connor's connection to Trinity College in the last years of his life.

S193. Gill, Richard T. "Frank O'Connor in Harvard." *Michael/Frank* [**S16**]. Ed. Maurice Sheehy. 38–49. O'Connor threw himself exhaustively into his teaching, lecturing on Irish literature or on the novel, and, most interestingly, teaching unorthodox writing courses which required students, for example, to gain class approval for the four-line themes they presented before proceeding to write stories.

S194. Solomon, Eric. "Frank O'Connor as Teacher." *Twentieth Century Literature* 36 (Fall 1990): 239–42. A former student, now a professor himself, reminisces about his greatest literature teacher, a brilliant "classroom performance artist" as lecturer.

S195. Stegner, Wallace. "Professor O'Connor at Stanford." *Michael/Frank* [**S16**]. Ed. M. Sheehy. 94–102. O'Connor was a memorable, devoted teacher: a powerful actor as lecturer and, in his fiction writing courses, a provocateur for students such as Larry McMurtry and Ken Kesey, who were as stubbornly convicted as the visiting professor himself.

Personal Recollections of the Man

S196. Brennan, Donal. "Reminiscences from France." *Michael/Frank* [**S16**]. Ed. M. Sheehy. 114–20. Discusses O'Connor's love of France, his many visits, his impressive knowledge of French literature, and his apt comparisons between Irish and French culture.

S197. Foley, Dermot. "The Young Librarian." *Michael/Frank* [**S16**]. Ed. Maurice Sheehy. 50–63. O'Connor's Pembroke Library assistant (who became an accomplished librarian) sheds light on the masks that O'Connor wore—his public persona, full of tempestuous energy and cast-iron confidence, is contrasted with his deep personal warmth and sympathy.

S198. Hendrick, Sean. "Michael O'Donovan's Wild Son." *Michael/Frank* [**S16**]. Ed. Maurice Sheehy. 5–15. A life-long friend describes O'Connor's exploits during the war years, his early literary and dramatic experiences in Cork, and his irreverence toward those who put on airs.

S199. Kennelly, Brendan. "Oration at Graveside." *Michael/Frank* [**S16**]. Ed. Maurice Sheehy. 165–67. Praises O'Connor for various reasons, most notably for being an inspiration "to all those who knew him."

S200. Lavin, Mary. "Visits to Michael." *Twentieth Century Literature* 36 (Fall 1990): 242.

S201. Lynam, Shevawn. "A Sparring Partner." *Michael/Frank* [**S16**]. Ed. Maurice Sheehy. 86–93. A friend recalls her many conversations with O'Connor about Ireland; his attitude was most often one of contempt toward the countless problems he perceived for the country he loved.

S202. Macmillan, Harold. "Foreward." *Michael/Frank* **[S16]**. Ed. Maurice Sheehy. vii-viii.

S203. Maxwell, Emily. "Michael and Harriet." *The Happiness of Getting It Down Right*. Ed. M. Steinman. 257–58. Provides insight into the collaboration which led to the 1996 publication of letters between her husband and O'Connor.

S204. O'Donovan, Liadain. "Michael O'Donovan, Frank O'Connor & Me." *Frisco* (December 1981): 31. By O'Connor's son.

S205. O'Farrell, Padraic. "Frank O'Connor." *Green and Chaste and Foolish: Irish Literary and Theatrical Anecdotes*. Dublin: Gill and Macmillan, 1994. Contains offbeat, humorous references to incidents drawn mainly from O'Connor's memoirs and Matthews' biography.

S206. Plunkett, James. "The Boy on the Back Wall." *The Boy on the Back Wall and Other Essays*. Dublin: Poolbeg, 1987.

S207. Sheehy, Harriet. (Harriet O'Connor). "Listening to Frank O'Connor." *Nation* (28 Aug. 1967): 150–51. Remembers her husband's continual "backward look"—in his lectures as teacher, his struggles in translating ancient poetry, his travels across the countryside, even his dreamlike process of discovering a story, he was always returning to Ireland and its people.

S208. Sheehy, Maurice. "The Platonist." *Michael/Frank* **[S16]**. 121–28. Although O'Connor purported to despise abstraction, Sheehy claims his understanding of truth and morality made him somewhat of an unknowing Platonist philosopher.

S209. Steinman, Michael. "Remembering Michael: A Talk with Thomas Flanagan." Interview with Thomas Flanagan. *Twentieth Century Literature* 36 (Fall 1990): 259–69. Flanagan discusses his friendship with O'-Connor and assesses O'Connor's literary criticism, his unfinished autobiography, *My Father's Son*, his Michael Collins biography, and, mainly, his reputation as a short story writer.

S210. Tracy, Honor. "King of the Castle." *Michael/Frank* **[S16]**. Ed. Maurice Sheehy. 1–4. Comments on the warm, generous, sympathetic spirit of Michael O'Donovan, as well as his serious, often opinionated convictions.

Inspired by Frank O'Connor

S211. Chalpin, Lila. "To Frank O'Connor." Ten-line poem of tribute and lament. *The CEA Critic* (magazine of the College English Association). (March 1969): 2.

S212. Jordan, Neil. *The Crying Game*. Screenplay for the film; published in *A Neil Jordan Reader*. New York: Random House, 1993. In his introduction, Jordan claims the interconnectedness of "Guests of the Nation" with Brendan Behan's *The Hostage* and his own *The Crying Game*.

S213. ———. *Michael Collins: Screen Play and Film Diary*. New York: Plume, 1996. O'Connor's book on Collins, which Jordan considers "still probably the best biography" (6), helped inspire his film.

S214. Kennelly, Brendan. "Light Dying: In Memoriam Frank O'Connor (Michael O'Donovan)." *Selected Poems*. New York: E.P. Dutton, 1972. 24–25.

Adaptations of O'Connor's Work to Other Media: Film, Stage, Television, Music and Radio Drama

S215. *Guests of the Nation*. Denis Johnston. Ireland, 1933. O'Connor himself played a small role in this silent film.

S216. Musical settings by Aloys Fleischman for O'Connor's poems: "The Student," "The Lover," "Autumn." Held by The Boston University Mugar Memorial Library.

S217. *Still Waters*. A play by John McGiffert. Based on O'Connor's story "Song Without Words." Circa 1945. Held by the Boston University Mugar Memorial Library.

S218. *When I Was a Child*. Stage adaptation of O'Connor's story "The Genius." Produced in New York, Dec. 1950.

S219. *The Rising of the Moon*. Film adaptation of O'Connor's story "The Majesty of the Law." Four Provinces Films, 1957.

S220. *The Martyr*. Adaptation of the short story for television, produced by G.E. Theatre in New York, 1954.

S221. *Larry*. Adaptation of the short story "My Oedipus Complex" for television by Geraldine Fitzgerald.

S222. *Orphans*. Adaptation of the short story for television, produced by G.E. Theatre in New York, 1956.

S223. *Country People*. O'Connor's radio adaptations of the stories "In the Train," "The Luceys," and "The Long Road to Ummera." Radio Eireann, 9 Dec. 1959.

S224. *Fighting Men*. O'Connor's radio adaptations of the stories "Guests of the Nation," "The Martyr," and "Private Property." Radio Eireann, 1 Feb. 1959.

S225. McKenzie, Neil. *Guests of the Nation*. Stage adaptation. Produced in New York, 1958. Text published by Dramatists' Play Service, 1960.

S226. *Silent Song.* Adaptation of the short story "Song Without Words" for television by Hugh Leonard, produced by BBC TV, 2 Feb. 1966. Italia Prize 1967.

S227. *Guests of the Nation.* A televised reading by the author on Radio-Telefis Eireann TV, 1964.

S228. Mayer, Paul Avila. *Three Hand Reel: Three One-Act Plays Based on Short Stories by Frank O'Connor.* New York: Dramatists' Play Service, 1967. ("Bridal Night," "Eternal Triangle," and "The Frying Pan.")

S229. Manning, Mary. *The Saint and Mary Kate.* Produced by the Abbey Theatre, March 1968.

S230. O'Connor, Sinead. "I Am Stretched On Your Grave." Song lyric adapted from Frank O'Connor's translation from the Irish. *I Do Not Want What I Haven't Got*, 1989.

Index

The following index includes proper names, topics, and themes. Works written by Frank O'Connor are followed by the abbreviation "FOC."

Contributors

JAMES D. ALEXANDER is Professor of English at the University of Wisconsin Center—Marshfield-Wood County, where he has taught composition and literature since 1964. His special interest in Frank O'Connor's writing led to two research ventures to Ireland. He has since published on O'Connor in *Ireland of the Welcomes*, in the *Journal of Irish Literature*, and in *Twentieth Century Literature*. His most recent article, in *Eire-Ireland* (Spring 1995), explains how O'Connor's narrative techniques altered when he wrote for *The New Yorker* magazine.

MEGAN DENIO, while pursuing a master's degree in English at the University of Nevada, Las Vegas, was awarded a scholarship to travel to Ireland to work on a thesis dealing with the Galwegian author Walter Macken. She has also taught English in Tashkent, Uzbekistan and plans further study and teaching of Irish literature and composition.

ROBERT C. EVANS, Professor of English at Auburn University at Montgomery, is author or editor of eight books and numerous essays. Although his main interest has been the literature of the English Renaissance, he also has published on critical theory, short fiction, and the *American* O'Connor—Flannery. Appointed Professor of the Year for his state in 1989 by the Council for the Advancement and Support of Education (Washington, D.C.), he has for a number of years focused on attempting to involve students in academic research. In 1997 he was named Alumni Professor at AUM.

ROBERT FUHREL is currently Professor of English at the Community College of Southern Nevada in Las Vegas. His main interests are Irish literature and history and Polynesian culture and language. He has taught in Florida, Samoa, and Hawai'i.

RICHARD HARP is Professor of English at the University of Nevada, Las Vegas, and is Director of Graduate Studies in the English Department. He is co-editor of *The Ben Jonson Journal* and has published books on Oliver Goldsmith and on Samuel Johnson's Dictionary. He has also written on Alice Milligan and her founding of one of the first Irish nationalist newspapers, *The Shan Van Vocht*. He is co-editor of the forthcoming *Cambridge Companion to Ben Jonson*.

JOHN KERRIGAN is a doctoral student of English and Irish literatures at the University of Nevada, Las Vegas. His master's thesis on Frank O'Connor was completed in 1995, and one of his current projects involves looking more closely at O'Connor's relationships with Yeats and Richard Ellmann.

MICHAEL NEARY has taught English at Stephen F. Austin State University for the past four years. He has published essays on Frank O'Connor and Sean O'Faolain in *Studies in Short Fiction* and on Mary Lavin in *Twentieth Century Literature*.

SHAWN O'HARE is an Assistant Professor of English at Carson-Newman College in Jefferson City, Tennessee. He is the editor of *Nua: Studies in Contemporary Irish Writing* and is currently completing a book-length study of Frank O'Connor's interest in dreams and *Here Comes Everybody*.

HARRIET O'DONOVAN SHEEHY was born in 1923 in Baltimore, Maryland. She met Frank O'Connor (Michael O'Donovan) at Harvard in July 1952 and they married in England in December 1953. They lived in Brooklyn Heights, Annapolis, and Palo Alto before moving to Dublin permanently in 1961. Their daughter Harriet (Hallie Og) was born in June 1958. After Frank O'Connor died in March 1966, his widow returned to Annapolis and lived there until September 1969, when she married Maurice Sheehy, a former priest of the Dublin Diocese and a close friend of the O'Connors. He died in August 1991. She now lives in Dalkey, County Dublin, where she continues to oversee the publication of O'Connor's works. The recently published book of letters between O'Connor and his editor at *The New Yorker* contains many photographs of her life with O'Connor.

MICHAEL STEINMAN is Professor of English at Nassau Community College in Garden City, New York. He is the author of *Frank O'Connor at Work* (Syracuse University Press, 1990) and the editor of *A Frank O'Connor Reader* (Syracuse University Press, 1994) and of *The Happiness of Getting It Down Right: Letters of Frank O'Connor and William Maxwell* (Knopf, 1996). He also edited a special Frank O'Connor issue of the journal *Twentieth Century Literature*, published in 1990.

VALENTINA TENEDINI is completing an M.Phil degree at Lumsa University in Rome. Her interview of Frank O'Connor's widow appears in this book, and her translation of O'Connor's novel *Dutch Interior* into Italian is in the final stages.

ALAN TITLEY, Professor of Irish language and literature at St. Patrick's College, Dublin City University, is the author of novels, stories, and plays in the Irish langauge. His selected essays (*Chun Doirne*) were published in 1996, and his selected essays in English on literary and cultural topics (*Nailing Theses*) will appear in 1997.

OWENE WEBER is Assistant Professor of English at Flagler College in St. Augustine, FL. She earned her doctorate at the University of Florida with a dissertation on O'Connor's presentation of women. She worked with the O'Connor papers even before they were deposited, helped arrange their trasnfer to the University of Florida library, and helped catalogue them after they were placed there. She is currently completing a book on O'Connor.

JULIANNE WHITE is a graduate student at the University of New Mexico, Albuquerque, taking her Ph.D. in the literature of the Victorian and Modern periods as well as in Rhetoric/Language. She has published poems, personal narratives, and academic papers in such journals as *Poet Magazine, English in Texas*, and two publications sponsored by the National Council of Teachers of English: *Women in Literature and Life Assembly* and *English Journal*. Her dissertation deals with the poetry of W.B. Yeats.

***

Curtis Bowden, John Burdett, Kathleen B. Durrer, Tasheka Gipson, Scott Johnson, Katie Magaw, Karey Oakley, Lane Powell, Michael Probst, Denean Rivera, Dianne Russell, Claire Skowronski, Gwen Warde, Claudia Wilsch, and Carolyn T. Young are graduate or advanced undergraduate students at Auburn University at Montgomery, as are Kelly J. Beyer, Clint Darby, Jeremiah Deneve, Heather Edwards, Earl Eidem, Jennifer Henderson, Cheri Norwood, Lane Powell, Douglas Scarborough, Angela Soulé, Kalicia K. Spigner, and Clinton Van Der Pool, Jr.

Burdett, Durrer, Johnson, Magaw, Probst, Skowronski, Wilsch, and Ondra Thomas-Krouse were participants in a 1997 seminar on Critical Pluralism held at AUM and sponsored by the Andrew W. Mellon Foundation, as were Timothy Francisco and Karen Worley Pirnie.